PENGUIN

CHAIM WEIZMANN

Norman Rose, born and educated in England, now lives in Israel and teaches history at Hebrew University, where he holds the Chaim Weizmann Chair of International Relations. His previous books include *Vansittart: Study of a Diplomat* and *Lewis Namier and Zionism*.

CHAIM WEIZMANN

A BIOGRAPHY

NORMAN ROSE

PENGUIN BOOKS

PENGUIN BOOKS
Published by the Penguin Group
Viking Penguin, a division of Penguin Books USA Inc.,
40 West 23rd Street,
New York, New York 10010, U.S.A.
Penguin Books Ltd, 27 Wrights Lane,
London W8 5TZ, England
Penguin Books Australia Ltd, Ringwood,
Victoria, Australia
Penguin Books Canada Ltd, 2801 John Street,
Markham, Ontario, Canada L3R 1B4
Penguin Books (N.Z.) Ltd, 182–190 Wairau Road,
Auckland 10, New Zealand

Penguin Books Ltd, Registered Offices:
Harmondsworth, Middlesex, England

First published in the United States of America by
Viking Penguin, a division of Penguin Books USA Inc., 1986
Published in Penguin Books 1989

1   3   5   7   9   10   8   6   4   2

Grateful acknowledgment is made to The Weizmann Archives for permission
to reprint Weizmann letters, some of which were previously unpublished.
Copyright © The Weizmann Archives, 1986.

LIBRARY OF CONGRESS CATALOGING IN PUBLICATION DATA
Rose, Norman.
Chaim Weizmann: a biography/Norman Rose.
p.   cm.
Bibliography: p.
Includes index.
ISBN 0 14 01.2230 3
1. Weizmann, Chaim, 1874–1952.   2. Zionists—Biography.
3. Israel—Presidents—Biography.   I. Title.
[DS125.3.W45R67   1989]
956.94′052′0924—dc19
[b]   88–32420

Printed in the United States of America
Set in Fairfield

For Tslilla

PREFACE

There is a curious gap in Zionist historiography that has unfortunately become more pronounced in recent years. Its simplified version would begin with Herzl and end with Ben Gurion (although since 1977 frantic attempts have been made to tack on Jabotinsky for good measure). Amidst the excitement and drama of Israel having to defend her independence by force of arms, the figure of Chaim Weizmann emerges, if at all, as a quixotic, elderly gentleman whose political ideas and style have become outdated, unfashionable, for some even positively harmful, and whose career has been consigned to a calm backwater rarely disturbed by an inquisitive public. In short, a political dodo.

Yet for anyone even remotely familiar with the subject this proposition is a patent absurdity. For almost a generation, from 1917, the year of the Balfour Declaration, until 1946, Weizmann, whether in or out of office, led the Zionist movement, dominating its councils and nursing it from political infancy to the responsibilities of statehood. Under his stewardship the history of the Zionist movement reads, despite its disappointments and setbacks, as one of the most remarkable political success stories of the twentieth century. Few leaders in the democratic world can equal such a record, and rarely has the popular image of the man so flagrantly contradicted the reality.

My first acquaintance with Weizmann was as an impressionable teenager in London in November 1952. With some friends I attended a commemorative rally for Weizmann, who had just died, at the Royal Albert Hall. Perched in the galleries, we gazed down at a packed auditorium to the dais where the pride of Anglo-Jewry was on display: captains of industry and commerce, distinguished academics, learned judges, dedicated communal and Zionist leaders. As they eulogized the late president of Israel their voices broke, some of them weeping openly, their spontaneous grief deepening the sense of loss of an already sorrow-stricken audience. This was a strangely impressive and stirring experience, though, in my youthful arrogance, my initial reaction was to consider how demeaning and unmanly (and perhaps un-English) it was for such eminent and sophisticated men of the world to display their emotions in public so shamelessly. But on the way home another thought struck me: what was the essence of this man who could move a mass audience to such demonstrations?

I then forgot all about Weizmann until I rediscovered him when I was a research student at the London School of Economics and learned, through his words and deeds, about the qualities that had endeared him to the audience at the Royal Albert Hall and made him one of the outstanding figures of his time. Even at one generation removed, his charm and wisdom and political wit still shone through. And if now, after writing his biography, I am aware equally of his faults and of his failings, I remain more than ever convinced not only that Weizmann is worthy of academic speculation but that his teachings have never been more relevant to the problems of contemporary Israel and the Jewish people. If this book helps to fill in the gap in Zionist historiography and restore Weizmann to his rightful place in the Zionist pantheon, it will have served a useful purpose.

ACKNOWLEDGMENTS

The writing of this book was dependent upon the good will and encouragement of many people, and during the course of my work I have incurred a great many debts. I am particularly grateful to the staffs of the numerous archives, libraries, and institutions that generously extended their facilities to me: the Archives of the Zionist Federation of Great Britain and Ireland; the British Library of Political and Economic Science at The London School of Economics; the British Museum Library and its Newspaper Collection at Colindale; the Central Zionist Archives, Jerusalem; the Chemistry Laboratories at Manchester University; the Institute of Historical Research, Senate House, London; the Kressel Collection at the Oxford Centre for Postgraduate Hebrew Studies; the Library for Humanities and Social Sciences and the National Library at The Hebrew University, Jerusalem; the Mocatta Library, University College, London; the Public Record Office, London; the John P. Robarts Research Library at the University of Toronto; the Weizmann Archives, Rehovot; and the Zionist Archives and Library, New York.

Crown copyright material at the Public Record Office is reproduced by kind permission of the Controller of Her Majesty's Stationery Office. I am also most grateful to the Trustees of the Weizmann Archives for allowing me to use material placed in their charge, including the late Richard Crossman's Notes (see also Bibliography). My thanks are also extended to the following institutions for permission to quote material of which they hold the copyright: the British Library of Political and Economic Science at the London School of Economics; the British Museum Library and its Newspaper Collection at Colindale; the Central Zionist Archives, Jerusalem; the Kressel Collection at the

Oxford Centre for Postgraduate Hebrew Studies; and the Zionist Archives and Library, New York.

My search for information led me to intrude upon the privacy of many individuals. For their understanding, frankness, and hospitality I wish to thank: Mrs. Batia Abromovitch; Sir Isaiah Berlin; Mrs. Elaine Blond; Lord Charteris; Mrs. Anne Crossman; Mrs. Jeannie Denman; Mr. Abba Eban; Mr. and Mrs. T. R. Fyvel; Dr. S. Levenberg; Mrs. Yisraela (Lichtenstein) Margalith; Sir John Martin; Mr. Yehudi Menuhin; Mrs. Norah (Schuster) Nicholls; Mr. Yehiel Paldi; Mrs. Dorothy de Rothschild; Mrs. Kitty Stein; Mrs. Strage; Mr. Shabtai Tevet; Mr. Ya'akov Tsur; Mrs. Lola Hahn-Warburg; Lord Weidenfeld; Mr. David Weizmann; Mr. Ezer Weizmann; Dr. Maidie Weizmann. I am also grateful to the Weizmann Archives for allowing me to use their extensive collection of photographs, painstakingly gathered from various sources, and view their collection of videotaped interviews, which included: Mrs. Yael Allingham; Mrs. Chani Bergmann; Mr. Joseph Cohn; Dr. Israel Goldstein; Dr. Ernst Joel; Mr. Yeheskiel Sahar; Mrs. Flora Solomon. I am particularly grateful to Mrs. Nechama Chalom, director of the Weizmann Archives, for her skill in guiding me through the material placed in her charge, and for her patience in replying to my countless queries. My thanks are also extended to Mr. Martin Gilbert, Mr. Tuvia ben Moshe, and Dr. Sasson Sofar, who provided me with valuable points of reference and information; and to Miss Inbal Rose who pursued further enquiries on my behalf. Dr. David Billis, Mrs. Nehama Chalom, Mrs. Helena Davis, Dr. Yitzchak Einav, Mrs. Diana Reich, Miss Inbal Rose, Professor Meir Verete, and Professor Eli Yoffe read the typescript, either in whole or in part. For their informed comments and advice I remain greatly in their debt.

The Leonard Davis Institute for International Affairs, the Research Fund of the Faculty of Social Sciences, and the Authority for Research and Development at the Hebrew University supported this project from its inception, acts of generosity for which I remain most grateful. I would also like to thank the officers of the Canada–Israel Academic Exchange Foundation and the University of Toronto for inviting me to spend a year in Canada where I began to write this book. The staff and students of the departments of Political Economy and History received me most warmly and ensured that my stay there was a pleasant and fruitful one. I wish also to acknowledge those authors and publishers (listed in the bibliography) for quotations I have used from works of which they hold the copyright. Allow me to put down in advance my apologies for those cases that I have inadvertently overlooked.

I am especially grateful to Robert Ducas, my agent, who accompanied and encouraged this project from its conception. Elisabeth Sifton deserves a special word of thanks. Her professionalism and expertise smoothed too many rough passages and saved me from some embarrassing errors; this book owes much to her skill and hard work. My warmest thanks are also extended to all those at Viking Penguin who helped in the preparation of this book, particularly Julie Dolin. Authorship is the loneliest of occupations, and perhaps only those who have experienced it first-hand can fully appreciate the necessity of being subject at all times to encouragement and support. I must, therefore, record my deepest thanks to my wife and daughter for sustaining me throughout this arduous project.

NORMAN ROSE

The Hebrew University, Jerusalem
January 1986

CONTENTS

Illustrations follow pages 174 and 366.

CHAIM WEIZMANN

A BIOGRAPHY

PROLOGUE

At five o'clock in the morning of Thursday, 30 September 1948, a C-54A Skymaster, a four-engine transport veteran from the Second World War now converted to civilian use and newly decorated in El Al colours, landed at Tel Nof, a military airfield some twenty-five miles south of Tel Aviv, after a non-stop flight of ten hours from Geneva.[1] On board were Chaim Weizmann and his entourage: Vera, his wife; Professor S. Zondek, his personal physician; Dr. Ernst Bergmann, director of the Weizmann Institute; and Dr. M. Simon, *chef de protocol*. Weizmann was approaching seventy-four years of age and recuperating from a serious eye operation, but he suffered no ill-effects from the tedious but uneventful flight. The crew, decked out in their dark-blue uniforms, had been respectfully attentive. Before he left the aircraft, Weizmann inscribed in its logbook the message: 'It has been a great privilege for me to travel for the first time in an Israeli plane so beautifully turned out and manned by such an amiable crew.' This nice human touch was characteristic of the man.

Weizmann's arrival in Israel was a moment charged with high drama. In the summer of 1947 he had left his home in Rehovot, a leader rejected by his movement, for a holiday in Switzerland. Now, little more than a year later, he returned as President of Israel's provisional Council of State. His august title was just recognition for his unique contribution to the Zionist cause: the creation of an autonomous Jewish state, the climax of his political career. Yet his reception at Tel Nof was not distinguished by great pomp or ceremony. Weizmann always professed disdain for the ostentatious display of the trappings of power, although he was not blind to its uses. In any case, the political situation was too grave to warrant such demonstrations. The ceremony was unpretentious yet dignified. A young Air Force girl presented Mrs. Weizmann with a bouquet of flowers. Then Weizmann stepped forward to embrace the representatives of the government, mostly old comrades, who had come to receive him: Eliezer Kaplan, Minister of Finance; David Remez, Minister of Communications; and especially the chairman of the State Council, Yosef Sprinzak. Senior officials from the Prime Minister's office, the Foreign Ministry, the Defence Ministry, and the Police Force were also in attendance. Having greeted his colleagues, Weizmann, accompanied by Vera, turned to inspect the small guard-of-honour of Israeli soldiers drawn up on the runway.* Then he and Mrs. Weizmann drove off, escorted by motor-cycle outriders and an armed guard, to their home in nearby Rehovot. The household staff at the Weizmann's house (known somewhat cheekily as the White House) had been in a state of nervous anticipation all morning. Drawn up on the steps, they welcomed the Weizmanns home. After some emotional greetings, Weizmann led his guests in for a communal breakfast. 'Not an enjoyable party', Mrs. Weizmann grumbled in her diary, 'tired to death.'²

After a short rest, Weizmann insisted on conducting a tour of the Scientific Research Institute now given his name. Accompanied by his confidant and the institute's chief fund-raiser, Meyer Weisgal, and

---

* Joshua Harlap, Weizmann's chauffeur and bodyguard, remembered the following incident. After the greetings,

the President hesitated, glancing nervously around and examining the faces of the people standing near him. A heavy silence fell. All eyes were fastened upon him. What was he looking for?

Joshua came forward a few paces from the spot where, wittingly or unwittingly, he had been hidden behind the car. The Professor [Weizmann] saw him and called, 'Come here, Joshua!' Suppressing his emotion, Joshua stepped up to the President and grasped his outstretched hand.

'Well, Joshua, it has come, the day has come, hasn't it? And now give me some earth.'

'Yes, Professor,' he answered in a low voice. He bent down and picked up a fistful, proferring it to his master, who placed his own hand beneath Joshua's to receive the soil. He then raised the handful to his lips.

And with his hand clenching the earth of Israel, the President walked towards the soldiers who were presenting arms and passed down the ranks.

The ceremony over, the car drove off—and the Professor's hand was still clenched.

See Shihor, *Hollow Glory*, 81–82. This incident went unnoticed by other observers of the scene. If apocryphal, its symbolic significance is nonetheless in keeping with the occasion.

its administrative director, Dr. Benjamin Bloch, he inspected the laboratories, pausing occasionally to question the young scientists on the state of their research. Moving from one building to another, he could not but notice the carefully landscaped gardens from which he always derived a special pleasure. He had watched the institute grow from its inception in the mid-1930s into a research centre of international repute. It was, as he often said, 'a monument'. But not just for him personally. It represented a wider vision. Early in his career he had perceived the synthesis between scholarship and national renaissance. 'Our best weapon is the spirit, and it is our duty to cultivate the spirit, to strengthen this weapon and keep it for the struggle for a better life. The [Hebrew] University should be our spiritual "Dreadnought": with it we could achieve greater successes than other peoples with their armies and navies.'[3] The institute personified his conception of the role Zionism could play as a force in Israel and in the modern world: erudition and vision combined with practicality and purpose, learning harnessed to the needs of society. 'Israel is a small country', he once observed, 'but it can be like Switzerland—a small country but a highly civilized one, a force for enlightenment and progress out of all proportion to its size.'[4] Although he was often impatient, at times bitterly critical, at the institute's pace and direction of development, he must have completed his inspection with a sense of deep satisfaction.

At four o'clock that afternoon the State Council met for its customary weekly session at the Tel Aviv museum in Rothschild Boulevard. Weizmann arrived an hour after its proceedings had commenced. Although there had been no prior announcement of his intended visit, the news of his presence filtered through to the populace and the streets of Tel Aviv were crowded with well-wishers gathered to applaud him. Dressed in a white suit, his eyes protected by dark glasses, Weizmann entered the hall with his party. The atmosphere was more formal than usual: those without ties and jackets were in a small minority—an unfamiliar sight in an assembly where the pioneering ethos, even in matters sartorial, was dominant. Members of the diplomatic corps were present, in particular the Soviet envoy, Pavel Ivanovitch, and the American special representative, James G. McDonald. Weizmann, leaning on the arm of Dr. Simon, approached the chairman's dais. As he entered the jammed hall, the assembly rose to its feet, acclaiming the President in a burst of spontaneous applause. Sprinzak guided Weizmann to his place of honour. He recognized some friends in the audience and waved to them. One witness felt that the meeting was not 'unlike one of the first sessions of the American Congress under the Articles of Confederation. On all sides there was great earnestness, and written clearly in the faces of most of the actors were marks of a long struggle.'[5]

Prime Minister David Ben Gurion introduced him to the members of his cabinet. The welcoming speeches by Sprinzak and Ben Gurion were brief and formal. Weizmann had prepared notes for this occasion, but, hands in jacket pockets, he spoke impromptu, in a low but clear tone, although at times trembling with emotion, expressing his thanks for this moving welcome. 'The great honour which you have accorded me,' he told his audience, 'bears an equally great responsibility. To the best of my capacity I shall endeavour to follow the ancient political principle which I adopted as my guide many years ago: "Zion shall be redeemed with judgement, and her converts with righteousness".'* For his colleagues in the struggle for independence, now laden with ministerial titles, he wished that 'they be strong and be favoured with wisdom', adding hopefully: 'Whatever political experience I may have gathered during the course of my life, I place at the service of the State.' 'We flew here,' he continued, 'in the first Israeli aircraft manned by young Jewish men and women, born here and abroad, united in the will to create and defend the State. I send my greetings to the young generation . . . which bears the brunt of battle and is sacrificing its youth.' His voice broke only when, in concluding his address, he recited the prayer: 'Blessed art Thou, O Lord our God, King of the Universe, who has kept us in life, and hast preserved us and enabled us to reach this day.'

Outside the hall a crowd of many thousands had congregated, waiting patiently for another glimpse of Weizmann. Clearly overcome by the warmth of his reception, he paused on the steps of the building and extended his New Year's greetings to his admirers. The *Palestine Post* later reported: 'As Dr. Weizmann left the Tel Aviv museum this evening after his reception by the State Council, a woman thrust an infant toward him and asked him to kiss it. She said her child would be blessed all his life if he were kissed by the first President of Israel.' He then returned home to Rehovot.

The dramatic, crowded events of 30 September 1948 marked the consummation of Weizmann's life's work. For at least a generation he had led, indeed dominated, whether in or out of office, the Zionist

---

* His favorite verse from Isaiah 1:27.

movement and Jewish communal life. As a child of eleven he had implored the Jews to seek their salvation in Palestine—'to Zion let us go!'[6] Now, at the age of seventy-four, old and exhausted, 'a myth in his lifetime',[7] he had returned to Zion as President of Israel, a sovereign Jewish state, the first for two thousand years.

ONE

FAIR BEGINNINGS

Chaim Weizmann's birthplace, the 'half-town, half-village' of Motol, stands some twenty-five miles north-west of Pinsk, 'a provincial metropolis' of thirty thousand inhabitants. Now incorporated as part of the Belorussian Socialist Soviet Republic, these landmarks were then situated in the province of Minsk, in the area generally known as White Russia, bordering the old kingdom of Poland. As Weizmann recalled, 'Motol was situated in one of the darkest and most forlorn corners of the Pale of Settlement, that prison-house created by czarist Russia for its Jewish population.'[1]

Imperial Russia's Jewish policy was trapped between the desire to exclude Jews from Holy Russia and the gradual expansion of Russian sovereignty into areas thickly populated by Jews chiefly as a result of the partitions of Poland in the late eighteenth century. The Pale of Settlement was its answer to this dilemma. By a *ukaz* of Catherine II in 1792, Jews were confined to certain territories along Russia's northern and eastern borders annexed from Poland in 1772. During the nineteenth century the system was institutionalized until finally Jews were permitted to settle in an area that included Russian Poland, Lithuania, Belorussia, most of the Ukraine, the Crimea, and Bessarabia. According to the census of 1897, almost five million Jews were concentrated in this zone of permitted settlement. Many of them had been forcibly herded into the Pale from their homes in outlying areas, often by the most brutal means. Some Jews were granted the right to reside outside the prescribed areas, but these were a pitifully small minority.

Even inside the Pale, the right of Jews to live anywhere was curtailed. Excluded from some of the larger cities—Kiev, Sebastopol, and

Yalta, for example (unless they succeeded in acquiring a special permit)—they were also subject to periodic expulsions from rural areas, particularly from those regions adjacent to Russia's western frontiers. Consequently Russian Jewry underwent an enforced process of urbanization so that by the turn of the century more than 80 per cent of them were either city or town dwellers. It is not by chance that the *shtetl* (small town) has gained such an exalted place in the Jewish folklore of the period. Dire overcrowding and impoverishment, often bordering on pauperism, were the normal lot of these unfortunate people. An English M.P. has left a graphic description of the plight of Vilna's 150,000 Jews at the turn of the century, their material conditions contrasting starkly with the city's reputation as 'the Citadel of Culture':

> There are probably few better places than Vilna in which to study a Jewish ghetto in all its original picturesque squalor and poverty. In many parts the streets are so narrow that only one vehicle can pass at a time. . . . At intervals along these narrow streets there are arched gateways leading into court-yards, round which the miserable dens and cellars in which the people live are clustered, and it is here that the housing conditions of the Jewish poor may be seen. . . . The walls of the houses were blistered and rotting, as if poisoned by the pestilent atmosphere within. Two and three families would be found in one miserable room or cellar rented at 45 roubles a year. They were mixed up together, regardless of age and sex and health. In one room I found a lunatic as a lodger among a family of four children. During my walks through the ghetto I was surrounded by a crowd of gaunt, curious, anxious faces—sad, careworn, hungry-looking people. Many openly begged alms. Some had trifles for sale. Others seemed to spend most of their time in the synagogue reading and rocking themselves into oblivion of their troubles.[2]

Shunned by the outside world, deprived of their most elementary civil and political rights, the Jewish masses in eastern Europe responded either by emigrating to more liberal countries or by following the chimera of revolution, or, in the case of the majority, by seeking refuge within their own tightly knit community. It was a world distinguished by extraordinarily rich tradition and culture. In a very real sense, the Pale constituted a sort of Jewish National Home. Confined to a single territory, bound together by a common language, sustained by an ancient and tragic heritage, united by the persecutions of a cruel adversary, the average Jew of the Pale was scarcely aware of the intellectual subtleties posed by such dubious concepts as 'dual loyalty' that so plagued his brethren in the West. Their everyday language, Yiddish, was inventive, infinitely varied, and generated a literature as rich as any in the world, while the last decades of the nineteenth century witnessed a vigorous revival of the Hebrew language, as both a spoken tongue and a literary form, itself a reliable indicator of a national renaissance. Weizmann, for example, wrote only in Hebrew to his father. East European Jewry possessed the superstructure of a national existence but without the solid foundation of a territorial base it could claim as its own.

Despite the abject poverty and despair, life in the Pale exuded a folksy attractiveness in retrospect, often shamelessly flattered by its literature. In fact, the security of this gigantic ghetto was illusory, and nothing should be allowed to mask the debilitating effects that such grinding poverty, political persecution, and racial prejudice had on those unfortunate enough to suffer them.

Many Jews, particularly from the intelligentsia, tried to escape the claustrophobic atmosphere of the Pale, by fleeing to western Europe where, since the Emancipation resulting from the French Revolution, new political and civil freedoms had prevailed that significantly altered the character of Jewish life. Yet having made the break they found themselves caught in a trap perhaps more deadly and insidious than the one they had abandoned, for inherent in the Jewish situation at this time was a great paradox: the principles of the French Revolution promised freedom and equality for all and held out the prospect of national redemption for oppressed minorities throughout Europe; yet if these principles were to be attained, how would the Jews safeguard their distinct and separate existence? Unlike other European national groups, they were unable to anchor their national survival in a legally recognized territory; all they possessed was a deep and powerful yearning for a land that had once been theirs but that they had never seen.

Of course, there were those who accepted assimilation into Gentile society, into the new Europe, as the most logical solution to the Jewish problem. In western and central Europe, where such a solution appeared feasible, they may have constituted the majority. Certainly the wealthy, the powerful, the ambitious tended to hold this view. But the process of emancipation was a sporadic and uneven affair, the pace differing from country to country, even province to province. Of more consequence, it did not formalize the equality of the Jewish community *per se* with other ethnic groups; it was a matter of individual, not corporate, entry into European society. Moreover, emancipation, apart from the immense benefits it advanced, also predictably bred the violence, not necessarily physical, of anti-semitism resulting from the intrusion of Jews into hitherto restricted areas. Often the cohesion and distinctiveness of Jewish communities offended the ethos of the incipient nationalisms which rejected parochial loyalties as divisive and hence dangerous to the coming social order. It can surely be no coincidence that the revolutions of 1848—'the spring of nations'—ushered in fresh outbreaks of anti-semitism in central Europe.

However convincingly Jews argued that these misfortunes were but the residue of medieval superstition and could be overcome by rational argument, their protestations contained a hollow ring. In the background there persisted a nagging suspicion that the assimilation of European Jewry, even if attainable, would be a drawn-out and painful process. None of this, however, touched upon perhaps the most pertinent point of all: why, in an age of rampant nationalism, should the Jews, of their own volition, abandon their national heritage? Was there not something degrading and humiliating in this spectacle? After all, had not the Declaration of the Rights of Man proclaimed, 'Sovereignty resides essentially in the nation as a whole; no group or individual can exercise any authority not expressly delegated to it or him'?

It has become a commonplace to link the revival of Jewish nationalism with its European counterparts. Yet the precise points of contact are more difficult to discover. Certainly the Greek struggle for independence and the Italian *risorgimento* must have had a profound impact. Both causes were adopted by liberal Europe, and both signified the fervent desire of ancient and once powerful nations to reassert their destroyed nationhood. The comparison with the first stirrings of Jewish nationalism requires no emphasis. The early Zionist writers Judah Alkalai and Zevi Hirsch Kalischer, though firmly wedded to the messianic tradition, were clearly influenced by contemporary historical experience. But the most striking example was the work of Moses Hess, a scion of an assimilated German Jewish family, whose book *Rome and Jerusalem* (1860) postulated that the only viable solution for the Jewish problem was the rejuvenation of Jewish national life in *Erez Israel* (Palestine). The title of his book, considered a Zionist classic, speaks for itself. Writing under the intoxicating impact of the reunification of Italy, Hess was captive, as were most of the ideologues of European nationalism, to the cloudy, romantic terminology of the age, but his message was clear.

It would be misleading either to exaggerate or to minimize the importance of these early Zionist propagandists. Their writings were not overnight best-sellers. Indeed, Hess's work was more popular a generation after his death than during his lifetime. Their significance lay in another direction. They recognized, however hesitantly, the *malaise* in Jewish life. The Emancipation had not solved the Jewish question, nor would it. In some ways it had sharpened it, made it more acute. To their minds, assimilation, whatever its superficial attractions, was in fact a pernicious and self-defeating doctrine. For what was at stake was not merely a matter of physical survival; it was essentially an affair of the spirit. In the midst of material plenty, possibly as a result of it, there had emerged a spiritual crisis of the first magnitude: the great inner conflict of personal identity which, to this day, still torments many Jews. There was, they argued, but one honourable way out of this quandary: the reconstitution of Jewish national life in the ancient homeland.

By the 1870s the Jewish condition in the West had changed for the worse. The idealism of the Emancipation had run its first course. In 1873, an obscure Hamburg journalist, Wilhelm Marr, published a pamphlet entitled *Der Sieg des Judenthaus über das Germanthum* (The Victory of Judaism over Germanism). It achieved instant success. The modern anti-semitic movement may be dated from the appearance of this virulent tract. Marr wrote his work during a time of severe financial and economic crisis in Germany, particularly in Prussia and Austria, in which a number of Jews had been implicated for indulging in irresponsible, speculative transactions. These misdeeds were interpreted as a diabolical Jewish plot designed to corrupt the German nation and bring down Christian civilization in ruins. The Jewish banking fraternity—the Rothschilds, the Warburgs, the Bleichroders, with their international networks and easy access to the leaders of government—provided a soft and highly visible target for the professional anti-semites and the easily duped. Marr played on deep-rooted prejudices to construct a fantastic ideology of national-racial purity. His rantings were embraced by an eager audience. By October 1880 a German anti-semitic league had been formed. A bitter period ensued. Jews were insulted in public; duels were fought and lives lost; and petitions were circulated to exclude Jews from schools and universities and disbar them from public life.

The disease spread to other countries. France spawned its own distinguished exponent of the new faith, Edouard Droumont. His book, *La France Juive* (1886), and his newspaper, *La Libre Parole*, kept emotions at fever pitch. As in Germany, an anti-semitic league was established. In Austria, Karl Leuger, a gifted demagogue and leader of the Christian Socialist Party, was elected mayor of Vienna on an anti-semitic platform. Nor was the new anti-semitism confined to politicians on the make, right-wing fanatics, or frustrated journalists. Left-wing intellectuals such as Pierre-Joseph Proudhon and Charles Fourier trailed along, invariably invoking the noblest of causes to mask their prejudice. It was with much justification that August Bebel condemned anti-semitism as the 'socialism of fools'.

The growth of racial anti-semitism raised questions of a fundamental nature for those Jewish liberals who had hitherto linked their future with that of European society in general. The pseudo-scientific teachings of Marr and his camp-followers erected barriers which were impervious to rational discussion. It was now a matter of genes, of preserving the purity of the nation's blood. A new dimension was added to anti-Jewish bigotry, at once arbitrary, unpredictable, and terrifying in its implications. Few believed at the time that it would lead eventually to genocide. But the popularity of the new philosophy deeply shocked Jewish intellectuals. If nothing else, intellectual honesty demanded an answer to the question whether or not assimilation was possible, not because the Jews did not want it, but because the majority would not allow it. Of more consequence, was emigration to other countries a viable solution? Or would this not merely transfer the problem from one land to another? Here was decisive proof that hatred of the Jews was not confined to backward Russia alone; the progressive West was also blighted by the same malady. As Weizmann later noted: 'In the West it was an open fight, in the East a conspiracy. The West preached liberty, the East practised repression; but East and West alike were enemies of the Zionist ideology.'[3] It was these developments, together with the intensification of the Jewish plight in eastern Europe, which stimulated the growth of Jewish national consciousness and gave an irresistible impulse to the consolidation of political Zionism as a force in the modern world.

At first, these questions troubled no more than a tiny minority. In a very real sense, the fate of the Jewish world would be decided in eastern Europe, and here developments followed a line parallel to those in the West but, predictably, with more brutal, violent, and widespread manifestations.

On 13 March 1881 Alexander II, the 'Tsar Liberator', was assassinated. (Among the revolutionaries was a young Jewess, Hesia Helfman; she was, however, only marginally implicated in the plot.) His successor, Alexander III, determined to avoid a similar fate, released the machinery for the suppression of dissident, revolutionary elements within his Empire. That Easter the Jewish community at Elizavatgrad, in southern Russia, was attacked; the wave of assaults on Jews and Jewish property that this inaugurated did not subside until the early summer of 1884. Hardly a major Jewish center escaped unscathed. And the statistics of violence were sufficiently alarming to prick the conscience of liberal Europe, although they fade in significance when compared with the horrors of our own age.*

Apart from the appalling physical consequences of these calamities, a moral reckoning had also to be made. There was little doubt that at the local, provincial level the authorities had abetted in the instigation of the pogroms. But it was also widely believed that they had been encouraged, even organized, by order of the highest government authority. The truth of this assumption has never been decisively proven one way or the other.[4] But it was certainly beyond dispute that the Tsarist regime had done nothing to deter the train of murder and pillage. If there was no satisfaction to be gained from the authorities, there was equally little to be obtained from Russian liberals and revolutionaries who claimed to perceive in the pogroms the first harbinger of social revolution, an uncontrollable outburst, as it were, by the Russian masses blindly exacting retribution for centuries of cruel exploitation. It was Vladimir Medem, a prominent Bund† ideologist, who

---

* Authenticated reports of the pogroms reached the West by the autumn of 1881. By the end of the year an estimated 215 pogroms had been perpetrated, mainly in southern and south-western Russia. At Korets, a fairly typical example, 1000 buildings were put to the torch and 39 people killed. These events were graphically described in the western press, and led to vigorous protests by some religious and lay leaders protesting the atrocities.

† The *Bund* (Allgemeiner Jiddischer Arbeiterbund in Lite, Poilnun, Russland, which is Yiddish for General Confederation of Jewish Workers in Lithuania, Poland, and Russia) was founded in 1897. Affiliated to the Russian Socialist Democratic Party, it viewed the Jewish problem as an integral part of the general class struggle and hence argued that the Jewish masses should cooperate in the revolutionary struggle against Tsarism. The Bund retained its Jewish identity as an organization but denied any national status for the Jews as being counter-revolutionary, apparently oblivious to the obvious contradiction.

coined the saying: 'Jewish blood spilt during the pogroms acts as oil on the wheels of the revolution.'[5] The pogroms were not a transient phenomenon. On the contrary, they evolved into an endemic feature of Russian life and were renewed with even greater intensity some twenty years later.

These atrocities killed any hope that Russia would evolve into a more tolerant regime. In May 1882 anti-Jewish violence was legally consecrated by a series of edicts that both tightened and expanded the existing legislation restricting Jewish rights. Known as the May laws, they were applied with particular 'savagery and ingenuity', and in this way it was hoped that 'our great ulcer', as one powerful Russian cleric put it, would be effectively eradicated.[6]

How did the Jews react to these disasters? The majority either remained where they were, kept at home by the force of inertia, or the fear of change; or, in ever increasing numbers, flocked westward, part of the great migratory movement that between the years 1881 and 1914 carried almost 2.6 million Jews from eastern Europe to the West, mainly the United States.

The pogroms provided the catalyst for the growth of the *Hibbat Zion* (Love of Zion) movement. This was not a homogeneous group. Young and intense idealists, the *Biluim* (an acronym for the Hebrew phrase *Beth Ya'akov lechu venelecha*: O House of Jacob, come and let us go), mingled with Jews who, though inspired by the national ethic, were not impervious to more material inducements. Influenced by a potent mixture of the old messianic-religious beliefs tempered by the new nationalist orthodoxy, the *Hovevei Zion* (Lovers of Zion) saw in Palestine the solution to the Jewish problem. Initially, the movement lacked a clearly defined, organizational structure. It possessed neither a precise programme nor a dominant leader. Groups, societies, circles of Jews met and debated. The atmosphere was evangelical:

> The meeting was very crowded. The throats of the speakers were sore from excess of talk and excess of smoke. The discussion was very stormy and went on for four or five hours. . . . Those participating in the discussion were solely concerned with the choice of the country of migration; there was no debate on whether or not Russia should be left for some other country in which an independent state would be established; it was not an issue. The meeting did not vote on a clear-cut resolution. But by the time we left the hall we ourselves were already enthusiastic *Hovevei Zion* . . . and had already formed the simple and absolute de-

cision to found a society of young people who would go to Erez Israel
and settle there.[7]

There was undeniably something of a populist, revivalist character
to the movement, at least in its early stages. The first settlers literally
got up and voted with their feet. Various attempts were made to coordinate their activities. In November 1884, at Kattowitz in Upper
Silesia, a loose administrative framework was agreed on. Committees
were set up in Odessa, Warsaw, and Berlin, and preliminary feelers
were extended to the Russian and Turkish authorities to facilitate
immigration to Palestine.

Although in the opinion of one observer the results of Kattowitz
were 'misty and puzzling', the Hovevei Zion could point to some substantial achievements. Their societies mushroomed, so that by 1885
they could count sixty such groups with a total membership of fourteen
thousand.[8] In Palestine, eight new settlements had been founded with
a combined population of two and a half thousand. True, the movement
was rudimentary and lacked all political sophistication, but it was the
forerunner of the modern Zionist movement.

European Jewry in both the enlightened West and the obscurantist
East had entered a period of deep crisis. 'My childhood,' Weizmann
later recalled, 'was passed in a world which was breaking up under
the impact of renewed persecution.'[9] Old patterns of behaviour were
disappearing, new ones emerging. Responses to the Jewish question,
once considered tenable, were now grudgingly discarded. It was a world
in desperate need of new answers to age-old problems, and decades
later the eminent historian Lewis Namier trenchantly described them:

> Israel has to face the practical problem of its existence and of its
> uncertain future—a stupendous process of reorientation in the oldest
> and most tenacious of races. Some of us find the solution in dissolution,
> others are determined actively to work for the 'miracle' for which we
> have hitherto waited. Orthodox Jewry is a melting glacier and Zionism
> is the river which springs from it; evaporation and the river result from
> the same process, and both are its necessary results.[10]

It was into this transient yet exciting and stimulating world that Chaim
Azriel, third child to Ozer and Rachel-Leah Weizmann, was born on
27 November 1874.[11]

* * *

Weizmann's father and mother emerge as the archetype parent-figures of Jewish tradition: kind, tolerant, observant, worldly wise, ambitious for their children. They had met when, as a youth, Ozer had arrived in Motol to pursue his religious studies. He himself was born in Syerniki, a nearby village even less grand than Motol. At Motol he lodged with his aunt Hanna, while his uncle, reb Shmuel Yitzchak, renowned as the local wit, supervised his religious instruction. One day when visiting friends, Rachel found there 'a fourteen year old boy, somewhat pale, with blue-grey eyes that penetrated the soul, and black curls around his head; a beautiful and attractive boy. In Motol, she hadn't seen anything like him'.[12] Despite strident protests from her family, who had already contracted a marriage arrangement on her behalf, 'she announced vehemently . . . that she loved Ozer and wanted him for a bridegroom'. Strong-willed and resolute, she soon made her parents capitulate before her determination. The young couple celebrated their engagement when Rachel attained the age of thirteen; her prospective bridegroom was just two years her senior.[13] The marriage was both happy and fruitful: Chaim remembered his mother as 'either pregnant, or nursing an infant'.[14] She bore Ozer fifteen children, twelve of whom, seven girls and five boys, survived to adulthood.

To an outside observer, Ozer was 'a quiet, reticent man, well versed in traditional Jewish learning and practice and of a natural gentility'.[15] Yet he clearly possessed sterner characteristics, his 'natural gentility' tempered by an inner authority acknowledged by his neighbours Jew and Gentile alike. There were about him, his son thought, the qualities of 'an aristocrat, an intellectual, and something of a leader too'.[16] This filial appreciation was shared by his contemporaries, for he was the only Jew to be elected *starosta* (headman) of Motol, a singular appointment for those times. A *maskil* (a Jew who followed the Enlightenment), his favourite reading was Maimonides, and on his bookshelves could be found the works of Gorki and Tolstoy, of modern Hebrew authors, Avraham Mapu or Peretz Smolenskin, Zionist literature, and even scientific textbooks.[17] It was a mark of his enlightened outlook that, despite his religious inclinations, he subscribed to a Russian radical journal with a deserved reputation as a paper that preached Jewish assimilation, but he supported it, his daughter recalled, because it also fought for Jewish rights in Russia and against religious fanaticism.[18] Acutely sensitive to the insecurity of the Pale, he would recite the *Birchat HaGomel* (a prayer to thank God for escaping from danger) several times a day. When asked why, he replied: Every day on his way to the synagogue he would meet gentile hooligans in the streets and he would be thankful that he was not beaten up or worse.[19]

His talents also extended to the synagogue. An amateur *chazan* (prayer-leader), he often led the community in prayers on High Holidays. Occasionally, angered by the petty bickerings of his congregation, he would ascend the pulpit, strike the lectern, and admonish the trouble-makers. He was a deeply observant man, but his was a religion not of blind obedience to his rabbi's dictates but of personal commitment to his faith. He abhorred the exploitation of religion for personal or political gain. His detestation of clericalism was to become a pronounced feature of his sons' political outlook.

Ozer Weizmann was also a subtle practitioner of the arts of village diplomacy, and developed an almost infallible recipe for success. As his son recalled: 'If a man insisted on telling him his side of the story he would listen patiently to the end and say. "From what you tell me, I can see that you are entirely in the wrong. Now I shall hear the other side; perhaps you are in the right after all".'[20] Patience and scepticism: these were invaluable lessons for his son to absorb. Apparently, he absorbed them well. One incident from his childhood stuck in his mother's memory for many years thereafter. Returning home from synagogue after prayers, Chaim and his parents passed by the house of one of the poorer residents of Motol. Through the window Rachel saw, standing on the table, her own silver candlesticks. Filled with anger at the theft, she wished to rush in immediately and retrieve her property. Chaim intervened: 'Today is a great festival, mother, do not embarrass those people on a holy day. It would be better if you wait until after the festival has ended.' Rachel listened to her son's counsel, though she never recovered her candlesticks.[21]

Chaim's mother, Rachel-Leah, appears in the family recollections as the proverbial Jewish matriarch, obsessively ministering to her brood's every whim. Demanding nothing but expecting everything, 'her hands were never idle—sloth was the only thing she hated'.[22] Forever in the kitchen—'"They've got to be fed, or they won't have the strength to shout"'—her daughter calculated that

she was busy twenty-four hours a day. She always had one or two babies and the small ones needed her care. She sewed and knitted all the clothes for the children. . . . The curtains on the many windows of the house were knitted or embroidered, and the tables were covered with tablecloths of her own creation. . . . In the summer, she would make jams of all kinds. . . . When father left town on business, she would continue his work from the house. And who knew as well as she how to bake all kinds of pastries for Shabbath or the festivals? And on Sundays, she would bake bread for the whole week.[23]

In contrast to Ozer, Rachel had little formal education and she was wholly literate only in Yiddish. A childhood attempt to acquire French had been frustrated by her grandmother. 'See child, don't be foolish! Your forefathers weren't in France and didn't know French, and your children will not be in France and will not speak French; why should you waste your time in unnecessary things like that?' Nevertheless, she remembered some phrases and short poems, and when in high spirits she would, to the delight of her children, recite them in French. Rachel developed intellectually in the wake of her children's experience. She insisted on learning Russian in order to follow the stormy political and literary arguments that increasingly preoccupied her children. When she seized upon *Anna Karenina* to improve her Russian, she was deeply impressed by the tragic heroine, but it was beyond her comprehension to grasp how 'such a feminine woman' could abandon her family and position for the sake of a grand passion.[24]

It was a boisterous household over which Rachel presided. The Weizmann clan 'roared and trumpeted, constantly erupting into a noisy babble of Hebrew, Yiddish, and Russian. They conducted multi-lingual quarrels and reconciliations; they emitted polyglot bellows of friendship and love, satisfaction and contentment'.[25] When her offspring had attained a measure of independence, she remained constantly on watch to protect her flock against arbitrary arrest by the Tsarist police, hiding Zionist and socialist subversive literature from their scrutiny and confronting these terrible figures of authority with, Chaim remembered, 'such dignity, and with such a sudden air of innocence . . . that she invariably disarmed the intruders'.[26] She apparently thrived on the excitement. Unlike Ozer, who died in his early sixties in 1911, Rachel-Leah lived to the venerable age of eighty-seven, and died in 1939, surrounded by her family, at her home in Haifa. She was a matriarch in the grand style who grew in stature in the eyes of her children once they had left home and dispersed throughout Europe. 'From Moscow to London we were drawn toward her.'[27]

Did she have a special premonition regarding Chaim's future? 'Leah-Rachel, you have borne a prince,' remarked a peasant woman after examining the child. No doubt the comment was little more than a polite sign of approval at the infant's health and glowing appearance.

But for some reason Rachel singled him out for preferential treatment, and sewed for Chaim shirts and nightgowns 'of specially fine linen or silk'.[28] Whether this was due to his delicate skin or simply because he was the favoured child, the 'treasure' of the family, it is impossible to say. It was an indulgence he maintained when he could afford to buy his own clothes.

Chaim's childhood was the world of the *shtetl*, and Motol, his birthplace, was typical of its kind. Virtually isolated from the outside world, it possessed neither railway nor paved roads nor even a regular postal service. Within its parochial confines two hundred Jewish families lived cheek by jowl with their more numerous Russian neighbours. The mainly Polish landowning gentry and the Russian peasantry surrounding them, despite at times an outward display of friendliness, constituted the worst possible combination for the Jews. Anti-semitism was endemic to both these classes, and their enmity was made clear to Chaim from the outset by his maternal grandfather, Michael Yikhael Tchemerinsky, who told how he 'had to kiss the hand of Polish noblemen and chant Jewish prayers for their pleasure, while . . . [he] was forced to climb a tree and imitate a cuckoo, on threat of being shot'.[29]

The contradictions inherent in *shtetl* life extended beyond the tensions of its inner being. Economically and physically inseparable from its environs, it lived in a spiritual world of its own, as remote from the Russian experience as one galaxy is from another. From the pages of Yiddish literature appears a portrait of a Jewish child, a typical product of the *shtetl*:

> He could not tell you a thing about Russia, about Poland, about Lithuania and its peoples, laws, kings, politicians. . . . But you just ask him about Og, King of Bashan, and Sihon, King of the Amorites, and Nebuchadnezzer, King of Babylon! Ask him about the Euphrates and the Jordan. He knew about the people who lived in tents and spoke Hebrew or Arabic. . . . He knew nothing concerning the fields about him, nothing about rye, wheat, potatoes, and where he got his bread from. . . . But he knew about vineyards, date palms, pomegranates, locust-trees . . . he lived in another world.[30]

Chaim himself, according to his own account, knew hardly a word of Russian until he was eleven.[31] Given the general thrust of their unique form of primary education, there is little need to emphasize the centrality of Palestine and the Return in the hopes and minds of the Jews of the Pale. These values were drummed into generation upon generation of Jewish children at *cheder* (school). Chaim began his education at the age of four. There was an immediate confrontation with his parents when he refused categorically to attend the normal classes designated for beginners. Instead, he insisted that rebbi Berl Bloch, a luminary brought in specially from Pinsk to tutor his eldest sister Miriam privately, should also teach him. He shut his ears to all rational argument. Eventually his rebelliousness paid off, and he too, at first, benefited from preferential treatment. Later, he reconciled himself to the system. 'If my *cheder* differed from others, it was perhaps in the possession of a family goat which took shelter with us in cold weather. And if my first Rebbi, or teacher, differed from others, it was in the degree of his pedagogic incompetence.'³² There was little finesse in these establishments. Perhaps his rebbi resembled Sholem Aleichem's Yudel the Scribe (or even Dickens's Dr. Wackford Squeers): 'Boys don't study with him; they're afraid. He hits . . . with a ruler over the hand. . . . I'm in school half a day. I study very little but I make up for it in slaps. From the teacher? No, from his wife.'³³ The rebbi, Avraham Yitzchak (known as the "Red" because of his red hair), was a notorious figure among the children of Motol. Portly and broad-shouldered, he was apt to doze during lessons, and, angry at being woken up to fulfill his duties, he would pinch and hit his pupils at their slightest mistakes. It was in this uninspiring atmosphere that Chaim studied the Talmud and Torah.

His biblical and Hebrew studies, however, were brightened by an exception to the rule: a teacher 'with a real enthusiasm' for his subjects that he succeeded in imparting to his pupils. Rebbi Avraham Mete-lenski (nicknamed the "Black" for his black hair) was clearly unique among his peers, a devoted teacher who was greatly admired by his young and impressionable students. A *maskil* and *Hovev Zion*, he in-troduced them to modern Hebrew authors, particularly Smolenskin and Mapu; conducted elementary classes in political science, explain-ing the nature of despotism and republicanism, of parliamentary de-mocracy and autocratic regimes; and discussed the social and political issues of the day. Although he was deeply religious, he shunned fa-naticism. He was innovative, open to change. On one occasion, he introduced into the classroom a textbook in Hebrew on natural science and chemistry: 'He would have us read with him some pages which seemed to him to be of special interest. We read, of course, and in the Talmudic chant hallowed by tradition, so that anyone passing by the school would never suspect that we were not engaged in the sacred pursuits proper to a Hebrew school.' They may not have comprehended what they were chanting, but it was Chaim's first introduction to the mysteries of chemistry. Metelenski made a profound and lasting impression on the Weizmann children. Particularly fond of Chaim, he quickly recognized the boy's intellectual potential and did all in his power to foster it. Chaim responded to Metelenski's imaginative methods, and he was widely considered as his prize pupil. Their friendship lasted until the rabbi's death.[34]

There were times when the Weizmann children were left to their own devices. Ozer's business ventures kept him away from home for long periods, while Rachel always had, or so it appeared, a new infant to care for or was engrossed in Ozer's business affairs. Perhaps for these reasons Chaim lived with his maternal grandparents for three years from the age of five, years that remained engraved on his memory.[35] 'I remember vividly those days—especially the winter mornings. Grandpa used to get up early, while it was still pitch dark, but the house was always beautifully warm, however severe the frost outside. First of all we said the morning prayers; then came breakfast.' Chaim would listen, lost in an enchanted world, while 'grandpa' regaled him with fabulous stories of Jewish heroes. One tale made a particularly forceful impression. When 'Sir Moses [Montefiore] came to Vilna, one of the oldest and most illustrious Jewish settlements in Russia, and the Jews of that community came out to welcome him . . . [they] unharnessed the horses and dragged [his] carriage . . . in solemn procession through the streets.' It was a wonderful story, one he never tired of hearing.

'Chaimke', as he was affectionately called, was terribly spoiled by his grandparents. Fruma, his grandmother, compared him repeatedly and favourably to 'an angel from heaven'. He was grandfather Michael's special 'treasure' and the old man would not hesitate to travel to Pinsk, a tedious and fatiguing journey in those days, to reward his favourite with a toy or sweets. In the winter, he would build snow-hills in the garden for Chaimke's amusement, tempting him with a primitive form of winter sports. Of the twelve siblings, Chaim alone enjoyed the advantages and disadvantages of an only child for these years. It is perhaps no surprise that he was deeply attached to his grandparents, for whom he could do no wrong. When Michael died in 1887, Chaim, then thirteen, could scarcely contain his grief. He was found huddled up in a corner of the yard crying, 'Grandpa hurts me.'

Michael Yikhael was devout to an extreme, and he scrupulously observed the minutiae of his religion. Some of this rubbed off on Chaim, who gained a reputation as an exceptionally religious child, so much so that Michael singled him out for a religious calling, dreaming, perhaps, of his grandson becoming a great rabbi in Israel. When it came time for Chaim to leave to study at the Gymnasium in Pinsk, Michael raised objections on the grounds that Chaim would neglect his religious duties, although he realized that Chaim had outgrown Motol. But Chaim promised faithfully that he would never succumb to the secular attractions of Pinsk: never, he declared, would he write on the Sabbath. Thus assured, Michael gave his consent.

Ozer must have been a remote figure to his children, mainly because of the obligations of his work. He was a *transportierer* in a business he had inherited from Michael Yikhael, and his work consisted of cutting timber and transporting it downriver to the port of Danzig, a journey of some 450 miles. He would work his way westward along the waterway system for the hundred or so miles to Brest, where he would manoeuvre his rafts onto the Bug River; the Bug would carry him to the Vistula, just north of Warsaw, and thence he would proceed to the Baltic coast. It was seasonal work: the cutting began in November, and the transporting of the logs went on all winter and summer, terminating the following autumn. Chaim often spent the long summer weeks on his father's enormous rafts, complete with cabins and kitchens, travelling almost as far as Warsaw and then returning home by train. His accounts of these journeys retain something of the flavour of a Wild West saga: navigating floods and shallows, thwarting the machinations of petty, corrupt officials, until finally and triumphantly the merchandise is delivered.

Motol was situated on a tributary of the Pripyet River and adjacent to a large lake, and Chaim could indulge in sailing, one of the few sports that captured his imagination as a youth—although perhaps more for the opportunities it offered him to express his qualities of leadership than for the actual physical satisfaction. His sister remembered:

> Pinkus, the old farmer, knew that before Chaimke's coming he had to repair the boats, for when he came the sailing season began. In our childhood we all learnt the art of sailing, and the beautiful lake in Motol often heard our singing. Other boats would go out with our boat, and Chaimke would captain this modest fleet. He would organize most of the children in one group, and they always looked up to him as a person of distinction, a superior being.[36]

Later he bragged that he 'could weather almost any storm in a primitive Russian boat. It's called *"douschegoubka"* [soul-killer].' 'Those were jolly times,' he recalled. [37]

Although Ozer's business fortunes fluctuated, they improved steadily overall, and his family, by the standards of the day, was fairly well-to-do. At peak seasons he employed between fifty and sixty workers, mainly gentiles, with whom he maintained amicable relations. He conducted his business affairs in an orderly manner. His accounts were meticulously kept, and his office even boasted printed stationery. The Weizmanns' annual income averaged $250–$300, not a princely fortune but enough to provide more than adequately for the family's material needs, especially as much of their food was home-produced. They lived on 'the right side of the tracks', as it were, or the right of the river that divided the wealthier, more established families of Motol from the poorer; and they attended the Old, rather than the New, Synagogue. Their house was a large wooden bungalow, consisting of seven rooms and a kitchen, with spacious, tall windows that provided plenty of light and air, in marked contrast to most of the houses in Motol. One entered the house via a wide veranda on one side, used for relaxation in the summer. On the walls, apart from the inevitable family photographs, hung pictures of famous European political figures: the great assembly at Berlin in 1878; Queen Victoria, her head covered by a shawl; even a print depicting the assassination of Alexander II. But pride of place was given to a portrait of Sir Moses Montefiore, that legendary figure who had come from far-away Britain to save the Jews of eastern Europe.

The house stood in its own grounds, surrounded on three sides by trees and marked off from its neighbours by a picket-fence. One remarkable feature was its flower-gardens, unusual for Motol, which Rachel tended with care. For Motol, it must have appeared a fine establishment.

On the Weizmanns' few acres of land they maintained some chickens, cows, a vegetable garden, and fruit trees; to attend this fair-sized estate, with its barns and stable, they employed a young Russian peasant. They were even able to afford house servants. 'Ahapa', an elderly Russian woman who had nursed Rachel as a child, helped also to nurse Rachel's children. Their devoted man-servant, Yakim, somewhat addicted to the bottle, remained with the family until they left Pinsk toward the end of the First World War. He fascinated the Weizmann children by teaching them Russian folk-songs. He held a particular respect for Chaim and during the First World War volunteered to go to London to take care of the by-now famous son.

Decently clothed and fed, nine of the Weizmann children eventually benefited from a university education, a prodigious feat for those times. This was not simply a manifestation of the Jewish search after learning, but reflected equally the considerable means at the family's disposal.

It was a close-knit family with a strong sense of mutual responsibility. When Ozer's parents died at a relatively early age, he accepted his two younger sisters, Bracha and Bila, into his household, and they grew up with his own children. The family followed a routine that consolidated the bonds between them. Every Friday, except in the most dire emergency, Ozer would return home to celebrate the Sabbath. The house was prepared and the candles lit. After everyone had changed into their Sabbath best, they partook of the traditional meal replete with freshly baked *chalot*, sweet wine, and Sabbath songs. Ozer would then retire to take a cat-nap. When he reappeared and took his place at the head of the table, the family would reconvene for what can only be described as a kind of collective reading evening. Ozer, 'with wrinkled brow from the effort', as his daughter Haya recollected, would study either the Gemorrah or something by Maimonedes, or even a book on Russian law. Rachel would immerse herself in her Yiddish stories. Miriam, the eldest daughter, and her fiancé, Chaim Lubzhinsky, would soak up the news from the latest journals or amuse themselves with contemporary Hebrew novels. The younger children, anxious not to be outdone by their elders, buried themselves in the Torah.[38] These scenes, touching in their combination of seriousness and gaiety, of tradition and innovation, were an integral element in Chaim's overall education.

Although Chaim left home at an early age, the strong family bonds were conceivably strengthened as a consequence of his new-found independence. His relationship with his parents continued on an even keel—allowing, of course, for inevitable, natural differences of opinion and outlook between generations. His sense of family obligation, his affection for his grandparents, parents, brothers and sisters were robust and mature enough to withstand the casual tensions that occasionally arose. Once he had achieved a degree of economic selfsufficiency, he felt compelled to ensure that his siblings' education was not disrupted for lack of financial means, even, at least on one occasion, to the point of conceding them priority over his fiancée's straitened circumstances.[39] And in 1921, when he was engaged in great affairs, he managed to send enough money to his sister Haya, then trapped in war-torn Moscow, to enable her to escape to Poland and eventually to Palestine. Although in later life he was given to moments of elation and despair, these moods may be explained more convincingly by the dramatic, kaleidoscopic course of his life than by sensational episodes in his childhood. His behaviour as a mature adult was normally idiosyncratic. Chaim never complained of a deprived childhood, although equally he never romanticized the circumstances of his upbringing.

TWO

APPRENTICESHIP

In the autumn of 1885 Chaim Weizmann left home to attend the Gymnasium in Pinsk. He was eleven years old. Of average height and slender build, his general demeanor imparts a seriousness in excess of his years. No trace of a smile lightens his countenance; perhaps such levity was frowned upon by photographers of the period. His face is oval, with highish cheekbones, and his complexion pale. His sharp and searching eyes, his most striking feature, gaze intensely off into the future. Fastidiously dressed (a habit he retained as an adult) in a frock-coat and a cravatte, his hair neatly trimmed and brushed, one hand carefully placed on a chair, the other clasping his hat, he appears as the epitome of middle-class respectability.

No other young Motolite had pursued his education outside the boundaries of his *shtetl*. Chaim's intellectual precociousness is amply confirmed in a letter he wrote to one of his teachers, presumably his Russian and Hebrew master, just before he departed for Pinsk. It is the first letter he wrote that has been preserved. 'A childish letter of a Motol boy,' he reminisced later, 'but it tells its own story'.[1] After proclaiming his allegiance to 'our sacred tongue . . . the Hebrew language', he reaffirmed his faith in his religion, no doubt intended finally to lay to rest the fears of his family and teachers: 'Do not imagine that when I attend the Gymnasium I shall throw off the garb of Judaism. No! On no account. I have determined in my heart to observe Judaism and I shall oppose the opinion of those who say that one becomes a doctor because he casts off his faith.' In a postscript Chaim demonstrated beyond doubt that, despite his years, he was well abreast of contemporary events, particularly in the Jewish world. 'I am sending you one of my ideas . . . AND THAT CONCERNS HEVRAT HOVEVEI ZION [The Society of Lovers of Zion] AND JERUSALEM WHICH IS IN OUR LAND. How lofty and elevated the idea which inspired our brethren the sons of Israel to establish the Hovevei Zion Society. Because by this we can rescue our exiled, oppressed brethren who are scattered in all corners of the world and have no place where to put up their tents.' After pledging his support for the Hovevei Zion, which 'sees the evil threatening us', and thanking 'the two patriots . . . Moshe *Montefiore and Rothschild*', Chaim excluded all countries other than Palestine as a refuge for the Jewish people: 'Let us carry our banner TO ZION AND RETURN TO OUR FIRST MOTHER UPON WHOSE KNEES WE WERE BORN. —For why should we look to the kings of Europe for compassion that they should take pity upon us and give us a resting place? In vain! All have decided: THE JEWS MUST DIE, but England will nevertheless have mercy upon us. In conclusion to Zion!—Jews—to Zion! let us go.'[2]

In view of his later British-oriented policy, both too much and too little has been read into this remarkable letter. At best, it was a child's recognition of the image Great Britain claimed in the eyes of persecuted Jewry and, indeed, in those of other oppressed national minorities: a highly civilized, humane, tolerant, liberal power whose sympathies and, conceivably, political support could be relied upon. Anglophile sentiment was a commonplace of Jewish intellectual life in eastern Europe, and Chaim, fascinated by his grandfather's yarns about Sir Moses Montefiore, had imbibed something of this sentiment.

But what makes the letter so extraordinary, for a boy of eleven, is its steadfast commitment to Zionism. There was nothing inevitable about this. Within the general context of East European Jewish life, the Hibbat Zion was something of a maverick organization, numbering, in 1885, some fourteen thousand of whom but a trickle eventually found their way to Palestine. Every Jew had to make his own reckoning. One of Chaim's brothers, reacting, one assumes, to the same stimuli, preferred the revolutionary path and died in a Russian penal colony at the end of the second world war. Nor, at this stage, could the Weizmann household claim to be Zionist. It was, as Chaim remembered it, 'steeped in rich Jewish tradition, and Palestine was at the centre of the ritual, a longing for it implicit in our life';[3] but the same could be said of hundreds of thousands of other Jewish families throughout the Pale.

Young Chaim's Zionism was a youngster's emotional, instinctive response to the condition of his people as he perceived it, reinforced by a traditional upbringing and youthful idealism and nurtured by stories he had picked up in his family circle. The sorry plight of the Jews, the pervading anti-semitism that warped every aspect of Jewish life, the interminable debates on the future of the Jewish people—all this was an integral part of the intellectual and emotional inheritance of Jews from the Pale. But Chaim remained totally dedicated, until the end of his life, to the credo he first enunciated at the age of eleven: 'Jews—to Zion! let us go.'

Compared to Motol, Pinsk was a bustling metropolis. Situated on the Pina River not far from its confluence with the Pripyet, and easily accessible to the great rivers Bug and Dneiper, it served as an *entrepôt* between southern and northern Russia and derived its wealth and importance from the timber and river trades. Certainly its libraries and hospitals, its factories and shops must have been a source of wonderment to the young and impressionable student. The mature Chaim Weizmann long retained a sentimental affection for Pinsk: 'Coming from Pinsk,' he was wont to remark, 'you are a guarantee of quick wit.'[4] Pinsk was a centre of Jewish learning and culture with approximately 70 per cent of its population being Jewish, and Zionist and Hebrew literature were in abundant supply. Pinsk was also a focal-point of Hovevei Zion activity, with an estimated 250 dues-payers in 1885.[5]

For about three years Chaim, his elder brother Feival, who was to learn lithography, and their aunt Bracha lodged with friends of the Weizmann family. Eventually, the economic burden of maintaining two sons away from home became too severe, and Feival was compelled to return to Motol to help run the family business; Chaim meanwhile accepted a job tutoring Saul Lurie, a son of one of the town's Jewish magnates, in return for which he received his daily keep and a sufficient income to cover his school expenses. He remained a member of the Luries' household until he left Pinsk in 1892.[6]

When Chaim returned home to Motol for the holidays it was a memorable occasion. His homecomings early acquired something of the mystique they retained in later years when he visited his family as a distinguished and influential man of great affairs. The house was carefully arranged, his room cleaned with special attention, fresh fruit was brought in for his benefit, and Rachel would prepare his favourite dish: barley and mushroom soup. His sister recalled,

> It was a festival for all of us, and for almost all the people of the town who regarded him as their favourite. At home, and in the homes of the uncles and the rest of the relatives, there were great preparations for his coming. . . . For Chaim in his youth was known for great wit, was light-hearted and happy, would artistically tell humourous stories, mimic every preacher and every rabbi . . . and everywhere he went he was the spirit of life.[7]

It was a trait of Chaim's—one that he exploited to excellent effect as a working politician and that singled him out from a majority of Zionist leaders—that he could expound on the most serious and weighty topics without losing his sense of humour. Witticisms and humourous anecdotes illustrated the lessons he conducted on Hibbat Zion to the children of Motol, in which he drew heavily on the tales of Avraham Mapu, founder of the modern Hebrew novel and himself a Hovev Zion: 'sometimes we felt ourselves alone with the heroes of these stories and lived through them'. As a consequence of these discussions, his young audience founded a Zionist group, the first of its kind in Motol. Chaim's career as a Zionist activist had already begun, at the age of twelve.[8]

His *barmitzvah* was, of course, an occasion of great rejoicing and family pride. As the day fell in November, during term time, it was celebrated in Pinsk and not in Motol. It was a modest affair: only his immediate family, close friends, and his rabbi, Shmuel Molkomeir, who taught him *Talmud*, attended. 'But, Blessed be His Name, it was enough honour for us,' recollected Rachel. 'Chaim's face glowed. He read his portion beautifully and his rabbi was overwhelmed with pleasure. The boy welcomed his guests in Russian and Hebrew. He spoke to them in an everyday, colloquial language, and it was then I felt that our Chaim had outgrown Motol. But when he spoke to me, it was the same Chaimel that I remembered as a small child.'[9] Here was a dichotomy that Chaim was to guard jealously in the future: his heritage as a *shtetl*-bred Jew complementing, not drowning, his experiences in the outside world, and vice versa. He preserved this delicate balance with, on the whole, a startling degree of success.

Inevitably, Chaim was drawn into Zionist youth activities in Pinsk, and these gradually absorbed much of his spare time. Violent discussions and lengthy arguments on Zionism and its alternatives with his fellow-students at the Gymnasium were a regular feature of his schooldays. Here also was his first initiation into the practical side of Zionist work: 'hour after hour I would go tramping through the mud. . . . I worked late into the night, but usually had the immense satisfaction of bringing in more money than anyone else.'[10] It was a drill he later perfected to a fine art, and he would claim, with some justice, the accolade of the greatest tax-collector in the history of the Jewish people.

Some letters survive from this period. Written to another of Lurie's sons, Ovsey, who, like Chaim, was studying away from home and in this sense was a kindred soul, they are somewhat pretentious in style and indulge in much name-dropping, perhaps understandable for a teenager eager to demonstrate his intellectual credentials. He recommended that Ovsey widen his general reading and tackle the works of Gogol, Turgenev, and Dostoevsky, novels which, one assumes, he had already ploughed through. As for himself: 'I . . . am now reading Weber—*The History of the Reformation*, and as fiction Machtet.'*

But the main theme of his message to Ovsey was on an entirely different plane. Be diligent and self-disciplined, he preached, for 'Laziness . . . is the basest of human failings; it brings in its wake a complete confusion in the human being, both in the moral and the physical sense, a complete demoralization.' Ovsey's parents were perturbed at his slow progress as a student, and Chaim spurred him on to greater efforts:

> If your work is satisfactory, try to improve it; if it is good—make it even better, for this is the main purpose of the happy years of your youth. I trust that you have already taken to heart everything your father has been saying about education in general and about reading in particular. The holidays are already approaching, and you ought to devote this free time to learning your history, a subject with which, as far as I remember, you are not very familiar as yet and which is essential to you, and to revising all you have learned up to now, in order that you may assimilate your subjects better in future. And remember mathematics and general reading, for the latter is essential too. When it comes to writing an essay, you must have the facts and ideas already well marshalled in your mind and not try to crib them from some book, for this is sheer waste of time and can never lead to anything sensible.

Never forget 'that great beneficial truth', he nagged his contemporary, who might well have been bewildered and discouraged by this unso-

---

*The references are to a Russian translation of Georg Weber's *Geschichte des Reformations-Zeitalters* (Leipzig, 1874) and to G. O. Machtet's novel *Zhid*, which treated with understanding a Jewish topic.

licited onslaught, 'that with an iron will and industry man can overcome all obstacles'.[11]

This was strong stuff for a youth of his years. Was he perhaps projecting his own anxieties onto Ovsey? Aware of the sacrifices his family was making on his behalf, he resolved not to ruin his relations with them by yielding to curable human frailties. His own routine was spartan: schoolwork; Hebrew studies; tutoring; and, for relaxation, his Zionist activities. He even began learning French and German, and once delighted his family by reciting Schiller's 'The Bell'. But whatever emotional difficulties or economic discomforts he encountered as a result of his prolonged separation from his family, he undoubtedly succeeded in his self-allotted tasks.

The qualities he tried to instill into Ovsey came more easily to himself. His own studies, as he modestly reported, were always 'going well', despite the scholarly airs of his instructors. Once again, there was a notable exception: his chemistry teacher, Kornienko. Apparently a scholar of some repute and 'a decent, liberal-minded fellow', he succeeded in stimulating Chaim's interest in his subject. 'Very possibly,' Chaim graciously recorded after mature reflection, 'I owe whatever I have been able to achieve in the way of science . . . [to] this gifted and fine-spirited teacher.'[12]

At the age of eighteen, a star graduate of the Pinsk Real-Gymnasium,[13] Chaim had to make a critical decision, one which confronted all young Jewish students bent on continuing higher education. He could remain in Russia, hoping to slip through the *numerous clausus* or, by trickery, to evade it. Or he could turn westward, as so many of his contemporaries had done. 'All my inclinations pointed to the West.'[14] In August 1892, fortified by the promise of further financial assistance from his parents, he crossed the German frontier at Thorn, a town on the Vistula some ninety miles south of Danzig, after making his last river journey on the great rafts. Characteristically, he fled the country of his birth without any official documents.

The substance of Weizmann's early years in Motol and Pinsk should be recognized as being decisive for his future. 'Pinsk . . . set the double pattern of my life; it gave me my first bent towards science, and it provided me with my first experiences in Zionism.'[15] He was, as he never tired of explaining, a typical product of the *shtetl*, but what set him apart from his contemporaries were the qualities he attempted to hammer into Ovsey: self-discipline; iron will; dedication; single-mindedness, even ruthlessness, when in pursuit of his goals—qualities that ran counter to the sterile practice of *shlimilishness* which permeated so much of *shtetl* life. Dreading he might after all fall victim to its allures,[16] Weizmann deliberately, consciously, excluded it from his life. Method and order were crucial factors in the success of his scientific career. Yet in a curious way, as a politician he could not escape his inheritance so easily. Something of the *shtetlnick* crept, reluctantly but noticeably, into his political style, at times much to the chagrin of his colleagues.[17] But for the time being, he set out for Germany intent on exploiting to the utmost the opportunities that awaited him in the West.

Whatever illusions Weizmann cherished about the West were modified by his first experiences in Germany. He arrived at the Polytechnic at Darmstadt 'a boy of nineteen', as he put it, 'naive, ignorant and impressionable'. He left, almost a year later, broken in health from 'overwork, malnutrition and loneliness', having suffered 'something approaching a breakdown' and with his lungs permanently damaged. The choice of Darmstadt was not entirely fortuitous. Two children from Motol, the Pollack brothers, having failed in their entrance examination for Pinsk Gymnasium, had been despatched to a Jewish boarding school in Pfungstadt, only a short distance from Darmstadt. Apparently they had been joined there by other Pinsk rejects. Their parents, eager that they should retain their command of Russian and Hebrew, persuaded the headmaster, Dr. Barness, to employ a suitable teacher. Weizmann fitted the bill. It being in all parties' interests, the arrangements had been duly made. The school provided Weizmann with food and board and a meagre allowance of 300 marks ($75) a year, in return for two hours' tuition a day.[18]

Weizmann's routine in Germany was as rigorous and demanding as the one he had abandoned in Pinsk—daily travel to and from the Polytechnic, intensive studies at a standard far higher than he had anticipated, and no less onerous duties as a junior teacher. The amount he had to catch up in his studies was considerable, particularly in physics and mathematics. His main subject was chemistry, and he registered for courses in agricultural, analytical, and organic chemistry, supplemented by laboratory work.[19] His day began at five in the morning and ended late at night, punctuated only by a make-shift lunch, 'a *brotchen*... and a piece of cheese, or of sausage', and supper, 'a wretched affair'. He wrote home far more picturesque descriptions of his life under Dr. Barness's austere regime, rendering his sketches in the style of Krilov's fables, much to the amusement of his family.[20]

Part of the trouble was that he was now transplanted to an environment totally at variance with his previous experiences. There was, firstly, a language barrier. He quickly discovered, to his 'astonishment and resentment', that his Pinsk Yiddish and even his self-acquired German had little in common with the German he encountered at university or in the street.

But far more traumatic was his first practical encounter with assimilated Jews or, as his headmaster grandly put it, 'Germans of the Mosaic persuasion'. When Weizmann, in all innocence, told one of his fellow-teachers that by nationality he was *ein russischer Jude*, he was met by 'gales of laughter. . . . A German, yes. A Russian, yes. Judaism, yes. But a Russian Jew! That was to him the height of the ridiculous.' But for Weizmann that was the very essence of his being. He was being treated to a convincing demonstration of the spiritual gap that separated him, and eastern Jewry, from the assimilationists in the West. For Dr. Barness, whom he evidently regarded as the epitome of the assimilated Jew, he developed and retained a violent antipathy, casting him off as 'an intellectual coward and toady'. He emphatically preferred the world he had left, with all its persecution and poverty. 'In Russia at least we . . . had a culture of our own, and a high one. We had standing in our own eyes. We did not dream that our Jewish being was something to be sloughed off furtively.'[21] He despised the philosophy of assimilation as demeaning, degrading, humiliating, and he often confessed, sadly, that he felt more at home in the company of gentiles than assimilated Jews. Despite his western education and his political sophistication, he remained, until the end, *ein russischer Jude*. Ultimately, this was the source of his strength both with his own people and with his gentile friends.

His feelings about assimilation were sharpened by the new anti-semitism then fashionable in Germany, and he was infuriated by those German Jews who refused to grasp the true dimensions of the problem confronting them. His own analysis was simple and to the point: 'If a man has a piece of something in his eye, he doesn't want to know whether it's a piece of mud or a piece of gold. He just wants to get it out.' Drawing on his experience as a scientist, he made the same point. 'I do not consider it a compliment to be called "the salt of the earth",' explaining: 'The role of salt from the chemical point of view is to salt somebody's soup. Salt has still another quality. It can be taken only in a definite concentration. The moment the solution is over-saturated, down go the salt and the soup.'[22] For Weizmann no deception was so fatal as self-deception.

The Pfungstadt interlude was an unhappy episode in his life, intellectually frustrating and personally distasteful. He remembered it 'without pleasure', for he lacked the warmth and encouragement, even flattery, to which he was accustomed and which he clearly craved. Isolated from his family and without any real friends, he was consumed by intense loneliness, for which there is no easy cure. He departed Pfungstadt 'without regrets'.[23]

In the summer of 1893 Weizmann returned to Motol, in desperate need of some kind of recuperation to prop up his spirits after the dismal experiences in Pfungstadt. Home cooking and the warmth and jollity of his family circle led the way to recovery. But his home-coming brought not only great excitement but also a measure of confusion. Somehow he had acquired in Germany a taste for croquet, and he insisted that his summer holiday be spent initiating his family into the refinements of the sport. With characteristic determination he inveigled the local carpenter to fashion mallets and balls and their handyman-gardener to prepare a suitable playing surface. The Weizmanns played croquet all that summer. Weizmann, naturally, was the supreme arbiter when disputes arose concerning the interpretation of this most sedate of bourgeois games. He usually came off best, exhibiting to the full his latent diplomatic talents, even when he was accused of religious sacrilege for daring to play on the Sabbath.[24]

If his move to Darmstadt was more or less by chance, Weizmann's second choice, of Berlin, was wholly by design. He aimed to study at the chemistry school at Charlottenberg Polytechnic, one of the most prestigious in Germany, where, under the directorship of Carl Liebermann, the organic chemistry laboratories were engaged in significant work on coal-tar derivatives. This would certainly be a giant step forward in his scientific grounding, and would bring him into contact with mature and reputable scientists and intriguing paths of research. Under the direct supervision of Alfred Bystrzycki, he was to explore the industrial potential for synthetic dyes, for which there was a growing commercial demand. In the Berlin laboratory, he also met another aspiring young chemist, Christian Deichler, with whom he was later to cooperate on research projects and the joint registration of patents.

Naturally there were some false starts. After a year or two at Berlin, Weizmann managed to engage the interest of a scholar-industrialist in one of his discoveries, apparently connected with his research on synthetic dyes. But the deal he hoped for fell through—alas, not before news of it had been received as a collective triumph for Pinsk Jewry and his family had toasted his success for forty-eight hours.[25] There were other disappointments.

It might be said that in Berlin Weizmann came of age, both as a scientist and as a Zionist. European university cities at the turn of the century were peppered with *emigré* student colonies. Berlin was no exception. He fell in with the Russisch-Juedischer Wissenschaftlicher Verien (Russian-Jewish Academic Society), a glittering circle of Russian Jewish intelligentsia which Weizmann described in his memoirs as 'the cradle of the modern Zionist movement'. Many of its members were to become his colleagues or opponents. Founded in 1889, four years before Weizmann's arrival in Berlin, it was a rallying-point for Jewish nationalists. It was an introverted, self-contained group, 'a kind of ghetto',[26] Weizmann thought, its members living in a world of their own without meaningful contact with, or even interest in, activities outside their universities or their society. For the most part without adequate funds and drinking only minute quantities of wine or beer, they found it impossible to find a permanent venue for their meetings and were driven from restaurant to beer-hall by proprietors exasperated with their puritanical habits. 'Friends,' Leo Motzkin, a founder of the Society, would plead, 'for God's sake drink more beer. Have some consideration for the Society.' Later they met regularly on Saturday nights at the Hotel Zentrum where, Weizmann reported, 'during lean periods, we could get beer and sausages on credit'.[27]

When they were flush, they would attend concerts of the Berlin Philharmonic, buying the cheapest seats in the 'gods'. Once, on hearing Beethoven's Ninth Symphony, Weizmann and his companions were so carried away that they joined in the choral accompaniment. The audience, shocked by this unseemly behaviour, tried in vain to hush them up. Fortunately, the conductor, Felix Weingartner, came to their rescue. Turning to the audience, and rising to the occasion, he began to conduct their singing.[28]

Their great forte were interminable discussions continuing into the small hours of the morning. The Zionists valiantly defended their views against their most formidable protagonists, the Jewish internationalists. Something of the fiery nature of these meetings, with an unexpected touch of humour often lightening the proceedings, can be gauged by the reminiscences of one of the participants, S. Levin. Parvus (A. L. Helphand), a noted Marxist theoretician and much-feared debater, Levin reports, was demolishing, demagogically but convincingly, the philosophy of nationalism. 'He grabbed hold of his own coat and roared: "The wool in this coat was taken from sheep which were pastured in Angora; it was spun in England, it was woven in Lodz; the buttons come from Germany, the thread from Austria: is it not clear to you that this world of ours is *inter*national and even a miserable thing like a coat is made up of the labour of ten different races?"' As he made this impassioned outburst, he accidently tore the sleeve of his international coat. Nachman Syrkin, a Zionist-Socialist 'whose eyes burned with rage and contempt', sprang up and shouted: 'And the rip in your sleeve comes from the pogrom of Kiev.' Undone by this challenging sentence, Parvus retired from the hall, accompanied by a tumult of applause from Zionists ecstatic at their unforeseen victory.[29]

Initially, Weizmann's contribution to scenes like these was modest. He was feeling his way, somewhat a country bumpkin who lacked the self-confidence to compete with city sophisticates on their terms. Young and inexperienced, plunged into a new and strange environment, oppressed by the notion that a mere chemistry student could never rival scholars of 'higher things', law or philosophy or economics, he may have been unnerved by his first months in Berlin. In time, he gained in boldness as he learned to recognize his powers and to assess those of his new companions realistically. Within a year, he was elected to the Society's executive committee.[30]

However much Weizmann found student life 'jolly and exciting',[31] he was determined to exclude its intellectual froth from the realities of his life. He perceived in many of his friends the rootlessness and aimlessness of the 'eternal student', a type he feared, detested, and pitied. Time-consuming discussions, debates, arguments could occupy only a limited, defined place in his activities. Not that he did not relish the social and intellectual life of the Society or benefit from it, but he was also a man of action who needed a concrete goal. This he found, for the present, in the laboratory and lecture-hall. As in Pinsk, he settled into a most punctilious schedule of academic studies and Zionist work. Driven by an urge to escape the fate of the ubiquitous Jewish *Luftmensch*, he eagerly embraced the discipline and order of scientific research. Later this not only provided him with economic independence and intellectual gratification, but also served as an anchor, a safe haven from the buffetings of political hurly-burly, where results were determined by rational analysis and decision and not by personal rivalries or unpredictable alliances. 'Chemistry is my private affair,' he confessed, 'an activity in which I rest from my public duties.'[32] The choice was never easy; his sense of public obligation inexorably pushed him deeper into political work. But early in his career, he decided: 'I don't want any vagueness, any duality that destroys my energy and tears me to pieces. I must regulate my activities in such a way that one thing (Zionism) does not interfere with the other (chemistry); I shall then be healthier and more creative. I shall work and there will be no more financial difficulties.'[33]

The 'financial difficulties' to which he referred were his most pressing problem in Berlin. He gave private tuition to boost his allowance of 100 marks a month, which barely sufficed to meet his needs, particularly when fellow-students, even more impoverished than he, tapped him for loans. There is a touch of desperation in his pleas, often in vain, to recoup his losses. To Leo Motzkin, a student friend, he wrote: 'The first is approaching, and I am unable to pay the landlady; I owe money to several persons who are causing me unbearable unpleasantness. I therefore beg you to let me have at least 30 marks, without fail. This is the only source on which I can count. . . . I am in terrible straits. . . . I have nothing to pawn. My compasses have long been in the appointed place [i.e. the pawnbroker's], and they are my only wealth.' It was apparently with some truth that he complained, 'I did not eat a single solid meal except as somebody's guest.'[34] Impecunity was and is a natural feature of most student life, and it continued to embarrass Weizmann for many years to come—even, strangely, when he had achieved status and a regular income as a university lecturer in Manchester. The evidence suggests that, despite his attention to detail, he was out of his depth when managing household accounts.

After two years in Berlin, Weizmann broke off his studies and returned home for a full year. By this time his family had resettled in Pinsk, mainly to facilitate Ozer's business requirements, and the initial process of adjustment was evidently difficult for the family. There was clearly a financial crisis of some kind. Ozer, as one means of coping with it, entered into a partnership with his son-in-law, Chaim Lubzhinsky, a talented businessman based in Warsaw; the association proved most rewarding and Ozer's business fortunes prospered. Lubzhinsky, a generous soul, helped to subsidize the education of the Weizmann children, including Chaim's.

Chaim's home-coming, after three years in the West, constituted something of a cultural shock.[35] 'After Berlin, Pinsk has made such a vile, repulsive impression on me that I find it unpleasant, even distasteful to share it . . . with you,' he wrote to Motzkin. 'There is nothing here and no-one: instead of a town—just an enormous rubbish-heap.' Ordinary Pinsk Jews were 'creatures devoid of all personality'. 'The so-called intelligentsia' he dismissed contemptuously as 'gossips' who indulged in 'avowedly innocent amusements'. And he would have nothing to do with the *jeunesse dorée* of Pinsk'. 'I could die of boredom,' he moaned. Even if one discounts the smart-aleck, arrogant tone of a youthful correspondence between two over-confident and quick-witted students, it is clear that Weizmann had outgrown his youth. Pinsk, shed of nostalgia, was, for the by-now worldly student, no more than a provincial backwater.

The great compensation was the reunion with his family, and so it remained during his periodical visits in later years. For its intellectual output at least continued to flourish, and heated arguments denouncing or advocating Bundism or territorialism or Zionism resounded throughout the house.

> The father, Ozer, gentle and studious, absorbed in a book in a remote corner, nodded in silent approval at the strong sessions which were proof of his children's awareness. Every now and then he would arbitrate with a truism from the Bible or a parable from the Sages. And the mother, while preparing mounds of their favourite foods, would come in and out, picking up terms and expressions completely unknown to her, aglow with pride at the abundant wisdom of her children and thanking God for His blessings.[36]

It was at one of these sessions that Rachel, bewildered by the conflicting data, remarked: 'Whatever happens, I shall be well off. If Shmuel [the revolutionary son] is right, we shall all be happy in Russia; and if Chaim is right, then I shall go and live in Palestine.'[37]

Although Weizmann complained of boredom, he could have had little free time to spare. First, and of the utmost priority, he had to rid himself of his military service, a burden that plagued all the Jewish youth of Russia. Often the most extraordinary measures were adopted to avoid conscription, in particular to evade the *"khappers"* (snatchers), press-gangs employed by the authorities to enforce the military quotas. Weizmann, by a combination of subterfuge and fast talk, managed to wriggle out of his military obligations, and he could, therefore, look forward to completing his education without interruption.[38]

Much time was invested in provincial Zionist work: debating, arguing, urging Jews in neighbouring villages to support openly the Hovevei Zion. In Pinsk, he cultivated a literary circle, 'national in character', and helped to establish a *cheder* in tune more with his spirit than with the spirit of the times. The new *cheder* was something of a revolutionary innovation for Russian Jewry, as the lessons were actually taught in the holy tongue Hebrew, instead of Yiddish. Naturally, it provoked an unholy alliance among anti-Zionists--the revolutionaries and Bundists, who staked all on the class struggle, and the ultra-Orthodox groups, who claimed a monopoly on Jewish educational and cultural activities and resolutely opposed any manifestation of Jewish nationalism as sacrilege, an unnatural tampering with the work of God, and who believed that Jewish redemption would come with the Messiah or not at all. But their agitation evaporated before the resoluteness of Weizmann and his supporters.[39] 'All this is not [achieved] without a violent struggle. . . . I have already succeeded in accomplishing something practical along our lines.' Nor did he neglect his chemistry. These months were spent profitably working at an oils-products factory in Pinsk owned by the Lurie family. All in all, he was not entirely sorry that he had stayed 'for the winter. For in spite of everything, I have managed to accomplish something!'[40]

Still, Weizmann craved the excitement of Berlin. 'What's the latest news?' he asked Motzkin. 'What's going on in our crowd? Which of our acquaintances has returned to Berlin? What is happening to the Society? . . . Have any Jewish students arrived? . . . Do send me some of the papers recently read in Berlin. At least their titles, if it is impossible to obtain the papers.' 'Never mind,' he consoled himself, 'it will be merrier soon, and it will be Berlin, too!'[41]

By the autumn of 1896 he had resumed his studies at the Polytechnic at Charlottenberg, where he stayed for another year. The Society continued to fill his world. Within its charmed circle he formed, as he put it, his first 'enduring and lifelong relationships'.[42] Foremost among them was his friendship with Leo Motzkin, his first political relationship. A gifted mathematician and seven years older than Weizmann, Motzkin, by virtue of his seniority and experience, overawed his young companion with the 'sweep of his vision'. Motzkin introduced Weizmann to the mature world of Zionism, to the subtleties of its politics, and he himself went on to a commendable career in Jewish and Zionist politics. Weizmann wrote later, 'He became . . . a *VereinsMeier*, a Johnny Joiner, frittering away his days and nights in innumerable little student gatherings, and taking with tremendous seriousness every minor incident in student political life.'[43]

Their correspondence reveals the enormous gap between their outlooks—Weizmann, impatient and eager to get on, the slightest hitch to his plans leaving him angry and perplexed; Motzkin, lackadaisical and easy-going, erratic, reluctant to reply to letters, perhaps to commit himself. Typically he sat on the fence during the bitter debate sparked off by the British proposal of 1903 to settle Jews in East Africa, the so-called Uganda controversy, unable to decide between his deep attachment to *Erez Israel* and the urgent need to help oppressed Jewry. Although they collaborated for many years, their early intimacy soon withered. Weizmann set his own standards as a fully committed Zionist, and he expected other Zionists, particularly those close to him, to live up to them as well. If they disappointed him, he repaid them with scorn and bitterness, lapsing into a ferocity of language that revealed his sense of betrayal. Motzkin progressed from being 'a very odd person' to a 'pathologically vain' one. At one point, in early August 1902, Weizmann bid him 'adieu', for he found Motzkin 'tired . . . and he doesn't do a single thing'. When they met again a few weeks later, Weizmann considered him 'repulsive. . . . I try to have little to do with him'.[44] Others were to encounter similar, if more refined, treatment in the future. Not many could match Weizmann's demonic energy or keep pace with his murderous work-rate, and Weizmann found this difficult to comprehend. It was one reason why he led his troops from afar.

One friendship withstood these trials. Asher Hirsch Ginsberg, known commonly by his literary pseudonym Ahad Ha'am (literally; One of the People), occupied a unique place in the consciousness of the Russian-Jewish intelligentsia and in the life of Weizmann. Weizmann thought of Ha'am, eighteen years his senior, as 'friend and comrade', 'adviser and teacher'. Born in 1856 into a prosperous, Hasidic family, Ahad Ha'am was marked by great intellectual distinction and linguistic talent. After a traditional upbringing, he declined to follow his father's wishes and become a rabbi and instead, having become a rationalist, abandoned all religious faith. Self-taught, without university education, he became in time the most renowned Hebrew essayist of his day, a writer with a precise and lucid style whose compositions unsettled the Jewish world and provoked incessant controversy. 'The appearance of one of [his] articles was always an event of prime importance. We read him, and read him again,' wrote Weizmann.[45] A member of the Hovev Zion Committee in Odessa, editor of the first Hebrew journal, the monthly *HaShiloach*, and the author of a number of highly influential essays, he wielded unrivalled authority, and his reputation went virtually unchallenged.

Ahad Ha'am's self-imposed mission was to strip away the illusions at the heart of the Zionist ideal. He was profoundly sceptical whether Zionism could resolve the Jewish problem as traditionally defined, with its manifestations of economic and social servitude and political subjugation. On the other hand, he held that Zionism could be decisive in solving what he called 'the question of Judaism'. He failed to produce a *magnum opus*, an organized, comprehensive work that encompassed, and might perhaps have refined, his teachings. But it is clear that his order of priorities was entirely at odds with that of the Zionist leadership. The titles of his best-known compositions reveal his bent: *Lo Zeh HaDerech* (This is not the Way), a critique of the methods and ideas of Hibbat Zion; *Emet MeErez Israel* (The Truth from Erez Israel), written after his first sobering visit to Palestine in 1891; and *Avdut Be-toch Herut* (Slavery in the Midst of Freedom), a devastating review of the plight of western assimilated Jewry. These penetrating studies allowed the Jewish intelligentsia no rest. Ahad Ha'am was not opposed to the creation of a Jewish political entity in Palestine or of a Jewish majority there, but he was unyielding in his criticism of the course adopted by Hibbat Zion and later by Theodor Herzl.

He was a subtle yet in some ways inconsistent ideologue: an almost perfect example of the enthusiastic sportsman standing on the sidelines, waving his team on to greater efforts yet declining all invitations to muddy himself. There was something of the intellectual snob about him. He was instrumental in forming, in 1889, the Bnei Moshe (Sons of Moses), a select, elitist group intended to aid Hibbat Zion but to which only the dedicated and worthy could aspire to membership. Weizmann joined this illustrious body in 1896. In 1897 Ahad Ha'am attended the first Zionist Congress where, in his own words, he observed its proceedings 'like a mourner at a wedding'. He never joined the Zionist Organization.[46]

Ahad Ha'am interpreted the Jewish problem as a collective crisis demanding not only an immediate political solution, but also, mainly, individual spiritual redemption, a more long-drawn-out affair but ultimately more solid and permanent. Zionist settlement in Palestine should be, must be, preceded by an intensive educational programme. Jews had to be spiritually prepared for the tremendous self-sacrifice required to create a national homeland in Palestine. In this way a new Jew would emerge, proud and deeply rooted in his Jewishness, supremely conscious of his Jewish heritage. This alone would guarantee the continuity of Jewish life in all its aspects, building, as it were, on the individual's Jewish consciousness to a new and more lasting level of national awareness. Haunted by the fate of other mass movements in Jewish history, those led by false prophets, Ahad Ha'am was fearful lest Zionism, opportunistic as all political movements must be, would pursue its material goals too quickly, tragically turning to ashes its achievements. Palestine might never compete materially with the West, but it could and should provide a spiritual centre for Judaism, for diaspora Jewry, and in this way stimulate Jewish national consciousness. The rest would follow. One institute of higher learning in Palestine, he postulated, is worth more than ten agricultural settlements.

There was a perceptiveness in the writings of Ahad Ha'am, a challenge to the conventional wisdoms, that often eluded those who took a more direct and simplistic approach and that made him compulsory reading for young intellectuals. He was among the first Zionist thinkers to pay attention to the dangers of the Arab question: 'If ever there comes a time when we shall have developed our life in *Erez Israel* to the point where we shall be encroaching upon them in a greater or lesser degree, [then we should not expect them] to yield their place easily.'[47]

Small, lean, and ascetic-looking, pedantic in personal habit and retiring by nature, sceptical and questioning, Ahad Ha'am was perfect material for a guru-figure. Weizmann, who referred to him as '*cher maître*', felt a special affinity to the man and his teachings, sought him out in times of crisis, and was consoled and comforted by him. After the British cabinet agreed to issue the Balfour Declaration in November 1917, Weizmann immediately went to Ahad Ha'am to let him in on the secret. The feeling was reciprocated: 'He always had a fondness for Weizmann . . . with whom he had a natural kinship'.[48] Yet however soothing the filial relationship was, Weizmann may have found something grating in Ahad Ha'am's perpetual carping, in his endemic pessimism and boundless scepticism, in his lack of positive passion. After their first recorded meeting, he noted: 'On the whole Ahad Ha'am makes a very pleasant impression as a European. He spoke about the Palestine cause with restraint, not too much, without heat and, or perhaps it only seems to me, with a little pinch of scepticism.' There was perhaps too much cool restraint for a hot-blooded creature like Weizmann. Although the academic in Weizmann delighted in the 'endless discussions' provoked by Ahad Ha'am's writings, the practical politician in him was faintly irritated by the lack of decisiveness and unworldliness of his 'teacher'. 'Of course he is not a "party politician" like me', Weizmann once pointed out, somewhat derisively. On occasion, Weizmann shrugged him off as 'a soul without a body'.[49]

Yet Weizmann's intellectual debt to Ahad Ha'am was enormous. Not that he accepted blindly all of his teachings,[50] but he built on their foundations. Throughout his career, even at the darkest moments, when the most horrific political events were threatening to overwhelm him, he never tired of explaining the spiritual and moral content of Zionism, its humanitarian and liberal values. Zionism was not just a political programme, not merely political activism, but a national liberation movement in the fullest and deepest sense of that much-maligned term, for it necessitated a spiritual regeneration in the lives of its adherents. If this were not realized, if Zionism succumbed to the political temptations of the moment, if it surrendered its humane and civilized principles for the sake of political expediency, it would lead to a corruption of the spirit that would eventually poison the body politic. All nationalist movements are egocentric in character, but Zionism dared at its peril to sacrifice all on its altar. Politics, yes. Pragmatism, certainly. Weizmann was not above wheeling and dealing in the great game; and he proved more adept at it than most. But he believed that all his manoeuverings and accomplishments would turn to dust should he abandon the ethical basis to his ideology that he first learned as a student of Ahad Ha'am. He never forgot this lesson and strived all his life to attain a working synthesis between the 'spiritualism' of Ahad Ha'am and his stratagems as leader of a political movement. The epithet Ahad Ha'amist clung to him long after he had outgrown his master's tutelage.

It would be difficult to exaggerate the importance of the Berlin period in moulding Weizmann's life. Reflecting later, he wrote: 'In Berlin, I grew out of my boyhood Zionism, out of my adolescence, into something like maturity. When I left Berlin . . . the adult pattern of my life was set. Of course, I learned a great deal in later years; but no fundamental change took place; my political outlook, my Zionist ideology, my scientific bent, my life's purposes, had crystallized.'[51]

Weizmann left Berlin in the summer of 1897 for the Swiss University at Fribourg to complete a doctoral thesis. Bystrzycki, his 'favourite professor',[52] under whom he had been working at Charlottenberg, had moved to Fribourg and invited Weizmann to join him there. In January 1899 he submitted his thesis, an extension of his researches into dyestuffs, and was awarded his doctorate *magna cum laude*.[53] That April he moved to Geneva, after a brief respite in Berne. By August he had obtained a position as a *privat-docent* in the University of Geneva. Once again, his contacts served him well, for he was concurrently appointed assistant to Karl Graebe, professor of chemistry at the University and a colleague of Liebermann from Berlin, and was made responsible for a section of Graebe's organic chemistry laboratory. As a *privat-docent*, the lowliest rank in the academic hierarchy, his duties included lecturing, but the post was non-stipendiary, and Weizmann depended for his livelihood on the number of students he could attract, each one contributing about fifty marks to his purse. In the event, fifteen turned up, five of whom were working for a doctorate. It was an auspicious start to his career and promised ample scope for both profitable research and academic advancement. No wonder that he was 'very pleased by the turn of events'.[54]

THREE

THE REBEL

On 29 August 1897 some two hundred Jewish men and women gathered in the municipal casino at Basel. They had arrived from points as distant as New York, Odessa, and Palestine to attend the first Zionist Congress. The preamble to the Basel programme read: 'Zionism aims at the creation of a homestead [*Heimstatte*] for the Jewish people in Palestine to be secured by public law.' Zionism, as a political force in the modern world, had arrived. Its inspirer and organizer, Theodor Herzl, rose to deliver his opening address. 'We are here,' he informed the delegates and the representatives of the world's press, 'to lay the foundation stone of the house which is to shelter the Jewish nation.' When he sat down, 'He received "the hosannas of a king, and men climbed over one another to congratulate him".'[1] Five days later Herzl confided to his diary: 'Were I to sum up the Basel Congress in a word — which I shall guard against pronouncing publicly — it would be this: At Basel I founded the Jewish State. If I said this out loud today, I would be answered by universal laughter. Perhaps in five years, and certainly in fifty, everyone will know it.'[2]

The figure of Herzl dominated these events. By any reckoning, he was a most improbable candidate to lead the Zionist movement. Born in Budapest in 1860 to a well-to-do, middle-class family, he moved, at the age of eighteen, to the bewildering and contradictory world of *fin-de-siècle* Vienna: elegant, sophisticated, cosmopolitan, intellectually stimulating, yet at the same time intolerant and violently anti-semitic, a centre of Austrian chauvinism jealously intent on preserving its prerogatives. Viennese society reflected in an exaggerated, hysterical manner the internal stresses of a multinational empire coming apart at the seams.

Herzl made his way in this *milieu*. A writer by trade, by the 1890s he was an established journalist of the most prestigious of all Viennese newspapers, the *Neue Freie Presse*, a minor playwright, and a widely read and popular *feuilletoniste*, a companion of those quintessential Viennese *literati* Arthur Schnitzler and Hugo von Hoffmannstahl. He was an extraordinarily complicated character. Torn between a doting, domineering mother and a neurotic wife, subject to fits of depression, fascinated by the sense of physical danger—he was involved in at least three duelling incidents—he possessed a vivid sense of high drama, and mapped out for himself the role of martyr, tragically to be realized, as 'the Parnell of the Jews'.[3]

Myth has it that the Dreyfus affair awakened him from his torpor as an assimilated Jew. The story, alas, as dramatic as Herzl's commanding presence, is merely legend. It was impossible to grow up in Vienna and remain immune from its anti-semitism. At the age of twenty-three he had resigned from his student fraternity, handicapped, as he wrote, 'by the impediment of Semitism'. It was abundantly clear to him that the Jews were 'living perpetually in enemy territory'. He concocted the most grandiose of schemes: the mass conversion of Jews to Christianity. He toyed with the notion of composing an overall survey of the Jewish condition, visiting, describing, analysing the state of Jewish communities throughout the world. He planned a trip to Palestine to inspect the colonies of the Hovevei Zion. This preoccupation affected his literary output. One faintly autobiographical play, *The New Ghetto* (poorly reviewed when it was eventually produced), had a strong Jewish theme: that of a Jewish intellectual who, failing to break into gentile society, seeks to preserve his integrity as a Jew and is killed in a duel for his pains. Its tragic *denouement* symbolized the fate of western Jewry.[4]

These thoughts, never absent from his mind, surfaced in Paris when he covered the trial of Alfred Dreyfus for the *Neue Freie Presse*. Slowly he came to believe in Dreyfus's innocence and in the conspiracy that had dragged him down. He witnessed that terrifying scene at the École Militaire in December 1894 when Dreyfus was publicly humiliated and degraded to the accompaniment of the menacing bays of the Paris crowd threatening 'Death to the Jews'. His latest biographer writes: 'In Herzl's eyes the scene was symbolic in a wider sense: the degraded man symbolized the Jew in modern society, conforming to its ways, speaking its language, thinking its thoughts, sewing its insignia onto his shoulders only to have them violently torn off on a grey winter morning.' It was 'merely the last straw'.[5]

These events roused Herzl into resuming his task to ease the plight of the Jews. And what more natural than he should first look for support among the great Jewish magnates of the West? His vain attempts to persuade the Hirsches and the Rothschilds have been well chronicled: no rapport was struck between this intense Viennese journalist with his burning sense of mission and the sceptical and haughty 'aristocrats of money' who refused to be convinced, content that their own philanthropic schemes for alleviating Jewish misery were sufficient, and even politically more realistic than Herzl's fantastic projects. And indeed Herzl's ideas must have sounded well-nigh incredible to his conservative listeners. Responding to a flight of inspiration, he set down his thoughts on paper in a 'Speech to the Rothschilds', intended to be read out in a family-council, though it never was; later it served as the framework for his celebrated pamphlet *Der Judenstaat*.[6]

The kernel of Herzl's classic was his demand for Jewish sovereignty 'over a portion of the globe large enough to satisfy the rightful requirements of a nation'. Anti-semitism, he argued, had no cure; assimilation was a mere pipe-dream. It made not a scrap of difference whether Jews lived in the progressive West or the oppressive East. 'We are one people,' he intoned, and subject to one fate. A mass exodus should lead, not to another diaspora, but to a territory the Jews could call their own: and a Jewish state. It was to be hoped that this would be welcomed by the gentile world, for it would remove a source of friction and tension within society as a whole. Had he any particular territory in mind? He left the question unanswered, or at least open to various interpretations: 'Shall we choose Argentina or Palestine? We shall take what is given us and what is preferred by the Jewish people.' It was typical of Herzl that, not content with enunciating a great ideal, he swept on to elaborate the administrative, organizational, and financial structure by which he intended to attain his goal. And to crown it all, he detailed the political and social content of his projected state.

This virtuoso performance was not greeted with universal applause. Better-known publishers refused to consider it; and it was only the optimism of Breitenstein, a small (non-Jewish) firm in Vienna, which ensured its publication.[7] In the West, the initial reaction was a mixture of bewilderment, shock, contempt, scepticism, ridicule, and apathy.

Press reviews were generally unfavourable. Anti-semites supported Herzl's thesis; the Jewish establishment, in the main, opposed it. The rabbis were particularly vocal in their hostility. Only among the Jewish intelligentsia did he gain some support, in particular from those already committed to the Zionist outlook.

The English, whose country Herzl had visited just prior to the publication of Der Judenstaat, accorded his pamphlet a warmer reception. Here there ran a deep vein of gentile Zionism dating from the Puritan revolution, and it made for a more sympathetic hearing. Typical establishment Jews—Claude Montefiore and Frederic Mocatta—reacted coolly to Herzl's challenge, but others, less inhibited, encouraged by the stability and relative tolerance of British society and fortified by the insularity of their position, accepted its main thesis. The famous Anglo-Jewish author Israel Zangwill met Herzl and was deeply impressed with the man and his ideas. He ensured Herzl an entrée into Anglo-Jewish society. A powerful Jewish merchant banker and Liberal M.P., Sir Samuel Montague, believed that Palestine could be purchased for the Jews for £2 million. In Cardiff, Herzl encountered a character straight out of the pages of fiction: Colonel Albert Goldsmid, commander of a Welsh Regiment, welcomed him with the words: 'We shall work for the liberation of Israel.' 'I am Daniel Deronda,' he explained.[8] The degree of Zionist support in Britain surprised Herzl, and later he and his successors attempted to capitalize on it.

Not surprisingly, it was among eastern Jewry that Herzl's ideas had the greatest impact. His theories, revolutionary in Paris or Vienna, were everyday currency in Vilna or Odessa. Indeed, Leo Pinsker's Autoemancipation (1882) had anticipated most of Herzl's basic assumptions. (When Herzl read Pinsker, shortly before the publication of Der Judenstaat, he noted 'an astounding correspondence in the critical part, a great similarity in the constructive one.'[9]) The leadership of Hibbat Zion reacted to Herzl with varying degrees of caution and enthusiasm, but the rank and file were less restrained. It was not so much the ideas that electrified them as the personality of their new champion from the West. The young David Ben Gurion later recalled: 'the messiah had arrived—a tall handsome man, a learned man of Vienna, a doctor no less—Theodor Herzl'.[10] Weizmann, now a mature student, was equally affected. 'It was an utterance which came like a bolt from the blue. . . . Not the ideas but the personality which stood behind them appealed to us. Here was daring, clarity and energy. The very fact that this Westerner came to us unencumbered by our own preconceptions had its appeal.'[11]

During the spring of 1896, when Weizmann was in Pinsk, his correspondence makes no allusion to Herzl or his tract, or even to Herzl's preparations to convene a great Zionist gathering. This is surprising, as Pinsk was a centre of Hibbat Zion, and Berlin, where Weizmann returned in the summer of 1896, boasted lively Zionist student groups. When the 'daring, clarity and energy' to which Weizmann referred came to fruition in that seminal event of modern Jewish history—Herzl's creation, the first Zionist Congress at Basel—Weizmann was not in attendance, though he had been elected a delegate for Pinsk. He was busy in Moscow trying, in vain, to sell one of his scientific discoveries.[12] Disappointed, he returned to Berlin.

Weizmann first saw Herzl at the second Zionist Congress a year later. He claimed later that he was not overly impressed: 'I cannot pretend that I was swept off my feet.' Although he admired and respected Herzl—his letters to him are couched with due regard to Herzl's position—he came to consider him 'naive', his Zionism a sort of 'superior philanthropy', and his emphasis on court politics too 'simpliste and condemned to failure'. What particularly distressed Weizmann was 'the touch of Byzantinism in his manner. Almost from the outset a kind of court sprang up about him, of worshippers who pretended to guard him from too close contact with the mob. I am compelled to say that certain elements in his being invited such an attitude.' Ironically, when Weizmann later assumed the leadership of the movement himself, there were those who would level the same kind of criticism against him. There is more than a touch of ambivalence in Weizmann's attitude toward Herzl. On Herzl's death in July 1904, Weizmann's final assessment of him, generous though it was, concealed a sting: 'At this moment all differences between us have disappeared, and I only have the image of a great creative worker in front of my eyes. I feel a great weight on my heart...and deep grief. He has left us a frightening legacy.' Even Herzl, Weizmann reflected, was unable to 'break the mold of his life.'[13]

It is a constant of political life, certainly of Jewish political life, that leaders, no matter how eminent, are subject to often unbridled criticism. Weizmann, throughout his life, and despite his unique achievements, knew this only too well: it particularly rankled when he was censured by his own constituents from the Pale. Yet Herzl, notwithstanding the controversies surrounding him, remained the idol of the Jewish masses, his image untarnished. His upbringing and background, his bearing and mannerisms, were so unlike the norm of eastern Jewry that his appeal to them was infinite. Not so with Weizmann. However far Weizmann distanced himself in his life style from the Jewish masses, he was comforted by the fact that he had sprung from them, that they had nurtured him. He was by no means a populist leader, and he disliked the gimmickery commonly associated with mass politics, but he was supremely aware of his origins as an ordinary Jew from the Pale. He never denied or concealed his background, or that it conditioned his behaviour and character. At times, he played to the gallery as a homespun Jew born and bred in the *shtetl*. This usually worked to his benefit in his relations with gentiles, but it did not carry the same weight with his fellow-Jews from eastern Europe. Unlike Herzl, he was one of the family, and therefore fair game for all comers. Weizmann instinctively appreciated this drawback and accepted it— perhaps as a sign of affection. He observed sardonically, 'When Herzl or [Max] Nordau blundered, the ghetto forbore to reproach a once truant and now penitent son; but let me make the slightest mistake, and the ghetto rises with a single shout: *"Weizmann, bist meshuga?"* [Weizmann, are you mad?]'[14]

Herzl gave the Zionist movement a recognizable form; its content remained a topic for furious discussion. These were the 'differences' to which Weizmann alluded. He took his cue from Ahad Ha'am who, from the outset, had registered profound unease at Herzl's emphasis on diplomatic endeavour. 'The salvation of Israel,' he asserted, 'will be achieved by prophets and not by diplomats.'[15] Herzl's proposed strategy was to obtain a charter from Turkey whereby 'the civil and military duties, [and] also the rights, of the settlers [in *Erez Israel*] would be specified'. His diplomatic forays brought him into contact with minor European royalty, with William II of Germany and Victor Emanuel of Italy, with Pope Pius X, and even with Vyacheslav Konstantinovich von Plehve, the Tsar's feared Minister of the Interior. But no amount of persuasion could convince Herzl's 'Monster', Abd al-Hamid II, Sultan of Turkey. Not even the prospect of Jewish economic aid to help cancel Turkey's foreign debts, the secret weapon in Herzl's armoury, had sufficient weight in the delicate interplay of political and ethnic forces at work in the Ottoman Empire. Nor would the Great Powers complicate their relations with Turkey for the sake of regularizing

Jewish settlement in Palestine. Thus, apart from some polite noddings of heads, Herzl's proposals went unanswered.

Weizmann was too much of a realist to view diplomatic Zionism in exactly the same dogmatic light as Ahad Ha'am did. Like other Zionists he anticipated a political *coup* and would have warmly applauded had one occurred. Hoping that the 'nervous attitude to political Zionism' would disappear and that 'a true understanding of its aims and tasks' would take root, he praised 'our dear untiring leader' during one of Herzl's excursions to Constantinople, and hopefully expected 'wide concessions'.[16] Yet Herzl's obsession with this aspect of Zionism, coupled with his noticeable lack of success, fostered Weizmann's growing disillusionment. By October 1902, after five years of the most intense efforts, all that Herzl could offer his fellow-Zionists was 'a very sad report'. Nor could the impatient Weizmann see any prospect of improvement in the future. Herzl appeared to him as something of a *dilettante*: flashy in style but lacking in depth, and particularly in concrete achievements. Now there was little Herzl could do right in Weizmann's eyes. 'How shockingly [he] defined Zionism and the Jewish nation,' he observed on learning of Herzl's evidence before the Royal Commission on Alien Immigration in July 1902.[17]

Weizmann, his own moods running hot and cold, was strongly affected by the apparent inability of the Zionist movement to rise to his own level of expectations. He left London after the Zionist Congress in August 1900 in a black humour, 'broken morally and physically' by the shallowness of its proceedings. He had attacked fiercely the influence of the rabbis and their presumptuous claim to a monopoly on educational and cultural activities. Weizmann put the case, too passionately for some, for 'Jewish national education'. 'If the rabbis come as representatives of the people, we welcome them. But if they come as representatives of the synagogue, then it's anti-Jewish—for there is no synagogue in Judaism! . . . I do not acquiesce to having the word "religious" inserted into our programme. The moment you do this you exclude a great part of the delegates from our Congress.' One incident particularly depressed him. Rumanian *emigré* Jews, marooned in London, demonstrated their plight outside the doors of Congress. The delegates raised a collection on their behalf. 'We all gave something of course; but the contrast between the grandiose talk of a Jewish State and the pitiful eleemosynary gesture for the stranded wanderers was utterly disheartening.'[18]

Weizmann's misgivings were shared by a growing number of young Zionist activists. From Munich, in the winter of 1900–1, a number of discontented Russian Jewish students called to convene a youth conference which, it was hoped, would give them a chance to express their anxiety about the manner in which Zionist affairs were being conducted. Weizmann seized this opportunity and turned it, eventually, into the first oppositionist group in the Zionist movement. Of course, he did not act alone. In Berlin, Leo Motzkin lent his support. Other friends—Martin Buber, the budding philosopher-theologian, and Berthold Feiwel, poet and journalist—were also heavily involved. This formidable collection of intellectuals made an impressive contribution to the Zionist movement, especially in the cultural field. Feiwel and Buber were instrumental in establishing in 1902 the *Judischer Verlag*, a publishing house that specialized in works on Jewish art and poetry; and both served as editor of *Die Welt*, the official Zionist organ founded by Herzl. These scholars were among the most enthusiastic advocates of an even more splendid project: the creation of a Jewish university. A restless group intellectually, they worked closely with Weizmann, and responded, at times reluctantly, to his leadership.

As a result of the Munich initiative, Weizmann was put in charge of the preparations to convene the conference. For this purpose an office was set up in his lodgings in Geneva. Assisted most ably by a group of young ladies drawn largely from the medical school at the University,[19] this project kept him busy throughout 1901. On the whole, he was well pleased with the progress made, though typically the all too frequent habit of his associates of 'talking paradoxes' irritated him. To Ahad Ha'am he confided that the point of the youth organization was to provide fresh terms of reference for those who found the old framework 'too narrow and uncomfortable'.[20]

His political activism sharpened his appetite for an open struggle with the Zionist establishment. For Herzl did not take lightly to these schemes, fearing they would jeopardize his negotiations with the Turks, which had then reached a crucial stage. But he was also extremely apprehensive—rightly, as it turned out—lest Weizmann's activities fragment the movement by introducing factional politics. He was especially concerned not to provoke the Orthodox Jews, who regarded educational work as their special prerogative, a view emphatically rejected by Weizmann as we have seen. Would Weizmann, therefore, as a loyal Zionist, abandon his project?[21] Weizmann attempted to put Herzl's mind at rest. At the youth conference 'we shall be concerned primarily with internal Zionist questions', not diplomacy or high politics. Many Zionists, he reminded Herzl, were unhappy at the 'dilatory and meditative approach to the solution even of domestic problems'. Should the conference not be held, he feared 'that many valuable forces will be drained away into the non-Zionist camp'.[22] To his intimates his language was less restrained: 'Dr. Herzl has no idea of Russian Zionism and of Russian Zionists. Dr. H. is being misled by various creatures, flatterers, "friends of the cause".' He was now quite prepared to fire the first shots in a 'war' on Herzl's leadership.[23]

Herzl met his rebellious follower in October 1901. Weizmann was keyed up for the confrontation: 'I shall not mince words tomorrow, and I will tell Herzl the unvarnished truth.'[24] But the meeting turned out differently. Herzl, in a previous note,[25] had already softened his opposition, and when Weizmann, supported by Buber, who accompanied him, pressed his advantage, Herzl withdrew his objections. The Youth Conference, now with the encouragement of the leadership (there was even talk of financial assistance), was scheduled to take place in December, just prior to the opening of the fifth Zionist Congress. This was a considerable victory for Weizmann and his coterie, but it must be attributed equally to Herzl's common sense and skill at averting an unnecessary confrontation.

The Youth Conference founded the Democratic Fraction. Its programme followed closely Weizmann's original plan proposed at a preparatory meeting the previous spring. It stressed practical development in Palestine and cultural and educational work in the diaspora (in Buber's phrase, *GegenWartsarbeit*); it repudiated the cult of the personality—a barb aimed at Herzl; and it declared in favour of factional politics, believing, optimistically, that it would lead to a healthy democratization of the Zionist movement.[26] This success was followed by another. The Fraction sent thirty-seven delegates to the next Zionist Congress where, with Herzl's agreement, a cultural committee was elected on a mandate that called for the 'education of the Jewish people in a national spirit [as] an essential part of the Zionist programme';[27] Weizmann and Ahad Ha'am were among its members. Not a great deal was accomplished by this committee apart from much discussion. Its lack of concrete results must have disappointed Weizmann, for he never ceased reiterating that he attached 'greater importance to practical work than to the theoretical side of the matter'.[28]

No sooner had the Democratic Fraction been established than it ran into trouble. Its two most prominent leaders, Weizmann and Motzkin, were quickly at loggerheads. Weizmann had been appointed head of the Fraction's Information Bureau in Geneva; Motzkin, in Berlin, was to chair a committee to formulate in detail its programme. Weizmann, consolidating his power base, together with friends founded a Zionist students circle, HaShachar (the Dawn), which was a focus for anti-Herzl agitation and missionary work among the Jewish student communities. Although Motzkin was senior to Weizmann in the hierarchy of the Fraction, at least in experience and reputation, he proved unequal to the contest. By the summer of 1902 Weizmann had emerged as the dominant force in the affairs of the Fraction, pushed forward by his single-mindedness, dedication, ambition. There is no evidence that he possessed outstanding organizational abilities. On the contrary, there was some criticism of him on this score.[29] But his energy and iron determination, combined with his sense of mission, were sufficient to carry the day. 'On the whole, Zionism does now exist: in spite of everything. . . . Our opponents will be wiped out in a few years' time. This will be brought about by life itself, and our movement is on the crest of a wave.'[30] For despite his disapproval of Herzl's methods, Weizmann's faith in the future of Zionism remained undiminished.

Also, Motzkin played into Weizmann's hands, sometimes acting in pique, and showing some ineptitude. He was no match for Weizmann, who scented his advantage and exploited his rival's weaknesses. Already wounded by Weizmann's harsh criticism of him at the Youth Conference—'in debate I always hit hard',[31] Weizmann acknowledged—Motzkin interpreted a harmless confabulation between Weizmann and Syrkin, a Zionist-Socialist, held without his knowledge, as uncomradely behaviour. In itself this was an incident of small consequence, yet it highlighted the tensions. After much petty wrangling, Motzkin succeeded only in exasperating Weizmann, who now referred to Motzkin's 'false enthusiasm and utter worthlessness'. Frustrated by Motzkin's lack of drive, Weizmann scornfully noted that '[he] has been revived from the dead'. Only eight months after its foundation, the future of the Fraction appeared in doubt. 'There is no Fraction,' Weizmann eventually despaired.[32]

On the political level relations were patched up sufficiently to allow the Fraction to appear as a more-or-less organized group at an important Russian Zionist conference in Minsk in September 1902. Weizmann, apparently a member of its steering-committee, the Permanenz Ausschuss, scored a success here: it adopted resolutions recommending cultural work in the spirit of the Fraction. One development, which he must have frowned upon, but for which he was indirectly responsible, was the appearance of the *Mizrachi* (religious parties) as a political group, ostensibly as a balance to his Fraction. This was to cause him a great deal of trouble later on, for other groups were to follow: better organized, more coherent ideologically, and more lasting than the Democratic Fraction. Only Motzkin had not changed. He walked about 'wearing a hang-dog look', his behaviour was 'foul', and he had become 'repulsive'.[33]

During those months Weizmann was undergoing an emotional crisis, the most severe of his life. Sometime in 1898 he had become engaged to Sophia (Sonia) Getsova, who was studying medicine at Berne, an active member of the Democratic Fraction and a close friend of the Motzkins. "Sonechka" had been introduced to Weizmann's parents, and during the summer vacations of 1898 and 1899 she had stayed with them at Pinsk. Weizmann had clearly entered into a firm commitment. Then, in November 1900, he met Vera Khatzman, an attractive nineteen-year-old student enrolled at the medical faculty in Geneva. Vera recalled that she was eating a meal at the Jewish Club 'when a tall, impressive man, with a fine, imposing head which was almost bald despite his comparative youth—he was only twenty-seven at this time—walked in and, standing with one foot on a chair, began to talk to someone. He was pale, dedicated, very frail yet serene, with a faintly ironic gleam in his eyes, mingled with deep and affecting sadness, and he seemed to carry all the burdens of the Jewish world.' Who is he, Vera enquired? 'Oh, he's just a Jewish intellectual,' her companion replied.[34]

Vera was quite different from most of the Jewish women students Weizmann had met. Her family came from Rostov-on-Don, far removed from the Pale, where they enjoyed special privileges in return for her father's long service in the Russian army. She knew neither Yiddish nor Hebrew. Her knowledge of Jewish history and tradition was limited. She had little interest in Zionist politics. Proud and remote, she was inclined to stand on her dignity. Unkind tongues described her as a snob. Weizmann found her 'quiet', 'retiring', 'pensive', 'almost sad'. He dubbed her *'princesse lointaine'*. It was an attraction of opposites, in terms both of ideological commitment and of emotional make-up.

Judging from his correspondence, he was bowled over by her. An extraordinary intensity of emotion and passion spilled over into his letters. He found their periods of separation unbearable. Once, when Vera was staying at Clerens-Baugy near Montreux, Weizmann, peevish at her absence, planned to cycle there and back from Geneva to join her—weather permitting, he added judiciously. 'Verochka,' he wrote on one occasion, 'I find it hard to be without you. I wish I could see you for at least a single moment. But you are so far, so far away.' And on another, he implored, 'Send me your picture but straight away, darling. I badly want to look at you at least in a photograph. Verusya, my darling, my sweet adorable one, my own.' 'I love you,' he confessed, 'I am deeply in love with my dear lovely Verusya.'[35]

The problem, stated simply, was that Weizmann was engaged to one lady while passionately in love with another and lacked the decisiveness to make a clean break. It took him almost two years before he extricated himself from this mess and finally reconciled the aggrieved parties—except of course Sophia and the Motzkins. His parents had come to regard Sophia as a prospective daughter-in-law, and he could not steel himself to tell them that Vera had taken her place until March 1903.[36] His relationship with the Motzkins and other Fraction members cooled considerably, for they considered his so brazenly deserting his fiancée as thoroughly dishonourable. The strain was intolerable. 'Nasty letters' began to arrive from Berne. His existence was 'one long torment, torture, anxiety, and upsets of all kind'. 'This has been poisoning my life,' he groaned.[37]

The combined effect of his personal crisis, his political agitation, and the pressures of his laboratory work was a drain on his health. He had never fully recovered from Pfungstadt, and these months added to his poor condition. He was forced to consult a lung specialist, and he began to complain that his 'eyes hurt'. 'It is difficult for me, Verochka, to live like this, and I am exhausted, exhausted, exhausted. An old man!' In November, when the controversy over the Youth Conference was at its height, he took to his bed for a week: 'A mountain of all kinds of filth, intrigues, dirt, a campaign against the Conference linked with a foul campaign against me personally . . . all this has broken me and shattered me completely.' Immediately after the Conference he consulted a doctor, who diagnosed 'neurasthenia and weakness of the respiratory organs', a condition not helped by his refusal to give up smoking. In July, he could lead only 'a vegetable existence'. The most trifling incident left him 'terribly irritable' and upset 'his equilibrium'. He saw everything 'larger than life', tending to overdramatize events. By October 1902, owing to the exertions of a propaganda tour of southern Russia, his condition was of 'general weakness and exhaustion'. The state of his health did not materially improve in time. His lungs—on occasion he spat blood—and eventually his eyes gave him most cause for worry.[38]

That Weizmann loved Vera deeply there can be no doubt. But he possessed a warm and affectionate and open nature, as his ardent correspondence to her amply confirms, and he craved similar demonstrations of love in return. Vera was unable to meet these needs. She was more restrained than he, possessed a calmer personality, and was less given to emotional outbursts. He had constantly to coax and prompt her into displays of greater affection—and, during his absences from her, to insist that his love for her had in no way diminished. Differences of age, temperament, background, and outlook were bridged only with difficulty. Yet they complemented each other, and Weizmann wrote with much justice that throughout the vagaries of his 'complicated existence, it was my wife who so organized things as to give me a stable and tolerably safe background'.[39]

Throughout his life rumours buzzed about Weizmann's relations with other women, and one cannot entirely discount the allegations. There was an impulsive streak to his nature. He was attractive to women and attracted by them. No doubt in Berlin and Geneva, in those tightly knit, introverted student communities, he sought female company and indulged in dalliances. His occasional 'flirtations' or 'infatuations' would give Vera reason for concern, though their relationship was stable enough to withstand these buffetings.[40]

Weizmann's first task was to educate Vera about Judaism and the niceties of Zionist politics. 'I always wanted to love the disciple in you ... to cleanse you, my joy, of all assimilation, to lead you into the movement.'[41] He impressed upon her the necessity of learning Hebrew and studying the Bible. And to round off her tuition, he recommended Nietzsche, whom he held in special reverence, and *Thus Spake Zarathustra*: 'This is the best and the finest thing I can send you.' 'So go on, my sweet,' he promised, 'and we shall read it regularly and without fail.'[42] The 'conversion', 'slow and painful', as Vera called it,[43] occurred in the summer of 1902. 'You have made me a Jewess,' she finally admitted. Weizmann was overjoyed, for it promised a harmonious intermingling of his ideology and his personal happiness, each fostering the other. 'Moreover, Verochka, since you became one with me in the

cause, too, since you told me that you are a Zionist, since then Verochka, our spiritual union has grown stronger, and what in other cases
springs from a passion, in our case, to my mind, has grown from a
spiritual affinity.'[44]

It was a remarkable feature of Weizmann's career that he coped concurrently, and on balance successfully, with the three main threads
of his life: his family, his science, and his Zionism. What kept him
in motion was something like the knowledge a juggler has who knows
that once he loses his rhythm his act will fail. Certainly Weizmann's
early career as a chemist progressed by leaps and bounds. He was
fortunate in that the first years of this century saw a rapid expansion
of the chemical industry, fuelled initially by the textile industry's need
to find chemical dyes. From the 1880s Germany, with abundant de-
posits of coal and potash, led the world in chemical innovations, particularly those relating to by-products of coal. By the 1890s, she had
acquired a near monopoly in synthetic dyestuffs, used in the production
of artificial fibres, photographic materials, drugs, plastics, new explosives, celluloid, and optical glass.[45] The field was wide open for an
ambitious chemist.

Weizmann's association with Christian Deichler, begun in Berlin
in the early 1890s, prospered. The main thrust of their research was
in dyestuffs chemistry. They published papers together and registered
joint patents. A contract at the Bayer works (later incorporated into
I. G. Farbenindustrie) gave Weizmann a steady income, estimated at
600 marks ($150) a month.[46] As in other fields, when excited by the
prospect of success, he drove himself hard: 'Yesterday I worked for 15
hours by the clock. At midnight I was still at the laboratory. Today I
have been here since 7 a.m.' In March 1902, he believed he was on
the verge of a major discovery, a process that would reduce the cost
of alazarin, a material basic to the manufacture of dyestuffs, by 30–
35 per cent. It proved a false start: the factory evaluation failed to
square with his own. He convinced himself that he was the object of
a swindle. His language turned sharper than usual: 'they are thieves
and want to drain the last drop of blood out of me. I shall try to resist.'
In the event, the affair petered out without benefit to anyone.[47] But
within a few years the range of Weizmann's scientific contacts and
associates had widened. In the spring of 1903 he was considering the

registration of a patent in the United States. The following year he accepted to do research, for a monthly salary of $75 and the promise of a share in the profits, for a Baku industrialist, Samuel Shriro, who dreamed of producing a colourless soap from oil waste.[48]

On only one occasion did Weizmann seriously consider abandoning the laboratory. In the summer of 1902, when his pet scheme for a Jewish university seemed to be foundering for lack of firm leadership, he raised this 'deadly difficult' possibility. Vera talked him out of it, apprehensive less he enslave himself financially to the Zionist movement as a paid official. Chemistry would provide not only a means of subsistence but also political and intellectual independence. Above all, in the longer run economic independence was the pre-requisite for their eventual *aliyah* (Hebrew: literally ascending, but meaning immigration) to Palestine. After acknowledging Vera's worldly advice, he left for Minsk to attend a Zionist gathering. 'All will be well,' he assured her.[49]

'I believe in the victorious force of the Idea, in the cogency of my arguments and of my Zionist life.' Like most men who dedicate themselves to a single cause, Weizmann was possessed by a sense of destiny, and it never abandoned him even during moments of deep crisis. He knew that eventually, 'The cause will summon me and I shall then come.'[50] This belief sustained him when he was engaged in grass-roots Zionist work, stumping the Jewish *shtetl* of the Pale. As he preached 'the Idea', with experience his reputation grew. He was an eloquent speaker and a formidable debater with a gift for the vivid phrase. Yet his trips to Russia usually left him dejected. Despite his popularity, the impression remains strong that he did not enjoy these expeditions. Time and again his letters voice unconcealed contempt for the cultural and intellectual standard of his people. He distanced himself, in mind, from his constituents and during these propaganda tours regarded the '"real world"... as a pageant'.[51] As a politician he did not require intimate contact with the masses to spur him forward. He was far more effective in restricted circles where he could exert the full force of his personality without fear of its evaporating in the delirium of a mass meeting. These public gatherings were not without physical danger. In April 1903, at a Zionist gathering at Minsk, he narrowly escaped arrest at the hands of the Russian police.[52]

Weizmann's main target was the Bund, an organization that aimed at the same constituency as the Zionists and was considered their most implacable foe. Preaching a revolutionary doctrine that Weizmann considered facile and an assimilationist view that he believed to be dangerous nonsense, the Bund presented a superficially attractive programme that he set out to destroy. One Bundist stalwart, Kolya Tepper, reportedly dogged his footsteps from meeting to meeting, trying to repair the damage Weizmann caused his party.[53] Weizmann described one of his triumphs in Warsaw in May 1903 thus: 'The speakers who came to the meeting are noted in Warsaw as "silver-tongued" orators; you should have seen how I wiped the floor with them. My address embraced the entire *Zionist* platform and lasted for three hours. The audience seethed, but listened benumbed.' After allowing the opposition to put its case, Weizmann 'took the floor . . . at midnight, and finished at four in the morning. The meeting had begun at 7 p.m. In brief, my resolution was carried by a majority of all against two. From 4 a.m., the Warsaw telephone was kept busy informing Jewry of the victory.'[54]

These battles, often extending over two or three nights, were paralleled by others in Geneva where Weizmann faced more serious protagonists: not only the Bund but its allies among the Russian Social Democrats, led by George Plekhanov and supported by the no less effective Julius Martov and Leon Trotsky. Weizmann expressed nothing but disgust for Jews who surrendered their intellectual integrity to Marxist dogma. The Bundists, whose ideology he saw as riddled with contradictions, roused his special ire, and he might well have agreed with Plekhanov's jibe that a Bundist was a Zionist who was afraid of seasickness.[55] They were, he thought, 'quasi-socialist, poorly assimilated as regards Judaism, degenerate, rotten, lacking in moral fibre [*moralischer Halt*]. . . . All the socialism of most of the local people, even the most outstanding of them, is merely a result [*Ausfluss*] of their own insignificance and individual weakness: they need the crowd to hide behind it, not to educate it.'[56] He met Plekhanov once in debate, in November 1901, when 'the General' was conscripted to rescue his troops, who were in danger of being vanquished. But 'Mr. Plekhanov was debunked and routed, and retreated in the most ignominious manner. . . . This had never happened in Switzerland before. Just think of it: Plekhanov, the favourite, the idol who is worshipped so. . . . I was in seventh heaven at having knocked out Balaam. I had been looking forward for an opportunity to come to grips with Mr. P. for a long time.' For Weizmann this was 'a tremendous triumph' that resulted in one hundred and eighty Jewish students joining the ranks of *HaShachar*. Plekhanov, outraged, demanded of Weizmann: 'What do you mean by bringing discord into our ranks?' 'Monsieur Plekhanov,' Weizmann rejoined, 'you are not the Tsar.'[57]

Weizmann's reputation thus secured, he was often alerted, via messages relayed from the Café Landolt, the most popular meeting-place of people in his Geneva circle, to hurry to some provincial Zionist society to aid in the contest against the Marxists. In this manner, he settled accounts in Lausanne with an old adversary, the Bundist Vladimir Medem.[58] February 1902 saw him in Munich for another gala debate lasting two nights. Weizmann opened the discussion: his paper went down 'excellently'; the opposition was 'insignificant', and it made no impact with its 'outworn phrases'. These intense all-night sessions left him prostrate. 'I am tired, tired, tired!' he complained.[59] But the effort was worthwhile, indeed essential. He regarded these clashes as a kind of holy war, the battles fought to save the souls of Jewish students from perfidy. And so, in a sense, it was.

But it was his efforts to establish a Jewish university that gave Weizmann most satisfaction. The idea, mooted initially at the first Zionist Congress, lay dormant until Weizmann and his friends breathed life into it as part of his great cultural campaign to rejuvenate the Zionist movement. In Weizmann's view there was also an immediate necessity for such an institution, given the increasing discrimination against Jewish students in Russia and elsewhere. He first raised the question in a serious manner at the preparatory youth conference in Munich in April 1901. This was the opening shot in a campaign which, in a broader sense, lasted his entire life: the Hebrew University in Jerusalem and the Weizmann Institute for Science in Rehovot are both living proof of his dedication to this concept. At any rate, for the two years 1901–3 the university project dominated his work. Its message was inscribed on the programme of the Democratic Fraction, and at the Zionist Congress in 1901 Buber and Weizmann moved a motion in its favour. Few Zionist gatherings could resist its allure, and favourable resolutions were carried at Minsk and Vienna. Weizmann wrote to Ahad Ha'am: 'I only joined the Cultural Committee [at the Zionist Congress] to tackle this problem. . . . I think there must be two institutions from the start: one in Palestine, devoted especially to

Jewish learning, another in Europe—a general university with a technical faculty and, of course, a chair of Jewish studies.' 'It will,' he enthused, 'be a synthesis of Yavneh* and Europe.'⁶⁰

Weizmann supervised the work with phenomenal energy from his office in Geneva: a questionnaire, known as the *Enquête*, on the state of Jewish academics and students in Europe was circulated; a pamphlet, *Eine Judische Hochschule*, prepared by Feiwel, Buber, and Weizmann was published late in 1902; a periodical, *Der Jude*, under their joint editorship, was planned to act as the organ of the Fraction and the mouthpiece of the university project; a committee of distinguished Jewish academics was formed; propaganda tours were undertaken to drum up support—Motzkin took in St. Petersburg and Moscow, Weizmann Kharkov, Rostov, Baku, Tiflis, Odessa, and Kiev; trips to London, Paris, and Brussels were planned. Weizmann canvassed an English politician, William Evans-Gordon: 'I should like to have the university in England, for that country is the most important focal point for us'. Both Herzl, who supported the project, and Weizmann believed, for practical reasons, that it should be located in western Europe, preferably Switzerland or England; and this despite a Congress resolution that it should be based 'only in Palestine'.

None of these plans materialized. In the wake of renewed anti-semitic violence in Russia in the spring of 1903, funds initially earmarked for *Der Jude* were diverted to aid victims of the pogroms. The frenetic activity for the university ground slowly to a halt, until finally the University-Democratic Fraction Bureau was shut down in February 1904.⁶¹ The project was virtually forgotten until Weizmann resurrected it again some ten years later.

The university provided Herzl and Weizmann with a common interest, and much of their correspondence dealt with this matter. Early on Herzl had indicated that he was 'very interested' in the project, and in July 1902 he undertook 'to achieve something practical'. Herzl's sympathy was, of course, of vital importance, but it did tend to diminish the significance of the Democratic Fraction as a ginger-group, for the university was probably the most salient aspect of its platform. Moreover, the affairs of the Fraction were not flourishing. Weizmann was unable to inject his own sense of urgency into his more dilatory col-

---

*The site of a Jewish seminary, situated approximately ten kilometres west of present-day Rehovot, founded after the destruction of the second Temple by the Romans in 70 AD. It became the spiritual and intellectual centre of Palestine Jewry, and a source of inspiration to the diaspora.

leagues. They were either tardy in replying to his letters, or lacka-daisical in carrying out instructions. The Fraction would not outlive his own enthusiasm for it. The tone of his language turned shrill; his temper grew shorter. He was fed up being the *'enfant terrible'*. 'Such indolence and utter indifference . . . None of the Fraction members write anything to me at all for the simple and very obvious reason that they said "Amen" to the Fraction a long time ago . . . the game is not worth the candle. Everything is so rotten that there is no hope of accomplishing anything.' He would waste no further time on 'a game of blind man's bluff'.[62]

Among Weizmann's associates in the Fraction, he most respected Berthold Feiwel, who cooperated loyally with him. About Martin Buber, he was more ambivalent. 'In a sense, it may be said that Feiwel gave to Zionism, losing himself in it, and Buber took from it, using it as his aesthetic material,' he wrote later. He also felt a strong, and potentially fatal, attachment to Zvi Aberson, 'the *Luftmensch par excellence*', as he called him, widely feared as a *"Bundistenfresser"* (gobbler-up of Bundists): 'a wonderful companion, gay [and] witty', possessing 'a brilliant mind' but lacking 'all sense of application'.[63]

Only to mention the names of the Fraction's stalwarts is to comprehend its problem. It was a lobby of quarrelsome, prickly, and un-disciplined intellectuals centered on the university cities of western Europe; it was an army with many aspiring generals and few soldiers. And, despite its pretensions, it lacked a coherent ideology, nor had it a mass following in eastern Europe. Did it believe the masses were even worthy of being led? 'God, what trash, what poverty of thought, what stupidity, pettiness and lack of everything,' wrote Weizmann, on one of his periodic tours. They were fit only for 'cannonfodder',[64] he said once, and he had no faith that the masses had regenerative qualities. Nor were they a source of positive inspiration for him; rather, he would have to save them from their own follies. They would have to be coaxed and cajoled, pushed and prodded by those who knew better. 'We ourselves are not a group of democrats,' he clarified, 'but rather *l'intellectuelle dans le sionisme [sic]*, if one may use the term'. It was ironic that the Democratic Fraction should bring 'aristocratic undertakings into being—an *Elite-Organ* [the projected periodical of the Fraction], *Hochschule, Kunstverlag*, etc'.[65]

The contemptuous, patronizing tone Weizmann employs to describe the inability of the Jewish masses to rise above their station and his emphasis on so-called elitist politics have been commonly ascribed, in philosophical terms, to the influence of Friedrich Nietzsche. Certainly, he was profoundly influenced by Nietzsche, who has been described by one eminent historian as 'the most influential thinker of his age', and Weizmann's letters for the period are laced with favourable references to him. *Thus Spake Zarathustra* was a best-seller in most European countries, and the German philosopher's biting criticism of the mores of contemporary bourgeois society captivated an entire generation of intellectuals.[66] Neitzsche's conception of the will to power as the basic drive of human behaviour might well have appealed to Weizmann. Was not his own behaviour decisive proof of Nietzsche's theories? Moreover, in a wider context, Weizmann saw Zionism primarily in terms of a self-liberating movement. Only the Jews could save themselves from the servility and slavery of the diaspora: they could not look for salvation in others. One can see an analogy: Nietzsche's 'Overman', who has overcome himself and his environment (Weizmann and his Fraction) and his 'Last Man', uncreative, conformist, hedonist (the Jewish masses).

There is no way of assessing the veracity of these conjectures, however appealing and logical, for Weizmann never explained the precise attraction Nietzsche held for him. It can be said that he was introduced to "elitist politics" as early as 1896 when he joined the *Bnei Moshe*, the *corps d'élite* inspired by Ahad Ha'am, whose personality and teachings were remote from Nietzsche's and who exerted a far more profound influence on Weizmann. In any case, put at its lowest common denominator, in mass politics one either leads or is led. Perhaps Nietzsche provided the ideological decoration, essential to his self-confidence as an intellectual, for Weizmann's predilection for leadership. Still, his intemperate outbursts denigrating the Jewish masses were the peevish, impatient, perhaps guilt-ridden, utterances of a young man in a hurry forced back into the painful reality of the Jewish world of the Pale after the relatively privileged existence he led in western Europe.

By the spring of 1903 that reality had taken a sharp turn for the worse. Weizmann, in Pinsk for the Passover celebrations, returned to Geneva in late April to hear the news of a terrible pogrom carried out at Kishinev, a pogrom proceeded by an anti-semitic press campaign and a stiffening of anti-Jewish policies on the part of the Tsarist authorities. On 19–20 April, when the Jewish quarters in Kishinev were attacked, forty-nine Jews were killed, hundreds were injured, shops were looted and considerable property destroyed. The blood-letting shocked western liberal opinion. Many Russians, including Leo Tolstoy, denounced the massacre. Chaim Bialik, poet of the Hebrew national revival, composed his best-known work, *The City of Slaughter*, with Kishinev in mind.

Kishinev was in some ways a key event that radicalized Jewish opinion; both the revolutionists and Zionists were strengthened as a result of it. Throughout the Pale panic spread; self-defence groups sprang up—in Pinsk, Weizmann's sister and brother, Haya and Moshe, were among its leaders.[67] Eleven years later, Weizmann imagined that he too had fought at Kishinev. 'In a group of about 100 Jews we defended women and girls, Jewish lives and property. We "slept" in the cemetery—the only "safe" place—and we saw 80 Jewish corpses brought in, mutilated dead'.[68] But no contemporary evidence supports this tale. On 22 April he was in Berlin, writing to Vera, while his first mention of Kishinev is on 27 April, having learned of the massacre from newspaper accounts in the West.[69] When he arrived in Geneva, Weizmann did his part to organize relief-work and speak at protest demonstrations.

Kishinev, like the pogroms of the 1880s, was a terrible reminder that the Jews remained powerless and vulnerable to the whims of anti-semites. Why, after six years of activity, had the Zionist movement been so singularly ineffective in converting the Jewish masses? Had it failed in its most elementary task as a national liberation movement? In the heat of the moment, it was plausible to question, as many did, the role the Zionist movement was playing, if any, in the calamitous events. Pessimists alleged that there was little to note on the credit side: no political breakthrough, no mass conversion to Zionism. These were the weighty issues to which Weizmann, aided by Feiwel, addressed himself in a lengthy memorandum for Herzl's attention.

A few months earlier Weizmann might have been confident of a favourable hearing, for, as he proudly boasted, his 'successes' had 'greatly impressed' Herzl.[70] Now some tension had crept back in their relations. Weizmann had indirectly associated himself with Ahad Ha'am's biting criticism of Herzl's romanticized conception of a Jewish Palestine, *Altneuland*. Enraged by this assault on his 'best book', Herzl enquired whether his infallible critic intended 'running for Pope'.[71] This controversy developed into a most acrimonious debate with Ahad Ha'am's 'cardinals' publicly cocking a snook at Herzl.[72]

Weizmann's essay—it ran to 6500 words—was a more reasoned, sophisticated discussion of the travails of Zionism. But it can only be read as an all-out attack on Herzl's methods and order of priorities. He reviewed, unfavourably, the state of world Zionism: in western Europe he detected only 'stagnation' and 'superficiality'; in Russia, young Jews were abandoning Zionism 'through revolutionary conviction'; regarding America, 'it is best to remain silent'. He again reiterated the demand for a serious investigation 'of Palestine and the adjoining countries'. In particular, he railed against the undue weight Herzl had awarded the *Mizrachi*: 'The *Mizrachi* know of only one kind of heroism, that of Orthodox dogmatism and dehumanized passive resistance.' He saw this as a major factor in explaining Zionism's dismal record. 'Their [the *Mizrachi*'s] horizon and perspective are so limited that they can have no understanding whatsoever of a modern approach.' Zionism was torn between the 'fanatically religious' *Mizrachi* and the 'narrow petty-bourgeois' path chosen by the others. This narrow division would bring catastrophe upon the movement. All that remained in Zionism, Weizmann complained, 'is denounced as atheistic, anarchistic, revolutionary . . . [and] driven into opposition'. Yet the Fraction remained the movement's only hope for survival: 'It alone is capable of assuming the struggle against the revolutionaries, which indeed it does. It alone is freedom-loving and socially enlightened. It extracts the Jewish essence from among the masses and pours it into a European mould. But what the Jewish essence is, the European Zionists refuse to comprehend; even the leadership has still to recognize it.' He refined this argument a few months later:

> One group conceives of Zionism as a mechanism, and is ignorant of its connection with the soul of the Jewish people. Consequently it seeks to 'manufacture' Zionism either through diplomatic journeys or through fund-raising appeals. Elements that are partly detached from living Judaism—the assimilated Westerners on the one side, and the Orthodox confined within their rigid formulae on the other—are incapable of a better understanding of the national cause.
>
> The other group, however, understands Zionism to be the life-giving force, both actual and potential: the free development of the nation finding its highest expression in the idea of statehood. . . .
>
> The great merit of leaders from the West came from their finding an instrument in the Congresses that proved appropriate. Tacitly, we made this pact: we would supply the content and it would be left to the leaders to create the external forms. I do not believe the compact was kept with equal responsibility by both sides. Whereas on our side

the political forms of the movement were being continually shaped into an organic force as a result of our Jewish content, for the West Europeans Zionism remained a cliché, completely devoid of Jewish content, unstable, wavering and hollow, finding its highest expression in so-called diplomacy, and in the 'Jewish Statism' that smells of philanthropy.[73]

Whether Weizmann actually believed that the Fraction had a future we do not know. For its failure he blamed his colleagues, 'the "activists"', who 'were asleep when they should have been in the vanguard'.[74] He was striking out at Herzl, yet he knew he possessed no trump cards to play.

So did Herzl. 'I am not over-sensitive toward a reasonable opposition,' he observed, 'neither do I want songs of praise sung to me,' but in no uncertain terms he condemned the Fraction for its divisive conduct. This, if persisted in, he countered, would ruin the movement. As for Weizmann, 'I regard you . . . as a person who has been temporarily misled, but nevertheless a useful force who will once more find his way back and proceed along the right road together with all of us.'[75] This was a condescending pat on the head to Weizmann, who had marshalled his facts admirably and presented his case with force and conviction. But Herzl's response accurately reflected the status of the Fraction in Zionist politics, as Weizmann knew only too well.

Still, the Fraction was highly significant for Weizmann's education as a politician. It raised him to the position of a leader, albeit of only a marginal pressure-group, whose word was listened to and whose advice was sought. It also gave him his first taste of the bitter-sweet concoction of authority and frustration inherent in leadership (more frustration than authority during these early years). He possessed a majestic vision and never doubted that his path was correct. While others vacillated, he plunged on impatiently, relentlessly, anxious to complete the task in hand but already perceiving the difficulties ahead. When events moved smoothly in his direction, he exuded an infectious optimism. His spirit soared: 'Am on fire. Full of hope.'[76] Thus buoyed up, he would bring to bear the full measure of his eloquence, his persuasiveness, his magnetic charm. Few could stand up to him when in full flight. If thwarted, however, he revealed less attractive facets of his nature: self-pity, pessimism, arrogance, pride, vindictiveness, pettiness. He would lash out at his opponents or his colleagues who failed to keep up with his pace. There was in him, as Richard Crossman has acutely noted, a 'combination of intellectual maturity and emotional instability'.[77] He never succeeded entirely in ridding himself of this failing, although in later years he managed to control it more effectively.

Nevertheless, he bent the Fraction to his will. He dominated its office in Geneva. (Of course, its organizational weakness worked to his benefit.) This was how he worked best, and would continue to do so in the future, in an intimate circle which he could dominate and in which he could infuse associates with energy, confidence and enthusiasm. He was always more at ease in an environment he could control than in a multilayered political organization. The Zionist leadership regarded him as no more than a 'gadfly'.[78] He did not yet possess the authority, the aura, that springs from success—but his qualities and potential were becoming more widely recognized.

During the summer of 1903 Weizmann's mood was grim. Apart from the dreadful state of Zionism, he was nearing a crossroad in his personal life. Geneva no longer promised certain professional advancement. His professor, Karl Graebe, was retiring, and with him went his assistants. Weizmann would have to look elsewhere to pursue his scientific career; and this impinged upon his relations with Vera, who had not yet completed her medical studies in Geneva.[79] But the real cause for his depression lay in his own sense of personal failure. All his plans to revitalize the movement had miscarried. The Fraction was in disarray, and however much he lambasted his associates he could not shirk his share of the responsibility. His last propaganda tour in Russia had ended miserably. The university project had foundered; *Der Jude* had failed to appear. It was one long procession of setbacks. Giving vent to his emotions, he blamed 'the disgusting swindle of philanthropic Zionism.' Pessimistically he wrote, 'I feel that we are descending into slime, heaven protect us, with everything in jeopardy . . . in my view Zionism as it is lived today is but a profanation of the idea.' He summed up the general situation on the eve of the sixth Zionist Congress in one word: 'awful [*schwach*].'[80]

FOUR

UGANDA AND MANCHESTER

On 22 August 1903, the night before the formal opening of the sixth Zionist Congress at Basel, Herzl wrote in his diary: 'My heart is acting up from fatigue. If I were doing it for thanks I would be a big fool. Yesterday I gave my report to the "Greater A.C."* I presented England and Russia. And it didn't occur to any of them for even a single moment that for these greatest of all accomplishments to date I deserve a word, or even a smile, of thanks.'[1]

The following morning, appearing exhausted and prematurely aged, he faced some six hundred delegates. The horror of Kishinev was uppermost in their minds. Herzl reported on his visit to Russia and his interview with Plehve, an initiative that earned him bitter resentment among the Russian delegates, optimistically interpreting Plehve's casual promises to alleviate the plight of the Jews. He recounted the failure of the attempted negotiations, encouraged by Joseph Chamberlain, the British Colonial Secretary, to effect Jewish settlement in the El Arish area of the Sinai.[2] He then told of a new British offer, which envisaged 'an autonomous Jewish settlement in East Africa with a Jewish administration, Jewish local government headed by a Jewish senior official, everything, of course, under the sovereign jurisdiction of Great Britain'. The new territory would never have 'the historic, poetical-religious, and Zionist value that even the Sinai peninsula would have had', and it could never dislodge the ultimate goal of Palestine. But the immediate hardship of Jewry was so

---

*The Greater Actions Committee, elected by the Zionist Congress, was responsible for the overall supervision of Zionist policy. The Smaller Actions Committee, which conducted Zionist policy on a day-to-day basis, was required to report to the GAC on a regular basis.

desperate that it called for radical, unconventional solutions. He asked the Congress to weigh the proposal carefully, to recognize the historical and political significance of the British approach: 'I believe the Congress can find a way to make use of this offer. The way in which this offer was made to us is bound to help, improve and alleviate the situation of the Jewish people without our abandoning any of the great principles on which our movement was founded.' Aware of discord within the Congress, he avoided asking for a clear-cut rejection or approval of the scheme but instead asked that a select committee examine the feasibility of Jewish settlement in East Africa.*[3]

Herzl's not entirely unexpected announcement dominated the proceedings.[4] Most delegates were prepared to follow his lead, some (particularly from the British delegation) with embarrassing enthusiasm: 'Three cheers for England,' cried Israel Zangwill, bringing the gathering to its feet in a burst of wild applause. But equally there was deep-rooted opposition, notably in the Russian delegation, representatives of those Jews whom Herzl, by his proposal, wished to rescue from other Kishinevs.

Max Nordau, Herzl's faithful aide, who at heart opposed the project, publicly came to his leader's rescue, pleading with the delegates to accept the proposal, not as a permanent solution, but as a *Nachtasyl* (temporary night-shelter). Eventually the Congress was persuaded to ratify Herzl's formula: when the roll-call ended, 292 delegates had voted in favour, 176 against, with 143 abstentions,[5] but it was a pyrrhic victory. Formal parliamentary majorities were no longer sufficient— passions ran too high. The map of East Africa was torn down from the wall behind the speaker's dais. The Russian delegation filed out to consider their position in closed session. Some delegates sat down on the floor and observed the traditional, ritual mourning for the dead. One man fainted; others wept. When Herzl tried to pacify them, he was met with a shout of 'traitor'. Soon after the Congress had dispersed, a radical student attempted to assassinate Nordau.

Herzl had to exert all his authority to convince the Russians to return to the Congress, to preserve the unity of the Zionist movement.

---

*This is popularly and inevitably referred to as "the Uganda crisis", and no amount of nitpicking by professional historians has yet shaken off the label. In fact, the original territories discussed with representatives of the British Government were some 40,000 square miles between Nairobi and the Mau escarpment, an area finally whittled down to 5500 square miles comprising the Gwas plateau to the north-east of the first mentioned zone. These lands lie clearly in Kenya.

He reassured them of his devotion to the Basel programme, to its aim to create a home for the Jewish people in Palestine, but he also reminded them of their duty to help the homeless, persecuted Jews of eastern Europe. They listened to him in stormy silence, but next morning they took their seats to hear his final address. Undeterred, he returned to the East Africa project, and emphasized again that it was but a temporary measure. Then, in a gesture of high theatre, he raised his right hand and recited in Hebrew, 'If I forget thee, oh Jerusalem, may my right hand forget its cunning.'[6]

The deliberations of the sixth Congress left the movement shaken and confused. Its unity could no longer be taken for granted. Not until the outbreak of world war in 1914 did the struggle between the so-called 'politicals', who followed Herzl, and the 'practicals' subside. In November 1903, at a meeting of Russian Zionist regional leaders at Kharkov, Meneham Ussishkin, the "iron man" of Russian Zionism, who had been absent from Basel but who was an implacable opponent of the East Africa scheme, threatened secession from the movement unless Herzl retracted and returned to the path of true Zionism.[7] Although nothing came of this manoeuvre, Ussishkin and his hardliners openly rebelled against the official leadership.[8] Ussishkin would no doubt have defined it as "war to the knife". It was Zionism's gravest crisis to date, and its repercussions were never entirely erased.

How did Weizmann react to these events? Judging from his memoirs, his attitude from the outset was clear-cut and decisive. He recognized, he wrote later, that of course 'this was the first time in the exilic history of Jewry that a great government had officially negotiated with the elected representatives of the Jewish people. The identity, the legal personality of the Jewish people had been re-established.' But following Herzl's sensational announcement 'a spirit of disquiet, dejection and anxiety spread through the Congress' which apparently also touched Weizmann; and when the Russian caucus met 'I made a violent speech against the Uganda project and swung to our side many of the hesitant', thus establishing a pattern for his future role: unrelenting opposition to the scheme, in which he and Ussishkin worked together; that he later played Ussishkin's trumpet in western Europe, there can be no doubt.[9]

But in fact Weizmann's initial, instinctive reaction to the Uganda proposal was more ambivalent than his recollections would have us believe. When the Russian caucus first convened, Weizmann expressed general support for Herzl's idea: he was attracted by the possibility of diverting the flow of Jewish emigration into an autonomous Jewish territory. For Weizmann it was imperative that the Zionist movement involve itself, somehow, in the regulation of Jewish emigration, lest the Jewish masses fleeing eastern Europe simply disappear into the morass of western society. He put a motion in this sense to the meeting, only for it to be rejected.[10] Consequently he declared that he would take 'a positive attitude' toward the British offer,[11] though he criticized the wider and more negative connotations of the scheme: it would scarcely convince the world community that the Jews were capable of running a country of their own, he believed, although he acknowledged the educative value it would have for the Jews actually engaged in it.

Weizmann's support for Herzl was at variance with his reputation as a young firebrand at odds with the Zionist establishment. And in fact his career as a "Ugandist" was a short-lived, temporary lapse. From this point on his memoirs are accurate. Yet his readiness to consider favourably the East Africa project is not surprising. Though it has become a convention of Zionist historiography to judge the Uganda proposal in a wholly negative, unfavourable light, it is clear that the project as argued by Herzl offered much to the movement. The Kishinev tragedy weighed heavily upon Weizmann's mind, as it did for most delegates. A responsible political leadership must address itself to the problems of the hour confronting the constituency it claims to represent. Herzl never denied the centrality of Palestine; indeed, he had made it clear that East Africa was but a temporary refuge. These were arguments convincing enough, at least, for Weizmann's father and brother Shmuel, who were to be counted among the Russian 'Ugandists'.[12] Also, Weizmann was too much a pragmatist to reject out of hand any proposal, however outrageous at first sight. If there was one political guideline that he followed faithfully, it was that there are no absolutes in politics: one must balance the advantages against the disadvantages before drawing a conclusion. Only after gauging the atmosphere at the Congress, and in particular the reaction of the Russian delegation, did Weizmann appreciate that on balance the Uganda proposal would cause the movement more harm than good.

During the plenary sessions of the Congress he watched and listened. He took no part in the great public quarrel, although he was active in the Russian caucus. Gradually, inevitably, the debate's tone and vehemence, the emotions it set loose, the logic of the opposition's arguments affected his judgement. He aired the hope: 'If the British government and people are what I think they are, they will make us a better offer.'[13] When Herzl's motion was put to the floor, Weizmann's hand was among those raised against it.

He explained his *volte-face* to a meeting of the *Nein-Sagers* immediately after the Congress had dispersed. 'Before the content of the project had been made clear to me I supported it; but in the course of the debate I discovered that it was of its essence that Zionism was to be transmuted. Then I turned into an opponent, for all that I am in favour of [controlled] emigration.'[14]

But the gist of his speech was an attack on Herzl's Zionist philosophy, a perennial theme of his. Herzl, he claimed, had transformed 'our entire programme at one go'. He had 'confused' his opponents, so much so that they hesitated 'to state whether the project was compatible with the Basel programme or not'. From all this Weizmann conjectured that:

> Herzl is not a nationalist, but a promoter of projects. He came across the *Hibbat Zion* idea and aligned himself with [it] for a period. Then when it failed, he reversed himself. He only takes external conditions into account, whereas the power on which we rely is the psychology of the people and its living desires. We, for our part, [always] knew that we were incapable of gaining Palestine in the short term and were therefore not discouraged when this or that attempt had failed. It is the people's consciousness that has [now] to be bolstered. There must be established a society to propagate the Zionist idea in its national form. . . . Cultural work must be put before all else.

Here is the leader of the Democratic Fraction once again. One should not doubt the sincerity of his criticism. There is a consistent theme in the complaint that can be traced back to his first days as the inspirer of the Fraction.

There were other, more practical reasons for his position. Weizmann was aware that if he persisted in his 'positive attitude' toward Herzl's plan, he would isolate himself from those elements in the Zionist movement who were essential to his survival as a political force. To align himself with the West against the East would be tantamount to political suicide. Prudence demanded that he keep a foot in the anti-Herzl camp. By opposing the East Africa plan he could raise his own status and, with the great cause of Palestinian Zionism to fight for, the Democratic Fraction would be revitalized. It would pioneer the new stage of the struggle: 'to work for a pure Zionism, a national Zionism, and devote all [its] efforts to the study of Palestine'.[15] His own power base secure, he could then cooperate with Ussishkin from a position of strength. Ambition, frowned on only by the naive, would thus serve the lofty principle he believed in, not contradict it. When the Congress elected a committee to report on the feasibility of the Uganda scheme, he accepted a place on it, presumably to act as watchdog over the interests of the 'national Zionists'.

It was typical of Weizmann that no sooner had he decided upon a new course than he pursued it with the utmost vigour. He planned to abandon the laboratory for six months and devote himself to Zionist affairs.[16] In his first directive to the Democratic Fraction after the Congress, he urged his followers to launch an anti-Uganda crusade throughout western Europe.[17] He was particularly concerned at the state of affairs in London, 'a most important and responsible centre',[18] where Zangwill was busy spreading his territorialist poison; Weizmann did not want it to fall by default to the Herzlians. He would test the earnestness of the British offer himself. His trip to London in the autumn of 1903 was organized as methodically as one of his scientific experiments. 'Dear Major,' he wrote to William Evans-Gordon, 'I am taking the liberty of asking you kindly to send me such Government reports, Blue-Books, and maps and descriptions that bear an official and authentic character.'[19]

This was the main purpose of his visit, but it was not the only one. His improved temper also led to activity on behalf of the moribund university project. Now he proposed inaugurating vacation courses— 'I visualize them for next summer in Zurich'—conducted by distinguished Jewish academics to keep the enterprise afloat until the time was opportune for more wide-scale activity.[20] And, sandwiched between these public duties, he would somehow sound out the possibilities of an academic appointment for himself.

Thus braced up he arrived on 8 October 1903 and took lodgings in Stepney in East London. He was appalled at the spectacle. 'I arrived today in this monstrous London, and have hardly managed to do a thing,' he wrote to Vera. 'I am terribly tired today. I have been rushing about madly, and there is slush here, foul weather, fog, din and uproar, and a language which is not entirely comprehensible to me. . . . I am now in Whitechapel. Lord, what horror! Stench, foul smells, emaciated Jewish faces. A mixture of a London avenue and Jewish poverty in the suburbs of Vilna.' He had also run out of money. 'Send me at least 60–70 francs,' he implored her, 'I made a grave mistake in my calculations'.[21]

But his politicking paid off well. (He must have conducted his talks in French or German, or at worst pidgin-English, but his fervour may have overcome this disability, for it did not prove to be a major disadvantage.) He met Evans-Gordon and Sir Harry Johnston, the Africa expert and one-time British Commissioner of Uganda, and found both sympathetic. Johnston dismissed Chamberlain as 'superficial' and his offer as 'frivolous'—sweet music to Weizmann's ears. Small wonder that he became convinced that the African project was 'as good as buried'. Immensely satisfied with his diplomatic accomplishments, he observed to Martin Buber, 'We, too, can be diplomats, eh?', adding unkindly, 'Herzl would have spoken already of *"gigantische Erfolge"* [huge successes]'.[22]

Weizmann encountered more opposition among English Jews than he had in the government. They were 'unenlightened and easily misled', he said, consumed by 'an African fever'. Zangwill, the ideologue of the East Africa scheme, knew nothing of Judaism or of the Jews, Weizmann now claimed. After a lengthy discussion, he dismissed and admonished him: 'You are the photographer of the Ghetto and not its psychologist.'[23] He also developed an antipathy to Leopold Greenberg, Herzl's chief agent in London and later editor of the *Jewish Chronicle*, a key figure in the negotiations with the British government. He, and his newspaper, adopted a hostile attitude towards Weizmann's activities which time did not mellow. Not one to cast grudges aside, Weizmann typically reciprocated in kind. 'I seldom read the *Jewish Chronicle*,' he remarked off-handedly more than thirty years after the East African affair.[24]

In this stronghold of Herzlian Zionism, Weizmann stumbled upon one staunch ally: Moses Gaster, *Haham* (chief rabbi) of the Sephardic community in England, one-time president of the English Folklore Society, and a vehement opponent of the Uganda scheme. For Weizmann Gaster was a rare windfall. He eventually helped to smooth Weizmann's academic path in Manchester, and periodically he would rescue his protégé from acute financial embarrassment with convenient loans. But he was also a useful, though unpredictable, political ally. Full of his own importance and inclined to stand on his dignity, he was also extremely ambitious, perhaps out of proportion to his real abilities. From the outset, Weizmann perceived that their relationship would be a difficult one. 'One has to be very careful with him', he warned Vera; he was an 'absolute rogue'.[25] For the moment, however, Gaster's ambition, his influence and many contacts, served Weizmann's purpose. Gaster cast himself in the role as Herzl's successor, an illusion Weizmann did nothing to dispel. Building on Gaster's authority and position and pride, he hoped to create an anti-Uganda front in London which, in alignment with Ussishkin's forces in the East, would destroy the scheme forever.

Less divisive by far were Weizmann's vacation courses in Jewish studies, which he had first thought of in Zurich and now realized in London—'Jewish Toynbee Halls', as they were called, in reference to the pioneer university settlement and social-service centre in the East End. This was a cause around which he rallied even those whom he had antagonized over East Africa—a political bonus whose significance could not have escaped Weizmann.[26] Even Zangwill agreed to cooperate with him; two other stalwarts of Anglo-Jewry, Joseph Cowen and Leopold Kessler, both Herzlians although less extreme than Zangwill, registered their approval. Herbert Bentwich, another leading figure in Anglo-Zionism, also lent his support. Gaster naturally agreed to conduct a course—in Bible criticism.[27] This was a rich harvest.

These accomplishments in a strange environment improved Weizmann's humour and raised his estimation of London as a political centre. 'The sun has smiled, and all my people have responded. . . . I am terribly pleased that I went to London, terribly pleased.' 'What an interesting city London is!' he concluded after four days in the capital. 'Darling,' he wrote to Vera, 'I have never in my life felt so well as here. It is not without reason that I was striving to get here. This is the hub of the world and, really, you sense the breathing of a giant, the city of cities.' His evenings were spent—invested really—in socializing. Even his financial situation looked brighter, albeit temporarily. 'Life here has proved far cheaper than I expected. Mainly because I am always invited out to dinner. I have dined at Gordon's, Gaster's (twice), Zangwill's, Kessler's, Bentwich's, and so on, and so on.'[28]

Shopping for Vera proved a mixed experience, though he managed to confirm a sterotype impression of the staid English. 'The English cannot understand at all how a man can buy articles of ladies' apparel. The sales girls were laughing at me. What a strange people!' Neither had he neglected his personal affairs. He made 'some *démarches*', he reported, and Gaster and Evans-Gordon promised to help him secure an academic appointment.[29] All in all, his first experience of London was an exciting one. He left after a week convinced that he could cut a figure in both Zionist politics and the scientific world in his newly discovered 'city of cities'.

Weizmann's prediction that the East Africa proposal was a non-starter turned out to be accurate. British settlers in Kenya joined the Zionist opposition in denouncing the scheme. Angry letters appeared in the press. A *Times* editorial intoned against the project in a language familiar to Herzl from the criticisms at the Congress. Other papers followed suit: one stigmatized the scheme as 'Jewganda'. These were signs that the British government could not ignore. If the Zionists did not want it and the British settlers were opposed to it, why pursue the matter further? The government's attitude cooled considerably. The Weizmann-Ussishkin alliance worked assiduously to keep up the momentum of opposition, though as usual the pace was too slow for Weizmann. 'I am awaiting your plan with great impatience', he pressed Ussishkin. 'Action is essential. I have tried to do everything in my power, but I feel that our Nay-Sayers are sluggish.'[30]

Ussishkin regarded his young accomplice in the West as a useful tool rather than an equal partner. He had refused to disclose to Weizmann the decisions taken at the conference in Kharkov, invoking the formal point that he was bound by the confidentiality of the proceedings.[31] When Weizmann learned of its resolutions from another source, he approved their militancy: 'the people rose to the occasion in the end with a radical resolution: either Africa or themselves'.[32] Despite this endorsement, Ussishkin's bulldozer tactics misfired: Herzl, refusing to be intimidated by the Russians, fought them on their own ground. Adopting a high tone, in December he charged his accusers with disloyalty and sabotage. Ussishkin did not appear at this confrontation, but his agents wilted before Herzl's aggrieved presence and sound arguments, and they departed empty-handed; their ultimatum — 'Africa or ourselves' — had been brushed aside. Weizmann was outraged at Herzl's methods — 'He is fighting the Russian Zionists in the shabbiest ways' — but it must have been abundantly clear that Herzl had outmanoeuvred them. Fight the system, Weizmann now urged, not personalities.[33] Fight it not by crash tactics or frontal assault, which offered little profit and courted disaster, but by indirection: consolidate your resources, feel out your opponent's weak spots, and then, when you sense the time is ripe, launch your attack. This was Weizmann's style for many years, and while it exposed him to accusations of over-subtlety, deviousness, or opportunism, it also paid off rich political dividends.

By December 1903 it was obvious, even to Herzl, that Jewish settlement in East Africa was no longer practical politics,[34] and the

Foreign Office now believed that it had blundered in promoting the scheme. Opposition to it was too vehement and too widespread. On 27 December Herzl informed the Greater Actions Committee that the British had withdrawn their proposal, 'owing to the difficulties they had encountered, especially through the absence of any enthusiasm and the creation of a hostile attitude towards the project on the Zionist side'.[35] This was Herzl's interpretation, no doubt intended to rein in the opposition on his own side. In fact, the British were more concerned about alienating their own colonists, and the territory they were now prepared to offer the Jews was far less attractive than the land mentioned in the original proposal.

At an extraordinary Zionist gathering in Vienna in April 1904, Herzl defended his position on East Africa, despite renewed threats by Ussishkin and company, but he was now merely going through the motions. A sick man, Herzl died at the beginning of July. The scheme lingered on for another year, until it was officially buried at the seventh Zionist Congress in 1905 after a negative report by the Africa Survey Commission.

The controversy over East Africa confirmed the centrality of Palestine in the Zionist programme. The Congress of 1905 resolved that only in *Erez Israel* could the Jewish people create a national centre. Those who thought otherwise, who rejected in principle the link between Palestine and Zionism, who believed that Zionism should foster Jewish national rights in any undeveloped country—the so-called territorialists led by Zangwill—ceded from the movement and set up their own Jewish Territorial Organization. Weizmann adopted an extreme position on this issue: even before the Congress had convened, he proposed to exclude such heretics from the Zionist Organization.[36] In the future, as the condition of world Jewry deteriorated, there were to be many other "Ugandas". He emphatically rejected them all as false panaceas. He was not oblivious to the sufferings of Jewry, nor blind to the need to devise temporary solutions to alleviate their plight. But settlement in Palestine had to take precedent over all other projects, however attractive momentarily, for only Palestine could provide the basis for a long-range solution of the Jewish problem, which Weizmann did not perceive solely in terms of anti-semitism or persecution.

One other unforeseen consequence of the African debate was to enhance the status of Great Britain in Zionist eyes. In the collective psyche of leading Zionists, it was already unique. 'England, great England, England the free, England commanding all the seas,' Herzl had enthused to a Zionist Congress in London, 'she will understand us and our purpose. From here the ideal of Zionism will soar higher and farther.'[37] Weizmann, as a child, had expressed a similar sentiment. His recent visit to London confirmed his impression and raised his expectations: 'if we are to get help from any quarter it will be in England'.[38] All this was pure instinct, reinforced by his unfortunate tendency, particularly when his mood was buoyant, to inflate the importance of his contacts.

The British government was certainly more receptive than other governments to Zionist arguments. The idea of settling European Jews in their ancient homeland of Palestine was viewed with great sympathy in certain political and intellectual circles in Britain. Ever since Oliver Cromwell had decided to allow the Jews to return to England in December 1655, the concept of the Return of the Jews to Palestine had been a topic for public debate, much of it highly polemical.[39] Nurtured on the scriptures and strengthened by a deeply felt bond with the Old Testament, an influential school of British politicians and publicists acted and felt as though they were fulfilling an historical mission when furthering the Zionist interest. One enthusiastic gentile Zionist, Josiah Wedgwood, recorded: 'When my ancestors hewed down the aristocrats at Wigan Lane and Naseby they were armed with the names of Aaron and Abner; and they rallied to the charge, calling on the God of Israel in the language of the prophets. . . . Toward such a people one has a feeling of awe, they are so well known, and yet so old and eternal.'[40]

There were political manifestations. In 1838, in the midst of a Great Power crisis in the Near East, Lord Palmerston had established a British consulate in Jerusalem with instructions to British representatives in the Levant to protect local Jewish communities, perhaps the first instance when British imperial policy merged with a benevolent interest in the fate of the Jewish community in Palestine.[41] This gentile Zionist tradition, hinted at in Disraeli's *Coningsby* and *Tancred*, found its most distinguished literary advocate in George Eliot and her novel *Daniel Deronda*. It was also represented by a colourful assortment of Victorian personages: Lord Shaftesbury, Laurence Oliphant, Colonel George Gawler, Colonel Henry Churchill, to name but the more prominent of them. Weizmann's contemporaries, Lloyd George and Balfour, Smuts and Milner, were the authentic heirs to this rich inheritance.

From its inception the Zionist movement had shown confidence in Britain by registering its financial instrument, the Jewish Colonial

Trust, in London. But the African episode had also shown that Britain would not hesitate to retreat from a sympathetic position should she detect a clash of interests between herself and Zionism, a point perhaps not sufficiently appreciated by Zionist politicians.

Weizmann's reborn enthusiasm for Britain resulted undoubtedly from a combination of his diplomatic triumphs and the advancement of his personal affairs. He had not yet reached a definite decision about his future, but as he confided to Martin Buber in October 1903: 'I have good prospects in England and I ought to be there for the sake of the cause'.[42] Yet his euphoria did not last long. His health took a sharp turn for the worse. In December he wrote of a 'constant temperature and a heavy cough'. He was coughing blood and complained of many sleepless nights. His health was 'totally ruined', and he thought that only a year's rest would repair it.[43]

His political expectations also remained unfulfilled. The plans to establish a university were jettisoned; even the vacation courses, which were to have taken London by storm, were abandoned. *Der Jude*, for lack of funds, remained a blueprint. Most significant of all, Weizmann's ambitious scheme to exploit the East Africa controversy in order to unseat Herzl and lead the Zionist movement back to Palestine had come unstuck. Although Weizmann believed that Ussishkin was the only Zionist leader who had not yet 'lost his head', Ussishkin never responded to his advances with an equal degree of warmth and trust; in principle, he opposed exploiting the Fraction as a pawn in the contest against Herzl, and scorned the party system as divisive and sectarian. He was engaged in a great national struggle, not in hole-in-the-corner political shenanigans. Abandon your 'scarecrow', he advised Weizmann.[44]

In any case, it proved impossible for Weizmann to mobilize the Fraction. The problems that had frustrated him in the past returned to thwart him now. None of his colleagues were infused with his zeal, with his intense sense of urgency; none were prepared to submit unconditionally to the crushing work load he wished to impose upon them. He wrote to his close friend Berthold Feiwel:

> We shan't achieve anything because we are all people with frayed nerves.
> . . . I cannot count on a scrap of support anywhere. I have to do everything myself. . . . Obligations assumed by other Fraction members have until the present never been fulfilled. They all know how to talk, to talk a great deal, and sometimes well, but no one is even partially conscious of his duties.[45]

He chided Martin Buber, one of the worst slackers:

> I cannot help feeling bitter about standing completely alone, as though abandoned, at critical moments; "we march together" only when everything works out well. . . . I too have made a resolve . . . after the Fraction Conference I am not going to lift a finger any more. I shall no longer accept any office.[46]

At yet another conference Weizmann tried desperately to galvanize the Fraction into a coherent political force. He braved student meetings, wrote directives, encouraged his friends, though with no illusion as to the outcome. To one of his young lady assistants, Catherine Dorfmann, he wrote: 'I am sending you the Fraction Circular. This is the last, and I consider it the Fraction's swan-song. At the conference I shall try and shake the dust from my feet. I don't want to be bothered with dead souls. The "youth" are as rotten as the old men.'[47]

The conference never materialized. In February 1904 Weizmann began to close down the joint office for university affairs and the Democratic Fraction. Losing the organizational framework for his political activity was a severe setback, but worse was to follow. He had planned a prestigious, grandiose propaganda campaign of the key Russian communities for April, a kind of last-ditch attempt to maintain the remnants of the Fraction as a going concern. When he arrived in Russia—at a particularly tense moment, when Russian reverses in its war against Japan had aggravated fears of renewed pogroms against the Jews (Weizmann, like most Russian Jews, hoped for a Japanese victory but feared its consequences)—his tour was called off owing to lack of funds. This was not an impressive demonstration of how the Russian Zionists viewed his value as a propagandist. Humiliated and depressed, he remained with his family in Pinsk most of April, celebrating the Passover festival with them and moping about the state of Zionism and the pitiful condition of Russian Jewry. He wrote to Vera:

> Every time I walk through the town I return with a broken heart. There is not a single animated face, not a single smile; all around there are only dead shadows. . . . Of course I shall work, Verochka, I shall work wherever fate takes me, for only cruel egoists who have silenced any voice of honour and conscience in themselves can fail to work for the Jewish cause. . . . One is compelled to marvel at the great moral force that lives in the hungry Jew. In such conditions others would have turned into beasts long ago.[48]

Everywhere he saw the triumph of territorialism. All the younger elements were 'for Uganda'. Zionist leadership, as he understood it, was at a low premium. It had become 'confused' and 'tangled': the veterans were squabbling, the new recruits 'occupy themselves with anything but Zionism'. As he felt the situation slipping from his grasp, his suspicions grew that his leaders were preparing to capitulate to the 'Ugandists'. When he heard of Herzl's victory over the rebels in Vienna, he knew the game was lost. 'We are once more on our own,' he concluded, 'their opposition to the Herzl regime has been broken.' Russian Jewry, aware, honest, productive, had been 'literally driven out of Zionism'. He left Pinsk 'broken' in spirit.[49] There was no hope now of reviving the Democratic Fraction or even of organizing a substitute working group in Russia.

Weizmann's reign as the uncrowned king of the Fraction had not been a happy one. Not that he lacked the attributes of a successful leader—a great vision, a pragmatic day-to-day policy, and sufficient energy to implement both—but he was unable to translate them into a profitable relationship with his associates and together take the Zionist establishment by storm. He was too impatient, too imperious; although he complained incessantly about his colleagues' shortcomings, his own peppery temperament made him an awkward taskmaster. Even at this early stage, it is apparent that he preferred subordinates to peers and would not countenance a subordinate role for himself.

During his stay in Pinsk, possibly as a result of it, he came to a decision about his personal future. The first contacts with English chemists had been made in October 1903 during his visit to London. Now, a few days before leaving for Russia, he received a firm invitation from William Perkin, professor of chemistry at Manchester University, to join him as his assistant.[50] Perkin was a foremost chemist in Weizmann's field (his father, Sir William, had produced the first aniline dye, known as "Perkin's mauve"), and Manchester was the centre of a great dye industry. This combination struck him as 'very advantageous' and the offer was tempting. On his way back to Geneva from Pinsk, he announced to a friend, 'I am going to live in Manchester'.[51]

No sooner had Weizmann made this decision than he was faced with an even more tempting prospect, which, if realized, would have turned his world upside down. The *Hilfsverein der Deutschen Juden*, a non-Zionist charitable organization whose teacher training college in Jerusalem was about to be inaugurated, was seeking a physics and chemistry tutor. Weizmann considered it a lowly post and not very well paid, but this was of little consequence for him in comparison with the great advantage of being in Palestine. 'I would accept [it] with great pleasure, and would be ready to move to Palestine at once instead of going to England,' he wrote. At his request, Ussishkin advanced his name as a candidate for the post, but the college refused to accede to this pressure. Its principal later recalled that the main reason for rejecting Weizmann was 'the impertinence of this young man who was amongst the leaders of the Fractionists against Herzl', though a contemporary report stated that the Hilfsverein refused Weizmann's services because he was a Zionist.[52]

So it was England as, if one may borrow the term, a *Nachtasyl* until Weizmann was prepared for life in Palestine:

> Perhaps this is *Gum Zu LeTova* [Hebrew: all for the best], so I shall pass through the English school too and then, being better prepared, come to my native land. I have made this the aim of my life. In England I shall try and fulfill the commandment *Vcyenatzlu et HaMitzrim* ['And you shall plunder the Egyptians'—Exodus 3:22] and learn everything that can possibly be put into practice in Palestine, especially in the field of colonization, etc.[53]

For a proud and ambitious man like Weizmann the last year must have been a nightmare. His political plans were in ruins; the university project had floundered; he was virtually unemployed; he had left Russia 'broken-hearted'; his relationship with Vera was complicated; his health was poor. Manchester was the one glimmer of light on the horizon; and it was with some truth that he wrote of 'his flight to England'. Nevertheless, his memoirs leave a misleading impression of his motives for coming to England.

> It was not, to be sure, real flight; it was in reality a case of *reculer pour mieux sauter*. I was in danger of being eaten up by Zionism, with no benefit either to my scientific career or to Zionism. We had reached, it seemed to me, a dead point in the movement. My struggles were destroying me; an interval was needed before the possibilities of fruitful work could be restored. Achieving nothing in my public effort, neglecting my laboratory and my books, I was in danger of degenerating into a *Luftmensch*, one of those well-meaning, undisciplined and frustrated "eternal students" of whom I have already written. To become effective in any sense, I had to continue my education in chemistry and wait for a more propitious time in the Zionist movement.[54]

The notion that Weizmann could retire, even temporarily, from politics and concentrate on his science is totally out of character. He was too political an animal to allow for sabbaticals, and this is borne out by the contemporary evidence. As he rationalized at the time, his continued 'participation in the cause' depended upon his leaving Geneva and moving to another 'large centre' where his talents would not be wasted.[55] Once he arrived in London in July 1904 and found himself in a more sympathetic and receptive *milieu*, he did not retire gracefully to the laboratory and ignore politics but again took up the activities initiated on his previous London visit. Only because of difficulties of acclimatization did he eventually tone down his political work, though never entirely. He was soon busy creating a new power base in England, where the competition was much weaker than on the Continent, to renew the attack on Herzlian political Zionism.

A few days before his intended departure from Geneva, his circle of comrades from *HaShachar* treated him to a *banquet de clôture*. There was a touch of nostalgia in the air. 'Friends arrive, bringing warmth and loving care.' His disposition improved. With his pals he attended a lake-side concert and wrote to Vera, then in Rostov, a farewell postcard signed also by his companions. There was a last-minute hitch when he found himself short of '300 roubles' for the journey and had to scrounge the money.[56]

In the midst of these preparations, on 3 July 1904, Herzl died. His death left the Zionist movement stunned and in a state of shock. Stephen Zweig wrote, 'It was not just a writer or a mediocre poet who had passed away, but one of those creators of ideas who disclose themselves triumphantly in a single country, to a single people, at vast intervals'.[57] Georges Clemenceau, not easily duped, eulogized: 'He was a man of genius, not to be confused with a man of talent. The Burning Bush and Revolutionary Sinai took shape in his appearance. There was a breath of eternity in that man.'[58] The sense of irreparable loss was common to both his admirers and his detractors. Weizmann, who shared the desolation, deeply distressed, his emotions on edge, still could not forget the coming struggle. 'I have only the image of a great creative worker in front of my eyes,' he wrote to Vera. 'I feel a great weight on my heart, the more so as you are not with me, and deep grief. He has left us a frightening legacy. . . . Verochka, put on mourning. We are all wearing it.' Instinctively, he perceived that Herzl's death had created a great void that perhaps he might help fill: 'Difficult times await me now. I feel that a heavy burden has fallen on my shoulders, and the shoulders are weak and tired.'[59]

Weizmann left Geneva on 6 July. His departure was the signal for a Zionist demonstration at the railway station, the participants united by grief and bereavement. He wrote to Vera: 'When the train moved cries of *od lo avdah* [from the Zionist anthem: 'Our hope . . . is not yet lost'] rose and mixed with the weeping, and something snapped inside of me. A line was drawn, a period of life came to an end. And ahead there is work, difficult work.' At this moment of deep crisis, with the weight of Jewish history bearing down on him, he feared for the unity of the Jews, at best a fragile thing, and vent his wrath on Jews who, he felt, had casually betrayed their heritage:

> I have one consolation: we are Jews, our destiny is different from that of any other people, we are a chosen nation, chosen in suffering, in torment, in feeling, and in our momentary but deep joys. I feel that some sort of ascetic attitude to life has begun developing in me, and I am afraid of it. We ourselves, and our personal future, do not frighten me in the least, and I am certain that everything will work itself out. But the general situation is getting worse and worse. In such moments there arises in me a terrible hatred towards "Jews" who turn away from Jewry. I perceive them as animals unworthy of the name *homo sapiens*.[60]

On the way to London, Weizmann stopped off in Paris to sound out Max Nordau. Their painful two-and-half-hour conversation moved him to tears. Appalled, he heard Nordau admit that he had never fully believed in Herzl's diplomatic methods. For various personal and political reasons, Nordau elaborated why he was unfit to accept Herzl's mantle and, flattering Weizmann, hinted that someday he was destined for the leadership: '*Sie sind aber zu jung!*'[61]

Weizmann landed at Newhaven on 10 July with eighteen shillings in his pocket and 'plenty of good intentions'. 'I managed perfectly well with the entry formalities, etc.', he reported to Vera. 'A real *gentleman*', he proudly appended in English.[62]

FIVE

NEW BEGINNINGS

Weizmann remained in London for only a little more than two weeks. Almost all his time was spent in renewing the political campaign he had initiated during his visit the previous winter, a strange way of demonstrating his alleged retirement from Zionist politics. Gaster, who aspired to Herzl's crown, was again his main contact, at whose home in Maida Vale he was a constant visitor.[1] He met the leaders of English Zionism but refused to involve himself in their intrigues and infighting. 'And what is your role?' he was asked. 'That of a bridge,' he replied.[2] He envisaged himself as chief liaison officer between the East and the West, but one whose allegiance was irrevocably committed to the Russians. He could have defined his task with greater candour as that of capturing this bastion of Herzlian Zionism from within. Periodically, and for some time to come, he reported to Ussishkin on the state of western Zionism and in particular on the internecine strife of British Zionism. This activity replenished his optimism. 'London will become a major Zionist centre, and from this point of view my arrival is important for me.'[3]

This conclusion was amply confirmed when he met for the first time high officials of the British foreign service. The East Africa question was still on the public agenda, for it had been recently debated in the House of Commons.[4] Lord Percy, Under-secretary of State for Foreign Affairs, had replied to a hostile motion in cordial terms, explaining that Britain had put forward the scheme also 'because of feelings of sympathy which ought to be felt by every Christian nation and which has always been felt by the British race'. Through introductions by Gaster he met Percy at Westminster, and Sir Clement Hill, Superintendent of African Protectorates at the Foreign Office.

Hill told him: 'If I were Jewish, I would oppose such a project absolutely. For a Zionist there is nothing to look for in Africa.'[5] Weizmann was delighted with his own performance. 'I can obtain an audience with Lansdowne [the Foreign Secretary] at any time,' he boasted to Ussishkin. 'As you see,' he consoled him, 'we can have our own diplomacy, without spectacular effects, but more solid. . . . If only it were possible to strike roots here and protect oneself from financial worries, then there is no doubt about the possibility of influencing English public opinion in our favour.'[6] To Vera he was even less inhibited: 'You will be amazed when you learn of the gist of my talks, and what I have achieved. I am convinced that I have achieved more than Herzl with all his diplomacy.'[7]

These were Weizmann's first diplomatic encounters of consequence. And although it was an outstanding success from his point of view, too much should not be read into them. There is no evidence, from their accounts, that Hill or Percy felt they were confronted by a major personality. They had simply met a Russian Jew who spoke little English and who was opposed to the East Africa scheme and confirmed most of their own suspicions about its practicability. No doubt his charm was on display, and he put his arguments forcibly and with his customary passion and incisiveness. But even the most cordial of Englishmen tended to regard him as a rather exotic bloom. Lord Robert Cecil, a true friend, wrote later of Weizmann's 'subdued enthusiasm' and the 'extraordinary impressiveness of his attitude'; but also of his 'rather repellent and even sordid exterior'.[8] Perhaps this was the most exciting of combinations. He still lacked the experience, the sophistication, the mystique of success, and above all the subtlety of language, to allow him to realize his full potential. It was a raw performance, but one full of promise.

Weizmann put one diplomatic foot wrong. In the traditional manner, he wrote summaries of the conversations which he then forwarded to Percy and Hill. He hoped his version would be ratified as official documents to be used later in the struggle against the advocates of the East African scheme. The Englishmen modified Weizmann's account; Weizmann was undeterred, since he considered their deletions immaterial and he was certain that 'the weapon against Africa is now perfected.'[9] If Weizmann had hoped to blow East Africa out of the water by revealing the sensational nature of his documents, he was to be disappointed. When the Greater Actions Committee of the Zionist Congress met in Vienna in August it decided to go ahead and send an expedition to East Africa, though with little illusion as to its outcome. The scheme was dying a slow death, though obviously too slow for the impetuous Weizmann, who would have drawn much encouragement had he known of Lansdowne's comment: 'We shall be fortunate if the project falls through.'[10]

Weizmann must have been desperately short of money. He had borrowed 300 roubles to leave Geneva, and he was forced to cadge an additional sum to attend the GAC meeting in Vienna. The income from his patents had dried up, and he relied on loans from the ever-obliging Gaster and his own brother-in-law, Lubzhinsky. For some time to come he would be out of pocket and be compelled to appeal to his friends' generosity.

Weizmann would have preferred to live and work in London, close to the political centre. Professor Sir William Ramsey of University College, London, had now made him a tentative offer, tempting but not definite. But on Gaster's advice, Weizmann decided on Manchester. Though he would begin as an unpaid assistant to Perkin, the prospects were bright: he could recommence his own research, take on students, and by Christmas could expect a paid fellowship of £50 per annum. There were 'even prospects of a Chair', he dreamed. Still, deep down he knew he was being banished to the provinces. 'It has an excellent laboratory and library, the climate is better, the town cheaper, and one can always move to London if the opportunity arises, *reculer pour mieux sauter!*'[11]

His initial impressions of Manchester surpassed his fanciful expectations. The town was 'interesting', the institute 'marvelous', the laboratories 'enormous', the libraries 'beautiful'. He found lodgings at Chorlton-on-Medlock, a short walking distance from the university. As a lowly recruit to the staff he was awarded a dirty and neglected basement laboratory. After much scrubbing and cleaning, he turned it into 'cosy and well-appointed' place for scientific research. Forever the diplomat, he made friends with Samuel Pickles, Perkin's assistant; Edwards, the chief steward of the laboratories; and Tom, his own lab boy—all essential cogs for the smooth running of his research.

The university was on vacation. Perkin had left for his summer holidays, and Weizmann lived 'almost incommunicado' until the beginning of term. He immersed himself totally in his work. Time passed quickly. 'I get up at 8–8.15, at 8.45 I leave for work, I come back at 1.30; at 2.30 I go out again until 5.30, then there is tea till 6 (five o'clock tea), then I work till 7. . . . I go for a walk till 8.30; then at 8.30 I have dinner; at 9.30 I still do some bookwork until 11–11.30, and then to bed.'[12]

His most pressing problem was to learn English. He had spoken French to Hill and Percy, German to Perkin, a primitive picture-sign language to Edwards and Tom. But he had an enviable facility for languages and applied himself diligently: he read the Bible in English, acquired copies of Macauley's works, and even studied Gladstone's speeches—a daunting exercise for the most intrepid of English-language students. He attended the theatre and saw 'a very good production of Julius Caesar. I would go more often if they were to present more Shakespeare here. It is very useful for the language.' Systematic as usual, he budgeted part of each day to these chores, learning whole pages of his chemistry text-books by rote. Within a few weeks he was able to communicate with his university colleagues. In time, he became fluent in English, though he never lost his Russian-Jewish accent and occasional grammatical errors would punctuate his flow of speech or composition. By June 1906 he was confident enough to pen his first letter in English.[13]

This form of semi-monastic existence could not last for long. As the months progressed, he became lonely and depressed, a condition aggravated by his enforced separation from Vera, who had remained in Geneva to complete her studies, and by his chronic lack of funds. Gregarious by nature, Weizmann sought stimulating company but did not find it. Manchester lacked the intellectual vitality he had enjoyed in Geneva and Berlin. 'Here there is nothing but plebs, plebs, plebs,' he sadly discovered. In vain, he searched for an agreeable 'intellectual milieu'. When he occasionally did venture out into society, he encountered only 'a very stupid rabble'. Anglo-Jewry, he hastily concluded, was superficial, materialistic, and devoted to money-grubbing; it lacked intellectual depth. After a year, Geneva still seemed a cut above Manchester, where 'the people . . . are rusty, or covered with soot like the city itself'.[14]

Nor could he fathom the peculiar habits of the English which, in a fit of temper, he compared unfavourably with those of the Turks. At times they were such 'blockheads'. Owing to 'a football game', he cried with astonishment, he could not find 'a single goy' to transfer his belongings to new digs.[15] Like most European intellectuals he demanded a serious attitude to life, even holidays. An English May Day was incomprehensible to him—nothing more than

a children's holiday, a festival of horses and donkeys. No mention of a workers' holiday. Not even the Social Democratic organizations observe May 1, and the factories keep working. On the other hand, they deck out all the horses. All the children (about 200,000) assemble in a huge square and are offered treats and entertainment by the city. They go from house to house, dancing and playing, receiving sweets and money. Then there is a donkey show, and the best (!) donkey (four-legged) receives a prize and marches in solemn procession through the city. That's all! England is an exception in everything. Besides these are very ancient customs, dating from time immemorial.[16]

In a no less serious frame of mind he examined the shortcomings of English society:

No one hurries in England and wheels turn slowly. The same is true of everything—their entire way of life—and this is why they have fallen behind. I must confess that we used to have false notions about the English and England. They have much that is good, but obtuseness prevails in everything. Well, God be with them. . . .

English society as such lacks the intellectual vigour one finds in Germany or France. The English Labour movement, with 1.5 million adherents, has not produced even one Jaurès or a Bebel. The country is governed by an oligarchy of the ancient hereditary nobility, and every-thing is made to fit the system. The main centres of education in England, Oxford and Cambridge, with their unrivalled resources and institutions, also incorporate countless relics from the Scholastic epoch. People like us, and myself in particular, find all this very difficult to accept.[17]

If he had placed his finger unerringly on the English *malaise*, he was also aware of the benefits English society bestowed upon him as a Jewish *emigré* from eastern Europe: freedom from physical persecution and the possibility of advancement in a tolerant and open environment. He had no doubt that the balance lay in his favour.

Baffled by the English, repelled by English Jews, Weizmann sought refuge among his own people. His social highlights were the Friday evenings he spent in the home of Joseph Massel, printer and Hebrew poet, 'a veritable angel'.[18] Here he could express himself freely, fluently, without inhibition, on familiar topics that absorbed him, to a sym-pathetic, admiring audience. A contemporary remembers him at a gathering in the house of another Hebraist, Isaiah Wassilevsky, where he sat hunched in an armchair, surrounded by bookshelves, defending Zionism, guiding the conversation along the desired lines in a 'low-pitched, guttural, slyly good-natured' voice.[19] .

These reactions are part of the normal pattern of behaviour among new immigrants when confused by a strange environment, and Weizmann's condition was magnified by his prolonged separation from Vera. During the period of their living apart, from July 1904 until August 1906, he wrote 468 letters, 335 of which were to Vera; at times, he was writing every day. Their correspondence makes strange reading. They were, as Weizmann confessed, 'both complex people',[20] and misunderstandings, reproaches, estrangements, reconciliations, mini-crises of one kind or another appear and disappear with bewildering frequency.

Vera was unhappy at the prospect of moving to Manchester. She hankered after Russia and wished to settle there after their marriage.[21] (She wrote later that her years in Manchester were among the most 'difficult' and 'depressing' of her life: 'dark days indeed, both spiritually and physically'.[22]) Naturally, she was also most concerned whether her medical degree (she graduated in May 1906) would be recognized in England. Weizmann was wildly optimistic on this score, assuring her that everything would work out satisfactorily. Gradually it dawned on them that English bureaucracy was no more accommodating than bureaucracies elsewhere: it was not until 1913 that Vera qualified for medical practice in England.

The built-in tension in their relationship never entirely vanished. Not that their love for each other in any way diminished, but their temperaments were in some ways incompatible. Vera never wrote enough to satisfy him—Are you testing me? he asked—and when she did, her letters were more often than not full of admonishments. On the other hand, he could never write enough to satisfy her—every day that passed without a letter was to her a sure sign of thoughtlessness.[23] It particularly pained Weizmann that Vera's relationship with his parents was strained. When she was in Russia, visiting her parents, she usually avoided Pinsk, despite Weizmann's assurances that his parents loved her dearly: 'Perhaps you really find it unpleasant to be in their company. After all they are my parents and not yours. . . . I am most fearfully upset, the tears are choking me. I felt very hurt and bitter after the letter from Mother, who loves you so much.'[24]

Vera, who expressed her emotions with great caution, feared that their separation had eroded the affinity between them, even if her love for him remained and his letters caused her great joy. Weizmann lacked any doubts of this kind. After visiting her in Switzerland, he wrote back, 'As the train began moving out of Zurich something snapped inside me; I was unable to calm myself throughout the journey. I so longed to go back to you Verusya, to be caressed by you.'[25]

They paid each other brief visits. Vera came twice to Manchester, in October 1904 and the winter of 1905. (Weizmann planned her journeys with frightening scientific precision: 'The best route is as follows: Berlin–Cologne–Ostend–Dover–London–Manchester. It is *absolutely impossible*, my child, to travel third-class from Cologne to London. The difference is about 30 marks, but also of two days. . . . Take a third-class ticket from Berlin to Cologne, you can travel by express; from Cologne a direct ticket to London via Ostend–Dover. You will have only three hours on board the ship.'[26] But these interludes of bliss were not sufficient to dispel the clouds of suspicion that gathered periodically around Vera in Geneva. Rumours reached her that Weizmann was thinking of breaking off their engagement and marrying someone else—an exploit for which there was a precedent. He denied the gossip. 'Who could be so interested in us as to have us married and divorced?' he queried. 'Someone is clearly keeping a watchful eye on us—may it go blind!'[27] Vera countered by further accusations of neglect and indifference, perhaps betrayal, and humiliated Weizmann by claiming the right of total independence, even financial independence, from him. Weizmann, his morale 'abominable' and his mood 'foul', was at a loss to understand what was happening to them. He sensed a change in their relationship: 'perhaps it is simply the realization that I am growing old' (he was thirty-one). 'I have always known that you don't trust me completely; but you didn't choose the right time to pile reproaches on me, some of them cruelly unjust.'[28] Two days later, after absorbing yet another rebuke, he replied in a most revealing passage:

> Surely it's not possible to love a man such as you picture me to be! At best it might be possible to pity me, provided one had once loved him. When I was in Geneva my life was richer, eventful. This is what I meant by glitter. I was a 'public figure'. You 'forgave' me a great deal for the sake of those moments when I interested you as a public figure. Now it's no longer so. I have become a quiet and hard-working drudge. For all my acquaintances, you among them I'm afraid, the glitter of former times has vanished. There is no reason to 'forgive' me; on the

contrary old grievances are recalled and counted against me! I have left the ranks, and, like a retired general, may be decorated for past deeds, if any. And that is all!

These days I am haunted by the conviction that I shan't live long. I keep driving the thought away, but, like a bothersome fly, it won't leave me. After all this, to hear words from you that caused me such self-humiliation: 'You will never take anything from me.'

Forgive my outspokenness. I too can suffer. The worst thing—the thing I cannot grasp—is that a person who loves could write in such a way. The moment my faith in your love is really shaken I shall consider my life as finished, to say the least. I have never, never used such expressions before; I hate them and am ready to despise myself for all that is seething inside me - but *c'est plus que moi*. My self-control refuses to function. I crave sweetness and warmth; cruelty and cold I have in Manchester enough.[29]

Although Vera claimed that Weizmann had misunderstood her and that her love for him remained unimpaired,[30] which was undoubtedly true, he had, in a moment of truth, unveiled a crucial dimension in their present and future relationship. Vera *was* enamoured, even intoxicated, with the 'glitter' of his public life. In some ways, its glamour, excitement, and prestige were more important to her than to him. It was a vicarious existence, for without Weizmann she could have hardly enjoyed these social benefits, and so she jealously guarded his station in public affairs against all detractors, equally for her own gratification as for his. This lay at the root of her snobbishness—an accusation levelled against her by even the most charitable of her acquaintances. Weizmann was aware of this about Vera from the outset. If he found it disturbing or exaggerated or embarrassing, it was the price he was willing to pay for his love for her.

They went ahead with arrangements for their marriage. On 23 August 1906, at Zoppot, near Danzig, with only Weizmann's parents and eldest brother and sister, Feival and Miriam, in attendance, they were finally married. All in all they underwent three marriage ceremonies: the first a religious ceremony in Zoppot, the second, a civil marriage in Manchester, and the third, another religious ritual in Manchester.

After spending some days with his family, which Vera found 'tiresome',[31] the couple travelled to Cologne to attend a meeting of the GAC—a working honeymoon. 'I remember chiefly my wife's extraordinary patience and understanding, and my feelings of guilt. I remember coming home—to the hotel, that is—at five o'clock one morning with a great bouquet of flowers and a basket of peaches as a peace offering.'[32] From these deliberations, they proceeded to a trip up the Rhine, third-class, to Switzerland, and thence by boat-train to Manchester. They arrived penniless, and were forced to borrow the taxi-fare, half-a-crown, from their friend Harry Sacher to get to their new lodgings in Parkfield Street, Rusholme.[33]

Weizmann's choice of accommodation was unfortunate: three dingy rooms in a badly-kept-up establishment. Vera 'hated it'.[34] The cold, the loneliness, the unfamiliarity added to her misery. These were difficult times, but, as Weizmann explained to Gaster, he was confident of overcoming them. 'I wish to take a flat by Easter, as living in lodgings is most uncomfortable, as well as expensive. I must save up to be able to buy furniture for two—three rooms at least. I hope to be appointed Examiner for London (Science and Arts), and this would perhaps yield 50—60 pounds. Things at home are going very badly, and I have to send off about 10 pounds a month; this is why we have to cut down to the degree that we don't allow ourselves anything at all. I take comfort in the thought that this period will not last very long, and that I shall be able to win my independence in this struggle. I have excellent prospects.'[35]

By the time Vera arrived in Manchester Weizmann's financial situation had vastly improved since his own departure from Geneva in 1904, although he complained that he was penniless and sought bridge-loans for many years to come. He was earning about £400 a year—£250 from the university and the remainder from private research at a local chemicals plant, and this sum increased annually. In addition, he had renewed his contact with the industrialist from Baku, Shriro, which put another £15 a month into his pocket. Shriro, however, proved quite unreliable, and Weizmann had cause to protest his wickedness when he lagged behind in his remittances.[36] For a brief period he believed that his financial problems were at an end;[37] but his responsibilities were continually mounting, particularly as he was syphoning off regular amounts each month to subsidize his siblings' higher education. Vera teased him, saying she had 'married his family, and not him alone'.[38]

At the university Weizmann advanced rapidly. Perkin was more than satisfied with his progress: 'These are the finest things done here during the vacation.' And when, in the autumn of 1904, he was informed that he would be appointed a Research Fellow, he threw caution to the wind, comparing this first rung on the academic ladder to 'a German Extraordinary Professor!' This was typical of Weizmann: when events began to move in his favour, his optimism tended to race ahead of reality. In fact, his progress was more than creditable without his imaginary embellishments. In July 1905, he was appointed Demonstrator in the organic chemistry laboratory with a handsome annual stipend of £100. Now, as Perkin's assistant, he was also responsible for the supervision of students' work, a bonus for any academic. Within less than a year he had consolidated his standing to a point where it would be difficult to dislodge him. His good fortune was a function of his research and teaching abilities and the confidence that Perkin placed in him.[39] Perkin in fact favoured him. He socialized with the Perkins, and referred to them affectionately as 'Ma and Pa'.

Perkin suggested that they collaborate on aspects of camphor research. Although this was a field outside Weizmann's current interests, he accepted the offer 'gratefully'. At the time, nothing came of this joint project (though later he produced a formula for artificial camphor), but two months later they successfully completed a piece of work on logwood and redwood dyes, a topic more familiar to Weizmann. He was also publishing papers, indispensable for academic respectability, in collaboration with Samuel Pickles. Expanding the scope of his academic activities, he planned to found a Chemical Society with Perkin as president and himself as secretary. In January 1905, he surmounted the last, most formidable obstacle of all. He gave his first lecture in English. 'No political speech I ever delivered, no matter how important and critical the issue, has ever affected me as deeply as this first lecture at an English University.' It was a huge success. The students gave him 'an ovation', Perkin was 'very pleased', and Weizmann, of course, was 'in seventh heaven'. From then on, the lectures were 'routine'.[40]

One of his students remembered him thus:

> Punctually the door on the left of the lecture-room bench opened, and a rather tall, erect person entered. His large head was bald, his face sallow, and he wore a closely clipped and pointed beard. With a suggestion of a friendly smile, the lecturer began and continued without interruption for an hour. . . . Walking back and forth and speaking without notes, he emitted a steady flow of pure organic chemistry, without personal touches or discussions on industrial application.
>
> Unlike most lecturers, Weizmann never stopped to help the sluggards. If you fell behind, you tried to catch up before the next lecture.

He spoke slowly, distinctly, and used good English with a slight accent. As sometimes occurs in all classrooms, there would be an occasional whisper or a mild demonstration of student humour. Then the lecturer would stop and look darkly at the culprit, but such interruptions were brief and gradually ceased.[41]

He was, by all accounts, a first-class teacher.[42]

The local dyestuffs factory where he worked on private research, the Clayton Aniline Company, was owned by a certain Charles Drey-fus, an *emigré* from Alsace who had become a local figure of note. An industrialist, active in municipal affairs, he was also a member of the executive of the English Zionist Federation (EZF) and president of the Manchester Zionist Association and the East Manchester Con-servative Association. He was to prove invaluable in promoting Weiz-mann's early career. Weizmann began work at Clayton's in January 1905. In general, his relations with his co-workers were amicable except for one, 'a dreadful person . . . a low and unscrupulous creature' whom, characteristically, he suspected of intriguing against him. Yet Weizmann was not entirely happy there; somehow, he felt as though he was prostituting his talents for vulgar, commercial gain. '*Schinderei*, chemistry perverted into alchemy,' he called it. Still, he soon adapted to the system: he had compelling reasons, not least of all Vera, for seeking his fortune as an industrial chemist. By April 1905 he had registered a patent, 'Improvements in the Manufacture of Camphene', under the name Charles Weizmann.[43]

Apart from affording Weizmann professional opportunities, Drey-fus was a pillar of the Anglo-Jewish, Anglo-Zionist establishment, far removed from the poverty of Manchester's ghettos. All doors were open to him, and through them Weizmann now also passed. The Dreyfuses went out of their way to ease Weizmann's path. They welcomed him to their home and introduced him to other stalwarts of the Manchester Jewish community. Weizmann accepted their hospitality graciously, but he was not enamoured of the society they kept. They lacked true Jewish spirituality, he thought, and worshipped materialism too heart-ily for his taste. Even their Zionism, philanthropic in character and patronizing in tone, lacked a firm ideological base. He was perhaps a trifle unfair in these generalizations. Nevertheless, 'An encounter with the artificial people here repels me, and I am filled with disgust when I meet the Dreyfuses. Why, I don't know, but this is how it is. They're such snobs.'[44]

Notwithstanding his preoccupation with his academic career and his ill-concealed dislike for the company of English Jews, he could not resist the temptation to try his hand once again at politics. From the beginning of his sojourn in Manchester he aimed at fashioning a political framework for continued Zionist work. In November 1904, four months after his arrival in Manchester, he addressed the Manchester Zionist Association, at Dreyfus's invitation, on the topic 'Political Movements of Jews in Russia.' He read his speech, which lasted for three hours, and despite his initial misgivings, he spent 'a pleasant evening'. Like most successful orators, he sensed the excitement of conquest and this spurred him on to greater efforts. His audience listened as 'under a spell . . . with rapt attention'. Naturally, they earned his admiration. 'This public, which always seemed so repulsive to me, was somehow different yesterday, more noble. My words stirred them, and at least for the duration of the lecture a bond was established between them, myself, and the whole mass of suffering Jewry.'[45] It was at one such meeting that Weizmann first met Harry Sacher, a journalist on the *Manchester Guardian* and related by marriage to the Sieffs and the Markses, the driving forces behind the chain-store Marks and Spencer, who was to be the first of his many younger activists and admirers in Manchester.[46]

This was the signal for his re-entry into political life, if indeed he had ever left it. No sooner had he arrived in Manchester in the summer of 1904, than he rushed off to Vienna for a meeting of the Actions Committee. He was disgusted with the proceedings. Petty men were desecrating the noblest of causes in a 'sea of intrigues. . . . We are standing amidst the ruins of the cause, and . . . the deceased contributed quite a bit to it. Herzl, *for his own sake*, died in time.' In despair he noted, 'It's much more difficult to fight Herzl when he is dead than when he was alive.' But, he vowed, 'My time will come, but later, later, when there will be nothing but fragments.'[47]

Was that time arriving? The key date was the forthcoming seventh Zionist Congress where a successor to Herzl would be elected. Here was a golden opportunity to crush the 'territorialists', even to deny them participation in Congress proceedings on the dubious grounds that, having contravened the Basel programme, they were 'unconstitutional elements'. 'I intend taking charge of the election campaign here in England', he bragged to Martin Buber. He turned up at the annual conference of the EZF in Leeds in January 1905 to inspect the *'Menschenmaterial'*: 'Rather poor, but better than I expected'. His ultra-Palestinian speech, given in Yiddish, was warmly applauded. Invitations rolled in to appear at other provincial centres. 'In short,' he noted, 'I am *lancé*,' even 'Greenberg and Cowen are wooing me'. That April a *Zionei-Zion* committee, the refurbished organizational structure of the *Nein-Sagers*, was set up with the avowed intention of influencing the election of delegates to the Zionist Congress. Gaster was its president and Weizmann joined the committee 'with a heavy heart', an emotion not borne out by his subsequent activities. [48]

Manchester sent Weizmann to the seventh Zionist Congress as her delegate, and the Zionei-Zion made substantial gains throughout the provinces, largely as a result of his propaganda work. When the Congress met at Basel in late July 1905, Weizmann's dream of unseating the Herzlians remained unfulfilled. To the Zionei-Zion's satisfaction, the East Africa proposal was finally rejected, a decision that caused Zangwill to lead his territorialists out of the movement to found his own Jewish Territorial Organization. This was a blow, though one not universally regretted in the movement. But to Weizmann's intense dismay, David Wolffsohn, a rich timber-dealer from Cologne and a close friend and follower of Herzl, was elected president of the Zionist Organization. For Weizmann, he was a mere cipher, a person of little consequence or ability. Referring to him disparagingly as the '*soicher*' (merchant), Weizmann harassed him relentlessly, not to say maliciously, at times overstepping the bounds of normal political rivalry. For the next six years Weizmann dedicated himself to ejecting Wolffsohn, that despised symbol of Herzl's legacy, from the leadership.

Weizmann returned to the public platform after this partial success, partial failure with renewed vitality. He unfurled the banner of the Zionei-Zion throughout the provinces (usually on weekends when he was free from his academic work): Leeds, Liverpool, Hull, Edinburgh. In Glasgow he met an audience of 3000. The message never changed: advocacy of practical work in Palestine, and opposition to any scheme for Jewish settlement outside the ancient homeland. 'Since the Congress,' he crowed, 'I have had over sixty meetings in various towns.' Having returned to the fray, he saw the internal Zionist debate in extreme terms as one between the children of light and the children of darkness. 'Zionism is becoming estranged, shallow and insensitive, descending from its democratic eminence to the baize-green table of plutocratic philanthropists, and perhaps as low as to the back-door of the elements dead to Judaism.'[49]

Such frantic electioneering thrust him into the vortex of English Zionist politics. This could hardly have been unintentional, despite his vow to remain aloof from parochial intrigues. He accepted with scarcely a whisper of protest official posts on Zionist committees, rising through the ranks from a place on the National Committee of the EZF to membership of the GAC in July 1905 to the vice-presidency of the EZF in February 1907. He worked in close association with Ussishkin, reporting to him regularly on the state of his campaign.[50] Inevitably, he was at odds with the leaders of Anglo-Zionism: Joseph Cowen was 'unstable', Leopold Greenberg 'plays politics', while Zangwill persisted in tired, cliché-ridden speeches which to Weizmann's ear sounded little more than 'kettledrums and trumpets for a crowd listening with bated breath to the announcement of a new kind of shoe-polish'. Even Gaster, with whom he was most closely identified, was either sulking or embittered.[51] 'It will require [but] a year to saw down these idols,' he promised Ussishkin.[52] In the event, it took him eighteen months to succeed in ousting the 'politicals' and promote Gaster to the presidency of the EZF—with the prize of a provincial vice-presidency for himself. This was a considerable victory for the 'practicals', though it had little lasting effect on the labyrinthine personal rivalries within the EZF. But Weizmann's reputation grew, chiefly as a manipulator and therefore as a coming man in Zionist politics.

Weizmann's sense of alienation was exacerbated by the English Jews' seeming apathy to the desperate plight of Russian Jews who were now trapped in the revolution of 1905. Pogroms were again reported in the western press. Weizmann's prediction—'The period of Russian revival will be written into Russian history in Jewish blood'—had become a frightful reality. His own family in Pinsk, and Vera's in Rostov, were in danger. Weizmann suffered with his brethren, his nerves in shreds. How could he teach chemistry to *goyim* when his own people were being massacred?[53]

His indignation spilled over when he learned that some of the great names of Anglo-Jewry, the Rothschilds and the Montefiores, had agreed that monies collected on behalf of Russian Jewish victims should not be used to facilitate their emigration to England. 'I spit on them,' this 'assimilated trash!' 'I sit here with a bleeding heart, without hope, without despair, without courage, without fear—a being turned to stone!' Yet he continued to exhaust himself in the north of England drumming up relief for the victims of Russian terror. At a mass demonstration in Manchester he appeared on the same platform as Gaster and Winston Churchill, then campaigning for the forthcoming parliamentary elections. Attending meetings, raising funds, passing resolutions, these were the kind of nebulous, lack-lustre activities he associated with assimilated western Jews. By implication, he was now part of the same decadent process. He wished to distance himself from it. Never would he succumb to the lures of western society and lose his identity. Time and again he referred to England as a temporary staging-post for his eventual *aliyah*. Only in Palestine could he truly fulfill himself; and only Palestine could provide a constructive answer to the plight of the Jewish people.[54]

Estranged ideologically and spiritually, Weizmann was also isolated in a more down-to-earth, practical sense. It was not that he existed in an olympian detachment from his surroundings, but he was an elitist in his political habits. He led no political group and possessed few, if any, intimate friends. He claimed to represent the Russian Jewish masses, but they had their own populist leaders—in Russia. For the fortunate few who had escaped to the West, he professed contempt. He told Ussishkin: 'Conditions here are frightful, in fact beyond description. You are dealing with the dregs of Russian Jewry, a dull ignorant crowd that knows nothing of such issues as Zionism. Greenberg and Co. have trained the local Zionists in accordance with English advertising methods.'[55] He even cut himself off physically from his despised electorate. Throughout his stay in Manchester he preferred to reside in the more prosperous, middle-class areas in the south of the city, far removed from the Jewish ghettos to the north. Did his conscience prick him about this behaviour? There can be no categoric answer; but one can certainly detect an inner restlessness and frustration in his conduct during these years.

By now, Weizmann was a local figure of expanding public reputation, worthy enough to appear on platforms with such dignitaries as Gaster and Churchill. The general elections of January 1906 afforded him an opportunity to extend the range of his contacts. Churchill, the Liberal candidate for North-West Manchester, a constituency which included Cheetham Hill, an area heavily populated with Jews, approached Weizmann, through his agent, to help swing the Jewish vote in his favour. Weizmann, although he acknowledged Churchill's influence, was reluctant to intervene so openly in British politics and simply referred the matter to Wolffsohn. Shortly afterward, he met with Churchill, who was returned with a majority of 1300 without the benefit of his good services, for a brief, introductory and uneventful talk.[56]

More significant was his meeting with Arthur James Balfour, leader

of the Conservative Party. They had first met briefly in January 1905
when Dreyfus, in his capacity as president of the local Conservative
organisation, had introduced them. Now, a year later, amid the bustle
of an election campaign, Balfour remarked to Dreyfus that he still
could not fathom the reasons for the Jews having rejected the Uganda
proposal. Perhaps also, as befits a shrewd political operator, he was
eager to dispell his image as the prime minister whose administration
had passed the Aliens Bill, an act of legislation clearly designed to
stem the tide of Jewish immigration. Dreyfus, himself a Ugandist,
magnanimously volunteered Weizmann's services to put the pro-Pal-
estine case. They met on 9 January at Balfour's election headquarters
(he was also contesting a Manchester seat) at the Queen's Hotel. The
conditions were hardly auspicious for a fruitful encounter. Balfour was
fighting for his political life (he in fact lost his seat) but throughout
the interview retained the demeanour of the imperturbable, cour-
teously attentive British aristocrat. Weizmann, on the other hand, had
to break down these barriers with his exotic appearance and imperfect
English. This meeting has since entered the annals of Zionist my-
thology. Yet no contemporary record of the occasion has been found,
nor is there any evidence that Weizmann was notably excited by it.
That night he penned, somewhat laconically: 'I had a meeting with
Balfour today, and had a long and interesting talk with him about
Zionism. He explained that he sees no difficulty in the attainment of
Palestine—only economic difficulties. We talked about territorialism.
I explained to him why this was not possible. We undertook to send
him a memorandum.' Some months later he added, in a note to Wolffsohn: 'He [Balfour] seems unable to understand why Rothschild, etc.,
are so hostile to Zionism. This had done much harm to Zionist policies
in England, because public opinion among prominent Christians is
influenced by Jews like Rothschild, etc. I tried to explain things to
him as best I could.'[57]

Balfour's first biographer, his niece Blanche (Baffy) Dugdale, who
was also Weizmann's confidante and friend, expanded on this encounter in her book, basing her account on both participants' memories. Weizmann's own memoirs add some details.

> I began to sweat blood to make my meaning clear through my English.
> At the very end I made an effort, I had an idea. I said: 'Mr. Balfour,
> if you were offered Paris instead of London, would you take it?'... He
> looked surprised.... 'But London is our own!' I said: 'Jerusalem was
> our own when London was a marsh.' He leaned back, continued to

stare at me, and said two things which I remember vividly. The first was: 'Are there many Jews who think like you?' I answered: 'I believe I speak the mind of millions of Jews whom you will never see and who cannot speak for themselves, but with whom I could pave the streets of the country I come from.' To this he said: 'If this is so, you will one day be a force.'

Shortly before I withdrew, Balfour said: 'It is curious. The Jews I meet are quite different.' I answered: 'Mr. Balfour, you meet the wrong kind of Jews.'[58]

This exchange had a strong impact on Balfour. Although not immune to traditional, pre-conceived opinions about the Jews regarding the extent of their so-called power and influence, Balfour felt that they were 'the most gifted race that mankind has seen since the Greeks of the fifth century'.[59] Now, for the first time, he had encountered a nationalist Jew who was capable of putting his case with intellectual depth, passion, and historical perspective, a combination bound to appeal to the inquisitive and sceptical Balfour. He told Mrs. Dugdale: 'It was from that talk with Weizmann that I saw that the Jewish form of patriotism was unique. Their love for their country refused to be satisfied by the Uganda scheme. It was Weizmann's absolute refusal even to look at it which impressed me.' Some days after their meeting, he wrote to a Jewish friend, an anti-Zionist, that Weizmann's 'intellectual qualifications' were not overstated by Dreyfus.[60] Balfour was swept away by the Liberal landslide. He did not meet Weizmann again for another eight years.

Weizmann was obviously delighted by his success at the EZF conference in February 1907. On behalf of his Russian comrades he had intrigued, successfully, to break the power of the 'politicals', Cowen and Greenberg, with whom, he now said, he found it 'nauseating to sit together', and had raised Gaster to the presidency. He anticipated a similar triumph at the eighth Zionist Congress due to convene at The Hague in August. Here he made his most memorable speech to date. 'I coined the phrase "synthetic Zionism",' he proudly announced, which he thought rallied the 'practicals' and eventually forced Wolffsohn's resignation.[61] This was not strictly accurate. The term had first been aired at the Helsingfors Conference in December 1906, and others at the Hague gathering voiced similar notions. But the slogan reflected Weizmann's order of Zionist priorities: Zionism would develop as an organic growth or wither on the stem; if he did not 'coin the phrase', he became its most passionate advocate, and it is rightly associated with his name.

During the set debate on 19 August, Weizmann rejected the narrow conception of the Herzlians and defined political Zionism in the broadest possible sense. For him, practical work in Palestine would be the lever to pry a Charter out of reluctant foreign governments. One was dependent on the other. The achievements, sacrifices, and experiences of the *Yishuv*—a slow and gradual process—would provide an irrefutable case for political power.

> None of us would wish to reject the great idea that Zionism is a political movement. But do not reduce politics to a mere approach to governments and to asking their opinion about Zionism. This will be of no use. We have already approached all the governments. We cannot start again on this tour.
>
> By political Zionism I mean that the Jewish problem should be put and stated as an international problem. We must say: Of course, the Jewish Question implies an international danger for the governments. We Jews claim our rights from the governments! And we say: We need your help; but we ourselves are also doing everything in order gradually to strengthen our position in the country which we regard as a home. Then the governments will understand us. Up to now no English statesman has been able to understand why the Zionist Congress rejected Uganda. . . .
>
> The opponents of political work say: We cannot take the risk of failure, for it will be said, not the attempts have failed, but Zionism has failed. But if you pursue such a policy you cannot do anything at all. . . . If we consider Zionism as an historic movement, we must put up with the idea that there may be momentary failures. . . .
>
> I conceive political Zionism as a synthesis of activities in all spheres; I consider practical activity to be the means of attaining the political aim, the Charter; and the Charter is to be the result of practical activity.[62]

As he described the occasion two days later to Vera, he spoke with 'unusual success and vigour', routing his opponents and basking in the warmth of 'a colossal ovation'.[63]

Was Weizmann pushing at an open door? This was the last public occasion when the divisions separating the two wings of Zionism were so clearly delineated. 'Practicals' and 'politicals' were convenient slogans, handy categories into which, helped by a touch of rhetorical exaggeration, one's opponents could be safely immured. Yet, without denying the clash in style or approach between these two wings, one can see that the differences were becoming blurred. This was not due solely to Weizmann's clarion-call. The Russian Zionists had been exerting steady and relentless political pressure on the leadership. Weizmann had merely expressed the same message in a more sophisticated and persuasive form. But the main arena was not in the conference hall but in Palestine. Here, the pioneers of the second *aliyah* were creating a new kind of reality. Inspired by their Socialist-Zionist faith, imbued with Tolstoyan theories, fascinated by Russian revolutionary principles though disillusioned by revolutionary practice, they were building a new socio-economic foundation in Palestine based on the dignity of Jewish labour. Although many later re-emigrated, the *Yishuv* grew steadily, so that by 1914 the Jews of Palestine numbered approximately 85,000, 12 per cent of its total population. Workers' parties, labour exchanges, insurance funds and medical aid, the *kibbutz* and *moshav* movements, Jewish self-defense [*HaShomer*], the new garden town of Tel Aviv—all had their origins during these years. Zionist banking services, the Anglo-Palestine Bank, were already available; and in 1908 the Palestine Office of the Zionist Organization was set up in Jaffa under the directorship of Arthur Ruppin. These activities were accompanied by a renaissance in the use of the Hebrew language, in danger of erosion by outside influences but fundamentally healthy and viable. Of course, much still needed to be done. The educational system, torn between the Hilfsverein (German), the Alliance (French), and the English, had come under heavy attack at the last Congress by Schmarya Levin, one of Weizmann's cronies. This was the heroic period in Zionist history, and Weizmann's 'synthesis' fed off it, though, as usual, the pace was never quite fast enough for him.

In August, immediately after Congress was over, Weizmann set off on his first visit to Palestine. Earlier in the year he had been challenged by Johann Kremenetsky, an associate of Herzl and owner of a large electric-lamp factory in Vienna: 'Weizmann, you talk too much. Why don't you go to Palestine to see what industrial developments are possible there?'[64] Of special interest were the prospects for the manufacture of essential oils, and as this tied in with his current research on the production of synthetic camphor and Kremenetsky was willing to finance the expedition, Weizmann agreed. During the spring vacation he went first to the south of France and Italy, where climatic conditions similar to Palestine's prevailed, and this also turned into a

sight-seeing jaunt. Monte Carlo was 'Real Hell': how could he escape
from 'this gang of elated scoundrels'? Rome was 'awe-inspiring, powerful, and beautiful' but *'tout passé'*: 'Feeble Jerusalem outlasted it';
Venice he found 'interesting and beautiful', but, he recorded sadly,
'my artistic sense is probably very feeble, and of course I cannot appreciate all these things.'[65]

Weizmann sailed from Marseilles for Palestine on 22 August. The
journey was divine: 'Wonderful sky, blue, blue sea, enchanting beauty.'
Two days later, in Alexandria, he detected 'Debauchery, licentious-
ness, passion, cupidity, greed for profit by plunder, murder, rape' in
the eyes of the natives. Then, owing to a quarantine, he lost ten days
in Beirut. 'My whole trip had been spoiled,' he grumbled. Finally, on
10 September, he disembarked at Jaffa: 'the sky and the sea are very
beautiful here, and the mood entirely different from ours'. He remained
in Jaffa only a day and a half, and was thankful to leave, for the locals
'concern themselves only with squabbles, gossip and homemade politics'. Depressed and constantly worried lest Vera, at home nursing
their first-born, Benjamin, could not cope with the myriad domestic
problems he had left behind—'Child, I shall never, never go without
you on such a trip,' he promised[66]—he toured Palestine for three weeks
in the company of Yehoshua Hankin, a veteran pioneer. Inspecting
the Jewish colonies, he came away inspired.

> It's worth a lifetime to glimpse the work of Jewish hands, to see how
> after twenty years of toil, former sand and swamp support flourishing
> orchards, to see Jewish farmers. I understood many things much better,
> more clearly: the potentiality of Palestine is immense. It is difficult to
> describe it, Verushenka; I must tell you all about it in the minutest
> detail, and transmit to you at least a little of the sunshine of Palestine.
> . . . My general conclusion is briefly the following: if everything pro-
> gresses so slowly, with such difficulties, the fault lies not with the *soil
> of Palestine*; nor even with the political conditions in the country (in-
> disputably difficult), but rather with *ourselves—and only with ourselves.*
> If our Jewish capitalists, say even only the Zionist capitalists, were to
> invest their capital in Palestine, if only in part, there is no doubt that
> the lifeline of Palestine—all the coastal plain—would be in Jewish
> hands within twenty-five years. No force in the world would then be
> able to destroy what was built.[67]

This was an important stage in Weizmann's Zionist education, for his
experience in Palestine confirmed his own practical philosophy: the

theory of organic growth. He summed up the Zionist programme in two words, *Geulath Ha'aretz* (redemption of the land), and remained faithful to it to the end of his career.

Weizmann also grappled with at least one aspect of the Arab question, the competition between Jewish and Arab labour, which was a highly controversial issue. For the Zionist there could be no redemption of the land except by the labour of Jews. Weizmann upheld this principle. He did not spell out its political implications, but he hinted at them. 'The Arab retains his primitive attachment to the land, the soil instinct is strong in him, and by being continuously employed on it there is a danger that he might feel himself indispensable to it with a moral right to it.'[68] One should not expect too much. At this stage, there were few who had plumbed the impenetrable depths of the clash between Arab and Jewish nationalisms.

Weizmann traversed the country by horse-drawn carriage and on horseback, from the colonies along the coastal plain—Rehovot, Rishon-le-Zion, and Petach Tikva—to Metullah, in northern Galilee. He saw Nazareth and Mount Tabor and gazed down upon the desolate Valley of Jezreel, destined to become the showpiece of Zionist endeavour. Eternal Jerusalem, where he made a public speech, he dismissed with the dead-pan comment of 'extremely interesting'. In Rehovot, where he was the guest of the Eisenberg family from Pinsk, they showed him a hillock just outside the colony: this Eisenberg property was the land he would later acquire and where he would build his home and the Sieff (later Weizmann) Institute. The tour exhilarated him, but he disliked the atmosphere in Palestine's towns. In a prescient mood, he noted, 'Here [in Jaffa] they don't leave one in peace for a moment, and literally tear you to pieces.'[69]

When he returned to London, Vera cross-examined him. 'Forget you are a Zionist and tell me what was so wonderful about Palestine.' He replied: 'It was magnificent.' Vera persisted, dissatisfied with this vague generalization. 'The air,' he expanded. 'It is difficult to understand without experiencing it. The air is crystal pure, so pure that you can look back over three thousand years of history.'[70]

What of the ostensible cause of his visit? Weizmann sent Kremenetsky a detailed report that, on the whole, favoured the establishment of small-scale plants. But unfortunately, nothing came of this enterprise. When Weizmann visited Vienna three months later, Kremenetsky informed him that he had no spare capital to invest in what he obviously considered to be a shaky venture. Weizmann's Jewish capitalists were playing true to form. 'Yes, my dear,' he wrote to Vera scornfully, 'he owns an enormous plant here in Vienna and there just isn't enough for Palestine.'[71] Still, the trip was not entirely wasted, and it served him well when he later returned to the theme of Palestine's industrial development.

The battle lines for control of the Zionist Organization were already being drawn up. In England, the Gaster-Weizmann alliance had scored considerable victories, but their authority was never absolute, and the Herzlians, led by Greenberg and Cowen, were on continual watch to recoup their losses. In Cologne, Wolffsohn, under constant sniping, hung onto power, his reputation always on the line. His negotiation with Turkey in November 1907, a repeat performance of Herzl's abortive efforts, brought him little credit, and collapsed when Wolffsohn was unable to match the Turks' inflated expectations of Zionism's financial power.[72] Had he succeeded, Wolffson might have moved on to consolidate his position; failure foretold renewed bids to wrest power from him.

In July 1908, revolutionary Turkish groups in association with discontented army officers seized power and compelled the Sultan, Abd al-Hamid II, to restore the Turkish constitution of 1876. It was widely assumed by outside observers that the Young Turk revolution heralded a period of reform and liberalization throughout the Ottoman Empire. Some Zionists, Weizmann among them, also believed that it would aid practical work in Palestine, easing the constraints that had hitherto restricted Jewish settlement there.[73] It was a golden opportunity which should not be frittered away. But Wolffson hesitated; and his opponents, the Russians, had no compunction about forcing his hand. They planted their own men in Constantinople—Victor Jacobson, a veteran colleague of Weizmann's from the Democratic Fraction, and Vladimir Jabotinsky, an outstanding young publicist—to soften public opinion in the Turkish capital. Wolffsohn acquiesced in this *fait accompli*, knowing full well that it weakened his authority and increased criticism of his passivity. The Russians pressed their advantage, proposing to shift the centre of the Zionist Organization's power from Cologne to Berlin and to expand the Executive Committee from three to eight members, thereby neutralizing Wolffson. This campaign came unstuck: Wolffsohn remained. Weizmann, though not directly involved, was privy to these stratagems and approved of them. For him, no doubt, they were part and parcel of his grand design to 'establish the organic link between East and West'.[74]

But Weizmann's expectations of the Young Turk revolution proved to be ill-founded. Far from leading to a liberalization of the Empire, the revolution adopted a narrow, repressive Turkish nationalism, and did not have sufficient strength to impose its authority on the peripheries of the Ottoman domains. Thus it encouraged the worst of both worlds: seeking to deny local nationalist aspirations, it had the reverse effect of stimulating them. In this sense, it worked against Zionism. A few years later, in 1913, Weizmann warned of the dangers of a renascent Arab nationalism. 'The Arabs are beginning to organize, though in a very primitive manner. They consider Palestine their own and have embarked on an intensive propaganda campaign . . . against the selling of land to "Zionists", the enemies of Turkey and the usurpers of Palestine. We shall soon face a serious enemy, and it won't be enough to pay just money for the land.'[75]

In Weizmann's own, more parochial sphere of activity, 'those tiresome English affairs' intervened yet again, this time to his detriment.[76] The shaky truce between the rival camps of the EZF broke down at its annual conference at Sheffield in February 1909. Gaster's presidency had not been a success: he was too rigid and too haughty to reconcile the quarrelsome factions. The rival Greenberg was elected to the London vice-presidency, defeating Herbert Bentwich, Gaster's favourite, by one vote; this was not only a political setback but also, perhaps mainly, a personal affront to Gaster, who resigned from the presidency, taking his followers with him. The Federation was effectively hamstrung.

At a public session during the Sheffield conference Weizmann called for reconciliation. 'Rotten London' was to blame for the impasse, he claimed, and he found most unsatisfactory an arrangement mooted in some circles that would leave Greenberg in control. What, then, did he propose: leaving the field to the Greenberg–Cowen faction, or continuing the executive that had just resigned? Weizmann's preference was to snatch the Federation from Greenberg's clutches in London and transfer it to a provincial centre—obviously Manchester, even though he would be accused of grabbing power for himself.[77]

Weizmann's suggestion was not acted upon. The Federation remained in London, paralysed by its internecine disputes. Gaster, behaving in a most undignified manner, refused to hand over the keys of office to his rivals.[78] To avoid total disintegration, another conference was called in March. The Gasterites boycotted it, and Charles Dreyfus was installed as a stop-gap president. There was no hope for a *rapprochement*. Gaster, now on the war-path and perhaps recalling Weizmann's speech in Sheffield, even suspected his loyal lieutenant of betraying him when Weizmann visited London but was unable to call upon him.[79] Gaster supporters were mobilized through the Order of Ancient Maccabeans whose Grand Commander happened to be Herbert Bentwich. The OAC was not presented to English Zionists as an alternative to the EZF; but its goal was to ensure the election of as many reliable delegates to the forthcoming Zionist Congress as possible, and Weizmann worked assiduously toward this goal.

When the ninth Zionist Congress convened at Hamburg in December 1909, Weizmann, now wielding great influence as chairman of the powerful Steering Committee, rose to the occasion. Yet instead of realizing his eagerly hoped-for triumph—the fall of Wolffsohn—his designs ended in a humiliating fiasco. Defending his policy skillfully, Wolffsohn attacked the opposition mercilessly and then, at the end of his address, announced that current conditions made it impossible for him to continue in office. The Congress gave him a sympathetic standing ovation. Despite this warning signal, Weizmann plunged on against him and, on behalf of his Committee, proposed a string of anti-Wolffsohn resolutions. They were shouted down. Deadlock ensued, and the session terminated in pandemonium in the early-morning hours of 31 December. It needed Wolffsohn, now riding on the crest of public acclaim, to restore the semblance of order: he was returned to office, and his personal standing strengthened. Small wonder that Weizmann, who had badly misjudged the mood of the Congress, described these events as 'a bad dream'.[80]

Weizmann left Hamburg with his reputation under a cloud. Baseless accusations were rife that he had rigged the Steering Committee's proceedings, and he was attacked in the *Jewish Chronicle*, what he called 'the yellow press', for uncomradely behaviour and for 'narrow-mindedness and incompetence' at the EZF conference.[81] His enemies had no difficulty in portraying him as an intriguer, and a not very successful one at that. In a strongly phrased letter to Wolffsohn, he demanded a ruling by a 'court of honour': 'I am not used to tolerating such insults from any Zionist or anybody else, let alone from you!' But the fact of the matter was inescapable: the under-dog, Wolffsohn, basked in public sympathy, while his assailant, Weizmann, retreated in confusion. Wolffsohn's threat—'You will all of you come crawling to me on your bended knees'—stuck in Weizmann's throat. He had a long memory in matters of this kind, and he bore his grudges with the utmost difficulty.[82]

Weizmann returned to Manchester beaten but unrepentant and continued to apply himself to Wolffsohn's overthrow. In England, the Maccabeans would be marshalled into a federation and replace the Wolffsohn-dominated machine in London. But Weizmann now looked wider afield. He corresponded with Rabbi Judah Magnes, the highly influential Jewish communal leader and Zionist luminary in New York, canvassing his support, and cast a net that encompassed Palestine, Constantinople, the United States, and the European centres.

> We in Europe are in touch with the Russians, Austrians, and some of the Rumanians. We have headquarters in Berlin with [Nahum] Sokolow at the head. We are about to publish a monthly, we have relations with Palestine and Constantinople, and want in this way to prepare for the Xth Congress, to offer to the Congress a programme, working plan, and Executive.

'Can we count on you?' he asked Magnes.[83]

In May 1910 Wolffsohn visited England, ostensibly to reconcile the warring factions, but in fact to press home his advantage. His blatant propaganda tour annoyed the Maccabeans, and the level of debate dropped to one of personal invective. Wolffsohn: 'The Executive was in need of businessmen rather than intellectuals.' Weizmann: 'Where is it written in the Bible that leaders must be timber merchants [Wolffsohn], shirt manufacturers [Cowen] and the Editor of the *Jewish Chronicle* [Greenberg]?' To which Wolffsohn replied tartly: 'It is not written that the leader must particularly be a Doctor of Chemistry.'[84]

Matters came to a head when Wolffsohn accused Weizmann of financial irregularities during his trip to Palestine in 1907. The accusation was groundless and Wolffsohn was eventually forced to retract it, but it stung Weizmann, and he had no compunction in airing a pun, in the worst possible taste, about Wolffsohn. 'I also heard a piece of news that Wolffsohn has syphilis and I made a joke about it: "*Wolffsohn ist sehr Erlich*"' (Wolffsohn is very honourable, or upright),* adding cruelly, 'It's all round Berlin already and will, I hope, reach Wolffsohn.'[85]

---

*The phrase is used in *er meint es ehrlich (mit ihr)*, meaning, his intentions (toward her) are honourable. The reference was to Paul Ehrlich, pioneer in medical research and winner of the Nobel prize, who had discovered an anti-syphilis drug.

This tasteless humour was a sign of weakness. Since the ninth Congress, Weizmann had failed to damage Wolffsohn politically, but his own conduct, even his personal integrity, had been scrutinized unfavourably. This demoralized him, and he even contemplated leaving public life. He would devote himself to his laboratory, he mused, and prepare himself for life in Palestine. He told Wolffsohn: 'we speak two different languages without hope of an understanding', and accused him of introducing 'the ancient and proven tactic of the Black Hundred [the notoriously anti-semitic League of the Russian People]'.[86] In June 1910, he resigned from the Greater Actions Committee, gave up his directorship of the Palestine Land Development Corporation, and ostensibly retired from the Zionist Organization. 'It was never my ambition to lead the movement', he assured Wolffsohn. 'My purpose was to prepare myself for Palestine.'[87] Of course, his abandonment of Zionist activity was an empty threat, and he continued his political work much as before, though perhaps a trifle more circumspectly. But the threat of resignation was a sword he would unsheath time and time again, whenever he sensed that he was being unjustly treated—which was often!

English Zionism stumbled from crisis to crisis, neither the Maccabeans nor the Federation receiving full satisfaction. Eventually, in February 1912, a Joint Council emerged to administer Zionist affairs. These petty disputes fatigued Weizmann. Gaster's paranoic suspicion of anyone who failed to bow to his wishes made him an impossible partner. 'He is an old politician and believes that everyone is an intriguer,' Weizmann noted after yet another *contretemps*.[88] As he saw no future in the London leadership, Gaster included, he relied increasingly upon his own inner circle. During these years he became the focal point for a number of young and talented Zionists: Harry Sacher, barrister and journalist; Leon Simon, civil servant and Hebraist; Simon Marks and Israel Sieff, directors of Marks and Spencer; Albert Hyamson, civil servant and Anglo-Jewish historian; Samuel Landman, later secretary of the World Zionist Organization. Above all, his relationship flourished with Ahad Ha'am, who had moved to London in 1907.

Then, in February 1911, Weizmann accepted the provincial vice-presidency of the Federation, this time with Cowen, hitherto his sworn enemy, as president.[89] This act can only be explained in terms of political expediency or, in other words, as a result of his recent political setbacks. Gaster, naturally, registered his intense disapproval: there could be no clearer sign that Weizmann was a turncoat. But, paradoxically, Weizmann's absorption into the English Zionist establishment was an indication of his growing self-confidence and his increasingly independent standing. He had learned the hard way that he could effect the changes he desired by using the EZF, not by tearing it down. Stealth would win where force had failed.

Yet the years of political struggle against Wolffsohn's regime, together with the impressive achievements in Palestine, had their effect in the end. At Basel, in August 1911, with Weizmann again prompting the players from behind the scenes as chairman of the Steering Committee, Wolffsohn resigned. His successor, Otto Warburg, an eminent botanist, was closely identified with the 'practical wing' of the movement, and his executive reflected the change in stewardship. Zionist policy went on much as before. To all intents and purposes the great debate between the 'practicals' and the 'politicals' had come to an end.

SIX

PERSONAL CRISIS— AND RECOVERY

The straitened circumstances of the Weizmanns' life in Manchester, which had at first so distressed Vera, were improving. Later, she described those early years to a close friend as 'the most wonderful epoch of our lives'.[1] From the three dingy rooms where they began married life they moved on to 'a tiny house' in Birchfields Road, and from there, in 1913, to a more substantial, middle-class residence in Brunswick Road, Withington, then 'almost a country lane. Initially, Weizmann furnished his home on a hire-purchase plan, paying off his debt with money he earned marking examination papers in his spare time.[2] Gradually, as their finances improved, they were able to live a model bourgeois life, hobnobbing with academic and local worthies. Nothing personifies their raised status better than a photograph of Vera taken at an academic garden-party in 1913. Fashionably attired in a dark dress with white ruffled collar, she gazes contentedly at the fine ladies feeling, looking, quite at home. By 1913, with Vera's appointment as medical officer for the Manchester clinic for expectant mothers, their joint income stood at about £1000 ($5000). For Weizmann, they were living 'in clover'. But their expenses were high. They were still supporting members of Weizmann's family who were studying in Europe and hosting them when they visited Manchester. They were continually hard up for that extra, elusive few pounds. Once, when Vera mislaid Weizmann's salary check of £100 in a bus, the family faced a deep financial crisis. As late as June 1914 Weizmann had to borrow £10 from Ahad Ha'am to tide him over until his salary was paid.[3]

In June 1907 Weizmann's first son, Benjamin, had been born. He was 'quite well-behaved . . . a *gentleman* . . . [and] the mother looks very well in the circumstances'. But as the child grew up, Weizmann worried that it was not easy in 'this English *Galuth*' to give his son a true Jewish education. 'Everything around is so terribly un-Jewish.' He lived in the hope that Benjamin would grow up in Palestine, an ambition, sadly, never realized. Benjamin benefited from his parents' social status, but there were tensions created by his father's public duties and his mother's social pretensions. Materially, he lacked for nothing. The Weizmanns were able to afford a nurse, Nelly, to administer to his needs, and a maid, Esther, to attend to the house. They spent their holidays at conventional middle-class resorts—Colwyn Bay in North Wales, or those like Grasmere with literary overtones in the Lake District, or, when funds were flowing, in the French Alps and Switzerland.[4] But soon Benji was proving a disappointment to his parents. Vera in particular complained incessantly of his waywardness. 'Could it be that he is lacking a father's authority?' Weizmann asked himself.[5] A pattern was being set for Benji's stormy relationship with his parents.

Weizmann's relations with his own parents had necessarily become more tenuous. On his periodic trips to Europe he saw those of his brothers and sisters who were studying in the West; and his brother Shmuel and sister Anna, a chemist, visited him in Manchester. But he made no more yearly journeys to Pinsk, and not until April 1911 did he return there for his first family reunion since 1904, passing through Warsaw on the way ('a depressing sight . . . 98 per cent starving and beggars, and 2 per cent feasting, over-eating, over-dressed in ultra-Parisian styles').[6] His father had been ill with pneumonia, and though Weizmann came somewhat reluctantly for the Passover celebrations, the family reunion went off 'very cheerfully'. Yet the moment Weizmann stepped into the streets of Pinsk his mood darkened. The Russian authorities had intensified their anti-Jewish restrictions, everything was 'impoverished and destitute, both materially and spiritually', and he could visualize only further catastrophes for Russian Jewry. In the autumn of 1911 the trial of Mendel Beilis, a Jew imprisoned on a trumped-up charge of ritual murder, began in Kiev, and its horrors were a fearsome reminder of Tsarist Russia's attitude to its Jewish population. Weizmann left Russia unhappy and confused, and he never returned to Pinsk. Three months later, his father died at the relatively young age of sixty. 'Naturally this grave loss will also impose new responsibilities on me. . . . I have had great anxiety during the past five months, and continue to have it.'[7]

Back in England, Weizmann found solace in one Manchester household: the Schusters'. Arthur Schuster, a converted German Jew, was professor of mathematics and physics at the university; he was later to become secretary and vice-president of the Royal Society. His wry sense of humour undoubtedly appealed to Weizmann,[8] and he was invaluable to Weizmann in aiding him to pick his way through the minefields of academic politics. He never committed himself to Zionism, though he never opposed it. Caroline, his wife, the daughter of English landed gentry, was fascinated by the vision of Zionism and captivated by Weizmann's personality, perhaps even a little in love with him; Weizmann was equally captivated by her. Both Schusters were devoted to the Weizmanns' welfare.

Caroline was seven years older than Weizmann, and he felt at ease in her company, with her mature, common-sense outlook on life. She responded sensitively, sympathetic to both his disappointments and his hopes, and to her he unburdened his most treasured thoughts.

Do you think I would have opened my mouth to speak about Zionism if I would have thought for a minute that you would not respect it, even if you may think it a dream . . . and shall consider it a privilege (what an awful word again!) much more than that, to be allowed into your house to be able to talk freely to you, heavens, to have *you* as a friend! One has to deserve it, and I feel that I could never deserve it. I can promise that I shall try to prove to you that the friendship is not misplaced. I shall try to become better, work harder, be purer and stronger. Let me come to your house more often.[9]

After one memorable encounter in January 1913, he returned home and wrote still more:

My dearest friend, guide, teacher, writer, mother, everything . . . I dare not go to bed for fear I shall not live through fully this beautiful moment in my life. . . . The few words you spoke this afternoon were so momentous that each syllable burnt me like fire and I was and still am trembling. . . . Friend, darling darling friend—I feel so weak and so strong, so sad and so joyful every little cell is awake in me, every little nerve vibrates. . . . You are a saint and my head burns when I look up to you, just as if I would look on a magnificent glacier in full sunshine.

'Don't you think I ought to go to Palestine now after all you said today?' he continued, and pledged: 'I shall work and toil and nothing shall be too hard for me. But you will always encourage me, won't you?'[10]

Weizmann also met the Schusters' daughter, Norah, and established a relationship with her that was equally complex. Many years later, when his memory was dimming, he wrote that 'as younger people ... [we were] on even more intimate footing'.[11] To Caroline he had promised 'to reclaim dear Norah, to get her to feel in unison and harmony with us'. He chose to define his relationship with her as that between 'a devoted brother ... [and] a dearly beloved sister'.[12] But he was clearly attracted to Norah, who was eighteen years his junior, on a quite different plane. Reclaiming lost souls for Judaism was, apart from the intellectual challenge, a gambit for Weizmann in approaching women who aroused him. So it had been with Vera; so it was with Schuster mother and daughter, and so it would be with others. When Norah moved to Cambridge in 1912 to continue her studies, Weizmann's ardent and educational letters pursued her, as he did himself on occasion. Once, to Norah's great astonishment, he declared that had he been single he would have asked for her hand in marriage, a proposal that she refused to take seriously. The truth was that Norah was embarrassed by his unrestrained, effusive affection, and she regarded his attempts to convert her to Zionism as faintly ridiculous. To her, he was a man of her father's generation, and she addressed him as Dr. Weizmann. When summoned to Birchfields Road for 'a private chat', she obeyed, unwillingly, eager not to offend him or her mother.[13]

At the beginning of February 1913 Weizmann was recuperating in Westcliff from a bout of influenza. On the weekend of 7–8 February, he invited Norah to meet him at Ahad Ha'am's home in Hampstead. Norah recalled that all evening the two men discussed Jewish politics. Finally, she decided to retire, and there came a tense moment as they said good night. Weizmann stood at the bottom of the stairs, 'looking into her eyes'. 'I thought you might be afraid of saying good night to me,' he remarked. He asked to kiss her and she agreed, wishing not to antagonize him. Only an 'innocent kiss' passed between them, and nothing further ensued. From then on his behaviour, she considered, was 'irreproachable' and 'the very soul of honour'.[14] The following afternoon, he wrote:

> Sunny Norah, When your train left, I felt so isolated in this cold big London and a fear overcame me that it is the last time I see you. I pray to God that my fear may prove wrong. ... I have no other claim on your friendship except the one which follows from a community of intellect, feeling and unity of purpose. The personal element which worried you so and created the present state of affairs is *eliminated* now and will never arise again.

His lapse, he tried to explain, resulted from the unbridgeable gap in their upbringing.

> British culture, freedom, greatness, strength and weakness. Who am I to fight all these giants. . . . I'm only a bundle of nerves, emerging from the gutter of the Ghetto. . . . What seems normal light to you, normal conditions, normal standards and canons . . . are foreign to me. . . . It was this difference and your intrinsic value and the 50 per cent Jewish blood in you which attracted me with such a violent force.

But he also knew that he was not only a casualty of the ghetto, but also a creature of Russian introspective soul-searching, an exotic hero who wore his emotions on his sleeve, unlike the strait-laced English. 'I made no secret of how I feel toward you. I have not hidden it from you and I am not an adherent of the semi-English, semi-spartanic virtue of hiding your feelings at any cost.' But then Weizmann returned to his mission of reclaiming her for Zionism.

> The feeling which you ought to have is not for *my* personality. I am a zero as such. But I represent to you a product of 2000 years in human suffering, of a downtrodden great race, which is making a gallant and bold attempt to free itself from chains, which have eaten deeply into its flesh. I am conscious of that with all my cells and nerves and for this representative I claimed your sympathy, your consideration, your tender mercies and your full friendship. It does not bind you to the cause I represent. Can you go so far? Do I ask for too much? It's the answer to those crucial questions which torment me. Is there anything ethically wrong in asking you? I think not, but I am at a loss: perhaps you apply "different" ethical standards.[15]

At this point Caroline Schuster intervened. Alarmed at what was developing between her daughter and her *protégé*, she asked Peggy (Edyth Goodall), her daughter-in-law and a well-known actress in Manchester repertory, to warn off Weizmann. Peggy did so, and then informed Norah of what she had done. For Weizmann this was a humiliating *coup de grace*, and he was deeply wounded. He now gave the worst possible interpretation to a conspiracy of three English ladies: it was damning proof that even English society, with its much vaunted political and economic equality, was closed to Russian *emigré* Jews with heavy accents. The half-Jewish Schusters—it was 'the 50 per cent Jewish blood' in Norah that had attracted him 'with such violent force'—were no different. They had been the first English family to open its doors to him, but even they would allow intimacy with foreigners only up to a point. Russia, Germany, France, Switzerland, England, what did it matter? The high and mighty English, patronizing and genteel, had the same prejudices as all the others, only they expressed them with honeyed phrases and impeccable manners. The Jews would always remain unwelcome outsiders. Weizmann put it: 'Having been born in the ghetto, one belongs to the ghetto all one's life.'[16]

Something snapped in his relationship with the Schusters. They 'are certainly charming people; nevertheless in those fundamental questions which constitute the centre of our whole existence they are strangers, indifferent, and moreover very remote'. He began to visit them less. 'Not because I love and respect them less. Nor have they changed their attitude one iota toward me, toward us. But it hurts me so much, and there is something bad coming into my feelings, something like envy and bitterness. I don't envy them, I envy the *goyim* who calmly devour the best we have and scream that we are exploiting them.'[17] Though he remained on close terms with the Schusters, their relationship moved to a different, more realistic plane.[18] In the summer of 1913 Caroline and Norah accompanied the Weizmanns to Vienna, where they sat stoically through the verbose, and to them incomprehensible, speeches of the eleventh Zionist Congress. And from there Norah continued with Chaim and Vera for a walking tour in the Tyrol.[19]

During the emotion-laden weeks when Weizmann's relationship with Norah was an issue, Vera and Benji recuperated in Cannes from attacks of pneumonia. For Vera, who had been ill since the previous spring, this was an especially difficult period. In December 1912 she had taken her medical finals while at the same time coping with Benji's illness and Chaim's academic problems (these days witnessed a crisis no less dramatic in his professional life). Weizmann's health deteriorated, and he was found to be suffering from 'bad neurasthenia and overstrain'.[20] The geographical distance between them compounded the emotional turmoil. But Vera could not have felt her marriage threatened, for Weizmann acknowledged its permanence even whilst he acknowledged his meetings with Norah (or Caroline). Norah, too, all innocence, had in fact mentioned her meetings with Chaim to Vera. Still, Vera was the aggrieved party, and Weizmann well knew it.

You should not think, child, that I shall become estranged from you. I really wouldn't be able to live without you. It always seems to you,

Verochka, that I love you less than you do me. Perhaps I love you differently, but this love is indissoluble and unshakeable. If, as you say, I became 'infatuated' this doesn't affect that love for you which is at the centre of my whole consciousness and existence. And the infatuations have passed. I have suffered and got over last year's incident and forgotten it, and I hope that you no longer think about it either. Please don't blame me, Verusya![21]

. This *crise de coeur* blew over, as would others in the future. It is impossible to state categorically whether or not Weizmann's "infatuations" reached physical consummation. The circumstantial evidence, rich in innuendo but scanty in fact, remains on occasion damning. But this is of secondary importance. Weizmann required love, tenderness, affection: if it could not be physical, it would be romantic, even ideological. His delicately balanced emotions, so often swinging between ecstasy and depression, were an uncontrollable force that demanded an outlet. He craved admiration; his self-confidence was in constant need of reinforcement. Highly impressionable young ladies were ready prey to his stormy but alluring temperament. To them, he gave full expression of his vision, his intellectual depth, and his undoubted charm—a heady combination. In return, they fed him the adulation that was essential to his well-being. Vera had gone beyond this stage, and indeed her strong personality was a ready match for his. His liaisons, at least so he rationalized, would strengthen the unique bonds between them,[22] and the history of their relationship suggests that this was the case. Vera's aloof, controlled disposition gave him a safe, if at times inhospitable, anchorage; if, occasionally, he would slip anchor, he did so confident that he could always return to a safe haven.

Serving two gods, 'the laboratory and Jews' street', was, as Weizmann never tired of pointing out, incredibly exacting. But whatever the difficulties, he never compromised his academic career. 'First, because I have many interesting problems in the workshop through which I could well make a name for myself. Secondly, because for the sake of Zionism, too, and especially of my role in the movement, I could not give up what I have achieved here.'[23] Also, he wished to secure economic independence, and the dream of earning a fortune from his patents was a constant factor in his calculations.

From 1904 to 1915, the Manchester years, Weizmann published

thirty-one papers, always in collaboration with other scientists. His reputation as a teacher grew. In the autumn of 1909 he was chosen to give a course in organic chemistry for medical students, his first introduction to biological aspects of chemistry. Apart from his traditional field of interest, dyestuffs, his industrial research focussed initially on processes for camphor-oil production, a line of enquiry with industrial implications. By the end of 1907 Givauden, a Swiss firm specializing in cosmetics, had licensed Weizmann's camphor patents.[24] After this success, Weizmann turned to a relatively new field: microbiology. From the spring of 1909 he began to spend his vacations at the Pasteur Institute in Paris.[25] By now he was investigating fermentation processes related to the production of synthetic rubber, potentially a highly profitable enterprise.

In early 1910, Perkin entered into a contract with Halford Strange, an entrepreneur with a working knowledge of chemistry, whereby he would place at Strange's disposal the results of his researches in return for a yearly retainer of £1000 plus royalties. Perkin, unfamiliar with the chemistry of producing synthetic rubber and scenting easy profits, drew Weizmann into the agreement. This suited Weizmann down to the ground. He received from Perkin a salary of £250 and a one-third share of the royalties.[26] Like Perkin, he saw the opportunity of rich reward and the prospect of financial security. Weizmann set about this new task with his customary energy. He conscripted the services of his distinguished professor at the Pasteur Institute, Auguste Fernbach, director of its Fermentation Laboratories. By December 1910 Fernbach too was under contract to Strange.[27] Research was to be carried out simultaneously in Manchester and Paris.

Their investigations did not, however, produce results of sufficient quality to warrant commercial exploitation. Strange, for the time being, backed away. Perkin, disappointed and out of his depth, renamed butyl alcohol, a necessary ingredient in the production of synthetic rubber, 'butyl futile', and advised Weizmann 'to pour the stuff down the sink'.[28] Before long Weizmann was quarreling with him and was at odds with Strange and Fernbach.

Despite the initial setback, Strange had decided to float a company, the Synthetic Rubber, Fusel Oil and Acetone Manufacturing Company, to exploit even the meagre results of the fermentation experiments. One encouraging piece of news was that the Admiralty were particularly concerned over the shortage of acetone. This augured well for the future of the new company. Perkin agreed to boost it, or rather its intended products, at a public lecture he was to deliver to the Society of the Chemical Industry in June 1912. Fernbach was also persuaded to lend his support. But Fernbach was more cautious, since his continued experiments with maize had had unsatisfactory results. Still, roused by the prospect of substantial profits and a place on the board, he composed for Strange's benefit a vaguely optimistic report.

What was Weizmann's position in all this conniving? His only contractual tie with the team was his by now outdated arrangement with Perkin. Yet new possibilities were unfolding: companies, shares, dividends, fat profits. Like his colleagues, he was blinded by the prospect of easy gain. Weizmann regarded himself, rightly, as Strange's key scientific figure in Manchester, complementing Fernbach in Paris. Perkin, relatively ignorant of fermentation chemistry, was now no more than an honoured passenger. But when Weizmann sought to assert his position, Perkin would have none of it. Whenever Weizmann suggested revising his own contract, Perkin hinted that the University Council would take a dim view of his being obliged to a commercial company. This was rank hypocrisy, in view of Perkin's own commitments, but he was senior to Weizmann and could pull rank. He threatened quite unambiguously that unless Weizmann withdrew his claims, his academic future at Manchester was in grave jeopardy.

Weizmann's anger at Perkin boiled over when he studied the text of Perkin's public lecture, in which Fernbach was lauded but Weizmann's own contribution virtually ignored. He planned, with Vera's backing, to circumvent Perkin by seeking a separate agreement with Strange and Fernbach and then presenting Perkin with an ultimatum: either he would have a more equitable deal, or it would be Perkin who would be left out in the cold. In an *échange de lettres* with Fernbach he concluded his scheme: he would receive 25 per cent of Fernbach's royalties plus £100 a year to be deducted from the salary Fernbach received from Strange. 'I hope my Verochka will be pleased,' he wrote to his wife. 'I kept in mind that you told me "to think of you during these business talks".'[29]

This plan sadly misfired, and Weizmann found himself an isolated party and the victim of a counter-intrigue. Strange, disturbed by Weizmann's independent conduct, persuaded Fernbach not to enter into any written contract with Weizmann until Perkin knew what was afoot. Perkin challenged Weizmann and informed him bluntly that a separate compact with Fernbach was out of the question. He would have to choose between academic life and commercial profit. Perkin spoke from a position of strength. Not only was he more influential than Weizmann in academic politics, but he had also received a letter from Strange that would have appalled Weizmann had he known of its contents:

> I [Strange] then told him [Fernbach] what I knew of Weizmann's history, of his proved tendency to lying in ordinary scientific matters, and his continual campaign for slightly more cash. Fernbach told me . . . that he felt it was unsafe that such valuable knowledge should be in the possession of a man of Weizmann's type without his having some direct interest in it. I told him of Weizmann's threats to you [Perkin], that he considered himself free to do what he liked with the information including rubber if he did not obtain satisfactory terms. I also told him of the promise not to do any outside work. . . . Fernbach has agreed to give Weizmann nothing in writing until we have discussed a joint plan of campaign. . . . When it is over I think the best plan will be to produce an agreement giving Weizmann the maximum we are prepared to agree to and if he doesn't sign fire him out. . . . Finally I have come to the conclusion that attempts to work in a friendly way with Weizmann only invite aggression on his part and in future I am afraid the policy with regard to him must be one of unmitigated firmness. The fact that we are not ready to deal with the situation for a few weeks will act in our favour as at present he has strained himself up to a mood of impudence and daring.[30]

Weizmann's scheme was collapsing around him. Fernbach would not quarrel with Strange and Perkin on his behalf. All attempts at a compromise failed, and Perkin, riding high and acting on Strange's advice, fired Weizmann. The open hostility between them was now common knowledge and subject to gossipy speculation in the senior common-room of Manchester University. Although Weizmann's university post was secure, Perkin's enmity filled him with apprehension, and he began to look elsewhere for work. He rejected Edinburgh but considered moving to Haifa, where an Institute of Technology was being planned. Perkin wished him well, hoping that 'the affair in Jerusalem [sic] would hurry up'.[31]

Weizmann's feud with Perkin could not have come at a worse time, for in December 1912 Perkin's election to the Chair in Chemistry at Oxford was announced, and the struggle for the succession to his position in Manchester began. Weizmann believed that he was a front-runner. Academically he had not put a foot wrong since his arrival in Manchester: his list of publications was impressive, his reputation as a teacher high. But he could expect no mercy from Perkin, 'a well-bred cat' who worked 'shamelessly' against him. Weizmann, he insinuated, was interested only in money-making; in any case, he was always talking about going to Palestine. For the short time that Weizmann was optimistic about his chances, he approached Fernbach and suggested they publish jointly their research findings in the hope that it would strengthen his application; his proposal met with an icy reception. He then informed Strange of his intention to submit to the University Council a copy of a draft agreement that he had recently received from Strange and that met with his approval, hoping to impress the authorities that his behaviour had been strictly above board. Strange, horrified at the naivety and implications of such a move, headed Weizmann off.

Weizmann now began to realize that his situation was without hope. A 'foreigner' whose candidacy had already been rejected by the Royal Society could not compete with such flawless pillars of university life. He sought guidance from eminent professors who were sympathetic to him, Samuel Alexander and Ernest Rutherford, and in particular from the Schusters. When they heard all the tawdry details of his story, they too were shocked and persuaded Weizmann to accept a compromise that seemed to them equitable given the exceptional circumstances. At the end of January 1913, Harold Dixon, a senior professor in chemistry, presented him with the *fait accompli*: Arthur Lapworth, Perkin's brother-in-law, would succeed to the professorship; Weizmann would be awarded a readership in biochemistry, a raise in salary (to £600), and an assistant (at £150).

When he first heard the news of this British compromise, Weizmann rejected it outright. He raced over to Schuster's for lunch and consolation. After the meal, he remained closeted with his friend for some time. Schuster calmed him down. Weizmann returned to Dixon that same afternoon to give his reply. 'I cannot afford to reject or accept proposals. I shall have to abide by the decision of the University. I consider your proposal as wrong in the interests of the University and as an offence to me. It will affect me in such a way that I shall try to get out of this place as soon as I can.'[32] Of course, there was nowhere else for him to go: Haifa was no longer a viable proposition.

In a curious way, this sad exercise in commercial greed and academic politics sobered Weizmann up. Inevitably, he attributed his defeat to the worst possible motives: treason, betrayal, and antisemitism (for which there was more than a shred of evidence). He told

Harry Sacher, who was in Cannes cheering up Vera, 'I'm certainly not going to sell Palestine for P's chair. The trouble is: Palestine is not ready for me, I have been ready for it for the last two years and tried my best to get a job there, but so far even Ahad Ha'am does not encourage me. I don't see anything for the next five years. In the meantime I might just as well spoil the Egyptians.' To Norah, he wrote: 'Everybody tries to comfort me in saying that it's difficult for a "foreigner" to get to the top in England. I do feel it rather deeply, but I promise you to take my beating calmly and continue conscientiously the work at College until my time comes and I can go to Palestine. . . . The awful part of Manchester life will be the complete isolation and solitude next winter.'[33]

Weizmann soon accustomed himself to his new position. His hyperactive imagination made his new title (Reader) the equivalent to 'a Professor at Oxford or Cambridge'. Still, he emerged from this fray a much wiser man. Although Perkin had behaved badly, Weizmann had played into his hands, allowing the prospect of quick rewards to warp his judgement. He had concealed from the university contracts which, if known, would have made his position untenable. Certainly, he was no match for a company promoter of Strange's calibre. In the future, Weizmann would be far more wary before committing himself to boardroom deals.[34] And, as luck would have it, he found other sources of financing his researches. Julius Simon, a wealthy Jew from Heidelberg and a friend of Weizmann's, agreed to back him in return for a share in the profits eventually deriving from the research. This was very much to Weizmann's taste. 'Both morally and physically [Räumlich] I'm completely separated and independent of the new professor', he breathed with an evident sigh of relief.[35]

At the beginning of this affair, when his work had been 'progressing splendidly', as he put it, Weizmann decided to put forward his candidacy for a Fellowship of the Royal Society.[36] Not only would membership be a dazzling achievement, but it would enable him to negotiate with the likes of Perkin, Strange, and Fernbach on an equal basis. The snag was that by the rules of the Society only British subjects could be elected Fellows. Undeterred, he did not hesitate to recruit Gaster's good services to exert pressure in high places to effect his naturalization as expeditiously as possible. Both Churchill and Herbert Samuel interceded on his behalf, and on 20 November 1910 he was informed that his naturalization had been granted.[37] His candidacy to the Royal Society, despite a list of distinguished backers, was, however, turned down, much to his chagrin. Did he lack academic distinction, or was there simply a general prejudice against foreigners? He never discovered the truth, although he took comfort from belief in the latter version.[38]

The three English ambitions he had set himself—a full professorship, admission to the Royal Society, and the consulship in Palestine—were never realized.[39] But there was always the compensatory excitement of Zionism. 'Zionist activities are an enormous comfort. It somehow lifts you above these little failures and one attributes less value to the "success" in a "strange land". It's not a mere autosuggestion, but I really find comfort in the thought, that my true ambitions are not in the Victorian university, but somewhere else and my real work is still before me.'[40]

Of course, this rationalization worked equally well in the opposite sense. Pure scientific research enabled him to 'really relax and forget all sorts of things', particularly disappointments in his Zionist world.[41] And he was still not prepared to abandon the laboratory for Zionism.

Offers were made: to join the SAC and work full-time in Berlin or to take over the Zionist office in Constantinople.[42] He was sorely tempted and flattered by these suggestions; he was fed up in Manchester and disgusted with academic politics. But he rejected the offers, convinced that either move would ruin his health and kill him in three or four years. He felt that his time had not yet arrived. First, he had to attain economic and political independence before he would consent to burn himself out for the Zionist movement. Only when he had 'achieved everything' in England [43] would he move to Palestine and devote himself exclusively to the movement. To act otherwise would be a confession of failure. His sixth sense spoke against leaving Manchester; so did Vera. And this proved decisive. She had just graduated from medical school, for the third time, and had begun to practice in Manchester. She disliked Germany, as did Weizmann, and refused to start all over again. Appealing to Weizmann's own inclination, she flatly refused to countenance her husband being relegated to the status of a paid Zionist organizer. 'Our road to Palestine will never go through Berlin,' she declared. 'I shudder to think of the possible results if I had yielded to the importunity of my friends and my momentary impulse', Weizmann later recalled gratefully.[44]

Of course, Weizmann was still a member of the GAC and as vice-president of the EZF he was heavily involved in the politics of that unruly body. Even when he was in Paris, fully engaged with scientific business, he rarely resisted an opportunity to further the Zionist cause. In March 1910 he met Lenin for a *tête-à-tête* at a Paris café on the avenue Orléans favoured by Russian *emigrés*. For two such historical personalities, it was an inconsequential meeting. Lenin pumped Weizmann about Sir Ernest Rutherford's researches and the socio-political views of scientists in general. Otherwise, they chatted about their Switzerland days like two veteran *émigrés*. '*Timeo Danaos!*' were Lenin's final words, echoing the mistrust of the more perspicacious of the Trojans: 'I fear the Greeks, even when they bring gifts.' Weizmann was more forthright to Vera. 'Boring our Zionists might be, they may not do great deeds; but they are true to the ideal and don't drink vodka when there is nothing to do. *Fonya Khazar!* (a derogatory Yiddish term meaning 'Russian filth').[45]

In March 1913, at a Zionist meeting in Berlin, it was decided to revive the idea of a Jewish University. Weizmann reported to Vera: 'The *clou* [chief attraction] of the Congress [in 1913] will be the creation of a Jewish University in Jerusalem, and the whole Zionist machinery will be put to work for the speedy implementation of this project.'[46] A committee was formed with those Democratic Fraction stalwarts Motzkin and Feiwel (Buber had retired from active Zionist affairs), and Weizmann was chosen to deliver the key address on the subject at the Congress. This was just the kind of medicine Weizmann needed to reinvigorate him after his recent disappointments, a golden opportunity to combine scholarly ambitions with Zionist vision. Dreaming of an academic institution in Jerusalem with himself installed as head of its chemistry department, he rediscovered the enthusiasm, the energy, the single-mindedness he had invested in the scheme ten years earlier. Once again he set off to organize, persuade, prompt, cajole, castigate the slackers, and was, as ever, irritated beyond measure by those who failed to concede the veracity of his approach. Living in '*Traumland*' (dream-land), as he himself called it, he envisaged the university as the Third Temple, a glorious monument destined to become 'the common property of a conscious people'. He conscripted new supporters, such as Paul Ehrlich, the Nobel prize winning immunologist—'a *very handsome Jew*, a sheer delight, a sort of saint'—and re-kindled old contacts such as Judah Magnes, with whom he was on most affectionate terms. On 8 September 1913 he delivered his 'Spiritual Dreadnought' speech to the Congress. With a university, he promised, 'we could achieve greater successes than other people with their armies and navies'. Instead of armaments, instead of dreadnoughts, the university could be the kernel of the Jewish national renaissance. He concluded with Fichte's words: 'What noble-minded man would not, by his acts and thoughts, sow seeds for the infinite, ever-growing perfection of mankind, to throw into Time something new, which never was before, that may remain for ever and become an inexhaustible source of new creation?'[47] The Congress rose to Weizmann's challenge and set up a commission to create 'a Hebrew University in Jerusalem'.[48] Weizmann's energy and enthusiasm and optimism fuelled this commission and turned its paper mandate into something real.

A Hebrew University in Jerusalem! What was Weizmann's conception of this fantastic undertaking? He knew what he didn't want. It was not going to be 'a *Stutzpunkt*' (foothold) of Germany in Palestine, a barbed reference to growing German ambitions in the area. Nor would he reduce it to the level of a 'second-rate Talmud-Torah', a transparent dig at the machinations of the *Mizrachi*.[49] At the Congress he had spoken of the university in the most general manner: as a focus for the rebirth of Jewish culture and science. But he was aware that he had to begin somewhere, from a particular point. He argued for the establishment of a medical school, with chairs in chemistry and physics, as 'the most practical, most important and most expedient' path.[50] He did not rule out a faculty for Jewish studies—indeed the pressure was great to found one—but it was his profound conviction that a medical school was 'of greater importance'. From this modest beginning would develop, organically Weizmann might have added, a full-blown university.

He fought hard to gain a consensus for this concept. Others countered that only a comprehensive university possessed sufficient glamour to capture the imagination and the resources of the Jewish masses, to say nothing of the Jewish moneybags. Ussishkin wanted to charge ahead without any time-wasting commissions. Another Russian Zionist leader, Yehiel Tschlenow, at odds with Ussishkin, was suspected by his rival of wishing to liquidate the project. Still others argued for a prestigious arts faculty. Some considered the scheme to be Weizmann's private fad, devised to gratify his academic ego. Many feared the project would divert badly needed funds from more vital activities, such as land purchases and economic development. Even Ahad Ha'am had reservations, prophesying that the establishment of a Jewish university would stir up the Great Powers. Weizmann took issue with his mentor: he refused to abandon Jerusalem simply because the Hebrew University and the Holy Sepulchre were 'incompatible'.[51]

One solid pillar of support was Schmarya Levin, the Zionist movement's outstanding propagandist and authority on educational and cultural matters. Levin, an Austro-Hungarian now resident in the United States, a member of the Zionist Executive and one of Weizmann's dearest friends from their student days in Berlin, was, in 1913, at the centre of the battle of the languages, a "war" fought to decide whether Hebrew or German would be the language of instruction at Hilfsverein-controlled institutions, which then included the Technicum (the institute of Technology at Haifa) and its secondary school. Weizmann too was drawn willy-nilly into this controversy. At a meeting of the Curatorium (the institute's Board of Governors), immediately after the Congress, Levin made a motion that Hebrew be the medium of instruction, and when it was rejected, Levin, Ahad Ha'am, and Tschlenow resigned. Weizmann, nominated as Ahad Ha'am's replacement, after some hesitation took his seat on the Curatorium.[52] Meanwhile, in Palestine the anti-Hebrew campaign roused the Jews there to defend their institutions. Its educational system threatened, its cultural heritage at stake, the Yishuv reacted passionately, at times with violence, and took the debate into the streets, on occasion compelling the Turkish authorities to suppress public demonstrations.

Weizmann was a Hebraist in principle, as he had made abundantly clear in his speech before the Congress. Any difficulties in using Hebrew would be easily overcome, he argued, as 'Hebrew is a flexible language'.[53] For him, the Technicum controversy was dangerous, for the furor resulting from this Kulturkampf considerably complicated his campaign for a university. A calmer, less volatile atmosphere would have smoothed the path and calmed his nerves. He was jumpy even with his closest collaborators, dubbing Simon and Sacher 'traitors' because they ignored, or were unable to comprehend, the true significance of the language struggle, arguing only that to finance Hebrew 'schools' was to divert funds from land projects and the university.[54] Yet there was something to this, at least in theory.

Weizmann's commitment to Hebrew put him at variance with the wealthy German Jews of New York, who were sympathetic to the idea of spreading of German culture in Palestine. This alone would not have caused him much grief, but it affected his attempts to win over the German-Jewish grandees of Wall Street and impinged on his relations with his biggest catch of all, Baron Edmond de Rothschild. Planning to 'draw [his] net around the Baron', he feared that the Technicum business would result in heavy losses for the university.[55]

He first met Baron Rothschild on 3 January 1914 at the baron's house in the rue du Faubourg Saint-Honoré, Paris. It was the beginning of a long and fruitful, if at times vexed, relationship with the Rothschild family.[56] Whereas Herzl regarded Rothschild as a rich novice, a *dilettante*, and was repaid in kind, Weizmann sensed that beneath Edmond's philanthropy ran a deep vein of personal commitment to the Jewish people and flattered him accordingly. Unlike Herzl, Weizmann could, when necessary, tune in to the Baron's wavelength, but it was not easy. He was a mercurial character, even to members of his own entourage. Weizmann's perceptive pen-portrait of him rings true:

> Something of a dandy, but full of experience and *sagesse*. Everything about him was in exquisite taste . . . and there still clung to him the aura of the *bon vivant*. . . . In manner he could be both gracious and brutal; and this was the reflex of his split personality, for on the one hand he was conscious of his power, and arrogant in the possession of it; on the other he was rather frightened by it, and this gave him a touch of furtiveness.[57]

The Baron was genuinely in favour of the scheme for a Hebrew University, provided he could get his own way with it. Weizmann had to trim his sails. A practiced drawing-room debater, he managed, though not without difficulty, to quell Rothschild's torrent of words and ideas, not all of which were expressed in logical progression, and to recompose them into an operational plan. 'If only you knew how difficult it is to describe a talk with the Baron. It's an *avalanche* . . . interrupted by interjections the whole time: *Vous comp., vous comp. (comprenez). Une université—c'est une chose dangereuse, pas un sou, mais institut c'est autre chose, vous comp. etc., etc. Il s'emballe.* But he's a wonderful old man!' Weizmann summed him up: 'He is a very wise old man, but a terribly *meshugener fish*.'[58]

Rothschild's idea of a research institute, 'where about thirty or forty good men would work at scientific research, publish it from Jerusalem and gradually attract pupils, and so in time form a university',[59] was not so far removed from Weizmann's conception of a medical school. Both men envisaged the Hebrew University developing from a smaller, prestigious, more specialized body; both appreciated that it was not possible to begin immediately with a full-scale faculty in all disciplines. The magic of Rothschild's name and the prospect of widespread financial support swayed Weizmann: he adopted Rothschild's basic premise, with the intention of tailoring it to suit the prejudices of the Zionist organization.

As a great international financier, Rothschild was mindful of the political cross-currents likely to disturb his enterprises and eager to preserve his anonymity in controversial projects. This applied also to Palestine: philanthropy was one thing, politicking quite another. He was also anti-German, on French patriotic grounds and railed against German ambitions in Palestine. In the language struggle his resolute defense of the use of Hebrew worked to Weizmann's advantage. Of Paul Ehrlich, whom he rated highly and regarded as his scientific *éminence grise,* Rothschild said: 'If Ehrlich works in Frankfurt, it is of no value to us; he will be eaten up by the Germans; were he to work in Jerusalem, it would be one of the greatest things for Judaism.' Of Nathan Straus, the German-American philanthropist, whom he saw as a potential partner, he remarked: '*Il faut dégager Straus des mains des Allemands; ils le mangeront.*'[60]

Weizmann was receptive to these sentiments on national and practical grounds. He had already won Ehrlich over. Straus, whose generosity was supporting a medical-centre in Jerusalem and an agricultural station at Athlit, was in touch with Magnes and was soon committed to the university project, as was Simon Flexner, bacteriologist and director of the Rockefeller Institute.[61] Weizmann had now to reconcile these practical achievements with the ideological niceties of the Zionist movement and the political sensitivity of Rothschild.

It was a mark of Weizmann's prodigious energy and persuasive abilities that by the summer of 1914 he had succeeded in welding these centrifugal forces into a stable whole. There was a price to pay: the incessant negotiations 'exhausted' him; the endless journeys were 'grinding him up'. After a particularly onerous session with the Baron in April, he returned to Manchester 'near collapse' for two days of solitude and recuperation.[62]

The scheme moved ahead. A site was located on Mount Scopus, a hill adjoining the Mount of Olives, which overlooks the Old City and the new Jewish quarters of Jerusalem to the west, and the Jordan valley and the Dead Sea to the east. Professors were scouted, salaries discussed. The tricky problem of finance was more or less regularized. Budgets of other institutes were scrutinized for clues; construction costs including equipment were eventually estimated at two million francs ($400,000), while the operating costs were put at half a million francs per annum. Rothschild was expected to meet the major portion of this budget. His contribution to the maintenance costs amounted to 150,000 francs; but he also promised half a million for the building costs. These were considerable sums. And together with the Zionists' contributions, roughly matching the Baron's, and another 100,000 francs from Straus, Weizmann, by July 1914, was confident that 'a solid basis' had been worked out.[63]

A stumbling block was Rothschild's narrow conception of what a research institute should be. At one time he wished to restrict it to microbiology, a notion quashed by Weizmann, who insisted that a scientific research institute worthy of its name could not exist without chairs in physics and chemistry. But on one point Rothschild was adamant: he felt unable to propagate its cause openly and immediately or even of lending his name for that purpose. This was unacceptable to the Zionists, and it flew in the face of their resolution taken at their last Congress. Weizmann knew that only a university backed by Rothschild, or the proclaimed prospect of one, would capture the imagination of the Jewish masses and empty their coffers.

The negotiations to wear down Rothschild were laborious. Egged on by Rothschild's private secretary, Gaston Wormser, to engage the Baron in a war of attrition—'*"luttez toujours"'*—Weizmann invoked the frustrated aspirations of 'thousands of our youth'. Finally, in April 1914, Rothschild agreed to a compromise formula: 'that we hope to *realiser le projet dans toute son intégrité*'. Unpredictable as ever, he then enquired how long this would take. Ten years, Weizmann replied. '*C'est trop long,*' Rothschild fired back. It was settled that Edmond's son, James, would henceforth represent his father in university matters. 'Very sensible and simple', concluded a relieved Weizmann.[64]

No sooner had Weizmann appeased Rothschild than he was faced by a revolt in the Zionist ranks. His most vocal critic was a young firebrand, Vladimir Jabotinsky, who headed the Russian office in charge of university affairs. Jabotinsky's criticism ran the entire gamut of Weizmann's achievements: he objected to Rothschild's conditions for a research institute, which he thought paralysing; to his contributions, which he considered inadequate; and even to his participation in the scheme, which he judged unnecessary. A 'modest university' was far preferable and more attractive for fund-raising. Most grandiose of all, he argued that by 1917 a Hebrew institution for teaching purposes should be opened and text-books and professors be introduced at the next Zionist Congress.[65]

These harsh and sweeping criticisms reflected a general disquiet about Weizmann's compromise recipe. Levin feared undue Rothschild influence; Ussishkin thought the plan 'naive'; Tschlenow was disappointed at Rothschild's gifts and believed the movement had more pressing goals for fund-raising. Only Ahad Ha'am counselled Weizmann to stand firm.[66]

There was in fact little choice. To have heeded the criticism would have implied renegotiating the agreement or abandoning the project, impossible alternatives for a man of Weizmann's temperament. He deployed for a counter-offensive. In a letter to the Smaller Actions Committee, he reconfirmed his outlook: '"The only beginning is the evolutionary way via the research institute." This can be proved, upheld and defended. I know this will "ignite" less than the false and misleading prospect of a fourth-class teaching institute which would have neither a practical . . . nor political and national importance. . . . We are falling into the same errors against which we have fought in Zionism for years.' Choosing Jabotinsky's stagy suggestions as the softest target, he subjected them to withering scorn:

> I shall assume that he cannot be serious after all; or does he consider me so stupid and perhaps so frivolous that I would embark on something which in its entire conception is calculated '*pour épater les bourgeois*'? That is easily achieved, it is cheap. It can be declared at the Annual Conference that we shall open a university in the Year of the Lord 1917. Better still, say straight away that we are already awarding diplomas—'Let all that are hungry enter and eat'; the future 'professors' can be dragged round the whole diaspora in cages and collect money, but this won't make it a university, only a monstrous blot.
>
> If the gentlemen believe they can conjure books, a language of instruction, professors, money, science, out of the ground, let them find bliss in their belief. *Épater les bourgeois* is easy; at the same time, however, it involves repelling the others, the perceptive ones, who are well aware of the value of a bluff and a one-day housefly.[67]

'Thank God', he flattered the members of the SAC, that your views are not identical with those of Jabotinsky's. To a 'dear friend', who had praised Weizmann's compromise with Rothschild, he described Jabotinsky's proposals as 'a bad *feuilleton*'—shades of Herzl![68]

By June he had managed to retie the undone strings. He convinced the SAC to adhere to his campaign plan, though not before he had threatened resignation from the university working committee. An Institute-University Curatorium was set up, with James de Rothschild as its chairman, with a first meeting scheduled for 1 August.[69] It had been, reflected Weizmann, 'the most difficult period' of his life and the 'most interesting'. He looked back on the past year with intense satisfaction: 'I started with nothing, and with the help of friends and through the *good, friendly* and *wise* support of the Actions Committee, got so far that the university project is taken seriously and worked for in circles which one could not have dreamed of a year ago.'[70]

In the summer of 1914 Weizmann was approaching forty years of age. By any reckoning, he was a major figure in Zionist affairs. If nothing else, his extraordinary performance over the university had propelled him into the front rank. A place on the Zionist Executive, the SAC, could have been his for the asking. But for all his worldly success and his achievements, and despite his doting circle of English admirers, he felt alone and isolated, rootless, as if living in a spiritual and physical vacuum. He was becoming Anglicized in habit, speech, and political style, a metamorphosis that would set him at variance with his colleagues. He personified the eternal outsider not only to those who watched his transformation with awe, but to himself. His confidant Judah Magnes, a staunch American ally in the university battle, received this instructive confession:

> Now I ask you to consider that quite for ten years I have lived away from the Jewish masses. England is very different from New York, where there is a mass of millions which perhaps bears within itself the seed of 'eternity'. As far as Judaism is concerned I live in voluntary exile, solitary, alone with my ideas, newspapers, books and . . . dreams. My days are passed in the service of something which, even if it is not un-Jewish, is at any rate 'non-Jewish'; my evenings 'at twilight', in short the so-called 'free' hours, belong to Zionism. I live an intensely Jewish life when I come into contact with friends, with the few given to me, whom I happen to meet in my wanderings. Sometimes, when my heart

becomes heavy, I take a ticket to London. For me this means to the street where Ahad Ha'am lives, and we pass an evening or two 'in holiness' and then we both withdraw into our solitude. . . . For me, too, the Zionist Organization, with all its faults, is not a party; and its aims have, unfortunately perhaps, become my world. . . . For me at least, whose life has stamped itself in such a specific manner, a mode of contact follows: to devote all one's strength to the service of Palestine, as the Englishmen here say: 'to keep your eye on the main chance'.

I would like to see one thing expressed differently: Palestine is not the pinnacle of Jewish effort but the focus, and without it the rest, the periphery, is incomprehensible.[71]

His solitariness, his aloofness, his detachment from his immediate environment, the private world of science and Zionism that succoured him—these were evident to most of his contemporaries even if not properly understood. Here is an impressionistic pen-portrait of Weizmann at the Zionist Congress in 1913, secure in the 'splendid isolation' he enjoyed; it is equally perceptive and misleading:

He gave the impression of studied indifference to what was going on around him. He was easily bored. He was still the promising young man who had joined in debate with Theodor Herzl . . . and with the followers of David Wolffsohn. . . . He was impatient with *pilpul* and sharp in procedure. He had a mordant sense of humour. . . . The older men dominated the caucuses. Dr. Weizmann stood in the rear of the hall, his eyes half-closed, listless. He was a ready debater and liked to speak; but in Vienna there was no drive in him. He seemed to be listening and waiting. . . . The last I remember of the Vienna Congress was the tired appearance of Dr. Weizmann reporting the nominations at the end of Congress.[72]

In mid-July 1914 Weizmann was in Berlin attending an ineffectual meeting of the Curatorium of the Haifa Technicum. He returned to Manchester on 22 July, planning to be in Paris at the beginning of August for the university talks and from there to move on to Switzerland for a family holiday. The first intimation that he was in the midst of an international crisis came on 28 July, the day Austria declared war on Serbia. His initial thought was for the safety of the Jews of Galicia and Poland.[73] Despite the crisis, he left for the Swiss resort of Champex on 30 July. Within a week Europe was at war, with Britain and her *entente* partners, France and Russia, ranged against the Central Powers, Germany and Austria-Hungary. Marooned in Switzerland, the Weizmanns made every effort to return home. Three weeks elapsed before they were able to catch a train for Paris, by which time the Allied armies were in full retreat. The massive German sweep through Luxembourg and Belgium to the Marne river and the French catastrophe at the Battle of the Frontiers in Lorraine gave them ghastly reminders of the horrors of war. They arrived in 'disturbingly quiet' Paris, visited Baron Edmond—'very sad . . . very calm', but confident in ultimate victory.[74] By 28 August the Weizmanns were back at Brunswick Road, Manchester.

SEVEN

TOWARD THE CHARTER

The speed with which Europe slipped into a general war caught the Zionists by surprise, as it did most European politicians. They were ill-equipped to deal with war: prudence dictated that they should adopt a strictly neutral policy, for European Jewry, defenceless and exposed, stood hostage to the fortunes of both hostile camps. As Palestine was under the protection of Turkey, soon to become Germany's ally, it was deemed even more prudent to take no action, to make no statement, that might antagonize the unpredictable Turks and endanger the physical existence of the *Yishuv*. These cogent reminders of the Jews' vulnerability were sufficient to convince many thoughtful Zionists. To have gambled unreservedly on the victory of one side, to play *va banque*, as it were, seemed to be the height of irresponsibility.

The cold logic of these premises was soon eroded by the passions of war. The nationalistic euphoria that encompassed Europe affected also the Zionists. German and Austrian Zionists defended the cause of their fatherlands with particular zeal. Shortly after the outbreak of war a German Committee for the Liberation of Russian Jewry, a quasi-government body, was founded. This was a popular cause: Russian Jewry wished to be liberated, even if by the Germans, and Russia, the ally of Britain and France, was world Jewry's despised enemy. Although neutrality was the obvious policy, some Zionists, impressed by the manifestations of German power, tended to interpret it as benevolent neutrality toward Germany. Also, the Zionists knew that any postwar settlement would resolve many international questions. How could they best profit from such a fluid and potentially hopeful situation? Every choice was fraught with uncertainty. Neutralism could antagonize either side or both. To declare unequivocably in favour of one side could lead to political suicide. In this delicate and complex situation, the Zionist Organization had to tread warily.

When the GAC finally convened in neutral Copenhagen in December 1914 to formulate an official policy, it was decided to retain the Central Office in Berlin, to resume the work of the Zionist Agency in Constantinople, and to open a bureau in Copenhagen; at the same time, links would be maintained with the Provisional Executive Committee for General Zionist Affairs (PEC) in the United States.[1] This patched-up compromise, which superficially conciliated all parties, was in fact quite unsatisfactory, even unworkable. In theory, the movement had retained its central, administrative framework and authority; in practice, competing agencies and bureaus were pulling in different directions. A power vacuum had developed, and it was only a matter of time and circumstances before it would be filled by a strong-willed personality with a clear-cut, decisive policy.

Weizmann fitted the bill. With the single-mindedness that had always characterized his public activities, he cut through these checks and balances, which virtually excluded any forward, positive policy, with hardly a second thought. He rejected the GAC's reading of the political map. To his mind, his colleagues had failed to analyse the situation 'deeply enough': they refused to comprehend the true nature of the 'historic forces' at work, and he condemned the activities of the Zionist Executive as 'impracticable and dangerous'. As for holding a conference in Copenhagen, he thought the idea 'entirely superfluous', even 'positively harmful', and promptly dissociated himself from its decisions.[2] From the outbreak of war he was firmly committed to a British victory (he was, of course, a British subject), and argued that the Zionist movement should pin its ambitions to the Allied flag. Like Herzl, who regarded England as 'the Archimedian point where the lever could be applied', Weizmann too believed that 'England will understand the Zionists better than anyone else'.[3] In the event of an Allied victory (and Weizmann could envisage no other outcome), Palestine would fall under British influence and the Zionists would be there at their side.

As early as December 1911, when speculating on the consequences of the Italo-Turkish war, Weizmann had recorded: 'The only way for us to approach the English is to show them how vital it can be for England to have a friendly and "strong" element in Palestine, in the Asian Near East in general, that we can be the link between England

and the Muslim world.'[4] Now, only two months after the outbreak of war, he wrote to Israel Zangwill: 'My plans are based naturally on one cardinal assumption, viz., that the Allies will win'. With victory, the Zionists could press their claim for 'an autonomous Jewish community in Palestine'. Britain would not turn a deaf ear to such a claim. Not only did Britain champion the cause of small nations, but in Palestine British strategic interests coincided with Zionist policy:

> Palestine is a natural continuation of Egypt and the barrier separating the Suez Canal from Constantinople, the Black Sea and any hostility which may come from this side. Palestine again lies on the junction of all the great railways . . . it will be the Asiatic Belgium, especially if it is developed by the Jews. We—given more or less good conditions— could easily move a million of Jews into P.[alestine] within the next 50–60 years and England would have a very effective and strong barrier [and] we would have a country.

Already, in the autumn of 1914, Weizmann was pre-occupied with the unity of world Jewry in order to proclaim to the nations of the world that 'we are one nation'. Only then would it be possible to appear before a future peace conference with 'definite demands'.[5]

Of course, Weizmann was not alone in advocating these ideas, though no one expressed them with greater pungency and consistency. English Zionists, naturally, took this line. Ahad Ha'am held the same view; Pincus Rutenberg, at first a Russian revolutionary, now a Zionist enfused by the vision of an entente victory, campaigned to raise a Jewish fighting force to fight alongside the Allies; Vladimir Jabotinsky advocated the same line.[6] Weizmann was also keen to win over American Jewry to his entente-oriented policy, no doubt believing that by so doing he would strengthen his own hand as well as secure a vital link in uniting world Jewry behind Zionist aims. At the outbreak of war, he conferred his blessing on the PEC, cementing his bonds with its leaders: Schmarya Levin, its inspirer and at the time the only general member of the SAC in the United States; its chairman, Louis Dembitz Brandeis, the noted jurist; and Judah Magnes, its vice-chairman.

American Zionism was then in its infancy. During the 1880s, Jewish immigrants from eastern Europe had brought with them the ideas of Hibbat Zion and had formed groups of Hovevei Zion in most of the large urban areas where they had settled. But it was only in 1898, after the first Zionist Congress, that the Federation of American

Zionists (FAZ) was established. Even then, the FAZ had an uphill struggle imposing its authority upon the autonomous Zionist groups and societies scattered throughout the United States; and it was plagued by organizational and financial difficulties. By 1914, out of an estimated Jewish population of three million, only twelve thousand Zionist activists were enrolled on its membership books, little more than 'a sect', in the estimation of one observer. This meagre showing was not, however, a true reflection of the extent of Zionist sympathy felt by the Jewish masses. 'I was amazed,' an eye-witness recalled, 'at the almost unanimous display of sentiment' expressed by the Jews of Manhattan's Lower East Side when they first heard the news of Herzl's death. Many American Jews pledged their allegiance to other large and powerful bodies—Hadassah Women's Organization, the Labour Zionist (*Poelei Zion*) organization, or the *Mizrachi*—which gradually strengthened their ties with the FAZ while retaining their formal independence.

The outbreak of war stimulated the growth and consolidation of American Zionism, although at no time during the war did it command the support of a majority of American Jews. The formation of the PEC on 30 August 1914 was a first step, and Weizmann immediately extended to it his warmest encouragement. Abandon 'all thought of any committee in Copenhagen', he argued, and allow the PEC 'to conduct all Zionist affairs until the arrival of better times', a far-reaching proposition that was turned down by his European colleagues. Conscious of the immense potential of American Jewry, he was determined to tap its vast reservoir of manpower, wealth, and influence for the benefit of Zionism. Any attempt to undermine the American Zionists' position or to slight their activities, particularly by their European rivals, he rebuked as 'a sin', confident that 'America will play an enormous role...when the interests of small nations are to be safeguarded' with the coming of peace.[7]

In much the same way as Weizmann wished to promote the Allied cause among Zionists, he was equally determined to erase the pro-German image with which the movement had been saddled. In wartime England, ugly attacks against foreigners and British nationals with foreign-sounding names, categories that included many Zionists and Jews, were an unfortunate by-product of the patriotic fervour that swept the country. Wishing to avoid the slightest trace of suspicion Weizmann stopped writing in German and advised his friends to do likewise.

The entry of Turkey into the war in early November 1914 gave an extra impulse to Weizmann's ideas. With the defeat of the Central Powers and their satellite, the Ottoman Empire (Palestine included) would be among the spoils. Prime Minister Herbert Asquith had made this abundantly clear in his 9 November speech at London's Guildhall in which he rang 'the death-knell' of Ottoman rule in Europe and Asia. The fate of Palestine was, of course, undecided, but the popular press had already begun to link its future with the Jews. Sympathetic letters were published in newspapers pleading for the restoration of Palestine to the Jews. H. G. Wells, in an open letter to Zangwill, asked, 'And now what is to prevent the Jews having Palestine and restoring a real Judaea?'[8]

However much events moved in accordance with Weizmann's thoughts, his own political standing was somewhat anomalous. Although his was a prominent voice in Zionist councils, he held no official position of real authority or power. (He was a member of the Greater Actions Committee, an unwieldy body of twenty-six worthies whose ability to direct or supervise Zionist policy was at a low premium because of the war, and vice-chairman of the English Zionist Federation, not the most prestigious of posts in the Zionist pecking-order. Members of the Smaller Actions Committee, the working executive of the movement, were scattered all over the world.) He preferred to be free of bureaucratic restraints so that he could pursue his 'reconnoitring work', as he defined his political chores, in an atmosphere conducive to his talents and personality: a charmed circle moved by his initiatives, owing allegiance to him, and held firmly in his grasp.

In England, there was no one to tie his hands in his political work. Even when the Russians Sokolow and Tschlenow (his two 'ow's') arrived in England at the end of 1914, they were overshadowed by Weizmann's commanding presence and the authoritative position he had made for himself. For the first months of the war he worked only with his own band of intimates: Ahad Ha'am in particular—'Practically nothing was undertaken without his knowledge or consent'[9]— and his Manchester friends. In November, a committee of Manchester dignitaries was formed which included Charles Dreyfus and Nathan Laski, but its activities were low-key. Gaster was reluctantly brought into the group. Weizmann kept his colleagues at the EZF, with whom his relations were at best strained, at a careful arm's length.

Weizmann's immediate aim was to unite the English Jews under an agreed programme as a prerequisite for advancing the Zionist cause. 'The position of the Jews in Eastern Europe and the future of Palestine and of Jewish Palestinian aspirations'[10] were the issues that would rally them to his side. His efforts at first met with a chilly response. '*Cher maître*', he addressed Zangwill, 'Would you like to lead in this great and critical moment?' No, replied Zangwill, unable to comprehend how the fate of Russian Jewry could be ameliorated 'by anything that happened in Palestine',[11] but he promised not to hinder Weizmann's work.

Nor was Weizmann more successful in bringing into line Claude Montefiore and Lucian Wolf, far more powerful figures than the unworldly Zangwill. Montefiore was president of the Anglo-Jewish Association, one of the two main organizations of British Jewry, and cochairman of the Conjoint Committee for Foreign Affairs, a body concerned with defending the rights of Jews abroad. Wolf, a scholar (he was founding president of the Jewish Historical Society) and journalist, sat on the council of the AJA and was a prominent member of the Conjoint Committee. During the war, Wolf, as representative of the Conjoint Committee, negotiated with the British government to secure Jewish rights in eastern Europe. Both he and Montefiore were dedicated anti-Zionists. They were not, however, the hard-hearted, unfeeling villains so often portrayed in the literature. Aware of the depth of Jewish suffering, they did their best to alleviate it. In March 1916, as a concession to the Zionists, Wolf proposed a formula to the Foreign Office that spoke of 'the historic interest' Palestine 'possesses for the Jewish people' and that would guarantee, should Palestine fall within the spheres of influence of Britain or France, Jewish civil, religious and political rights with 'reasonable facilities' granted for Jewish immigration and settlement.[12] But the two men resolutely turned their faces against national self-determination for the Jews: the very concept was anathema to them. Against this rock, all subsequent bargaining broke down.

Protracted but fruitless negotiations with 'the Wolves'—Weizmann's label—began in November 1914. Weizmann was in a pugnacious mood. 'I am going to fight openly and *sans trêve*, but before opening the fight we shall attempt everything to rope in those Jews and work with them harmoniously. If they don't come they will be removed from their pedestal.'[13] Conferences followed, to no avail. In August 1916 the Rothschilds interceded and contrived a meeting between Wolf and Weizmann, but again with no result other than to deepen the suspicion and antagonism on both sides. 'Our interests *clash*,' Weizmann judged, 'and no paper formula can bridge over a gulf which is widening every day.' He would dispose in his own way of these self-appointed *shadlanim** who impertinently claimed to speak for all Jewry. 'We shall certainly denounce these . . . people who have in the most critical period of Jewish history betrayed the national interests of the people.'[14] He had put his finger on the chink in his political armour: the internal divisions of Jewry, which compounded the weakness of the Zionist movement. The ideological differences between himself and 'the Wolves' flared into open hostility in the spring of 1917.

Rallying English Jews to a Zionist programme, however innocuously phrased, seemed to be a hopeless task, but Weizmann also encountered unexpected obstacles within his own camp. His official ranking in the Zionist organization was not high enough to allow him to negotiate authoritatively on behalf of the movement or to commit it to any definite course of action, and his burst of independent activity during the first months of the war must have raised some eyebrows among his so-called seniors. At any rate, Sokolow and Tschlenow were despatched to London to supervise the political work that Weizmann had monopolized. There was also little coordination between Weizmann, still feuding with Greenberg and Cowen, and the EZF. When in February 1915 the EZF, without consulting him first, called for the reconstruction of the SAC and the removal of the central office from Berlin to The Hague, he took umbrage and resigned from its executive, a protest without real meaning but which symbolized the state of relations between himself and other English Zionists.[15]

Of greater significance was the clash between Weizmann and the American Zionists. In Palestine, the Turks began to crack down on the *Yishuv*. From November 1914, alarming reports from Palestine of widespread famine and the mass deportation of Jews reached the West. Weizmann, with three sisters and one brother in Palestine, was torn with anxiety,[16] but in America, Magnes and his colleagues panicked. In urgent cables Weizmann was asked to take 'no important steps' without prior consultation with them; all the tribulations of the *Yishuv*

---

*From the Hebrew meaning, literally, 'pleaders', used to refer to Jewish notables who interceded with the rulers of their country on behalf of their community.

were laid at his door because of his openly pro-British activities. This was a great nonsense, as Weizmann was quick to point out: the idea of Jewish restoration in a British-protected Palestine was an open secret and had been freely discussed in the Jewish and general press for some time; Turkish policy could not be attributed to it. In fact, Weizmann had been unusually discreet in his parleys. What particularly distressed him was the attitude of Schmarya Levin, whom he held in the highest regard. Levin was not prepared to accept unconditionally Weizmann's British-oriented policy and had publicly taken him to task on this score. They even stopped corresponding, though Levin hastened to explain that he had no wish to embarrass Weizmann with letters from an Austrian citizen.[17]

Throughout this time, Weizmann was canvassing British politicians. This proved far more rewarding, and luck—vital for any aspiring politician—smiled. In early September 1914, at a garden party of one of Vera's associates, a Mrs. Eckhard, Weizmann was introduced to an elderly, distinguished-looking gentleman with a majestic beard and piercing blue eyes. Weizmann did not catch his name. Where do you work? he asked. The *Manchester Guardian*, replied Charles Prestwich Scott, its celebrated editor. A few days later Weizmann visited Scott at his elegant home, 'The Firs', at Fallowfield. He launched into an anti-Russian tirade followed by an exposition of the Zionist case. Scott was impressed: 'I would like to do something for you.' He was certainly in a position to do so. An intimate of Lloyd George and other members of the Liberal government, Scott regarded Whitehall for the most part as an unlocked door through which he entered as if by right. Weizmann was not blind to this. 'I had a long talk with C. P. Scott . . . today and he will be quite prepared to help in any endeavour in favour of the Jews.' 'Scott carries great weight,' he calculated, 'and he may be useful.'[18]

In some ways Zionism, particularly a Jewish national home under British auspices, was an unlikely cause for Scott to champion. A Liberal anti-imperialist, he had in the past strongly opposed 'forward' foreign policies. Weizmann was not always certain whether he could rely on Scott to press the case for a British commitment in Palestine,[19] but he need not have worried. Weizmann clearly struck the right chord with his account of Jewish suffering, of the messianic dream of Zionism, of the vision of a tiny, persecuted people re-establishing their nationhood after two thousand years. In Weizmann's personality, these aspects of Jewish history knitted together naturally, and Scott was won over. Weizmann turned repeatedly to him, not only to seek political advantage but also for personal guidance.

Soon after Turkey entered the war, Weizmann wrote to Scott. His aims were clear-cut:

> Don't you think that the chance for the Jewish people is now within the limits of a discussion at least. I realize, of course, that we cannot 'claim' anything, we are much too atomized for it, but we can reasonably say that, should Palestine fall within the sphere of British influence and should Britain encourage a Jewish settlement there as a British dependency, we could have in 25–30 years about a million of Jews out there, perhaps more; they would develop the country, bring back civilization to it, and form a very effective guard of the Suez Canal—perhaps be a valuable protection against an aggression from Constantinople.[20]

And a few days later, after another frank conversation,

> It is the first time in my life I have 'spoken out' to a non-Jew all the intimate thoughts and desiderata. . . . In this cold world we 'the fanatics' are solitary onlookers, more especially now. I shall never see the realization of my dream—'the 100% Jew'—but perhaps my son will see it. You gave me courage and please please forgive my brutal frankness. If I would have spoken to a man I value less, I would have been very diplomatic.[21]

Scott's *Manchester Guardian* developed into a pro-Zionist organ. For Scott, Weizmann commanded the two essentials of genuine statesmanship: that 'rare combination of the idealistic and the severely practical':

> What struck me . . . was first the perfectly clear conception of Jewish nationalism—an intense and burning sense of the Jew as Jew; just as strong, perhaps more so, as that of the German as German or the Englishman as Englishman—and, secondly, arising out of that, necessary for its satisfaction and development, his demand for a country, a homeland, which for him, and for anyone sharing his view of a Jewish nationality, could only be the ancient home of his race.[22]

Had Scott been aware of it, Zionism had long since penetrated the portals of the *Guardian* building in Cross Street. Harry Sacher, a member of its editorial staff, was an early convert: in 1907 he and Weizmann had been accredited by the paper to cover the eighth Zionist Congress at The Hague. Two other senior members of the staff were also pledged to Zionism, apparently converts to Sacher's convictions: Herbert Sidebotham (he wrote under the labels *Candidus* or *Scrutator*), a military commentator, viewed Palestine mainly through a strategic-imperial perspective, while William Crozier (later editor) found in Zionism, according to a colleague, a 'secular but profound fulfillment of his strongly scriptural imagination'. (Sacher and Sidebotham, joined by Israel Sieff and Simon Marks, were later to form the nucleus of the British Palestine Committee whose monthly, *Palestine*, led the campaign to swing influential British public opinion behind Zionism.) At first, the *Manchester Guardian* was restrained, perhaps out of deference to government susceptibilities, and only a few memorable editorial comments or, here and there, the odd reference to the strategic importance of Palestine appeared. It was only after the issuance of the Balfour Declaration that the newspaper adopted an openly pro-Zionist line.[23]

True to his word, Scott lobbied Lloyd George. Zionism was not a new topic for the Chancellor. His firm of solicitors had drafted the Zionist memorandum on the East Africa scheme, and, as he told Scott, he was drawn to Zionism by 'sympathy on the common ground of small nationality'. This was not merely playing with words. Lloyd George was of Welsh origin and had been brought up in Caernarvonshire, where he imbibed the maxims of Welsh nationalism; a Nonconformist intrigued by the mystique of Jewish survival, the vision of Zionism appealed to the romantic in him. It also appealed to him on sound strategic grounds. He first met Weizmann at one of his working breakfasts in January 1915, with Herbert Samuel, President of the Local Government Board and the first practicing Jew to sit in a British cabinet, also in attendance. Lloyd George later told Dorothy de Rothschild, 'When Dr. Weizmann was talking of Palestine he kept bringing up place names which were more familiar to me than those on the western front'. Impressed by Weizmann's personality, he prophesied to Samuel, 'When you and I are forgotten, this man will have a monument to him in Palestine.'[24]

A month before the Lloyd George breakfast, Scott had engineered an interview between Weizmann and Samuel. Weizmann viewed this first encounter with much trepidation, and it is doubtful whether he would have taken the initiative in promoting it, since he had thought of Samuel as a typical product of that class of assimilated English Jews which he so disliked. But Samuel astonished him. Without elaborating, he told Weizmann that his own plans were more ambitious than Weizmann's: 'big things would have to be done in Palestine', he hinted. 'Messianic times have really come,' Weizmann wrote to Vera.[25]

Weizmann would have been even more amazed had he known of Samuel's 'reconnoitring' activities among his cabinet colleagues. On 9 November, immediately after Britain's declaration of war against Turkey and a month before he met Weizmann, Samuel had buttonholed Sir Edward Grey, the Foreign Secretary, and discussed the future of Palestine. Samuel spoke like a true Zionist, though he made clear that he had never been one officially, and indeed he had studied the topic with the conscientious thoroughness that characterized his career. He argued on traditional Zionist lines for a Jewish state in Palestine and, as a responsible cabinet minister eager to secure British imperial interests, argued that it should fall under British protection. Grey concurred, as did Lloyd George, whom Samuel met briefly the same day.[26] After seeing Weizmann, Samuel translated these ideas into an official memorandum entitled 'The Future of Palestine', which was placed before the cabinet at the end of January 1915. Its reception was mixed. Grey, Lloyd George, and Haldane, the Lord Chancellor, registered varying degrees of approval.[27] Asquith thought it 'dithyrambic' and mused as to how this 'lyrical outburst' could proceed 'from the well-ordered and methodical brain of H. S.', concluding that 'it is a curious illustration of Dizzy's favourite maxim that "race is everything"'.[28]

At the same time, Weizmann renewed his acquaintanceship with Balfour. Their discussion, as might have been expected, was 'more academic than practical'. Balfour confessed to Weizmann that he shared many of the anti-semitic prejudices of Cosima Wagner. Weizmann took this provocative statement in his stride; he too, he acknowledged, was 'a cultural anti-semite'. But whereas he agreed with Mrs. Wagner as to her facts, he disagreed profoundly as to the conclusions to be drawn from them: 'The essential point which most non-Jews overlook, and which forms the very crux of the Jewish tragedy, is that those Jews who are giving their energies and their brains to the Germans are doing it in their capacity as Germans, and are enriching Germany and not Jewry, which they are abandoning.' As the Jews withdraw from Jewry, the Germans and other communities react against their assimilation with anti-semitism: 'The tragedy of it all is that whereas we do not recognize them as Jews, Madame Wagner does not recognize them as Germans, and so we stand there as the most exploited and misunderstood of peoples.' Only a revived Jewish nationalism in Palestine would re-establish the status of the Jews and create 'a type of 100 per cent Jew'.

Balfour listened attentively. He was very moved—according to Weizmann, 'to tears'. Was there 'anything practical' to be done? he asked. No, replied Weizmann, nothing could be done while the guns were roaring. But when the military situation was clearer he would, with Balfour's permission, come again. 'He saw me out into the street, holding my hand in silence, and bidding me farewell said very warmly: "*Mind you come again to see me, I am deeply moved and interested, it is not a dream, it is a great cause and I understand it*".'[29]

Samuel's caveat that the British government would not consider any proposal without the backing of 'international Jewry' only confirmed what Weizmann already knew. This explains his perseverance with the Wolf-Montefiore group. He would even have settled for an uneasy truce, on his terms, had they agreed. Still, Weizmann intended to bring heavier guns into play: the Rothschilds. Not all the English Rothschilds were potential Zionist activists. Leopold de Rothschild, younger brother of the first Lord Rothschild, and his son, Lionel, opposed Zionism and joined forces with the Conjoint Committee. But the senior branch of the family, headed by Walter and his younger brother Charles, were gradually drawn into the Zionist net. Much of the early missionary work with them was due to the enthusiasm of Dorothy de Rothschild, who had married James, Baron Edmond's son, in 1913. Then only nineteen years old, she 'combined charm, intelligence and more than a hint of steely resolution'. She was on excellent terms with her father-in-law and devoted to upholding the ideals cherished by her husband. Weizmann contacted her in early November 1914. Dorothy, he discovered, was 'genuinely interested' but 'utterly innocent' of the questions raised. But she promised to sound out the opinions of her relatives and to mull over the problems he had elaborated.

Here was a golden opportunity for Weizmann to display his talents as mentor, a role he relished. Dorothy served as his confidante, a role flattering for her and useful for him. But beyond the bare political expediencies of their relationship, Weizmann appreciated that her commitment to Zionism was genuine, and there developed a true friendship rooted in a common ideal. He enlightened her about the state of the Jews, about Zionism, about Palestine. The Rothschilds, he claimed, had a special responsibility to alleviate the plight of their people. 'People like you, your good husband, your father-in-law could at present save the situation and help transform a nation, which is suffering the tortures of the damned, into a great factor of real human civilization.'[30]

Weizmann pursued the Rothschilds. At the end of December he proceeded to the Rothschild mansion in Paris on the rue du Faubourg-Saint-Honoré. Baron Edmond had already been alerted to the visit by Dorothy. Still, Weizmann must have been surprised at what he heard: Edmond now sounded more Zionist than the Zionists. Rely only on yourselves, he entreated Weizmann. Do not take the assimilated English Jews, of Montefiore's ilk, into your confidence: they are of no value and are not to be trusted. Prepare the ground carefully with the British government. Work secretly through a small committee to avoid leakages and sabotage. Reveal your plans to the general public only when they are mature. Perhaps, he ventured, the time was ripe to secure the charter Herzl had fought for. He assured Weizmann of his support. This was most encouraging. Weizmann could not have defined his own political *modus operandi* more succinctly or accurately.[31]

Moreover, Baron Rothschild introduced Weizmann to the formidable Lord Bertie, Britain's abrasive and opinionated ambassador to France. Here the response was far cooler, revealing the natural scepticism of the 'professionals' as opposed to the well-meaning intentions of their political masters. 'An absurd scheme,' he ruled. Bertie let slip an important qualification, however, which could not have escaped Weizmann's notice: Neither France nor Russia would be welcome as neighbours of Egypt, the fulcrum of British power in the Near East. But if not France or Russia, who would step into the power vacuum in Palestine? Bertie left the question unanswered, remarking only, 'This scheme, like many others, is a counting of chickens before the issue of war'.[32]

Through 'Dolly' Rothschild, Weizmann met her distant kinswoman by marriage Lady Crewe, daughter of the Earl of Rosebery, whose wife was a Rothschild. Lady Crewe's husband, the Marquess of Crewe, secretary of state for India, had already professed sympathy for Zionism, but his wife was more reticent. She had the apparently justified reputation of being 'snobbish and *mondaine*', of having objectionable manners but of being 'good-hearted', 'brilliant', and 'serious'.[33] Weizmann's violent anti-Russian outbursts had left her with the impression that he was pro-German. She was soon won over. Before long the educational missives began to arrive. 'We claim to be treated as normal human beings, capable of entering the family of nations as equals and to be masters of our own destiny,' Weizmann wrote to her. Lest there be any misunderstanding, he clarified: 'We equally hate anti-semitism and philo-semitism. Both are degrading.' He sent her a few books on the movement: 'Perhaps you may find time to glance through them.' Apparently they had the desired effect. By March 1916 Lady Crewe was overheard informing Lord Robert Cecil, 'We are all "Weizmannites" in this house.'[34]

Through his contacts with the Rothschilds Weizmann met Cecil, then parliamentary Under-secretary of State for Foreign Affairs, in August 1915. 'I am not a romantic,' he told the aloof Englishman, 'except that Jews must be romantic, for to them the reality is too terrible.' Cecil, after listening to Weizmann's arguments in favour of a British presence in Palestine, noted for his colleagues' attention: 'It is impossible to reproduce in writing the subdued enthusiasm with which Dr. Weizmann spoke or the extraordinary impressiveness of his attitude, which made one forget his rather repellent and even sordid exterior.'[35]

In the Mayfair *salons* of the Rothschilds and the Crewes, and later of the Astors, whom he also came to know well, Weizmann began to move in the stratosphere of high politics in Britain: select dinner-parties and fine talk, idle chatter and good manners, impeccable breeding whether the background was land or money. The list of those privileged to attend was restricted, though minor adjustments were made here and there. There was no question of Weizmann being accepted as an insider in this rather incestuous *beau monde*, and however flattering, he would have rejected such an accolade. This was his strength. He enjoyed and exploited their society but was not seduced by it. For them, he was a tolerated outsider, a Russian-born Jew, a naturalized British subject who could raise them above their day-to-day cares with his vision of the restoration of the Jews in Palestine. For him, this was sufficient. At one dinner-party Nancy Astor, in her inimitable way, made much the same point. 'Don't believe him!' she exclaimed, glaring at Weizmann. 'He's a great charmer. He will convert you to his point of view. He is the only decent Jew I have met.'[36]

Through his socializing he was put in touch with a bevy of politicians, government officials, journalists, and academics who were either in government or close to the centres of power: Balfour; Reginald McKenna, Chancellor of the Exchequer; Lord Bryce, the jurist, historian, and Liberal statesman; Lord Robert Cecil, a leading Conservative and, from 1916, Minister of Blockade; Leo Amery, a rising Conservative luminary; Neil Primrose, Lady Crewe's brother, undersecretary at the Foreign Office, and later government chief whip; Theo Russell, diplomatic secretary to Grey and Balfour. He became acquainted with Wickham Steed, foreign editor of *The Times*, and it was at the Astors' that he met Philip Kerr (later Lord Lothian), editor of *The Round Table* and destined to become Lloyd George's powerful private secretary. Kerr and Amery had been members of Lord Milner's *"Kindergarten"* in South Africa (later to coalesce as the Round Table group), a cluster of high-minded imperialists presided over by Milner, a member of Lloyd George's war cabinet, who straddled the worlds of academia and politics. It included Lionel Curtis, a founder of Chatham House (The Royal Institute of International Affairs); Geoffrey Dawson, editor of *The Times*; John Buchan, writer, Conservative politician, and finally Governor-General of Canada; Reginald Coupland, an Oxford don; and Sir Alfred Zimmern, a close friend of Harry Sacher's since their student days together at New College and now an academic expert on international affairs. Weizmann was on close terms with some: Amery, Kerr, Buchan, Coupland, Zimmern; others, like Curtis and Dawson, he scarcely knew. Their corporate influence has been much exaggerated, but in the crucial year 1917 the Round Table took a favourable view of Zionism, [37] and many of those associated with the group were to hold key positions in government. All in all, this was a splendid catalogue of names for Weizmann's social-political calendar. He had manoeuvred himself into easy talking-distance with impressive and influential people who were in a position to directly guide government strategy on the Middle East in general and Palestine in particular.

Weizmann's hobnobbing with Britain's political élite, begun in the winter of 1914–15, occurred because of his special blend of fortuitousness and a keen eye for the main chance. It was in the nature of a social snowball gathering momentum and size as it rolled, or was guided, from one *salon* to another. But what did all this amount to in concrete political terms at the time? Not a great deal. In Weizmann's perceptive phrase, it was just reconnoitring work. There was no hint of a British commitment; merely expressions of sympathy from some individuals at the idea of the restoration of the Jews to Palestine with British support. The British would discover Zionism in their own time and for their own reasons. The most that can be said at this stage is that, at the official level, the question had been placed before cabinet ministers and, provided they read all their briefs conscientiously, they would be conversant with the proposal. When the issue was mentioned in cabinet by Samuel in March 1915, it was passed over in silence.[38] Still, Weizmann was adroitly preparing the groundwork for a favourable political opening that he could not yet envisage but that he felt intuitively was bound to appear.

Weizmann described himself during these months as moving in a 'dreamlike trance'.[39] Certainly, the flurry of meetings he initiated, the consistent message he proclaimed, and his faith in an eventual British victory together give the impression of a man in a state of extreme political exaltation. Perhaps he believed that time was short, that, as most military experts predicted, the war would be won in a few months and the peace-making could begin. By the end of 1914 this comforting theory had been killed in the mud on the western front. The armies of both sides confronted each other in a series of trenches and fortifications strung from the coast of northern France to Switzerland. All that could be expected was a protracted and terrible war of attrition. In February 1915 there was another brief moment of hope as Britain launched the expedition to Gallipoli with the intention of taking Turkey out of the war. Instead, another slogging match ensued that was not to end until the evacuation of the Allied forces in the winter of 1915–16. Despite titanic efforts of both camps, the military stalemate prevailed until the spring of 1918. Deprived of the glory of a decisive knock-out blow, politicians sought other, political advantages. This ultimately worked to the Zionists' benefit, though how best to exploit it was a problem of a quite different order.

By the spring of 1915 Weizmann began to emerge from his 'trance'. Once more, when highly motivated he summoned up phenomenal reserves of energy. He had taken on an extra teaching load at Manchester University; he was constantly travelling to London and Paris for his political activities; and what spare time he could find was spent 'drilling religiously' to repel an invasion. There were his usual complaints of frayed nerves, lack of time, and working in a vacuum. Nor did his frequent absences from home improve his temper, or Vera's. 'Depression', he diagnosed, 'is also a form of insanity and very common with people suffering from an overdose of Zionism.'[40] These handicaps were compensated somewhat by his friendship with Ahad Ha'am, with whom he could relax on his frequent visits to London.

From the spring of 1915, politics took a back-seat as Weizmann's time was taken up more and more by scientific work. The War Office, in a routine circular, had invited British scientists to report all discoveries likely to be of military value, and as a matter of course Weizmann submitted his fermentation process, hoping to attract the attention of the authorities because of the relatively large quantities of acetone and butyl alcohol it realized. On 9 February 1915, William Rintoul, chief research chemist at Nobel's Explosives, visited Weizmann's laboratories. Suitably impressed by what he saw, he recommended the process, after further exploratory tests, to his superiors. Nobel's were sufficiently interested to make Weizmann a concrete offer. There was talk of £3000 'cash down'. Weizmann, on Rintoul's advice, hurriedly registered his process under the patent laws. Nothing resulted from Nobel's offer, for an explosion occurred at their plant at Ardeer, Scotland, which set back their plans and prevented them from undertaking new projects. Instead, Rintoul brought the process to the attention of his old chief, Sir Frederick Nathan, now seconded to the Admiralty as adviser on cordite supply. Weizmann's process had attracted great attention because of an unprecedented shortage of acetone, an essential ingredient in the manufacture of cordite, the propellent explosive used by British forces. Vital for the manufacture of munitions, if used in the correct proportions it increased the smokeless quality of the gunpowder; it also had the effect of lowering the temperature of the explosion, thus reducing the erosion of gun barrels and permitting the firing of more rounds per barrel. These factors were of crucial importance to the British war effort, and the need to ensure a cheap and plentiful source of acetone had become a matter of national urgency. The Admiralty was the first ministry to take an interest.

Nathan realized immediately the potential of Weizmann's process and set in motion a programme for the large-scale manufacture of acetone. This was splendid news for Weizmann. What had eluded him a few years earlier was now within his grasp: recognition, fame, even fortune. But, perhaps conscious of his delicate position as a foreign-born national, he refused to enter into talks on financial recompense but left the question of remuneration to the discretion of the

Admiralty: he would make no claim, he said, while Britain was at war. And 'should the Admiralty continue to manufacture acetone by this process after the war I leave it to them to fix my remuneration.'[41] This was a rash decision that he would soon regret.

Weizmann found the people at the Admiralty 'exceedingly nice . . . and very go ahead'. Nathan, his immediate boss, 'was very interesting to talk to', though Weizmann tactfully avoided the topic of Zionism with him. Nathan ushered him into the presence of Winston Churchill, First Lord of the Admiralty. 'Well, Dr. Weizmann, we need thirty thousand tons of acetone. Can you make it?' Weizmann, taken aback at this Churchillian query, responded with a studied, academic reply on the technical difficulties of producing such large quantities.[42]

The acute shortage of acetone led the government to seek out other suppliers. Strange, who continued to employ Perkin and Fernbach, put the findings of his research team at the disposal of the government. In April 1915 a contract was signed, and Nobel's fermentation plant at Kings Lynn was put into operation using Fernbach's bacillus on a potato mash. The results were extremely disappointing, producing on average only half a ton of acetone a week.

On the other hand, Weizmann's process was a huge success. Since his break with Strange's team, he had continued his researches independently, aided by Julius Simon's generosity. After many experiments, Weizmann found, on an ear of corn, bacteria that suited his purposes: *Clostridium acetobutylicum Weizmann*, nicknamed bacillus B-Y (*B* for bacillus, *Y* for Weizmann); when turned loose on a mash of corn, bacillus B-Y caused it to ferment rapidly, producing a solution that contained butanol, acetone, and minor quantities of ethyl alcohol (twice as much butanol as acetone, but three times more acetone than alcohol). These solvents could then be separated in pure form by a relatively simple process of distillation.[43] Although it was not appreciated fully at the time, these ingredients were vital to an assorted range of industries: high explosives, plastics, synthetic rubber, petroleum, and aviation fuel. It was this process that so excited Rintoul and Nathan.

Nicholson's gin distillery in Bromley, East London, was the site of Weizmann's first large-scale experiments. These proved so successful that in September 1915 the trials were upgraded and transferred to the Navy's cordite factory near Poole, Dorsetshire, using 15,000-gallon fermentation vats. Meanwhile, Scott informed Lloyd George, now minister of munitions, of Weizmann's discovery. Quickly, Lloyd George, too, conscripted Weizmann, independently of the Admiralty (a strange reflection on the bureaucratic process in wartime Britain). Distilleries geared to the Weizmann process were soon to be found scattered throughout the British Isles: at Bromley, Kings Lynn, Poole, Belfast, and Ardgowen. Before long a plant was established in Toronto; and when the United States entered the war two distilleries were set up in Terre Haute, Indiana. In time, the Weizmann process was exploited in India, and France and Italy took a keen interest as well.[44]

By any reckoning, Weizmann was now involved in a large-scale industrial operation. In February 1916, an annual production of 30,000 tons of acetone was planned. Initially, the fermentation process was dependent upon a regular supply of maize, most of it imported from the United States. When Germany opened her campaign of undeclared submarine warfare with the intention of destroying Britain's food-supply, this source became unfeasible and the situation critical. Weizmann turned to substitutes: horsechestnuts in Britain, rice in India. Groups of schoolchildren scoured the English countryside for 'conkers', suddenly an important war *matériel*; it was rumoured that Queen Mary herself partook of the national hunt.[45] These substitutes were only partially successful, and in time, under the pressure of events, the bulk of the acetone production was moved to North America, where the supply of maize was plentiful.

Seconded from Manchester University for essential war work, Weizmann was drawn by force of circumstances to London in the autumn of 1915. Eleven years previously he had gone reluctantly to Manchester, certain that he was being banished to a provincial backwater; now, by government request, he returned to the centres of power, his personal standing considerably enhanced. By September the major details of his transfer to London were agreed upon. He first took rooms in Chelsea, at 3, Justice Walk, a bachelor-apartment that he shared with Jabotinsky. When Vera and Benji joined him three months later, they moved to more spacious accommodations in Kensington. By October 1916 he had acquired a lease on a house in Addison Road, just west of Holland Park. An enormous leap forward from the conventional respectability of the middle-class dwelling the Weizmanns had abandoned in Brunswick Road, 67, Addison Road was an imposing detached fifteen-room mansion designed in neo-classical style, with an impressive portico entrance, a fine gravel courtyard, and extensive gardens at the back. Acquiring a pile of this scale suggested Weizmann's appreciable rise in income, or at least the firm expectation of one, and bound its owners to a gracious style of living which they happily adopted. It was here that their second son, Michael, was born in November 1916. Three years later, when their lease unexpectedly ran out, they moved to 16, Addison Crescent, a larger but less impressive establishment a few minutes' walk away.[46]

Weizmann's future was still uncertain; he was roaming uncharted territory. Unlike the *salons* of Mayfair, the corridors of Whitehall were unfamiliar to him. To guide him through this maze he relied very much on the good offices of Scott, who served him well. In September 1915 he was appointed honorary technical adviser on acetone supplies to the Admiralty, with a two-year research grant of £2000 per annum. At the same time he entered the employment of the Ministry of Munitions as chemical adviser on acetone supplies with a salary of £1500 a year plus a £500 allowance for removal expenses from Manchester to London. The ministry also undertook to equip new laboratories for him at the Lister Institute, London. The following April he was appointed superintendent of the government laboratories at the institute, with the status of adviser on research work connected with acetone production.[47] These opportunities enabled him to develop his research on butyl alcohol, the other chief by-product of his fermentation process. By converting it into benzene, toluene, and methyl ethyl ketone he provided other substantial contributions to Britain's war effort. But never far from his mind was the future of Zionism. 'If all that succeeds,' he confided to Dorothy de Rothschild, 'it would help our Palestinian work very considerably and perhaps the Jewish star will bring some luck this time.'[48]

Weizmann's responsibilities were now considerable. With his distilleries dispersed over the British Isles, he was constantly on the move, overseeing his fermentation process. He was also charged with the preparation of bacillus B-Y and the training of bacteriologists to carry out his process. Naturally, he was concerned with maintaining the highest standards. Pedantic in his personal and scientific habits, he would not countenance slovenliness in others. His attitude did not always win him friends, but it earned him respect. He was also unduly sensitive to his position as a foreigner, for which his titles were some compensation. All in all, his period in government service, which lasted until June 1918, was for him a refreshing experience in the art of wielding authority.

It was not all plain sailing. Weizmann was on terms of mutual distrust with Lord Moulton, an eminent jurist who now served as

Lloyd George's director-general of explosives supply. Nor was he in favour with Christopher Addison, Lloyd George's parliamentary private secretary. These gentlemen missed few opportunities to queer the pitch for Weizmann. When Moulton refused to authorize Weizmann's visiting France on government business, Weizmann, frustrated and unable to cope alone, called in his protector, Scott. At a luncheon party, Scott challenged Lloyd George: was Moulton simply jealous? or did Moulton, and by implication Lloyd George, suspect that Weizmann would pass on valuable information to the enemy? Lloyd George brushed aside this ridiculous assumption and sanctioned the trip. Even so, these annoying pinpricks continued. Again Weizmann appealed to Scott: 'It is impossible for me to go on a day longer if matters are not definitely settled'. Only when Nathan was transferred to the ministry of munitions, where he managed to neutralize Moulton's hostile attitude, was a workable compromise attained.[49]

The question of Weizmann's payment for his fermentation process was also causing him acute anxiety. He had long regretted his reckless promise to waive his account until the end of the war. Considerable sums were involved. He reckoned that the Italian royalties on acetone alone, excluding butyl alcohol, should net him £400 a week, while in the United States, where he did not patent his process until January 1920, 'hundreds of thousands of pounds' were at stake. Chancellor of the Exchequer McKenna told him in March 1916 that it was considered preferable to pay him a lump sum rather than royalties. This was in principle acceptable to Weizmann, but he wished the sum to be sufficient to realize him an annual income of £2000: this would have meant an award on the order of £50,000. In addition, he still hankered after a professorial appointment and, looking still further into the future, requested that the patent rights in other countries remain his. Scott, his counsellor in these matters, found these suits 'reasonable', and he fought Weizmann's battle, badgering those in authority on his behalf. Scott noted that these difficulties 'were preying upon [Weizmann] and destroying his working powers'. 'My own position,' Weizmann reflected, 'is not secure. I cannot help thinking that I am living in *false prosperity*, which may come down like a pack of cards at any time.' This issue seemed to drag on, '*ad infinitum*', with Weizmann sensing that it was slipping beyond his reach.[50]

Weizmann appeared before the reward committee in June 1917. He told Scott in a letter in September that the Admiralty had decided to pay him a royalty of £4 per ton of acetone produced during the war.

'For the time being the worries are over and that is something.' But the precise details of the agreement remain obscure. Was Weizmann referring only to his Admiralty contract or also to his work at the ministry of munitions? In *Trial and Error* he noted, somewhat derisively, that he had been granted 'a token reward' of 'about ten shillings' a ton, netting him a total of £10,000. Unless the Admiralty changed its mind, there is an obvious discrepancy here. Estimates of acetone production during the war vary from 15,000 to 30,000 tons, with the probable figure closer to 30,000, though not all was produced through the Weizmann process. At the rate of £4 per ton and taking the lower estimate, he would have realized about £60,000. Neither does he make any allusion to monies received, if any, for that other valuable by-product, butyl alcohol, or even for the considerable quantities of acetone produced abroad. This whole episode remains cloudy. What is transparently clear, however, is that Weizmann emerged from the first world war relatively free of economic worries, financially independent, and with substantial sums of money at his disposal.[51] With his newly found fortune came an appropriate change in his life style.

One factor that was causing Weizmann profound anxiety at the time, and that certainly accounts for the delay in determining his payment, was the activities of his pre-war collaborators, Halford Strange and Auguste Fernbach. Since their attempts to produce acetone at Kings Lynn had proved startlingly ineffective, the government decided to cancel their contract. Strange reacted by claiming legal rights over Weizmann's method, in fact arguing that Weizmann had infringed their patent and filched their process, a calumny he aired in government circles. But although it planted suspicion in the minds of some— Moulton, for example—the government decided to turn over the Kings Lynn distillery to Weizmann. He was delighted but wary. He wrote to Lloyd George, 'I am sure you will appreciate that I cannot go into their works and do what they have failed to do unless I feel quite satisfied that there is already a record of the fact of such failure which will prevent them from alleging, after I have worked my process at their factory and attained satisfactory results, that my process is in any way identical to theirs.'[52] He submitted to the ministry all documents and correspondence relating to the dispute, apparently to everyone's satisfaction. By June 1916 the Kings Lynn plant was producing acetone under the Weizmann process.

When Weizmann appeared before the reward committee he was cross-examined at length on these points. Patiently he explained the differences between his maize process and the potato process of his rivals. It was a convincing performance. His audience, he gratefully acknowledged, was 'extremely fair and friendly'. He had won this round of his battle with Strange and Fernbach. But there would be more to come, for they refused to concede defeat. The legal niceties of the case were involved and confused, and it dragged on, to Weizmann's despair, until February 1926 when, in an action in the English courts, he was entirely vindicated.[53]

It was Lloyd George who first put out the now well-worn legend that the British government's commitment to a Jewish National Home, the Balfour Declaration, was awarded as a prize for Weizmann's wartime work. Weizmann discredited it: 'history does not deal in Aladdin's lamps'.[54] Yet the link between the acetone process and the Balfour Declaration is clear enough. Weizmann's contribution to the British war effort was considerable. The shell shortage, a national scandal, had been a factor in breaking up Asquith's Liberal administration in May 1915; his process greatly eased the situation in that it assured a plentiful and cheap supply of acetone. By February 1917, the production rate at the main British distilleries had reached 228 tons monthly, while in North America 2563 tons were produced during the first eleven months of 1917.[55] It is difficult to believe that his spectacular achievement had no effect on the attitude of civil servants and politicians toward him. He did not have to convince Lloyd George or Balfour of Zionism, but he did have to convince them, as a Russian-born Zionist Jew, of his personal integrity, of his loyalty, of his trustworthiness. (Paradoxically, the Strange–Fernbach cabal against him eventually worked in his favour, for he was totally cleared of all their spurious charges by a government committee.) That he earned the confidence of British leaders there can be no doubt. How else can one explain the extraordinary decision to send him as chief British representative on a secret diplomatic mission to Gibraltar in July 1917? These developments fall neatly into place, for as the pace of his scientific work slackened toward the beginning of 1917, the rate of his political activity quickened as the general political climate turned in the Zionists' favour.

On 6 December 1916, with the wartime coalition government in a state of crisis, Lloyd George was summoned by the king, George V, and asked to form a new government. By the following day he had succeeded in his task. His administration, in varying combinations, was to rule until October 1922. He assumed the premiership at a bleak moment in Britain's war fortunes: bloody stalemate on the western front; conspicuous failure at Gallipoli; crisis in the war at sea; rising prices and increasing industrial unrest at home. Did he see a single ray of hope? When, in January 1917, Neil Primrose, chief Liberal whip, asked Lloyd George, 'What about Palestine?' the premier replied, with a smile, 'Oh! We must grab that; we have made a beginning.'[56] For Sinai–Palestine was the one theatre of operations where British armies were actually advancing, cautiously but steadily. In December 1916 El Arish, a large town commanding the coastal route to Palestine on the north-east tip of the Sinai peninsula, was occupied; the following month Rafah, some twenty-five miles farther north, was captured. The British were poised to conquer Palestine.

The outbreak of hostilities with Turkey was not requisite to stimulate British interest in Palestine. Ever since the British occupied Egypt in 1882, their eyes had been turned not only toward the upper reaches of the Nile, but also toward the Sinai peninsula and Palestine. Bound to the traditional policy of safeguarding the territorial integrity of the Ottoman Empire, the British had hesitated before committing themselves to the revolutionary path of partition. But as the war progressed, British reluctance faded. Asquith had already hinted at a change. In a series of so-called secret agreements during 1915 and 1916, considerable areas were prised out of the Ottoman Empire to the benefit of the Allies—on the assumption, of course, that they would emerge victorious from the war. But until Lloyd George came on the scene, no British minister had dared to 'grab' Palestine with such certitude.

While Weizmann was enthusiastically and on every occasion putting the case for a British protectorate for Palestine, the British were painstakingly weighing up their interests in the area. In April 1915, a high-powered inter-departmental committee, the de Bunsen committee, met to consider British desiderata in asiatic Turkey.[57] Its conclusions regarding Palestine were by no means cut and dried: in the event that the Empire was dismembered, they said, Palestine was to be allocated to a British zone, mainly for strategic reasons, as a kind of land-bridge between Egypt and Mesopotamia and the Persian Gulf, but also so as to exclude France from areas important to British interests. However, the committee recognized the snags involved if Britain claimed unilateral control over Palestine: it was a country 'whose destiny must be the subject of special negotiations, in which both belligerents and neutrals are alike interested'. This did not rule out the possibility of a British presence, perhaps preponderance, in Palestine, but it did not guarantee it.

Subsequent British diplomacy was characterized by a similar caution. Immediately following the committee's report, an approach was made to Sherif Husayn of Mecca to determine what the territorial and political price would be for Arab participation in the war against Turkey. The chief British negotiator, Sir Henry McMahon, had been briefed on the committee's findings; and the reservations he imposed on Arab demands, especially in respect of Syria and Palestine, were loosely phrased. Indeed, his tortuous language has invited political and historical controversy that rages to this day. Arab apologists contend that in return for Arab participation in the struggle against the Turks, McMahon 'pledged' Palestine as part of a great Arab state destined to arise at the end of the war. The British, supported throughout by the Zionists, have consistently and resolutely denied this interpretation, claiming that it was never their intention to include Palestine or the 'more northern coastal tracts of Syria' in an Arab state. Nor, they added, would they have acted to the detriment of their ally, France. A close reading of the contemporary records bears out the British version.[58]

In conjunction with the approach to Husayn, the British reviewed the future of the Middle East with their allies. No doubt they intended to dispel any future misunderstandings or charges of double-dealing. Ironically, they had the reverse effect, for the result of these *pourparlers*, the Sykes-Picot agreement, a much maligned and abused document, has since become a byword for wicked imperialist plots. This agreement between the British and French governments (in its first stage it also included the Russians) attempted to reconcile their divergent interests, spelt out as zones of interest and areas of more direct rule, with a measure of Arab independence as promised to Husayn— a not altogether happy exercise. Regarding Palestine, it kept roughly to the provisions of the de Bunsen committee report, calling for an international regime in part of western Palestine, while claiming control of the Haifa bay area and predominant interests in the Negev and Transjordan for Britain. None of these agreements, letters, or committee findings mention Zionism or its exploitation to advance British interests.

These arrangements, necessarily tentative until the successful conclusion of the war, represented, inevitably, a compromise among conflicting views. One British official whose influence was apparent throughout this season of bargaining was Sir Mark Sykes. Sykes moves ubiquitously through these scenes. He was drafted by Lord Kitchener onto the de Bunsen committee; he acquainted British officials in the Middle East as to its findings; and he lent his name, as chief British negotiator, to the agreement with the French. He himself wished to see Palestine fall within a British sphere of influence, for traditional imperial considerations, and he could envisage no practical way of obtaining this aim other than by ensuring British dominance there. Sykes has been portrayed as the classic illustration of that truly authentic figure of British public life, the amateur.[59] Heir to an estate at Sledmere, Yorkshire, he had travelled extensively in the Near East in his youth. He was not conversant with its languages—Arabic, Turkish, or Persian; he had no formal training in oriental studies nor as a professional diplomat. None of this tarnished his reputation. A prolific author and a skillful cartoonist, and moving in the right circles, he came to be recognized as an expert on the area.

At this stage, the Zionists barely entered into the calculations. Not that Zionism was an unknown quantity. Its aims had been aired in the press; Scott was pressing its case, as were other publicists; Samuel's memorandum had provoked mixed comment in government circles; Weizmann and his *coterie* were pursuing their 'reconnoitring' work with commendable enthusiasm and unexpected success. But none of this amounted to a breakthrough. British politicians and officials may have been aware of Zionism, but British policy was formulated without relation to its demands. Zionism had affected the fringes of British political life; it had yet to penetrate to the core of government thinking.

Something of this nature began to occur in the early months of 1916. The negotiations with France had a sobering effect on the British. The extravagant nature of France's ambitions and her obduracy in procuring them stimulated fresh, perhaps latent, ideas in British government circles. Official voices speculated on the political interests of the Jews in Palestine. Perhaps, it was mooted, Zionism should be incorporated somehow in the final arrangement with the French, if not as a means of totally excluding them, then at least as a way of strengthening the British position in the Middle East. Simultaneously, reports reached the Foreign Office that an Allied, preferably a British, declaration recognizing Jewish aspirations in Palestine would procure world Jewish sympathy to the Allied cause, then much in question, particularly in the United States, where the Jewish community deplored the alliance with Russia.[60]

Sykes, who in the past had displayed many of the genteel, anti-semitic traits so common to his class, now took note of Zionism. He familiarized himself with Samuel's memorandum, and Samuel introduced him to Gaster, who taught him his basic lessons in Zionism. Prevalent in these circles was a rather pathetic belief in the international omnipotence of Jews. Robert Cecil, a sound friend of Zionism and an idealist to the end, thought it was impossible to exaggerate 'the international power of the Jews'.[61] Agitated by the hostility of Jewish opinion and impressed by the growing power of the Zionist movement in America, the Foreign Office turned to Lucian Wolf for advice. He, unrepentant anti-Zionist as he was, submitted his pro-Zionist formula in March 1916. Sir Edward Grey, who until then had showed no more than a conventional regard for Zionism, now wished to improve on it. He instructed his ambassadors in Paris and St. Petersburg to represent to their accredited governments that, in the course of time, 'the Jewish colonists in Palestine . . . may be allowed to take the management of the internal affairs of Palestine (with the exception of Jerusalem and the Holy Places) into their own hands'.[62] This instruction, which can only be interpreted as a reincarnation of Herzl's charter, must have received the support of Asquith, who only a year earlier had rashly despatched Samuel's memorandum to the wastepaper basket. Other ministers—Crewe, McKenna, Balfour, Cecil, Samuel, Lloyd George, Kitchener—approved, or would have approved had they known its details.

Nothing came of Grey's initiative. The Russians rendered it lukewarm support; the French, for reasons of their own, killed it. But now, by the spring of 1916, the British government was prepared to embark on a Zionist-oriented policy. Troubled by the adverse attitude of American Jewry to the Allied cause; impressed by the strength of Russian Zionism; persuaded of the infinite power of world Jewish opinion; and, in some cases, touched by a deeply felt sympathy for Zionism, the British were moving toward the policy first advocated by Weizmann at the outbreak of war. They were doing so at their own tempo, for their own reasons, and, so far, without any formal contact with the Zionist movement. The favourable political constellation—the convergence of Zionist and British interests—that Weizmann could not have foreseen but that he was to exploit with consummate skill and timing was already apparent eighteen months before the issuance of the Balfour Declaration.

Weizmann was fully employed in his laboratories and distilleries in 1916, though not to the exclusion of all else. In January, at the Hotel Grand Central in London, he helped to set up the Zionist Executive for England, a body that included, among others, Jabotinsky, Ahad Ha'am, Sokolow, and the Greenberg–Cowen faction. Its meetings were irregular, its activities low-key, and it died a natural death a year later.[63] Sometime in April Weizmann got wind of the shift in British policy from Samuel, but it did not, as might have been expected, galvanize him into action. Perhaps he was too busy in his laboratories, or perhaps he was still chasing the chimera of Jewish unity, waiting hopefully for the outcome of further discussions with Lucian Wolf (talks that broke down in August).[64] A month later, the Zionist Executive decided to present their case to the government.[65] Sokolow was the chief draftsman, with Weizmann lending a hand only in the final stage. For the first time, the petition for Palestine as the Jewish National Home was put forward. It remained, for the moment, a paper demand. Never submitted formally to the government, it appeared later, in April 1917, when the Zionists passed on their 'programmatic statement' to Philip Kerr, Lloyd George's secretary.

In the midst of these activities, at the end of August 1916, Weizmann received a strange summons from the War Office requiring him 'to join for service with the colours' that September. He replied posthaste, pointing out that he was already in government employ and had been 'badged [engaged in essential war work] practically since the beginning of the war'. After due verification of these facts, Weizmann's military obligations were waived, and he was left free to follow his other pursuits.[66]

There was little urgency in the Zionists' own policy. Were the leaders at a loss to know what to do? They were, in a sense, whistling in the dark, hoping that something would turn up that they could exploit to their advantage. Weizmann's eye was fixed on the eventual peace conference. But his approach was flexible enough to exploit any eventuality that would allow the Zionists to press their claims. There was no contradiction here. One eventuality, he hoped, would lead to the other.

EIGHT

THE CHARTER

Lloyd George's elevation to the premiership in December 1916 gave Weizmann his opportunity. Unshackled by prejudices of the past, Lloyd George inaugurated a period of vigorous and decisive leadership. In foreign policy he was his own master, much to the consternation of the stiff professionals at the Foreign Office. His predecessor, Herbert Henry Asquith, had noted, 'He does not care a damn for the Jews or their past or their future, but thinks it will be an outrage to let the Holy Places pass into the possession of "agnostic, atheistic France".'[1] This was less than fair. True, Lloyd George was determined not to let Palestine fall to France— an aim shared by others—but he did care about Zionism and he remained its faithful friend both in and out of office. Moreover, he rightly saw no contradiction between the uses he could make of Zionism and his genuine sympathy for it. Weizmann would not have faulted Lloyd George on this score, for his mind worked in much the same way, though naturally his order of priorities was different.

In January 1917 Lloyd George decided to 'grab' Palestine. In March, he wrote to his brother that the news from Palestine was 'thoroughly cheerful. I am looking forward to my Government achieving something which generations of the chivalry of Europe failed to attain.'[2] In April he gave unambiguous instructions to Sykes, then about to depart for Egypt, to include Palestine in the British zone, adding that nothing should be done to hinder the Zionist movement and the 'possibility of its development under British auspices'.[3] He had adopted Zionism, and whether by chance or design he gathered round him men of a similar outlook: Milner and Jan Christiaan Smuts in the war cabinet; Sykes and Amery, attached to its secretariat, an informal brains trust submitting weekly summaries of the world situation; and William Ormsby-Gore, their assistant, who also served as Milner's parliamentary private secretary. Philip Kerr, his own private secretary, was a receptive and sympathetic figure who acted as a dependable channel of communication with the prime minister. (Kerr's influence, which has sometimes been exaggerated, was recognized as considerable. Balfour once asked him whether Lloyd George had read a certain memorandum. 'I don't think so,' was the answer, 'but I have.' 'Not quite the same thing is it, Philip—yet?' said Balfour mildly.[4] When the Zionists submitted their 'programmatic statement' in April, one hopes it did not suffer the same fate.)

Sykes had begun his Zionist education under Gaster, and this tuition was reinforced by his acquaintance with Aaron Aaronsohn, a colourful Palestinian Jew of whom Leo Amery wrote, 'If all the Jews in their own country turn out as sturdy, frank-looking fellows as he, Zionism will certainly be justified.'[5] A prominent agriculturist, the discoverer of 'wild wheat', he was among the founders of the anti-Turk espionage ring Nili, which from 1915 supplied intelligence to the British. Though not always in tune with the official Zionist line, Aaronsohn was in regular touch with Sykes and the war office. Among British military figures, impressed by the bravery and dedication of Aaronsohn's group, who began to view Zionism in a more favourable light were General Sir George MacDonogh, director of military intelligence; Professor Charles Webster, one of his aides; and Colonel Richard Meinertzhagen, chief field intelligence officer to the Egyptian Expeditionary Force (later to become chief political officer in Palestine).

The awakening of these men to Zionism coincided with the intensification of the campaign to form a Jewish Legion to fight against Turkey alongside Allied forces in Palestine. Its predecessor, the Zion Mule Corps, had fought gallantly at Gallipoli, but had been disbanded in May 1916 after the evacuation of the peninsula. Now Jabotinsky, the driving force behind the idea, strove to reconstitute a Jewish fighting unit. His enthusiasm, frowned upon by the Zionist Executive as likely to compromise Zionist neutrality, was upheld by Weizmann, and he recommended Jabotinsky to Sykes as 'an excellent fellow, highly intelligent, honest and very energetic'; but, as Sykes noted and Weizmann agreed, Jabotinsky's *'idée fixe'* would have to wait for a more opportune moment.[6] Still, the discussion generated about a Jewish Legion coincided neatly with the realization that the Zionists could also contribute politically to Britain's future role in the Middle East.

Concurrently, these themes were being brought to the attention of a wider audience as the Zionists stepped up their propaganda campaign. A collection of essays entitled *Zionism and the Jewish Future* (1916), with a foreword by Weizmann on 'Zionism and the Jewish Problem', a thinly veiled attack against the assimilationists, sold 3000 copies, a respectable enough sale. It secured an enthusiastic notice in the *Manchester Guardian*: of all constructive war aims 'none can compare in intrinsic importance and nobility with that of Zionism'.[7] A British Palestine Committee was formed, dominated by Weizmann's colleagues from Manchester. Their weekly, *Palestine*, the first issue of which appeared on 26 January 1917, had inscribed on its banner: 'The ... Committee seeks to reassert the ancient glories of the Jewish nation in the freedom of a new British dominion in Palestine.' *Palestine*, on occasion, ran ahead of Weizmann in its demands and its shrill tone, but it served him as a useful stalking-horse and fulfilled an invaluable propaganda service. By the beginning of April Weizmann could write to Sokolow, though not without a touch of exaggeration, 'Here last week practically every paper wrote about Jewish Palestine under British Protectorate. ... There can be no doubt that the feeling here is very strong.'[8]

Circumstances could not have been more propitious for the Zionists when, in January 1917, Sykes sought out more representative leaders of Zionism than Gaster. He consulted James Malcolm, a British subject of Armenian descent, and a well-known spokesman for Armenian nationalism, yet another of Sykes's pet causes. Sykes, his imagination on fire, was already weaving the tapestry of a born-again Middle East constructed on the revived nationalisms of Judaea, Armenia, and Arabia, and beholden to Britain. His Armenian contact-man, Malcolm, one of those fly-by-night characters of history, led him to the leaders of the third dimension of his master plan, to Weizmann and Sokolow. They first met on 28 January. Weizmann pleaded earnestly 'for Zion' leaving Sykes intrigued and favourably impressed. It was agreed to hold a full-scale conference. To prepare Sykes, the Zionists handed him the latest version of their statement. Drafted chiefly by Sokolow, it contained the following formula: 'Palestine to be recognized as the Jewish National Home, with liberty of immigration to Jews of all countries, who are to enjoy full national, political and civic rights; a

Charter to be granted to a Jewish Company; local government to be accorded to the Jewish population; and the Hebrew language to be officially recognized.' On 7 February, at 11.30 in the morning, the parties convened at Gaster's house in Maida Vale, under his chairmanship, with Weizmann, Sokolow, Herbert Samuel, Lord Rothschild, Joseph Cowen, Harry Sacher, and Herbert Bentwich in attendance. Facing them—in a private capacity, he insisted—was Sir Mark Sykes.[9]

From this point on the shadow-boxing ceased and the real negotiations began. The Zionists pressed strongly for a British protectorate and were adamant in their opposition to any form of international control for Palestine. Rumours had reached them that some kind of a deal might be in the offing with France. This, Scott had counselled Weizmann, 'would be fatal both for you and for all of us'. Lloyd George was told the same thing.[10] Sykes played this card very close to his chest. He could not elaborate on the Anglo-French agreement; but he hinted that a British protectorate was not out of the question for the area south of Haifa, excluding the Jerusalem–Jaffa corridor. At any rate, he assured his nervous listeners, the government had managed to keep open the Palestine question. His description of the borders of a British protectorate held no appeal to the Zionists. Some, including Lord Rothschild and Sacher, argued for a Jewish state. For the moment, these were theoretical debating points. On one issue, all were in unison: that Zionism would flourish best under British patronage.

Sykes urged the Zionists forward. Time was short. With British forces deployed before Gaza, the Palestine question was becoming acute. He reviewed the dangers. Arab nationalists were claiming all Syria, including Palestine, though he was optimistic that an accommodation could be reached with them. In particular he warned against the international ramifications: Russian and Italian interests, and above all French claims, in the Middle East. He proposed that the Zionists nominate one of their number to put their case to the French. This exacting task was allotted to Sokolow. Weizmann approved; in fact he had suggested a kind of roving diplomatic commission for Sokolow even before the conference.[11] It was a natural choice, for Sokolow was senior to Weizmann in the Zionist hierarchy. Still, for Weizmann it was a fortunate choice, since Sokolow's diplomatic forays abroad allowed Weizmann himself to confirm his position as commander of British Zionism when Britain was about to become the arbiter of Palestine. It was also fortunate for Zionism that Weizmann's 'reconnoitring' of the past three years had prepared him for this task. In the transactions that followed he seized his opportunity with all the confidence of a seasoned diplomatist endowed with exceptional gifts. Weizmann, with sound instinct, regarded the conference at Gaster's home as 'an historic one'. From it emerged the Balfour Declaration.

On 11 February 1917, four days after this meeting, Weizmann was elected President of the English Zionist Federation. At Weizmann's insistence there were no other nominees. He was equally determined to pack the Executive with his own supporters and to ensure that the resolutions adopted expressed a definite Zionist purpose on the lines that he was pursuing. Clearly, in the coming negotiations he wished for a free hand unencumbered by ambitious competitors or harmful dissent. Already, he had had occasion 'to tell [Gaster] off once or twice . . . [he] thinks that he has got the monopoly now'.[12]

Sykes had sounded out the Zionists, he said, in a private capacity. This transparent deception was an accepted part of the game, and both sides played it in the coming weeks. 'The Zionist negotiations with Sir Mark Sykes are entering upon their final stage,' Weizmann wrote to Scott on 20 March. Yet he was troubled. The French had their claims, and 'although Sir Mark is very keen on the Zionist scheme I cannot help feeling that he considers it somewhat as an appendix to the bigger scheme with which he is dealing—the Arab Scheme.' Sykes had already hinted at the Arab difficulties. Weizmann was now convinced that this was a real obstacle, and agreed to Sykes's proposal that he go to the Middle East to smooth the path with the Palestinian Arabs. Scott dissuaded him from doing so, at least until the government had committed itself to a pro-Zionist declaration,[13] and Weizmann remained in London at the centre of events. The negotiations with the government moved into a higher gear. Before long, Weizmann received confirmation of Sykes's misgivings from more authoritative political sources.

He met Balfour on 22 March. The Foreign Secretary raised the stock objections that French and Italian ambitions would prohibit a Jewish home in Palestine under British protection. If all else should fail, perhaps an Anglo-American condominium would be the solution? Weizmann did not warm to this proposal: two masters were worse than one. Still, Balfour was a convinced Zionist. Zionism was, an astute commentator noted, the one subject he really cared about. At a cabinet meeting that week he professed himself 'freely in favour of Zionism'. Weizmann claimed, without hesitation, that Balfour 'is in full sympathy with our aspirations'.[14] At the same time, Weizmann bumped into Lloyd George at the Astors'. Come and inflict yourself upon me, he enjoined Weizmann, 'take [me] by storm'. They breakfasted together, with Scott as intermediary, on 3 April. Scott recorded in his diary that the prime minister was full of Palestine. 'It was to him the one really interesting part of the war. . . . He was altogether opposed to a condominium with France, to which Weizmann was no less hostile. "What about international control?" he asked. Weizmann said that would be a shade worse as it would mean not control but mere confusion and intrigue.' He floated Balfour's idea: '"What about joint control with America"? Weizmann said he could accept that. The two countries would pull together. "Yes", said Lloyd George, "we are both thoroughly materialistic peoples".' Two weeks after this promising conversation, a cabinet subcommittee convened to consider British territorial claims at the conclusion of the war. It recommended that Palestine, whose borders were to embrace the Hauran region and the area up to the Litani river, be included in a British protectorate, an aim, the committee pointed out, that necessitated revision of the Sykes-Picot accord. Small wonder that Weizmann counted on the prime minister's 'full sympathies' as well as Balfour's.[15]

If the change in the British government in December 1916 had worked to the Zionists' benefit, so also did other external events. The March revolution in Russia allowed the Zionist movement there greater freedom of activity. It grew in size, and in the ripe imaginations of outside observers its influence, in fact minimal, blossomed. Perhaps it, too, could be harnessed to the Allied cause. Would not a pro-Zionist declaration win over the Jewish masses, help mobilize the pro-entente forces in Russia, and effectively block the movement agitating for a separate peace with Germany? As 1917 progressed, this fanciful idea captured many adherents in Whitehall. Analogous thoughts were considered regarding the position of American Jewry. A statement sympathetic to Zionism would give American Jews, some of whom were indifferent about the outcome of the war, a stake in an Allied victory. Perhaps, then, American Jews would lean on the Wilson administration to soften its much publicized non-annexationist policy in favour of one advocating a British protectorate for Palestine? With the entry of the United States into the war in April 1917, these conjectures took on a special significance.

Weizmann did not have to be persuaded of the importance of Russian and American Jewry. But unlike his British friends, he suffered from no illusions about their power or influence. He had supported the American Provisional Executive Committee from its inception in August 1914. From April 1917 his correspondence with Brandeis, its chairman, increased in both volume and frankness. The American Zionists, now free from the strictures of neutrality, had no inhibitions about supporting Weizmann's policy. The Russians were more problematical. But the Zionist axis that linked Washington, Moscow, and London acted as a powerful stimulant upon British policy makers.

In mid-April Scott heard from a reliable source close to the French foreign office that an agreement had been reached that allotted Palestine north of a line drawn between Acre and Tiberias, including the Hauran, to France, while the remainder was to be internationalized. Without hesitation, he passed this information on to Weizmann.[16] Shocking as the news was, it could not have been totally unexpected. Rumours to this effect had been circulating for some weeks. (At the 'historic' February conference with Sykes, the Zionists had tried vainly to ferret out these details.) For Weizmann, it was the worst possible solution, 'a Solomon's judgement' that mutilated Palestine, making Galilee French and putting Judaea under international control.[17] He resolved to kill it without delay.

On 21 April, five days after receiving Scott's message, Weizmann cabled Brandeis relaying the bad news. He urged upon Brandeis the only satisfactory policy for the Jews everywhere: a 'Jewish Palestine under British protectorate'. Arguing that since both the United States and Russia were proclaiming anti-annexationist principles, the Jews should press for an international agreement that Britain should hold Palestine in trust for them. 'The Zionist Organizations ... trust implicitly British rule and they see in a British Protectorate the only possibility for a normal development of a Jewish Commonwealth in Palestine.'[18] Brandeis was asked to put this view before his government.

Brandeis was in a unique position to do so. His relationship with President Woodrow Wilson has been described as one of 'enduring friendship'.[19] Brandeis had provided much of the legal argumentation for Wilson's controversial anti-trust campaign, and they remained on close terms. Even so, it was an uphill task to convince the President of Zionism. He remained, at best, 'vaguely sympathetic', while his secretary of state, Robert Lansing, would not even commit himself that far. Wilson relied more on Colonel House, his confidential adviser, on such matters. At any rate, it was not until the late autumn of 1917 that it was possible to elicit a positive response from Wilson.[20] Still, Brandeis was on the spot, active and willing to press the Zionist case. He did not stint his services, and played an invaluable role in the new Zionist diplomacy.

One of Brandeis's conspicuous successes was with Balfour, who was in Washington in the spring of 1917 on an official visit. In view of the deteriorating situation, Weizmann was most eager that Brandeis should lobby him. They met at a party at the White House. Balfour later remarked that Brandeis 'was in some ways the most remarkable man he had met in the United States'.[21] Balfour was already committed to Zionism, but Brandeis's unequivocal message that American Jewry supported Weizmann's policy could only have strengthened his conviction.

Weizmann himself, prompted by Samuel, had gone off to lobby Lord Robert Cecil, minister of blockade and Balfour's deputy at the Foreign Office. In the classical tradition of *haute diplomatie*, the Sykes-Picot agreement was not mentioned; instead the discussion turned on an arrangement that was supposed to exist between Britain and France. Once again, Weizmann reiterated his theme that, in a world based on the principle of national self-determination, only a British protectorate would suit British and Zionist needs, as this could not be interpreted simply as a British 'annexation of Palestine'. There could be no question of French control, as the French imposed the '*esprit français*' on the peoples they ruled. Nor was internationalization acceptable: it was a solution fraught with danger, for apart from the inherent weakness of dual control it would also weaken the defenses of Egypt. Cecil patiently heard out this lecture, occasionally prompting his visitor with an apposite question but voicing no disagreement. When they parted, he said, 'there are considerable difficulties in the way but that it would strengthen the position very considerably if the Jews of the world would express themselves in favour of a British protectorate'.[22] The hint was obvious.

Had Weizmann but known it, the Sykes-Picot agreement was the least of his worries—as far as the British were concerned. By now, even Sykes was beginning to have second thoughts. Lloyd George, the real director of British foreign policy, thought of it merely as an encumbrance. He was searching for a face-saving formula to wriggle out of it, and Weizmann provided him with one. On this point at least, Weizmann was preaching to the converted.

Sokolow was not. His task was to create a favourable atmosphere for Zionist claims in Paris, Rome, and the Vatican. From mid-April until mid-May Sokolow moved among the European capitals drumming up support. In Paris, the French agreed in principle to the Zionists' 'programmatic statement', though without referring to the eventual suzerein power in Palestine. Later, Jules Cambon, secretary-general at the French foreign office, wrote to Sokolow expressing 'sympathy for your cause, the triumph of which is bound up with that of the Allies'. At the Vatican, where the ground had been prepared for Sokolow by Sykes, a prominent Anglo-Catholic, he had an encouraging interview with Cardinal Gasparri, papal secretary of state, and was received by the Pope, Benedict XV: 'We shall be good neighbours,' he was told. On 12 May, he met the Italian premier, Paolo Boselli, who assured him of Italian sympathy should the Allies take a positive initiative on Zionism.[23] Sokolow's mission, often overlooked in the wake of Weizmann's achievements, made a substantial contribution to the international recognition accorded to the Zionist programme during 1917.

Weizmann was aware of the delicacy of Sokolow's task and of the 'great skill' with which he discharged it. But Sokolow's dilatoriness often put him on edge, and he was concerned that, despite Sokolow's unquestioned talent for diplomacy, he had made a grave tactical error in showing the French the 'programmatic statement', which had not yet been submitted formally to the British government.[24] Weizmann's nightmare was that the French would seize the Zionist card and play it to their imperial advantage in much the same way that he hoped the British would. The Zionists alone were too weak to wreck French designs. For this, they needed to stiffen the British resolve, a task Weizmann assigned to himself.

In fact, despite the complexity of the international situation, his chief adversaries were to be found in the Jewish world, as he had long suspected. For Weizmann this was 'The Enemy from Within'.[25] In public, he expressed extreme confidence that his plans were about to mature. He was probably in one of his elated moods, for the government, as yet, had made no firm decision. On 20 May, he told a conference of the English Zionist Federation that the final ideal of the movement was the creation of a Jewish Commonwealth in Palestine.

During the intermediate period, the Jews, he hoped, would be allowed to develop Palestine under the wings of that 'mighty and just Power' Britain. He went on: 'I am entitled to state in this assembly that His Majesty's Government is ready to support our plans.'[26] Thus committing the British government in public provoked his 'bitterest opponents'. He had already warned of the dangers of a '*Bruderkampf*',[27] and it now broke out in full fury. Four days after his speech, *The Times* printed a statement on behalf of the Conjoint Committee that unequivocally rejected the Zionist solution. Regarding Palestine and Jewish rights, it would go no further than Wolf's formula.

Weizmann's response was immediate and sharp. His reply appeared in *The Times* on 28 May, reconfirming 'the fact' of Jewish nationalism while categorically rejecting the claim of 'Messrs. Alexander and Montefiore' (joint presidents of the Conjoint Committee) to speak for all Jewry. Supporting him were letters from Lord Rothschild (which he himself had edited) and the chief rabbi, Joseph Hertz, figures whose authority in Anglo-Jewry went virtually unquestioned. For Weizmann, this showdown was coming at a most appropriate moment; he could not have timed it better had he tried. Lloyd George had no use for the Wolf formula, which was too vague to suit British policy. Nor were 'the Wolves' representative in any meaningful sense: a revolt against the rule of 'the Grand Dukes' had been brewing for some time, and the present controversy confirmed their isolation.[28] *The Times* itself came out strongly in favour of the Zionists. Wickham Steed, its foreign editor, had met Weizmann a day or two earlier when they discussed 'the kind of leader which was likely to make the best appeal to the British public'.[29] While clearly not a government organ, the standing of the newspaper was such as to impart to its views an official imprint. But of greater consequence, the Jewish Board of Deputies, one of the parent bodies of the Conjoint Committee, disowned its offspring and, in a dramatic vote on 17 June, condemned the committee's anti-Zionist statement, declaring that the committee had lost its confidence. Shortly afterward the committee was dissolved.[30]

This was a great victory for Zionism and in particular for Weizmann. He had taken the lead in the struggle against the committee and had triumphed. It confirmed his position not only as the leader of British Zionists, but also as the representative voice of English Jews. To the British government this enhanced his personal status, already secure owing to his war work. Here, by logical extrapolation, was incontrovertible proof of what it wished to believe: that the Zionist movement dominated international Jewish opinion. Weizmann was now a figure to be courted, to be used as an instrument of British foreign policy. Promoted from the ranks, so to speak, and flattered by the attention shown him, Weizmann was more than content to play this game so long as it advanced Zionist interests. In July, he was sent by the British government as their chief representative on an extraordinary mission to Gibraltar: to foil American attempts to inveigle Turkey into a separate peace.

This trip was, as Weizmann later described it, 'opéra bouffe' from start to finish.[31] Henry Morgenthau, former American ambassador to Constantinople, had persuaded his government to allow him to negotiate a separate peace between Turkey and the Allies. Morgenthau had influential contacts in Turkey and he believed that he could exploit the well-known differences between the pro-German Enver Pasha and his rival, Taalat Pasha. The British were highly sceptical of his chances, but, for the sake of good relations with their raw American partners, agreed to play along.

Weizmann had got wind of Morgenthau's errand from Brandeis. The news alarmed him: would the Americans conduct the negotiations on the basis of 'an integral Turkey'? Could the Turks agree to anything less? This ran directly counter to Zionist and British policies which, in their different ways and for their own reasons, were already committed to the break-up of the Ottoman Empire. Weizmann took a strong line. To his chief contacts in the Foreign Office, Sir Ronald Graham and William Ormsby-Gore, he denounced the American initiative as detrimental to British, and Zionist, interests, for it would leave German influence paramount in Turkey and particularly in Palestine. Instead, he proposed sending 'a Zionist whom we can trust' to head off Morgenthau. The British fell in with this ploy, but Sacher, Weizmann's original choice, was unfortunately indisposed, and Weizmann found that he had in fact volunteered to undertake the mission himself.[32]

Weizmann was deeply concerned at the active interest the German government was now showing in Zionism and the ways in which it could be manipulated to suit German policy. Articles in the German press had highlighted the world-wide importance of the Zionist movement and warned against the dangers of a Jewish Palestine under Britain, while emphasizing the necessity of retaining Palestine, a Jewish Palestine, under the protection of the Central Powers. There were stories, not entirely unfounded, that the Germans would declare their

Weizmann's
father, Ozer

Weizmann's mother,
Rachel-Leah

Weizmann, aged eleven,
Pinsk, 1885

Family group, 1904. Standing (left to right): Masha, Anna, Moshe, Zinaida, Feivel, Fruma, Chaim, Gita, and Samuel Weizmann. Sitting (left to right): Haya (Weizmann) Lichtenstein, Avraham Lichtenstein, Rachel-Leah Weizmann, Ozer Weizmann, Miriam (Weizmann) Lubzhinsky, and Chaim Lubzhinsky. Children, sitting: Mina and Yehiel Weizmann.

Members of the Democratic Fraction at the Fifth Zionist Congress, December 1901. This is the only known photograph in which Weizmann (second row from front, on extreme left) and Herzl (same row, centre) appear together.

Vera Weizmann

Chaim, Vera, and Benji Weizmann outside their home in Brunswick Road, Manchester, England, 1913

The Zionist Commission travelling through Palestine, April 1918. From left: Captain Eric Waley, unidentified man, Ze'ev Gluskin, Mordecai Hacohen, Leon Simon, Sylvain Levi, Israel Sieff, Joseph Cowen, Weizmann, Major William Ormsby-Gore. Standing, on train, from left: David Eder, Walter Mayer, Aaron Aaronsohn, Jules Rosenheck.

Foreign Office,
November 2nd, 1917

Dear Lord Rothschild,

I have much pleasure in conveying to you, on
behalf of His Majesty's Government, the following
declaration of sympathy with Jewish Zionist aspirations
which has been submitted to, and approved by, the Cabinet.

"His Majesty's Government view with favour the
establishment in Palestine of a national home for the
Jewish people, and will use their best endeavours to
facilitate the achievement of this object, it being
clearly understood that nothing shall be done which
may prejudice the civil and religious rights of
existing non-Jewish communities in Palestine, or the
rights and political status enjoyed by Jews in any
other country."

I should be grateful if you would bring this
declaration to the knowledge of the Zionist Federation.

Facsimile of the Balfour Declaration of 2nd November 1917

ABOVE: Facsimile of the Balfour Declaration

BELOW: Weizmann leaving a reception held in his honour at New York's City Hall, 5 April 1921.

ABOVE: Laying of the
cornerstone for the Hebrew
University, Mount Scopus,
Jerusalem, 1918

TOP RIGHT: Weizmann and
Nahum Sokolow

MIDDLE RIGHT: Weizmann
and Lord Balfour in Palestine

BOTTOM RIGHT: David Lloyd
George, the guest of honour
at a meeting of the Zionist
Federation presided over by
Weizmann, at the Savoy
Hotel, London, 1931

Weizmann, in Arab headdress and a three-piece suit, with Feisal, June 1918

Weizmann relaxing at Merano, Italy, 1926.

Weizmann touring Rhodesia, May 1932.

ABOVE: Weizmann, surrounded by Jewish notables, at the Chicago Century of Progress Fair, July 1933. Meyer Weisgal, with cane and cigar, promised Weizmann $100,000 for Jewish refugees if he would make an appearance at the fair on Jewish Day.

ABOVE: Weizmann with David Ben Gurion and Moshe Shertok, at the St. James's Conference, London, February 1939

LEFT: Stephen Wise presenting Weizmann with a signet ring that belonged to Herzl, at the Biltmore Hotel conference, New York, May 1942.

Weizmann, while travelling in the United
States, February 1940

With the stars in Hollywood, June 1941.
From left: Gene Raymond, Vera, Louis B.
Mayer, Jeanette MacDonald, Weizmann.

support for Zionist aspirations. In June Weizmann had brought these disturbing reports to the attention of the Foreign Office. He wrote to Graham that perhaps the time had now arrived for the British government to recognize openly 'the justice of Jewish claims on Palestine'. Graham concurred. So did Balfour, when persuaded that such a statement need be no more than a general assurance of sympathy. On 19 June he saw Weizmann and Rothschild, and suggested that they submit a formula for consideration by the government.[33] This was a considerable step forward. Ten days later Weizmann left for Gibraltar determined to stymie the Morgenthau mission lest it ruin the chances of a British declaration.

It developed that he had little to fear from Morgenthau, whose expedition, Weizmann noted, had been arranged in a typical '"American way", i.e., a lot of "external trappings", and a great deal of pomp—and zero inside'. Weizmann, after an exciting journey to Gibraltar via Madrid escorted by British intelligence officers (one a 'very smart' lady who arrived in a 'big luxury car') and tailed by German agents, discovered that Morgenthau's intentions were 'very vague, and no amount of discussion and question could elucidate any definite plan or programme'. After this, Morgenthau revised his position and called his mission off. Weizmann reported back to Graham that on no account should Morgenthau be given *carte blanche* to roam the diplomatic field as he thought fit, and that, as he had told Morgenthau, in no circumstances would the Zionist Organization be implicated in his amateurish negotiations. Morgenthau's mission had collapsed under the weight of its own incompetence; Weizmann gave it the final push.

His trip was not entirely wasted. He enjoyed a few days' rest at Algeciras—'It's extraordinarily beautiful here'—while in Madrid he met Max Nordau, who was, he reported, 'delighted by our work in England'. Even Morgenthau's delegation was not a total disappointment, for it included a young Zionist, Felix Frankfurter, a distinguished professor of law at Harvard who was influential in liberal, intellectual circles in the United States, and who later became one of Weizmann's close supporters. But his trip to Gibraltar was important in another, wider sense. It signalled Zionism's coming of age as a factor in the calculations of the powers, certainly in the eyes of the British. Inevitably, Weizmann's personal standing was considerably enhanced. Here was a foreign-born Zionist leader actually advising the Imperial War Cabinet—his report on the mission was later circulated as a cabinet paper. Zionist correspondence was now being transmitted through official channels. Both he and Sokolow were in fact proxies of the British diplomatic service, advancing the cause of Zionism by serving British interests. By the late summer of 1917 Zionist and British policies had converged, if only for a fleeting moment.[34]

Weizmann was by now convinced that the time was ripe for a public British government commitment to Zionism. No sooner had he returned to London from Gibraltar than the Foreign Office asked him to go to Paris, where an inter-Allied conference on the Balkan situation was in progress. The French had softened their stand on Palestine, he surmised, with Cambon's letter as proof. The British, he gathered correctly, had already decided to press the Palestine campaign to a successful conclusion. Together with Sokolow, he met with Balfour and Lloyd George. The British leaders were debating among themselves the feasibility of despatching American troops to the Turkish front; Weizmann was willing to 'expedite matters' by bringing into play the Brandeis group—his 'American firm'. 'George and Arthur,' he reported to Ahad Ha'am, '[had] a very positive attitude towards our cause and a strong desire to receive the *nachlah* [Hebrew meaning estate, i.e., Palestine] as soon as possible. They hope that things will start to move in the near future.'[35]

Back in London by the end of July, Weizmann, again with Sokolow in tow, organized the London Zionist Political Committee to advise on the conduct of political affairs. In mid-August a London Zionist office was opened at 175 Piccadilly, organized by Simon Marks, who no doubt also financed the move.[36] Weizmann was creating his own organizational framework, staffed essentially with his own people, and placing before the Zionist Executive a comforting *fait accompli*.

The first draft of the Zionist Declaration was sent to Balfour on 18 July. In Weizmann's absence, Sokolow took the lead in formulating it. After toning down the demands of the maximalists—led by the duo from the *Manchester Guardian*, Harry Sacher and Herbert Sidebotham, who were already claiming a Jewish state—Sokolow presented a text that included 'the principle that Palestine should be reconstituted as the National Home of the Jewish people' and an obligation by the British government 'to secure the achievement of this object'.[37] This draft, together with two other amended versions (by Balfour and Milner) were brought before the war cabinet for consideration on 3 September. Milner had rephrased a vital passage, substituting 'the establishment of a home for the Jewish people in Palestine' for the original. Even this concession did not satisfy the war cabinet, which met in the absence of Lloyd George, who had succumbed to ptomaine poisoning, and Balfour, who was still in Scotland on holiday, but in the presence of Edwin Montagu, Secretary of State for India.

Montagu was not a member of the war cabinet. But as the only Jew of cabinet rank he had been invited to this meeting to state his views. Unlike his relative Herbert Samuel, he was an implacable anti-Zionist, and it was because of his most vehement opposition that a favourable decision was shelved until the cabinet had made further soundings in Washington.[38] When Weizmann heard this news, leaked to him by Amery and Ormsby-Gore, he vented all his anger against 'the "dark forces" in Anglo-Jewry' that dared once again to thwart the true desires of Jewry. He wrote to Philip Kerr:

> This time they have mobilized their great champion, who although a great Hindu nationalist now, thought it his duty to combat Jewish Nationalism. It is, I confess, inconceivable to me how British statesmen still attribute importance to the attitude of a few plutocratic Jews and allow their opinion to weigh against almost a unanimous expression of opinion of Jewish Democracy. . . . When these gentlemen come out into the open they are always defeated; they are therefore working in the dark and we are powerless to do anything against them You are aware no doubt that a 'declaration' is before the War Cabinet. This declaration of Palestine policy has been approved by Mr. Balfour and the P.M. Still it is hung up owing to opposition of a few Jews, whose only claim to Judaism is that they are working for its disappearance.

As a parting thrust, he added that the delay was harming not only the Zionist interest but also British policy.[39]

While Weizmann railed against the dark forces of plutocratic Anglo-Jewry, he must also have had in mind other forces, equally dark, working against him inside his own camp. Russian Zionism, which had nurtured him, was balking at his London-oriented policy. Pleading the principle of neutrality, and refusing to jeopardize the *Yishuv*, again subject to Turkish persecution, or the fate of two and a half million Jews living under the rule of the Central Powers, Tschlenow, the leader of Russian Zionism, refused to agree to Weizmann's programme. Russian Jews distrusted the motives of the British government, he warned, for it had supported the hated Tsarist regime and at the same time revealed a naive belief in the good intentions of the newly installed Provisional Government. At the very moment when Weizmann most needed world Jewish support, his Russian comrades denied it to him.

Both Weizmann and Sokolow strived to change Tschlenow's mind.

To an All-Russian Zionist conference held in Petrograd in early June 1917, Weizmann had sent a message pleading for an 'integral Jewish Palestine under British Trust', but it had been disregarded.[40] On 1 September, discouraged and 'very depressed', he appealed yet again to Tschlenow:

> I expected more support from your Conference, not publicly but at least privately. But Russian Zionism is far too eclectic, far too much under the banner of the Soviet of Worker's Deputies. . . . What is significant is that there is a policy of almost hostile 'neutrality'. . . . The result of this policy will be that in the end we shall find ourselves completely friendless. And if you are putting your hopes in a peace conference— I don't stake as many hopes on it as you do—then it is important to bear in mind that you need strong friends who could defend the Jewish position . . . you must support our work more intensively. . . . Otherwise we'll fall between two stools. . . . I cannot change my attitude, being a very one-sided person, but I can give up the work and pass it into the hands of more 'many-sided' persons. With Nahum Osipovich [Sokolow] we have been working hand-in-glove, and also with Asher Isayevich [Ahad Ha'am]. I admit they are calmer and of more equable temperament, but as to work in England, the lion's share has fallen on my shoulders, and that's perhaps why I am more sensitive.[41]

Once again, his plea was in vain. The sad truth was that the Zionist world was split. Its 'Anglo-Saxon' components—Britain, South Africa, Canada, and the United States—stood with Weizmann, while European Zionists followed a policy of what Weizmann dubbed 'almost hostile "neutrality"'.[42]

While he was squabbling with the Russians, Weizmann was also involved in a bitter controversy in Britain. In late July, the War Office announced that an independent Jewish fighting unit was to be formed, an infantry regiment carrying the Shield of David as its badge and destined to serve on the Palestine front.[43] Although Weizmann never took the initiative in this matter, he had supported Jabotinsky's campaign for a Jewish Legion from the outset. In April, Lloyd George had hinted that it would not go down well with British public opinion if the Jews were not willing to fight for Palestine. Don't worry, Weizmann had assured him, 'they will fight and fight well'.[44] But the Jewish Legion was a highly controversial and delicate issue.

There were approximately 20,000 Russian Jews resident in Britain who were eligible for military service but owing to the fact that they were not British subjects were not liable for call-up. Legislation, never implemented, was placed before Parliament that offered them the choice of either serving in the British army or being deported to Russia to serve there. This proposal attracted unwelcome attention and threw into question, by spurious implication, the loyalty of the Jewish community as a whole. A Jewish Legion, recruited from volunteers, offered an honourable way out. Nevertheless, the War Office announcement was greeted by a chorus of disapproving voices combining both Zionist and anti-Zionist feeling. Most were agreed that placing Jews in a separate category would imply that their contribution to the war effort until now had been negligible; unlike Catholics or Methodists, they had to be bribed into making the supreme effort. Or, as others argued, was this not yet another miserable concession to the Zionist lobby? Among the Zionist leaders, Weizmann found himself isolated. Even his closest collaborator, Ahad Ha'am, took issue with him: 'You know my point of view in principle. Although it is highly advisable to have Jewish soldiers at the Palestine front, they should be in British (or, if possible, American) units and not in a separate Jewish regiment. I consider the latter to be an empty demonstration, the result of which may prove disastrous both to Palestinian and, generally, Turkish Jewry and to our future work in Palestine, if, after all, it is not occupied.'[45]

The same day he received this rebuke, 17 August, Weizmann tendered his resignation from all his Zionist offices.[46] Hurt and frustrated, and facing the crisis concerning his renumeration for his acetone work, he felt unable to cooperate any longer with colleagues who refused to view the great affairs with which he was dealing in a wider perspective. He confirmed his retirement two weeks later in letters to Sokolow and Ahad Ha'am.[47] Ahad Ha'am replied immediately:

> We never elected you and we cannot accept your resignation. Your personal qualities and external conditions have made you the symbol of Zionism in the eyes of the public. You were chosen by the conditions of life, and these conditions will dismiss you when the time comes, when full victory or defeat will render the continuation of your work no longer necessary. [Resignation would be] an act of treason [and] from a personal point of view . . . would be moral suicide.[48]

In fact, Weizmann's resignation was a passing tantrum, an empty demonstration devoid of real content, a triumph of nerves over matter. He continued to attend meetings, press his views, write letters: one can detect no appreciable slackening off in his activities. Eventually he retracted. Still, the 'suspicion, envy and . . . fanaticism' that he felt surrounded him rankled.[49] He must have been aware of the malicious gossip that dogged him. One of his intimate friends wrote to another: 'In general I agree that this Declaration business is of no very great importance, and I do my best with my own little circle to keep the sense of proportion. It's not hard, because they take a pretty similar view. I'm inclined to think that W. has outlived his usefulness as a Zionist leader. He has got to break with Jabotinsky or with us.' Stage whispers were rife that he was enamoured with 'imperialism and militarism'.[50] In this venomous atmosphere, Weizmann derived his greatest comfort from Scott, who had heard of the crisis. For him to resign, he encouraged Weizmann, would be a real misfortune: 'You are the only statesman among them.' Grateful for Scott's sympathy, Weizmann pressed home his advantage: 'My hands would be very much strengthened if the declaration . . . could be obtained as soon as possible.' Would it be possible to talk over the situation with Lloyd George? he asked Scott.[51]

The heat was soon removed from the Jewish Legion controversy. A compromise was reached whereby Jewish battalions would be attached to the Royal Fusiliers. In any case, despite the rancour of the dispute, Weizmann persisted in his main task: to attain the Declaration. Immediately after the war cabinet meeting of 3 September he cabled Brandeis, calling in American help. But President Wilson's first response was disappointing. Weizmann was at a loss to understand what had happened. Knowing full well that without American support the British would be reluctant to move, he urged Brandeis to make greater efforts. On 24 September, Brandeis was able to cable back that he had met the President who now expressed 'entire sympathy with declaration'.[52] Weizmann himself was busy lobbying his British friends. Scott, naturally, was his chief prop. But he also saw Balfour and Smuts, whom he found as cordial as ever; he remained in contact with Philip Kerr; and he was still working hand-in-glove with Sykes, with whom he helped compose a memorandum for the war cabinet's benefit.[53]

On 28 September Scott succeeded in bringing Weizmann and Lloyd George together, 'for two–three minutes'. Weizmann reiterated how urgent it was to issue the Declaration without further delay. Lloyd George agreed. He ordered his secretary to place the question on the agenda of the next cabinet meeting, scheduled for 4 October.[54] The day before, Weizmann and Rothschild sent to Balfour yet another reminder of the case for a pro-Zionist statement: 'We, therefore, humbly pray that this declaration may be granted to us.'[55]

When the cabinet convened the pro-Zionist forces, with the exception of Smuts, were in full attendance. But so also was Montagu. Once again, making a vehement onslaught, he succeeded in holding up the Declaration. It was a last-ditch stand. Balfour spoke most strongly in favour, elaborating the Zionist case dispassionately but incisively, warning of the dangers of allowing Germany to pre-empt a British move. Lloyd George and Milner were of the same mind. Apparently, at one stage of the proceedings a messenger was despatched to summon Weizmann to appear before the cabinet to state his views, an act without precedent, but fortunately for constitutional niceties Weizmann could not be located in time. 'Perhaps,' he ruminated later, 'it was better so. I might, in that setting, have said something harsh or inappropriate.' Eventually, it was decided to poll Anglo-Jewry, its anti-Zionist and Zionist factions, as well as to gain Wilson's agreement, before finally approving the Declaration. Did Montagu sense that this decision, eminently fair, would not kill the Declaration but only postpone it? Just after the meeting, he wrote to Lloyd George: 'You are being misled by a foreigner, a dreamer and idealist, who . . . sweeps aside all practical difficulties.'[56] It was the kind of compliment Weizmann could live with.

This situation was tailor-made for Weizmann's persuasive, manipulative talents. He had nothing to fear from the British. Scott told him that Lloyd George and Balfour were 'immovable', Milner 'favourable';[57] Smuts could also be relied upon. Montagu, his chief bugbear, sailed for India on 18 October, where he achieved greater success with the Montagu-Chelmsford reforms. Weizmann had defeated the anti-Zionist establishment in May: they had nothing to offer but a rehash of already discredited arguments. The way was open to mobilise widespread support. In the United States Wilson, at last, registered his approval. In Britain, Weizmann orchestrated a propaganda campaign to convince the government that Zionism enjoyed mass support. By late October three hundred Jewish organizations had passed unanimous resolutions in favour of the Zionist programme. To Sir Maurice Hankey (secretary to the Committee of Imperial Defence and Imperial War Cabinet) Weizmann wrote: 'Our opponents . . . are entitled to speak in their own name only, but have no right to speak for the Jewish masses whose hopes, aspirations, ideals, and sufferings they do not share.' When the war cabinet finally met on 31 October only Curzon raised an anti-Zionist voice, but not loudly enough to disturb the prevailing consensus. The fifth and final draft of the Declaration, substantially the Milner-Amery formula, was endorsed, taking the form of a letter from Balfour to Lord Rothschild:

> I have much pleasure in conveying to you, on behalf of His Majesty's Government, the following declaration of sympathy with Jewish Zionist aspirations which has been submitted to, and approved by, the Cabinet:
>
> 'His Majesty's Government view with favour the establishment in Palestine of a national home for the Jewish people, and will use their best endeavours to facilitate the achievement of this object, it being clearly understood that nothing shall be done which may prejudice the civil and religious rights of the existing non-Jewish communities in Palestine, or the rights and political status enjoyed by Jews in any other country.'
>
> I should be grateful if you would bring this declaration to the knowledge of the Zionist Federation.[58]

While the cabinet was in session, Weizmann waited impatiently outside. Sykes brought him the document: 'Dr. Weizmann, it's a boy.' Weizmann had wanted a more clear-cut commitment. As he put it: 'I did not like the boy at first. He was not the one I had expected.' But there could be no mistaking the historic nature of the occasion. After telephoning the news to Vera, he made his way to Ahad Ha'am to share with him the excitement of the moment. That evening, in his library at Addison Road, Weizmann joined his more intimate friends in a Hasidic dance to celebrate the great event.[59]

The Declaration has been generally recognized as Weizmann's most substantial achievement, as his personal masterpiece. His name and the Declaration are indissolubly linked. His ascendancy over the Zionist movement, though never unchallenged, was complete, recognized as such by Jews and gentiles alike. The Charter, which had eluded Herzl, was bestowed upon him, and he inherited Herzl's mantle as the greatest figure in the Jewish world. His mother, attending a Zionist demonstration in Russia, was hailed for having given birth to 'the Emancipator'.[60] Weizmann accepted his new position with hardly a qualm of doubt, as though it were his aristocratic birthright. He had been waiting a long time for this moment, following his star, believing in his destiny to lead his people.

The Declaration was a milestone in Jewish history. For the first time since the destruction of the Jewish state in 70 AD, a Great Power had publicly recognized the national identity of the Jewish people. For despite the misty phraseology of the Declaration there can be no doubt what was in the minds of its architects. The evidence is incontrovertible. All envisaged, in the fullness of time, the emergence of a Jewish state. Even so, it was, as Weizmann has noted, a 'bitter pill to swallow'. He would have preferred a more tightly worded formula, along the lines of the first draft. As it was, he viewed the Declaration as 'the Magna Carta of Jewish liberties', comparing it with the Declaration of Cyrus the Great calling on the Jews to return to Jerusalem to rebuild the Temple.[61] He was also unhappy at the dual obligation implicit in the final text, not for its own sake but because it implied oppressive Zionist intentions. And what of the British commitment to administer Palestine, which had been Weizmann's goal since the outbreak of war? There is no mention of it. These were serious drawbacks. A more dogmatic mind might have rejected the final draft, holding out for maximalist aims. Weizmann took it, knowing that it nevertheless 'represented a tremendous event in exilic Jewish history',[62] digesting the unpalatable fact that unless he grasped the opportunity now it could easily slip away for ever. The swiftly moving events of 1917 offered little respite for introspective debate. As befits a political artist, he had a finely honed sense of timing.

The Declaration fulfilled few of the grandiose expectations invested in it by its authors. Four days after the letter was sent to Lord Rothschild, on 6 November, Lenin seized power in Russia. By the following March the Soviet Union had concluded a separate peace with the Central Powers at Brest-Litovsk. The Jews high in Bolshevik circles were violently anti-Zionist. Any pro-Zionist declaration was anathema to their credo, and they casually consigned both Britain and the Zionists to the rubbish-heap of history. Russian Jewry had enjoyed a brief moment of freedom. Its political influence, always negligible, was now nonexistent. In the United States, the Declaration had little visible effect on American policy. Lansing and the State Department never warmed to the idea, and Wilson, sympathetic in private, would not support the Declaration in public until August 1918. Britain's allies, France and Italy, were also reluctant to voice public expressions of support, and did so only several months after the Declaration was issued. Georges Clemenceau, the French prime minister, was content to accept it as a clever piece of wartime propaganda, a sentiment shared by many others.[63]

Of course, the Balfour Declaration was received with enthusiasm by Jews everywhere, except for dedicated anti-Zionists. Britain's reputation certainly rode high with the Jewish masses. But as their influence on world events was marginal, this could hardly be said to have served British interests in any meaningful way. On the contrary, it soon became apparent that the Declaration was a burden not an asset to Britain's international relations. Even the strategic-imperial argument that the Declaration paved the way for a British protectorate over Palestine, which had always been Lloyd George's aim, has, on reflection, a hollow ring. For a result of the war was that Britain was in effective control of a strip of territory from Egypt to the Persian Gulf, and it is reasonable to assume that Lloyd George's inventive mind would have hit upon another excuse for 'grabbing' Palestine if he had needed it. The Declaration was for him a convenient pretext, not a *sine qua non*, for claiming Palestine. In any case, many ministers, Balfour included, were by no means convinced that Britain should carry the added burden of Palestine. What, then, induced the government to issue the Balfour Declaration?

Lloyd George described 1917 as the most critical year in the history of the British Empire.[64] Victory over the Germans was far from assured; indeed defeat often seemed closer at hand. Desperate situations require unorthodox answers. On more than one occasion Lloyd George had surprised his colleagues with his unconventional dictates. In the Balfour Declaration, surely one of the most improbable acts in the history of British foreign policy, his cabinet had contrived a wartime expediency that, it was believed, would swing world Jewish opinion behind the Allies and, it was hoped, strengthen the British position in any future bargaining over Palestine. They had surrendered to a myth of our times: the omnipotence of the Jewish lobby. At the same time, Lloyd George, Milner, Smuts, Balfour, Robert Cecil, and many of those who served them genuinely believed in the revival of Jewish nationalism in Palestine. In their own way, these gentile Zionists were no less committed than their Jewish brethren. They had held this view before the cataclysmic events of 1917, and they would continue to hold it long afterward.

It was fortunate for Zionism that these leaders also believed in Weizmann. For them he personified the spirit of the Return. His burning faith in Zionism and his unadorned Jewishness harmonized in a charismatic personality that bewitched friend and foe alike. Weizmann, recognized one British minister, 'could charm a bird off a tree.'[65] His approach to politics—casual yet serious, not without a touch of humour, flexible yet never losing sight of the ultimate goal—reminded the British of their own tradition. He spoke to them in a language they could readily comprehend; he adopted a political style with which they could easily identify. In fact, he was the only Zionist leader they took seriously.

Until the advent of Lloyd George's coalition, Weizmann's demands had been far in advance of those of the British and they were also out of tune with the official Zionist leadership. Although Weizmann claimed to speak for Zionism, he did so as a minority voice. He could rely on unstinting support only among English Zionists. Sokolow, resident in London throughout the war, rendered him invaluable help. In America, Brandeis's group rallied to him, but others opposed him. Even Schmarya Levin, one of his favourites and a considerable influence among American Jews, took issue with him. The Russians, perversely, stuck to their policy of 'almost hostile "neutrality"'. Zionists in Central Europe refused to accept his entente-oriented policy. It was only after the issuance of the Balfour Declaration that the movement rallied round him, graciously acquiescing in a *fait accompli*.

In a sense, Weizmann was more successful with the British government than with his own constituency—a recurrent theme in his career. Until early 1917 his contacts with British politicians had been confined mainly to his 'reconnoitring' activities or else were connected with his scientific work. They had found no expression in official contacts between the government and the Zionist movement nor in any government policy decision regarding Palestine. They had been useful in softening the opposition, but of limited political value. Yet gradually, for their own reasons, some of them totally misplaced, the British came to realize that Zionism could also advance their own interests. Weizmann's pro-British policy merged with Britain's pro-Zionist policy in the figure of Lloyd George.

When the Zionists' negotiations with the government began in earnest in February 1917, it was by no means a foregone conclusion that they would terminate in a pro-Zionist declaration. This goal could have evaporated at any stage of the proceedings: the intervention of the Conjoint Committee; the passionate, neurotic outbursts of Montagu; the lack of an initial, positive response from the United States; dissent within the Zionist camp. Above all, the British had all manner of things on their mind in 1917 other than a pro-Zionist declaration. But Weizmann's persistence maintained the momentum of the negotiations, and this swung the balance in favour of Zionism. From the outbreak of the war in 1914 he had followed with dogged consistency his pro-British line, pulling sceptics along with him. His faith in the rightfulness of his policy inspired others and allowed the British no respite when they might have faltered. 'We were persuaded,' admitted Smuts, 'but remember it was Dr. Weizmann who persuaded us.'[66] Weizmann later recalled that during 1916–17 he had conducted 2000 interviews. This number seems unlikely, but it was not the quantity of his essays in persuasion that counted but, rather, its quality. The celebrated historian Sir Charles Webster, who as a junior official in the War Office saw him in action, recorded:

> With unerring skill he adapted his arguments to the special circumstances of each statesman. To the British and Americans he could use biblical language and awake a deep emotional undertone; to other nationalities he more often talked in terms of interest. Mr. Lloyd George was told that Palestine was a little country not unlike Wales; with Lord Balfour the philosophical background of Zionism could be surveyed; for Lord Cecil the problem was placed in the setting of a new world organization; while to Lord Milner the extension of imperial power could be vividly portrayed. To me who dealt with these matters as a junior officer of the General Staff, he brought from many sources all the evidence that could be obtained of the importance of a Jewish National Home to the strategical position of the British Empire, but he always indicated by a hundred shades and inflexions of the voice that he believed that I could also appreciate better than my superiors other more subtle and recondite arguments. This skillful presentation of facts would, however, have been useless, unless he had convinced all with whom he came into contact of the probity of his conduct and the reality of his trust in the will and strength of Britain.[67]

In Webster's view, Weizmann's feat was the greatest diplomatic coup of the First World War.

In this way, the focus of Zionist activity shifted from continental Europe to London. A new chapter had opened: Zionism had moved into its Anglo-Zionist phase. In these circumstances no one was better qualified than Weizmann to lead the movement. But although a dominant figure, indeed in Britain the key personality, he was by no means the unchallenged leader.

Weizmann, more than any other Zionist leader, was responsible for the Balfour Declaration, an act of immeasurable consequences. For the Zionists it led to the establishment of their state. For the British it inaugurated one of the unhappiest episodes in their imperial history. Weizmann attempted in vain to bridge the gap. And so there began for him a period full of promise but also of intense frustration. One cynic noted that the process of whittling down the Balfour Declaration began on 3 November 1917. Weizmann, in his darker moments, would have concurred.

NINE

PALESTINE AGAIN

O ur wish,' Lord Robert Cecil told a packed London Opera House on 2 December 1917, 'is that Arabian countries shall be for the Arabs, Armenia for the Armenians, and Judaea for the Jews.' London Jews, mainly from the East End, had flocked to this meeting to thank the British government for the Balfour Declaration. On the platform were gathered a most imposing array of Jewish leaders—Weizmann, Sokolow, Lord Rothschild, Samuel, Zangwill, Gaster, Dr. Hertz; they sat together with the accredited representatives of the government—Cecil, Sykes, and Ormsby-Gore. It was a striking display of the extravagant hopes entertained by the Jewish masses. Weizmann, who shared those hopes, was also aware of the pitfalls ahead. His message to this enthusiastic audience was sober and realistic. There could be no doubting the historic significance of the occasion, he told them, but, equally important, the Jewish people must rise to the challenge and responsibilities now thrust upon them. The Declaration was but a framework; it must be filled with content by their own effort or else it would remain merely a fine-sounding principle. Before the gathering dispersed, he asked the audience to repeat Psalm 137: 'If I forget thee O Jerusalem, let my right hand forget her cunning,' and sing 'Hatikvah' and 'God Save the King'.[1] Weizmann never ceased to preach this judicious message, however unpopular it was in some circles.

Forever impatient, Weizmann was keen to push ahead: to create facts before a peace conference convened. Only four days after the Declaration was issued, on 6 November, he floated the idea of sending out a commission to Palestine to advise the British authorities on matters relating to the welfare of the Jews in Palestine and the establishment of the Jewish National Home. By mid-December he had concrete proposals submitted to the government. Apart from the general principle of establishing an organized Zionist framework in Palestine recognized by the British administration, two issues particularly concerned Weizmann: he was eager to pre-empt any hostile reaction from the Arabs, to tone down any friction, to remove any misunderstandings at the source—quite conscious, as any perceptive politician must have been, of the need to reach an agreement with Arab nationalists; and he was also determined about the foundation of the Jewish University. In Weizmann's mind these two issues were not entirely unconnected. 'That is the one great project which if set in motion now . . . would clearly symbolize before the eyes of the world our relation to our country and also the spirit in which we desire to enter Palestine.'[2]

Weizmann wished the composition of the commission to be as representative of world Jewry as possible. He kept Brandeis fully informed, but the Americans were unable to participate, owing to the United States' continuing neutrality in the war against Turkey. (The Russian Jews, though duly appointed, were left stranded in their country, so they, too, failed to appear.) Without design, the commission was heavily weighted in favour of the British: Weizmann; Leon Simon, his friend; David Eder, a psychiatrist; Joseph Cowen, a clothes manufacturer; and Israel Sieff, his Manchester colleague, who also acted as its secretary. James de Rothschild was also attached to the commission, while William Ormsby-Gore served as its liaison officer with the British authorities. The Allies were represented in the form of Sylvain Levi, professor of Sanskrit at the Sorbonne, 'an avowed anti-Zionist', in Weizmann's estimation; and Commendatore Levi Bianchini, an amiable companion inclined to put Italian interests before those of the Zionists.[3] There was no question as to who dominated this group.

On 4 March, the day he left for Palestine at the head of the commission, Weizmann was received by the king. At the last moment there was a slight *contretemps*. Some Foreign Office officials, influenced by reports of Arab hostility to Zionism, attempted to prevent the meeting. Weizmann nonetheless insisted that it take place. Balfour, with his usual finesse, overrode his staff and supported Weizmann. Wearing a top hat and a morning suit, Weizmann was presented to King George V at Buckingham Palace. The king was preoccupied about the fate of his cousin Nicholas in Russia, but he dutifully extended his sympathy to Zionism and wished Weizmann well in his endeavours. That afternoon, equipped with warm letters of recommendation from Lloyd George and Balfour and fortified by an encouraging interview with Smuts, Weizmann departed for Paris,[4] thence to Rome and Taranto, where his party embarked for Alexandria.

In Alexandria, Weizmann met the local Zionists: Palestinian refugees, 'lively... complicated... [but] reliable', and the Egyptians, 'frivolous, green, superficial'. He made the acquaintance of General Sir Gilbert Clayton, chief political officer to the Egyptian Expeditionary Force: 'He does *not* see any obstacles to our work.' He also found time to address Jewish soldiers in Cairo. A young Jewish solicitor on his way to Palestine, Horace Samuel, observed the encounter:

> Lolling at a table, with his hands deep in his trouser pockets, he just spoke to them easily and racily and familiarly, in their own and his own native Yiddish, getting his points well away with that idiomatic shrug and gesture which constitute one of the most integral parts of the language.
> The audience responded to a man. They were all his, body and soul, ready to leap into his pocket at the first word of command. As he walked across the camp, the men, like rats after the Pied Piper, just followed him, to the long-drawn-out wistfulness of the *Hatikvah*.[5]

After spending about three weeks in Egypt, the commission members left by the coastal railroad for Palestine. In the evening of 4 April 1918, they arrived in Tel Aviv. In Palestine, the military situation had stabilized. General Edmund Allenby, commander of the Egyptian Expeditionary Force, had conquered Jerusalem on 9 December 1917, the Christmas present Lloyd George had promised to the British people. By the spring of 1918 Allenby held a line a few miles to the north of Tel Aviv. But any thought of another breakthrough had to be shelved. The great German offensive on the western front had shattered sections of the Allied front, and it was not to be finally stemmed until mid-July. In the meantime, reinforcements were hurriedly rushed to Europe to arrest the German advance. Allenby's forces were also depleted. All thoughts turned to northern France, where the decisive battles of the war against Germany were being fought. This was not the most propitious moment to badger the authorities about the Balfour Declaration.

Weizmann encountered a disturbing tendency among many of Allenby's officers and administrators. Either they were scarcely aware of the existence of the Balfour Declaration, or else they viewed it as an irritant to be neutralized or disposed of as expeditiously as possible. Many had been reared in the so-called Cairo-Khartoum school, which envisaged a pan-Arab union throughout the Middle East under British tutelage.[6] The Balfour Declaration did not fit into this ambitious scheme, nor did the activities of the Zionist Commission, which some regarded as an intolerable affront to their designs. Niggling incidents demonstrated the resentment: a reluctance to recognize Hebrew as an official language, or the astonishing fact that the Balfour Declaration was not officially published in Palestine until May 1920. Overall this amounted to barely concealed hostility.

Wyndham Deedes, Allenby's senior intelligence officer, showed Weizmann extracts from that notorious anti-semitic forgery called *The Protocols of the Elders of Zion*. What is this rubbish? Weizmann asked. 'You will find it in the haversack of a great many British officers here—and they believe it!' came back the reply.[7] It was common currency at the time, not only among the naive, to link the Bolshevik revolution with fantastic theories of a Jewish world conspiracy. The British military administration in Palestine thus gained a deserved reputation for being anti-Zionist which in some cases spilled over into anti-semitism. Ronald Storrs, governor of Jerusalem, was a prime butt of Zionist accusations. Well-known as an orientalist and amateur musician, widely read in the classics and modern literature, airing his erudition at the drop of a hat, Storrs himself commented on the quality of his colleagues among whom were 'a cashier from a Bank in Rangoon, an actor-manager, two assistants from Thos. Cook, a picture-dealer, an Army coach, a clown, a land valuer, a bo'sun from the Niger, a Glasgow distiller, an organist, an Alexandria cotton broker, an architect, . . . a taxi-driver from Egypt, two school-masters and a missionary.'[8] Before long Weizmann was complaining bitterly about the local administration run by mediocre officials and second-rate juniors. He told Balfour that the British government had to clarify its policy. 'All sorts of misinterpretations and misconceptions were put on the declaration. The English, they said, are going to hand over the poor Arabs to the wealthy Jews, who are all waiting in the wake of General Allenby, ready to swoop down like vultures on an easy prey and to oust everybody from the land. . . . You will therefore realize, dear Mr. Balfour, that we found ourselves in an atmosphere very unfavourable to our work.'[9] These strictures, first raised in 1918, remained to poison thirty years of British rule in Palestine.

Weizmann stayed a few days at Allenby's headquarters, a German hospice in Bir Salem near Ramleh. He struck up an easy working relationship with Allenby, whom he found straightforward and likable. But Allenby would not exceed the conventions of military administration; without express instructions from London he would rule on no political decision designed to alter the *status quo*. This soldierly approach caused some tension, and Weizmann exploited what is known as the Petach Tikva incident to clear the air. This Jewish settlement, founded in the early 1880s, was situated close to the front some ten miles north-east of Tel Aviv. Contrary to a prior agreement, the British military authorities, suspecting that valuable intelligence information was being leaked to the Turks via the colony, ordered the immediate evacuation of all its civilians in April 1918. Weizmann, who was prepared to accept the decision on grounds of military exigency provided due notice was given to allow the evacuation to proceed in an orderly fashion, protested strongly at what he viewed as a flagrant infringement of a previous understanding. He was particularly incensed because the military were not evacuating two neighbouring Arab villages, closer to the Turkish lines. This smacked of outright discrimination. Weizmann raised the issue with Allenby over dinner. Allenby listened sympathetically, and Weizmann pressed his advantage to review the entire spectrum of relations between the authorities and the Zionists.

> You can measure your conquest by one of two yardsticks [he told the general], either in square kilometres . . . or else by the yardstick of history. If this conquest of yours be measured by the centuries of hallowed tradition which attach to every square kilometre of its ground, then yours is one of the greatest victories in history. And the traditions which make it so are largely bound up with the history of my people.[10]

Weizmann felt he had dented Allenby's military reserve, but his appeal had little lasting effect. After an enquiry, the decision to evacuate Petach Tikva was upheld, and before long Zionist relations with the British administration had reverted to the usual norm of mutual suspicion.[11]

Weizmann discovered at least one kindred soul in Wyndham Deedes, a British general who rose to high rank in the colonial service. Deedes, a saintly man who spent the last years of his life helping the poor of London's East End, was profoundly impressed by Weizmann and attracted to Zionism on religious grounds. With him Weizmann felt he could 'speak freely, dream freely'.[12] But the gap between Zionist expectations and the ability of the British to match them was enormous. Ormsby-Gore, a true friend of Zionism, as Weizmann well knew, wrote to Maurice Hankey, the cabinet secretary: 'No one admires Weizmann more than I do, but he is at times too fanatical and too partisan and uncompromising. He wants all Jews to be 100 per cent Zionist and few even here can stand quite so strong a dose.'[13] Most members of the British administration of Palestine were also unable to stand so strong a dose. Weizmann, it must be remembered, was an accomplished diplomat, master of the tactful phrase, the soothing word, the winning smile. Others who followed in his footsteps were less skilled. The mainly East European leaders of the *Yishuv* viewed every bureaucracy with the utmost suspicion; British colonial experience was not geared to deal with such awkward, demanding, and intelligent subjects. They lived and operated on two different planets. Schmarya Levin put the dilemma in the following way: 'Of course, you [Sir Arthur Wauchope, high commissioner of Palestine in the 1930s] cannot understand. You were born and lived in a free country. We were forced into the ghetto. For you, an authority was your natural friend and protector. For us, authority was our declared enemy. When I went to school, I learned the irregular verbs quicker than regular verbs.'[14]

At the end of April Weizmann spoke to a group of Arab notables at a dinner held by Storrs in Jerusalem. According to Storrs, it was 'an eloquent exposition of the Zionist creed', in which Weizmann emphasized that the Zionists came in peace, that they were returning home, and that there was plenty of room for both peoples. The Mufti of Jerusalem, Kamel al-Husayni, replied politely. But can they be trusted? Weizmann pondered. In any case, 'I feel that I do not need to concern myself with the Arabs any more; we have done everything that was required of us, we have explained our point of view publicly and openly: *c'est à prendre ou à laisser.*'[15]

Weizmann knew the Arab question required careful tending; it would not simply disappear. And on the way out to Palestine the issue had been the subject for preliminary discussion among the commission members. When he arrived, Weizmann found the Arab problem 'far more acute here than in Egypt or in London'. Anti-Zionist propaganda was rife. The Arab world of Palestine was being called 'to awaken from its torpor, and to rise up in defense of its land, of its liberty, of its sacred places against those who were coming to rob it of everything'.[16] The British were attempting to clarify with Arab leaders the implications of the Balfour Declaration within the context of general

British policy. As early as January 1918 they had despatched Commander David Hogarth, and Oxford don, now director of the Arab Bureau at Cairo, to enlighten Sherif Husayn on these vexing questions. Husayn was outwardly accommodating, expecting that he would realize his full ambitions at the peace conference that would follow the end of the war.[17] It was now considered advantageous that Weizmann should follow suit: arrangements were put in train for him to meet Feisal, Husayn's son, who was leading an Arab army east of the Jordan. Toward the end of May he left Palestine on his mission, hopeful that he could persuade the most prominent of Arab leaders of his Zionist programme.

Accompanied by Ormsby-Gore, Weizmann sailed round the Sinai peninsula in a tramp steamer from Suez to Akaba. His companion succumbed to dysentery, and Weizmann, escorted by Colonel Pierce Charles Joyce, British agent at Akaba, continued by foot, camel, and car to Feisal's headquarters at Wadi Waheida, on the Transjordanian plateau north of Akaba.

> Here I was, on the identical ground, on the identical errand, of my ancestors in the dawn of my people's history, when they came to negotiate with the ruler of the country for a right of way, that they might return to their home.... Dream or vision or hallucination, I was suddenly recalled from it to present-day realities by the gruff voice of a British sentry: 'Sorry, sir, I'm afraid you're out of bounds.'

His talks with Feisal were most satisfactory.

> He is the first real Arab nationalist I have met. He is a leader! He's quite intelligent and a very honest man, handsome as a picture. He's not interested in Palestine, but on the other hand he wants Damascus and the whole of northern Syria. He talked with great animosity against the French, who want to get their hands on Syria. He expects a great deal from collaboration with the Jews! He is contemptuous of the Palestinian Arabs whom he doesn't even regard as Arabs.[18]

Weizmann returned to Palestine convinced that he had taken a giant step forward in resolving the Arab question, and indeed in a few months' time his efforts were formalized in a written agreement between the Zionists and Feisal. But like the British, Weizmann overrated Feisal's capacity for leadership. When confronted with the demands of his own militants on the one hand and the exigencies of the Anglo-French alliance on the other, he proved to be a broken reed. And Weizmann could operate only in the framework prescribed for him by the British. Still, his achievement, in this restricted context, was considerable. If Palestinian Arab nationalism would accept Feisal's leadership, he had brought off a great coup. The signs were not auspicious. Local hostility to Zionism was growing. By the end of 1918 a rabid anti-Zionist campaign was afoot in Palestine. Slogans proclaiming that 'Palestine is our country' and 'The Yarmuk will run with blood and Palestine will not be given to the Jews' were widely circulated. [19] For the moment, Weizmann counted on Feisal's reining in his own extremists.

Of one thing he was certain: the Arab question was 'the central problem', and he was by no means sanguine that a satisfactory solution was feasible. He was playing a poor hand dealt to him by Feisal and the British. Even so, he thought in terms of a solution 'more radical and on a larger scale' than the generally accepted one. [20] Later, when Palestine had settled into the routine of the British mandate, he was determined to make his constituents face reality. 'Palestine must be built up without disturbing a hair of the legitimate interests of the Arabs. The Zionist Congress must not confine itself to platonic formulae. It must recognize the fact that Palestine is not Rhodesia, but that 600,000 Arabs are there who, from the point of view of international justice, have just as much right to their life in Palestine as we have to our National Home.' [21] Yet Weizmann's plea for mutual compromise found no echo on the other side. The hopes he placed in Feisal were to prove illusive, a brief, transient moment of optimism in Jewish-Arab relations.

When Allenby first heard of the request for a ceremony to symbolize the spirit of the National Home, he was amazed: 'But we may be rolled back any minute!' Weizmann replied: 'This will be a great act of faith — faith in the victory which is bound to come and faith in the future of Palestine.' On 24 July, before an audience of six or seven thousand people, the foundation stone of The Hebrew University was laid on Mount Scopus in what Weizmann described as a 'simple and dignified' ceremony. He was the only speaker. He promised that the university would be open to all, irrespective of race or class:

> Our Hebrew University, informed by Jewish learning and Jewish energy, will mould itself into an integral part of our national structure which is in process of erection. It will have a centripetal force, attracting all that is noblest in Jewry throughout the world; a unifying centre for our

scattered elements. And inspiration and strength will go forth to revivify the forces latent in our distant communities. Here the wandering soul of Israel shall reach its haven; its strength no longer consumed in restless and vain wanderings, Israel shall at last remain at peace within itself and with the world. There is a Talmudic legend that tells of the Jewish soul, deprived of its body, hovering between heaven and earth. Such is our soul today; tomorrow it shall come to rest, in this our sanctuary. This is our faith.[22]

So, from his student days in Switzerland when he had first led the agitation for this unlikely project, his quest had led him to a remote hill overlooking Jerusalem and the Dead Sea. From London, his teacher and collaborator Ahad Ha'am, expressing also his own feelings, wrote to him of a university which will become 'the true embodiment of the Hebrew spirit of old, and [will] shake off the mental and moral servitude to which our people has been so long subjected in the diaspora. Only so can we be justified in our ambitious hopes as to the future influence of the "Teaching" that "will go forth out of Zion".'[23] With this act completed, Weizmann felt it was time to return to London.

Despite the difficulties and the 'nervous tension' that 'lasts from early morning until late at night',[24] he had much cause for satisfaction. He had breached, or so he thought, the wall of Arab hostility, and he had launched his 'spiritual dreadnought'. But the vagueness of British policy in Palestine continued to concern him. It was, he felt, wrapped in confusion, pulling in every direction—toward the Arabs, the Zionists, the French—without any firm directives from the centre. He placed his faith in the new Arab–Zionist *rapprochement* (an optimism shared by some British officials), but he warned Balfour that without careful nursing from the British it would turn to dust. He pleaded for the abandonment of the Sykes-Picot agreement, which he perceived as the fount of all evil: 'It forms a centre of political intrigue which obscures the true vision and runs counter to the principle of real self-determination as expressed in the Zionist and Arab movements. The continuance of this agreement and all that it stands for is a constant source of embarrassment here.'[25]

Weizmann was uneasy at leaving Palestine, not only because the political situation appeared to him fraught with danger, but mainly because he saw no one capable of replacing him in the delicate interchanges between the *Yishuv* and the British authorities. Over two months he had attained, 'with blood and sweat', a position of respect and influence. 'What will happen when I leave? Who is to replace me? I'm simply terrified at the thought that all this hard work will be placed in jeopardy.'[26] His fears were well-grounded. None of his subordinates was suitable. And indeed a vacuum emerged when he left. In early 1919 Ussishkin joined the commission and assumed its leadership in October. If Weizmann wielded a rapier, Ussishkin hacked away with a sabre. His *modus operandi* was direct and blunt, as personified in his war-cry: 'Well done—badly done—DONE!' Or as Schmarya Levin once remarked, he 'never racked his brains for syntheses, since he was never aware of antitheses'.[27] Eventually, Weizmann solved this problem by elevating his own men to positions of power in the *Yishuv.* This did not always enhance his reputation in Palestine, but it considerably eased his constant war of attrition with the authorities in both Jerusalem and London.

Weizmann was favourably impressed with the development of the *Yishuv*—'An independent Jewish life is no longer a fairy tale'—but he had no time for its factional politics, and believed its leadership to be politically immature and out of touch with reality, noting, 'The Jews here are meddlesome and tactless.'[28] He was not oblivious to the criticism levelled against him by the leaders of the *Yishuv*, for they too had surrendered to the inflated hopes conjured up by the Balfour Declaration. But it was his task, as a responsible leader, to guide them back to earth. David Ben Gurion, the most prominent of the Palestine labour leaders and one of his most vocal critics, had asked him: 'Why didn't you demand a Jewish state in Palestine?' Weizmann patiently explained: 'We didn't demand one because they wouldn't have given us one. We asked only for the conditions which would allow us to create a Jewish state in the future. It is simply a matter of tactics.'[29] Ben Gurion at heart recognized the validity of Weizmann's argument, but his rebuke revealed an underlying tension that stemmed also from Weizmann's imperious temperament. Weizmann consistently underestimated the political strength of the *Yishuv*, in particular that of its labour groups. He refused them representation on the Zionist Commission, favouring his own hangers-on. Criticism mounted that he was weak and compromising in his relations with the British, a theme that haunted him for the rest of his political life. He eventually reached an accommodation with his Palestine labour critics, but they remained uneasy associates.

During his crowded months in Palestine, Weizmann had little time for socializing. He met Bella Berligne, the twenty-two-year-old daughter of a prominent Zionist, and she has been described (in an anon-

ymous biographical note) as an 'intimate friend'; at any event, he
conducted a frank, at times ardent, correspondence with her.[30] Otherwise, Palestine worked its own magic spell on him: 'And so in the
evening after a heavy day, I sometimes walk alone on the beach near
Jaffa and the sea. The evenings here are marvellous, even after a hot
day. Absolute calm reigns. The wonderful Palestinian sky, the beautiful
sea, the great silence—then indeed one seems to hear the voices of
the dead rising from the tomb, the voices of our prophets, sages and
judges foretelling the future.'[31] But inspiration apart, his five months
in Palestine convinced him of the need to face its cruel reality: 'Oh,
what a difficult road and how many lives will yet go in creating the
"*Home*"!... We shall have to create our Palestine with pain and torment. *Ça vous ronge le coeur*!... But I haven't wavered for even a
second, neither in my faith nor in my work. Indeed, faith is essential,
and those without faith had better not come here, they would only be
a burden.'[32]

By the beginning of October 1918 Weizmann was back in London.
One of his first tasks was to re-organize the London office of the
Zionist Organization. In Palestine he had complained incessantly about
its inefficiency. Sokolow's 'even keel' and general passivity were 'poisoning' his life: 'Perhaps you could hit Sokolow on the head so that
he wakes up'.[33] New premises were acquired at 77, Great Russell
Street, near the British Museum, and the organization was put on a
more businesslike footing. He resumed his 'reconnoitring', now from
a position of greater authority. On Armistice Day, 11 November, he
lunched with Lloyd George, in the circumstances a 'confused visit'.
When he saw Balfour on 4 December he argued for the 'free and
unfettered development of the Jewish National Home in Palestine'
under British trusteeship, 'so that we should be able to settle in Palestine about four to five million Jews within a generation, and so make
Palestine a Jewish country'. 'There is room in Palestine,' he added,
'for a great Jewish community without encroaching upon the rights of
the Arabs.' Balfour agreed. Three weeks later he put the same view
to the prime minister. Weizmann's policy was still linked to a British
trusteeship for Palestine, the abrogation of the Sykes-Picot agreement,
and his dubious compact with Feisal.[34]

There was indeed much to do. The Peace Conference was due to
convene in January. But already, unknown to Weizmann, a tentative

understanding on the Middle East had been reached among the Powers. At the beginning of December Clemenceau visited London for talks with Lloyd George. No official record of this conversation was kept, but Maurice Hankey noted its contents in his diary: '"Tell me what you want," asked Clemenceau. "I want Mosul," said Lloyd George. "You shall have it," said Clemenceau. "Anything else?" "Yes, I want Jerusalem too," continued Lloyd George. "You shall have it," said Clemenceau.... Thus and thus is history made!'[35] The original Sykes-Picot agreement was crumbling; a more fashionable one was taking its place, based on the new realities of the aftermath of the war: the British conquest of Palestine, Syria, and Iraq; French ambitions; above all, the need to preserve the Anglo-French alliance in both Europe and the Middle East. This would prove to be disastrous to Feisal and would hurt Weizmann's policy. In the tremendous conflict of interests between the Great Powers and the aspiring nationalist movements, whether Arab or Zionist, the balance moved inexorably in favour of the former.

Meanwhile, encouraged by Balfour, Weizmann concluded an understanding with Feisal. They met at the Carlton Hotel, London, on 11 December for a preliminary discussion that Weizmann found 'most satisfactory'. Four weeks later, on 3 January 1919, they appended their signatures to an agreement that called for the 'closest possible collaboration' between Arabs and Jews in the development of 'the Arab State and Palestine'; it agreed that there would be 'definite boundaries between the Arab State and Palestine'; it envisaged the implementation of the Balfour Declaration and 'large-scale' Jewish immigration while protecting the rights of the Arab peasants and tenant farmers; it also provided for Jewish economic assistance to the Arabs, and a united Jewish-Arab front at the Peace Conference. There was no mention of a Jewish state. Feisal added one proviso: 'If the Arabs are established as I have asked . . . I will carry out what is in this agreement. If changes are made, I cannot be answerable for failing to carry out this agreement.'[36] Later, Feisal's adviser T. E. Lawrence—perhaps now cloaked in his guise as a British intelligence officer—was suspected of being less than frank to Feisal about the full extent of Zionist aspirations or the real purport of British undertakings.[37] But it is clear that a basis, however shaky, existed for a Jewish-Arab accord: the Weizmann-Feisal talks; the agreement; and a confirmatory letter, dated 1 March 1919, from Feisal to Felix Frankfurter, all pointed in the same direction.[38] Whether Feisal was powerful enough to deliver the goods, or whether the French and British would allow him to do so, was a different matter.

These were matters over which Weizmann had no control. He had to play the hand dealt him as best he could. Although his personal authority among British politicians was unrivalled, it had yet to be ratified officially in Zionist circles. The only titles he held were President of the EZF and membership of the GAC. On 22 January 1919 he was co-opted onto the Zionist Executive, but only after furious scenes with Sokolow, who claimed such procedures were unconstitutional and hence invalid.[39] By the strange quirks of Zionist politics, it was not until July 1920 that Weizmann was finally installed as President of the World Zionist Organization.

Weizmann left for the Versailles Peace Conference on 4 January 1919. The Zionists had prepared their case thoroughly. After much re-drafting—their initial proposals had been rejected by Ormsby-Gore as too extremist—a final memorandum was submitted to the Peace Conference on 3 February.[40] This amounts to the Zionists' first draft for the British mandate, and it asserted the historic right of the Jews to return to Palestine. Reiterating the demand, supported by world Jewry, that Britain should act as the mandatory power, it specified the duties and obligations of the mandatory power and the representative Zionist bodies. Boundaries were also delineated. Starting at a point south of Sidon, the boundary moved eastward to the Litani River and then dropped south-east until a point just west of the Hejaz railway; from there it followed a line west of the railway until it reached Maan, thence to the Gulf of Akaba; to the south-west, the frontier followed the international line from Rafah to Akaba. These proposals proved to be starting points for long, protracted, and at times bitter negotiations. The final draft of the mandate was not published until August 1921,[41] to be ratified only in the summer of 1922. As for the final frontiers of mandatory Palestine, these were hardly dependent upon the quality of the Anglo-Zionist debate but, rather, the result of hard bargaining between Britain and France. On all scores Weizmann was forced to retreat from his original positions.

. Paris during the Peace Conference was crowded with delegations and lobbyists, all with their specific demands and expectations, adding to the excitement of the moment. Weizmann, staying at the 'very pleasant and quiet' Hotel Plaza, found it 'hard to grasp what is being "done"—it's mainly developing connections'.[42] He had little faith in the ability of the conference to frame a lasting peace. Colonel Richard

Meinertzhagen, now a member of the British delegation to the conference, urged him to strike at once and demand Jewish sovereignty in Palestine. Weizmann refused, believing the time was inopportune for such an extravagant demand, calculating that it would wreck the concept of 'Mandatory Zionism' which he considered the only practical course. When President Wilson granted him an interview, Weizmann restated his case, explaining the Jewish position in Palestine, the intricacies of the Arab problem, the pressing need for Britain to assume the mandate—'Yes, I know all that. I only wish the British were prepared to take over all we want them to', and the difficulties with the French —'I am with you there. We have no community of thought.'[43]

On 27 February he appeared before the Supreme Council of the conference, commonly referred to as the Council of Ten. Sokolow opened the Zionist case, acting, Weizmann thought, 'as if two thousand years of Jewish suffering rested on his shoulders'. But the delegation also included Sylvain Levi, who had been foisted on them by the Quai d'Orsay and who, when his turn came, praised the Zionism of the pre-1914 era, but roundly attacked the proposals now being put forward. They would exacerbate the Arab question, he claimed; Russian Jews, and 'explosive element', would introduce 'dangerous' ideas into Palestine; and, of most concern, the concept of a National Home would sharpen the question of dual loyalties. Weizmann and company were taken aback at this onslaught. As luck would have it, Lansing turned to Weizmann and asked him to define the National Home. 'I replied briefly and forcefully, and the general opinion was that Levi had been demolished... it was a marvellous moment, the most triumphant of my life!' He had saved the day. His speech, Balfour reflected, was 'like the swish of a sword'. Balfour and Baron Sidney (Giorgio) Sonnino, Italian foreign minister, congratulated him. The French remained silent, though later they issued a statement indicating that they would not object to Britain's assuming responsibility for Palestine. After they had filed out of the chamber, Levi offered his hand. Weizmann spurned it: 'All is over with us. You have betrayed us.'[44] Assimilationist Jews who sought to sabotage the National Home were, for him, the bottom of the barrel.

Thus began a period of intense activity for Weizmann. He was constantly on the move between London, Europe, and Palestine. In October he was back in Palestine, though only just—the military authorities wished at first to refuse him entry, a blunder straightened out by Meinertzhagen appealing over their heads to the Foreign Office.

He exploited the occasion to rectify some of the damage caused by Ussishkin who, in his dealings with the British, displayed an attitude of 'overbearing intolerance with a contempt for compromise'. On an average, he saw 'fifteen and twenty people a day, slept three—four hours a night—mainly because, by then, I was so tired that sheer fatigue kept me from falling asleep'. For the first time in his life he acquired a bodyguard, Avraham Shapiro, 'an amiable and decent man'. He never ceased reminding the authorities of their duty to help facilitate the establishment of the National Home. On his return to London in January 1920 he lobbied Lloyd George to include within Palestine's northern border the headwaters of the Litani River and the Hermon watershed, essential for the National Home's economic development—an unsuccessful exercise, as it turned out.[45]

By late March 1920 he had returned to Palestine, this time taking Benji with him. Politically, the situation had changed dramatically. The Powers were due to meet at San Remo to work out a treaty with Turkey. In order to forestall any decisions inimical to their interests, Feisal's advisers had persuaded him, against his better judgement, to proclaim the autonomy of Syria, including Palestine, with himself as king—an illegal act, in the eyes of the Allies. The Arab Middle East was in turmoil. In Iraq and Egypt nationalists were demonstrating against foreign rule. Nor did Palestine escape the unrest or the violence. On Weizmann's arrival in Egypt he was deluged 'by a torrent of depressing news. Killings in Upper Galilee; more attacks by armed bands on Metullah: the Jews defended themselves, six were killed, among them Trumpeldor . . . demonstrations in Jerusalem; the administration frightened and therefore crawling to the Arabs; a desire to dissolve the Jewish Battalion; a desire to get rid of Meinertzhagen; in a word nothing but bad news all along the line.'[46]

Worse was to follow. Before Weizmann left Palestine on 10 April, anti-Jewish excesses had erupted in Jerusalem, mainly in the Old City, leaving six Jews dead, many wounded, and much property destroyed, including synagogues. He fired off two indignant telegrams to Lloyd George demanding a commission of enquiry. The overwhelming majority of British officials, he reckoned, considered the Balfour Declaration a catastrophic policy mistake and were doing their utmost to undermine it. They were sabotaging closer relations with the Arabs, he asserted, while their protégé, Feisal, was no more than 'a broken reed'. 'There are so few Meinertzhagens and Deedeses,' he fulminated, 'the only Englishmen who have come up to the mark; the rest are wolves and jackals!'[47] Perhaps he had in mind General Sir Louis Bols, the senior British officer in Palestine, who was entirely convinced that the Zionist Commission 'should be broken'. Allenby, whom he met in Cairo to set the record straight, described Weizmann's mood: 'He was in a state of great nervous excitement, shedding tears, accusing the administration of being anti-Zionist and describing recent events as a pogrom.'[48]

Weizmann was particularly outraged at the arrest of Jabotinsky, director of the political department of the Zionist Commission, for organizing Jewish self-defense in Jerusalem: 'they could just as well convict me', he cried. But, much to the dismay of the *Yishuv*, he refused to take any precipitate action to secure Jabotinsky's release, relying instead on patient negotiations. At heart, he held a sneaking admiration for Jabotinsky's courage: 'Anyone meeting a lion on the other side of the street would run away,' he said, 'except Jabo, who would beckon it with his finger.' But he thoroughly distrusted Jabotinsky's judgement, who from prison was conducting an anti-Weizmann campaign, and in time he came to detest his politics. Already, in 1920, he was 'convinced that J. is not normal. I regret it deeply... something is eating him up all the time and he is becoming impossible.' Nevertheless, he spared no effort to rescind Jabotinsky's conviction.[49]

Weizmann's conclusions from these distressing events were unequivocal. In the short run, he fought strongly to retain the Jewish Battalion as a local militia to defend the *Yishuv*. In the long run, he was more convinced than ever that the military administration of Palestine had run its disastrous course. It was time to adopt a clear-cut policy directed from London, and not from the mess-halls of the British army in Palestine. The soldiers had to go, to be replaced by a civil administration which saw as its duty the implementation of the Balfour Declaration. It was in this frame of mind that he set off for San Remo.

The principal business of the conference was the Turkish treaty. Its main outline was finally approved, and, despite a rearguard action by the French, the Balfour Declaration was included in it. The mandates for Palestine (which by inference included Transjordan) and Iraq were assigned to Britain; for Syria (with Lebanon) to France. This was a great victory. In mandatory Palestine Britain was obligated, in Weizmann's opinion by 'public law of the world', to put into effect the Balfour Declaration. The precise terms of the mandate, yet to be formulated, were to be submitted to the League of Nations for ratification. There was no firm agreement over borders. Immediately after San Remo, Lord Curzon, the British foreign secretary, noted, 'The boundaries... are to be determined at a later date'.[50] There was no doubt that the territories east of the Jordan would be included in the British mandate, but would the provisions of the National Home apply to them? There was no guarantee. The Zionists had been pressing for rights in western Palestine and an area beyond the river to points close to the Hejaz railway. Nothing, however, had been settled. In practical terms, the Balfour Declaration applied to the area west of the Jordan under British military administration, O.E.T.A. (Occupied Enemy Territory Administration) South. The frontier question dragged on for another two years of Anglo-French wrangling. In the final analysis, the borders of mandatory Palestine reflected the interests of the two Great Powers, not the ambitions of the Zionist movement.

The San Remo decisions not only clarified the Zionist position, but also complicated it. The French now felt free to oust Feisal from Damascus and impose their own rule in Syria. By July this had been accomplished. A year later, in August 1921, the British installed Feisal as king of Iraq, thus repaying their debt to the Hashemites. Weizmann's agreement with him, always problematic, was now an historic relic. The cohesiveness of Arab nationalism, never robust, had been shattered. In Palestine, the events of March–April were but the prelude to decades of mounting violence. Palestinian Arab nationalism took a more belligerent course, its batteries recharged from Feisal's tragedy.

For Weizmann, San Remo was another in his string of triumphs. Lloyd George took leave of him with the words, 'Now you have got your start, it all depends on you.' Weizmann agreed: 'a new era' had begun. He wrote to Vera: 'Your untiring support enabled me [to do the] work.' Since the March riots he had kept his head, refusing to be side-tracked by his own hotheads. He refused to be led down the road of barren confrontation. His policy of 'Firmness, Quietness, and Tact' had paid off. Despite the setback, he inspired confidence from the outset, displaying true qualities of leadership. We must 'hold firm', he told the Zionist Executive. 'We shall be severely tried in the next few months, but I feel that this crisis will bring us new light.... Keep up your courage and don't be detracted from your work for one single moment.' Small wonder that he left San Remo in a mood of boundless optimism. 'One chapter has ended in a most dramatic way, and now the construction of the New Palestine begins!'[51]

On 30 June 1920 the military administration came to an end and

Sir Herbert Samuel arrived in Palestine as its first high commissioner. General Bols handed him a receipt: 'one Palestine complete'. Samuel added: 'E. and O. E.' (errors and omissions excepted).[52] Weizmann had worked for Samuel's appointment for some time.[53] During the March disturbances Samuel's attitude had disappointed him: 'He is altogether too cautious . . . and will need a big shaking up before he understands the real situation.'[54] But the idea of a Jew sympathetic to Zionism and prominent in British political life as the first civilian governor of the Jewish National Home was immensely attractive and politically useful. Weizmann could count unreservedly on Wyndham Deedes, who would join Samuel as his chief secretary. He was also eager that Meinertzhagen, who had been a pillar of strength throughout these troubled months, should remain in a key post in the civilian administration. This did not work out, and Meinertzhagen returned to London. Still, from Weizmann's point of view, Samuel and Deedes were an excellent team. He could look to the future with confidence.

TEN

BETWEEN PALESTINE, PINSK, AND WASHINGTON

Weizmann first met Louis Brandeis in June 1919 when Brandeis was passing through London on his way to Palestine. He 'makes an excellent impression', Weizmann reported to Vera. 'It's a pity that he's sixty-three years old already and only came to us after he had given his strength to others, to strangers.'[1] Brandeis, now profiting from his enhanced authority and prestige as a justice of the Supreme Court, the acknowledged leader of American Zionism with the power of American Jewry at his back, who owed nothing to European Zionism and stood above its sectarian politics untainted by its rivalries and squabbles, had emerged, in the eyes of his devoted followers, as the most suitable candidate to guide the Zionist Organization at this critical juncture in its fortunes.

After spending July in Palestine, Brandeis returned to London for a meeting of the GAC. He was dismayed at the parlous state of Palestine: its backwardness, its large-scale unemployment, the incompetence of the Zionist Commission, the anti-Zionist prejudice of the British authorities there. He reported to an astonished GAC that Jewish immigration to Palestine should be discouraged until malaria was controlled and that all available funds should be directed to this purpose. But the main issue before the gathering was to consider various drafts of the mandate, and in particular article four, which spoke of 'an appropriate Jewish agency' to be recognized 'as a public body for the purpose of advising and co-operating with the Administration of Palestine in such economic, social and other matters as may affect the establishment of the Jewish national home and the interests of the Jewish people in Palestine.'

When the GAC resumed its deliberations in late August, Brandeis's delegation proposed that the Zionist Organization be recognized as the 'Jewish Council [i.e., agency]'. It would be free of non-Zionist elements, for to their minds mixing believers with non-believers would only hinder the development of Palestine. Weizmann, representing the London leadership, opposed this concept, wishing to exploit all Jewish bodies interested in furthering the development of the National Home, even the Jewish minority councils in eastern Europe. Brandeis got his way. One of his lieutenants, Julius Simon, drafted a resolution stating that the Zionist Organization should be recognized as the Jewish Agency and that 'the co-operation of all Jews' should be secured. Weizmann wished to add the words 'and Jewish organizations', but Brandeis, chairman of the session, vetoed this suggestion. When Simon's resolution was finally put to the floor, Weizmann argued furiously against it. There was a hung vote. Brandeis, perplexed, ordered that Jacob de Haas, known in some circles as his *éminence grise*, be brought to the meeting to cast his vote and decide the issue. Nobody protested — a mark of Brandeis's authority — and the GAC waited in silence until de Haas was found to do his duty. In this manner Brandeis ensured that his view prevailed, and the Zionist Organization was duly recognized as the Jewish Agency, the formula that was eventually incorporated in the final draft of the mandate.

After this 'totally unparliamentary procedure', as even Simon called it, the meeting ended in confusion. Weizmann boiled over. 'We shall never forget this vote,' he assured Felix Frankfurter.

> Zionism is built on one and only [one] fundamental conception and that is Jewish Nationalism, which means unity of purpose of all Jews, the purpose being [the] return of the Jews to Palestine and setting up there a Jewish life 100 per cent. . . .
>
> That will give us the Jewish National Movement capable of producing the National Home. All that is creative in Jewry will be absorbed by the National Home, the rest will become English or American or whatever it chooses to be. . . .
>
> . . . but you are 'practical' and 'careful', you cannot afford to take any risks, because you have got positions to lose — in contradistinction to the *sans-culottes* who have nothing to lose.

His parting shot was cruel. 'Brandeis could have been a prophet in Israel. You have in you the making of a Lassalle. Instead, you are choosing to be only a professor in Harvard and Brandeis only a judge in the Supreme Court.'[2]

Already one can detect the two diametrically opposed concepts of Zionism held by Brandeis and Weizmann. Brandeis was an American liberal, unversed in Jewish heritage, who had to rediscover the Jewish people. He embraced Zionism at the age of fifty-six, but it was a Zionism spawned from the American experience, its ideals and standards. He once remarked, 'We must develop Palestine in the spirit of Anglo-Saxon manhood.' How unlike Weizmann, whose Jewishness was rooted in his childhood in Motol, whose Zionism sprang from the essence of Jewish life in the diaspora, integral to his very being. But beyond these grave philosophical, ideological divisions there lurked a personal factor of some consequence: Brandeis was the one serious competitor to Weizmann's leadership.

All these issues coalesced at the London conference in July 1920. The *Jahreskonferenz* was the largest gathering of Zionists since the Congress of 1913. At it Weizmann had both to justify his policy and to ensure its continuity. This was not an easy task. For one thing, in his casual, off-handed, superior way, he had antagonized many of the leaders of the *Yishuv*. Once he had noted, 'It will be extremely difficult to find people who were able to negotiate with the British and also to reach an understanding with the Jews. With all modesty, I may say that I am the only "synthetic" type to fit this situation.'³ *Yishuv* leaders such as Ben Gurion and Berl Katznelson did not take kindly to patronizing insinuations of this nature, and they now took the occasion to criticize severely his policy as being too weak, blurring Zionist true goals, treating the Jewish people and the *Yishuv* as incompetent. Weizmann could hardly have been indifferent to this opposition. But it was not a serious challenge, particularly as another Palestinian, Yosef Sprinzak, proclaimed, 'The political victory at San Remo made up for all the errors.' Nevertheless, sensitive to any form of criticism, he responded frankly and firmly at a mass demonstration at the Albert Hall: 'You tell us what we have not done. Jewish people, what have *you* done? Victories are not won merely by a *grand geste*'.⁴

The real threat, however, came from Brandeis or, rather, from those pushing him forward. Julius Simon, Weizmann's pre-war benefactor, came to him with a proposition. 'Chaim, you have rendered an immortal service to the cause of Zionism. Now I ask you to crown your work by offering leadership to Brandeis.' Weizmann heard him out in stony silence. When Frankfurter heard of this advance, he observed to Simon: 'You could not have said anything worse.'⁵ Deep policy differences soon emerged. Weizmann had laid down three tasks before the conference: to approve a plan of operations; to devise a means of raising sufficient monies to put the plan into effect; and to adapt and reshape the organization to meet its new challenges.[6] Brandeis might have agreed with the definition of the tasks, but he profoundly disagreed with the tactics to be employed in realizing them.

Brandeis introduced a novel dimension to Zionist politics. He argued that the Balfour Declaration and the San Remo decisions had cleared away the political obstacles to Zionism, and now that a political base had been secured, the movement required 'builders', not 'propagandists'. As Schmarya Levin caustically put it: 'Not a single Jew should settle in Palestine until the last mosquito has been banished.'[7] Consequently, the Americans proposed, unsuccessfully, to abolish the Zionist Commission and replace it by a Jewish Advisory Council. Brandeis also submitted wide-reaching administrative proposals to alter radically the structure of the Zionist Organization. Instead of one central authority, he suggested a number of virtually autonomous centres. In effect, this meant the decentralization of the movement, diminishing London's position as the main centre, and increasing the powers of the national Zionist bodies, particularly those in Jerusalem and New York. For Weizmann, this was an absurd proposition. All his experiences, from the Balfour Declaration to the Zionist Commission to the San Remo conference, had indicated precisely the opposite: that the political stage, far from being over, was only just beginning. Never before was there a greater need for political unity of the Zionist movement.

Brandeis's conception led him into deep waters. His dispute with Weizmann centered on the role of the *Keren Hayesod* (Palestine Foundation Fund), intended as the financial instrument for the development of Palestine, which was set up at the last session of the conference with a capital of £25 million (yet to be raised). Brandeis favoured the separation of investment funds for specific development projects from donations intended for the general public services—administration, education, health. To his mind, investment corporations, staffed by experts, would inject a 'business-like' and 'efficient' approach to the development of Palestine, hitherto conducted in a sloppy manner by the officials of the Zionist Organization; authority over these investment bodies should rest ultimately with the national Zionist federations. And as American Jews were expected to make the most substantial contributions, effective control would remain with Brandeis's group.

Weizmann was not blind to the shortcomings of the Zionist movement or of its enterprise in Palestine. But he was entirely convinced that Brandeis's far-reaching proposals were tantamount to asking the World Zionist Organization to commit suicide. Brandeis obviously held a contrary view, equally convinced that his innovatory ideas would revitalize a sick body. Weizmann, forever personalizing his politics, tended to believe that Jacob de Haas, Brandeis's chief adviser and previously Herzl's private secretary, was responsible for his deviationism. De Haas had never concealed his dislike of Weizmann or his displeasure at Weizmann's newly acquired stature.[8]

Personal relations between the two protagonists deteriorated. The so-called Brandeis-Reading pact brought matters to a head. Brandeis, a justice of the Supreme Court, had suggested to Lord Reading, lord chief justice of England, that the Zionist Congresses be suspended for a number of years to allow breathing space to a new, practical, more business-like executive to conduct the affairs of the National Home free from petty political rivalries. The executive would be formed of seven members: four Zionists (Weizmann, Sokolow, Brandeis, and Bernard Flexner, a Brandeisian) and three British non-Zionists (James de Rothschild, Sir Alfred Mond, and Sir Robert Waley Cohen). Having seemingly reversed his previous position, Brandeis, innocently, assumed that Weizmann would approve of this transparent ploy. But Weizmann killed it before it got off the ground. Brandeis felt betrayed, humiliated. A proud man, he took umbrage, and no amount of mediation sufficed to bring them together again. 'Dr. Weizmann,' he said, 'you are not a man with whom I can work.'[9] One can only speculate whether Weizmann fabricated this crisis in order to force a showdown. Certainly, it would not have been out of character with his capacity for political manoeuvring and his sense of timing to know when to strike.

But whatever the explanation, it is clear that Brandeis's premises struck at the very root of Weizmann's conception of Zionism. Weizmann coined the slogan 'Washington versus Pinsk'. There could be no identity of interests, he claimed, between European- and American-born Zionists, those champions of 'Yankee Doodle Judaism', who could only calculate the Jewish renaissance in sterile terms of accountancy. How could one evaluate the contribution of the *kibbutz* movement in barren figures of profit or loss? The true goals of Zionism could be realized only by a concerted effort of all the Jewish people, not by the approval of American "time and motion study" experts. The Zionist movement had to remain united and strong, feeding off the vitality, the faith, the hopes of the Jewish people. Brandeis was, he said, cut off from the Jewish masses; he had no conception of their deepest aspirations. Weizmann vowed that he would not play Clemenceau to Brandeis's Wilson.[10] He drove his point home to Samuel: 'he is so un-Jewish in his outlook, in his feelings, and has never attempted to realize the deep causes which have moved the Jewish masses towards Palestine. He is a colonizer purely and simply. He happens to colonize Palestine.' Schmarya Levin put it in a different way. When Brandeis told him that 'the bank must be controlled by experienced businessmen and not by propagandists and politicians', Levin responded: 'Long live the Hebrew language.'[11]

Ostensibly, Weizmann had scored an impressive victory at the London conference. He was elected President of the World Zionist Organization and the *Keren Hayesod* was established on his terms. He had retained power and ensured that London would remain the centre of Zionist operations. But Brandeis and his supporters returned to America disgruntled and unrepentant. At a convention of the Zionist Organization of America in Buffalo in November 1920 resolutions were passed that overturned the London decisions and regulated the activity of the *Keren Hayesod* in America on Brandeisian lines. This amounted to a virtual declaration of war on London, and Weizmann reacted vigorously to the challenge. He hinted at resignation, but from a position of strength, not weakness. He told Frankfurter, 'The position is becoming daily more untenable'. 'Gentlemen,' he questioned the American Zionist Executive, 'do you expect the President of the World Zionist Organization to act as promoter of private companies?' Over everything, he confessed to Bella Berligne, 'hangs . . . the pall of an almost unavoidable split with America'.[12] It was clear that he could no longer postpone a trip to the United States to confront the mutineers on their own ground.

Weizmann arrived in New York, his first visit, on 2 April 1921 to a rapturous welcome. He came, in his own words, as 'a Jewish Columbus . . . to re-discover Jewish America'.[13] New York Jewry flocked to greet him. From the Bronx and Brooklyn the cars arrived, flags flying and horns blaring. He landed at the Battery, where a motorcade awaited his party to conduct them via the streets of the Lower East Side, lined with excited Jews, to the Commodore Hotel. Soon afterward he was guest of honour at a reception at City Hall. The spontaneity of this unprecedented demonstration was heart-warming and encouraging, even though a 'magnificent mood of anticipation' had been orchestrated by a local pro-Weizmann committee, 'rebels' in the eyes of the American Zionist establishment.[14] Weizmann brought an impressive retinue with him: the great German physicist Albert Einstein, to awaken American interest in the Hebrew University and as a symbol of world Jewry working amicably with Weizmann; Ussishkin, the ironman of Zionism, to allow no compromise on principle; Leonard Stein, his personal assistant, a skilled draftsman at exploring every avenue of compromise; and reinforced by Schmarya Levin, the darling of the Yiddish-speaking masses, who joined his group in New York.

No effort was spared to obtain a reasonable settlement. But after two weeks of intensive, at times acrimonious, negotiations, Weizmann realized that there was no hope of achieving harmony. Egged on by Levin, he decided to break with Brandeis. By virtue of his authority as President of the WZO, he announced the establishment of a *Keren Hayesod* bureau in America and opened the campaign by donating ten pounds from his wallet: 'Take this and proceed,' he ordered Emanuel Neumann, its first director.[15] This was tantamount to the opening of hostilities. Despite his pledge, he had decided after all to play Clemenceau to Brandeis's Wilson, cutting Brandeis down to size in much the same way as Clemenceau had savaged Wilson's authority at Versailles. He was confident of success. The Jewish masses looked to him, their folk-hero from Pinsk, not to Brandeis, the austere judge from Boston. He wrote to Sir Alfred Mond:

The masses of American Zionists and Jews have nothing in common with B. and his group, which is only a small oligarchy of men with a certain social position in this country but without influence on Jewry, with the exception of a few assimilated, non-Zionist or anti-Zionist Jews. Ninety-five per cent of American Jewry are those who understand a 100 per cent Zionism full-blooded, and are ready to follow and give money to such a Zionism and no other. . . . B. is an American first and a Zionist only a few minutes in the day, and therefore has lost touch with Jewry and with the actualities of Palestine.[16]

While this drama was unfolding, in May 1920 anti-Jewish riots had broken out in Palestine, leaving forty-seven Jews dead and one-hundred-forty-six wounded. (Forty-eight Arabs were also killed and seventy-three wounded, mainly by British troops quelling the disorders.) Herbert Samuel, in an attempt to pacify Arab feeling, had temporarily suspended Jewish immigration, to a mighty cry of anguish from the Jews. For Weizmann this only fortified his belief that the political base of the National Home was fragile to an extreme and still required careful attention. He attended the fateful Cleveland conference in June more convinced than ever that his was the right course.

The Cleveland convention of the ZOA resulted in a resounding victory for Weizmann. He attended the sessions though he did not participate in them, influencing the proceedings through his presence. The crucial vote went 153–71 in his favour. Brandeis resigned his position, taking with him his cohorts, the giants of American Zionism: Judge Mack, Felix Frankfurter, Stephen Wise, Abba Hillel Silver. Weizmann left the Organization in the faithful hands of his disciples: Louis Lipsky, Morris Rothenberg, Abe Goldberg, a less glamorous group but one more representative of American rank-and-file Zionists. 'As you are aware,' he reported to Herbert Samuel, 'I had to perform a very painful operation on the American Zionist Organization.' Evoking the emotive imagery of a corrupt, venal group bent only on maintaining its own privileged position, he went on:

> The ground for the revolution was amply prepared. The rank and file of American Zionists were utterly dissatisfied with the leadership and everything was almost completely demoralized. For a year the A.Z.O. has done nothing, and in that way has destroyed confidence not only in itself, but in Palestine and in the World Zionist Organization. For practical purposes [it had] ceased to exist. They had no plans, no money, no friends. There was Brandeis with a few of his friends and sycophants, the latter always ready to do their master's bidding, quite detached from the great mass of Zionist adherents, enshrined in Washington or in Boston, simply preaching a negative policy, criticizing mercilessly and ignorantly everything and everybody, with the deplorable result that Palestine and Zionism have been discredited. . . . The leaders have lost faith in themselves and in the people. Brandeis tried to force his negative programme on us by all the brutal methods of which only Tammany Hall politicians are capable. . . . It was a bitter struggle, but it is over now.[17]

In time, many of the Brandeis group returned to the fold, but in the meantime they glowered from the sidelines. Weizmann, undeterred, strengthened his grip in America and exploited the occasion to become acquainted with American political habits. He saw President Warren Harding, paid a courtesy call on Brandeis, and undertook a vigorous campaign tour of North America, the first in a long series. His prime purpose was to fill the coffers of the *Keren Hayesod*. In this he was less successful than his first optimistic evaluations: $4.5 million had been promised; by November $.75 million was actually raised.[18] Still, even this was far in excess of the sum Brandeis had promised him. Weizmann's odyssey had begun: tapping the resources of American Jewry to provide for the needs of Palestine.

Weizmann's quarrel with Brandeis had been a bitter one. It had been fought on decisive issues of principle that were to determine the character of the Zionist movement and the *Yishuv*. For Weizmann this was a life-or-death struggle and he fought it with no holds barred, employing every weapon in his political armoury, often blackening his opponents' reputation in the wildest terms. After having engineered Brandeis's defeat, he wrote to Emanuel Neumann, director of the *Keren Hayesod* in America, admitting, 'some of the criticisms of the Brandeis group were true: I always said so'; but, he continued remorselessly, the remedy they offered was 'a mere palliative'.[19]

Weizmann had underestimated neither his opponents nor the forces at his own disposal. At the decisive moment, Brandeis had proved to be a man of straw, an 'invisible force' in Weizmann's estimation, who allowed his minions to conduct his battle for him, for 'owing to his position' (the Supreme Court was then in session) he had not appeared at Cleveland.[20] In his resignation letter, Brandeis wrote: 'We who believe in those principles and policies cannot properly take part in any administration of Jewish affairs which repudiates them.' He would join his followers 'as humble workers in the ranks' until the time came 'when the standards which we seek to establish will be recognized as indispensable to the attainment of our great end'.[21] Weizmann's victory was complete. And it could not have escaped his notice that having vanquished Brandeis he now stood in splendid isolation as President of the WZO, without a real competitor to harry his policies or threaten his position.

Weizmann returned to England aboard the SS *Celtic* at the beginning of July 1921. He arrived in the middle of a first-class crisis. While he had been settling accounts in the United States, events in Palestine and the Middle East had taken a sharp turn for the worse. Samuel's initial impression, that 'The country is so quiet that you could hear a pin drop,' proved to be wildly optimistic.[22] Kemal Ataturk's struggle against the Turkish treaty imposed at Sèvres in August 1920 introduced a further element of political instability in the region. Other indigenous nationalist movements took heart from Turkey's rejection of the Allied settlement. Palestinian Arab hostility intensified, and the lack of an agreed Anglo-French policy compounded the uncertainty. The decisions taken at San Remo rested on shifting sands. With the mandate yet to be formulated and ratified, it would take immense effort and skill to capitalize on Weizmann's 'great triumph'.[23]

In the autumn of 1920 Feisal's elder brother, Abdullah, appeared in Transjordan at the head of an Arab force with the declared intention of marching on Damascus and restoring his brother to the throne. Ever since the French occupation of Syria in July 1920, Transjordan was something of a no-man's land, caught between the British presence in the west and the French in the north. Samuel, to forestall menacing French moves, had suggested sending British troops to occupy the area up to the Hejaz railway, a proposal firmly rejected by the Foreign Secretary, Curzon.[24] Now, with Abdullah breathing revenge in the Transjordanian desert, the situation had altered radically. A prince of the Hashemite family, widely considered as puppets of British policy, was threatening to upset the Anglo-French accord. Despite Curzon's reluctance, the British had no option but to intervene more decisively in the future of Transjordan, for the dispute in the Middle East had European ramifications of great consequence, which made it imperative for Britain and France to preserve their alliance.

These events coincided with the transfer of responsibility for the mandated areas from the Foreign Office to the Colonial Office, now in the energetic, restless hands of Winston Churchill. Churchill hardly hesitated. He proposed to separate Transjordan from Palestine, creating in fact an independent political entity, and to set up Abdullah as its ruler; here the British mandate would apply except for those clauses pertaining to the establishment of the Jewish National Home. The Zionists, already suspicious of British intentions, had noted Samuel's speech to a gathering of six hundred Arab sheikhs at Es-Salt in Transjordan in August 1920 when he had hinted at a possible separation of the two territories. 'What about our eastern border?' asked a worried Weizmann. His question remained unanswered. The uncertainty mounted. On 1 March 1921, three days before Churchill was due to leave for Cairo for a key conference to settle the affairs of Iraq and Transjordan, Weizmann wrote him a lengthy appeal pleading for the inclusion of all Transjordan as part of the Jewish National Home. Weizmann's arguments had no effect. The essential decisions had already been taken.[25]

From the Cairo conference, Churchill made his way to Jerusalem.

Weizmann was especially anxious that the British minister be introduced to the new Palestine, to see the *chalutzim* (Jewish pioneers) at work and dispel any notions that they were tainted by Bolshevik tendencies. Churchill toured the colonies and was greatly impressed, but his visit was marked by violence and by anti-Zionist demonstrations. The Arabs submitted to him a memorandum demanding the abrogation of the British government's pro-Zionist policy. Churchill rejected their petition in the most forthright manner.[26] He was among the staunchest defenders of the government's policy, and he lost no opportunity to assure the Zionists that he was a true friend. If, occasionally, he failed to live up to their expectations, this was not because of an erosion in his basic sympathy to Zionism, which had strengthened as a result of his visit, but rather because of his perception of his duties and obligations as a British politician. Weizmann would encounter this phenomenon many times in the future.

Samuel's behaviour was also giving Weizmann much cause for concern. In March 1921, he had appointed Haj Amin al-Husayni as Mufti of Jerusalem, a post that carried not only spiritual authority but also great financial and political power. Haj Amin, an incurable anti-Zionist, had been tried *in absentia* for his part in the 1920 riots and sentenced to fifteen years' imprisonment. He had fled Palestine. Now he returned covered with glory. This was a monumental blunder on Samuel's part, but, at the time, Weizmann was more concerned by Samuel's decision to temporarily suspend immigration in the wake of the May 1921 disturbances and, still more, by his June speech, which placed a most limited interpretation on the Balfour Declaration.[27] 'Honour him, but suspect him,' he advised, choosing as his text a popular Hebrew proverb.[28] But he refrained from criticizing Samuel in public, not wishing to exacerbate relations with the British government. He consoled the Zionist Congress: never forget that "Samuel is the High Commissioner for Palestine and we are High Commissioners for *Erez Israel* [the Land of Israel]'.[29] In private, however, he wrote 'openly and with a brutal frankness'. He told Herbert Samuel that there had been 'a shifting of political values . . . which momentarily obscure the vision of British statesmen.' He hoped this was a passing phase, but the tendency to ignore the Balfour Declaration and the San Remo decisions 'destroys the political foundation on which we have been building. . . . It seems that everything in Palestinian life is now revolving round one central problem—how to satisfy "and to pacify" the Arabs. Zionism is being gradually, systematically, and relentlessly "reduced"'. 'My dearest Friend,' he wrote to Wyndham Deedes, 'Of the Balfour Declaration, nothing is left but mere lip service. . . . I shall most probably resign at the next Congress, as I cannot assume any responsibility before the Jewish people'. Please consider this letter as an *ad memorium*, he added, hoping, no doubt, that Deedes would register his message with the higher authorities.[30]

This steady erosion of the Balfour Declaration obligations—or 'whittling down', as Weizmann was wont to put it—had to be brought to a halt. Shortly after his return from America Weizmann attended a high-level meeting at Balfour's house in Carlton Gardens. Those present included Lloyd George, Churchill, and Hankey. Weizmann was determined to extract from the ministers a re-affirmation of Britain's Zionist policy. He told them the Declaration meant an 'ultimate Jewish majority'. Yes, chorused Lloyd George and Balfour, we always understood it to mean 'an eventual Jewish State'. Weizmann went on to condemn Samuel's speech and the 'representative government' plan for Palestine—again to gestures of approval. Only Churchill, a conspicuous minority of one, proved obdurate, defending Samuel and his ministry's policies.[31] Weizmann had every cause to be satisfied with his performance, for this was political lobbying of the highest order. Yet it was a transient success, and it revealed the fundamental weakness of the Zionist position. Weizmann knew this when he spoke of converting 'diplomacy . . . into politics'.[32] Despite the genuine sympathy of Lloyd George and Balfour, British policy continued to send out shockwaves in the Zionist direction.

Throughout the coming year Weizmann absorbed yet more blows. In the autumn of 1921, the Haycraft Commission published its report. Having investigated the May riots, it concluded that Arab hostility and discontent were caused by Jewish immigration and by the Jews' conception of Zionist policy. The whole tone of the document was highly critical of Zionist aims and methods.[33] It was the first of a long series of similar government statements. In August, a Palestinian Arab delegation arrived in London for talks with the British; they remained for almost a year. To discuss what? cried Weizmann.

> They asked me to put in a phrase that the Zionists don't intend to create a Jewish State in Palestine. I refused to do so and gave them a chief reason that we cannot forswear such a possibility, which might

or might not arise in some future generation. I told them at present we are building Palestine, but it may be that the Jews may be in the ascendancy there, that neither they nor anybody else have a right to stop us.

The Arabs refused to meet Weizmann face to face. In a fit of pique, he referred to them as 'blackguards' and 'trash'. Only after Churchill's intervention was a joint meeting arranged. It was not a success. Weizmann spoke moderately, in favour of a dialogue and mutual compromise, but his manner was condescending, in 'the nature of a conqueror', noted one official; 'I think he despises the members of the delegation as not worthy of protagonists'. In fact, the Arabs had nothing to offer Weizmann or the government except a total reversal of the Balfour Declaration policy. No amount of cajoling by Churchill, or readiness to compromise by Weizmann, could shift them from their absolutist position.[34]

In Weizmann's view all this shilly-shallying was inevitable, given that the ratification of the mandate still hung fire. If the mandate, the legally accepted basis for Zionist activity in Palestine, could be presented to the world community, and the Palestinian Arabs, as a *fait accompli*, opposition to Zionism would inevitably lessen and, he hoped, in time disappear. Ataturk's rebellion, and difficulties with the French and the Americans, gave anti-Zionist forces in Palestine and London a breathing space to gather strength to defeat the British government's Zionist-oriented policy. It had taken two years of the most pettifogging negotiations to formulate the provisions of the mandate, but by August 1921 the final draft was ready. Despite its 'imperfections and lacunae', which Weizmann readily admitted, he could be more than satisfied with the finished product,[35] for it met most of the Zionist requirements, confirming the 'historical connection of the Jewish people with Palestine', a phrase to which Weizmann attached great importance, and recognizing the Zionist Organization as the Jewish Agency for Palestine, defining its status and functions in favourable terms.

Of course, Weizmann hardly acted alone in drafting the mandate. He was well served by experienced advisers and draftsmen of the highest calibre, in particular Benjamin Cohen, a Brandeis man who remained in London, and Leonard Stein. He found sympathetic partners on the British side, Eric Forbes-Adam and Robert Vansittart, who, at least on one occasion, acted independently of Curzon's instructions to the Zionists' advantage.[36] But Weizmann was the mainspring, and his was the final word. He resolved the problems, unravelled the knots. Lloyd George, Balfour, Churchill, Smuts, Milner, even Curzon, paid attention when he spoke. They listened to his pleadings with respect and consideration, out of an esteem and admiration that they bestowed on no other Zionist leader.

By the summer of 1922 the struggle over the mandate was moving to its climax. In June, the government published a summary of its discussions with the Arab delegation and Zionists, together with a statement of policy; this was the famous Churchill white paper — drafted by Samuel.[37] It re-affirmed that the Balfour Declaration 'is not susceptible to change'. But it then redefined the Declaration, not in the enthusiastic, positive terms previously expressed by Lloyd George and Balfour, but in more limiting phrases. Although it recognized that the Jews were in Palestine 'as of right and not on sufferance', it viewed as 'impracticable' the proposition, expressed by Weizmann at the Paris Peace Conference, that Palestine would become 'as Jewish as England is English'.

The same month, the Lords voted in favour of a motion that questioned the validity of the mandate, despite a brave maiden speech by Balfour, newly created an earl. The vote was not binding on the government, but it came as a rude shock to the Zionists, highlighting as it did the depth of anti-Zionist feeling in England. But this was the last spasm of the anti-Zionist lobby, for the time being. On 4 July the Commons, in a debate on the Colonial Office vote, registered overwhelming approval of the government's Palestine policy. In a powerful speech, Churchill rallied the House behind the government's obligations.[38] Three weeks later the League of Nations ratified the mandate which effectively limited the Jewish National Home to the area west of the Jordan.

These tense weeks had put Weizmann under a tremendous strain. Immediately after the League's decision, he escaped to Gornergrat, 'climbed a glacier and was happy'. Had he fulfilled his destiny? 'You are right,' he wrote to his sister, Miriam,

> the Mandate was written for the greater part with my own blood, but who knows, perhaps this is the purpose of my wandering all my life, from Motele to London, to accomplish this great task; when I look at the Jewish community here, and in all the Western countries. when I remember the destruction in the East, my heart freezes, and I come to the conclusion that only the Chosen Ones who have acquired all their moral strength from the only true Jewish source — only they are pre-

pared and fit to assume the burden of work for the sake of others, and they will succeed in reviving the dry bones. So let us not complain of our destiny: it may be difficult, but it's beautiful![39]

These shifts in British policy were a far cry from Weizmann's original hopes. He grudgingly accepted the limitations, as did the Zionist Executive, out of a sense of *force majeure*: 'Under the adverse circumstances we shall loyally abide by it'. To suggest that by so doing Weizmann had abandoned the *Endzeil*, the final aim, of Zionism, the establishment of a Jewish state, is absurd. He was not given to empty, theatrical gestures more relevant to grand opera than to practical politics. Even Jabotinsky acknowledged Weizmann's achievement as 'without parallel as a personal performance', recognizing that the mandate did not 'exclude our most remote goal—even a Jewish state'.[40] Weizmann could not have phrased it more succinctly. With all their drawbacks, the white paper and the mandate provided a workable framework to bring in Jews, develop the *Yishuv*, create a National Home. Should the Jewish people respond to the challenge, a state would follow. He had continually to guide his own people back to reality.

> What did it [the Declaration] mean? It did not mean a Jewish State. Not because I or you did not want a Jewish State; not at all. I do want a Jewish State. I trust to God that a Jewish State will come about; but it will come about not through political declarations, but by the sweat and blood of the Jewish people. That is the only way of building up a state. No other way is known to me in all the history of the world. It is the golden key which unlocks the doors of Palestine and gives you the possibility of putting all your efforts into that country.[41]

Despite his frustration, Weizmann had every cause to feel satisfied. His current successes were, in some ways, far more substantial than the Balfour Declaration. In 1917, he had skillfully exploited a favourable political situation; between 1918 and 1922 he found himself swimming against the political currents. Impeded by hostile forces from all sides, he had taken the Balfour Declaration, 'an act of faith', and turned it, through the mandate, into a practical instrument of policy recognized by public law. Moreover, his ambition since 1914 had been attained: Britain assumed responsibility for Palestine as the mandatory power. He had achieved all this against colossal odds.

Opposition appeared from all quarters. After the balmy days of Feisal, Weizmann had to deal with the more militant Palestinian Arabs. Fortunately for him, their political ineptitude, their striking incapacity to conduct their politics in the British style, played into his hands. Demanding everything, they got nothing. As long as Weizmann could rely on their intransigence, his path was fairly smooth. More disturbing was the change in the climate of British opinion. An effective Arab lobby was now active in Parliament. The Northcliffe press was openly anti-Zionist, while Beaverbrook was conducting a public campaign for Britain to 'evacuate Mesopotamia and Palestine bag and baggage *and at once'*. At times, this paper war was scarcely distinguishable from anti-semitism. Who is this '"Mysterious Chaim"', asked the *Daily Express*, who has inveigled the innocent and unsuspecting British into the mire of the Middle East? Why should the British taxpayer pour money into Palestine? Or British baronets separate quarrelsome Jews and Arabs?

Much of this insidious propaganda focussed on the so-called Rutenberg concession. Pincus Rutenberg was the author of a hydro-electric scheme crucial to the industrialization and economic development of Palestine. He had been active in Russian revolutionary politics and had served in Kerensky's administration, though later he had been imprisoned by the Bolsheviks for his pains. But his name, his origins, his background told against him. He was perfect fodder for an anti-semitic, anti-Zionist campaign linking Bolshevism and Zionism. Provocative questions were raised in Parliament; inflammatory articles appeared in the press. Eventually, the Rutenberg concession was granted, and in 1923 he established the Palestine Electric Company. But it was with some justification that Weizmann commented on 'an anti-Semitic Crusade' being waged against the National Home.[42]

Weizmann met this demagoguery face on, pointing out its flaws, explaining patiently the facts regarding the Zionist effort in Palestine and the devious methods employed to sabotage it. He also proved adept at parrying the opposition from within, though he did not have an easy ride at the Zionist Congress at Carlsbad in 1921. Brandeis was still a force to be reckoned with, even if Brandeis himself had retired. Criticism of Weizmann's authoritarian, egotistical manner was rife. Rutenberg, writing to him in a different context, expressed a widely held opinion about his distinctive political style: 'The interests of our unfortunate people became in your mind equivalent to the interests of petty advertising of your ephemeral successes, of your personality. . . . To denounce you publicly would be to shatter the only beautiful illusion which our long-suffering nation has preserved.' There were always those ready to denounce his leadership as opportunistic or defeatist or vain-glorious, or all three. But he vanquished them, securing a resounding endorsement, 348 votes to 58, of his programme.[43]

Weizmann defended his policies resolutely and with unbounded confidence. But it was typical of him that at the same time, fed up with the personal attacks on him and anxious to pay back the ingratitude shown him, he often hinted at resignation. He never did resign; his sense of duty prevailed. He *knew* that he was indispensable to the Zionist movement if it was not to squander the triumphs of the past years. No other leader was more suited than he to meet the specific challenges of the moment: to unite the Jewish people behind the Zionist experiment in Palestine; to deal with the British government; to reach a *modus vivendi* with the Arabs. He would not abandon his destiny. When he next met the Congress, he called for a world Jewish 'alliance for *Erez Israel*'. Whether it would emerge, he would not prophesy, 'But I believe it is the highest duty of the hour to extend our hand toward such an alliance.'[44] His struggle to enlarge the Jewish Agency had begun.

❦

ELEVEN

THE BENEVOLENT DESPOT

D o you know what a nightmare is?' Weizmann asked the American Zionists in 1921. 'It is the budget of Palestine.'[1] This nightmare haunted him throughout the 1920s, for despite its astonishing political successes the Zionist Organization was virtually bankrupt. Without adequate finance the future of the National Home was bleak: there could be no land purchases or settlement, no productive absorption of new immigrants. By 1923 almost 32,000 Jews had entered the country. The third *aliyah* (wave of immigration) was distinguished by its high ideological tone, its devotion to the ideals of Jewish labour and socialism, its pioneering ethos. But it was in the throes of a deep crisis: widespread unemployment; hunger in the countryside. These grim facts determined Weizmann's political activity. He knew that without obtaining funds from Jews all over the world and in particular the United States, the Jewish National Home in Palestine would remain a dubious adventure. Risky experiments would not secure for long the good will of the British government or the patience of the Jewish people. He had to prove that Palestine was a worthy investment, not necessarily in cold figures of profit and loss, but in terms of the Jewish *renaissance*. Superficially this message held little appeal to hard-headed businessmen or practical politicians, but it was Weizmann's singular talent to convince the sceptical of the impossible. He proposed to expand the Jewish Agency to include sympathetic non-Zionist Jews. Only by mobilizing world Jewry would he ensure the future of Jewish Palestine. This issue had first appeared in the early stages of the controversy with Brandeis. The British favoured it: article four of the mandate spoke of it.[2] Now Weizmann returned to the idea, determined to bring it to a successful conclusion.

It was a proposal that still provoked furious controversy. Many Zionists were not prepared to dilute the purity of their movement by an influx of organizations and individuals whose only virtue was the possession of fat bank balances, who had no ideological commitment to Zionism, and whose incorporation into the structure of the movement might subvert its national and democratic character. Only with the greatest difficulty did Weizmann counter these weighty arguments, but at a meeting of the Actions Committee in the autumn of 1922 he was empowered to explore the possibilities of realizing his scheme.[3]

American Jews were the key. From 1923 to 1928 Weizmann visited the United States six times, 'eating my way from coast to coast', as he put it.[4] In time, he came to dread these exhausting, frustrating, unpredictable trips—'a horrible prostitution of the movement.' 'Why are things so difficult this time?' he wrote to Vera in February 1923. 'It is as if I were climbing a steep mountain and must wearily gain the summit in the hope of beholding the "Promised Land"'. Once in New York, the game began: 'journalists, photographers, badgered, pestered'. 'But the boredom and dejection are unbearable, the loneliness interminable. Do write to me often, my darlings,' he implored his family. And then he would set off on his pilgrimage, discovering America by train, raising support and spirits in towns and cities on the way. These one-day stands followed each other with soul-destroying regularity: reception committees and speeches, breakfasts, lunches, teas, and dinners, all strikingly similar in appearance, content, and taste.[5]

When irritated with his European confrères, Weizmann liked to compare the 'simple and natural' American Jews who 'respond to the Zionist ideal' with their European counterparts: 'complex, intellectually perverse, sophisticated and incapable of action'.[6] The truth was more complicated; while he often found American Jews more compliant with his views and responded readily to their desire to perceive in him a new messiah, they at times irritated him with what he thought was naivety, unbounded self-confidence, assertiveness, and an axiomatic conviction that the future lay with them. The 'good graces of the Babbitt millionaires' flaunting their 'Yankee Doodle Judaism' often drove him to despair. It annoyed him that they likened Europe to 'a run-down museum which is up for sale', as he recorded.[7] He soon discovered that American Zionism and Jewry were no less 'complex' and 'perverse' than their European counterparts, and equally given to personal rivalries and schismatic politics. The sheer size of the United States also complicated Weizmann's task. He complained that the farther west one travelled, the more difficult Zionist work became, moving, as it were, from the sophisticated, international-minded East Coast into the isolationist heartland. Yet he found useful allies in Chicago—Albert Epstein and Benjamin Harris, both industrial chemists—while in New Orleans he made the acquaintance of the 'Banana King', Samuel Zemurray, head of the United Fruit Company, who proved 'profitable for the Funds'.[8] These were the initial contacts. Over the years, he became a familiar figure to the Jewish communities of North America from Toronto to Dallas and New York to San Francisco.

When Weizmann arrived in America in the spring of 1923 he saw his main task to win over the pillars of the Jewish establishment on the eastern seaboard, in particular Louis Marshall and Felix Warburg. Marshall was perhaps the most influential voice in the American Jewish community, a New York lawyer, president of the American Jewish Committee, among the founders of the American Jewish Joint Distribution Committee (the Joint), founded in 1914 to relieve the suffering of Jewish war victims, a staunch defender of Jewish minority rights in eastern Europe. Weizmann first met Marshall at Versailles where he was a member of the American Jewish delegation to the Peace Conference. Outwardly a representative of assimilated American Jewry, Marshall was, Weizmann felt, more closely identified with Jews and Judaism than some avowed Zionists—Brandeis, for example. He had even learned Yiddish to familiarize himself with the problems of the Jewish masses, which must have especially commended him to Weizmann. Warburg was a different kettle of fish. A scion of the German banking family, he had married into the investment house of Kuhn, Loeb. Known as the 'Black Prince', he was imperious by nature, exasperatingly self-opinionated, and a well-known philanthropist.[9] Escorted in America by these two notables, Weizmann was certain he could carry through the Jewish Agency project.

His 1923 trip was a brilliant success, Weizmann believed. Substantial amounts of money were raised for the *Keren Hayesod*: $1.5 million in cash and pledges of an additional $1 million. Not only was the budget until the end of the year covered, but 'all the deficits will be wiped out', he reported. His presence also helped to mollify American Zionists after the Brandeis crisis. He persuaded Warburg, who earlier had succumbed to anti-Zionist gossip, to contribute $10,000 to the Hebrew University and to visit Palestine to see for himself the progress the *Yishuv* had made. Lastly, and most significant of all, he established the most friendly relations with Marshall. He had every reason for immense satisfaction. New York Jews, he proudly announced, 'won't give money to anyone else'.

> Yesterday there was a meeting here [Philadelphia], and all the leaders of assimilation and our most powerful opponents live here . . . everybody of importance was present. Against my wont I spoke at length . . . altogether I spoke for three hours. The chairman declared that he had never understood Zionism in his life, and that what I had said *is the nearest thing to prophecy I have heard.* One passionate opponent got up in protest against the banal questions that were being put to me and said, *I have heard enough; please ring me up and tell me what I have to give.*
>
> All the Jews, beginning with Marshall and Warburg and down to the East End, talk about nothing else but the height to which the matter has been raised, and everything will come—people and money. [10]

In the event, it took Weizmann far longer to put the Jewish Agency together than he had at first anticipated, and acute financial crises continued to threaten the movement. In his excitement and self-satisfaction, he failed to evaluate correctly the complexity of the American Jewish scene. Still, he returned to Europe with his head swimming. He was spoiling for a fight. Comparing his current achievements in finance and development with the Balfour Declaration in politics, he warned his associates: 'I am coming to the Congress with powder dry and armour shining.' [11]

When the Congress convened in Carlsbad ('which I can't stand') in August 1923, the controversy about the Jewish Agency dominated its proceedings. Opposition to the scheme was widespread. Typically, Weizmann agreed to a compromise that was flexible enough to allow him to continue his efforts, and ultimately he prevailed. For this concession, which allowed him to open negotiations with non-Zionists while at the same time stipulating that a world Jewish congress would shortly convene to ratify the results, he exacted a price, excluding from the new executive those who had opposed him: Motzkin and Ussishkin. After some prompting by himself, a resolution was then moved to general acclaim expressing 'profound gratitude and heartfelt appreciation' for Weizmann's 'extraordinary achievements in the service of the Zionist movement'. 'If our movement had no other attribute of a government,' Weizmann complained half-seriously, 'it had at least the first prerequisite—an opposition.' Exhausted by these squabbles, he retired from Carlsbad 'a broken man, tired both mentally and physically', to recuperate for a few days in the solitude of the Italian Alps.[12] By the end of the year he was back in America, campaigning again for his Jewish Agency.

Weizmann was obsessed with the notion that whenever he was absorbed in saving the movement in one place, incompetent forces were sabotaging it elsewhere. During his absences from London or Jerusalem or New York, the dyke would burst and then he would have to rush back to stem the flood. 'Our dear comrades in London' were sapping his 'powers and life's blood . . . as soon as I leave they apparently start their quarreling, confusion, intrigues and trouble-making, and forget about work.' His 'comrades' in Palestine or America, he held, were equally disrespectful of his feats. After a particularly unsavoury episode, he unburdened himself to a close friend:

> I can hardly describe to you how sick and tired I am of all this. May God help me to arrange things somehow and then leave, leave, leave — to eat dry bread and water, but not to have to bother with all this any more. Jews must still languish as slaves, they do not deserve to have their own country! They have taken a pure and holy cause and desecrated it![13]

Of course, he never left — or at least not of his own free will. He vowed to do so on countless occasions, at times 'irrevocably'. But the cause was too 'pure and holy', too sacred for him to forsake it to the bungling hands of his critics. All they could do was 'Protest! Demand! Insist!' He dismissed this crude formula contemptuously, calling his opponents mere novices, unversed in the sophisticated world of real politics and diplomacy. Left to their own folly, they would ruin his magnificent achievements. Their incompetent politics, their gaucherie reinforced his estimation of himself as indispensable to the viability of the Zionist movement: 'They will perish' without me, 'as soon as I turn my back . . . everything will fall apart'. He confided to Vera:

> Yes, a heavy task fell to my lot, and this makes your life and mine bitter at times, but aren't you my friend and my beloved wife? You yourself would not want my work turning to failure after I've carried the burden of this sick Palestine for so many years. I know that no other man in the world would have been able to accomplish anything like this — I know it even though I do not suffer from megalomania.[14]

Often, he behaved with a cavalier indifference toward his colleagues. He was loath to indulge in horse-trading to retain the presidency of the movement: either they accepted his tactics or else they could do without him. He insisted that his executive be one he could work with or at least one that would not work against him. At the Congress in 1925 he stalked out before the final session when the delegates failed to endorse the executive he desired. Ben Gurion denounced his departure as a 'gesture of contempt'.[15] But again Weizmann prevailed. He could afford such gestures, the meaning of which was crystal clear to those who resisted him. Inevitably, they bowed to his wishes—usually grudgingly and with a bad heart. During the 1920s, Weizmann was as close to being the complete autocrat as it is possible to be in a democratic movement.

His adversaries played into his hands, for whereas he threatened to resign but never did, they executed their threats. In 1922 Weizmann replaced Ussishkin as chairman of the Palestine Zionist Executive with one of his *protégés*, Frederick Kisch. Ussishkin, a powerful figure who personified the spirit of no-compromise, was a permanent thorn in his side. They squabbled interminably, neither of them, when the occasion demanded it, fighting 'chivalrously'.[16] Weizmann was no less conscious than his critics of the hostility of the Palestine administration, but he was equally aware of the faults of the movement he led. Unlike them he did not view the situation in black and white. 'The boot is on the other foot as well,' he pointed out.[17] Kisch, born in India, a colonel in the Royal Engineers, was the ideal candidate for a most delicate post. He could negotiate with the British on equal terms and formulate the more outrageous demands of the *Yishuv* with suitable diplomatic nuances. Together with Arthur Ruppin, the 'father' of Jewish settlement in Palestine, a reliable team was formed that served Weizmann well.

Weizmann mollified Ussishkin, to a degree, by offering him the presidency of the Jewish National Fund. He was less successful with Jabotinsky, a more tempestuous character and a far more serious foe, whom Weizmann considered as a likely contender for his throne, perhaps the only one of real consequence.[18] Jabotinsky swept into opposition in January 1923 and two years later founded the World Union of Zionist Revisionists, isolating himself by the unbridled, demagogic nature of his tirades. Cooperation with him seemed no longer feasible. He thrived 'on our difficulties', Weizmann complained, and made capital from 'the inherent weakness of the situation'. 'Disgusted' by his irresponsible antics, Weizmann kept Jabotinsky at an arm's length from the centres of power and influence.[19]

Accused by the radicals of 'selling Zionism to the rich for their gold', by the *Mizrachi* of degrading religion, by Jabotinsky of being 'a cunctator', Weizmann was under general siege. Periodically, he would respond:

> Looking at all this, one can only stand amazed. Good God, what a cacophony! And I ask myself: '*Qu'est-ce que je fais dans cette galère?*'
>
> What's the use of all this nonsense, and what's the point of this tilting at windmills and phantoms by men who are drunk with mere words. . . . All this is so gross and clumsy that it's difficult to understand the mentality behind it and one must accept the idea that it is not at all a question of mentality, but that we are dealing here with hysterical, helpless people!

Claiming that he had created a new kind of Jewish statesmanship—'I am a Jewish statesman, and you, Mr. Gruenbaum [his radical critic] are a creature of assimilation'—he went on:

> There is no royal road to Palestine. Whoever prefers an easier road should go to Uganda or the Crimea or wherever they like. Often we shall conquer, often we shall sustain defeat. We will build stone by stone in Palestine till the time comes when once more a tribunal will sit before which we will be able to formulate demands. . . . Then your future leader will appear before this tribunal and you will be able to rely on work accomplished, small perhaps, but healthy, and honest, and genuine. For this time you must wait with patience and courage as becomes an ancient race. . . . Do not clamour for ephemeral successes that, like a boomerang, will afterward turn back upon your work. I can only proceed along this road, for it is bound up in my faith and in my experience. If you want a quicker route, then you will have to choose another leader.[20]

Much of the criticism directed against Weizmann hinged on his relations with the British government. His detractors portrayed him as being weak, pliable, prone to compromise, too much of a trimmer. The high hopes generated by the Balfour Declaration had not materialized. Yet no one was more aware of this than Weizmann. The struggle over the mandate had been accompanied by what appeared in Zionist eyes to be an all-out assault by the government on the National Home. From 1921 until 1923 proposals to institute a Legislative Council in Palestine, to form an Arab Agency, and to include Palestine in an Arab Federation followed each other in rapid succession. Nothing came of these ideas, owing to the obduracy of the Arabs, who resolutely set their face against any concession—even if it would have awarded them a tactical advantage—that implied recognition in principle of the Balfour Declaration or mandate. Weizmann was inclined to allow the Arabs to set the pace, counting on their inflexibility to kill the proposals at birth. He saw no reason needlessly to exacerbate relations with the British. Until he was certain that the government intended 'to break faith' he would not worry his head 'with fancies'. On the other hand, he could not ignore Zionists and Jews who expected a vigorous response from their leaders. Weizmann at times conciliated, as over the Arab Agency; on other occasions let fly; 'the inclusion of Palestine in a political sense in a Federation of Arab countries,' he warned the Colonial Office, 'would... be disastrous, if not fatal, to the Zionist Movement.'[21]

It infuriated Weizmann that his critics held him personally responsible for the formulation of British policy. The halcyon days of the Balfour Declaration, when Zionist and British interests ran fleetingly together, were over. Territorially, the British Empire was at its zenith. From Egypt to the Persian Gulf to India, London controlled the destinies of tens of millions of Arabs and Muslims. For responsible British politicians the fundamental issue was painfully clear: how to balance their commitment to Zionism against their wider imperial interests. Weizmann's ability to turn these incontrovertible geo-political facts to his advantage was extremely limited, and it became even more so as the international situation deteriorated. Given this context, Weizmann's achievements appear all the more remarkable. He was involved in a holding action, playing for time to allow the *Yishuv* to consolidate itself, to present itself as a going concern, as a political fact that could not be wiped off the map. Aided by none of the conventional trappings of power, endlessly intoning the legal and moral obligations of the mandate, an increasingly worthless formula, to a bored audience, he had to rely on the force of his personality.

Weizmann was also a victim of the political upheavals in Britain. In October 1922 Lloyd George, his staunchest ally, was compelled to resign, never to hold office again. Balfour, really a spent force, now decorated the House of Lords. The Conservative Bonar Law, with close ties to Beaverbrook, replaced Lloyd George. His administration, bent on retrenchment, inaugurated a reappraisal of Britain's Palestine policy. After extensive investigations, in July 1923, the cabinet agreed to continue with the policy of the Balfour Declaration but mainly for reasons that stressed Palestine's strategic importance for the Empire.[22] As Weizmann knew, this was a double-edged sword that could as easily be wielded against Zionism as on its behalf. In January 1924 he encountered an entirely new phenomenon: James Ramsay MacDonald at the head of a minority Labour government. Labour, with no experience of government or the management of foreign affairs, was an unknown quantity to the Zionists. As it happens MacDonald had visited Palestine in 1922 and had been favourably impressed, particularly by the *chalutzim* and the communal settlements.[23] But each change of government induced a slight *frisson* in Zionist hearts. 'There is a new Government,' Weizmann reported on hearing of Stanley Baldwin's succession as prime minister of a Conservative administration at the end of 1924, containing 'two or three reactionaries, anti Zionists and even anti-Semites.' These were the 'Pharaohs who "know not Joseph"', in Weizmann's pertinent phrase; and they would multiply over the years.[24] Happily, Baldwin appointed Leo Amery as Colonial Secretary, with Ormsby-Gore as his Under-secretary. This was a familiar team of dedicated gentile Zionists with whom Weizmann was on the best of terms.

However harshly he criticized his own people, or whatever obstacles the British raised, Jewish Palestine developed steadily according to the Weizmann principle of building 'stone by stone'. By 1925, 82,000 immigrants had entered the country, constituting approximately 15 per cent of the population. Determining the rate of immigration was a matter that caused continuous friction with the authorities. Weizmann opposed arbitrary restrictions on Jews entering Palestine. In 1919 he spoke of 'bringing into the country [a] hundred thousand productive working Jews' to pave the way to 'a Jewish Commonwealth'.[25] But it would be done in an orderly, regulated fashion. He was conscious that Palestine lacked the economic infrastructure to absorb large numbers of immigrants without causing hardship and unemployment that, in the long run, would be counter-productive to the development of the *Yishuv*. Yet always he returned to the *chalutzim*, those standard-bearers of the Jewish revolution, for 'They would build roads, drain marshes, dig wells, plant trees . . . [lay] the foundations of the National Home.' There was something faintly Tolstoyan in his attitude:

> The backbone of our work is and must always be agricultural coloni-
> zation. It is in the village that the real soul of a people—its language,

its poetry, its literature, its traditions—springs up from the intimate contact between man and soil. The towns do no more than 'process' the fruits of the villages.

He censored any attempt to duplicate diaspora life in Palestine, warning that the National Home could not be built on the model of the ghettos of eastern Europe. Speeches elaborating these themes earned him the ire of the so-called 'capitalist' class of immigrants (those who could show a minimum capital ranging from £200–500) and their defenders.[26] He did not under-rate the importance of this *petit bourgeois aliyah*, its capital, or the commerce and light industries it developed. But he was not to be deflected from his vision; his order of priorities was clear.

Immigration was the life-blood of the *Yishuv*. Weizmann accepted the yardstick of 'economic absorptive capacity' as laid down in Churchill's white paper, a flexible formula the application of which involved him in endless, frustrating debate not only with the British, who put a narrow interpretation on it, but also with the leaders of the *Yishuv*, who wished to stretch it to breaking point. Periodically, he met with the officials of the Colonial Office to lay down the guidelines of a joint immigration policy. The results in the 1920s went 'far to satisfy' Zionist needs, and were, in the opinion of one authority, a further indication of Weizmann's ability to squeeze the maximum out of adverse circumstances.[27]

Coupled with immigration was the question of land purchases. Here again, there was immense frustration. The Zionists expected the so-called state lands to be placed at the disposal of the National Home. The great 'scandal' of the Beisan *jiftlik*, only the most conspicuous example, illustrated Weizmann's predicament. These vast tracks of land (about 490,000 dunam, or 122,500 acres) were supposed either to remain fallow, pending a rather protracted government survey, or to be purchased (about 110,000 dunam, or 27,000 acres) by 'bona fide cultivators', mainly Bedouin, at nominal prices from the Palestine administration. Not until 1928 were certain parcels of land in this potentially fertile district released for purchase by Jews.[28] Areas not under direct government supervision were equally problematic. The neglected valley of Esdraelon had been the subject of negotiations with its absentee landlords, the Sursuq family of Beirut, since before the First World War. In 1920 the contacts were renewed. In the eyes of some Zionists this was a risky business venture that smacked of bad management, for there were no readily available funds to cover the considerable outlay involved in the purchase. Nevertheless, Weizmann approved the project. Impatient telegrams were despatched to America. 'I am willing to undertake to make a special effort and I have already written to some friends in America about this matter.' Eventually the valley (Emek Jezreel) was acquired at a cost of more than £700,000; it developed into the agricultural showpiece of the *Yishuv*.[29]

When in Palestine, time permitting, Weizmann would visit the settlements and the newly acquired areas in which he had invested so much time and energy. These tours often assumed the character of a royal progress. On the roads he was greeted with cries of '*Yechi Weizmann!*'—'Long live Weizmann!' Kisch remarked, 'It has been a great happiness to see the tremendous popularity of our chief.' In Tel Aviv for the New Year celebrations of 1924, thousands of youths congregated outside his residence to convey their greetings. When he appeared, he was drawn into the throng of dancing and singing *chal utzim* to shouts of 'Long live our leader'. At Ein Harod, he told the *chalutzim* that he had two tasks: to create the minimum political conditions to develop the National Home, and to find the means to ensure its viability. His companions sensed that he was refreshed and reinvigorated by the warm reception given him.[30]

Immigration and land were the sinews of the National Home. But it would have been out of character had Weizmann concentrated only on these issues. On 1 April 1925 he realized one of his most cherished dreams: the Hebrew University was officially inaugurated at its site on Mount Scopus. The original building, Grey Hill House, had been renovated to house the institutes of Microbiology and Natural Science; together with an Institute of Jewish and Oriental Studies and the Jewish National Library, containing 90,000 volumes, the nucleus of the university was assured.

Everything had been prepared with scrupulous care. A wooden platform was constructed to accommodate the guests for the opening ceremonies: its strength was tested by *chalutzim* dancing an energetic *hora* and its security guaranteed by the Haganah, the Jewish defense organization. The festivities were held in a natural amphitheatre on the eastern slopes of Mount Scopus, set against the splendid panorama of the mountains of Judaea descending steeply to the river Jordan and the calm, shining waters of the Dead Sea. In the far distance could be seen the mountains of Moab and Gilead.

The ceremonies began in the late afternoon. Lord Balfour, the guest of honour, clad in the scarlet gown of the chancellor of Cambridge

University, created a tremendous stir. He was followed on to the platform by Allenby and Samuel. There were the inevitable speeches, some of them 'rather straining people's patience'. Weizmann was observed plucking at the sleeve of Rabbi Kook hoping to cut him short, but the Chief Rabbi angrily disengaged himself and continued. Weizmann was 'deeply moved'. He told the audience of 12,000:

> Our faith has been justified. . . . A university is nothing if it is not universal. It must stand not only for the pursuit of every form of knowledge which the mind of man embraces, but also for a commonwealth of learning, freely open to all men and women of every creed and race. Within the precincts of these schools political strife and division cease and all creeds and races will, I hope, be united in the great common cause of searching for truth, in restoring to Palestine the thriving civilization which it once enjoyed, and in giving it a place of its own in the world of thought and learning.

In the evening, the guests assembled for dinner. Allenby, recollecting the hectic, dangerous days of 1918, assured his audience, 'The confidence of this civilian [Weizmann] helped to maintain the confidence throughout my army.'[31]

In the winter of 1925 a crisis had been brewing in Weizmann's relations with Vera. When they set off together to Palestine for the opening of the Hebrew University in April, taking Benji with them, Weizmann hoped the trip would be 'a renewal'. 'It seems to me that this is going to be our second honeymoon', he promised her.[32] Three months after their return to England, in mid-July, they closed down their London home and separated. Weizmann went to live with his friends George and Emily Halpern, when he was not travelling abroad on business. Vera, together with Michael, moved to the Continent, staying at various resorts until March 1926. Benji began his studies at Jesus College, Cambridge. Not until April 1926 did the Weizmanns decide to reopen the house on Addison Crescent and resume a normal family life.[33]

It is difficult to ascertain the precise reason for the break-up, if there was one. None of Vera's letters for these months have survived. Certainly, both parties were depressed and in bad health: they spent the first month of their separation taking the cure at fashionable spas, Vera at Châtel-Guyon, Weizmann at Wiesbaden. Vera in particular had been run down since the beginning of the year, and her moodiness continued to distress Weizmann. It appears that it was she who took the crucial decision to separate, and it was her reluctance to return to London that spun out the crisis. Weizmann, a victim of his own passionate temperament, conscious of his own faults, uneasy at the consequences of Vera's humour, pursued her, eager to rekindle their relationship, and believing, hoping, the crisis would pass, would be the prelude to a happier and more stable partnership. 'I was heartbroken . . . coming back afterward to an empty house,' he wrote to her. 'Verochka, you must put yourself in good shape. I hope that our house is not "The Cherry Orchard." Not everything has been destroyed, and we shall either go back home or build something new — won't we, Verochka?'[34]

Weizmann's love for Vera had not eroded. He could not envisage being with anyone else. But in some ways their lives moved in two different circles. Both possessed strong personalities, his stormy, hers more subdued. Weizmann, constantly preoccupied with great affairs, had little time to spare for the niceties of domestic life; and Vera, haughty and remote, pulled back from meeting him half-way. Weizmann was aware that his behaviour was far from being blameless. Two weeks after their separation, he confessed:

You need have no doubt that I love you exceedingly, respect you and appreciate you. I wonder if now, *par les temps qui courent*, there are many couples where such harmony, understanding and respect reign. Recently, owing to circumstances beyond our control, it has been difficult. Both of us, I confess, especially I myself, buckled under, and it was this that introduced that factor into our lives, about which you write so justly in your letter. I have therefore decided firmly to pull myself together, to get my health improved, and you will see, my dear, that everything will be all right again, and I shall make my Verochka happy once more. In twenty days' time it will be nineteen years since we were married, and it's almost twenty-five years since we met. We shall celebrate it together and with God's help this will be the end of this unfortunate *intermezzo*.[35]

The twenty days elapsed without a reconciliation. They met occasionally, in Paris, but the winter of 1925 drifted by with no change in their situation. Vera continued to mope. Weizmann, fed up, reacted more impatiently than in the past. 'The main thing is that you must be cheerful, then we shall have a home, and shall all be together. If, on the other hand, you are going to eat yourself up, then I prefer to live like a gypsy.' And the final thrust: 'Our home was best of all, even during the time you didn't take much care of it.'[36]

By the spring of 1926 the storm had blown itself out. The house at 16 Addison Crescent was re-opened, the family re-united. Weizmann carried on travelling extensively, attending meetings, fulfilling his duties as President of the World Zionist Organization; Vera resumed her role as a social-political hostess; Benji and Michael continued to fret at their stunted home life. Before long, Vera was complaining again, uneasy at Weizmann's handling of the boys' education—as he saw it reproaching him 'unjustly', 'angry with the Zionists', and generally 'depressed'.[37] But there were to be no more separations by choice. Both had learned to compromise.

One contributory factor to this sad episode must have been Weizmann's propensity to form *liaisons* with other women. This was not a decisive factor for Vera, as she was sufficiently confident of her position as his wife, but she would have been less than human had his flirtations not wounded and humiliated her. In the early 1920s he had formed an attachment with Bella (Bellochka) Berligne, daughter of a trusted Zionist who had been employed as a nurse in Palestine at the end of the war. Some years later he became intimately involved with Lola Hahn-Warburg, daughter of the banker Max Warburg. Then, in December 1926, at a reception in New York he met Hanna Rovina, later the first lady of the Israeli theatre, whose rendering of *Eliyahu Hanavi* moved him to tears. The familiar syndrome began. 'Dear Anna Davidovna," he wrote, 'I shall weep bitterly if you don't keep it [their assignation]. . . . I intend to convert you to our faith—the Jewish one.' Two days later he assured Vera, who was far away in London, 'Yes, a heavy task fell to my lot, and this makes your life and mine bitter at times, but aren't you my friend and companion and my beloved wife? . . . I shall soon be with you, next to you, in peace. We are good people, both of us!' He signed off, 'With ardent love, your good and bad husband, Chaim.' Three days later, after some schoolboyish behaviour at an after-theatre soirée, he explained to Anna Davidovna, 'It was the last time that I was seeing you on the stage—and this time they spoiled it for me. . . . Do not judge me, dear, it is difficult for me to leave. *Partir c'est un peu mourir!*' From Chicago he wrote: 'I am looking at the lake, I hum *Eliyahu Hanavi*. . . . This tune does not leave me for a minute since our parting in N.Y.' But the cardinal point was still unresolved: 'You and I have not in fact agreed finally about Zionism. . . . I want very much for you to understand everything.' His *liaison* with Hanna Rovina continued for many years. Yeheskiel Saharoff (Sahar), Weizmann's private secretary and personal bodyguard in the late

1930s, recalled that every time Weizmann returned to Palestine he would say: '"Let us go to Rovina." I used to take him to her house. I remained in the car . . . and after half an hour he came out.'[38]

Weizmann's relations with women were not always on this plane. In the autumn of 1925 he made the acquaintance of 'Baffy' (Blanche) Dugdale, Balfour's niece. Lewis Namier was the go-between. In his rooms in Chelsea, 'not the most auspicious surroundings', he improvised a dinner-party to bring them together which despite organizational mishaps was a great success. Baffy's political usefulness could not have escaped Weizmann's notice. Highly intelligent, a political animal to her last breath, she was related to some of the most powerful political clans in Britain: the Campbells, the Balfours, and the Cecils. Born into the British political élite, she knew everyone who mattered. Baffy succumbed to Weizmann's charm. In time, she became the most ardent gentile Zionist of her generation, admitted to the inner circle of Zionist policy-making bodies. She acted as Weizmann's confidante and as an informal channel of communication with the government, transmitting messages, divulging cabinet secrets. Working in close harness with her great friend Namier, they formed a gifted intellectual partnership that was scarcely equalled before or since in the history of Zionism, and it served Weizmann well.[39]

In the spring of 1926, as he was being reconciled with Vera, another heavy load was lifted from Weizmann's mind. 'The affair'—the accusation brought by Strange that Weizmann was not the true inventor of the corn-starch fermentation process—was heard before the English courts, and Weizmann was totally vindicated. From Merano he unburdened himself to Caroline Schuster: 'The miserable allegations' had been disproved: 'I have won. They had to withdraw everything, and so I am freed from a nightmare. . . . I was worn out after this miserable business and so came here for ten days.'[40] For a public figure like Weizmann the repercussions of this tedious, protracted litigation had extended beyond the issue of his personal and scientific integrity, important though this was. And there were also mundane considerations, for considerable sums of money were at stake. The Weizmanns had become accustomed to, and enjoyed, a modish, expensive style of life. Fortunately, they were not deprived of the means to pursue their tastes; their powers of endurance were never put to the test.

* * *

After the riots and the political uncertainty of the early 1920s, Palestine was calming down. Samuel reported to the government in 1925 that Palestine was 'the most peaceful place in the Middle East'. Weizmann thought he was too cautious, however, and was not satisfied with his emphasizing the policy of equality of obligation between the Arabs and Jews, for the Zionists interpreted the mandate as giving definite priority to the establishment of a Jewish National Home.[41] Still, the progress made in Palestine under Samuel's guidance had been considerable: public administration, finance, transport, health, agriculture, industry, education had taken their first steps into the twentieth century after centuries of decay under Turkish rule.[42] Much of this was an effect of the influx of Jewish capital, manpower, and technical skills. And Samuel, sympathetic and receptive to the Zionist ideal, and in the name of sound government, afforded these developments every encouragement. He completed his term of office in July 1925. Deedes, to Weizmann's intense disappointment, had resigned two years earlier. Weizmann used to quip: 'Never wish for the death of a *goy* in case you get a worse one in his place.' Who would replace the tested and congenial team of Deedes and Samuel?

To everyone's astonishment, field-marshall viscount Herbert Plumer, one of the few British generals to emerge from the First World War with his reputation intact, was appointed. 'With his receding chin, ruddy complexion, bushy moustache and monocle . . . and he was by no means tall',[43] he resembled more the cartoon character Colonel Blimp than an enlightened colonial administrator. But appearances were deceptive. 'He seems to be without prejudice,' Weizmann divulged to Kisch. 'He made on me an excellent impression as a benign, quiet and well-disposed gentleman, who has been quite properly coached by somebody in our affairs.'[44] He was also a tough, no-nonsense soldier. When the Arabs complained that he stood to attention during the playing of *Hatikvah*, he countered by offering to help them acquire a national anthem of their own. He refused to kowtow to Arab threats. 'Gentlemen', he assured an Arab delegation who had said they could not 'be responsible for public order' should a Jewish military parade take place, '*I* am responsible for public order.' Hoping to trap this political innocent into making a compromising statement, someone had asked him, What is your policy? He replied without guile that he received instructions from His Majesty's Government and carried them out 'with what exactness he could'.[45]

The policy of the British government was simply to administer Palestine with as little fuss and expenditure as possible. Budgets were pared, garrisons were allowed to run down. Plumer's eccentric methods of conducting negotiations, although they earned him respect, did not solve the Zionists' problems. They were still frustrated by a Palestine administration that on occasion did not disguise its hostility to the Zionist experiment, and a government in Whitehall whose order of priorities did not always square with their own. Plumer, like Samuel, could never move fast enough for them.

In one respect, the situation seemed to improve. Already in 1924 Weizmann had judged that the Arab question had 'lost a great deal of its acuteness'. On every occasion he drove home the same message: the necessity to 'make terms with this people'.

> We have told the Arabs, and we mean it, that we come to Palestine not as conquerors but as a people returning to its home. We shall not take from them any of their possessions, neither shall we take from them their language or their culture. We shall cooperate with them. We shall do everything to help them fructify the land from the Euphrates to the river of Egypt.[46]

Here again, he railed against his own 'hotheads' who were sabotaging his efforts. Unlike some of the so-called experts, Weizmann sensed that the Arabs could not be fobbed off by the economic benefits that accrued to them from the development of the National Home. During the controversy over an Arab Agency, he did not rule out the possibility of 'a real constitution' for the Arabs, on condition that they pledged to uphold the mandate. In 1926 he contributed £200 to the *Brith Shalom*, an organization founded by leading Jewish intellectuals to promote Arab-Jewish understanding on the basis of bi-nationalism, a future state in which each community would preserve its autonomy in domestic affairs while united by a common Palestinian interest. Later, when he felt the group was exceeding its original programme and advocating compromises of too far-reaching a nature, he branded them as 'extreme pacifists . . . who would like to scuttle and give up everything', more dangerous than Jabotinsky's revisionists.[47] Prepared for mutual concessions, he searched for moderate Arab leaders, but in vain. In a flight of fancy, he hoped that the Sephardic Jewish communities would act as a bridge to them or, equally illusionary, that Rothschild money would buy their support, a form of activity that led one of his aides to claim that Weizmann 'didn't really understand the Arabs'.[48]

In fact, the Arab question had lost none of its acuteness; during the mid-1920s, it was merely quiescent. Divided among themselves, alienated from the *Yishuv*, bitterly hostile to Zionism, intensely suspicious of British intentions, the Palestinian Arab leaders viewed these years as an interregnum. Also, they must have been greatly fortified by the travails of the *Yishuv*, in the throes of an economic-financial crisis that threatened its very existence. With a little more patience, perhaps it would disintegrate of its own accord.

The most striking indication of the plight of the Zionist movement was the shocking revelation in 1927 that more Jews left Palestine than came in. Three years earlier, the Grabski reforms in Poland had forced many petty traders and merchants out of business, and many of them were Jewish. Their entry to the United States was severely curtailed by quota regulations passed in 1924 that limited potential immigrants on the basis of their national origin; in 1925 only 10,000 Jews entered America, while 35,000 found their way to Palestine. This large influx of lower-middle-class immigrants, men and women who were light years away from the pioneering ethos of the *chalutzim*, contributed to the Palestinian crisis. Unemployment, strikes, industrial unrest shook the *Yishuv*. 'I have no bread,' Ben Gurion proclaimed, 'I have a dream.' Weizmann was equally frank, but characteristically he packaged his dismal message in a more attractive wrapping. Addressing demonstrators in Tel Aviv, 2000 of whom were unemployed, Kisch reported, 'He made no fair promises such as he could not execute and told the bitter truth that immigration must be slowed down, yet told it in such a way as not to give rise to depression'.[49] He tended to lay the main blame for this abysmal state of affairs on American Jews: they had the manpower and possessed the money to retrieve the situation, but neither was forthcoming.[50]

At the Zionist Congress in 1927 the argument ran the other way, and Weizmann's methods came under heavy attack: apart from his weak line with the British, it was claimed that he managed an inefficient, wasteful administration, squandering funds that in any case were in short supply, discriminating between rural and urban development. Weizmann bent, slightly, to these censures. His friend Harry Sacher was elected to the Palestine Zionist Executive in the hope of encouraging a more thrifty regime. The Jewish labour movement in

Palestine remonstrated against Sacher's brief to refrain from establishing new settlements until existing ones were consolidated. But Weizmann was more conscious than his critics of the need for parsimony. After all, he collected most of the money. Yet whichever way he turned he found himself under attack. When he arrived in Palestine in October he encountered 'a few of them [his critics] gnashing their teeth', but he vowed to 'do everything' to assist Sacher in implementing the new policy. Everything depended, however, on 'finding the means'. He may well have repeated the cry he first made in July 1920: 'Jewish people, what have *you* done?'[51]

Weizmann's most pressing task was to raise money. In May 1927, he declared that within a month 'the Zionist Executive in Palestine . . . will find itself in the bankruptcy court.'[52] He explored all avenues to escape this fate. He called on the Midland bank for a loan of £400,000; he scoured Wall Street; he approached the League of Nations for an advance of £1.5–2 million. Despite some promising starts, nothing materialized from these exertions,[53] but some relief was forthcoming: in December 1927 an issue, fully subscribed to, of Palestine 5 per cent stock was released by the Bank of England. The £4.475 million were used mainly to purchase capital assets—railways—for the government; but sufficient remained for other investments, mainly the construction of a modern port at Haifa.[54] Toward the end of 1928 the crisis receded. Immigration figures were again positive—the acid test. A relieved Weizmann noted, 'We could begin to draw breath.'[55]

Weizmann viewed fund-raising as an unpleasant, even humiliating, but necessary chore. He considered it 'ungenerous, un-Zionistic . . . to smirch' the reputation of American Jews with 'the libel that they are purely money-getters'; by implication, of course, this besmirched his own reputation. But 'even if it were so, it would be of greater value than the singing of *Hatikvah* in the Polish parliament', for no money could be collected without 'instilling Zionism into these people', without stimulating their collective responsibility for the future of Palestine.[56] Now, in July 1924, he found that the 'Babbitts' were diverting their wealth from the *Keren Hayesod* to a utopian scheme concocted by the Soviet government to settle Jews in the Crimea. Territorialism in any guise roused his deepest hostility, for were they not 'projects of despair' designed to transfer the Jewish problem to other lands, not to solve it?[57] And Russian patronage of the scheme only compounded his antagonism. Yet to voice his opposition too vehemently would mean a break with those American Jews he was so eager to welcome into the Jewish Agency. He had to feel his way. The fragile alliances he formed between Zionists and non-Zionists on his periodic visits tended to wither away during his absences. The creation of his enlarged Jewish Agency was a sisyphean, frustrating task that called for a cool head and steady nerves. It took Weizmann the best part of six years to accomplish.

Relations between Weizmann and the American non-Zionists were replete with agreements, heartfelt promises of cooperation, even a 'Pact of Amity'. Felix Warburg, unexpectedly, proved a tower of strength. Weizmann, the family's biographer wrote, 'fascinated Felix and mesmerized . . . Frieda [his wife]'. In January 1927 Warburg contributed $50,000 to alleviate the plight of the unemployed in Palestine. He was behaving 'splendidly', thought Weizmann, 'like a brick', helping 'in every possible way', useful 'both in word and deed'.[58] There would be less idyllic periods in their relationship. With Marshall procrastinating, 'Brandeisism raising . . . its head again', and Weizmann's opponents in the Zionist Organization pursuing obstructionist tactics, it was not until July 1928 that he managed to achieve a decisive breakthrough. By then he was 'dead tired of it all. . . . [I] told them I shall only stay if I get a clear majority without abstentions.'[59]

After more than a decade of intensive Zionist activity, sacrificing himself on behalf of ungrateful colleagues, he was clearly at the end of his tether. Pleasing Vera, who had been complaining of the 'treachery, deceit, dishonesty and arrogance' of his colleagues and had been nagging him to resign, he added: 'I hope it will be refused, and I shall be able to leave this place [Berlin] on Wednesday.' Fortunately, after 'a very serious debate [and] in great solemnity', the Actions Committee voted overwhelmingly in favour of the Agency, 41–4. 'I think the thing will be carried through and I am certain that a new era will begin.' Just to keep everyone on their toes, and perhaps also to assuage Vera, he announced his determination 'to withdraw [at the] next Congress'.[60] As it happened, the next Congress would be the setting of one of his greatest triumphs.

The year 1929 started badly for Weizmann. In ill health and physically exhausted, he was bed-ridden at Ruthin Castle sanatorium in North Wales for more than a month, *hors de combat*. Although his victory at the forthcoming Congress was assured, his pitch was queered until the last moment by opponents conducting a vigorous campaign against his policy; and even by colleagues unable to comprehend the issues at stake. Gossip, relayed by Vera, spoke of a possible Brandeis–Jabotinsky alliance; an old and trusted comrade, Isaac Naiditch, now revealed himself as 'fickle'; Harry Sacher's behaviour seemed unsportsmanlike. He could deal with his refractory friends, but the thought of fire-eaters like Jabotinsky endangering the future of the Zionist movement was sufficient to reinforce Weizmann's sense of national responsibility and to dispel any notion of his abandoning the field. 'If I go away,' he reflected, 'the movement is likely to become extremist and [this would] lead to most serious consequences.'[61]

When the Congress met at Zurich at the end of July 1929, both sides trotted out their stock arguments: the proposed Jewish Agency would either hasten the development of Palestine by the influx of greater resources and manpower, or it would debase the character of the Zionist movement without any guarantee that non-Zionists would rise to the challenge. The impassioned debaters were merely going through the motions. By an impressive majority of 230 votes against 30 (with 45 abstentions), the Congress ratified the Agency scheme. Representation on its bodies would be divided equally between Zionists and non-Zionists.

The first session of the Council of the enlarged Jewish Agency was held at the Tonhalle, Zurich, on Sunday, 11 August, graced by some of the most famous names in world Jewry: Einstein, Leon Blum, Sholem Asch, Herbert Samuel, Louis Marshall, Felix Warburg, Lord Melchett, Sir Osmond d'Avigdor-Goldsmid. They were present at Weizmann's bidding, for there could be no doubt as to who was the chief architect of this remarkable accomplishment. When Weizmann rose to address the Council, the audience stood, as one man, to acclaim and applaud him. He proclaimed 'the unity of Israel': 'We never wanted Palestine for the Zionists; we wanted it for the Jews. The living, evolving Judaism of Palestine is no party matter. The Balfour Declaration is addressed to the whole of Jewry.'[62]

This was an event of historic significance for Jewry and a personal triumph for Weizmann. Weizmann's Congress of 1929 had taken Herzl's Congress of 1897 a crucial stage further. Even Ussishkin recognized that Jewish nationalism had entered a new era, and acknowledged Weizmann's vital accomplishment in bridging the gap between the Jewish world and Zionism. Already President of the Zionist Organization, Weizmann was now also elected President of the new Jewish

Agency. His reputation enhanced, his prestige unrivalled, without challenger or peer, he dominated not only the Zionist movement, but also the politics of world Jewry.

After these exertions Weizmann retired to Wengen, a resort in the Bernese Oberland, filled with 'a sense of peace and achievement'. Arthur Ruppin noted, 'He is quite cheerful and looks better than he did at the Congress. Today [19 August] he told me he would like to settle in Jerusalem and devote himself to the university.'[63] On the morning of 25 August a telegram arrived interrupting the tranquility of his holiday. It contained the first news of violence that had erupted in the Old City of Jerusalem two days earlier and that in the coming days would sweep over Palestine. The traditional Jewish communities of Hebron and Safad were attacked by Arab marauders with particular savagery. In all, some 472 Jews were either killed or wounded. Weizmann was 'struck as by a thunderbolt'.[64] But this was just the first of a series of blows that would threaten his achievements and undermine his position. Louis Marshall, his chief collaborator and prop in the Jewish Agency, died on 11 September. By the end of the year, an economic crisis of unprecedented severity had enveloped the western world, drying up funds and resources that Weizmann had counted on to sustain Palestine. He was facing the gravest crisis of his career: the virtual collapse of Anglo-Zionist relations coupled with an all-out onslaught on the National Home.

TWELVE

THE CHIEF

When, on 11 August 1929 at Zurich, Weizmann opened the Constituent Assembly of the enlarged Jewish Agency he had so painstakingly created, he was approaching his fifty-fifth birthday.* He had reached the height of his power, influence, and success, and the Jewish people hailed his achievement and recognized his leadership. He was indeed their uncrowned king.

Weizmann even radiated a regal air, and he did nothing to dispel it. How many references, not all flattering, were made to his 'royal household', his 'court'? ('It's like accompanying royalty to a command performance,' noted one aide as they entered the concert hall to hear the Palestine Philharmonic Orchestra in Rehovot in 1947: 'I feel a bit silly in this *galère*'.) He possessed in abundant measure what the French call *présence*, the power to impress by the sheer fact of being present. He was also physically imposing. Just under six feet in height (his passport reads 1.82m) and well-proportioned, he inclined in middle age to a slight portliness that only added to his stately appearance. He had balded prematurely. His head was broad at the upper parts and tapered off at the chin and jaws. He sported a goatee, grizzling with age. He had dark, expressive eyes that brightened when his mood was buoyant, a rather large nose, and a sensitive mouth; he smiled easily, with a wry, all-knowing, at times sardonic, gaze. His hands were well-kept and expressive. His overall appearance, which was described as 'mephistophelian', suggested to one perceptive observer a more humane Lenin.

Everyone who came into contact with Weizmann, opponents no

---

*For references in this chapter, see Notes, p. 485.

less than supporters, recognized his extraordinary qualities. He has been favourably compared to such diverse personalities as Thomas Jefferson, Lenin, and Jean Jaurès. Smuts thought him the greatest Jewish leader since Moses. Lloyd George believed that his would be 'the one name that will be remembered in Jewish history a thousand years from now'. He captivated Balfour. For Churchill, he was the 'ablest and wisest leader of the cause of Zionism'. Lawrence of Arabia assured the doubting Dr. McInnes, Anglican bishop of Jerusalem, that Weizmann '[is] a great man whose boots neither you nor I . . . are fit to black'. Truman regarded him as a most exceptional figure and an outstanding statesman. Ben Gurion called him 'the Chosen One'. Jabotinsky once wrote, 'As long as Zionism needs diplomacy and statesmanship, Weizmann must remain the leader.' The list of celebrated names and lyrical praise could be expanded indefinitely. There was another side to this coin, though it amounted to much the same thing: a *Daily Express* front-page lead article of 28 October 1922 was headlined: 'The Mystery of the Great Chaim', 'the genius' who lured Britain 'into the morass of Palestine', 'one of those master-minds who dominate the destinies of nations'. An Englishman once told him, no doubt intending it as a compliment, 'You know, Dr. Weizmann, there is no Zionist movement, but there is your devilish ingenuity.' But whether a revered leader or a diabolical master-mind, Weizmann clearly belonged to the elect of his generation.

Not only his achievements and rare gifts but also his style of life set him apart from his colleagues and the people he chose to lead. By the 1920s Weizmann was a man of considerable means, financially secure and independent. The royalties from his patents, registered mainly in Europe and the United States but also in Japan, Australia, India, Morocco, and South Africa, were bringing in a regular and expanding income. His friends Simon Marks and Israel Sieff, executives of the famous retail store chain Marks and Spencer, more experienced and worldly than he in the realm of high business, were on hand to guide his investments. He dealt in safe government securities or U.S. bonds, and in other reliable stock—Imperial Tobacco or Tate and Lyle, and of course Marks and Spencer shares—which he reputedly bought at nominal prices. He and Vera also possessed investments in Palestine (estimated assets in 1944 were put at £32,000) and India. The precise state of his fortune is difficult to ascertain, but by the late 1920s he was dealing in hundreds of thousands of dollars. In 1926 he received a cheque for $70,000 from his acetone and butyl alcohol patents in the United States: 'Do buy yourself a car, Verochka,' he pleaded. By 1929 he reported that his Butacet Corporations bonds alone amounted to £103,000 ($515,000).

He adjusted easily to his wealth. He maintained a magnificent establishment in Addison Crescent—serviced by a butler, a chauffeur, a nurse-governess, a cook, and maids—which, under Vera's loving eye, developed into the most select of Zionist political *salons*. He travelled first-class and stayed at the best hotels; drove in his Rolls Royce, rarely used public transport, and was 'frightfully extravagant' about taxis. He smoked the best cigars, not those 'coachman's cheroots', and bought his cigarettes at an exclusive shop, The Egyptian, in Bond Street, where he would order his favourite brand, Viafidis, five hundred at a time. Much of his diplomacy was conducted over the tables of the Savoy Grill.

Weizmann gained the reputation of being something of a dandy, 'a Beau Brummel', one acquaintance said. He would order his suits from his tailor, Samuel and Son of Savile Row. 'Drop in,' he entreated Vera, 'and order me a nice summer suit according to your taste . . . [from] a thin woollen, dark grey, nice cloth.' He bought his handkerchiefs at Doucet's, Paris, inevitably '*le plus dernier cri*', or at Hamboro's, London, the coloured kind that 'I always buy'. He acquired his underclothes at the same chic establishments: 'Buy me two silk *caleçons* [pink was a favourite colour], I have the vests, but no shorts. They know my measurements,' he assured Vera. His clothes cupboards at home were bursting with shirts, socks, ties, and accessories. Although he lacked a visual artistic sense, he knew, even in old age, a bad tie when he saw one. When his doctor entered his room wearing 'an ugly yellow tie', Weizmann ordered him to remove it and choose a more tasteful one from his collection.

Weizmann relied heavily on Vera's taste, which was modish to an extreme. Vera, always exquisitely attired, bought her clothes at the dress shop run by her niece, Eva Lutyens (née Lubzhinsky), or else scoured the Paris shops with her sister, Rachel Blumenfeld. Weizmann revelled in his wife's refined stylishness, her 'extravagant simplicity'. 'Always be elegant' were among the last words he spoke to her.

If Weizmann aspired to elegance in his personal attire, he sought it also in his immediate environment. He lived graciously and surrounded himself with handsome objects. He took a keen interest in the planning of the lawns, the flowers, the shrubberies, the trees that today beautify the Weizmann Institute and House and that have made these carefully tended gardens one of the horticultural showpieces of contemporary Israel. He abhorred carelessness, untidiness, lateness. He was obsessed by cleanliness. As a lecturer he would break off his demonstrations five minutes before the end in order to scrub the laboratory benches. At the institute, he was often observed picking up cigarette butts from the paths, as an example to his staff. Later he wrote, with a touch of justified pride, 'By now every chauffeur in Palestine knows that the Sieff Institute is one place in Palestine where one does not throw cigarette ends on the floor, but in the receptacles provided for that purpose'. Neither did the Zionist Congresses escape his fastidious eye. 'I shall be most grateful if you will tell the organizers . . . that it is most essential to have the Congress externally beautiful and more hygienic than it was last time, and see that order and cleanliness are really kept.'

Weizmann was not an intellectual in the accepted sense of the word. In the main, he arrived at his political conclusions instinctively rather than as the result of intensive, systematic study. He was 'one of those creatures who have a sixth or seventh sense in sniffing what is in the air'. Again: 'He was not an analytic, but a synthetic thinker, and presented a pattern or amalgam of elements, not the essence of each separate component isolated, taken apart, and looked at by itself.' In his youth he read widely. He greatly enjoyed Yiddish literature. Russian authors—Pushkin, Turgenev, Tolstoy, Krilov—were familiar to him. Knowledge of Schiller, Goethe, and Heine was part of his German education; and he admired the short stories of Guy de Maupassant. But as he grew older and became increasingly preoccupied with his political and scientific work, he found less time for general reading, devoting his few free hours to catching up on the latest scientific developments and essential political material. On occasion he turned to escapist literature, John Buchan or Conan Doyle; or literature with a pronounced social-political content—Upton Sinclair or Howard Fast. In his bedroom at Rehovot he kept within easy reach works by Dickens, George Eliot's *Daniel Deronda*, and Charlotte Brontë's *Jane Eyre*, together with that loaded polemic *Guilty Men* and a harmless *Child's History of England*. The Old Testament provided him with much comfort, particularly his favourite reading from it, the Book of Isaiah. At the height of the blitz in London, Weizmann was noticed resting calmly in the shelter of the Dorchester Hotel reading Isaiah in Hebrew.

He was a sporadic theatre-goer, and usually critical of what he saw. Shaw's *Widowers' House* failed to impress him, while he found Sheridan's *The Rivals* 'very boring'. Charlie Chaplin's art entertained him, but, unlike Vera (who regularly frequented the Curzon Cinema), he had little time for motion pictures. His sense of the visual arts was deficient, though when in Amsterdam he paid lip service to Rembrandt's 'Nightwatch': 'The colours seem to light up the whole grey room.' The art that appealed to him most was music. Mozart's *Magic Flute* left him 'as happy as a child'; Chaliapin's singing in *Boris Godunov* he found 'immensely' enjoyable. He most admired Beethoven, whose third symphony, the 'Eroica', was his particular favourite, and Brahms. In 1936 he invited Arturo Toscanini to Palestine to conduct the opening concert of the newly formed Palestine (Israel) Symphony Orchestra. In old age, the maestroes came to him: Yehudi Menuhin and Leonard Bernstein were honoured guests who conducted and played for his benefit at Rehovot.

He shunned most forms of sport. (A swimming pool was installed in his estate at Rehovot, but he hardly ever used it except to sit by it with a soft drink.) Mountain walking was the notable exception. He began to indulge in this activity before the First World War, and he kept it up fairly regularly until the late 1930s when ill health forced him to retire. He loved the mountains. Their strength and serenity enabled him to relax and to unwind, especially immediately before or after a Zionist Congress. 'It is so lovely here, and we are doing a great deal of walking and climbing, that the nerves got into condition again.' He was forever searching for a glacier to explore. 'We had a wonderful holiday,' he reported once from Merano, 'the weather was wonderful, and we used it well. We climbed the highest peaks in the Dolomites— Schlern, Sella, Marmolata—and took many shorter trips.' Weizmann had an understandable tendency to embellish the hardships endured on these expeditions. Norah Schuster, brought up on the rigours of twenty-mile hikes in the Lake District or the Peaks of Derbyshire, was shocked at the levity of the Weizmanns' attitude to serious mountain walking when she accompanied them on a tour in the summer of 1913. Against her inclination, she was treated to refreshing drinks of wine at every inn, and long pauses for hot lunches. When the Weizmanns decided to take the train from St. Bernard's Pass to Pontecina, she refused point blank. 'A sissy tour', she recollected, 'they only managed ten miles a day.' In his last years, his favourite resorts remained those picturesque villages perched in the mountains between Lake Geneva and Montreux, the haunts of his younger days, in particular Glion and Vevey.

In the early 1920s Weizmann discovered the Sanatorium Stefanie in Merano, high in the mountains of the South Tyrol above Bolzano. Almost every year he would spend a few days or weeks here, relaxing, re-charging his batteries, recuperating. For despite his outwardly robust appearance, ill health plagued him for most of his life. Calm and methodical in the laboratory, outside it he succumbed to frequent bouts of nervous tension and depression. He drove himself hard, but he tired easily and was unable to relax. If he could only control his nerves: 'How I envy people without nerves! Life in this world is simpler and easier for them.' At times, he found it difficult to sleep. In his late fifties, he began taking a mild drug, Gardenel, or a popular night-drink, Ovaltine, to help him through sleepless nights. In his early thirties, he was haunted by approaching old age, by 'the conviction that I shan't live long... it won't leave me'. Later, when Alice Ivy Paterson, Orde Wingate's mother-in-law, used to read his palm, all that interested Weizmann was the length of his life line: 'Will I live long enough? How long will I live?' The untimely death of his father could only have strengthened his fear that he might die young.

Often he sank into depressions. 'This dark mood is still upon me, and nothing can ease it. The sensation of sadness and oppression is limitless and affects my well-being. . . . In this state I always feel worthless, and this depresses me even further.' Benji coined the expression 'fogs' for these attacks. They would seize him sometimes for hours, sometimes for days. He would become maudlin, deeply melancholic, and introspective, retreating into his shell to brood endlessly. Unable to come to terms with his own overheated emotions, he would lash out at the world, searching out everyone's shortcomings. A close family observer was particularly struck by the extremes of his temper: he was capable of the most wonderful optimism and then the black depression, the 'fog', would descend to blanket all. These 'fogs' persecuted him all his life.

Ever since his painful experiences in Pfungstadt as a student, which weakened his constitution, he was prone to physical ailments. After the First World War he began to complain of enflamed eyes and difficulty in reading; neither glasses nor eye-drops eased his distress. Toward the end of the Second World War he realized he was suffering from glaucoma. No amount of treatment or surgery could arrest the disease, and the last years of his life were spent in near blindness. At times his disabilities would accumulate in what amounted virtually to a physical breakdown. The year 1929 began by his spending a month, from mid-January, at Ruthin Castle, where he had his teeth pulled. These were painful operations, and he recovered slowly. 'My appetite isn't bad,' he wrote to Vera, 'but [I have] a general malaise. . . . Every second day I get an arsenic injection.' Later in the year he still complained of physical exhaustion: 'I have no reserves left at all.' His tonsils were enflamed; his kidneys were not functioning properly (his doctor prescribed insulin treatment and a strict diet); and he suffered from an irritation of the bladder. He lost weight. 'Since January I have been a semi-invalid and I do not know how much longer this will last.' A month later he was at Zurich in the thick of Zionist politics, presiding over the creation of the enlarged Jewish Agency.

This was not the only such episode. In the spring of 1937, with the Peel Commission about to propose the partition of Palestine, Weizmann was again at a low ebb. His doctors ordered him to rest for three months, which was clearly impossible. Facing a crisis with the British government and rebellion in his own ranks, he hung on until the autumn, bending the Zionist Congress to his will. That November his doctors confined him to bed: 'Accordingly I'm here [Paris] but don't wish to be disturbed.' 'I am quiet, sleep a lot, eat little and read the Bible.' A year later he was taking the cure at Cauterets in the Pyrenees: 'a glass of milk every two hours . . . strict diet and treatment: water, baths, etc.' And in the autumn of 1942, at the height of his bitter controversy with Ben Gurion, he was compelled to retire to a health resort in the Catskills to recover from a severe attack of nervous exhaustion. Failing health and increasing years took a heavy toll on his powers of leadership.

There was no question of who ruled at 'Oakwood', 16, Addison Crescent: Vera, who 'spoke only to God when she deigned to speak at all', reigned. She acquired the house in 1919 when their lease expired on 67, Addison Road. Through the excellent connections of Simon Marks, a mortgage of £2500 was arranged—redeemed three years later. Vera redecorated the house, put in central heating, and had everything in order in time for Weizmann's return from the Paris Peace Conference. Later she availed herself of the expertise of Robert Lutyens, the architect son of Sir Edwin Lutyens who had married Weizmann's niece

Eva Lubzhinsky, in restyling the interior of the house. This was her domain where she imposed her tastes, her standards, her values. The Rothschilds and Astors and Crewes had provided her with tantalizing glimpses of how great London houses should be run: she would do equally well, if on a more modest scale. London society intoxicated her: but it was, in one observer's view, society with a capital S. Even her closest friend thought her 'a tremendous snob', noting that her great quality was her 'imitativeness'. After an evening out, she would remember the menu, the order of the dishes, the *placement* at dinner, the way a bathroom was appointed or the style of a drawing-room. 'She was a jackdaw who picked up and took home with her the memories of all that was smart and elegant in the world she met and turned Addison Crescent into the most elegant mansion, beautifully appointed and of course beautifully managed.' She introduced order and stability and style in Weizmann's life. In this refined if sometimes uncongenial atmosphere, Vera wrapped Weizmann in a protective cocoon against the coarse intrusions of his political life.

Weizmann unquestionably enjoyed the splendid home Vera had created, with all its ceremony and paraphernalia, and pandered to her acting the role of *la grande dame*. In time, he came to accept it as an integral part of his life. But at heart, unlike Vera, he appreciated that it was a means to an end and not the end itself. He might well, in desperate moments, have turned one of his favourite sayings on himself: *C'est à prendre ou à laisser*. And he must at some level have found it difficult to relax in this stilted atmosphere, for while Oakwood provided him with a dignified setting for the world of *haute politique*, it erected a barrier against his most intimate companions. Meyer Weisgal tells the following story.

> Weizmann received me joyfully and in a moment of recklessness invited me to tea at Addison Crescent. . . . Mrs. W. was not at home. About a half an hour before I was to leave she arrived. Weizmann, with bubbling warmth, said in Russian: 'Verochka, you know Meyer, don't you?' She froze like a turnip and replied: '. . . I don't recognize him.' Weizmann could only flinch.

If boon companions such as Weisgal or Schmarya Levin, with whom he could unbend and swap stories in Yiddish, were frozen out, so too were the Palestinians. Here was a political, not merely social, price to pay. Weizmann was increasingly dependent on the Palestinians for political support, but they and Vera lived on two different planets.

The thought of those colonials tramping through her drawing-room with their open-necked shirts and crude manners, speaking Hebrew or Yiddish or at best broken English, did not raise Vera's spirits. They were guests, but on sufferance, not as of right. The distance that separated Weizmann from his followers was not always of his making.

Vera's *ménage* was regarded with a mixture of awe, admiration, and bewilderment, sometimes with resigned amusement, even by those closest to the family. Mr. Paine, the butler, with his refined accent, whom Leon Blum dubbed 'the admirable Crichton'; Miss Usher, the nurse; Bishop, the chauffeur; the parlourmaid and the housemaid and the Russian cook only added to the confusion. The running of the household reminded a close friend of Benji's of *Brideshead Revisited*: with Benji he would seek out Nurse in one of the upper rooms to take tea with her. But Chaim and Vera Weizmann were not Lord and Lady Marchmain. Whatever Vera's aspirations, Weizmann took her way of life in his stride, raising no objections, conscious of its drawbacks while luxuriating in its benefits.

Vera has been described as a 'harsh and ambitious and rather heartless woman', as 'an iceberg' who 'would not have wept at the fall of Jerusalem', as 'an absolutely honest woman with very high moral standards, with great integrity' who 'detested lying'. All this was in marked contrast to Weizmann's 'warm, affectionate, *folksmenschlich*' temperament, who was also, according to some witnesses, 'a bit of a villain and often deceitful'. There can be no doubt that, by his own lights, he genuinely loved her: the stream of passionate endearments he lavished upon her form a permanent theme of their life together. He constantly pampered her, bringing her presents from fur coats to halva, and he was forever appeasing her moods and suspicions, declaring his love anew. Apart from the incident in 1925, when they separated for a few months, there was no major crisis between them. It is true that on occasion he sought excitement elsewhere. But Vera nursed him and protected him, cared for him and defended him; she was his sheet-anchor. 'You see, Vera was—whatever you think about her—a very, very good wife. She gave herself to him: she dedicated herself to him . . . she was utterly devoted to Chaim . . . and he depended on her.' The stability and order that Vera provided were essential to his well-being, to his ability to function effectively as a politician and leader.

Weizmann's relations with his sons, Benjamin and Michael, were equally problematical. Like most men of affairs, he had little time to spare for his family. He was constantly travelling or attending meetings; even when at home, his thoughts were frequently elsewhere. 'I have finished packing, and have been sitting for a while talking to Benji, who looks sadly at my luggage.' There was a bitter truth to Benji's complaint to Vera in January 1937 'that it is high time this family was taken in hand by somebody, otherwise the Jews may have a National Home but we shall have none at all'. Weizmann's recurrent absences from home left Vera free to impose her own values on their sons' upbringing. Benji, born in 1907, spent his formative years entirely under her influence. Early on he showed signs of rebellion; an acquaintance of those years remembered him as 'a very naughty boy'. In 1916, Michael was born (apparently a difficult birth); the same year the family employed the services of Jessica Usher as his nurse. Miss Usher remained with the Weizmanns until 1938, gradually assuming the tasks of a general factotum and becoming a dominant force in the boys' upbringing. Miss Usher was present on a day-to-day basis to attend to the boys' needs; Vera laid down the general principles of their education. This was not the happiest of combinations.

Miss Usher, in her own way, also had a mission in life.

> I felt it my job as a Christian to come into that family and to give those boys as far as possible a normal life because Jews are so cruel to their children. Jews have all these customs they impose upon them. Jews expect so much of their children and I wanted to give those Jewish boys as far as possible a normal English life.

She was, in a real sense, anti-Jewish in that she disliked what she conceived to be the Jewish ethic. She was also no Zionist and shared, perhaps played upon, the boys' resentment of their father for devoting himself to Zionism and taking himself away from them. It was a most extraordinary situation: a woman of strong anti-Jewish prejudice, totally indifferent to Zionism, bringing up the children of the leader of world Zionism. A close and dear friend of Vera's thought Miss Usher 'a malign influence', and worked hard, in vain, to have the family get rid of her.

She was of course extremely efficient, and a trained nurse. For one thing, she cared for the family when they were ill. 'Benji, Michael and Vera and Chaim, because they were Jews, were always ill. Jews make a great thing about illness and indeed Jews actually enjoy illness ... each member of the family used to have their own thermometer and [were] keen on having their temperatures taken.' Before long, particularly as a result of the parents' absences from home, she became indispensable to the smooth running of the household, attending to almost every problem. 'Did you appoint the staff?' she was once asked. 'Yes, in the end, finally the staff were always coming and going and I had to do this. I had to pay the wages, I had to pay in the cheques to the parents' accounts, and to the boys' accounts because Vera didn't have the time.' Often, in order to ensure the normalcy of Benji and Michael's upbringing, she would bring them 'to Chippenham where [her] brother was an engine driver and lived in a cottage and had a huge alsatian dog and the boys could run free in the fields'. Miss Usher may have inflated her position in running the household, but her influence was considerable, did not lessen with time, and was regarded by most outside observers, and finally by Benji himself, as being harmful rather than beneficial. Benji, when fully grown, wrote of 'Nurse's disgraceful behaviour. . . . It is my firm conviction that we have had a Rasputin in the house for far too long.' The following year, 1938, Miss Usher retired from service after a nervous breakdown.

Vera complemented Miss Usher's work in her own way. She determined that her children were to benefit from an education that befitted the family's status, and so it was governesses at home, prep school, public school—Westminster for Benji, Rugby for Michael—and Cambridge. If it was *de rigueur* for the children of gentlefolk to take music lessons, so too would the Weizmann children. 'She was cracked, Vera, about the boys' becoming musicians. Neither boy had an ounce of music in him and yet Vera insisted that they should do their piano practice, particularly poor Michael.' Her regime was strict and lacked warmth and understanding. When Benji begged Vera to remove him from Westminster, where he was having a 'hard time', she refused. Nor was the atmosphere at home conducive to inviting friends, for if they came they were bound to cause offence by some innocent action. Playing cricket on the front lawn at Oakwood, for example, was frowned upon by Vera as a breach of etiquette.

Benji suffered most from this state of affairs. He was unable to fit into any recognized framework, either at his studies or later at work. He possessed a rare gift for languages and had only limited scientific abilities; still, he wished to emulate his father as a successful scientist, and Weizmann encouraged him, coaching him, pushing him forward. The result was confusion. He drifted from one course to another, as later he was to switch jobs. He hit back in the only way left open to him—by increasing disobedience and eventual estrangement from his family. 'Come home as soon as ever you can safely leave your affairs,' Norah Schuster pleaded to Weizmann in 1923, 'Vera is . . . in danger of a bad nervous breakdown. If you knew the way he [Benji] spoke to his mother you would boil into rage.' Benji's frustrations were directed primarily against Vera. Whenever they were together there would be 'furious rows'. He teased her about her English pronunciation and accent, a shrewd blow, for Vera had an unfortunate habit of letting slip an occasional malapropism: 'You're a couple of street orchids,' she would chide her children.

In 1937 Benji married Maidie Pomeranz; three years later a son, David, was born. The marriage brought a modicum of stability to his life, but he continued to be a source of concern to his parents. He was in a state of permanent rebellion against his surroundings. In January 1937, he wrote to Vera:

> I know you have always felt that I have treated you badly and been a bad son. Surely you must realize that if I have adopted such an attitude in the part it is because I always felt that not only did you never try to understand me but you always tried to prevent me doing what I wanted to. After all one sets out with certain ambitions and ideas of what one wants to do and study and when one sees other people studying and getting a profession it makes me very bitter that at their age I was not provided with the same facilities.

He drank heavily, verging at times on alcoholism. In 1940, suffering from shell-shock, he was invalided out of the army. He divorced Maidie in 1952 and finished his life farming in Ireland and the Channel Isles. Weizmann was mortified at Benji's behaviour: 'This is a generation that does not read or think,' he complained to Vera, 'a Jazz generation.' His own son had turned into a *Luftmensch*, that despised creature of his youth. He was heard to refer to Ernst Bergmann, his close scientific collaborator, as 'my *ben yachid*' (only son). Benji blamed Weizmann for abandoning him to Vera, to the cruel fortunes of life without adequate guidance and due care, but most of all for transfering his fatherly love from his son to the Jewish people. 'What was he to these people,' he murmured to Meyer Weisgal over Weizmann's grave, 'that he was never to me.'

Michael coped better. He was more resourceful, more forceful, more resilient than Benji. He was less introspective, less prone to self-pity; and he possessed that touch of ruthlessness, noticeably lacking in Benji, that distinguished much of his father's social-political activities. On the surface, he was everything that Benji was not: handsome, clever, gregarious. He had the reputation of being 'a man about town'. Vera adored him. Weizmann followed suit, though occasionally he entertained suspicions that behind the outward brilliance lurked a dangerous superficiality: 'no trace of the "smart Aleck" about him', Weizmann hopefully conjectured after one misunderstanding. Michael was killed in 1942 while on an air force mission over the Bay of Biscay. Thus, in the most tragic circumstances, his life was cut short before he could fulfill the great expectations invested in him. His memory lived on, glorified and revered in the minds of his parents.

Despite the striking differences between them, on one point Benji and Michael were in unison: they wished to have nothing to do with their father's Zionism. When Abba Eban, a fellow-undergraduate, approached Michael at Cambridge to join the University Zionist Society, he was fobbed off with the rejoinder, 'We have enough Zionism at home.' Benji was no less estranged. In January 1937, again at odds with Vera, he considered volunteering to defend the Spanish Republic: 'it is the only cause I know worth fighting for'. Six months later he was turned back at the Spanish border, just barely escaping imprisonment. It remains one of the saddest aspects of Weizmann's history that both his sons were alienated from his life's mission. Later, he regretted that they had been educated at 'some British college. That was one of my mistakes, perhaps the worst of them.' In a moment of truth, at the height of a major crisis with his sons in November 1937, he wrote to Vera:

> I feel I ought to write to you these lines; I am tongue-tied and speaking is very painful to me just now. You must not think that I have in any way changed toward you; neither my love nor my affection or respect have suffered any diminution, but in the same time I know that nobody and nothing can relieve me from my suffering except the end for which I am praying. What has happened I don't know. Something has snapped in me and the whole mechanism is out of gear and running out.
>
> Perhaps I have borne too heavy a burden and am now paying the unavoidable penalty. Perhaps it is being borne upon me that I have neglected my own small family for the sake of the larger which I have been trying to serve so faithfully. Benji and Michael each one in their own way are witnesses of my defeat. I have in my own clumsy way tried to make partial amends, but it is no good. We speak different languages and we have different standards of values, we are strangers; they not only belong to another generation, but almost to another category. I am a lonely man standing at the end of a road, a *via dolorosa*. I have no more courage left to face anything—and so much is expected

from me. The disappointment about Michael may in itself be a comparatively minor event, but it comes at the end of a long chain of severe shocks which was my misfortune to receive of late.

Forgive the inadequacy of these words, but my heart is like a lump of ice. I can only sit still and wait and wait!

Nothing personifies Weizmann's terrible predicament more than these heartrending words.

However difficult the strains within his immediate family, there was nothing Weizmann relished more than going to Palestine for extended family reunions, particularly, if he could, for the Passover or Chanukah celebrations. By the early 1920s, his mother, five sisters, and three brothers were resident in Palestine. The centre of family life was in Haifa, at 4, Melchett Street, 'a large stone building with a wide terrace supported on stone pillars', nicknamed 'the fortress'. The great man of affairs, who held the fate of the Jewish people in the palm of his hand, was a constant topic for family discussion, his activities carefully scrutinized, his policies heatedly debated. The family basked in his glory, and it was impossible to escape his presence when he was there. His nephew, Ezer Weizmann, recalled the atmosphere: 'Uncle Chaim is coming, Uncle Chaim intends to visit, Uncle Chaim is ill, Uncle Chaim is better, Uncle Chaim succeeded, Uncle Chaim failed, Uncle Chaim convinced, Uncle Chaim thinks, Uncle Chaim said.'

When he arrived, the reckoning would begin. Furious discussions erupted as to whether the latest Zionist ploy had been a success or a failure, for Weizmann had to justify his policies in his own domestic forum, a kind of mini–Zionist Congress, with the right wing represented by his youngest brother, Yehiel, and the leftists defended by his sister Haya. Naturally, Weizmann spoke *ex cathedra*, and the adults paid attention even if they withheld their agreement, while the youngsters 'sat in the corner drinking in every word of the night-long discussions'. But the Weizmanns were a jolly as well as a serious family. Weizmann was a famous wit, his sense of humour best expressed in his native tongue, and one Yiddish word or phrase, one evocative gesture, would set the family laughing. In this congenial atmosphere, which flattered and spoilt him, it was simply fun to be in his company.

News of his intended arrival electrified the Jewish community of Haifa no less than the family. When it was Passover, as Ezer Weizmann recalled it,

The *seder* would be presided over by Grandmother, in her majestic splendour, with Feival, her eldest, on her right, and Chaim on her left. All eyes rested on Grandmother and Uncle Chaim, through whose joint presence the room and the family and the Feast of Freedom all seemed to acquire an added dimension of omnipotence. Of course, Uncle Chaim did not belong to us alone. While we were reading the *Haggadah* and hungering for the *kneidelach* [dumplings], the people of Haifa began to gather outside for their share of Weizmann the Great.

All this was to Weizmann's liking. He lapped up the affection and warmth. Like a true leader, not lacking in exhibitionism, he took up his rightful position on the balcony to acknowledge the cheering crowds calling 'We want the President.' He would then descend to join his people, 'graciously allowing the circle of *hora*-dancers to surround him, singing along with them in homespun fashion'.

These were moments of true pleasure. He was always conscious of the distance separating his life-style from that of his family and the *Yishuv*, and his family detected in him an inner reserve, which he did not deny and which Vera guarded jealously. He never broke down the barrier, but these family get-togethers lowered it somewhat. And Weizmann, now rich and famous, contributed regularly to the family exchequer, indeed felt a special responsibility to maintain their welfare. He did not stint himself in effort or thought, but misunderstandings were inevitable, since he conducted these operations by remote control, by letter or cable, using his influence and contacts to secure his relatives jobs when necessary; sometimes these benefits smacked of largesse bestowed by a generous *patrón* upon the needy, or at least so it appeared to the recipients. There was undue sensitivity on both sides. When accused of neglect or indifference, Weizmann found it hard to contain his hurt feelings. 'I guessed long ago that I am considered a "bad" brother, but it was interesting to hear it today from Mariya (his sister), who incautiously blurted it out.' But these were passing squalls that blew over as quickly as they arose. Nothing could damp the deep love and affection that Weizmann felt toward his family, which sustained him and which was reciprocated.

Weizmann, Sir Isaiah Berlin has judged, was 'an irresistible political seducer'; a charmer of the highest order. Most who came into contact with him would have endorsed this judgement. He possessed extraordinary powers of elucidation, of simplifying the complicated, of penetrating to the root of the matter, of convincing the sceptical with that bewitching mixture of paradox and ironic wit that was his hallmark. Anthony Eden, no friend of Zionism, remarked that 'he would see ministers and turn them inside out', which perhaps explains why Eden was usually so reluctant to see him. 'He was a brilliant talker with an unrivalled gift for lucid exposition,' admitted Ronald Storrs, no favourite of Weizmann. 'Did he not explain Einstein's Relativity to my sister and myself at luncheon until for a moment I dreamed that even I understood?' 'His methods of argument were a curious combination of subtle ingeniousness, as a scientific searcher after truth, with the stabs of epigram or some challenging generalization.' These gifts blossomed in the intimate atmosphere of luncheon or dinner parties, or restricted meetings, or a quiet *tête-à-tête*. He possessed a unique ability to kindle the imagination of those with whom he came into contact, to impart to them his faith in the destiny of the Jewish people and the significance of its survival. 'A terrible political flirt', he would turn on the charm to conquer those, Jews and gentiles alike, he felt could advance his cause. In these circumstances, he was indeed 'irresistible'.

Weizmann was fluent in many languages — most competent in Yiddish, Russian, and English, while his German was more proficient than his French, his Hebrew was good, and he had a working knowledge of Italian. When conversing he was known to switch from one language to another, to the consternation of his collocutors. He was an ingenious improviser, concocting his own words in German, an idiosyncrasy that made him fascinating to listen to. But Yiddish was his preferred choice. Whenever the occasion allowed, he lapsed into his mother tongue. He was never so relaxed, so fully at ease, so much at home, less inhibited, so gossipy, as when chatting with his mates from the *shtetl*. Here there were no hidden meanings, no cunning idiomatic traps; everything was understood without superfluous comment or explanation. He was in his natural element, and he revelled in it. Lewis Namier once said that Meyer Weisgal was Weizmann's court jester. He meant to be unkind, but in fact he was paying Weisgal a great compliment.

The language Weizmann used was peppered with *bons mots*, rich in humour. Referring to the 'Prontras', delegates at a Zionist Congress who could not make up their mind, he was reminded of the Russian peasant woman who needed warm weather for lifting the potatoes and cold spells to dry the land: '"We must pray for a warm frost", she said.' 'Miracles do happen,' he once noted, 'but one has to work very hard to achieve them.' Occasionally, his English usage took a public-school turn: '[I] am beastly fagged out', he complained after a strenuous trip abroad. One of his most appealing traits was his ability to laugh at himself. 'Call me anything except "Mr. President",' he instructed his bodyguard, Joshua Harlap. 'At present I'm nothing but the president of a world organization of *Schnorrers*, although it is a fairly large one.' 'Yes,' he confessed as first President of Israel, 'I'm just a symbol who plays the cymbals.' His language was always racy and amusing, at times obscene. He was heard to refer to his military ADC as that 'pompous potz'. But his favourite expletive was that expressive Yiddish word *schmock*, which he was wont to use to decorate those of his colleagues with whom he happened to be at odds, usually a lengthy list.

If he was a natural conversationalist, he found greater difficulty in expressing himself on paper. 'You know that my journalistic capacities = 0, and I always have to drag things as though out of glue.' His correspondence, though a fascinating human and political document, full of insight and lit by his brilliant turns of phrase, lacks literary merit. There are few descriptive passages; he rarely strays from his Zionism, or his science, or his personal problems. His correspondence is almost as one-dimensional as his politics.

To help him compose his lengthy memoranda or prepare his set speeches (though he often discarded the text at the last moment and spoke impromptu), he kept on hand a talented group of draftsmen: Lewis Namier, Leonard Stein, Baffy Dugdale, Moshe Shertok, Abba Eban. Nor was Weizmann an orator in the grand manner: he was certainly no tub-thumper. 'His voice was not resonant. He had few gestures. He used no groping introductions or exalted perorations. He hated the impersonation of emotion. . . . He was not made for stage effects.' In this sense, he was not in the same class as his friend Schmarya Levin or his rival Vladimir Jabotinsky. An admirer presented him with a copy of *The Art of Public Speaking*, but he failed to digest its contents. He spoke, often extemporaneously, in a low voice, his audience straining to hear him, and he shied clear of demagogic tricks. He would discuss the issues with his audience rather than rant at them. But he could be effective, even spell-binding: his sincerity, his controlled passion, his *hadar* (majestic aura) enthralled his listeners. He also knew how to inspire them: 'We are reproached by the whole world. We are told that we are dealers in old clothes, junk. We are perhaps the sons of dealers in old clothes, but we are the grandsons of prophets. Think of the grandsons, and not of the sons.' He was, after all, Weizmann the leader, the statesman, the interpreter of his people's needs, the advocate of their aspirations. More than anyone else, he spoke in the name of the Jewish people.

After a particularly good performance, he would wait for the compliments. '"How was it?" he asked', recounted Maurice Samuel, Weizmann's literary collaborator. '"Tremendous!" He was pleased. It was, I think, exactly the word he wanted.' In time, he grew accustomed to the limelight and expected, as of right, to be the focus of attention, whether at a dinner-party or on less formal occasions. He soaked up praise. It raised his spirits and spurred him on to greater efforts. He was not bamboozled by it, nor deceived by the idle flattery of hangers-on attempting to curry favour. The compliments had to ring true, be spoken from the heart by those whose opinion he valued. Then he would respond, satisfied that he had really done well. 'He will sit and purr and want to be purred at. It can grow tiresome; but we go along, we realize he's just recharging.'

As a scientist, Weizmann was extremely disciplined, allowing nothing to interfere with the strict timetable he imposed on himself and others. 'Occasionally he would receive scientists at the Zionist office and at such times it was as much as anyone's life was worth to intrude, however pressing the matter.' This habit caused much friction and criticism. But his political routine was more flexible, particularly as he grew older. Shertok, a martinet in such matters, complained that 'Chaim is prepared to sit and discuss every free hour that he has from other meetings and is surprised when you tell him there is something urgent to be done.' Most of his aides rather enjoyed his informality. Arthur Lourie recalled

Weizmann, the kindly chief who would start the working day by inviting you down to his room in the Great Russell Street office for an early morning cup of tea, at which the invariable greeting was, 'Well, what's wrong now?' And generally there was plenty! This would be the preliminary to a quiet and intimate 'schmooz', than which there was nothing that Weizmann enjoyed more, in which he would talk about his politics and people, about his childhood home in Motele near Pinsk, about the past and about the future.

Later in his career he took to cat-napping in the afternoon to help carry him through the day, and took unkindly at being awakened without due cause: 'It was quite unnecessary to disturb my afternoon slumber by telephone,' he reprimanded an over-zealous Lourie, 'which always gives me a jar.' He also became somewhat lackadaisical in his habits. As a young man he had been known to forget his best waistcoat in a hotel room. When he was older, he developed a tendency to stuff pieces of paper, often containing important information, in his pockets or elsewhere, and then to forget where he had placed them. On one occasion, he left a letter, in which was set out the Jewish Agency secret code, on the desk of William Ormsby-Gore, the British colonial secretary. He could be indiscreet in conversation, letting slip in the heat of the moment secrets best left unsaid. Namier commented: 'If Weizmann was in partnership with the Almighty he would try to keep some small thing secret from him and then tell it to the first American journalist who happened to come along', characterizing him as 'unsystematic, indiscreet, self-indulgent and whimsical'. Nahum Goldmann, too, reacted to his lack of organization and contempt for routine: 'For you, each day is Genesis, and the world is recreated every twenty-four hours.' All this could be extremely embarrassing. His minions tolerated these lapses, since while they complicated life, they were a small price to pay for Weizmann's leadership. On the other hand, he chaired his meetings in what is popularly assumed to be the 'Anglo-Saxon way'. He kept strictly to the topic under debate and maintained orderly discussion, handling heckling coolly and quickly putting down repetition or what he considered to be foolish talk. This down-to-earth approach was quite out of tune with the verbose histrionics that characterized most Zionist politicians.

There was another side to his efficiency. He lacked, in one admirer's words, 'true collegiality'. 'Subtle, impressionable and untrustworthy, he could and would let you down.' He harbored grudges and interpreted criticism as personal enmity. He used people, exploited them, and then discarded them, not so much out of spite as for reasons of expediency, *raison d'état*. Ussishkin soon 'outlived his utility'; Sokolow bored him 'to tears'; Selig Brodetsky, a leading English Zionist, he treated with contempt; Namier and Stein were often outraged, and left stranded by his political manoeuvring. Julius Simon knew that when Weizmann called him 'darling', the bill would soon follow. Even Baffy Dugdale was the victim of a misunderstanding. And Weizmann all too often thought in terms of plots and intrigues against him. He seemed to be embarrassed by the constant necessity of explaining his actions, and those who opposed him did so at their peril. 'You could see the interest leave his face if he disagreed with you.' In this way, he carelessly stimulated opposition. A born autocrat, he preferred to play a lone hand. His mind leaped rather than plodded. Impatient at the second-rate, he did not suffer fools gladly. He was bored by intellectual *poseurs*, cutting them short with the riposte, 'It's time to go to bed.' He wished to be stimulated intellectually, without having to spell out every word. He would take Isaiah Berlin on walks in his gardens in Rehovot: 'You always understand what I say. For you, half a sentence is enough,' he told Berlin. A natural leader, he was suspicious of those who might challenge his authority. He did not surround himself with yes-men: his inner court comprised immensely able, talented, and intellectually independent collaborators. But they were subordinate to him: they offered no threat to his position as leader. It was noted, ironically, that Weizmann's *bureau* was run by three non-Jews: Lewis Namier,* Baffy Dugdale, and Doris May.

Lewis Namier, an acute observer who worked side by side with Weizmann for twenty years, wrote somewhat critically of his chief's political style:

> First, he must never be allowed to go into a conference alone; because when he returns he knows what he has said, but has hardly any notion of what the other people said. Secondly, pursuing broad lines and fundamental ideas, he fails to drive the things to a point; he does not coin the bullion into hard cash. The impression is produced, but unless there is someone to translate it into positive terms it evaporates without leaving positive results.
>
> The worst of Chaim is his incredible lack of self-discipline. A most important matter may have to be dealt with but, if he is not in the mood, or if he wants to go home for tea, or if his sons are back from school, he will leave the office, and not do the thing; occasionally he is like an impish naughty child and likes to upset the apple-cart to then see others struggle as they straighten out the mess.

Weizmann straddled the two worlds of science and politics: a political artist, impressionistic, impetuous, emotional, visionary? or a cool scientist, bound only by the calculations of his scales and test tube? In him, one confidante discovered 'a strange, though effective, mixture of method and order—his scientific training, with a finely-honed intuition—his artistic-political sense'. He was forever compar-

---

*Although Namier's parents had converted to Roman Catholicism when he was a child, Namier himself was proud of his Jewish origins and was a passionate Zionist. His countless enemies in the Zionist organization were only too eager to classify him, spitefully, as a 'non Jew', seeking revenge for his barbed comments about them.

ing the honesty of the laboratory, where facts were facts, with the wheeling and dealing of political survival, adjusting from one to the other. 'Weizmann goes for a stroll in the institute whenever he has to make a chemical analysis of the political situation.' He fell back on his science to illustrate his political philosophy. 'I am an adherent of the cellular theory,' he told Israel Zangwill. 'It is essential to create the first cell, which should in itself contain the future of the poly-cellular organism, which may grow out given normal conditions.' His golden rule was, 'In politics, like mechanics, you can only get out of things what you put into them.' 'And what are you doing?' Lord Peel asked him, finding him busy in his laboratory. 'I am creating absorptive capacity,' he replied. Unlike Herzl, he did not theorize in a systematic manner about the forms the future Jewish state would take: its con-stitution, party system, administration, or army. These questions were too abstract for his scientific mind, his organic approach to Zionism.

His wit, if illuminating, could also be wounding and cruel. All too often, his colleagues were the butt of his undisguised contempt. 'I am all alone here. . . . There's a rumour that Sokolow is here, but nobody has seen him. If I want to take a decision, I stand in front of a mirror and hold a conference with my reflection, and that is how the "organ-ization" is run.' He was, of course, duty bound to cooperate with the elected bodies of the movement. He did so; but at times with a notable lack of enthusiasm.

> I take a benevolent but very detached interest in the A[ctions] C[ommittee]. . . . In reality I know what will happen. As soon as I have made my statement they will get a fit, the flood-gates of eloquence will open, I shall be barged into; they will argue with me thinking I'm the Mandatory Power. In due course I shall be called a traitor. Being already hardened and immunized against such an appellation we shall part company on most affectionate but nevertheless decisive terms . . .
>
> I don't see why we could not do it by correspondence. I'm prepared to write to the A.C. and be called names in absentia, which may be more convenient for both sides. They can be more outspoken and I need not listen to it.

The *Yishuv*, he once grumbled, consists of six hundred thousand 'ex-Presidents and ex-Secretaries of Zionist societies', each with their own policy.

For all that, no other Zionist leader inspired such devotion and love. Few could withstand his potent combination of overpowering charm, sparkling intelligence, and penetrating wit. A *raconteur* of the first order, he hypnotized his audiences. In politics, he possessed the Midas touch, a special kind of magic. He radiated success. Above all, the policies he pursued were eminently reasonable, logical, humane; they fulfilled the needs of his people within the context of his time. Mercurial and contradictory, his portrait should perhaps be painted in the style of the *pointillistes*, one dab after another, the whole being harmonious. Baffy Dugdale wrote that he was touched by genius,

> but what a curious genius his is—rising to greatest heights, then by some foolish, unpremeditated act undoing his own work and making one wonder whether it is instinct—or intellect—which is uppermost in him. . . . But when one is with Chaim one feels the infinite nobility of soul—the vast intellect—and knows that here is one of God's instruments. But was there ever a man more full of human weaknesses, as well of human power of suffering? In Chaim there is *everything*.

Weizmann held that Zionism was a genuine revolutionary movement in that it set out to transform in the most radical way Jewish life in the diaspora. This monumental task demanded fixity of purpose and iron resolve. He called himself a 'fanatic', relegating to secondary importance anything that might interfere with his mission: 'The only way to achieve things is to put on blinkers and then go on to achieve them.' It was for this reason that he castigated those negative factors of Galut life which he saw transmitted to Palestine. He condemned shoddy workmanship, 'Levantine' standards, speculative land purchases, the rise of a Jewish Palestinian *petit bourgeois* class. 'Zionism,' he told Congress, 'is a protest against Dzika and Nalevki [or Whitechapel or the Lower East Side].' These home truths earned him much criticism, in Weizmann's eyes 'hatred,' but he was not deterred. He persisted in proclaiming his message. Zionism was not merely a national liberation movement in the political sense; no less significant was the revolution it heralded in the social and economic life of the Jewish people.

Weizmann sprang to the defense of the pioneers, the *chalutzim*, on every conceivable occasion. Accusations that they were kept children, *Kostkinder*, a drain on the movement's resources, filled him with rage: 'There is an invisible capital which the *Keren Hayesod* does not invest, in overwork, in energy, in hunger and in malaria. Items not found in the budget.' His fierce support for the pioneers appalled some wealthy donors to the Zionist cause, but he was not moved by their prejudice. For him the *chalutzim* were the true bearers of the Zionist revolution, its most authentic and original expression. 'They are my army,' he proclaimed. 'Without them I am not President of the World Zionist Organization.' Allegations that he was fostering Bolshevism in Palestine he dismissed as cheap demagogism. 'They do not want to see that . . . on the fields of Deganya, Nahalal, Petach Tikva and Hedera, there is a beginning of the solution of the problem.' He was no hairshirted socialist, nor even one of the gentler variety; his mode of living gave the lie to such an outrageous thought. He would take great pride in conducting his visitors through the fields and orchards of Mishmar HaEmek or Nahalal, singing their praises, and then retire thankfully to the splendour of his palace at Rehovot. But he was at one with the Jewish Palestinian labour movement on many issues: how to develop the *Yishuv*; the role of Jewish labour; the priority of national capital.

Weizmann's religious habits would have shocked the orthodox wing of the Zionist movement. He thought of himself as 'a deeply religious man, although not a strict observer of the religious ritual', while others observed in him 'a natural piety'. He was observant, conforming to the traditions he had learned as a child, but he interpreted them in an individual, common-sense way as befitted a nineteenth-century liberal, a product of the Enlightenment. He attended synagogue on the High Holidays, enjoyed the festivals, and meticulously conducted the Passover service in Hebrew. But he took pleasure from these events as much for their social gaiety and cohesiveness as for their religious content. True religion could not be imposed from above. Genuine orthodoxy, as his father practiced it, he understood; Jewish clericalism he would never tolerate. He was resolutely opposed to the rule of the rabbis. Any attempt to turn the Zionist movement, or later the state of Israel, into a bastion of religious orthodoxy, of rabbinical dogma, met with Weizmann's emphatic disapproval.

Quite early in his career he had protested at the harmful influence of the rabbis, at the undue weight given to the *Mizrachi* in Zionist councils. Toward the end of his life he wrote to Harry Truman that it was never the intention 'that Palestine should become a "religious" or "theocratic" state'. His memoirs clarify the vexed problem of religion and state, and his own attitude to it:

> I think it is our duty to make clear to them from the very beginning that whereas the State will treat with the highest respect the true religious feelings of the community, it cannot put the clock back by making religion the cardinal principle in the conduct of the State. Religion should be relegated to the synagogue and the homes of those

families that want it; it should occupy a special position in the schools; but it shall not control the ministries of state.

I have never feared really religious people. The genuine type has never been politically aggressive. . . . It is the new, secularized type of rabbi, resembling somewhat a member of a clerical party in Germany, France or Belgium, who is the menace, and who will make a heavy bid for power by parading his religious convictions. It is useless to point out to such people that they transgress a fundamental principle which has been laid down by our sages: "Thou shalt not make of the Torah a crown to glory in, or a spade to dig with." There will be a great struggle. I foresee something which will perhaps be reminiscent of the *Kulturkampf* in Germany, but we must be firm if we are to survive; we must have a clear line of demarcation between legitimate religious aspirations and the duty of the State toward preserving such aspirations, on the one hand, and on the other hand the lust for power which is sometimes exhibited by pseudo-religious groups.

Weizmann stands out as a leader in the history of Zionism in that he led no party or faction; he led the movement or he did not lead at all. His one experience of factional life, the Democratic Fraction, had not been very successful. It was not that he was incapable of infighting—far from it—but he found it distasteful, beneath his dignity: he would not submit to the party machine; in his aristocratic way, he felt it would only hinder his style. On public platforms he would adopt his characteristic pose: slumped over the table, left hand on brow, gazing off into space. The parties would come to him, and he would deal with them *primus inter pares*. After all, had he not risen to the top almost in defiance of the official leadership?

Weizmann never seriously considered creating a party machine of his own. There was something faintly old-fashioned in his approach, as though he was unable to comprehend the new trends in politics and diplomacy. Life with Weizmann, one aide remarked, was 'permanent drama', a continuous summit conference; but it would be summitry in the style of the Congress of Vienna. He rarely pandered to public opinion: he controlled no newspapers; conducted interviews in an offhand, indiscreet manner, as though they were of little consequence; rarely exploited the radio. He lacked the popular vulgarity essential to a mass politician. He could only be a statesman—he was fitted for no other role.

As the Zionist movement matured, and party divisions hardened, Weizmann nonetheless found himself increasingly dependent upon party support to maintain his position as leader. He forged a working alliance particularly with the Palestine Labour Movement and to a lesser degree with sections of the General Zionists. But it was an uneasy partnership, as between primadonnas competing for the limelight. There was more than an element of *l'état c'est moi* in Weizmann's attitude to the Zionist movement. When the Zionist Congress forfeited his services, in 1931 and 1946, he was shocked, in a state of stunned disbelief at the impertinence, the *chutzpah*, of his critics. What would become of Zionist policy without him? What charlatan dared to usurp his position? What utter irresponsibility to endanger the destiny of the Jewish people in such a reckless way!

If Weizmann had one political *idée fixe*, it was his faith in the connection between the Zionist movement and Britain. This runs through his career from the unformed, intellectual gropings of the boy of eleven to the mature reflections of the elder statesman. London, he surmised on his arrival in 1904, must become a major centre for Zionist activity. Yet those early years were difficult ones as he grappled with the problems of a new immigrant. How often did he moan about England's intellectual poverty and pine for the stimulation and excitement he had left behind in Berlin or Geneva. In 1905, he wrote to Vera: 'The English Labour movement, with 1.5 million adherents, has not produced even one Jaurès or a Bebel.' And in another letter the same year, 'I must confess that we used to have false notions about the English and England. They have much that is good, but obtuseness prevails in everything. Well, God be with them.' Soon, however, he appreciated that what he had derided as a weakness of the British system was in fact its great strength.

It was in the sedate drawing-rooms of Manchester academics that he first learned the art of talking to British gentiles in their own language, of exposing his brand of Zionism to them in a manner compatible with their own values. Forever adaptable, he was already discarding the heavy-handed, overbearing, continental style of polemics that revelled in crushing the opposition with ideological sledgehammers, for a lighter though no less serious touch. He preferred minds uncluttered by ideological dogma; he suspected doctrinaire programme-makers. An empiricist by profession, he applied the principle also to his politics, and he found it among British politicians. Lloyd George's well-known quip, 'I am a man of principle, and expediency is one of them,' would have appealed to him. 'There is no *Derech HaMelech*, no "royal road" to Palestine,' he once told the Zionist Congress. British statesmen responded easily to his brand of vision laced with pragmatism. Listened to with respect in these august circles, he in turn responded to them. 'The English Gentiles are the best Gentiles in the world,' he said in 1911. He admired the system they represented: its flexibility, its stability, its social decorum, its quiet self-confidence, its clannishness, its lack of doctrinal strife. He succumbed to its mystique. Comparing the qualities of Oxford and Berlin universities, he concluded:

> Oxford is irrational, it is multiplied, it overlaps; it is twenty universities in one. It gives room for a smaller number of students than Berlin, it costs much more than Berlin. From a scientific point of view, it lacks much in comparison with Berlin. But it made England, Egypt, India, Canada and Australia. From the walls of Oxford there gaze down upon the students hundreds of years of science and tradition. When the student comes to Oxford, he finds that in his dingy room lived this and this great man, and he is inspired by it.

When Weizmann was lionized by London society, he of course delighted in the flattery and attention showered upon him. Although he often claimed a preference for the company of gentiles to that of assimilated Jews, there is no truth to the hoary legend that he was seduced by the advances of the British ruling class, that he readily succumbed to a process of 'anglicization' that somehow compromised his integrity when he was presenting the case for Zionism. As he himself put it, he shunned the prospect of becoming 'a hyphenated Jew'. Opportunities were not lacking for his absorption into the British political elite—perhaps a knighthood for his wartime services or, later, a safe seat in Parliament on behalf of National Labour. He rejected these gifts out of hand. Not only would they have signified a betrayal of his life's work but, unlike the assimilated Jews, he knew that he could never compete with the British on their terms. The source of his attraction for them was not an acquired English manner but his unbridled Jewishness. Richard Crossman wrote:

> The attraction of Weizmann for the British was precisely that he was the most Jewish Jew we had met. He impressed us *because* he was not Western, *because* he was not assimilated, *because* he was utterly proud to be a Russian Jew from the Pale, *because* he had no feeling of double loyalty, *because* he knew only one patriotism, the love of a country that did not yet exist.

Weizmann, in a mischievous mood, would no doubt have agreed with the fictional narrator of Gregor von Rezzori's novel *Memoirs of an Anti-Semite*:

> Besides, the specifically Jewish quality in Jews had never repelled me so much as the attempt—doomed from the start—to hush it up, cover it over, deny it.... One related to Jews in the same way as an Englishman to foreigners: one assumed they would not act like us. If they did so nevertheless, it made them look suspicious. It seemed artificial. It was unsuitable... the point at which our hair stood on end was when Jews revealed in their social pretensions their desire to belong to us. Not because we might have feared compromising ourselves by accepting them as our own but, rather, because the attempt was so feebly presumptuous.

Weizmann, the Zionist revolutionary, embraced conservativism in his attitude toward the British Empire. He based the Anglo-Zionist alliance in 1917 on a presumed community of interests between the British Empire and the Zionist movement: 'The welfare of Zionism is intimately linked up with the strength of British policy in the East,' he wrote to Balfour, 'and I feel that London, Cairo, Jerusalem and Delhi are very intimately connected and the weakness of a link in this important chain may have serious consequences.' He was too realistic to believe that this identity of interests could be permanent, but he wished to preserve it long enough to consolidate the National Home and enable the *Yishuv* to stand on its own feet. It surprised him how quickly the British came to regard the Palestine mandate as an encumbrance and no longer as an asset, and it disappointed him how slowly the Jewish people responded to the challenge of the Balfour Declaration, to this act of faith. Lloyd George had warned him at San Remo: 'You have no time to waste. Today the world is like the Baltic before a frost. For the moment it is still in motion. But if it gets set, you will have to batter your heads against ice blocks and wait for a second thaw.' Weizmann had no answer to this advice. He could only cry: 'Where are you Jewish people?'

Weizmann believed the British to be supremely gifted politically. They had learned the necessity of compromise; they practised with consummate skill the apophthegm that politics is 'the art of the possible'. But his reliance on Britain was based not only on the mystique of British greatness, or his belief that Britain was the most civilized and tolerant of the Great Powers. It stemmed primarily from his obsession with the political weakness of the Jewish people. And he often doubted the corporate political wisdom of the Jewish people. For all their genius, they were, to his mind, nonpolitical: too impatient, too obstinate, too rigid, too doctrinaire, too emotional. Almost his last recorded words were on this theme:

> You see, the Jews are a small people, a very small people quantitatively, but also a great people qualitatively. An ugly people, but also a beautiful people, a people that builds and destroys. A people of genius and, at the same time, a people of enormous stupidity. . . .
>
> We Jews can do something very good, something which can be an honour to us all and to all mankind. But we mustn't spoil it. We are an imperious people and we spoil and sometimes destroy what has taken generations to build up.

It took much effort and sacrifice, a protracted and painful process, to attain the degree of national maturity necessary to establish the National Home and eventually to create a state. If the Jews had to have a tutor to prepare them for this task—and in the context of international relations of the period there was no other option—Weizmann preferred to have the British over all other candidates.

The National Home was still in the nature of an experiment; there was no guarantee of its success. Persecuted Jewry, in the main, saw its future in western Europe or North America rather than in Palestine; the *chalutzim*, the idealists, were a pitiful minority. Zionism needed the protective umbrella of the British Empire until it had attained national maturity. Weizmann was wont to say that whenever he interviewed high political personages in London he kept his fists clenched: 'If ever I opened them they would see that I've got nothing.' He argued:

> Whatever revolutionary methods I adopt in getting the Jews into Palestine, I can't do it without the support of Great Britain. And if I want British support, I've got to win the confidence of the British Government. I've got to take the ruling class at its face value. I've got to put the best interpretation on everything it says. Because, if I don't, where am I?

From the outset, he had no illusions about the turn British policy was taking. But he was caught in a cleft stick, for every other alternative appeared far worse. In private, he did not mince words with the British, and criticized them, often with the most unrestrained language, when the occasion demanded it. Ben Gurion witnessed these scenes: 'I was often present when he spoke to cabinet ministers and to those in high places, and I was always astounded by the inner forcefulness, sometimes even aggressiveness, of his manner.' He wished to preserve the alliance and defended it, 'with my tongue in my cheek', before his own people. 'I did it deliberately because the connection between our work in Palestine and the British was and is precious to me.' In return, he was berated, often in the most vicious manner, by his constituents for his moderation. 'They want me to go to Downing Street and bang on the table,' he remonstrated. 'I could get in, and bang on the table once, and that would be the end of it.' Downing Street, he recalled, was his *via dolorosa*.

In time, the convergence of British and Zionist interests, upon which he had based his policy, no longer held. From the mid-1930s Anglo-Zionist relations moved inexorably toward a crisis point. Weizmann refused to lose faith. His policy revolved around two axes: either resuscitation of the mandate on its original premises, or partition, to establish a Jewish state in treaty relations with Britain. 'Who wants us?' he asked the Zionist Congress in 1946. 'Who runs after us? Are there countries which implore us to come under their wing? True, it is difficult to work with Britain. I know that only too well. . . . But I do not as yet see on the political horizon any countries eager for the privilege of building up the Jewish National Home.' He found it unbearably painful to even contemplate a break, let alone an armed clash, with Britain. 'It is axiomatic to me,' he wrote in March 1947 to a close associate in Palestine, 'that we can do nothing and we shall not succeed unless we re-establish confidence between the Movement and the British Government and the British people.'

It may well be that during these years he sadly underestimated the power of the *Yishuv* to fend for itself and that it was no longer as reliant as it had been once on the patronage of Great Britain. Even so, he refused to forget the immeasurable debt the Jewish national movement owed to Britain. Britain helped 'to lay the foundations of Jewish independence'; without Britain 'we would be nowhere, and many of our people who, at present, lead a good life in Palestine, and are making their contribution to the rebuilding of the country, might have been burnt in Auschwitz.' 'It hurts me,' he went on, 'that our people are not sufficiently grateful. Gratitude has always been a trait of the Jews, but their manners have deteriorated like everybody else's.' It was literally his dying wish that Anglo-Israel relations be restored to their former glory. It is fitting that his last recorded letter was to the Anglo-Israel Association:

A new era has begun, but the record of British support for our national aspirations will for all time remain a significant chapter in the annals of the British and the Jewish peoples. As one who has been closely associated with that phase from its inception, I heartily welcome your efforts to give new meaning and content to this historical relationship by promoting understanding, goodwill and constructive cooperation between Great Britain and the State of Israel. . . . May your efforts be crowned with success.

THIRTEEN

YOU HAVE SAT TOO LONG AT ENGLISH FEASTS

Communal tension began to mount in Palestine in September 1928. On the Jewish day of atonement, 24 September, a screen used to divide Jewish male and female worshippers at the Wailing Wall was forcibly removed by the police at the request of the Arabs who complained that it was an infringement of the religious *status quo* guaranteed by the mandate. Religious separatism fanned by national passions—a most explosive combination—enveloped the dispute, and within a year it led to the violence of August 1929.[1] The scale and ferocity of the outbreaks came as a rude shock to the Zionists. In the so-called Marienbad memorandum, composed immediately after news of the riots reached Europe, they set forth the salient shortcomings of British policy, with a demand that Whitehall stand firm by its mandatory obligations. Weizmann despatched urgent telegrams to the same effect to Ramsay MacDonald, now again prime minister, and Lord Melchett, head of Imperial Chemical Industries and joint chairman of the enlarged Jewish Agency. By 27 August he was back in London from his retreat in Switzerland, having postponed surgical treatment, to salvage something from the train of disastrous events that had overtaken the *Yishuv*.[2]

On 28 August he saw Lord Passfield (Sidney Webb), the Colonial Secretary, and a week later, in Geneva, where the Assembly of the League of Nations was in session, he met with Ramsay MacDonald. Weizmann's message was clear: the British government must not be 'deflected from [its] settled policy', it should issue 'a complete restatement of policy. . . . The Jewish people must know how the government will react!' But already there were disturbing symptoms of vacillation at the ministerial level. Weizmann had hotly attacked the Palestine administration, particularly its policy of disarming special Jewish constables, and on the general grounds of its hostility to Jews and its incompetence, and he demanded the suspension of two high officials, Harry Luke, the chief secretary, and Archer Cust, his assistant. He was especially riled at the tone of the official communiqués that spoke of 'clashes' between Arabs and Jews when they should have condemned the Arab attacks on Jews outright. Passfield's initial sympathy to these complaints quickly evaporated. It soon became apparent that he was being run by his officials—a conclusion confirmed by his wife, the redoubtable Beatrice Webb, who herself took a somewhat detached view of the riots, telling Weizmann: 'I can't understand why the Jews make such a fuss over a few dozen of their people killed in Palestine. As many are killed every week in London in traffic accidents and no one pays any attention.' Perhaps this attitude might have rubbed off on her husband. Ramsay MacDonald later told Weizmann: '[Passfield] is old, in some ways efficient, but he has the mind of a German professor and an indestructible belief in the experts who sit in the C.O.' For his part, Passfield regarded Weizmann as a 'rather formidable' personality to whom all doors were open, unlike the Arabs who were 'not represented, they are nowhere'.[3]

None of this boded well for the Zionists' future. Weizmann had no doubt about the basic antipathy of a majority of the officials in both Palestine and London; he had remonstrated against this phenomenon since 1918. On balance, they were hostile to Zionism and out to sabotage the National Home. Their influence was so widespread and pernicious, their prejudices so deep-rooted, that cooperation between the Zionists and the government became virtually impossible. In the past, strong ministers, a Churchill or an Amery, had held their anti-Zionist subordinates in check. Now Weizmann was dealing with Passfield, himself a civil servant by training and instinct. It was like a nightmare come true.

There is some truth in this hypothesis, as well as some exaggeration. But the precise historical truth is less important than how the Zionists perceived their position. They believed they were being attacked tooth and nail, and they acted accordingly. Yet one unexpected factor worked to the Zionists' advantage, the inherent weakness of the government elected in May: a minority Labour administration, dependent upon Liberal Party good will for its survival, beset by acute economic and social problems at home and pressing international questions abroad, it was particularly vulnerable to political pressure.

Weizmann played this card for all it was worth. Parliamentary friends from all parties, mobilized by Baffy Dugdale and Namier, rallied to his cause. Lord Balfour, although bedridden, was 'waiting for the signal when he can be of some use'. Richard Meinertzhagen wrote to his uncle, Lord Passfield, castigating the Palestine administration and calling for a full and impartial enquiry into its actions. The government had already reached a similar conclusion. At the beginning of September, Sir Walter Shaw was appointed to head a commission to investigate the immediate causes of the riots.[4]

Weizmann was not entirely satisfied by this move. He wanted a clear and unequivocal statement that the government intended to carry out the mandate 'in the spirit and in the letter'. Vague declarations of good intent, and a commission of enquiry that would turn into a 'purely whitewashing business', were certainly not enough. He feared that the commission, puffed up by its own importance, would exceed its terms of reference and question the mandate itself, without exposing, as he wished, the culpability of the Palestine administration. He vowed this must never happen. Perhaps Meinertzhagen would agree to serve on the commission to see 'that justice is done'? But in particular he pressed that the commission be granted judicial powers to hear counsel, who could then call and cross-examine witnesses under oath.[5] In the event, Meinertzhagen remained in North Wales, bird watching, while Weizmann's legal requests were only partially met.

When Weizmann saw MacDonald and Passfield he put forward his maximalist programme: full implementation of the mandate; a liberal immigration policy, allowing 15,000–20,000 Jews a year to enter Palestine; a generous economic and fiscal strategy; greater Jewish participation in Palestine's defense forces. Nor did he rule out a round-table conference. But first the Arabs must be told that the Jews have 'come *to stay*'; only then would negotiations with them be meaningful. The ministers listened sympathetically, but gave nothing away.[6] Weizmann, his physical resources spent, left to recuperate at Merano, where he remained throughout October.

The winter of 1929–30 brought him no respite. Rumours continued to reach him that the Shaw commission, despite the prime minister's assurances, was indeed exceeding its brief. Prompted by Weizmann and Baffy, his parliamentary friends arranged for a letter, signed by Lloyd George, Smuts, and Balfour, to appear in *The Times* on 20 December, reminding the government of its obligations and suggesting that another body be appointed to deal with major policy issues on Palestine. This was a remarkable exercise in public relations, but it had little effect on the train of events.

Meanwhile, Weizmann had to perform one of the saddest duties of his life. Early in March 1930 he travelled to Fishers Hill near Dorking, Surrey, where Balfour lay dying at the home of his brother, Gerald. He was Balfour's last visitor outside of the family circle. Their farewell, witnessed by Baffy, was 'brief and silent'. Balfour, frail and too weak to talk, acknowledged his friend's presence by lifting his hand to touch Weizmann's bowed head. After a few moments, Weizmann departed, choked with emotion. Balfour died on 19 March, and in synagogues throughout the world ceremonial candles were lit and the prayer of remembrance, *Ha'askara*, was chanted in his memory.[7]

At the end of the month, the Shaw Commission's report was published. It confirmed all of Weizmann's worst expectations. Harshly critical of Zionist activities in Palestine, it absolved the administration there from responsibility for the disturbances, saw no serious grounds for complaint against the Mufti, Haj Amin al-Husayni, and concluded that the violence was not premeditated but a spontaneous outburst by a discontented, landless class. According to this interpretation, the fundamental cause of the disorders was the Arabs' frustration at seeing their political and national aspirations thwarted by a Zionist-oriented policy.[8]

Two days after learning of the contents of the report, on 28 March, Weizmann and other Jewish leaders were invited to lunch with MacDonald and Passfield at the House of Commons. The Prime Minister was apologetic: 'Imagine my position. Here is a report and I have got to say it all means nothing.' Weizmann, his hackles up, tore into the Palestine administration: it was responsible for the 'pogrom', and he would attack it without mercy, he promised. 'It's a fight between a Jew and a goat,' he told the startled ministers, between progress and stagnation. There was no need for experts, 'only a certain amount of good will'. MacDonald, ready for compromise and admitting that the report was 'very bad', proposed sending to Palestine 'one big man who carried great weight in international circles, who would . . . wash out this report,' someone 'who has Palestine in his bones'. Smuts was his choice.[9]

This was a tremendous boost for Weizmann. Ever since his days as a member of Lloyd George's war cabinet, Smuts had been a committed gentile Zionist. Weizmann held him in the highest esteem and had pushed his candidacy to replace Plumer as high commissioner, though with no success. Smuts, for his part, believed implicitly in Weizmann's star. Recently, he had lobbied British ministers, warning them not to tamper with history: no Empire could afford to be unjust to the Jews, he expounded, invoking the terrible example of Russia. 'I shall always be your friend and help you,' he promised Weizmann, 'because I am honour bound to help and I believe in it.'[10] Whether Smuts possessed any real influence over a British cabinet must remain highly speculative, but there was a certain mystique attached to his name and certainly he was no party hack. Widely regarded as a world statesman, respected by most politicians, honoured by the general public, he could always be relied on to drop the right words in the right ears at the right time. Perhaps by a process of transference, Weizmann had a *penchant* for believing in the ability of 'great personalities' to retrieve lost situations. In the future, he would turn to Smuts time after time.

To Weizmann's consternation, MacDonald spoke in one voice, his government in another. Smuts was eventually discarded because of his spirited pro-Zionist views and replaced by Sir John Hope Simpson, an experienced but colourless colonial administrator and an unknown quantity.[11] Weizmann, naturally, wanted to make Hope Simpson's acquaintance before he left for Palestine. Having arranged this with Passfield, he hurried back from Merano especially for the meeting only to discover that the colonial secretary had reneged on his promise.[12] Was this malice, or second thoughts, or merely a misunderstanding? Weizmann assumed that Passfield's officials had yet again intimidated their chief. At any rate, he felt badly treated. He was not used to slights of this nature from British ministers. He told Passfield: 'One thing the Jews will never forgive, and that is having been fooled.'[13]

Worse was to follow. On 15 May, 2350 certificates for Jewish labour immigrants (those whose employment was guaranteed by the Zionist Organization) were suspended by the Palestine administration pending the completion of Hope Simpson's investigation. This struck at the Zionists' most tender nerve, and seemed an extraordinary act of folly in view of the round of assurances MacDonald had given Weizmann. Clearly, the Colonial Office was up to its tricks again. Weizmann shot off a number of protestations. Using the good offices of Malcolm MacDonald, the prime minister's son, who in these difficult days proved to be a resolute friend, he warned, 'There is I fear nothing left to me but to call my constituency and inform them that the Mandate is not being complied with and tender my resignation'. He was indeed under terrific pressure from many Zionists to do so. Saddened and 'ashamed for England, which I love and respect', he refused to lose 'hope or courage'. He would not abandon the search for a reasonable compromise.[14]

Ramsay MacDonald, too, was eager to avoid a showdown. In particular, he was concerned at the adverse effect the Palestine controversy was having on Anglo-American relations which, in any case, had taken a sharp turn for the worse in the late 1920s owing mainly to the impasse in naval disarmament talks between the two powers. Weizmann cautioned him: 'Palestine influences Jewish public opinion . . . [and] American Jews are very critical', adding politely, 'they trust the word of a British prime minister and are anxious to see those words confirmed by deeds.' MacDonald was most sensitive on this point. He handled Anglo-American affairs personally and was committed to promoting friendship between the two powers, an aim he laboured hard, and with much success, to attain. Weizmann continued to let fall gentle hints that if British policy persisted in undermining the mandate, 'he could no more stop [the protests] than you could stop Niagara'.[15] It was an effective card when played discreetly and skillfully.

Already reeling from the effects of the new restrictions on immigration, the Zionists received yet another body-blow when the government issued an official statement that virtually endorsed the Shaw report.[16] No amount of good will on the part of the Jewish Agency could withstand this kind of pressure, nor could Weizmann continue indefinitely defending the government tongue in cheek. His dilemma was acute. He would meet with MacDonald or Passfield, nail them to the wall, only to discover later that the civil servants had unravelled his work. The effect was 'devastating', and his work seemed akin to punching a pillow. 'The spirit of co-operation of which you speak so well in your letter,' he wrote to Malcolm MacDonald, 'does not exist in the Colonial Office at present. They not only place us constantly before *faits accomplis*, but they do so, if you will allow me to say so, to your own father.' Could he have pursued an alternative policy? Resignation, wild threats, dramatic gestures? What would he have gained? What would the Zionist movement have achieved? After due consideration, Weizmann informed Malcolm MacDonald, 'We shall wait patiently and try to do our best in the interregnum'.[17] Trying 'to do our best' meant reminding the government of its obligations, diligently and forcibly.

On the surface, the signs were encouraging. Malcolm MacDonald worked assiduously and successfully to defer some of the government's legislative proposals to restrict Jewish land purchases. In July, Passfield broke the ice and renewed contact with Weizmann, assuring him that the government only wished well of the National Home. In fact, he hinted, the Hope Simpson report would work to the Jews' advantage, for it would provide an 'authoritative reply' to Arab accusations. Weizmann, now wary, retorted that 'our conception of the National Home was that of a great Jewish settlement. To that end we should seek to pack as many Jews into Palestine as was at all possible.' But he exploited the marginal improvement in the atmosphere to resuscitate the so-called Rutenberg proposals, which called for an overall Arab-Jewish settlement as the basis for a comprehensive arrangement, while guaranteeing the rights of the Jewish Agency under the mandate.[18] Nothing materialized from these plans. As the summer passed into autumn, there was no substantial improvement in the Zionist position.

During these months, Lord Passfield had been subject to mounting pressure from the Palestine administration. If the government could be accused of dithering and fumbling in its policy, the same could not be said of Sir John Chancellor, the high commissioner, who held rigid views on the future of Palestine. Throughout the crisis he stressed the need for drastic changes in the structure of the mandate, changes that envisaged the termination of British rule and consigned the *Yishuv* to the status of a permanent minority.[19] Weizmann was aware of Chancellor's hostility, of his constitutional programme which, if realized, would ultimately 'destroy the policy of the National Home'.[20] But he could not be certain of the extent of his influence. However Weizmann juggled the odds, the troika of Chancellor, Hope Simpson, and Passfield offered only dismal prospects.

On 24 September Passfield wrote to his wife, Beatrice, 'The whole Palestine proposals were approved today,' noting in a moment of presentiment: 'Whether we can anyhow avoid a shriek of anguish from all Jewry I don't know.' He imparted the general features of the new policy to Weizmann a week later. Weizmann refused to commit himself until he had studied the documents in detail, but his aide, Namier, commented: 'the general character of the discussion showed a certain *empressement* on the part of Lord Passfield, as if to soften things and put a sugar coating on the very bitter pill. Our attitude was one of extreme restraint.' On the other hand, Passfield thought the Zionists' attitude 'very reasonable and amicable'.[21]

Very little could now be achieved to avert a break. Weizmann bade 'farewell' to Passfield on 13 October after yet another barren session. In the late afternoon of Friday, 17 October, the statements were delivered to the Zionist headquarters at 77, Great Russell Street. Namier was on hand to receive them. He took them immediately to Weizmann, who was waiting with other leaders at Lord Melchett's office in the I.C.I. building on Millbank. There was a feeling of despondency in the air. In Weizmann's car returning to Addison Crescent, Namier turned to him and said: ' "We have reached rock bottom; we must . . . say our political 'Shema Israel' [Hear O Israel]." And then I quoted to him Kelvin's words to King Francis I: "*Nous conservons nos âmes et attendons la main forte du Seigneur*".' Later that evening Baffy joined them, and 'it was as if we were sitting in mourning'.[22]

The papers that Namier had brought to Weizmann were the government's statement of policy (later to achieve notoriety as the Passfield white paper) and the Hope Simpson report. Both these documents, which envisaged drastic restrictions in the scale of Jewish immigration and land purchases in Palestine, and far-reaching constitutional proposals, were extremely damaging to the Zionist cause.[23] The white paper in particular was formulated in a manner to cause offence to Jews. Even Beatrice Webb, no friend of the Zionists, judged, 'The statement . . . is a badly drafted, a tactless document'. Weizmann was left with no option but to resign. At a press conference on 20 October he announced publicly his departure from office as president of the Jewish Agency and the World Zionist Organization, issuing a manifesto, 'In a Solemn Hour', to the Jewish people. With him went Lord Melchett, joint chairman of the Council of the Jewish Agency, and Felix Warburg, chairman of its administrative committee.[24] At one blow, the framework of Anglo-Zionist relations had been shattered. And the future and reputation of its great advocate hung in the balance.

The 'Jewish hurricane' that the Webbs had prophesied now blew at gale force.[25] Organized by Baffy, opposition leaders—Baldwin, Amery, Austin Chamberlain, and Churchill—rallied to the Zionists. Eminent legal names questioned the validity of the government documents. Smuts protested. From Wales, Lloyd George thundered that the British people were not 'scuttlers', whether in India or in Palestine. An influential group in the parliamentary Labour party, led by Commander Joseph Kenworthy and Josiah Wedgwood, revolted against their government's policy. Palestinian labour leaders were in touch with their British counterparts. Ernest Bevin, the powerful trade-union leader, who was running a candidate in a by-election at Whitechapel, told his contact, Dov Hos, that he would 'instruct my boys' to vote against the government if the white paper were not amended. Anti-British demonstrations swept the Jewish communities in London, Poland, the United States, South Africa, and Palestine. In New York, plans to exert economic and political pressure on the British government were rumoured to be under consideration—a warning light for Mac-Donald.[26]

MacDonald, by now 'very vexed', could not remain indifferent to this violent reaction. Not only was it threatening to strain Anglo-American relations, a corner-stone of his foreign policy, but it had already destroyed the national consensus that had hitherto dominated on the Palestine issue, and transformed it into a topic for acrimonious inter-party bickering, a development his administration could ill afford. Some form of compromise was inevitable; and the first gesture came from MacDonald himself, a sure sign of weakness. After assuring Weizmann that 'the difficulties' were of the most minor character, merely 'words, interpretations upon words, assumptions of what is or is not inevitable', that the whole sad affair was 'in the nature of a storm in a tea cup', he invited Weizmann to a meeting 'to enable cooperation to continue'.[27] They met, over lunch, on 6 November. MacDonald, tired and overworked (he was also involved in preparations for the London naval treaty, negotiations for an Egyptian treaty, and a settlement in India, apart from being in the thick of the world economic crisis), announced that the cabinet had decided to appoint a special subcommittee 'to consider the situation in Palestine' with Jewish leaders. Malcolm interjected: was it to consider the white paper? Ramsay replied dramatically: 'There is no white paper.' Weizmann remained noncommittal, claiming that he would first have to consult with his colleagues, particularly the Americans. As usual, Weizmann had kept the Americans fully informed; but owing to procedural difficulties negotiations with the British government began without them, though American observers were present.[28]

Weizmann, like MacDonald, had little option but to compromise. No precedent existed for any government abrogating a command paper, no matter how contentious. The most Weizmann could hope for was that it be amended in such a way as to render it meaningless. And, in his view, this was the point of the Anglo-Zionist mini-conference that met from mid-November until the end of January 1931, holding, in all, six sessions. Arthur Henderson, the Foreign Secretary, acted as its chairman, and, as a special favour to Weizmann, Malcolm MacDonald was drafted as his personal assistant. 'He has our complete confidence,' Weizmann effused to the Prime Minister, 'and if you will allow me to say so, our most sincere affection and respect. We should like him to be present as a link between us and the cabinet delegation, and still more as a link between us and yourself.' Conveniently, the day the conference opened, 17 November, a debate on Palestine took place in the House of Commons that enabled Weizmann's friends — Lloyd George, Amery, Walter Elliot, and others — to remind the government of its obligations and its precarious position.[29]

The discussions were involved and at times highly technical. Issues of high policy were dealt with by Weizmann; the details were ironed out by Namier and Stein in what the former termed 'the flea-catching memorandum'. Weizmann wished to exploit the crisis to wipe the slate clean and start from scratch. He turned over the idea of transferring responsibility for Palestine from the Colonial Office to the Foreign Office so that, as Namier put it, he could deal with 'infinitely more intelligent officials' and escape from 'Passfield and his clique'. The matter needed 'careful handling', but the Foreign Office balked at the proposal and it was dropped. At the same time, Weizmann worked to neutralize the ruinous influence of the Colonial Office by extending the terms of reference of the Henderson committee and converting it into a forum for major policy decisions regarding the National Home. The Colonial Office sabotaged this idea too, interpreting it as an intolerable affront to their authority. There were limits to the readiness of the British government to listen to him.[30]

Weizmann had to feel his way very carefully. His political antennae, always sensitive, were tuned in to the government's weaknesses, which he exploited without compassion; but he knew that it would be impolitic to overstep the mark. Not so some of his colleagues, or those who sought to replace him. At his back stood an outraged Jewish world. Voices far more strident than his were raised. Weizmann's opposition, more adept at scoring obscure ideological debating points than at patient negotiating, alienated the government instead of convincing it. Their shrill protests grated sharply on British ears. Jabotinsky's Revisionists, especially, delighted in 'pointing out all the iniquities of the government' in the most hysterical terms. Ramsay MacDonald, nettled by their intemperate lobbying, gave expression to a widely held opinion:

> I do not want to lose my patience with the Zionists but they try it greatly. They have gone very near to destroying any influence they have by their policy. They know perfectly well what we are trying to do in the face of great difficulty much of which they have created... friend after friend is being alienated, and I have had reports from Geneva which are anything but encouraging regarding their conduct there.[31]

This standing deficiency of Zionist diplomacy—an inevitable one, given the democratic nature of the movement—placed Weizmann under tremendous pressure. On the one hand, it was a pertinent reminder that he could go so far and no farther; on the other, it limited his room for manoeuvre and undermined his efforts to attain a reasonable solution.

During the current negotiations he steered successfully between these risky alternatives. He left most of the day-to-day haggling to his competent aides, Namier and Stein, and intervened only when major questions were at stake. On 4 February 1931 the cabinet ratified the final draft of the conference's concluding document, known as the MacDonald letter. There was one last hurdle to surmount. 'We want it made clear,' Weizmann briefed the Prime Minister, 'that the letter to me containing the authoritative interpretation of the White Paper shall be the basis of the law in Palestine.' Putting it as bluntly as possible, he went on: 'If a question is put to you in the House tomorrow, then you can still put matters right.... We are dealing with an administration [in Palestine] in which we have no confidence, and in which I think you should not have any yourself.' MacDonald acceded to these requests. The letter was laid before the Council of the League of Nations as an official government document, despatched to the high commissioner as a cabinet instruction, and tabled and recorded in the proceedings of parliament.[32]

Weizmann had every cause for deep satisfaction. The MacDonald letter was an important milestone in the history of Anglo-Zionist relations, even if it only repaired a breach caused by the government's inconsistency of policy. Although it did not abrogate the Passfield white paper, it constituted in fact the legal basis for the administration of Palestine for the next nine years. But also it heralded a period of unprecedented growth and expansion in Jewish Palestine. Immigrants and capital flowed into Palestine on a scale undreamt-of before. In a very real way, the economic and political future of the National Home was secured during those years. Of course, outside factors contributed—in particular there was the tragically negative factor of anti-semitism in Germany and eastern Europe. But without the letter, without the change in the psychological atmosphere (personified not least by the appointment of Sir Arthur Wauchope as high commissioner), Palestine would have been unable to absorb either the immigrants or the capital in such quantities. In short, it provided the *Yishuv* with breathing space.

Weizmann had also restored the Anglo-Zionist partnership, but it would never return to its previous degree of harmony or trust. The after-effects of this unhappy episode lingered on. Too much suspicion had been sown, too many words spoken in anger: the crisis was an omen for a dark future. Weizmann knew that his *bête noire*, the world of hostile British officialdom, remained on guard in London and Jerusalem, biding its time, waiting to recoup its losses. For them, the Passfield white paper had merely been pigeon-holed, not overruled. Nor could he be certain that a favourable political constellation—a highly vulnerable government that was easy game for a skillfully orchestrated campaign of public pressure—would again offer itself. 'The British are sports,' he took for granted. 'We had a fight and we shall shake hands after it is over.' But he could not afford to let his vigilance slip for a moment. Only five months after the MacDonald letter was issued he was complaining bitterly of official indifference to its rulings.[33]

The 'Jewish hurricane' that had so alarmed Passfield also struck at Weizmann. Throughout the crisis his leadership was under relentless, at times vitriolic, attack from those who sought to stiffen his policy or wanted to replace him. This had severely limited his diplomacy, causing endless delays with time-consuming and often futile consultations. In Palestine, Rutenberg, chairman of the National Council of the *Yishuv*, the *Vaad Leumi*, unable to adapt to Weizmann's 'system of work', was, Weizmann thought, playing 'the dictator' and needed taking down 'a peg or two'. 'He's a splendid fellow and a good engineer,' responded Weizmann, 'but he is hopelessly naive,' thereby terminating the discussion.[34] Rabbi Judah Magnes, chancellor of the Hebrew University, was also interfering unnecessarily, he thought. He was already at odds with him over the pace and course of development of the university. Now Magnes's connection with Brith Shalom led him into murky political waters, for which Weizmann had no doubt that he was quite unsuited. News reached Weizmann that he was negotiating independently with the Arabs, proposing to limit Jewish immigration and hence jeopardizing the possibility of an eventual Jewish majority in Palestine. As Magnes's ideas for a Jewish-Arab *rapprochement* filled Weizmann with horror, he translated them in practice as total capitulation to the Arabs, the abandonment of 'political Zionism'; he reacted somewhat strongly: 'that hypocrite, that Tartuffe! Magnes lightly abandons the Balfour Declaration. He did not bleed for it, he only gained by it!' When someone had the temerity to compare Magnes to Jesus Christ, Weizmann retorted, 'no wonder the Jews crucified him'. As for the Palestinian Arabs:

> Believe me, I know [them]. If we give way now we may as well pack up. . . . I too believe in an agreement with the Arabs; it is necessary for us, for the Arabs and for the English, but all three parties must assist and—give and take. So far we have done all the giving, have already explained to the Arabs what we are prepared to do, and that over the fresh graves of our brethren. The Arabs have not even once expressed regret for what has occurred. [35]

Meaningful negotiations between Jews and Arabs could take place, Weizmann believed, only when it had been clarified beyond peradventure to the Arabs that the Balfour Declaration and the mandate were irrevocable. Another political innocent, Albert Einstein, who had lent his support to Magnes's utopian thoughts, remained unconvinced by this diatribe, to Weizmann's intense displeasure. [36] His anger was all the greater because he did not need prompting from the likes of Magnes or Einstein on the need to attain a *modus vivendi* with the Arabs. It was perfectly clear in his own mind how to proceed: he had, since the late autumn of 1930, been in touch with Abbas Hilmi, the ex-khedive of Egypt, hoping to use his services to meet Abdullah and other 'moderate' Arab leaders. Nothing materialized from these schemes, even though Weizmann invested much energy and money in them, a fact that could not have improved his temper. [37]

But all were agreed that the Arab issue, after lying dormant for several years, had re-emerged in all its acuteness. The German Zionists were pressing for a new approach. In America, the Brandeis group had rejoined the Zionist movement and was reinforcing the anti-Weizmann agitation. Felix Warburg, 'a marvellous man' and supposedly Weizmann's chief prop, was now backing Rutenberg and increasing 'the chaos from day to day', Weizmann reported, with a nonstop stream of criticism, much of it founded on hearsay. 'Is [Rutenberg] such a sweet baby?' Weizmann asked Warburg who had hinted that Weizmann should run the Zionists as Warburg, apparently, ran his banking house. 'You ask me to become a Moyshelini [Mussolini]. He is impossible in Jewry. . . . I could not do it, because I believe in persuasion and education and not in compulsion.' Fatigued by this incessant carping, Weizmann compared himself to 'the Rock of Gibraltar (which, by the way, already has a tunnel bored in it)'.[38]

If those who could be considered his traditional allies were causing him trouble, his permanent opposition, the *Mizrachi*, the so-called Radicals, and Jabotinsky's Revisionists were exploiting the situation for all it was worth. Jabotinsky was his most dangerous foe, the only rival of sufficient stature to replace Weizmann. Recently revisionism in eastern Europe had gained considerable support, leading Jabotinsky to believe he could 'conquer' the Zionist Executive. Up to his demagogic and fire-eating tricks again, he had revived the disputatious question of the *Endzeil* (final aim) of the movement, which Jabotinsky eventually defined as a Jewish state on both sides of the River Jordan. For Weizmann this was so much intellectual froth, totally irrelevant to the real needs of the Zionist movement. Its only practical result would be to excite the Arabs and antagonize the British. 'To me,' he stated, 'a pronouncement is real only if it is matched by performance in Palestine. The pronouncement depends on others, the performance is entirely our own. This is the essence of my Zionist life.'[39]

When the Actions Committee of the Zionist Organization met in Berlin in August 1930 Weizmann declared bluntly that as a Jewish majority in Palestine could not be attained in the immediate future, and as the imposition of minority rule was unthinkable, it was pointless to demand a Jewish state now. He wrote to Felix Warburg:

> If a Jewish State were possible I would be strongly for it. I am not for it because I consider it unrealizable. If Palestine were an empty country, the Jewish State would have come about, whether we want it or not. Palestine being what it is, the Jewish State will not come about whether we want it or not—unless some fundamental change takes place which I cannot envisage at present. The propaganda which is carried out in certain Zionist circles, like the Revisionists, for a Jewish State, is foolish and harmful, but it cuts no ice, and you could just as well ask for a Jewish state in Manhattan Island.

Claims for a Jewish state would, Weizmann believed, only lend credence to the calumnies being spread that the Zionists intended to expel the Arab population by force. For the present, he fell back on the formula of a bi-national state, 'provided it was truly bi-national'. 'Equality in rights between partners as yet very unequal in numbers requires careful thought and constant watching. Palestine is to be shared by two nations; one is there already in full strength, while of the other so far a mere vanguard has reached it.'[40]

These plain home truths sounded very much like heresy to Weizmann's critics. But to argue, as some did, that Weizmann was opposed to a Jewish state is to make an allegation that will not stand serious examination. When the time came, there would be no more forthright champion of Jewish statehood than he. But he was far too cautious and pragmatic a politician to commit himself irrevocably in advance. In 1931, he might well have cast himself as an erudite teacher attempting to discipline an unruly and ignorant class.

Weizmann arrived in Basel at the end of June 1931 fully conscious of the coalition of forces planning to pull him down at the forthcoming Zionist Congress. The ranks of his supporters had thinned out. *Mapai*, the main Palestine labour group, favoured his remaining in office, even though opinions were divided. Ben Gurion, its leading figure, and others felt that Weizmann should withdraw gracefully, of his own volition, for a limited period, a self-sacrificial act that would ultimately serve Weizmann's interests and the movement's. Nahum Goldmann, then a Zionist radical, remembered that he had reached 'a gentleman's agreement' with Weizmann on this point. For months Weizmann had been hinting at resignation. '[He] is determined to leave,' Namier recorded. No doubt the thought of a temporary retirement from active Zionist politics was immensely alluring. Apart from the fact that his doctors had been urging him to take a prolonged rest, Weizmann needed time to put his personal affairs in order, to devote himself more to his family, perhaps to return to his laboratory, to invest more energy in the affairs of the Hebrew University. But he vacillated, unable to make the final break. Few are the politicians who retire of their own free will. Many friends were counselling him to remain, fearful of the repercussions his retirement might bring, nourishing his image of himself as indispensable to the movement.[41]

Sokolow opened the Congress on 30 June. The following day, Weizmann defended his stewardship of the movement in a lengthy address; it was, he told the delegates, 'his final report'. Presenting himself as Herzl's successor, he listed the substantial achievements of the National Home, claiming categorically that the MacDonald letter had effectively neutralized Passfield's white paper and restored the *status quo*. He emphatically denied having neglected the Arab problem:

> The Arabs must be made to feel, must be convinced, by deed as well as by word, that whatever the future numerical relationship of the two nations in Palestine, we on our part contemplate no political domination. But they must also remember that we on our side shall never submit to any political domination. Provided that the Mandate is both recognized and respected, we would welcome an agreement between the two kindred races on the basis of political parity.

Only steady progress in land settlement, education, and immigration would create the conditions for far-reaching political demands:

> The walls of Jericho fell to the sound of shouts and trumpets. I never heard of any walls being raised by such means.
> I have heard other critics of the Jewish Agency sneer at what they call the old *Hibbat Zion* policy of 'another dunam and another dunam, another Jew and another Jew, another cow and another goat and two more houses in Gederah'. If there is any other way of building a house save brick by brick, I do not know it. If there is any other way of building up a country, save dunam by dunam and man by man, and farmstead by farmstead, again I do not know it.[42]

Despite some memorable passages, Weizmann's speech contained nothing new, certainly little to keep his critics at bay. An avalanche of criticism fell. Jabotinsky pitched in, attacking Weizmann's record on every point, insisting that the Zionist movement declare for a Jewish majority on both sides of the Jordan. Rabbi Stephen Wise, Brandeis's man, taunted him cruelly: 'You have sat too long at English feasts.' In anger, Weizmann left the hall. 'This speech is invalid from the legal and parliamentary viewpoint,' he protested to Motzkin, the chairman of the session, who had sat listening to Wise's tirade. Chaim Arlosoroff, the rising star of the Labour party, bravely came to his rescue, earning Weizmann's eternal gratitude. 'You spoke in such a manner that it was much more than a speech. It was a great historic deed. And I am happy to feel that there is someone who will at one time (I hope soon!) be able to continue the true and unsullied policy.'[43]

That same day, 3 July, in an interview to the Jewish Telegraphic Agency, Weizmann defended his policy:

> Parity does not mean a bi-national state, which is vague and does not necessarily imply parity. I have no sympathy or understanding for the

demand for a Jewish majority. A majority does not necessarily guarantee security. . . . A majority is not required for the development of Jewish civilization and culture. The world will construe this demand only in one sense, that we want to acquire a majority in order to drive out the Arabs.[44]

No statement could have been more skillfully formulated to produce the most tremendous ruction.

Was this not an act of bravado on Weizmann's part, challenging the delegates to follow him on his terms, or to find their own way? He was clearly struggling for political survival. Toward the end of Congress, he received news that Ramsay MacDonald wanted to renew his contacts with the Zionists. Ben Gurion and Namier flew from Basel to meet the MacDonalds, father and son, at Chequers on 12 July. After reviewing the whole range of Anglo-Zionist relations, they obtained MacDonald's agreement to the concept of parity with the Arabs in any future constitutional arrangement for Palestine.[45] From Weizmann's point of view the mission was a resounding success. But for his opponents it only confirmed the impression that he was still feasting at English tables. In any case, Namier was an extraordinary choice as a Zionist emissary. Although he hero-worshipped Weizmann, he detested most other Zionists, his contempt matched only by his tactlessness in highlighting their iniquities. Weizmann's reliance on him could not have raised his credibility as a leader.

In fact, the interview with the Jewish Telegraphic Agency sealed Weizmann's fate. Even Arlosoroff thought it politically damaging. A vote of censure was drawn up regretting Weizmann's statement. No amount of behind-the-scenes manoeuvring convinced Weizmann of the need to retract. 'Please don't go to the trouble,' he told Goldmann. 'Try to get your resolution adopted by the assembly.' By 123 votes to 106 (Labour and a sprinkling of General Zionists remaining faithful), the motion of censure, in fact a vote of non-confidence, was passed. At this dramatic moment Weizmann sat on the platform 'like a Buddha', his face frozen. Jabotinsky sent a note to Vera: 'I am proud of my friends.' Vera replied: 'Thanks for the condolences. We are not dead yet.' Immediately after the vote, the Weizmanns left the hall, the scene of 'this ghastly nightmare', accompanied by their closest friends.[46]

Weizmann returned for the closing session. The occasion was witnessed by Weisgal:

Suddenly two ushers opened a side door and the figure of Weizmann, tall, stately, his expression grave, emerged, followed by a hundred or more delegates of the Labour Zionist wing. . . . The atmosphere became electric. An ovation began, spreading in waves from the galleries to the hall, and thence to the platform. The whole Congress was engulfed in it. Weizmann remained seated. The applause gathered volume and continued till he was compelled to rise from his seat. It was the signal for a renewed acclamation. The delegates wept and in effusive continental fashion embraced and kissed each other.[47]

The following day he left for Bad Gastein. Shocked by the enormity of the betrayal, of what he saw as a presumptuous act of *lèse-majesté*, he was in desperate need of rest and time to reflect on his future.

The Zionist Congress shrank from drawing the consequences of Weizmann's dismissal. Jabotinsky's bid to conquer the executive ended in failure. Humbled and disappointed, he stormed out of the conference hall taking his revisionists with him, tearing up his delegate's card on the way. Sokolow, who had dogged Weizmann's path since the days of the Balfour Declaration, was elected President. Weizmann dismissed 'the Panjandrum' contemptuously: 'Being a quasi Jewish Historian he is duly impressed by the fact that the Jews have been waiting for 2000 years and thus he is in no hurry.'[48] One wit compared him to an empty clothes-stand waiting for Weizmann to return to hang his coat on. The Zionist Executive, too, reflected continuity. Two Labour members, Arlosoroff and Berl Locker, were elected, as was Selig Brodetsky. And of course Sokolow, closely identified with Weizmann, presided. Even to the politically naive it was apparent that although Weizmann had gone, Weizmannism remained.

While recuperating at Bad Gastein, Weizmann was visited by a Labour Party delegation—Ben Gurion, Sprinzak, and Arlosoroff— supposedly to coordinate policies for the future. Sprinzak urged him to lead a progressive bloc within the Zionist movement. Weizmann refused, content, at this stage, to nurse his wounds in private, not air his grievances in public. But he maintained close links with the Labour leaders, particularly with the young Chaim Arlosoroff, whom he came to regard as his natural heir. He had much time for reflection. Despite his brave face, he admitted that he was 'completely broken, with a grave wound and a gaping emptiness in my heart'. Giving free rein to his tendency to personalize his politics, he saw 'old, proven Zionists contaminated by vanity, jealousy, vindictiveness, and pettiness.' His opponents were animated by 'hatred, vendetta, trickery and treachery'.

Inexplicably, George Halpern, a close friend, had been 'the main assassin', while his one-time student rival, '"old" Motzkin, played Pontius Pilate'. But what of the future?

I ask myself: is there a place at all for me in this organization? For years now I have stood almost alone, and my views are not even those of my friends. Again I ask myself: shall I start to work . . . for this would naturally lead to a fight against all that is loathsome, or shall I devote my strength to some great constructive work in Palestine . . . to a task which is free of Zionist politics and intrigues? And — let the dead bury their dead! I wrestle with myself fiercely and bitterly but have not yet found an answer.[49]

FOURTEEN

ENFORCED RETIREMENT

A the age of fifty-seven, Weizmann now returned to science after an absence of fourteen years. He rented rooms in High Holborn, London; equipped them as a laboratory; engaged Harold Davies, his assistant from the war, to help him re-establish his position; and began digesting the latest advances made in his field. But his ambitions ran higher. Even before his dismissal from office he had canvassed Albert Einstein, the most eminent of the governors of the Hebrew University, about the possibility of becoming academic head of the university, in which case he could divide his time between research in Jerusalem, the Agricultural Research Station at Rehovot, and a scientific institution in England. Einstein supported such an arrangement. But hints soon reached Weizmann that no budget was available for such an ideal compact. In fact, the plan was never seriously discussed. Weizmann, who had created the Hebrew University almost single-handedly, the indefatigable fund-raiser who had rescued the institution time and again, believed, not without cause, that he was being slighted outrageously. He saw his enemies in Jerusalem at work, notably the chancellor of the university, Magnes, to whom his presence there would be uncongenial. Left with no alternative, he concentrated his scientific work in London, where it cost him approximately £600 a year to run his laboratory. At the same time, he began gathering material for his memoirs.[1]

For a number of years he had been watching the development of the Hebrew University with growing disillusionment and estrangement. The controversy was reminiscent of his battles before the First World War. He wished the university to establish firmly its reputation as a post-graduate institution devoted to research of the highest order, before proceeding to graduate teaching. But, under the guidance of Magnes, the university had moved quickly into the field of undergraduate studies. Perhaps this would have been tolerable to Weizmann had Magnes shown himself to be a capable, efficient, judicious administrator. He had many fine qualities: he was an eminent rabbi with a distinguished record of public service, popular in the United States, strong in public relations, and a key figure in raising monies. But Einstein and Weizmann concluded that he lacked experience in running a first-class academic institution. Together they worked to clip Magnes's authority, to break his 'autocracy' and install an eminent scholar as academic head of the university. It was an uphill struggle, for Magnes commanded support among faculty members and in the governing bodies of the university. Relations between Weizmann and Magnes deteriorated steadily, and were not improved by Magnes's frequent and uncalled-for irruptions into politics, which infuriated Weizmann. By early 1932, Weizmann had seemingly lost all desire 'to get tied up with the university', to put his head into such 'a hotbed of intrigue'.[2]

But another possibility emerged: a School of Agriculture of the Hebrew University, to be based in Rehovot in association with the Jewish Agency's Experimental Station and placed under Weizmann's overall direction. The Board of Governors ratified a proposal for such a school, and an opening date was set for October 1933. Then nothing further occurred. Difficulties, not entirely unexpected, intruded: finding suitable staff and defining their status, and inevitably lack of money.[3] After much clarification it became obvious that the time was not opportune to implement the decision. Once again, Weizmann was left without an academic base in Palestine. But another opportunity came his way that was to satisfy his most cherished dreams.

Israel Sieff's son, Daniel, had died in tragic circumstances, taking his own life at the age of seventeen in February 1933. Weizmann knew him well. He was a contemporary of Michael's and had shown early promise as a scientist. One afternoon, when walking with Sieff in Hyde Park to console him, Weizmann began to expand on the fascinations of science. Suddenly he turned to his friend: 'If you want a memorial for Daniel, why don't you build a scientific institute named after him? I will be its first director.'[4] Sieff warmed to the idea and, together with his kinsfolk, the Markses and the Sachers, pledged financial support for the project. Weizmann chose Rehovot, then a small village some fourteen miles south of Tel Aviv, as its site, for the very practical reason that it lay adjacent to the Agricultural Experimental Station. (Weizmann was fond of spreading the story that he had been drawn to Rehovot because it adjoined Yavne, where, after the destruction of Jerusalem by the Romans in 70 AD, a great seminary had arisen, a place of learning renowned as the spiritual and intellectual heart of Jewry, spreading its inspired message throughout the Jewish world. But his pleasing explanation had probably been tacked on as an afterthought.) By April the foundation-stone had been laid. Exactly a year later, on 3 April 1934, at a modest ceremony, the Daniel Sieff Research Institute was officially inaugurated. 'The purpose of this institute,' Weizmann asserted, '[is] pure scientific research in all fields of agricultural and biological chemistry. It hopes, at the same time, through the application of modern scientific methods . . . to contribute to the development of Palestinian agriculture.' Inscribed over its gates was the legend: 'Work for this Country—Work for Science— Work for Humanity', which expressed succinctly his own philosophy. Typically, Weizmann insisted that it appear in the three official languages of Palestine: Hebrew, Arabic, and English. Some days later, jubilant at his achievement, he wrote to his bosom friend Lola Hahn-Warburg, 'My institute is built up; work will start there on the 15th [April] . . . [it] is a real gem.'[5]

It was, indeed, Weizmann's institute. He was not going to repeat the mistakes of the Hebrew University. No facet of its activities escaped his microscopic scrutiny: fund-raising; budgetary decisions; salaries; staff appointments; research programmes; building plans; landscaping the gardens. His sister Anna joined the minuscule staff of ten scientists.[6] Ernst Bergmann, a young and promising organic chemist, was brought, via Berlin and London, to be his right arm, relieving him of much of the tedium of the institute's day-to-day administration. Their relationship deepened to such a degree that the armchair psychologists among Weizmann's acquaintances believed they had discovered his 'substitute son' (Bergmann was four years older than Benji). Weizmann was, as ever, constantly travelling, and the way he ran the institute by remote control led to misunderstandings and some misgivings. Bergmann's scientific reputation was not matched by administrative ability; inexperienced in financial and organizational matters, his casual attitude eventually compelled Weizmann to impose a tighter system of book-keeping and general supervision, reinforced by a threat to terminate Bergmann's contract unless he mended his ways.[7] Other, more substantial differences later arose relating to the nature and purpose of the institute's research projects. But, for the moment, they cooperated happily and fruitfully.

Initially, the institute's researches followed Weizmann's own predilections. Work was resumed on his fermentation processes with their industrial implications in plastics, high-octane aviation fuel, and synthetic rubber. Using his pre-war experiments in dyestuffs and camphor-oil production as starting points, he planned, tentatively, to establish a pharmaceutical plant in Palestine with his Swiss contacts. Synthetic foodstuffs was another field that attracted his attention. Fruit Chemistry Ltd. was set up, with himself as chairman, to produce citrus-fruit concentrates. Professional contacts in Paris, his brother-in-law, Joseph Blumenfeld, and in Chicago, Albert Epstein, a world-renowned expert in food chemistry, allowed Weizmann to entertain bright prospects of international marketing potential. 'Some capitalists are already after us,' he happily reported to Vera. By the autumn of 1936 he was busy establishing fund-raising committees of Friends of the institute to secure its financial independence and academic future.[8]

Weizmann had originally conceived the institute as 'an integral part of the Hebrew University', or at least working in intimate cooperation with it. What he had failed to achieve in agreement with the university authorities he would obtain by his own efforts, presenting his short-sighted fellow academics with a *fait accompli*. Then it became clear that this admirable plan was doomed to failure.[9] He was still at odds with Magnes. His relations with Felix Warburg, who took Magnes's part, suffered. He also clashed with his erstwhile ally Einstein who, fed up at the Magnes group's filibustering tactics regarding his proposals to reform the university, resigned from the Board of Governors, hinting that Weizmann was exploiting him as a cat's-paw in his political battle against Magnes. Weizmann reacted sharply: Einstein 'seems to be acquiring the psychology of a prima donna who is beginning to lose her voice!'

In April 1934, the Hartog committee, which had spent months investigating the university's affairs, submitted a report that led to reforms being instituted and Magnes's powers severely curtailed. But it was in the nature of being too little too late, though Weizmann was able to rejoice that Magnes's 'dictatorship has been broken'. Nothing of substance had changed. He still regarded the university 'bosses' as 'savages'. 'Candidly, I have lost all confidence in the possibility of improving things there unless really radical measures are taken.' But the main bone of contention was the university's hostile attitude toward the Sieff Institute as his private personal domain. To add to the tension, accusatory fingers were pointed at him for filching funds destined for the university's coffers. Weizmann was deeply wounded by the university's attitude toward him, and the chances of a genuine *rapprochement* were slender. In any case, the "Family" (the Sieffs, the Markses, and the Sachers), who held the purse strings, wished the institute to preserve its independence, and Weizmann was content to respect their wishes as they coincided with his own. Although he never severed his connection with the Hebrew University—his emotional attachment ran too deep for that—henceforth he devoted himself unreservedly to the glory of the Sieff Institute, where he could work in peace as a free agent.

Weizmann's involvement with the institute meant that he was spending longer periods in Palestine. He went for a three-month stay in November 1934, and again the following winter. After so many years and innumerable visits, he was now viewed in Palestine not as an honoured guest but as a potential immigrant. Living there in fact came as something of a shock. What he saw appalled him: grossly inflated land prices; shoddy standards of workmanship; the selfish pursuit of material comforts. 'Our whole system of education is in need of reorganization and profound readjustment,' he wrote. He was witnessing the emergence of a *petit bourgeois* society devoid of the old pioneering values. Desolated by the experience, he conceded, '[we] do not live here [in Palestine] from free choice, but because of Zionist duty'. Later he told Namier, 'We have made a mistake. We ought to have gone to live there ten years ago.' Namier replied, 'It was not for me to tell you so, but [T. E.] Lawrence said to me fifteen years ago, "One does not build the National Home by living in a villa in Addison Road".'[10] In time, Weizmann toned down his pessimism, though he remained as critical as ever. From the outset of his career he had been unable to compromise with those who failed to live up to his standards.

The Weizmanns settled into a daily routine. They rented a bungalow—two small bedrooms, a living-room, and an enclosed verandah—and brought along their excellent Swiss cook.

I am alone in the house, Vera has gone to Tel Aviv to a cinema. I was too tired to join her, I was working the whole day. There is nothing else to do here but to work, so I am staying in the Lab from 9.15 in the morning until 7.30 evening with a break of an hour or so for lunch. I am not going away much from R[ehovot]. Sometimes people come to see us here, but we don't encourage it too much.[11]

Vera felt the change most. She so much 'wanted to have things like in London'. But she was already planning something much grander than London. Land was purchased; a famous architect, Eric Mendelsohn, was engaged, and work began on a mansion befitting her idea of the Weizmanns' station. It was to rise on a neglected hillock overlooking the institute to the west, in a derelict citrus grove on the outskirts of Rehovot, with a magnificent panoramic view of the Judaean hills to the east. This was Vera's special mission. Building commenced in the summer of 1935. For the next two-and-a-half years she waged a war of attrition with Mendelsohn on practically every aspect of the house, from indirect lighting to the size of the rooms, and usually prevailed. The costs rose steadily, from an original estimate of £12,500 to almost double that amount, to which must be added the cost of the land, another £5,000. Eventually, all the obstacles were surmounted: the removal of their furniture, insurance premiums, even the paving of a road to the house for security reasons. In December 1937 they moved into their new home. 'It is a lovely house,' Weizmann remarked, somewhat laconically. 'Vera has been working like a Trojan from the very first moment'.[12]

An imposing, three-storey edifice of white stone, the Weizmanns' house presented a novel architectural spectacle in mandatory Palestine. The politicians called it 'the White House', the locals dubbed it 'the Palace', while the children of Rehovot saw it as the fairy-castle of their story-books. Only Benji, less flatteringly, referred to it as 'the White Elephant'. It must have appeared as the last word in luxury, particularly its swimming pool flanked by the two wings of the house. Weizmann's library, a long, rectangular room which led to the patio surrounding the pool, was full of his personal mementos: presents he had acquired over the years, a miniature edition of the Bible on his desk, autographed photographs from his admirers, an entire wall of books ranging in interest from Judaica to organic chemistry to political biography. And dominating the whole was Sir Oswald Birley's striking portrait of him. The drawing-room, tastefully fitted, was adorned with a number of splendid works of art: a Persian silk carpet; a tenth-century T'ang dynasty horse; Ming statuettes; paintings by Utrillo, Dame Laura Knight, and Reuben Rubin, and an intriguing painting of Vera reclining, aristocratically, on a sofa. A bust by Jacob Epstein surveyed the dining-room, spacious enough for the most lavish of parties. From the hall, a majestic spiral stairway led to the bedrooms and guest rooms. The Weizmanns' bedroom suite, overlooking the Judaean hills, was spacious, with sufficient built-in closets to house their extensive wardrobes. On either side of the bed stood small bookstands crammed with serious and popular tomes, some of which, on closer inspection, proved to have false bindings, perhaps one of Vera's touches.

If Weizmann scarcely interfered in the planning and furnishing of the house, he took a keen interest in the exquisite gardens that set off his home to perfection. His chief gardener, Yehiel Paldi, had previously worked for the King of the Belgians. Weizmann insisted, Paldi recollected, that the gardens include 'long paths' so that he could conduct his guests for intimate talks in what he imagined to be 'the English style'. Baffy Dugdale, the first guest to stay at the house, was quite carried away: 'Here was the noblest modern house I have ever seen . . . perfectly expressive of its owners. Like them, it is a national possession, and I believe is so looked upon by all Palestinian Jewry.' It has since acquired the status of 'a stately home', a national shrine open to visitors.[13]

After the debacle of 1931, Namier had advised Weizmann to steer clear of politics, of 'those frogs born of the slime of the Seventeenth Congress'. Weizmann rated Namier highly but thought he lacked judgement,[14] and Namier's advice must have seemed great nonsense. A leader of Weizmann's calibre cannot opt out of politics. Every conversation he holds, every letter or article he writes, every meeting he addresses, even his physical presence at an informal gathering, has a political connotation. Was he even capable of retiring from Zionist work? No sooner had he escaped from the humiliation of the Basel Congress than he was urgently summoned to save the Jewish Colonial Trust from bankruptcy and aid Sokolow in the first contacts with the government, tasks that he fulfilled, grumbling as he went, before returning to his family on holiday. He reassumed the presidency of the English Zionist Federation, which accorded him some political leverage. In February 1932, he left for a four-month trip to South Africa 'to keep Palestine from collapsing'. The visit was a huge success (£100,000 was collected) even though he contracted ptomaine poisoning from 'a kosher kitchen which . . . was bacteriologically very unkosher'. Typically, he compared the life of the animals at the Kruger

National Park—unmolested, protected, benefitting from a bountiful home—with the abysmal state of his own people.[15]

In the spring of 1933 Meyer Weisgal implored Weizmann to come to Chicago for twenty-four hours to speak on Jewish Day at the World's Fair. 'What's in it for the movement?' Weizmann asked. '$100,000', Weisgal promised. Weizmann arrived on 3 July, spoke for ten minutes before an audience of 160,000, and duly received his reward earmarked to aid Jewish refugees fleeing Europe, ample compensation for the American razzle-dazzle at the Fair which he found distasteful.[16]

Weizmann's increasingly frequent incursions into politics were frowned upon by his sons as 'dangerous bits of backsliding', but he was pushed forward by his own inclination and the force of international events. Unlike many of his contemporaries, he had read *Mein Kampf* and he had not the slightest doubt as to the malignant significance 'of those comic-manic perorations, those crude commonplaces, those pseudo-scientific biological and historical generalizations', just as he was convinced that its author was mentally unbalanced.[17] The fate of the Jews under Nazi rule now became his most immediate concern. In Hitler, anti-semitism had found a passionate believer whose ruthless devotion to his twisted cause heralded a tragedy without parallel in recorded history. And the steady growth of Nazism in Germany had encouraged anti-semitic movements elsewhere. From the early 1930s Jewish and other refugees sought safety in the more liberal West, the trickle swelling into flood after Hitler's accession to power in January 1933. A month earlier, on his last visit to Germany, Weizmann warned the Jewish community of Munich, 'Hitler means every word,' advising them to flee the country. The following March he spoke publicly of Germany relapsing 'into barbarism', claiming that enlightened opinion in the West opposed 'the forces of reaction'— hoping this would induce the Nazi leaders to adopt a policy of restraint. Then in October 1934, he appeared as 'the chief elder of Zion', to use his cynical appellation, in an action brought by Swiss Jews against the distribution of *The Protocols of the Elders of Zion*.[18]

Hitler's rise to power, nightmarish in its prospects, reinforced Weizmann's conviction that Palestine alone could provide a long-term solution to the Jewish problem. In November 1933 he wrote to Felix Warburg:

> The world is gradually, relentlessly and effectively being closed to the Jews, and every day I feel more and more that a ring of steel is being

forged round us. . . . It is all inescapable, and every ounce of my energy . . . is going toward the consummation of that end [Palestine]. Everything else is a palliative, a half-measure, and merely postponing the evil day.[19]

The years 1933–35 witnessed a sharp rise in Jewish immigration into Palestine: 134,640 authorized immigrants, a truly dramatic increase from the overall figure of 247,404 for the period 1921–35. The problem was how to absorb them productively. 'Will they be able to push new roots into the hard soil of Palestine? Or will they end their lives here in a sort of exile, forever bewailing the past and unable to reconcile themselves to the present?' Weizmann's views on this matter had not substantially altered. He still thought that Jewish labour redeeming the soil of Palestine was the highest expression of Zionist self-realization. Now, this mainly middle-class immigration was disturbing the equilibrium between town and village. It was impossible to dictate the manner of their absorption, but new, untested forms of development, attractive 'garden-townships' like Nahariyah, which combined light agricultural work with a modest urban existence, proved most successful. At times, he considered selecting the immigrants, weeding out those 'unsuitable' for life in Palestine. But, as he fully realized, the situation was too critical for such fine distinctions.[20]

In his own field, Weizmann spared no effort to lure world-famous Jewish scientists, now stripped of all their honours and possessions, to make their home at the Sieff Institute or the Hebrew University; but his efforts were usually in vain. Fritz Haber and Richard Willstaetter died in exile in Switzerland. Others preferred the great universities of the West or, incomprehensibly, those of Turkey. He told Einstein, potentially the most prestigious catch of all: come to the Hebrew University, 'all you need is pencil and paper and a quiet corner'. But Einstein, like his eminent contemporaries, did not wish to take such a revolutionary step. In any case, soured by the Magnes controversy, he wished only to distance himself from the university. He found his 'quiet corner', but in' Princeton. In a sense, this was a luxurious pastime. As Weizmann recognized, the German catastrophe was so horrendous that 'even so great a man as Einstein fades into significance beside it'.[21]

Weizmann, beset by a feeling of helplessness, was convinced that only a concerted effort, the mobilization of the Jewish people in a meticulously planned campaign, could relieve the refugee problem in a meaningful way. It became his prime concern. In May 1933 he joined the Executive of the Central British Fund for German Jewry. That September the Zionist Congress, convening in Prague, nominated him to head the Jewish Agency's Central Bureau for the Settlement of German Jews. Unable to refuse, despite a professed reluctance to become involved again in Zionist politics, he obtained the assurances he desired: 'My work is completely independent and has nothing in common with Sokolow, who gave an undertaking that he was not going to interfere.' Master of his own domain, he acquired an organization and staff in Jerusalem and London which accorded him considerable political leverage, a benefit he exploited discreetly.[22]

After eighteen months of intense activity as head of the Central Bureau, he summarized its achievements, modest in relation to the overall tragedy but substantial in their own right. As he reported to his American and British colleagues, sixteen thousand German Jews had been productively absorbed in Palestine: academics, professionals, artisans, petty traders. Retraining programmes had been set in motion, cheap loans issued, veteran settlements strengthened and new ones established. A Department of Youth Aliyah had been founded under the directorship of Henrietta Szold, a particularly responsible and sensitive task. The cost of running these projects ran into the millions of dollars. But no matter how much time and energy were invested, or monies collected, or immigrants absorbed, these, as Weizmann was painfully aware, were merely drops in the ocean as Hitler remorselessly tightened the noose around German Jewry's throat.[23]

Weizmann's work brought him into contact with James McDonald, the official responsible for refugee affairs at the League of Nations. Weizmann, who had preferred Viscount Cecil for the job, described him as 'a small man, and an American to boot'. Still, he cultivated McDonald assiduously, and canvassed, successfully, to place Cecil on the Refugee Commission and to secure the appointment of Norman Bentwich, an English Zionist, as McDonald's assistant for Jewish affairs.[24] He looked further afield than Palestine to settle displaced Jews. The hoary question of Transjordan was again aired. Conversations were held with the French authorities to permit Jewish settlement in the Lebanon and Syria, but, fearing Jewish irredenta, they were prepared only to discuss, half-heartedly, the acquisition of lands 'somewhere in the north, in the region of the Euphrates'.[25] Palestine remained the only viable option.

Weizmann worked concurrently to alleviate the plight of the Jews inside Germany. After Hitler's rise to power, he met Mussolini twice, in April 1933 and February 1934, to solicit his help. The Italian dictator, then at odds with Germany over Austria and anxious to avert the 'disaster' of a 'victory of barbarism', appeared to show much sympathy for Weizmann's position: 'You are very wise,' he acknowledged. Mussolini did not hesitate to broach wider issues, telling Weizmann, 'You must have a Jewish state.' 'A great concept,' Weizmann agreed, '[it] is the Archimedian fulcrum.' But the burning problem of German refugees remained unresolved. Mussolini's motives for wooing the Zionists were part of a wider pattern to replace Britain as the dominant power in the eastern Mediterranean, which would allow him to appear as a new, more understanding patron of the National Home. Weizmann was too astute to be taken in by so transparent a policy. In any case, he would never exchange Rome for London. 'The Romans', he reminded Mussolini, 'destroyed [the Jewish state] *en toute pièce*', and he kept the British fully informed of these conversations. 'Dictators,' he reported to Ormsby-Gore, 'must always go *crescendo*. . . . There is, of course, a good deal of *braggadocio furioso* in all these blusterings. . . . He will fail in the end, as he must, but (like Hitler) he will cause a great deal of sorrow and distress in the world first.'[26] Nevertheless, retaining Italy's good will was essential, both in the general context of European politics and for the pressing reason that Italian ports were important staging posts for Jewish immigrants to Palestine.

Although he was out of office, Weizmann had never been busier. Apart from his scientific labours, he was still lobbying ministers and consorting with governments, raising funds around the world (his name guaranteed the highest rewards), and grappling with the German problem. For all practical purposes, he had never abandoned full-time Zionist work. But he refused to sully himself by associating with the Zionist Executive, that 'inefficient . . . untruthful and self-advertising' lot, 'trading with my old clothes', and wasting the 'public money' he raised. 'I see them [as] self-satisfied, complacent . . . basking in the sun of their exalted positions,' he wrote to Chaim Arlosoroff and Ben Gurion, continuing, 'And added to all this, there is the atmosphere of undisguised hostility toward myself which emanates from these people.' Under continuous pressure, particularly from the Labour groups and his American supporters, to return to Congress politics, he was not to be tempted. He told Arlosoroff: 'My time has either definitely passed, or it will come only much later on.' In any case, he was 'pretty busy' in his laboratory. To his American supporters, he explained that 'My present intention . . . is not to attend the Congress [of 1933] at all. . . . Congress politics seem to me to be of the highest degree of irrelevance'.[27]

He wrote these words in May 1933. A month later, *en route* to Chicago, he heard that Chaim Arlosoroff, aged thirty-four, had been assassinated while strolling with his wife on the beach at Tel Aviv. Weizmann had thought of 'Arlo', by now a prominent leader of Mapai and head of the political department of the Jewish Agency, as his most natural heir. From 1931 they had worked closely together, the younger man consulting Weizmann and in general following his line, though preserving his independence of mind. Weizmann was shocked beyond belief at the tragedy. 'The vision of him doesn't leave me for a moment. . . . Among the young—the most gifted!'[28]

Suspicion for the murder fell upon the Revisionists and their splinter groups. For some time they had been conducting a vicious campaign of vilification and calumny against Labour leaders, inciting their supporters to violence. Weizmann, indicting the Revisionists with every conceivable political crime, now held them responsible for Arlosoroff's death.[29] Even if a Revisionist had not actually pulled the trigger, the group had certainly fostered an atmosphere of virulent hatred that made the crime possible. But in his wrath Weizmann drew wider conclusions. He saw fascism rife in Palestine and the Revisionists resorting to 'terroristic tactics'. Arlosoroff's murder, he claimed, was also aimed at him. The guilt was general. Not only was the Revisionist press 'stained with this blood', but so also were the '*Mizrachi*; *and* the General Zionists, *and* the President [Sokolow], who was elected by Revisionist votes!' Weizmann had long urged the movement to curb Revisionist excesses, but it had remained indifferent to his pleas. Now it was reaping a bitter harvest. He saw no possibility of cooperation with a morally and politically bankrupt leadership. 'Patriotism is the last refuge of the Nobody!' he decreed, into which category he consigned 'the Motzkins [and] Ussishkins' as well as the Revisionists.[30]

When the Zionist Congress met at Prague in the last week of August 1933, Weizmann pointedly took his holiday at Zermatt. 'Prague does not leave me in peace,' he complained. 'I am being pushed and pulled. I receive telegrams and phone calls every day, they want me to come there and take control.' He refused. He told the Labour leaders Sprinzak and Ben Gurion:

I am bound to say that I'm horrified to be identified in any way with this Congress. . . . To sit with those people in Congress is in my humble

opinion tantamount to political suicide, apart from the abhorrence which
I feel—and which you must feel—to breathe the same atmosphere
with the Revisionists and their supporters.

He could not 'work in the Organization as long as it is ruled by fascism'.
Harsh though his judgement might be, it was sincerely and deeply
felt. He would serve Palestine in his own way, through doing 'really
constructive work' at the Sieff Institute and alleviating the plight of
Jewish refugees, independently of Sokolow and his ilk. His decision,
disappointing to his admirers, was cheered by his family and "the
Family" which backed his institute.[31]

Yet force of circumstances drew Weizmann back to Zionist leadership. The murder of Arlosoroff led to a radicalization of *Yishuv*
politics. 'The Jews are torn into pieces,' he observed in despair. On
the verge of fratricidal war, Palestinian Jewry presented a miserable
spectacle of disunion and internecine hostility. Efforts were made to
calm the hotheads, but to no avail. Talks between Jabotinsky and Ben
Gurion, despite some progress, eventually collapsed. A split was inevitable, and in the spring of 1935 Jabotinsky announced his intention
to set up his New Zionist Organization. Weizmann would no longer
have to breathe a poisoned atmosphere.[32]

Within the Zionist movement there was widespread dissatisfaction
at Sokolow's lack-lustre performance. Ben Gurion thought him a talented, erudite journalist, but quite unsuitable for political work: when
he did intervene in these matters 'he was simply ridiculous. No one
took him seriously.'[33] But the international situation had never been
more serious. Anti-semitism was rampant in Europe; Germany, in
March, had flagrantly violated the disarmament clauses of the Versailles treaty, an ominous sign for the future, while Italy, having consolidated her grip on Libya, was openly preparing to embark on her
Abyssinian adventure. More than ever before, Zionism needed a leader
of recognized world stature to represent its interests. There were vague
suggestions that Ben Gurion might fill the gap, but to his credit he
recognized that he was not yet suitable; nor, he insisted, was it a
propitious time to replace Weizmann.[34]

The Palestine Labour Party wanted Weizmann back. Over the
years they had become the key element in Zionist Congress politics
and by 1935 they commanded the support of 48.8 per cent of the
delegates.[35] They had not abandoned Weizmann in 1931; in 1933 they
had lobbied for his return; now, in 1935, they were in a position to
crown him, should he desire it. Ben Gurion, a critical admirer, put

it like this: 'He is a *great man*. There is a holy flame in him. He has a magnificent record. And he has an enormous reputation in the English-speaking world. He is trusted by the British Government, and Britain's trust in us is an important condition for our political success.'[36]

Others had reached the same conclusion. Stephen Wise, a powerful voice in American Zionism who had attacked Weizmann without mercy at previous Congresses, now reversed his position and pledged fealty to a Weizmann presidency. Labour and other groups, the General Zionists and *Mizrachi*, past opponents who were now prepared to acquiesce in Labour's initiative, constituted an unbeatable combination that guaranteed Weizmann the maximum of political support. And the Revisionists were not there to cause trouble. Obstacles of a different nature were also cleared aside. Israel Sieff arrived at Lucerne with a special aim: to convince Weizmann to return to political office. Two years earlier he had insisted that Weizmann devote himself to the Sieff Institute. Now British cabinet ministers had told him that the Abyssinian dispute might lead to an Anglo-Italian war in the eastern Mediterranean, placing Palestine in the centre of events. The pattern of the First World War should repeat itself—with a genuine Anglo-Zionist partnership. Only Weizmann could turn this to positive account.[37]

While this consensus was emerging, Weizmann vacillated. For one thing, family considerations held him back. His sons were reluctant to lose him again, while Vera would not forgive the humiliation of 1931. But he also recoiled from taking the decisive step, from putting his head back into this hornets' nest. He shuddered at the thought of indulging in degrading political accountancy, of endless, sterile discussions. If he were given a free hand, *carte blanche* to clean up the mess without fear or favour, to choose his own colleagues and pursue his own policies, it would be a different proposition.[38] Searching for a reasonable compromise, Weizmann proposed that he enter the executive to direct its political activities, retaining Sokolow as a figurehead president who would know his place and not intervene in matters beyond his competence. The delegates rejoiced at this noble gesture. But Vera quashed it, unable to swallow the notion that her husband would play second fiddle to Sokolow, even if only in matters of protocol. Perhaps Weizmann had counted on Vera's sense of the proper, for he now demanded total independence, with a kind of private politburo staffed by his own appointees. He would be responsible to the executive but not part of it, and he would brook no interference by individual members in his work. This was a desperate ploy. Weizmann's backers would not accept him as a 'political dictator', nor would they abandon the idea of forming a broad coalition. He was given the choice either to remain an ordinary soldier, in effect to remain in retirement, or to serve in the executive under Sokolow, or to become president bound by the accepted rules of the game.[39] He took the presidency. On 3 September 1935, to general acclaim and assurances of loyalty, Weizmann was unanimously elected (with only six abstentions) President of the World Zionist Organization and the Jewish Agency.

Weizmann returned to office in vastly changed circumstances. No longer able to dictate terms as he had done in the past, he found his room for manoeuvre severely curtailed. In the early 1920s, the Zionists had followed him with an enthusiasm that set few limits on his talents and ability and gave recognition to his outstanding political achievements. In time, the movement matured; more conscious of its collective strength, it was less willing blindly to follow him. Nowhere was this more evident than in his relations with Mapai, the Palestine Labour party, whose leaders were among his warmest admirers. But they were equally conscious of his faults. Weizmann had built his political power on personal contacts and influence, on the charismatic appeal he held for all sections of Jewry. A moody and volatile loner, he was given to intense personal likes and dislikes which, occasionally, coloured his political judgement. And he had stamped on the movement a highly individualistic style of leadership which, though it had its uses, was now considered outdated. Mapai's power, on the other hand, rested not on shifting sands but on grass-roots political activity in the *Yishuv*, on a political machine and knowing how to manipulate it to good effect. Yet both parties needed each other. Weizmann's political future hinged on retaining Mapai's trust and support, for no stable executive could be formed without them. Mapai required his immense prestige and authority to unite the movement; a workers' party, it required that touch of class, that air of majesty that Weizmann alone could bestow upon it, legitimizing its political coming of age. With a great international crisis brewing, with European Jewry under siege, Mapai understood that it would be folly to disavow his unique talents.

It was not a love-match but a *mariage de convenance*. Mapai did not wholly trust Weizmann, and now spoke from a position of strength. The centre of gravity of Zionist affairs was moving toward Jerusalem. Ben Gurion was now chairman of the Jewish Agency Executive, the major figure in *Yishuv* politics, and challenging for the leadership of the movement. Lacking in charm and a sense of humour but possessing many of Weizmann's other traits, he represented the buoyancy and self-confidence of the *Yishuv*, the conviction that Palestine Jewry, by its own efforts, could guarantee its future. Did Weizmann really understand these problems? Was he not too remote from the bread-and-butter issues that were determining the character of the *Yishuv*? Too set in his ways, too ready for compromise, too overeager for agreements? To be on the safe side, Berl Locker, a member of the executive, was sent to London to act as his watchdog, though like so many who came into contact with Weizmann he soon succumbed to the great man's charm. Other Labour leaders, Yosef Sprinzak and Moshe Shertok (Sharett), were also to be numbered among Weizmann's retinue. They shared his pragmatism and were impressed by his *savoir faire* and often surprised at his aggressiveness in his dealings with the British. Suspicious, yet conscious of the benefits he would bring them, they approached him gingerly, aware that if they came too close they would fall into his embrace.

For his part, Weizmann was more in tune with Labour than with any other group. Although no socialist, he had defended the *chalutzim*, supported land settlement, encouraged the use of national capital, railed against the Palestinian *petit bourgeoisie*. Yet for all his sympathy, he found it demeaning to submit to any kind of collective leadership. His scheme to reorganize his political machine, to bring in the reliable Namier, transfer dead-wood like Brodetsky, exclude the *Mizrachi* and other enemies, foundered on the coalition politics of Mapai. And so it would be in the future. Other differences, more personal in nature, were to emerge, particularly with Ben Gurion. Still, the Weizmann–Mapai alliance, based on self-interest as well as a unity of purpose, dominated Zionist politics for the coming decade and led the movement to eventual statehood.

FIFTEEN

STANDING ROOM ONLY

From the autumn of 1935 the international situation steadily deteriorated, crisis following crisis, sweeping Zionism and Jewry into the maelstrom, placing them on the defensive in a struggle for bare survival. Weizmann, brought up on sound liberal principles—the rationalist, the humanist, a nationalist not a raving chauvinist—was horrified by the barbarous and corrupt atmosphere. In May 1938, after the *Anschluss* and with the Czech crisis simmering, he confided to Blanche Dugdale:

> I am distressed that the Jews don't understand the apocalyptic nature of the times. . . . Part of us will be destroyed and on their bones New Judaea may arise! It is all terrible but it is so—I feel it even here [in Rehovot], and can think of nothing else. . . . A new leader should arise in Israel now who should sound the call; we are already old and used up, I'm afraid.[1]

At the Zionist Congress in 1935, Weizmann asked for a year to devote himself solely to political issues. His other commitments were too great for such a sharp break, however, nor was he, by nature, able to jettison projects that he had initiated and that he saw as his personal responsibility. Immediately after his re-election, the Board of Governors of the Hebrew University convened at Lucerne to ratify the breaking of Magnes's autocracy: his administrative and academic duties were drastically reduced, and he was installed as an ornamental president. Weizmann continued as chairman of the Board and accepted the position of dean of the science faculty with a *carte blanche* to organize it as he saw fit. On paper, it was a complete victory, but Weizmann had little time to consolidate it: he was preoccupied with politics, and he also had to nurse the Sieff Institute to maturity. He never cut himself off from university work, but the institute took first preference. As before, he intervened in every aspect of its activity, securing its finances, extending its research programmes, attending to the welfare of its staff.[2] Weizmann did this full-time job on a part-time basis, for by now he was engrossed in his political work.

The position of German Jewry had worsened. In September 1935 the Nuremberg Laws deprived German Jews (including those of one-quarter Jewish descent) of their citizenship and forbade intermarriage between Jews and German gentiles. Fresh efforts were needed to sustain this persecuted Jewry. Emergency plans to raise funds were put in motion, and a Council for German Jewry was set up under the chairmanship of Samuel. Much of its activity depended upon smooth cooperation between Zionists and non-Zionists, a matter for consummate diplomatic skill, as each side was a stickler for its rights. In all this, Weizmann represented the Jewish Agency's interests, arguing for the primacy of Palestine in any overall solution.[3] In fact, since Hitler's rise to power 30,000 German Jews, roughly one-fifth of the total immigration into Palestine, had been successfully absorbed. To maintain this momentum, vast sums of money were needed, and to prevent its being swallowed up in a wasteful bureaucracy was not the easiest of tasks. But above all else, a favourable political atmosphere was essential.

Weizmann arrived in Palestine in November 1935 to spend the winter in the gentle climate of Rehovot. The political climate was less inviting. The Italians had attacked Ethiopia on 3 October, raising the spectre of Anglo-Italian hostilities in the Mediterranean, which boded ill for the National Home. Weizmann speculated: if the Ethiopians were victorious it would signal the triumph of a native people over a European power; if the Italians won it would mark a decline in British prestige; either alternative would give heart to Zionism's enemies. The repercussions of the war were felt throughout the region. In Egypt and Syria, violent nationalist agitation in the winter of 1935–36 led to concessions by the imperial powers and new treaties of friendship with the nationalists. Would Palestine go the same way? Weizmann had no doubt that 'Our work in Palestine . . . will be gravely affected'. In November, Arab leaders in Palestine, their national spirit revived, put forward extreme political demands: the cessation of Jewish immigration; a ban on all land sales to Jews; and self-government for Palestine based on the Arab majority. Reporting to Blanche Dugdale, Weizmann noted: '[We are] surrounded by peoples seething with discontent . . . and this has its repercussions here; there is a tension, an uneasiness, in the air.'⁴

Even without prompting by the Arabs, the mandate government had long been committed to the idea of a legislative council, and in December 1935 Wauchope announced his intention to implement the proposal. Weizmann had consistently opposed this scheme with every colonial secretary since Passfield. This negative stand placed him in a complicated position, for here was the leader of the Zionist movement—itself perhaps suffering from a surfeit of internal democracy—adopting a typically *colon* attitude toward self-government, laying himself open to charges of being anti-democratic, which was very far from the truth. But Weizmann was not prepared to endanger the *Yishuv* by conceding it to Arab extremists. Asserting that to impose self-government arbitrarily on Palestine contradicted the letter and spirit of the mandate, he had perfected the 'parity of representation' formula and, in 1931, sold it to Ramsay MacDonald.⁵ He returned to it, as a fallback position, whenever the government re-opened the question.

At the same time, as Weizmann wrote to Namier, he had 'authentic information' that the government was contemplating new legislation restricting land sales and immigration quotas. This attack against the National Home conjured up images of the Passfield crisis. Weizmann's relations with Malcolm MacDonald, who as Colonial Secretary and later Dominions Secretary was also involved in these plans, cooled. From the dependable ally of 1931, MacDonald was now showing himself as 'a broken reed'. Harsh words were also reserved for Wauchope, hitherto a shining example of what a high commissioner should be. When they met at the end of January 1936, Weizmann, in an impassioned outburst, accused him of taking this action when the Jews 'were simply drowning in their own blood'. We will resist this policy, he warned, and 'fight to the last ditch'.⁶ Confident that he had shaken Wauchope, he decided to return to London to fight the government on its own ground. But already he was thinking in more revolutionary terms than simply killing the latest proposals. Polish and German Jews, on the verge of a terrible catastrophe, were in need of a more radical solution.

On the eve of his departure, he revealed his thoughts to Stephen Wise, setting out the guidelines of a great debate that would absorb Zionism for the coming decade. His instinct was as sure as ever. Adapting his policy to the changed circumstances of the time, he grasped that Zionism had outgrown its total dependence on Britain.

He was still feeling his way. He had no pat solution, only a gut feeling that Zionist policy was at a crossroads.

> I feel that now is the time to reopen the whole of our problem and with much more force, because of our achievement in Palestine and because of the critical situation of our people, than we did in 1916. . . . I think it could make a powerful appeal to civilized humanity.
>
> As a necessary corollary to such a formulation of the problem I consider the opening of Transjordan and the establishment of some sort of organization which may be less than a state, but certainly more than what the Jewish Agency is now. Only if we possess a certain amount of executive power shall we be able to conduct our business properly; we have grown too large for a merely voluntary organization. At present the executive power and income are in the hands of the British; the difficulties and responsibilities rest on us. This is becoming increasingly untenable. [7]

Weizmann arrived in London on 8 March, a day after Hitler marched into the Rhineland. 'Everybody is so busy with Germany that they cannot bother about us,' he moaned, a recurrent complaint for the next several years. Still, his gentile friends had on their own initiative organized debates in Parliament that roundly criticized the government's policy in Palestine. [8] Weizmann was not overjoyed by this display of independence, believing it might antagonize the government, but he exploited it to good advantage. Informed opinion held that the government's policy had been dealt a death-blow. A fortnight later, the cabinet agreed to postpone implementation of the proposals, pending further clarifications with the Arabs; in fact this was the *coup de grace*. There was even speculation whether Wauchope or Jimmy Thomas, the Colonial Secretary, would resign. Baffy Dugdale had decided, 'It is not fit that the future of Zion should be in the hands of a drunken ex-engine driver [Thomas]'. [9] By the time Weizmann left for Rehovot on 25 March, the assault on the National Home had been successfully repulsed.

Two months later Weizmann was in London again, dealing with a situation far more explosive than unwelcome constitutional innovations. His brief respite in Palestine had been marred by the outbreak of the so-called Palestine disturbances. On 19 April 1936 serious rioting had flared up in Jaffa, the culmination of months of mounting tension between Jews and Arabs. This was the prelude to a period of great violence and one of permanent crisis for the Zionist movement. The following day an Arab National Committee was set up and a general strike declared throughout Arab Palestine. On 25 April a Supreme Arab Committee was established, subsequently known as the Arab Higher Committee, headed by the Mufti, Haj Amin al- Husayni. Its demands were a rehash of the November memorandum. In this manner began the Palestine disorders, which were to continue intermittently until the outbreak of the Second World War.

There could be no doubt that the Arabs were out to strangle the National Home. Weizmann's initial reaction was that he must stiffen Wauchope's resolve, 'no surrender to Arab intimidation' was the gist of his message. A firm hand, cool nerves, and energetic action would serve both Zionist and British imperial interests. But it soon became apparent that the British were set on a different course. A Royal Commission of Enquiry was proposed: a well-worn recipe for vacillation. Weizmann contemplated boycotting it, since his experience of commissions of enquiry in the past inspired no confidence in yet another futile exercise in fact-finding. 'What was the commission going to investigate?' he asked Baldwin. By the time Weizmann arrived in London, on 17 May, it was already too late to influence the government's decision. The commission was a fact of life, and its terms of reference were communicated to the House of Commons by Thomas. Making a virtue of necessity, Weizmann bowed to the inevitable. His policy now was to squeeze every possible advantage from an unhappy situation. Provided the commission did not cut at the roots of the National Home, he would not withhold his cooperation.[10]

The commission's brief was clear and far-reaching: it was instructed to investigate the underlying causes of the disturbances and the manner in which the mandate was being implemented, and to make recommendations to rectify any alleged grievances of either Jews or Arabs. It was a most distinguished body. Chaired by Lord Peel, the other commissioners were the ex-ambassador to Germany, Sir Horace Rumbold (vice chairman); two experienced colonial administrators, Sir Laurie Hammond and Sir Morris Carter; a top civil servant, Sir Harold Morris; and an Oxford don, Reginald Coupland, Beit Professor of Colonial History.[11] By July they were ready to begin work, but they had to wait patiently in England until November, for they could not commence their enquiries until law and order had been restored in Palestine.

These were tense weeks for the Zionists. With the Arabs on the offensive and the British clearly planning something, Weizmann felt the need to seize the initiative and not simply wait upon events dictated by others. One dramatic stroke could turn the tide his way. On 9 June he met Nuri al Sa'id, Iraq's ambitious foreign minister, who had promoted himself as a mediator in the Palestine dispute. What was needed to bring peace, Nuri insinuated, was a signal to allay Arab fears: perhaps a voluntary suspension of immigration. Weizmann later regretted that he did not oppose this suggestion 'as vehemently as I might have done'. Exploiting Weizmann's lapse, Nuri passed on his version of the conversation to the British. The following day, at a Zionist meeting, Weizmann suggested that the Jewish Agency 'should offer *itself* to suspend immigration for a period' as a gesture of good will. This proposal was violently rejected by everyone present except Mrs. Dugdale. Ben Gurion's opposition was the most vociferous. Not only would it split the Zionist movement, he said, but it would instantly provoke civil war in Palestine, for it would no longer be possible to restrain the *Yishuv* from retaliation against Arab provocations. Weizmann retreated. He would do nothing to split the unity of Jewry, 'our chief asset'. Having covered his tracks with his colleagues, he then had to explain his *faux pas* to Ormsby-Gore, his old friend who was now Colonial Secretary. Weizmann vehemently denied Nuri's story, but the evidence speaks against him.[12]

What was Weizmann up to? If he was merely flying a diplomatic kite, it had been unceremoniously shot down, and with no great credit to him. The Mufti had made it perfectly clear that he would accept no compromise formula from the Zionists; he would not even cooperate with the Peel Commission, demanding first total capitulation. Or was this simply one of Weizmann's well-known indiscretions, a slip of his persuasive but loose tongue which he was unable to control?

Whatever the explanation, his friends in Mapai took fright. It corroborated their impression that Weizmann, perfectly at ease in the drawing-rooms of London, had lost contact with the prevailing spirit in the *Yishuv*. They continued to exploit the immense benefits his presence bestowed upon the Zionist movement, but this distressing incident confirmed for them the necessity of scrutinizing his every move, of holding him in tight rein.[13] For Weizmann, the very idea of anyone daring to supervise his diplomacy was an affront. He never accustomed himself to overseers breathing down his neck. But the unpalatable fact remained: he was no longer the free agent of happier, bygone days. Ben Gurion and his comrades trembled at the thought of Weizmann indulging in his beloved *tête-à-têtes*. Henceforth, he would be accountable to them. 'The king is absolute,' Weizmann observed, adding bitterly, 'so long as he does what we [Mapai] want.' In October, unable to contain himself, he wrote to Shertok: 'I have had enough of this passive role. . . . We are here being reduced to an Embassy; we are given orders to see this or the other man, but our suggestions remain unheeded. If times were not so critical I would . . . have left the Executive high and dry; but times being what they are one is a prisoner.' As for the future, he wouldn't touch the executive with 'a barge pole'.[14]

Mapai was aware that it could not afford to push Weizmann too far. It had to pamper him, to create the illusion that his hands were free, not the easiest of stratagems to play on a politician of Weizmann's acumen and temperament. There was an element of bluff on both sides, for neither party could really do without the other. Fully conscious of their strengths and weaknesses, Weizmann and Mapai persevered in their uneasy partnership, in the long run fruitful to the movement even if nerve-racking for the participants.

On 12 October the Arab general strike was brought to an end. It was in fact breaking up under its own weight. Hurt by its economic effects, the Arabs were looking for an honourable way out. The British, in a display of strength, poured 20,000 troops into Palestine, a tardy move that nevertheless earned Weizmann's admiration. But the British also acquiesced in the intervention of outside Arab rulers to resolve the dispute, a face-saving formula for the Palestinian Arabs but a crude exercise in 'bazaar politics' for Weizmann. The Zionists viewed this development with extreme disquiet, for, as Namier put it, 'If the Arab Kings had a right to intervene to stop a strike, next time they could intervene to start one'.

Other busybodies were also intervening. Samuel had drafted an overall solution that would have limited Jewish immigration to 40 per cent of the total population. 'A dangerous precedent', Weizmann noted, for it set unpredictable and erratic political guidelines to immigration policy which should be based on ascertainable economic facts. Clearly, the disturbances had opened a veritable Pandora's box. Weizmann's premonition that 'fundamental issues of policy' were now at stake was more than justified.[15]

At 10.30 in the morning of 25 November 1936, at the Palace Hotel, Jerusalem, Weizmann opened the Jewish case before the Peel Commission. He gave evidence for two-and-a-half hours. By all accounts, it was a memorable performance. Speaking as though the full weight of Jewish history rested upon his shoulders, he summoned up all the artistry at his command to win over the English gentlemen who faced him. He defined the Jewish problem in one word: 'homelessness'. East of the Rhine, the Jews had become 'the flotsam and jetsam of the world': 'almost six million Jews . . . in that part of the world are doomed to be pent up in places where they are not wanted, and for whom the world is divided into places where they cannot live, and places into which they cannot enter. . . . They are doomed, they are exasperated, they are in despair.' But the disease of Nazism had also spread to the West. In Paris, he had again heard the dreadful cry: '*Mort aux Juifs*'. In all quarters, he detected a nervousness, an uneasiness among the Jews, 'a minority everywhere, a majority nowhere'. He traced the historical and cultural attachment of the Jews to Palestine, the cardinal factor in preserving the peculiar state of the Jews: 'we have never forgotten it; we have never given it up'.

Outlining the course of gentile Zionism in Britain from Cromwell to Palmerston to Balfour, he denied that the Balfour Declaration was a rash wartime expedient given lightly without serious reflection. Quite the contrary, it was a solemn undertaking, deeply considered, rooted in British tradition. It was, he explained, 'the Magna Carta of the Jewish people'. And what did it mean, what was 'the ultimate goal? 'At that time and, speaking in political parlance, a Jewish State.' He reviewed the unhappy story of relations with the mandatory power, illuminating it with an anecdote from the Passfield era.

In 1930 Lord Passfield, a very practical man, a great economist, told me: 'But Dr. Weizmann, do you not realize there is not room to swing a cat in Palestine?' I do not want to be facetious, but many a cat has been swung since then, and the population of Palestine has increased, since that particular talk, . . . by something like 200,000.

Weizmann touched on the attempts to reach a *modus vivendi* with Arab nationalism, but '[our] hand which was repeatedly stretched out was always repelled'. The Arabs, he argued, had not achieved 'one hundred per cent satisfaction out of the war', but they had gained enormously: the Hejaz, Iraq, Transjordan, Egypt, Syria. All 'we have [is] this small land to work in'. Your task is complex, he told the commissioners, and you meet at a dark moment in Jewish history. 'I pray it may be given you to find a way out.' In a typical, parting gesture he presented a copy of Ahad Ha'am's works to the commission's secretary, John Martin.[16]

Weizmann returned home that evening 'happy' and 'relieved'. He received telephone calls, cables, flowers from well-wishers, visits from friends, congratulating him on his success. His appearance had been dignified, the manner and content of his speech first-rate. He had excelled himself. The commission had listened to him in rapt attention and with sympathy. The *Yishuv*, the Jewish world, basked in his glory. Vera recorded in her diary that the news of his achievement swept 'over the whole country and the morale of the poor people went up by leaps and bounds'. Mapai need not have worried. His reputation as the great envoy of his people took on a fresh lease of life. Peel later recorded that only Weizmann's evidence had impressed the commission. Looking back, Ben Gurion regarded his testimony as 'the most profound and penetrating analysis ever given to the plight of the Jewish people.... I do not think there is in the whole of Zionist literature anything as profound, as awe-inspiring, as penetrating, or as true.'[17]

The following day Weizmann returned home from the commission 'pale, sad and worn out'. Giving evidence in camera, he had been subjected to a testing cross-examination for three hours, a startling contrast to the brilliant monologue he had delivered the previous day. Vera noted his state of mind. 'We shall have to make concessions', he reported. 'They are convinced that our case is a good one, but the imperial interests are of the first consideration; they can't afford to quarrel with the Arabs.' Unable to enforce the peace and equally unable to guarantee it, the British were going slow in Palestine. He envisaged a freezing of the National Home, with the Jews relegated to the status of a permanent minority. Lord Peel had asked him:

> 'Can you and we take upon us the responsibility of bringing in thousands of Jews without giving them a proper protection?' Ch.— 'We think in different categories, my Lord. The Jews protected in Poland would prefer to live unprotected in Palestine.' At these words Hammond had tears in his eyes.

Rumbold butted in: 'When will the J. N. H. be finished?' 'Never,' said Chaim, 'England is never finished.'[18]

After Weizmann's pessimistic account, great gloom spread over his listeners. But it was early days yet. The commission was still fishing, searching for an answer. Perhaps, after all, Weizmann had sown more deeply than he realized when he had reminded the commissioners in the most emphatic way that the 'ultimate goal' of the Balfour Declaration was a Jewish state.

On 23 December, at another in camera session, the question of cantonization, a topic then much in vogue, came up. Coupland explained, 'Perhaps . . . instead of having a bunch of cantons, you could have two big areas, developing the possibilities of self-government'. Weizmann was sceptical. He refused to be drawn, despite being pressed to do so by Peel: "I do not really understand the proposal. . . . If there were a definite suggestion before me, I would do my level best to consider it.' Coupland returned to the theme on 8 January 1937, this time in a completely clear and unambiguous manner. Supposing, he mooted, there was no prospect for peaceful harmony between Arabs and Jews, what practical alternative might there be? He offered one, revolutionary in concept:

> To terminate the mandate by agreement, and split Palestine into two halves, the plain being an independent Jewish state, as independent as Belgium . . . and the rest of Palestine, plus Transjordania, being an independent Arab state, as independent as Arabia.

Hammond interjected, 'With a British *entente*.' Weizmann replied:

> Yes, I appreciate that. Permit me not to give a definite answer now. Let me think of it. . . . Of course, it is cutting the child in two. . . . I appreciate the spirit in which the suggestion has been put to me, and perhaps, I may be given the opportunity of coming back to it.

Thus began the great debate on the partition of Palestine.[19]

Weizmann's muted reaction to Coupland's proposal disguised his real feelings. Immediately after the session, he took his private secretary, Yeheskiel Saharoff, for a walk on Mount Scopus to clear his head. He became very excited, highly emotional. 'I foresee the destruction of European Jewry,' he cried, 'and therefore the proposal is so important. No matter how big it will be—we shall be our own masters. We could save a lot of them.' Saharoff 'had never seen "the chief" in so exalted a mood . . . his voice would be suddenly choked by emotion and his eyes filled with tears. All his love for his people, all his love for England, rushed to the surface.' His life's labour, everything he had toiled for, was now within his reach: 'The Jewish state was at hand.'

At the end of January, elated and keyed up, Weizmann met Coupland at Nahalal, a cooperative farm in lower Galilee which he held in special esteem. It was a cold, wintry day as they made their way along the muddy paths to a hut where they were to be closeted together until evening. Coupland, in his academic way, was turning over a number of alternatives, partition among them. Weizmann put the pertinent question: could Britain, given the precarious nature of her strategic situation, any longer guarantee the conditions necessary for the healthy development of the National Home? In Weizmann's view, clearly not. There remained one viable proposition: partition of the mandate territories. Convinced at last, Coupland finally said to him: 'There needs to be an operation; no honest doctor will recommend aspirins and a hot-water bottle.' At dusk, they emerged from their confidential talk. Weizmann turned to a group of settlers waiting expectantly nearby: 'Chevra [comrades], today we laid the basis for the Jewish State!' He then left for Haifa to inform his mother of the good news.[20]

Weizmann became resolutely committed to partition. He grasped immediately that Coupland's proposal had killed the old mandate and that it could not be resuscitated artificially. 'The Jews would be fools not to accept it, even if it were the size of a table-cloth. This Chaim strongly feels,' recorded Baffy on 1 February. The passing of time only strengthened his conviction, obsessed as he was by the fate of European Jews. He carried his London Zionists with him. He even listed additional converts: Leon Blum; Leo Amery—'could . . . [we] call it Judaea'; and a prize catch, Wauchope himself.[21] But he had to move cautiously. Opposition to the scheme, which by the early spring was common knowledge, was widespread. Naturally, the Revisionists fulminated against it. 'Froth and show', derided Weizmann. Jabotinsky's evidence before the commission had contained 'many good and new points, but the good isn't new and the new isn't good'.[22] A broad coalition of Zionists, from the extreme right to the extreme left, including the religious groups and some sections of Mapai, opposed the idea of partition, either invoking the sacred principle of the indivisibility of Palestine on national-religious grounds or else espousing high principles of working-class solidarity.

Weizmann appreciated their apprehension and suspicion, but he was convinced that they could no longer shackle themselves to outmoded policies. Events had overtaken them and they had to adapt accordingly. His own tactics were clear. Partition must not be regarded as Zionist-inspired, but rather as a scheme foisted upon them which they were prepared to consider for want of a better alternative. This required a most delicate touch, which the Zionists were not always capable of applying. Even Weizmann overstepped Shertok's modest bounds by his overt 'enthusiasm for the project'.[23]

Weizmann's most immediate concern was to construct a pro-partition coalition at the forthcoming Zionist Congress, and to achieve this he needed the support of Mapai, among whose leaders Ben Gurion was of crucial importance. At a meeting of the Mapai central committee at the beginning of February 1937, Ben Gurion argued for 'a positive radical solution', an aphorism denoting acceptance of the principle of partition, and envisaged an eventual Jewish state in treaty relations with Britain. He was quick to point out, however, that he would not accept partition 'at any price' or 'under any conditions'; only if given sufficient territory and real sovereignty would it be 'the solution'. In fact, nothing of substance separated Ben Gurion's approach from Weizmann's. Both leaders favoured the concept of partition and were of one mind regarding the conditions, territorial and otherwise, necessary to make it workable from a Zionist point of view. They were also in agreement regarding the tactics to be employed in attaining their joint aim: to allow the British to take the lead, with the Zionists allowing themselves to be pulled reluctantly after them.

But Ben Gurion profoundly distrusted Weizmann's ability to negotiate a satisfactory partition. In a series of ill-chosen and violent phrases, he claimed that Weizmann was the worst possible choice to conduct the political negotiations. 'In my opinion,' he told his Mapai comrades, Weizmann 'is the most dangerous figure in Zionism'. He could not be relied upon. Unable to control his emotions, Weizmann would blurt out in public his enthusiasm for partition, thereby conceding the initiative to the British while at the same time fomenting an internal crisis in the Zionist movement. Ben Gurion shuddered at the thought of an unchaperoned Weizmann roaming the corridors of Whitehall (and indeed three members of Mapai's central committee— Moshe Shertok, Dov Hos, and Berl Katznelson—were quickly despatched to London, to be joined later by Ben Gurion himself). Something of these remarks must have been leaked to Weizmann in London, for on 2 March Mrs. Dugdale noted 'the growing rift between Chaim and Ben Gurion who is making the most foolish and intransigent speeches. . . . We all try to soothe Chaim, who is very angry.' By April, Ben Gurion had calmed down, appeased no doubt by Weizmann's diplomatic performances which contradicted his own grim forecasts. However, it was not until late June that Mrs. Dugdale felt confident enough to record that 'Ben Gurion will now stand or fall with Chaim,' even though some of his colleagues remained staunchly anti-partitionist.[24]

Weizmann fell under attack from all quarters. In America, Felix Warburg was threatening the break-up of the Jewish Agency, claiming that a small Jewish state would undo twenty years of effort and building in Palestine. In London, the *Jewish Chronicle* denounced partition as 'an evil and intolerable thing', impossible for any decent Zionist to support. Weizmann reacted angrily:

> I can see from the news . . . that the floodgates of demagogic eloquence are wide open and the zealots are gnashing their teeth and clenching their fists. I suppose I'm the 'traitor' [i.e. author of the scheme]. The zealots have since time immemorial brought misfortune on the heads of our people, but I am sure they will not succeed this time. Either the project of division (which is not *my* proposal) is sound and 'viable', then it will be accepted, or it is unsound, then we shall all reject it. To make political capital out of the thing before we know how it looks is folly, but you cannot save people from their own stupidity. I can hear my old friend Uss.[ishkin] raging and tearing about 'Uganda'. But it won't wash. . . .
>
> It is the reality of life as against the obscurantism of a few who may sway certain delegates at the Congress but who will be disavowed by the stern facts![25]

To Stephen Wise, he pleaded for unity and cool heads, elaborating his own position, defending himself against the slanderous accusation that he had sold his Zionist birthright for a mess of British pottage:

> Partition is not *my* project; it has never been and never will be my project. It was sprung upon me in the last hour of the four secret sessions. . . . I refused to give an opinion off-hand; I consulted my colleagues; and I think I am speaking the truth when I say that our general conclusion was: Here is a new line of thought—an audacious proposal; it contains in it the germs of a great future, but also grave dangers; everything will depend on the details. . . . We felt that it would be wrong to let the thing go by default by simply saying 'No'. . . . We should have fallen between two stools, and taken upon ourselves the responsibility for almost certain failure within the next twenty-five years.
>
> I may be wrong in all this. Perhaps I am too close to the events themselves, too steeped in them, to have an unbiased judgement. But I do feel that to return to the old machine, which is a constant source of friction . . . would be like going back to bondage.

He continued, reaffirming his life-long faith:

> It is our destiny to get Palestine, and this destiny will be fulfilled
> someday, somehow. Our present task is to get a fulcrum on which to
> place a lever, and if we are capable, within the area allotted to us, of
> bringing in 50,000 to 60,000 Jews a year for the next twenty years or
> so . . . then our job is to make the best of such an opportunity in our
> own house, with our own forces, as a small sovereign State, leaving the
> problems of expansion and extension to future generations. There is
> no absolute in this world; everything is in flux. This is my own honest
> conviction, but I would repeat to the world we stand uncommitted. . . .
> It may be either a Solomon's judgement or a Caesarian operation: it
> depends on how it is carried out.[26]

At immense cost to his physical and mental resources, Weizmann
formed a workable pro-partition alliance that would follow his lead at
the Congress in August. But his energies were also directed to building
up support among British politicians. On 8 June he dined with Sir
Archibald Sinclair, Amery, Clement Attlee, Josiah Wedgwood, Victor
Cazalet, and James de Rothschild, with Churchill as the guest of
honour. Lloyd George was unable to attend, but he promised to abide
by the decisions of the group. Weizmann put the case for partition.
With the exception of Amery, all those present opposed the scheme.
Apart from the countless technical difficulties involved, they regarded
it as a concession to violence, a confession of failure, a triumph of
fascism—a disastrous example for a great imperial power to set. Wedgwood argued for 'six months of resolute government'. Churchill, apparently quite inebriated, turned to Weizmann and declared: 'You know,
you are our master—and yours, and yours [pointing to other members
of the party]—and what you say goes. If you ask us to fight, we shall
fight like tigers.'[27] Weizmann had bargained for a more enthusiastic
reception. Churchill's warning that the government were 'a lot of lily-
livered rabbits' and would surely betray them again rang true in his
ears, given the turn of international events.

Baffy Dugdale saw the Peel Commission's report, which was made
available to her by Walter Elliot, a cabinet minister and her close
companion, at the Savoy Grill 'about midnight' on 22 June. 'Nothing
in all this that cannot be adjusted by negotiation', was her first reaction.[28] Two weeks later, on 7 July, the document was released to

the less privileged public. Weizmann's immediate impression was favourable.

> On the whole it is not bad. The boundaries . . . are more skimpy than I thought and what I was a definitely given to understand.
>
> Somebody asked me what he should write about the boundaries. I advised him to place at the head of the article: 'standing room only!'
>
> On the other hand it is a beginning of a new chapter in Jewish History. The kingdom of David was smaller; under Solomon it became an Empire. Who knows? *C'est le premier pas qui coute!*[29]

Yet, at the moment of greatest need, Zionist cooperation with the government was gravely endangered. Weizmann's first request for an advance copy of the report had been refused. 'So you want to strangle us in the dark?' he snapped at his friend Ormsby-Gore. 'We shall fight you from San Francisco to Jerusalem; what you are doing is an unfriendly act.' No amount of pacification by Ormsby-Gore, hitherto one of Weizmann's favourites, availed. Of more significance, the government, although it had endorsed the partition plan, also proposed to restrict immigration to 8000 for an eight-month period beginning in August. This threw the Zionists into utter confusion. Ben Gurion ranted against the 'bloody British'; Weizmann fired off his protests. But nothing would move the government. The clause on immigration remained as a most dangerous precedent. The Zionists' minimum conditions for a Jewish state—full sovereignty preceded by a short transitionary period; and substantial additions of territory, particularly the inclusion of Jewish Jerusalem and the Negev—were left unfulfilled.[30]

Weizmann left London on 22 July to attend the Zionist Congress. But first, he was in need of relaxation. Planning 'a four or five days' "tramp" in a Ford with [Michael],' he felt the need to 'get out of London; my brain is just reeling and I shall have to face a heavy barrage at the Congress.'[31] On 1 August he arrived in Zurich to persuade Congress to accept the principle of partition. The British, he felt, had let him down, and he was by now 'quite obsessed with that distrust of British good will which had burst into flame' when he had learned of the government's immigration restrictions. Nor could he have gained much comfort from the debates in Parliament, where the report was roughly handled, and the call had gone out for another inquiry before presenting a definite scheme.[32] Yet his own faith in partition was as firm as ever. He had recognized immediately the revolutionary character of the proposal. Never before had a great power lent its support to the concept of a Jewish state. In politics, one has to seize the opportune moment lest it slip away forever. 'You cannot turn the clock back,' he warned his coterie.[33] And delay could be fatal. Convinced that only a Jewish state could offer an immediate, viable cure for the afflictions of European Jewry, and supported by Ben Gurion and Shertok, he prepared to extract from a grudging Congress consent to his policy.

On 4 August 1937 he rose before a capacity audience in the Tonhalle to deliver his key speech. The Jewish position, he reminded them, can be rendered in a saying of the Talmud: 'If the jug falls upon the stone, woe to the jug. If the stone falls upon the jug, woe to the jug.' Then followed a passionate, emotional attack upon the British government.

> I say this, I, who for twenty years have made it my life-work to explain the Jewish people to the British, and the British people to the Jews. And I say it to you, who so often girded at me, and attacked me, just because I had taken that task upon myself. But the limit has been reached. We cannot even discuss such proposals, there is no psychological criterion for immigration [among the 'palliatives' proposed by the commission should partition prove impracticable]. Gates are opened or closed on definite principles. I say to the Mandatory Power: You shall not outrage the Jewish nation. You shall not play fast and loose with the Jewish people. Say to us frankly that the National Home is closed, and we shall know where we stand. But this trifling with a nation bleeding from a thousand wounds must not be done by the British whose empire is built on moral principles—that mighty empire must not commit this sin against the People of the Book. Tell us the truth. This at least we have deserved.

At this point, overcome with emotion, he asked for a recess of five minutes.

Returning to the rostrum, Weizmann refused to discuss the Peel Commission's partition plan. It 'is unacceptable [prolonged applause]. I speak of the idea, the principle, the perspectives which the proposal opens up'. In appraising the principle, he laid down two basic criteria. 'Does it offer a basis for a genuine growth of Jewish life?... of our young Palestinian culture... for rearing true men and women, for creating a Jewish agriculture, industry, literature, etc, in short all that the ideal of Zionism comprises?' This, he pointed out, might have been sufficient for 'our great teacher, Ahad Ha'am'. But times had changed, and it was necessary to apply another test: 'Does the proposal contribute to the solution of the Jewish problem—a problem pregnant with danger to ourselves and to the world?'

The shadow of the impending Jewish tragedy lay across Congress. None felt it more than Weizmann, and he succeeded in imparting his foreboding to the delegates.

> I told the commission: God has promised *Erez Israel* to the Jews. This is our Charter. But we are men of our own time, with limited horizons, heavily laden with responsibility toward the generations to come. I told the Royal Commission that the hopes of six million Jews are centered on immigration. Then I was asked: 'But can you bring six million to Palestine?' I replied, 'No. I am acquainted with the laws of physics and chemistry, and know the force of material factors. In our generation I divide the figure by three, and in that you can see the depth of the Jewish tragedy: two millions of youth, with their lives before them, who have lost the most elementary of rights, the right to work.'
>
> The old ones will pass, they will bear their fate, or they will not. They are dust, economic and moral dust in a cruel world. And again I thought of our tradition. What is tradition? It is telescoped memory. We remember. Thousands of years ago we heard the words of Isaiah and Jeremiah, and my words are but a weak echo of what was said by our Judges, our Singers, and our Prophets. Two millions, and perhaps less: *Sche'erit Hapleta*—only a remnant shall survive. We have to accept it. The rest we must leave to the future, to our youth. If they feel and suffer as we do, they will find the way, *Beachrit Hayamim*—in the fullness of time.[34]

Although not by temperament one of the movement's great orators, he had, by every account, delivered a most stirring oration. Instinctively he had struck the right chord, sensing the mood of the audience and expressing it, spontaneously, in thrilling language animated by the force of his emotions. 'It was not a speech,' Baffy recorded that evening, 'it was an inspired utterance.'

> He will never rise to these heights again—we shall never hear the like of it again. . . . Looking back on yesterday, when Lewis [Namier] and I were preparing a few bones of the skeleton which he brought to glorious life, I think one of the greatest moments of privilege of my life should be that when he came out to the balcony where we were working— apologized for interrupting—and said: 'Children, I shall probably put in a few words about the Messianic hopes.'

It will prove, Baffy Dugdale promised, 'the birthday of the Jewish State'.[35] Weizmann knew he had done well. On the drive back to the hotel, he relaxed, full of self-satisfaction, seeking none of the compliments he usually craved after a big occasion.

At the end of a week of heated debate, the Zionist Congress adopted, 299–160, a resolution rejecting the Peel scheme but empowering its Executive to negotiate a viable proposal with the British government. It was a great triumph for Weizmann. Attempts to discredit him—a secret protocol had been dramatically produced at one of the sessions purporting to expose him as a British agent—wholly misfired. At one point, Weizmann, no longer able to stomach the criticism, decided to quit the Congress. Vera put her foot down. 'No, Chaimchik, you are not leaving,' she ordered. He stayed until the 'prontras', the waverers at Congress, those who prayed 'for a warm frost', had been won over.[36]

After the delegates had dispersed, Ben Gurion wrote to Weizmann.

Dear and venerated Chaim:

I am very, very sorry, much more than I can express in words, for having caused you yesterday, before the close of the Agency session, distress and suffering.* I have loved you all my life; all Jews have loved you since those great days of the Balfour Declaration. But you were sevenfold dearer to me when I saw you after the 17th Zionist Congress [1931]. In your distress and humiliation a new Weizmann revealed himself to me then—not Weizmann the leader, the magician and charmer, but Weizmann the man, full of pain, wounded, writhing in his anguish and conquering, with supreme moral heroism, his personal ambition, putting himself as an ordinary, devoted soldier at the service of the Movement that had wounded him.

After I had the privilege of working closely with you, I saw you in a new light. I never was a blind follower of yours, and I never will be. I did not always agree with you; whenever I felt I had to oppose you, I did so; if in the future I again see a need to oppose you, I shall do so again.

But even in the fury of battle my feelings of love and veneration for you were not diminished by one iota. I know that you are the champion of the Jewish people, not because you have been elected . . ., but because you were born for it; the 'Schechinah' [divine presence] of the Jewish people rests upon you. And, during the last few months, when the great hope of establishing a Jewish State began to glimmer, I saw this 'Schechinah' shining all over you with a great and new light, and a new power

---

*Ben Gurion is referring to an incident at a meeting of the Jewish Agency when, apparently, he interfered with Weizmann's attempts to conciliate Felix Warburg, who was resolutely opposed to partition. In this connection, Weizmann writes of 'unpleasant discussions' at Zurich. See WL, xviii, nos. 165, 186, 190.

of youthfulness revealed itself in you, with grace and charm to an extent invisible to my eyes before. And although, even in those months, I have sometimes disagreed with you on one detail or another, I know that this time you are bearing upon your shoulders a historic burden not borne by any other Jew for the last two thousand years. I also know that every one of us now, more than ever before, stands by you with all his heart and with all his might so that you may succeed in carrying out the stupendous task imposed on you by the historic destiny of our people — the renewal of the Kingdom of Israel.

The task imposed on you now is, in my view, greater and more difficult than the burden of the Balfour Declaration. The hindrances and pitfalls on your road are now more manifold than ever . . . and there are also more enemies, not only from the outside, but also from the inside. Our enemies have been joined by the cowards and the blind. But if the number of our opponents has grown, so has our strength — our strength in the country, our strength in the Jewish people, and our strength in the world. And you are the personal focus of this strength. There is no other man or circle of men in the Jewish people that can compare with you. I do not believe the superficial theory that history is made by personalities. But I do believe that unique personalities are the emissaries of the collective energies of nations and of classes in history. The Zionist enterprise and Zionist vision have beamed all their light on their supreme emissary, and this light is growing apace. . . .

There are in Erez Israel one hundred thousand Jewish workers, and I am one of them — and no more than that. As one of them, you are dear to me as the Chosen One of the people; as one of them, I know that I must stand by you, and as one of them I pray for your success.[37]

Yet within three months Weizmann's policy, to all intents and purposes, was in ruins. Now that a Jewish state was practicable politics, he became its most consistent advocate. But, through his sources in government circles, mainly Baffy's friends, it became known to him that the cabinet was under severe pressure to backtrack on its previous obligation. A most formidable alliance had emerged to fight partition. The Foreign Office warned in unequivocal language that it would provoke dire consequences in the Arab and Moslem world, while the chiefs of staff, hypnotized by the dire prospect of general hostilities against an exposed empire, argued that a peaceful Mediterranean was necessary to reduce the burden of Britain's military commitments.[38] This implied terminating the Arab rebellion, if possible by agreement with its leaders, not fanning it to a greater degree of violence.

In September 1937 — the same month that Lewis Andrews, a high official in the Palestine administration, was shot and killed leaving the Anglican Church in Nazareth—the first pan-Arab Congress convened at Bluden, Syria. Referring to Zionism as 'a cancer' that had to be eradicated from 'the bodies of the Arab countries', the Congress warned Britain in no uncertain terms that she would have to choose between Arabs and Jews, otherwise Arab support in times of crisis could no longer be counted upon and the Arabs would seek a new alliance to protect their rights.[39] With Germany and Italy waiting in the wings, the hint was clear enough.

The terms of reference of the technical body that arrived in Palestine in April 1938 to recommend boundaries for the proposed Jewish and Arab states, the Woodhead Commission, did not preclude the possibility of abandoning partition. Zionists christened it the "Re-Peel Commission".[40] Weizmann described the Arabs' attack on partition as 'a veritable Witches' Sabbath'. He asked Ormsby-Gore: 'What are the real intentions of the government?' The Jews, he declared, would never 'exchange their Polish or German ghettos for an Arab one'. In a desperate fling, he appealed to the British sense of fair play. 'To throw us to the dogs may seem good *"Realpolitik"* to some [but] it would certainly not add to the spiritual armament of the Empire.' In an age when power politics counted, this kind of political talk sounded increasingly anachronistic, but Weizmann was being forced into a *cul-de-sac*. As he told the American Zionists in December 1937, in the circumstances partition was 'the only solution we have'.[41]

The old mandate of 1922 had died at the hands of Peel, for he had not only proposed partition, but had also recommended a series of so-called 'palliatives' which included a ceiling on immigration (the figure of 12,000 a year was mentioned) and restrictions on land purchases. If, eventually, the British government reneged on its commitment to partition, it would continue the mandate on the basis of a thorough revision of its previous interpretation, inevitably to the detriment of the National Home. Nor could Weizmann hope for any improvement in the foreseeable future. As the international situation steadily deteriorated, the British need to assuage the Arab world increased. In this game, the Zionists were but an expendable pawn that the British, perhaps conscience-stricken but rationalizing that they had no alternative, would have to sacrifice.

Like two well-rehearsed actors, the Zionists and the British spoke their lines with absolute conviction, manoeuvring on a crowded stage toward an inevitable confrontation. There was little room for subtlety or finesse in Weizmann's diplomacy. In blunt terms, he warned Ormsby-Gore of the repercussions of the government's shilly-shallying, not least to his own position, which 'may become untenable'.

I know the Jewish people fairly well and I am confident that 95% of Jewry would accept Partition on the basis of an improved proposal of the Royal Commission, but they will not take a mutilated project which may be concocted in the offices of the Palestine Government! Should an attempt be made to force such a proposal upon them, then the group of Zionists which has been leading the movement for twenty years in the spirit of cooperation with Britain which you yourself helped to instil, must go into the wilderness.[42]

But the Colonial Secretary, himself favourable to partition, was outgunned by the Foreign Office, the chiefs of staff, and the Palestine administration.

SIXTEEN

THE DOCTRINE OF TEMPORARY EXPEDIENCY

In November 1937, the same month the Foreign Office launched its broadside against Palestinian partition, Weizmann was tormented by a grave crisis concerning his sons. Remote from his political world, they were giving him the dreadful feeling that he had failed in his parental duties. In Paris, he was confined to bed by his doctor, as his condition was 'rather low', and put on a strict diet—'all the good things are forbidden'. He slept a lot, ate little, and read the Bible: 'Jacob was a great cheat, I think! No wonder the children of Esau don't like us.'[1] By the end of the month, sufficiently recuperated, he set out for Palestine; again his sons were left behind to fend for themselves.

Although Weizmann had visited Palestine many times before, this trip held a special significance. He and Vera were about to move into their new home in Rehovot. Everything was prepared. Their servants had gone on ahead, accompanied by 'masses of our luggage and our silver, etc'. But please, Weizmann entreated, he wanted it to be met at customs, for 'I would like it to arrive in Rehovot without Arabs pinching it'. Within a short time their London home was put up for sale.

Moshe Shertok, now head of the political department of the Jewish Agency, remarked that Weizmann's move to Palestine symbolized the end of 'the Balfour era'. It was generally agreed among Weizmann's intimates that not much remained of the famous Balfour Declaration. Introducing Baffy (Balfour's niece) to some of his friends, who had asked, *sotto voce:* 'Who is this distinguished lady?', Weizmann said, in his usual sardonic tone, 'She is what is left of the Balfour Declaration.'[2]

Weizmann saw his task to salvage something from his great, but now sadly faded, achievement.

Weizmann found little in Palestine to improve his mood. Arab violence had escalated sharply after the publication of the Peel Commission's report. The British reacted vigorously: they deposed the Mufti, Haj Amin al-Husayni, and disbanded the Arab Higher Committee. In October, Haj Amin, disguised as a Bedouin, fled his sanctuary in the holy shrine *al-Haram al-Sharif* to the Lebanon, where he continued to conduct a campaign of terror against the *Yishuv* as well as against those Arabs who dared to oppose him. Bodyguards were appointed to protect Weizmann, now a necessary imposition, for it had been reliably reported that the Mufti's bands had put a price of £2000 on his head.[3] Whenever he travelled around the country, he did so under heavy armed escort. His own family would not escape without casualties. In July 1938, Tuvia Dounie, his sister Gita's husband, was killed in Haifa by Arab rioters as he came to the rescue of a wounded Arab policeman. Two months later his youngest brother 'Chilik', and his nephew, fourteen-year-old Ezer, were injured when their car overturned after being fired at on the main Tel Aviv–Haifa highway at Beth Lydd. He had learned to expect these hit-and-run terror tactics from the Arabs, whose nationalism he now regarded as 'totalitarian in nature, shallow, aggressive and arrogant', a shoddy imitation of its European models.[4] But it was beyond his comprehension that Jews should adopt the same despicable methods. He blamed the Revisionists for needlessly escalating the violence. Since the spring of 1937 the Irgun Zvai Leumi, the military arm of the Revisionists, had been responding in kind to Arab terror, their actions reaching a horrible climax in July 1938 when bombs set by the Irgun exploded in a market in Haifa, causing the deaths of fifty-six Arabs and three Jews.[5]

Weizmann was not a pacifist. When Wauchope asked him how he would deal with rebellious Arabs, Weizmann replied abruptly, 'Hang them!' though later he judiciously softened his position.[6] From the early 1920s he had known and approved of the activities of the Haganah (the defence organization of the *Yishuv*, run by the Jewish Agency). In 1923, just before Easter, he had warned the Jewish defence force to prepare itself for any emergency, authorized funds for arms purchases, and used his extensive contacts in Europe to open doors for Eliyahu Golomb (whom he nicknamed 'Voroshilov'), the driving force behind the Haganah.[7] He recognized the need for the Jews to have a legitimate defence organization in Palestine, one that was responsible to the democratic, national institutions of the *Yishuv* and would act within the parameters of Zionist policy as defined by its elected leadership. But he abhorred the anarchy of terrorism—an insidious, corrupting manifestation of the nationalism he upheld which, if allowed to flourish, would tear apart the moral and political fabric of Zionism. Ultimately, he saw it as the crazed acts of desperate, irresponsible men, the work of a lunatic fringe who, by their insane provocations, brought their cause into disrepute. Above all, he regarded it as morally corrupting and politically counter-productive, a suicidal combination. He never deviated from this view, and when, in the tragic circumstances of the Second World War, terrorism again raised its ugly head his voice would continue to condemn it in the most forthright terms.

The Revisionists operated in a limited world of their own, outside of his jurisdiction as leader of the Zionist movement. But there were ominous signs that elements in the Haganah were also losing patience, aiming to redefine their declared policy of *Havlagah* (self-restraint) and to adopt a more activist line. This would not have been to Weizmann's liking. He had no compunction about Jews establishing new settlements or bringing in immigrants in defiance of the Palestine administration's decrees, or equipping and training the Haganah to defend the *Yishuv* from Arab attack, for these were legitimate activities that served Zionism and raised its moral tone. But he knew how thin was the line that divided activism, which he could justify, from senseless violence, which he could not. His differences with the leadership of the *Yishuv* over the freedom of action to be enjoyed by the Haganah remained, and deepened, in the course of time. Weizmann was dealing with an increasingly impatient generation that all too often came to regard his strictures as antiquated irrelevancies.

Fortunately, this discord was pasted over, temporarily at least, by one of the more picturesque characters to enter his life. At the end of May 1937, Orde Wingate, a British eccentric in the captain's uniform of an intelligence officer, offered, in an unofficial and often thoroughly indiscreet way, his services to Weizmann. Brought up in a Puritan household—'He felt the Divine presence'—Wingate, in his biographer's view, adopted Zionism as he would a religious faith. 'Lucky for us that Wingate's fanatical Zionism gets the better of his sense of duty as an Intelligence Officer,' remarked Baffy. 'He is clearly one of the instruments in God's hand.'[8] To cope with Arab terror, Wingate proposed organizing Special Night Squads composed of Haganah members with a stiffening of British officers and NCOs. His policy: active defence. The SNS would seek out raiders in the countryside, lie in ambush for the gangs, and, whenever possible, destroy the rebels in their village bases. His tactics proved outstandingly successful. Wingate (known simply as *HaYadid*, the friend, in Zionist circles) canalized Haganah enthusiasm into paths beneficial to the British and ultimately of immense profit to the Haganah. This was the kind of activism Weizmann could live with: responsible, accountable, coordinated.

Wingate's extreme, partisan views were a considerable source of embarrassment to his superiors, however, and in consequence he was posted out of Palestine in May 1939. He thought Weizmann 'a prince in Israel', the only genuine leader Zionism had produced.[9] In turn, Weizmann admired Wingate's martial qualities and personal integrity, though he thought him politically naive, even dangerous. He tolerated Wingate's ungovernable temper with its violent undercurrent, but diplomatically turned a deaf ear to his preposterous political suggestions. In March 1944, Wingate, promoted to major general, was killed in an air crash in Burma, never to fulfill his life-long ambition to command a future Jewish army. Despite their differences, Weizmann's deep attachment to him and his family had never slackened, and his wife, Lorna, and her mother, Alice Ivy Paterson, came to be numbered among his lady confidantes.

Weizmann required no prompting from Wingate or others that the situation in Palestine in 1937 was grave. He was already considering more drastic measures. On 17 February 1938 he arrived in London to impress upon the government the need to persevere with its decision to partition Palestine. He could not have arrived at a less opportune moment. The cabinet was in the midst of a major crisis. On 20 February Anthony Eden, whom Weizmann had never met, resigned as Foreign Secretary to be replaced by Lord Halifax, who from Weizmann's viewpoint proved to be more accessible and, surprisingly, exhibited 'something of the quality of understanding that A.J.B. [alfour] used to display'. Weizmann trod the familiar path among government ministries—interviewing, arguing, persuading, pleading—but with meagre results. Ministers' minds were elsewhere. Since February, German pressure to coerce Austria into her orbit had been mounting steadily. The Austrian crisis was on the boil, to culminate in the *Anschluss* on 12 March. Two days earlier Weizmann had met the Prime Minister: 'Why are you so uneasy?' Chamberlain asked. 'Why do you worry so much? We are committed to partition.'[10] But Weizmann discerned that partition, if not dead and buried, had entered upon the terminal stage of a brief illness. What remained? Even the Jews failed to grasp 'the apocalyptic nature of the times. . . . Part of us will be destroyed and on their bones New Judaea may arise! It is all terrible but it is so—I feel it even here, and can think of nothing else. . . . A new leader should arise in Israel now who should sound the call; we are already old and used up, I'm afraid.'[11]

He returned to Palestine in a despondent mood. He had met the leading lights in British politics but his magic had failed to stir them as it had in the past. 'I find myself dealing with Pharaohs who "know not Joseph",' he explained to John Buchan, now Lord Tweedsmuir, Governor-General of Canada. 'Everything here just now seems to be overlaid with a kind of "surrealism"—what in other terminology might be called the doctrine of temporary expediency, opportunism.'[12]

Since the beginning of 1938 Weizmann had been dropping hints of an emergency, crash programme 'to buy more land, occupy it and hold it'. And if the Jews were to be treated as scapegoats, he announced to the *Vaad Leumi* (National Council), it would be necessary to create a force strong enough to offer resistance. Victor Cazalet, a sympathetic M.P. close to Weizmann, told his parliamentary colleagues that if partition were abandoned 'the Jews will declare themselves an independent state . . [and] produce 100,000 young men to look after their own frontiers.' In April, Weizmann wrote to Baffy on the same theme, now proposing to buy 'as much land as we can', to arm '20,000 men to begin with', to acquire 'a few aeroplanes', to prepare 'for the manufacture of munitions', and to grow enough 'foods and fibres' to become self-sufficient—a comprehensive master-plan which would cost £2 million.[13]

What was Weizmann after? Surely not a *coup d'état* against the British, a move so beset with perils as to contradict flatly his entire political outlook. But the world situation was critical: the ghastly spectacle of Austrian Jewry humiliated by Nazi thugs told a gruesome story. Where, if not in Palestine, could these unfortunate people seek refuge? But how was Weizmann to shift British policy, make them aware of the magnitude of the problem, shake them out of their complacency? He reflected, perhaps relying on their legendary sense of fair play, that:

Our diplomatic efforts with the British may have some effects but nothing is more impressive than the creation of solid facts and when the British see our seriousness and our determination in this respect they will value it and perhaps appreciate it deeper than our mere talking about it. . . . I believe we can do it.[14]

Yet as the summer progressed it became increasingly clear that not even 'the creation of solid facts' would save the Jews.

Jewish refugees were fleeing persecution in central and eastern Europe only to discover that wherever they turned they encountered quotas and restrictions, bureaucracy and red tape, instead of open doors and assured havens. In 1935, Palestine absorbed more Jews (61,854) than the combined efforts of the United States and the British Empire. The relentless expansion of German power, resulting in ever greater numbers of refugees, goaded President Franklin D. Roosevelt into convening an international conference at Évian, France, in July 1938, which would, it was hoped, propose concrete measures to resolve their plight. Weizmann thought the gathering 'a waste of time' and guessed, accurately, that the thirty-two participating nations would be governed by narrow-minded national interests and not by humanitarian considerations. As if to substantiate his sixth sense, Britain insisted that Palestine be excluded from the agenda. Weizmann was pressed to attend, but did not do so, suspecting the hostility of the British delegate, Lord Winterton, and the lack of understanding of the American, Myron Taylor. However, Jewish Agency representatives, among them Golda Meyerson (Meir) and Nahum Goldmann, did attend its barren sessions, submitting documents and statistics emphasizing the importance of Palestine. After days of tedious deliberations, only tiny Santo Domingo agreed to accept 100,000 refugees. Otherwise investigatory commissions were set up to explore the possibilities of territories such as British Guiana or Rhodesia or the Philippines absorbing large numbers of Jewish refugees. These exercises in 'territorialism' earned Weizmann's scorn; he knew they were worthless, raised only to divert attention from Palestine.[15]

The results of Évian were virtually nil. The United States and Britain relaxed their restrictions but only marginally so, and those fortunate enough to gain entry were still only a relative few. In a perverse way, the failure at Évian served Zionist interests in that it accentuated the primacy of Palestine. Not that the Zionists would have opposed Canada's adopting a more liberal refugee policy, to take a most notorious example.[16] But as Weizmann had always argued, Palestine provided not only a refuge for persecuted Jews but also a genuine home where they could flourish as a nation. If the free, democratic countries of the world remained largely impervious to Jewish cries for help in their moment of greatest need, was it not decisive proof that only Palestine, only a Jewish state, could resolve the Jewish problem in a positive and creative manner? Nevertheless, however convincing his case and with whatever moral conviction he put it, Weizmann could only stand by helplessly and watch the misery of his fellow Jews. This mass of human suffering was an agonizing reminder of his people's tragedy that allowed him no respite.

In August 1938 Weizmann took the cure, 'a complicated one', at Cauterets in the Pyrenees. At the age of sixty-three, these cures had become a yearly ritual. The monkish routine was strict. He rose early, drank the mineral waters, bathed in the hot springs, endured spinal and stomach massages, had his nose syringed and his ears blown out, slept much and read little, drank a glass of milk every two hours, and retired at ten. The results justified the effort. He lost weight and felt 'better generally'. Clementine Churchill, who was also staying at Cauterets, sent her regards, and he chanced upon Lady Crewe but unfortunately failed to recognize her. Otherwise he was left to the not so tender mercies of his doctors and masseurs.[17]

Throughout these summer months Weizmann fought strongly to keep the idea of partition in Palestine alive. His price for the Zionists' agreement to this remained high: aiming to scotch persistent rumours that the British government had abandoned the scheme, Weizmann told Malcolm MacDonald, Colonial Secretary since May, that there could be no whittling down of the Peel Commission's proposals; quite the contrary, the Jewish state would have to be large enough to absorb a million-and-a-half Jews within a few years. When he appeared before the Woodhead Commission, he repeated the same message.[18] From June until September the talks with MacDonald continued.

In the background, the Czech problem was building up to a climax. Ever since the German absorption of Austria in March, the Germans, through their surrogates, the Sudeten German Nazi Party, had been threatening the unity of Czechoslovakia by demanding greater autonomy, in fact annexation to Germany, for the Sudeten areas of Czechoslovakia, which bordered on Germany and which contained some three million ethnic Germans. The danger that the Czech crisis might spill over into a European war was uppermost in the minds of the cabinet, and to avert that catastrophe they had not hesitated to pressure the Czech government into making concessions to the Nazis. Within this context, the Palestine problem was more than just a minor irritant, for the British were holding down almost as many troops in Palestine as they could offer to France in the event of European war.[19] Moreover, in the Mediterranean the Italians were undermining the British position, while in the Far East the Japanese, now at war with China, were threatening vital British interests. British resources were stretched dangerously thin. The imperatives of imperial policy dictated cutting obligations outside Europe to a bare minimum at the least political cost. Naturally, the British would have preferred to reach an agreement with their disputatious partners, but if this should prove impossible— and by now it was clear that the obstacles were virtually insurmountable—they would not balk at behaving toward the Zionists as they had behaved toward the Czechs.

On 6 August MacDonald arrived in Jerusalem on a snap visit. He found the Palestine administration's views regarding a political solution 'at sixes and sevens',[20] but he still favoured partition, if practicable. Still, since Arab extremists were setting the pace, he knew the chances of securing agreement to it were all but nonexistent. He floated the idea of an Arab-Jewish conference under British auspices, in the circumstances an empty gesture more than an act of policy. Weizmann too was making gestures. His final statement to the Woodhead Commission was nothing more than 'a record before the bar of history'. Woodhead asked him, 'Then you think we are wrong?' 'I do,' replied Weizmann. 'Time alone will tell,' answered Woodhead. It was patently clear that Weizmann could expect nothing from the commission.[21]

As a last resort, the British had no option but to impose their own settlement. Toward the end of September, with Europe on the brink of war and trenches being dug in the parks of London, MacDonald drew up an emergency wartime programme for Palestine. It included the abandonment of partition, the suspension of immigration, and the continuation of British rule, as far as possible in accordance with the mandate.[22] The Czech crisis passed, but the shadow of war remained, and MacDonald's crude and unpolished blue-print also remained, for future reference and refinement. MacDonald imparted to Weizmann the flavour of these ideas at three meetings during the same week while Chamberlain was negotiating the fate of Czechoslovakia with Hitler. At their third meeting, at Addison Crescent, at which Weizmann was accompanied by Ben Gurion, Vera and Baffy waited anxiously in the adjoining room playing bezique. The gist of the conversation, Baffy noted, was a complete sell-out: no partition but an emasculated mandate. 'We are all stunned. Ben Gurion's first reaction—and mine—was that the Jews will fight, physically, rather than go back to the Mandate. . . . Chaim said nothing much.' But when Weizmann met his executive, on 21 September, he was in a fighting mood. For him cooperation with Britain had always been as 'the Rock of Gibraltar'. Now MacDonald was betraying them, and the *Yishuv* would find itself in 'a death trap'. He told them, 'There would be no Jewish state unless we ourselves made it.' From now on his policy would be one of 'uncompromising hostility to Britain—to work, silently at first, toward arming and preparation, which in time (he knew not how long) would enable Jewry to pursue its own policy in the Middle East.' As for MacDonald, he would never negotiate with him again. After Weizmann had left the room, Ben Gurion tried to calm the waters. To break with MacDonald meant in effect to break with the British government, and this, in present circumstances, should be avoided for as long as possible. Ben Gurion's moderation prevailed, for the time being, over Weizmann's militancy. Negotiations continued. But in Weizmann's eyes, MacDonald had committed the cardinal sin: he had dishonoured his friendship and fallen from Zionist grace.[23]

Weizmann's rancour stemmed also from a sense of personal betrayal; it could not be measured simply in cold terms of a political setback. His whole political world, the philosophy that had governed his political behaviour, had collapsed around him. He had gambled everything on the British connection, and it had failed him in his hour of greatest need. It was not he who had broken faith but the British. The great democratic principles for which they stood, the moral superiority they gloried in when comparing themselves to the dictatorships, were as dust. They too would sacrifice the Jews on the altar of political expediency. He was still tied to the British, but now only as a last resort because he had nowhere else to turn. His brave talk of an independent Jewish policy, at least for the immediate future, rang hollow in his own ears. The glorious days of the Balfour Declaration were gone forever.

On 30 September Baffy came down to breakfast to read in the newspapers that 'in Munich honour died'. The implications for Zionism were clear. Weizmann feared that Chamberlain would appease the Mufti in much the same way that he had appeased Hitler. Jan Masaryk, the Czech minister in London, advised him to buy a house with three storeys: the first for Hailie Selassie, the second for Masaryk, and the third for Weizmann himself. When the Zionists convened the following day, Mrs. Dugdale recorded that there was no dissent from the general view that 'we cannot yet resist by arms—we can only work by every means, fair and foul (all is *kosher* now), to buy land, bring in men, get arms. And in two—three—four years we will bring the Jewish State into being.'[24]

The Woodhead report was published on 9 November. Its conclusions, though expected, were nevertheless a severe blow. Pronouncing the partition of Palestine impracticable, the best scheme it offered reduced the Peel Commission's proposals to a rump state of approximately 400 square miles on the coastal plain. At the same time, the government proposed convening a round-table conference, inviting also representatives of the Arab countries; if the parties failed to reach a settlement, it would impose its own solution. This was nothing more than 'a piece of bare-faced cynicism', Weizmann raged at MacDonald. There would be no tampering with the mandate, he warned, except 'over our dead bodies'.[25]

That night, 9–10 November 1938, there occurred in Germany an organized pogrom against Jews, the infamous *Kristallnacht*. Synagogues were gutted, property was destroyed, and 50,000 Jews were placed under arrest. Western public opinion was shocked, but sympathetic editorials would not save European Jews. As news of the horrific events in Germany spread, Weizmann addressed a Zionist meeting at the Anglo-Palestine Club in London. He formulated Zionist policy for the coming months: 'Partition', he told his audience, 'has been killed by the new commission.' 'The struggle . . . before them was a struggle of their rights under the Balfour Declaration and the mandate . . . especially their right to immigration, subject only to economic capacity, without any political limitations—avowed or hidden.'[26] He had already received enough hints to know that it would be an uphill struggle. In the meantime, he found himself involved in a most bizarre diplomatic venture.

'I felt that they are right who say that the Jews are all-powerful,' Baffy Dugdale commented when she first learned of Weizmann's new Turkish connection, adding, 'and yet—*how* impotent!' His contact was a certain Sami Gunzberg, Ataturk's dentist and *homme de confiance*, who had contacted him to suggest that the Turkish government was eager for a loan; sums between £50 million and £60 million were mentioned, for in their naivity the Turks evidently believed that the Zionists controlled vast fortunes. Nothing, it seems, had changed since the days of Herzl. Weizmann was prepared to consider having the Zionists make some contribution, far more modest, of course, in the hope that the British, appreciating the strategic bonuses it would bring, would also give aid to Turkey. He was already weaving grand schemes: with Turkey in her pocket, Britain could safeguard her imperial interests by constructing an 'outer circle' of allies—Turkey, Iran, and Afghanistan—and, with a strong *Yishuv* guarding the eastern Mediterranean seaboard, would have nothing to fear from a hostile Arab world.

With high hopes Weizmann arrived in Ankara on 27 November to pursue this Turkish connection. Prior to his departure, Lord Halifax had hinted that British and Jewish interests coincided at the Bosphorus. But the trip was inconclusive, for Weizmann had simply not read the political map correctly. The 'outer circle' strategy was certainly attractive, and its kernel already existed in the so-called Saadabad non-aggression pact of July 1937, of which Turkey, Iraq, Iran, and Afghanistan were signatories. But for the British it made more sense to implement it without the Zionists complicating matters and causing friction. In this way, the entire area from Egypt to India would fall into their orbit. In any case, for reasons of their own Mediterranean policy, they did not begin serious negotiations with the Turks until the spring of 1939, concluding a mutual assistance agreement in May. They were not dependent on Weizmann's manipulations to conduct their grand strategy, and he returned to London on 11 December empty-handed.[27]

Weizmann was still the undisputed leader of the Zionist movement. In the field of Anglo-Zionist relations in particular he towered above any of his contemporaries or rivals. He had led the Zionist movement to its greatest triumphs. Could he now save it from impending disaster? But time had taken its toll. He was more nervous, more easily agitated, more prone to emotional outbursts than in the past. Perhaps he sensed that his long period of leadership was approaching its end. All this, compounded by his lack of administrative discipline, reflected on his powers. He clashed repeatedly with his closest advisers. Baffy Dugdale witnessed the process. At times she had seen Weizmann so infuriated that all work in his office had to cease while 'all tried to soothe him'. 'Chaim calmer', she would note later with obvious relief. Deploring his inability to co-operate with any outspoken colleagues, she sadly concluded that he was 'a *bad* team driver. They all feel some grievance.'[28]

Baffy herself was not immune from Weizmann's suspicions. On 16 December 1938,

> Chaim spoke to me beforehand in a most extraordinary manner—about a 'cloud' between us. Also declared that Vera had said to him that I had told her that Namier had criticized Chaim as being 'weak' with Malcolm [MacDonald]. There is not a word of truth or substance in this, and I was terribly upset that Chaim should be ready to swallow an allegation that I was making mischief between him and Namier. But what can Vera have said—and *why*? Why Chaim's sudden unmistakeable suspicion and hostility towards me?... Chaim's violent animosity against Lewis [Namier] burst forth in black rage.

A few days later, the situation had improved, much to Baffy's relief. She wished only that 'this miserable misunderstanding... be left behind.'[29]

Whatever Vera's motives for relaying this piece of gossip, it was undoubtedly true that Weizmann's behaviour was causing concern to his colleagues. The immediate issue was whether or not the Zionists should participate in the conference in London convened by the government to discuss the crisis in Palestine. Initially, Weizmann argued for boycotting it unless the government, as a sign of good faith, agreed to allow 10,000 German and Austrian children into Palestine. An emotional issue at the best of times, this assumed a particular significance after *Kristallnacht*. He told MacDonald, 'We shall fight you from here to San Francisco, and when I say fight I mean *fight*.' MacDonald asked, 'Do you mean I am to go to the House on Friday and announce that you will not come to the conference?' 'We shall have saved you the trouble,' Weizmann replied. But before long, he began to have second thoughts. MacDonald was quick to detect this, and reported to the cabinet that whereas Namier resolutely opposed the London discussions, Weizmann 'had been a bit shaken'. The same day that MacDonald drew his conclusion, 16 December, Weizmann decided in favour of going to the conference. At a Zionist meeting, he argued, as Baffy reported, that 'it was in the Jewish interest to participate... however terrible the situation was. He was not going to endanger the slender chance of drawing from the conference what he could by refusing the invitation now.'[30]

In the coming weeks, Namier was not alone in noticing Weizmann's lack of firmness. He told Baffy that the 'criticisms . . . were widespread— far too weak, many points going by default, and a subservient manner.' Peter Rutenburg, head of the Palestine Electric Corporation and a member of the *Vaad Leumi*, took the analysis a stage further: Weizmann 'was "all broken to pieces" . . . but must be preserved in leadership as "there is no other Weizmann"!' These observations must be taken with a pinch of salt. Namier was valuable to Weizmann in many ways, but he lacked judgement, balance, and finesse. He was not a policy-maker, but a diplomatic technician. Still, it was apparent that Weizmann was floundering. He knew what he wanted, but not how to attain it. Neither did the other Zionist leaders. Unable to challenge Britain, powerless to compete in the world of *Realpolitik*, all they could do was to fall back on the increasingly anachronistic language of moral values and past obligations.[31]

The cabinet was aware of the Zionists' predicament and exploited it. MacDonald admitted that the Jewish children from Austria and Germany could be absorbed in Palestine without 'causing injury to anyone's interest'. But the balance of opinion was against him. No step should be taken, it was thought, that would inflame an already volatile situation and endanger the forthcoming conference. Halifax bluntly defined the government's aim as ensuring 'that the Arab states would be friendly toward us'. Chamberlain and MacDonald were unimpressed by Weizmann's bluster, and they brushed aside his threat of a boycott. The Zionists, they reasoned, had no alternative but to attend the talks and ultimately to acquiesce in an imposed settlement. All other options were closed to them. As one minister put it: 'The Jews are driving down a one-way street.' Eventually, it was decided to allow the children into Britain, no doubt on humanitarian grounds but also to sap Zionist resentment.[32]

Meanwhile, it was common knowledge that the Palestinian Arabs were feuding among themselves as to the composition of their delegation. Without their active participation the conference was doomed, and this seemed to Weizmann a most convenient outcome. For a brief period, he had doubts whether the gathering would materialize at all, doubts that were strengthened by persistent rumours of an imminent German attack in the West. Undeterred, MacDonald invested every effort to ensure the presence of the Palestinians, though he was unable to achieve this until after the conference had actually begun. The war scare worked very much to the detriment of the Zionists. The chiefs-of-staff issued a persuasive memorandum urging, for high strategic reasons, an agreement favourable to the Arabs. MacDonald pursued the same theme in cabinet. By the end of January 1939, the government had before it a fairly detailed scheme which would later blossom into full growth as the May white paper.[33]

After much soul-searching by the *Yishuv*, the London conference opened at St. James's Palace on 7 February. There was something inherently false about the entire spectacle. The magnificent setting of the royal palace, the punctiliousness of the opening sessions, the stiff formality of the occasion—all served to mask the distasteful fact that the main decisions had already been taken, in principle if not in detail. As the Arabs refused to sit down with the Jews, two conferences proceeded simultaneously, with the British passing messages back and forth. This, too, placed the conference in a most peculiar light in Zionist eyes, since it made the British take on the role of Arab spokesmen, leaving the Arabs as silent spectators, in a sense content to watch the verbal battles fought between the Jews and the British. The net effect of the conference, which continued until mid-March, was to polarize the parties' existing attitudes. An air of futility enveloped the proceedings, best expressed by Namier, who wondered why MacDonald did not read out '*Alice in Wonderland* or *Bradshaw*; either would have made a long speech, would have been restful, and for relevancy would have equalled some of his own performances'.[34]

When Weizmann met with the Jewish delegates two days before the opening, he had emphasized that there were only 'gradations' in British government policy, none of them satisfactory to the Zionists, whom MacDonald wanted 'to go very, very slowly'. There had been talk of halting the 'irritant' of Jewish immigration to Palestine or at least of reducing it to a minimum; Weizmann, however, as though to highlight the gap separating the sides, defined the Jewish objective as securing 'large-scale immigration', a goal on which there could be no compromise, for any concession would to be to sacrifice 'so many thousands of Jewish lives'. If the Arabs would agree to an overall settlement, there was room for flexibility; if not, deadlock would ensue. There were limits even to cooperation with Britain to whom, it must never be forgotten, the Jews owed an 'historic debt of gratitude'. Since Weizmann had been brutally frank, no delegate retained any illusion as to the probable outcome of the conference: it would, in Weizmann's words, 'fill the cup of Jewish suffering'.[35]

Weizmann himself addressed the conference on 8 February. In the main, he rehashed his evidence before the Royal Commission, and time had not eroded his gift for a vivid phrase. All talk of paralysing the National Home was so much idle chatter, he argued. 'You cannot stop an organic growth; you cannot stop a plant from growing; you cannot stop the sun from turning round. Only Joshua succeeded in doing it, and I am afraid I cannot attempt it.' Halifax and MacDonald congratulated him on 'a moving and logical speech'. Even rabbi Moshe Blau, representing the anti-Zionist *Agudah*, shook his hand and congratulated him warmly: 'All strength to you.' But logic and emotion were no longer of sufficient weight to balance Arab hostility. Throughout the conference, Baffy concluded, the Jews took 'all the dialectical honours'. It made not the slightest impact on the outcome. The Arabs were implacably opposed to any notion of compromise, and the British drew the only conclusion: to put into effect the programme they had fashioned well before the conference had convened. This included draconian restrictions on Jewish immigration and constitutional proposals for a Palestinian state in which the Jews, in effect, would have the status of a permanent minority.[36]

The conference had run into a dead-end, as Weizmann feared it would. Almost from the outset the Zionists had been debating whether or not to break off the talks. Weizmann had hesitated, hoping against all the odds to salvage something, but now it was clear that there was nothing to be gained by further negotiations. He had tried everything— logic, emotion, moral pressure—but to no avail. He had attempted to mobilize the pro-Zionist lobby in the United States, only to learn through Baffy's contacts that Roosevelt intended to stand by Chamberlain. He had sought out Smuts, but to no effect. Zionist sympathizers in Parliament, led by Amery, had found the Prime Minister indifferent to their pleas. Chamberlain told Weizmann that he would have liked to have handed Palestine over to the Jews, 'but his advisers had made out an unanswerable case'.[37] It was somehow fitting that the day the conference died, 15 March, the Germans marched into Prague, destroying the Munich settlement. On 21 March, they annexed Memel. Two weeks later, the Italians conquered Albania. The Zionists had no answer to these punishing blows. In the face of mounting German and Italian aggression in Europe, it was clear that the British government would seek to rid itself of its embarrassing obligations elsewhere.

Neither Weizmann nor Ben Gurion attended the final session; the nature of the government's proposals was such as to make their presence seem undignified. MacDonald matter-of-factly submitted the details of the new policy: immigration was to be restricted to a maximum of 75,000 for the coming five years and then renewed only with Arab consent; crippling restriction on land sales waş envisaged; and finally, a Palestinian state, in treaty relations with Britain, was to be established after a transition period of ten years. There were additional flourishes: the possibility of a federal solution, or that independence would be withheld until the British government was entirely satisfied that Arabs and Jews could work together. But the overall effect was, for the Zionists, of an unmitigated disaster. MacDonald made clear that these proposals were final, inviolate. There was no discussion, and the delegates dispersed. The following day, Weizmann bade farewell to the Panel, the Jewish delegation to the conference:

> All that was happening was an episode, one more turn in the ups and downs that their people had known. They had wonderful hopes and these had been partly shattered. They would build them afresh. They had waited for thousands of years, and they would plod along another five years.[38]

These weeks had been among the most disagreeable of Weizmann's life. He had sustained a considerable political set-back and was convinced that worse was to follow. Exhausted, all his energy spent in barren discussion, he prepared to leave for Palestine. He could register one, small success: the government decided to postpone publication of its statement of policy for a short period, mainly for its own reasons but also because Weizmann's parliamentary friends and the Americans had hinted broadly that it would be advantageous for all concerned to do so. Weizmann promised Chamberlain that he would exploit the time 'to explore the possibility of a Jewish-Arab agreement', an exercise that complemented British efforts to persuade the Arab states to accept their new policy. Neither Weizmann nor the British succeeded in their mission. The Arabs, clearly encouraged by the British attempts to woo them, refused to lower their price for an agreement, and in these circumstances there was nothing of substance that Weizmann could offer.[39]

Weizmann's stay in Palestine tended to narrow his perspective on the political forces working against Zionist policy. This was perfectly understandable. He soaked in the atmosphere of the *Yishuv*, at that time witnessing the most harrowing scenes of so-called illegals attempting to break the British blockade. 'Untold tragedies are being enacted along these coasts,' he wrote to Leo Amery.

> Boats overloaded with refugees from German concentration camps are floated about for weeks on end . . . their passengers starved and afflicted with the diseases of hunger and exhaustion, among them women and children of tender age. Some of these boats were recently seized by British patrol vessels, dragged to Haifa and then pushed out again to the open sea with their human cargo, although it was known that they were not seaworthy and that their provisions would not enable them to hold out for more than a few days . . . When desperate Jews are fleeing in leaky boats to the land of their supposed National Home no dictates of humanity, no doctrine of political asylum ensures them admission.[40]

He could not explain British policy in rational terms. Should the government continue its heartless policy, it would 'divest itself of its moral and legal right to govern Palestine. They will have to rule the Jews with force and not by the consent of the people.' Surely the government realized that the *Yishuv* would oppose 'laws and regulations' that closed the National Home at a time 'when millions of Jews are undergoing a sadistic persecution such as the world has not known since the darkest ages'. Why jeopardize the loyalty of the *Yishuv*, or ignore its manpower and technical and scientific know-how, a visible and valuable asset in times of war? Fear of antagonizing the Arabs was an inadequate explanation, for it was evident that in the event of war the Arab world would depend upon Britain and would seek the protection of the democratic countries against the threat of Germany and Italy.

Instead, Weizmann found comfort in a highly personalized explanation: there was 'a regular cabal organized by the enemies of the Jews'. The centre of this intrigue, he believed, was the British embassy in Cairo, presided over by Sir Miles Lampson, 'a blind tool' in the hands of his capable oriental secretary, Walter Smart, 'an avowed opponent' and the brother-in-law of George Antonius, a Christian Arab publicist close to Palestine nationalist circles. The conspiracy encompassed the officials of the Palestine administration and was rounded off in London in the figure of George Rendel, head of the middle east department at the Foreign Office.[41] There was some truth in Weizmann's theory, for these people were vociferous in their opposition to a pro-Zionist policy, but their arguments were only one piece of the intricate jigsaw-puzzle Chamberlain was assembling. And contrasted with the need to erect an effective diplomatic front in Europe, the

Zionist question was of little moment. Against the 'unanswerable case' Chamberlain's chief advisers had made, Weizmann had no convincing policy to offer.

By 10 May he was back in London, determined to make one last effort to stay publication of the statement. On the following evening he saw Chamberlain and MacDonald at the House of Commons. 'What the Arabs were after was [the Jews'] very blood,' he told the startled ministers. 'They wanted their lives, their houses, their gardens. . . . The tragedy of it would be that the law would be on their side, and British bayonets would be there to help them achieve their purpose.' Weizmann added, for good measure, 'that his mother was already preparing his *trousseau* for the Seychelles'. Chamberlain expressed his deep regret and offered his utmost sympathy, but nothing more. As Weizmann prepared to leave, MacDonald, who had remained discreetly silent throughout these exchanges, invited him to tea at his country house, Hyde Hall, in Essex. Weizmann's first inclination was to refuse. He no longer had anything in common with MacDonald, once a good friend but now an utterly despised figure. MacDonald had 'betrayed' him with a rubber smile and was worthy only of his 'contempt, disgust and hatred', he thought. Still, embarrassed at MacDonald's persistent overtures in the presence of Chamberlain, he finally acquiesced.[42]

Whatever remained of their personal relationship was surely destroyed as a result of this tea-party, which left Weizmann 'shattered'; 'it was the worst afternoon of his life'. Never had he spoken 'so rudely and so straight to any man and . . . it left a bitter taste in his mouth'. He accused MacDonald of rank hypocrisy, of treachery, of handing the Jews over to their assassins. No, Weizmann replied, in answer to an indignant rebuttal, 'I have never called you a coward.' He swept on, challenging the government to bring the issue before the International Court at The Hague, pitying Chamberlain, 'the innocent victim of specious advisers'. 'All this talk about strategic necessities,' he continued, 'was just bunk.' In this savage attack, all of Weizmann's pent-up rage poured out, and the hapless MacDonald could not defend himself with any spirit. 'I advised him not to shed crocodile tears', Weizmann explained later to Vera, 'but you can spit in his face and he'll say it's raining.'[43]

It was a pointless confrontation, except in so far as it drained Weizmann's seething emotions. But it was highly symbolic in the sense that it personified the absolute collapse in relations between the Zionists and the British. Dealing well with Britain had always been

Weizmann's special province, his trump card. Now the British had weakened him, perhaps fatally. He had been their staunchest ally, but in undermining his position, they were fanning to life more extreme elements in the Zionist movement.

On 17 May the government published its statement of policy, a document that achieved instant notoriety as 'the May white paper'.[44] It contained no surprises, its proposals following closely those already communicated to the Zionists. On the whole, the British press thought it 'fair', 'logical', 'sound', and 'a supremely wise act of statesmanship'. True, Geoffrey Dawson, editor of *The Times*, called it 'folly', but his paper's editorial policy failed to follow his line; only the *Manchester Guardian* termed it 'disastrous'. The Mufti, supported by other Arab leaders, rejected it, as it failed to give the Arabs a Palestinian state. In Palestine, the *Yishuv* demonstrated against the new policy, and planned a campaign of civil disobedience. Crowds in Tel Aviv and Jerusalem chanted 'If I forget thee O Jerusalem', while banners were raised proclaiming, 'We shall never surrender to the government's policy.' On occasion, the police intervened with batons to disperse unruly elements, and shots were reported to have been fired. But the most telling, defiant challenge to the white paper was the establishment of twelve new Jewish settlements in Palestine during the month of May.[45]

Weizmann could not alter the government's policy, but he could soften its impact. There was perhaps some relief that the white paper had finally been published. The blow had fallen, and now the Zionists could harry the government in public, thrusting aside all previous inhibitions about breaching the protocol of confidential debate. Once again, Weizmann turned to the United States. The power of American Jewry, financial and political, had yet to be tapped to the full. It had proved a potent factor in the First World War; could it not be utilized to even greater effect in these crisis-laden months? But the Zionist lobbyists had a negligible effect on American policy. Roosevelt himself expressed doubts as to the legality of the white paper but in the last resort took no practical steps to undermine Chamberlain's policy. He would not unnecessarily complicate his relations with the British for the sake of the Zionists, whatever his scepticism.[46]

Lack of an active, positive American response was a special, though not unexpected, disappointment. It meant that Weizmann was compelled to work mainly through British channels, a more familiar milieu, and he laboured ceaselessly to pack the press with critical letters and brief his supporters in Parliament for the forthcoming debates. In both these tasks he chalked up notable successes.[47]

In the Commons, he scored a particular triumph. On 23 May, after two days of intensive debate, the House divided on party lines only for the government to discover that its normal majority of 250 had eroded to a mere 89, virtually a vote of no confidence.[48] Amery was 'the high spot' of the first day's debate, Churchill of the second. Weizmann cabled Churchill, whom he had coached personally: 'Your magnificent speech may yet destroy this policy.' Words fail me [to] express my thanks.'[49] But of course it had no such effect. The government might have been shaken by the hostility displayed by Parliament, but it did not flinch from carrying out its declared policy.

However much Weizmann railed against the white paper, its provisions could hardly have taken him by surprise. He had been aware of British intentions for at least a year, since the summer of 1938. Even the much-lauded Peel Commission report contained 'palliatives' that now found expression in the May white paper. For all that, Weizmann acted as though under a traumatic shock. What rankled most were the spectres of an Arab veto and a permanent Jewish minority in Palestine. No Zionist could accept this. It was not simply a question of crippling the National Home, however iniquitous this alone might be—the Yishuv, as Ben Gurion promised, could look after itself[50]—but the fate of European Jewry was at stake. Weizmann, like the entire Zionist leadership, was living under an intolerable emotional strain. The Jewish world he had known in Europe was threatened with extinction. A horrified spectator, he looked on as it disintegrated, powerless to render his persecuted brethren effective aid. He was overpowered by the moral righteousness of his case, yet forced to bow to callous administrative and political dictates.

Weizmann wished to believe that the current crisis was a transient phase in his long *affaire* with the British, a 'sort of mental and moral aberration', as he put it, brought on by the exigencies of the international situation. When the emergency disappeared, so too would the white-paper policy, he hoped, and Anglo-Zionist relations could then proceed along the path he had mapped out long ago. In his public declarations after the publication of the white paper, this train of thought can easily be discerned:

Are we to be disappointed in this darkest hour? I do not believe it. I do believe that very soon there will be a revulsion of feeling, and these temporary necessities, these 'administrative expediencies' of which we have heard so much, will disappear, and that the Britain we know, the Britain which believes in the sanctity of treaties, the Britain which condemns unilateral breaches of promises, this Britain will emerge from the fatal mistake into which it has been led by some temporary aberration.

He offered no facile solutions, no false panaceas. All one could do was to carry on as before, 'bringing in people, reclaiming swamps, building up industries'. This would be the most telling answer to the pusillanimous Chamberlain and the faint-hearted MacDonald. Encouraging his audiences, he entreated them never to lose hope:

> Long before the Balfour Declaration, God has decreed that our destiny is bound up with Palestine, and against this decree, all decrees of humans, however mighty they may appear to themselves and at the time, are as naught; they will blow away like chaff before the wind. [51]

In cold political terms the Zionist leadership, Weizmann at their head, knew that some form of compromise was inevitable. They suffered no illusions as to the intentions of the British government, and they comprehended fully the motives pushing it forward—though they rejected them outright. They argued cogently that the British consistently exaggerated the Arab threat to their security and underestimated the contribution the Zionists could make to imperial defence. But these strictures remained purely academic until put to the test. When hostilities finally broke out, it was too late to reverse the policy. In any case, the Zionists knew that in the event of war immigration would be restricted; they were confident, rightly as it turned out, that they could evade the restrictions on land sales; while the prospect of a Palestinian state ten years in the future and dependent for its establishment on Arab-Jewish co-operation seemed sufficiently remote as to exclude it from the realms of political reality.

For the British, the white paper was a kind of insurance policy, from their point of view essential in the circumstances of 1939. What the Zionists vehemently objected to was being compelled to pay an exorbitant premium for a policy of dubious propriety; and the violent manner and expression of their rejection reflected their hopelessness and frustration on the eve of the holocaust. Both the Zionists and the British were pursuing national interests as they perceived them. It was an unequal clash of opposites, for the Zionists, though they possessed most of the trappings of statehood, lacked the decisive attributes of national power. Weizmann could only tell his constituents to hang on until better times. Not, perhaps, a very inspiring message, but no responsible Zionist could offer a better one.

How to neutralize the white paper? That was the most pertinent question facing the Zionists. Weizmann, prepared to clasp at the flimsiest of straws, looked also to the League of Nations. It was the slenderest of chances, but should the League reject the white paper, Britain would be entangled in interminable legal wrangling if she wished to gain international recognition for the new policy. He canvassed his friends on the permanent mandates commission, flattering this feeble group that it was the one objective body in a distracted world capable of meting out true justice. His pleadings came to naught. Eventually the British, supported by France, stymied his lobbying with comparative ease.[52] Far more hopeful was the case for federalism, which Weizmann now began to espouse with much enthusiasm. This option had not been explicitly excluded by the white paper, and, nursed along by Weizmann, it soon found many influential advocates both in and out of government: the Peel Commissioners; *The Times*; the Archbishop of Canterbury; Lord Lothian; Lord Lugard; and Walter Elliot, to name but the more prominent of them. Even MacDonald was prepared to consider 'some form of federation', while Lord Halifax inclined also in the same direction. Leading Conservative Party officials told Weizmann that they, too, were searching for a more constructive way out of the impasse, as they could ill afford a repetition of the parliamentary debates of May, which had been a considerable source of embarrassment, in political terms a virtual catastrophe.[53]

Weizmann met Professor Coupland at his Oxford home on 20 June. Joined by Lord Lugard the following day, the trio drafted the details of a workable federal scheme for Palestine. In Weizmann's view this meant the Zionists would have full control over immigration, a fair margin for territorial expansion, and, initially at least, parity in the governing bodies of the federation. Under these conditions, the National Home would continue to grow. He was convinced that in the circumstances this was the right path to take. 'It seems to me to be the first ray of light which has pierced the fog of the White Paper policy'. By the beginning of August, Walter Elliot felt able to forecast that federalism had 'come so far forward as the final goal, as to monopolize the picture'.[54] This was too sanguine. Even while the idea of federalism was gaining ground, the forthcoming immigration quota was cancelled, owing, the British explained, to the large influx of so-called "illegal" immigrants—reminding the Zionists that hostile officialdom still wielded its baneful influence.

Still, the picture of events since 17 May was not one of unrelieved gloom. Parliament had protested; some ministers were wavering; federalism was making new converts. Yet there was a singular lack of urgency on the part of the federalists, for they would come forward with their proposal only when it became clear that the white paper had failed. How long would this take? Weizmann departed for his cure on the Continent, confident that he had done everything he could, yet uneasy that the initiative lay with Coupland and his group and not with him.

While he was resting at Cauterets, contemplating these thoughts, he heard the news of his mother's death at the age of eighty-seven. Weizmann's adult life had been spent remote from her influence, meeting her only occasionally on his visits to Russia or Palestine, yet he always retained his childhood image of her as the proverbial Jewish matriarch, the centre of family life, calm, resourceful, radiating inner strength and confidence that drew together the diverse elements of her family. Her death 'came as a terrible shock. To her children a mother is always young'.[55] He commiserated with his family in Palestine but was unable to join them to share their familial grief. In two weeks' time, on 16 August, the twenty-first Zionist Congress was due to convene in Geneva.

When the Congress assembled, it did so under the shadow of war, in Weizmann's words in 'an atmosphere of unreality and irrelevance'. It was the shortest Congress on record. Weizmann reviewed the events of the past years, concluding, 'We have not failed, we believed in Britain.' And indeed, for all the anger, the frustration, the wild talk, none of his critics could offer a viable, alternative policy.

A great row broke out over the question of illegal immigration into Palestine. Rabbi Abba Silver, the ebullient American leader and an outspoken critic of Weizmann, condemned it, to Congress's immense displeasure, arguing that the time was not yet ripe for the confrontation with Britain that it was bound to provoke. The much-respected Palestine Labour leader Berl Katznelson answered him, endorsing the 'illegals' in the most forthright words, to Congress's great delight. Even more, he roundly criticized Weizmann for failing to grasp the true significance of the white paper: 'the old Zionist policy of dunam after dunam . . . is no longer relevant to our times'.[56]

Weizmann turned to Ben Gurion and said: 'Not a helpful speech.'

Ben Gurion replied: 'The best Zionist speech yet made here.' Weizmann's eyes turned to 'small hard stones'.[57] Was there a Labour conspiracy to force his hand on this delicate issue? It was not that Weizmann opposed illegal immigration, as everyone knew, but that he wished to bring in the maximum number of immigrants with the minimum amount of publicity. By 22 August, these controversies had been engulfed by the impending world calamity, for on that date news was received that a non-aggression pact had been signed between the Soviet Union and Germany. Its significance was clear, and Congress acted swiftly to wind up its affairs.

Weizmann met the delegates, some of whom he would never see again, to deliver his farewell speech. He spoke simply, in Yiddish.

> There is a darkness all around us and we cannot see through the clouds. It is with a heavy heart that I take my leave. . . . If, as I hope, we are spared in life and our work continues, who knows—perhaps a new light will shine upon us from the thick black gloom. . . . My heart is overflowing.
>
> We shall meet again [prolonged applause]. We shall meet again in common labour for our land and people. Our people is deathless, our land eternal. There are some things which cannot fail to come to pass, things without which the world cannot be imagined. The remnant shall work on, fight on, live on until the dawn of better days. Towards that dawn I greet you. May we meet again in peace.

On the platform, he embraced Ussishkin and Ben Gurion 'as if he would never let them go'. As he prepared to leave the hall, Congress rose to applaud him, and many delegates had tears in their eyes as hundreds of hands were stretched out towards him. 'Never shall I go through a more moving scene,' wrote Baffy.[58]

Late in the evening of 24 August, the Weizmanns, accompanied by Baffy, set out for London in their Rolls Royce. Twenty-five years ago he had made the same journey in vaguely similar circumstances. How different were his expectations and hopes then? In 1914, sensing that monumental achievements were within his grasp, he had seized his opportunities with the healthy instincts of a natural statesman to set the Zionist movement in the direction of eventual nationhood; in 1939, after many successes and not a few disappointments, he was engaged in a fateful holding-action to secure his earlier triumphs. In Paris, the travellers absorbed the gloom and apathy at the approach of war. 'Certainly "ce n'est pas gai" to be in France during mobilization.' Weizmann saw Blum, who held out the slenderest of chances for peace.

By 29 August the Weizmanns were back in London. That day he sent a letter to Chamberlain pledging that 'the Jews [will] stand by Great Britain and will fight on the side of the democracies' and placing 'Jewish man-power, technical ability, resources, etc.' at the disposal of the British government. 'The Jewish Agency,' he went on, 'has recently had differences in the political field with the Mandatory Power. We would like these differences to give way before the greater and more pressing necessities of the time.' Weizmann was calling for a temporary truce, hoping, in one observer's phrase, to put 'the White Paper into refrigeration and create conditions in which it would appear after the victory as a grotesque and unseemly anachronism.'[59]

At dawn on 1 September German troops crossed into Poland. The following day, Chamberlain replied to Weizmann in a stiff note that did not auger well for the future. He thanked Weizmann for his offer of help, but 'You will not expect me to say more at this stage than that your public-spirited assurances are welcome and will be kept in mind,'[60] At 11 a.m. on 3 September, after dramatic scenes in the House of Commons, Britain declared that a state of war existed with Germany; six hours later, France followed suit. The guns were not to cease firing for another five-and-a-half years, years that would witness the most terrible catastrophe ever to afflict the Jewish people.

SEVENTEEN

ONLY REBUFFS
AND HUMILIATIONS

In his letter to Chamberlain, Weizmann had pledged to subordinate the Zionists' current 'difficulties' with the British government, given 'the more pressing necessities of the time'. He had no doubt about this course of action, and few took issue with him. Ultimately, the future of Zionism, of the National Home, of the Jewish people depended on an Allied victory over Nazi Germany: this goal transcended all others. And with victory, would not Britain remain the paramount power in the Middle East, the decisive voice in a post-war settlement that would determine the fate of Palestine?

But this viewpoint became increasingly difficult to sustain in the face of the British resolution to proceed with the directives of the white paper at almost any price. All the old, threadbare accusations against Weizmann were trundled out: his excessive Anglomania, his outmoded parliamentarism, his surrender to British interests. In the eyes of his accusers, he was the personification of appeasement. These charges wounded him deeply, the more so as they struck him as patently unjust. In private, the British were often the hapless victims of his unbridled tongue; in public, his language was no less cutting, though more restrained. But he would not give moral comfort or political advantage to Hitler by criticizing Britain publicly when she was engaged in a life-or-death struggle against him. He knew the limitations of his diplomacy: he knew his need of the British was greater than their need of him. Orde Wingate once rebuked him: 'You ought to go into Winston's room and *demand* a Jewish army! You ought to bang the table! Why don't you do that?' Weizmann replied, 'I could do as you say, and I might even achieve something by doing it, but I could only do it once, and I want to see Winston Churchill many times.'[1]

This rejoinder highlighted the insuperable dilemma that confronted the Jewish Agency under his leadership, a dilemma from which it never fully escaped until the end of the war. Strategically, all parties claimed a common goal: the defeat of Nazi Germany. Yet they found little or no common ground to define the Jewish contribution toward the realization of that goal. No matter how much pressure the Jewish Agency exerted or how cogently Weizmann argued its case, they were ultimately dependent on the good will of the British government, as British ministers were only too keen to point out. Ben Gurion's celebrated slogan, 'We shall fight the White Paper as if there were no war, and the war as if there were no White Paper', expressed, regardless of its inspiring rhetoric, the fundamental weakness in the Zionist position.

Still, the Zionists hoped to put the white paper 'in abeyance', as Namier airily put it. Despite MacDonald's stinging denial of Namier's wishful thinking, Weizmann detected a 'certain willingness' on the part of the government to provide the Jewish Agency with facilities, mainly communications and travel arrangements, to carry out its work in wartime. In the late autumn of 1939, Weizmann readily acceded to the government's request that he travel to France and Switzerland on scientific business. But nothing, apparently, could melt the 'glue' that was gumming up Jewish efforts to cooperate effectively with the government. Weizmann's offer to place 'Jewish man-power, technical ability, resources, etc.' at its disposal remained very much a dead letter.[2]

The first major confrontation occurred over the promulgation of the white paper's land-transfer regulations in February 1940. For some time there had been unmistakable signs that the government was set on implementing these: immigration into Palestine had been severely cut, and then the quotas for the period October 1939–March 1940 had been cancelled; the link between land and immigration policies was obvious. Weizmann was already thinking in terms of a mass immigration after the war,[3] an unattainable aim unless sufficient land was made available. At the end of November, on the eve of a trip to the United States, he attempted to clarify the situation with Halifax.

> Is the land law to be promulgated, or is it for the time being to remain in abeyance? Are the Jews in Palestine to be treated as suspects, or as people whose loyalties and readiness to serve deserve to be encouraged?

Are political considerations rooted in the white paper to be allowed to defeat schemes of practical assistance in the conduct of the war, or are British war interests to prevail?

Halifax's reply was brought by special messenger to Weizmann's suite in the Dorchester Hotel. His aides gathered round as he read it. Namier glanced over Weizmann's shoulder and remarked, 'This is bad'. In a cold, stiff statement, Halifax ruled that 'It is not possible to modify or postpone the application of the white paper policy.' He reminded Weizmann: 'So far as this country is concerned, we are putting our whole energy into a life-and-death struggle with Nazi Germany, the persecutor of Jewry in Central Europe, and by ridding Europe of the present German regime we hope to render a supreme service to the Jewish people.'

This must have shattered whatever hopes Weizmann had entertained that the government might nullify its policy. The following morning, 20 December, he left for America. From Lisbon, he sent Halifax a reminder that Britain was fighting to preserve the 'moral values forming the very foundations of our civilization'. How, he wondered, did the shabby treatment of the Jews square with this lofty aim? Clearly it did not; but, trapped by the rules of a game not of his making, he pledged yet again 'unconditional' support for the Allies.[4]

What remained for Weizmann was another futile exercise in backstairs lobbying. Opposition leaders were contacted, as Churchill had been, a natural focus for any Zionist canvassing: now a member of the war cabinet, his prestige greatly enhanced, his speech denouncing the white paper was forever engraved on Zionist memories. If anyone could mount a successful counter-attack against the white paper, it was surely he. Weizmann had met with him on 17 December to discuss the projected land legislation. Weizmann told him, 'You have stood at the cradle of the enterprise. I hope you will see it through,' adding that it was his hope that after the war the Jews might build a state in Palestine with three or four million Jews. Churchill replied: 'Yes, indeed, I quite agree with that.'[5]

By late December it appeared as though he had intervened decisively. News reached Baffy Dugdale and Namier that 'the little rabbit' (MacDonald) had suffered a 'thorough trimming'. They considered it was a hopeful end to the old year. Baffy recorded in her diary: 'The Lord shall reign on Zion's Hill.'[6] But the extent of MacDonald's 'trimming' had been exaggerated. Churchill battled valiantly against him;

but he refused to press his opposition to the point of a cabinet split, and predictably he found himself isolated among his colleagues.[7] Fighting back, MacDonald ensured that the legislation was finally approved in cabinet on 12 February, 1940. The comparative ease with which Churchill's challenge had been mastered signaled an ominous portent of things to come.

The regulations, promulgated on 25 February, constituted a devastating, in theory fatal, blow to Zionist plans. Out of an estimated 10,429 square miles only 519 (378,080 acres) were set aside for unrestricted Jewish land purchases, and these included the large urban areas of Haifa, Tel Aviv, and Jerusalem. Mass demonstrations now swept the *Yishuv*, which often were dispersed in a most brutal manner. Weizmann demanded a judicial enquiry into the 'outrages'. No action was ever taken. In a phrase that illustrated the helplessness of his position, he reserved the right to publish details of police brutality as soon 'as this can be done without injury to our common cause'. He viewed these deplorable events from New York, cut off from the events he had hoped to control. Lacking tangible power, he fell back on words, relying on his moral authority. To his old friend Lord Lothian, now British ambassador in Washington, he wrote that the regulations reduced the National Home to 'a ghetto' and condemned Palestine to 'stagnation'. He had no wish to embarrass the government, but he would never acquiesce in an 'illegal' and 'wholly unjust' action that even as a temporary expedient was useless.[8] His protest duly delivered, the regulations went into force. But in fact Weizmann's prognosis proved correct, though perhaps not in the sense he meant it. Although the regulations had a serious effect, they by no means brought Jewish land purchases to a halt. Legal ingenuity discovered loopholes that enabled the Jews to continue to acquire land in the prohibited and restricted areas, though on a reduced scale. Various sources estimate that during the war Jewish land possessions increased by approximately 61,250 acres.[9]

The war contributed to Weizmann's moody temperament, which was in any case prone to rapidly alternating humours. But he was not alone in suffering fluctuations of the spirit. All the Zionist leaders were under terrific pressure, which increased as the war progressed, and their behaviour, which to outsiders often appeared hysterical, reflected the intractable nature of the problems they faced but were unable to solve. Even Weizmann's relations with Baffy, usually conducted on an absolutely even keel, became unbalanced. Shortly before

Christmas 1940 they quarreled over a trivial matter, 'a piece of tattle' that Weizmann had overheard and that seemed to impugn his capacity for leadership. Baffy, eager to clear the air, visited Weizmann at the Dorchester:

> He talked from 3.30 to 5.00 without drawing breath, the most extraordinary jumble of thoughts, accusations (of Gestetner and others), of descriptions of his lonely position in Jewry, the faults and findings of his colleagues (e.g. Lewis), in fact of everything under the sun, some of it showing his greatness, some showing his smallness, all of it showing that he is under an almost intolerable strain. When at last he had done, I did my best to disentangle the parts that bear on our personal relationship and explained to him the point at which I thought they had gone wrong, in October and November, when he began to neglect the office for the laboratory, and Vera had let out to me that he thought we were 'bothering' him. I told him I must reserve the right to speak of him as I chose behind his back. . . . We parted friends of course. But the whole episode has been an experience which I shall not forget.[10]

Other friends and colleagues were less fortunate: Weizmann was clearly living in a state of high nervous tension. When in the summer of 1940 the danger of a German invasion of Britain seemed imminent, it was suggested to the Weizmanns that if the Germans succeeded in their plans the first person they would kill would be Churchill, the second Weizmann. Vera acquired some Veronal pills to forestall such a contingency. Some months earlier Weizmann had drawn up a new will, bequeathing his house in Rehovot, after his children's death, to the Jewish people, 'as a sort of "Chequers", or as a museum'. He ensured that some of the Zionist archives would be transferred to Canada, and personally requested his comrades (Leonard Stein, Arthur Lourie, Lewis Namier, and Moshe Shertok) to gather the material relating to his 'forty years' work' for the movement. These were sensible precautions, but late in May he rejected outright Baffy's suggestion that he remove his centre of operations to the United States 'to preserve himself for the movement', claiming that he would be more useful in London 'both as a Zionist leader and as a chemist'.[11]

On 10 May 1940 the Germans launched their great offensive in the west. In the space of six weeks their Panzer divisions had cut through France and stood poised to strike across the English Channel. By mid-June the Allied forces lay broken and scattered, their remnants evacuated from the beaches of Dunkirk, and Hitler was master of the Continent from the Atlantic to the Vistula. As the German armies swept forward, Weizmann gave expression to his darkest thoughts in a letter to Meyer Weisgal, whom he had recently appointed his personal representative in the United States:

> I can only trust that you and our friends in America will take counsel together, bearing in mind the terrible and indisputable fact that European Jewry, with very few exceptions, has been practically blotted out, so that the whole responsibility henceforth falls on America. The *Yishuv* is still intact, and I hope it may remain so, and that Italy will not join the Germans. But who knows? [Italy entered the war on 10 June.]
>
> The foundations of everything in which we believe, and for which we live and work, are rocking, and unless the onslaught of the German hordes is stopped in time, we shall all go under. I am confident that it *will* be stopped in the end; but when and at what cost, and what havoc may have been wrought meanwhile, no one can say. It is such thoughts as these that govern one's life at present, and everything else seems to have receded into the background.[12]

A new Dark Age had descended on Europe; and millions of Jews, whose fate Weizmann had prophetically foretold, found themselves in the grip of a barbarism more terrible than any known in recorded history.

These tumultuous events raised Churchill to the premiership of a new wartime coalition that was confronted with the gravest crisis in Britain's history. Zionist circles heaved a huge sigh of relief that 'the old gang' had finally been pushed aside. Churchill, who could always be counted upon, was supported by 'friends' of Zionism such as Arthur Greenwood (minister without portfolio), Archie Sinclair (Secretary of State for Air), Duff Cooper (Minister of Information), Leo Amery (Secretary of State for India), Herbert Morrison (Home Secretary), Ernest Bevin (Minister of Labour), and Albert Alexander (First Lord of the Admiralty), while even Clement Attlee (Lord Privy Seal) had moved 'closer to us'. In the cabinet reshuffle, the despised MacDonald was shunted aside to the Ministry of Health and later 'banished' to Canada as High Commissioner. The new Colonial Secretary, Lord Lloyd, was, in Shertok's words, 'brilliant', 'unstable', 'ambitious', 'inflexible', 'slightly mad', though Ben Gurion thought him 'an honest and sympathetic man'.[13] Had 'the Dead Hand' been lifted at last? The initial signs were encouraging. With Britain's military and political fortunes at their nadir, government relations with the Zionists were bound to improve. Reassuring messages were relayed through Randolph Churchill that his father would now take a more positive view toward Jewish offers of help.[14]

There was certainly room for optimism. Yet Weizmann knew it was pointless to indulge in wishful thinking. No government, not even Churchill's, would formally rescind the white paper—the example of Passfield had not faded from his memory. He was equally aware that governments came and went but that the officials endured, seemingly forever. Nothing could dent their hostility. For the moment, the most he could do was to chip away here and there until he had effectively nullified the white paper. Yet even at the outset of the war he fixed his eye on a wider goal, one that he had pursued tenaciously since the Peel proposals. When he met Roosevelt in Washington in February 1940 he revived the idea of an independent Jewish state. Roosevelt characteristically enveloped his supplicant in a friendly and comfortable atmosphere, which Weizmann all too readily interpreted as agreement with his sentiments, while disclosing little as to his true thoughts.[15] With Roosevelt apparently sympathetic and Churchill an old and trusted gentile Zionist, Weizmann hoped to promote Zionism as an Allied war aim through these dominant personalities whose prestige increased as the war progressed. Only they could break down the barriers of opposition, unravel the red tape, and impose their will on the bureaucrats.

But personalities, however charismatic, would not decide the central issues. Even when reinforced by the loyal Smuts, the Churchill–Roosevelt duo was unable to overcome the ingrained enmity of their officials. Nor, in the case of Roosevelt, is the evidence entirely conclusive that he wished to do so. Although Churchill fought valiantly for Zionism throughout the war, he fought largely in vain. His powerful and persuasive interventions, reinforced by the authority of his office, came to naught against the combined weight of his chief military and political advisers, who time and again turned his arguments back to the same incontrovertible point: any far-reaching concessions to the Zionists would severely, perhaps fatally, damage Britain's imperial interests in the Middle East and probably throughout the Muslim world. This reasoning was sufficiently compelling to remind Churchill of where his true duty lay.

Weizmann clung to these will-o'-the-wisps not only out of a misplaced conviction but also for lack of a better alternative. For the time being, he exploited Churchill's good will by renewing his offer of Jewish help. On 29 May 1940 he forwarded to Churchill a comprehensive programme outlining how the Jews could contribute to the British war effort.[16] Point by point he elaborated the same proposal that Chamberlain had cold-shouldered at the beginning of the war. Promising to mobilize 'the economic, military, political and technical resources of the Jewish people in Palestine and elsewhere for the British cause', he singled out supplies, economic warfare, and propaganda for special mention. Regarding military aid, he proposed:

(a) We can raise several divisions in Palestine and elsewhere for service with the British army. We have in Palestine about 30,000 men who have had some training either as auxiliaries to the British Force there or in European armies. (b) We can organize an Air Force unit (squadron) . . . (c) We can help with Military Intelligence.

For every Zionist, the right of the Jews to arm and defend themselves, to raise an independent Jewish fighting force in a war against their most vicious persecutor, was axiomatic. 'If we have to go down,' Weizmann clarified to Lord Moyne, 'we are entitled to go down fighting, and the Mandatory Power is in duty bound to grant us this elementary human right.'[17] Chamberlain's initial response to this, which had left Weizmann bitter and frustrated, was the beginning of a protracted and dreary controversy that did not change with the advent of Churchill; indeed, it lasted until the final stages of the war. Equally disheartening was the attitude of the British authorities in Palestine, who clamped down heavily on the activities of the Haganah, seemingly intent on crippling its operational capacity and destroying its morale. Perhaps the most glaring case was the arrest and detention in October 1939 of forty-three members of the Haganah for possession of arms. Many of these men had served with distinction under Wingate during the Arab disturbances, but they were now condemned to long terms of imprisonment, and it was only after a prolonged public campaign that the detainees were finally released, as a gesture of good will, in February 1941.

Despite these difficulties, the response of the *Yishuv* to the war effort was remarkable. By the end of September 1939, out of a community of less than half-a-million, 136,000 Palestinian Jews—90,000 men and 46,000 women—had enrolled through the Jewish Agency for some kind of essential national service, the vast majority of the men specifically mentioning their readiness to serve with the British army. The British reaction to this impressive display was niggardly. The figures speak for themselves. By mid-1941 only 9000 Palestinians, including seventy officers, had been absorbed into the British forces.[18] When, in the autumn of 1939, the first official call came for Palestinian Jews to join British units the numbers requested were small, and, of more consequence, the volunteers were to be enlisted on a basis of strict numerical parity between Jews and Arabs. As the Arabs scarcely responded, the Jewish contribution was reduced to a bare minimum. In December Weizmann renewed his offer of 'a Jewish division' to Field Marshal Sir Edmund Ironside, Chief of the Imperial General Staff. Of course, he accepted the fact that the higher command posts would be staffed by British officers, preferably 'sympathetic' ones (a proposal warmly endorsed by Wingate, who had already carved out for himself the role of commander of the future Jewish division), but he requested that the junior officers should 'include a strong contingent of Palestinian Jews'. Ironside, who had revealed much understanding in private conversations with Weizmann, now spoke in his official voice. Accepting Weizmann's offer 'in principle', he added that 'other implications . . . will have to be taken into consideration'. The British stuck to their principle of parity, much to the Zionists' chagrin.[19]

On the face of it, Weizmann's programme was an extremely attractive one. If acted upon it would have released tens of thousands of British soldiers for duty elsewhere and would also have established, in an area of vital strategic importance, an industrial-arms complex of inestimable value to the war effort. Yet, despite the gravity of the situation, in early September, Hore Belisha, Secretary of State for War, vetoed the formation of independent Jewish units, explaining to Weizmann that Britain's real problem was lack of equipment, not men.[20] Although Weizmann was disposed to accept this clarification, or at least not to challenge it openly, many Zionists, less accommodating than he, saw in it only another manifestation of British ill will. Still, the British excuse should not be rejected out of hand. Fully equipped mass armies do not spring up overnight. After the neglect of the interwar period, shortage of supplies was a real, even if at times an exaggerated, issue.

But there were other, in the long run more telling, considerations. With the passing of time it became abundantly apparent that the British were moved mainly by political motives. Any obligations incurred to the Jews would unquestionably provoke the hostility of the Arab, perhaps Muslim, world, while the political implications of maintaining a Jewish force, commanded by its own officer corps, were too radical for the government to sanction. It was General Barker, commander of British forces in Palestine, who voiced this attitude most violently. He informed Ben Gurion that the Haganah 'were preparing for rebellion against Great Britain' and that 'he felt it his duty to smash that organization'. General Sir Alan Brooke, Chief of the Imperial General Staff, made much the same point, if more politely, when he briefed the British military representative in Washington, General Dill, who was girding himself for an interview with Weizmann.[21] The generals' views were but a reflection of much deeper currents prevailing in government circles and the Palestine administration. In this sense, it made not a scrap of difference whether one 'banged on the table', as Ben Gurion, Namier, and Wingate at times wished to do, or used the less histrionic Weizmann style. As always, the British would be guided first and foremost by their perception of their own interests. In the First World War, Weizmann had persuaded them that they and the Zionists shared a common interest. Perhaps he believed that in the Second World War he could, if allowed sufficient time and leeway, perform a similar sleight-of-hand. However, it was absolutely clear to him that he could not badger the British into agreement. At least his more level-headed approach guaranteed continuity in Zionist diplomacy, a vital ingredient to a successful outcome of his lobbying.

'The walls of Jericho fall, but at what a moment!' Baffy recorded on 28 May 1940. Weizmann had just left Brendan Bracken, Churchill's go-between with the Zionists, who had told him that 'the P.M. is telling Lord Lloyd that no obstacles are to be put in the way of the Jewish war effort'. Bracken was not the most reliable of sources: he had a tendency to enrich his findings, and the Zionists had an unfortunate tendency to build on his embellishments—a dangerous combination. In fact, Lloyd gave away little when he met Weizmann. Claiming that 'a real *risorgimento*' was astir in the Arab world and that any precipitate move would set it ablaze, he aired the idea of separate Jewish and Arab units under 'one British umbrella'.[22] This was a tiny step forward, but it signified a change from the bleak days of MacDonald.

Weizmann quarried on, pursuing the matter further with Lloyd and Eden and, more importantly, when he lunched with Churchill himself. On the first anniversary of the war, 3 September 1940, Churchill gave 'his blessing for the Jewish Army'. Also, Baffy noted, 'there will probably be a "Desert Force" (Jewish) destined to strike up at Libya from the south. This is Orde Wingate's idea and it is hoped that he will train them.' Ten days later Weizmann clinched Churchill's 'blessing' at a meeting with Anthony Eden and Lloyd. Baffy summed up the occasion:

> A great Day! . . . all our demands are granted. There is to be a Jewish Fighting Force of 10,000 men, of whom three to four thousand to be recruited in Palestine, and national status and recognition granted, as to the Poles and Czechs. The Walls of Jericho have fallen, fallen! I looked in at the Dorchester about 5 p.m. and found Chaim just back from this interview, elated and solemn. He said, 'It is almost as great a day as the Balfour Declaration.' [23]

The results of these parleys were submitted to the war cabinet and summarized by Lord Lloyd in a letter to Weizmann.

> You will be authorized to recruit 10,000 Jews for incorporation in Jewish units in the British Army. Not more than 3,000 of these will be drawn from Palestine. The remainder will be drawn from America or wherever else you can recruit them. Each recruit will have to produce a guarantee that he will be accepted by his country of origin after the war. These Jewish units, including their officers, will be trained in the United Kingdom, the officers being selected by yourself or your representative with the approval of the War Office. No guarantee can be given as to the theatre of war in which the force . . . will be employed. Equipment will be provided by His Majesty's Government as and when their resources allow. [24]

Lloyd called for strict confidentiality, noting that nothing could be done before the presidential elections in the United States. Preparations were put in motion to create the force. A liaison officer, Brigadier Alec Lee, was appointed, and shortly afterward Brigadier Leonard Hawes was commissioned as its commander. Weizmann's programme appeared to be on the brink of realization.

Although Lord Lloyd's letter contained the essence of Weizmann's demands, its rigid framework revealed some of the government's hesitations about authorizing an independent Jewish force. The Foreign Office, the Colonial Office, the War Office, and in particular the Middle East military command all harboured serious doubts as to its overall utility to British policy, and all would work, in their different ways, to reverse the decision or empty it of real content. Nor could their fears have lessened after hearing the cries of the Revisionists that a Jewish fighting force should be used to 'gatecrash' Palestine, or Ben Gurion's insistence that it must fight in Palestine, or even

London Conference, 1939

Weizmann in his laboratory at the Sieff Institute, Rehovot, May 1938

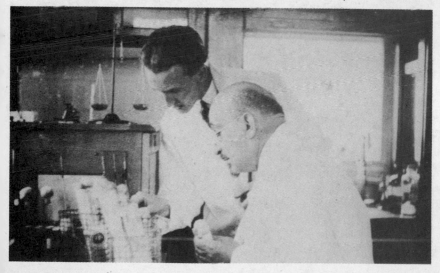

Tea-time at Kibbutz Geva, 1946

Weizmann's tour through Emek and Galilee, 1944. Inspecting a guard of honour of Jewish settlement police at Nir David.

Weizmann and Vera voting in
Israeli general election,
25 January 1949.

Weizmann being sworn in as first President of
Israel by Yosef Sprinzak, 17 February 1949.

Opening the Twenty-second Zionist Congress
at Basel, December 1946. It was the last
Congress that Weizmann attended.

Weizmann presenting a Torah scroll to
President Harry S. Truman, May 1948.

Weizmann in Washington, 1948

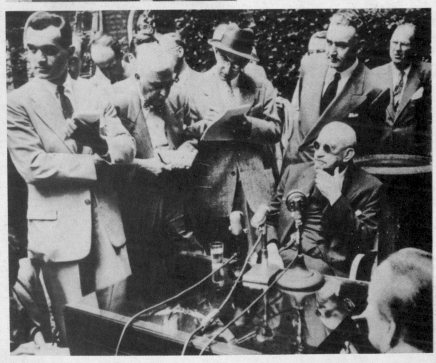

Reviewing Israeli troops at Be'er Sheva, March 1949. Weizmann is holding the arm of Yigal Alon, commander of the Palmach, and is escorted by a helmeted Chaim Bar-Lev (later chief-of-staff of the Israeli army).

Weizmann and Vera at Israeli army maneuvers, 1950

Vera, with Michael's wings on her hat

Weizmann and his entourage inspecting his new Lincoln limousine, presented to him by Henry Ford II,-November 1950.

The Weizmann house, Rehovot

Benji Weizmann

Michael Weizmann

Weizmann and Vera in the
library of their home at
Rehovot

Weizmann relaxing with his
grandson, David.

Weizmann's outburst to Eden in January 1941 that two million Jews would enter Palestine by the front door after the war.[25] Still, the idea of 10,000 Jews fighting in 'Jewish units' was a seductive one, and the Zionists, allowing their wish to be father of the thought, interpreted it as allowing for a force of divisional strength. Flags and badges, national anthems and regimental music, even the status of rabbis, became subjects for weighty discussion. Lloyd soon brought the parties concerned down to earth. 'Ill, and very irritable', he bluntly informed Weizmann in early November, 'no force had been intended, only units in British Army'; later he told Namier, equally frankly, 'No, no one ever talked of a division; it is units.'[26]

Lord Lloyd died on 4 February 1941: it fell to his successor, Lord Moyne, to bring the issue to a head. Churchill needed much persuasion before agreeing to an adverse decision. To the last, he remained unimpressed with the arguments made to him: 'Wavell [commander-in-chief, Middle East], like most British military officers, is strongly pro-Arab,' he wrote to Moyne. Nor did he trust Wavell's judgement, having overruled him once: 'All went well, and not a dog barked.' But with the British position in the eastern Mediterranean close to disaster in the spring of 1941, Churchill did not want unnecessary complications. 'Therefore,' he instructed Moyne, 'Dr. Weizmann should be told that the Jewish Army project must be put off for six months, but may be reconsidered again in four months. The sole reason given should be lack of equipment.'[27]

Whether Weizmann swallowed this explanation, as has been suggested, is not entirely clear. Had he lacked political antennae, there might be some justification for believing that he did, but no one could level that charge against Weizmann. Throughout his career he displayed an artist's sensitivity to nuance in political debate. It is likely that the government's true motives were as obvious to him as to his critics. As he wrote to Felix Frankfurter at the time, 'The main reason for not arming the Jews is political and bound up with appeasement of the Arabs.'[28]

The controversy in Zionist circles centered on tactics. Perhaps, Weizmann reasoned, the British government's postponement could be turned to some advantage. Ventilating the contents of Moyne's letter in restricted circles in the United States and Britain would have the effect of nailing down in public the political pledge that a Jewish fighting force would one day be created while emphasizing the nonpolitical nature of its current postponement—thereby, it was optimistically believed, manoeuvering the government into a position from which it would be difficult to retreat in four months' time. True, this was the slenderest of hopes. But apart from bluster and threats, what alternative remained? Namier, now vociferously criticizing him on this issue, concluded a lengthy censure by noting to Baffy, 'This matter has to be handled in the most careful and gingerly manner . . . so far from playing on a good wicket, we are in a tight corner. We have to move with supreme caution and not in a spirit of exuberant optimism.'[29] This was akin to preaching to the converted.

On 12 March 1941, the eve of Weizmann's departure for another trip to the United States, 'a miracle' occurred. He went to Downing Street to say farewell to Brendan Bracken, only to find himself ushered in for an impromptu chat with Churchill. Churchill confessed that whenever he saw Weizmann he felt 'a twist in his heart'. 'As their thoughts were 99 per cent the same', he continued, there was little need for a long conversation, but he reassured Weizmann that the decision regarding the Jewish fighting force had only been postponed, not reversed. Turning to greater matters, the post-war settlement, Churchill told Weizmann

> that he was thinking of a settlement between us and the Arabs after the war. The man with whom we should come to an agreement is Ibn Saud. He, the P.M., would see to it and would use his good offices. I. S. would be made the Lord of the Arab countries, the 'Boss of the Bosses' as he put it. But 'he would have to agree with Weizmann' (he put it that way) with regard to Palestine. 'I will see you through', the P.M. said.

In *Trial and Error*, Weizmann records that Churchill added, 'Keep this confidential, but you might talk it over with Roosevelt when you get to America. There's nothing he and I cannot do if we set our minds on it.'[30]

Time would prove this an over-sanguine evaluation, but Weizmann was clearly impressed with Churchill's off-the-cuff remarks, interpreting them as a commitment to support a Jewish state after the war. Just before he was about to board his aircraft at a secluded airfield near Bournemouth, he sealed a résumé of the conversation in an envelope and sent it off for safe keeping to his friend, Sigmund Gestetner, 'to be opened in case something happens to us on our trip'. These were perilous times, and Churchill's pledge must be preserved at all cost for posterity. As in a last will and testament, he swore before all 'to the truth of this statement'.[31]

By the spring of 1941, the British position in the eastern Mediterranean had been gravely weakened. In a swift and ruthless campaign, German armies occupied Yugoslavia, Greece, and, in a daring airborne operation, the island of Crete, inflicting heavy casualties on British land and sea power and compelling the evacuation of the remnants of the British expeditionary force to Cyprus and Egypt. As the Greek débâcle unfolded and General Rommel's Afrika Corps advanced into Libya toward Egypt, the British government made some concessions to the Zionists. Generous in relation to previous decisions, they nevertheless fell far short of Zionist expectations.[32]

In the autumn, on his return from America, Weizmann renewed the campaign but once again encountered acute disappointment. Pleading shortages in shipping and equipment, Moyne put 'the matter of a Jewish contingent into cold storage for the present'. This was only partially accurate. When the cabinet discussed the question, some ministers voiced apprehension at equipping 'troops of doubtful value'. This dubious assumption was reinforced by a widespread fear that any armed Jewish force would be used to solve the Palestine problem along Zionist lines once the war had ended. Why, the ministers and generals rationalized, should they train and equip a Jewish unit only for it to be employed against British interests? As an alternative the government proposed to expand the conscription of Jewish 'technical personnel (doctors, engineers, etc.)'; and, as a further sop, to encourage the enrollment of additional Palestinian Jews, though only for local and police duties. The idea of a Jewish fighting force was again rejected. Weizmann appealed in vain to Churchill and angrily rebuked Moyne: 'the floor is littered with broken promises'. Small wonder that he complained about the 'Buffs and Rebuffs' (the Palestine companies were attached to the East Kent Regiment, 'the Buffs') he had endured from the government.[33]

The situation did not materially alter until the summer of 1942. Prompted then by Rommel's renewed advance into Egypt, the British government eventually decided to abandon its principle of strict numerical parity and to form a Palestinian Regiment with separate Jewish and Arab battalions. Although the Zionists considered this 'a real step in the right direction', it was not until the autumn of 1944 that the disparate Jewish units were welded together into a truly Jewish fighting force, one that met in some measure the original demands first raised by Weizmann in September 1939. Weizmann thanked Churchill 'most warmly', sending him a sketch of the proposed flag: 'two horizontal blue stripes on a white background with the Star of David in the centre'. 'We hope to see our young men follow it into battle alongside the Union Jack'. Ben Gurion, in a generous lapse, later admitted that the credit for securing the JFF 'must go largely to Weizmann and Moshe Sharett [Shertok]'. But it had taken four long and tedious years to tear down the walls of Jericho.[34]

Weizmann's wartime career was not only marked by acute public disappointments, but also touched by personal tragedy. In the early morning of 12 February 1942, he and Vera were waiting in the lobby of a hotel in Bristol, about to leave for another trip to the United States, when Weizmann was called to the telephone. At the other end, Simon Marks read out the text of a telegram from the Air Ministry informing him that Michael, captain of a Whitley bomber on anti-U-boat patrol, had been reported missing in operations over the Bay of Biscay. The Weizmanns hurried back to London, where they were consoled by their friends. Baffy saw them three days later: 'Chaim very natural, poor Vera frozen stiff.' They held out against all odds that Michael would be found. Their nephew, Ezer, then training as a pilot in the RAF, unwittingly raised their hopes when a friend of his sent a postcard to his father, Chilik, who was staying at the Weizmanns' home in Rehovot, which was seen by Vera: 'We met your son, he is flying and he sends you his love.' The effect must have been shattering.

Michael was lost, and Benji was invalided out of the army with shell-shock. Vera was particularly affected by the tragedy, and her recovery was slow, 'like a wounded bird trying to fly', Weizmann recorded. Only the birth of their grandson, David—'a bright spark', in Weizmann's words—afforded their own intimate family circle some sense of continuity.[35]

After 'a month of martyrdom', Weizmann set off on the third of his wartime journeys to the United States. (In all, he spent some twenty-one months in North America.) Even at the outset of hostilities, it was clear that America's role in world affairs would be enhanced as a result of the war, and Weizmann was also aware that Roosevelt, though he had acquiesced in the white paper policy, had voiced vigorous doubts as to its validity and efficacy. With the fate of the Jewish people hanging in the balance, American support would be decisive. As in the First World War, he aimed to mobilize United States support for Zionism and unite American Jewry behind Zionist aims.

So began again the odyssey he had first undertaken in the 1920s: hectic timetables, crowded meetings, fatiguing coast-to-coast expeditions. Though not crowned with success, his mission gave substantial support to American Zionism. He called upon his close associates Weisgal (his 'personal representative'), Wise, and Lipsky to effect 'a real *union sacrée*' among American Jewry. This was easier said than done. It was essential not only to bridge the gap between Zionists and non-Zionists, but to reconcile the deep personal rivalries that divided the Zionist leadership. Stephen Wise could now be counted upon, but his fiery adversary, Rabbi Abba Hillel Silver, was more unpredictable: 'Put not your trust in princes,' he urged, thinking of Roosevelt and Churchill, and perhaps also of Weizmann. A Republican in his sympathies, he was not above weaning the Jewish vote away from the Democrats if Roosevelt should refuse to use his influence to soften British policy. As the overwhelming majority of American Jews voted the Democratic ticket, this amounted to virtual heresy, particularly for Wise, a Democrat who was close to Roosevelt's inner circle. Weizmann viewed the exploitation of Zionism as a cat's-paw in American politics with horror, but he could not control Silver, whose militancy and rhetorical skill—his populist harangues were, more often than not, greeted with rapturous applause—were painful thorns in his side.[36]

When Weizmann met Roosevelt in February 1940, he advanced the cause of an independent Jewish state, and with Roosevelt nodding agreement he believed he had cause for satisfaction. But it was difficult to hold the American Jews in tight rein, particularly from London. It soon became evident that he would have to invest much time and energy in monitoring the American scene. On his return to London, he bared his thoughts to Richard Meinertzhagen, who noted: 'His aim is to secure substantial backing in America as anti-semitic feeling in Britain is so strong as to give small chance for progressive Zionism. At the end of this war it is [his] intention to secure American co-operation and influence in Palestine and demand Jewish sovereignty.'[37]

In the spring of 1941, Weizmann took in the Grand Canyon, Yosemite Valley, Arrowhead Springs, Los Angeles and Hollywood—which he found 'controlled by Jews' and rather vulgar—San Francisco, Washington, and Toronto, as well as the eastern establishments of New

York and Boston. Summing up his impressions he found 'a very sound sentiment for Palestine' among American Jewry that, unfortunately, the Zionist Organization was unable to exploit owing to 'undue friction' in its machine. The Jewish upper middle classes, he thought, were either 'aloof' or 'hostile and ignorant', and as the Zionist educational programme was rusty, little headway was being made among them. He did not exclude himself from blame: twenty years of carrying the heaviest burdens had left him, like so many of his colleagues, 'tired and oppressed'. Turning to matters of state, he reflected realistically but sadly that 'not one iota of difference' separated the officials of the state department from their counterparts in the foreign or colonial offices: they were 'interchangeable', 'tainted with an anti-Zionist bias' that affected the President, Secretary of State Cordell Hull, and his deputy, Sumner Welles.[38] The anti-Zionist glue-pot was as evident in Washington as in London.

Weizmann's advocacy of a Jewish state to Roosevelt was consistent with his views since the days of the Peel report. He never deviated from his belief that there would have to be partition, but early in the war another alternative was put to him. In October 1939, through the auspices of Namier, Weizmann met with Harry St. John Bridger Philby, explorer, orientalist, and confidante of Ibn Abdul Saud, over luncheon at the Athenaeum in London. Weizmann knew Philby from old and did not trust him. His first dealings with him had dated from the early 1920s. Before he knew Philby personally, Weizmann had recommended him to Samuel for a post in the Palestine Administration, which, needless to say, he did not fill. Then Philby had once offered him an extraordinary job: the premiership of a joint kingdom of Palestine and Transjordan under the kingship of Abdullah—an admirable idea, perhaps, but one which spoke of an over-ripe imagination out of touch with political reality. Desultory contacts with him continued in the late 1930s but yielded nothing of substance. Weizmann saw him as an 'adventurer and enemy', 'a political *dilettante*', a 'concession hunter'; the Colonial Office spoke of him as 'an absolute liar and a dangerous man'.[39]

Philby now proposed that 'western Palestine should be handed over completely to the Jews', with its Arab population being transferred elsewhere; in return, the Jews should try 'to secure for the Arabs national unity and independence', which could be achieved 'under Ibn Saud alone'. With 'extensive financial help' from the Jews (Philby mentioned £20 million), the deal could be completed. Weizmann listened, was prepared to consider the 'economic advantages', but would make no binding promises, as 'we had not the power "to deliver the goods"'. Nor would he make any commitment that conflicted with 'our loyalties toward Great Britain and France'. They agreed to explore the issue more thoroughly, Weizmann with his contacts in the United States and Britain, Philby with Ibn Saud.[40]

The tortuous negotiations that followed the Athenaeum talks, with their conflicting reports and interpretations, bore out Weizmann's basic evaluation of Philby. But Weizmann was induced to lend credence to the plan, more than it deserved, because of unambiguous hints he received that Churchill and Roosevelt would back it: Churchill's scheme for making Ibn Saud 'Boss of the Bosses', with Roosevelt's help, was very much in his mind when he pursued these matters in the United States. In the presence of Sumner Welles, Roosevelt, in June 1943, touched upon the plan though without mentioning it by name.[41] Indeed, from Weizmann's point of view any scheme that promised 'western Palestine' was singularly attractive, particularly as both Britain and the United States were receptive to the idea or at least did not reject it outright. Even the idea of creating an Arab federation, which would ensure a role for a Jewish state in western Palestine, would not have deterred him. This concept had been common currency for a number of years, and on different occasions both Ben Gurion and Weizmann had supported it, hoping in this way to lessen Arab hostility.[42] Thus he had good reason for exploring this avenue, and it would have been irresponsible of him had he not done so. Perhaps also, at the back of his mind, he dreamed of repeating his great *coup* of 1919, with Ibn Saud now playing Feisal's role.

Yet nothing materialized from these parleys except misunderstandings and mutual recriminations, although all parties remained in contact until the end of 1943. Throughout, Philby displayed great arrogance, claiming falsely that he could persuade the king of the plan's benefits. But Ibn Saud refused to be drawn into any meaningful negotiations, even, apparently, blacklisting Philby; and this outlandish affair finally petered out when Roosevelt's special emissary to Ibn Saud, Colonel Hoskins, reported that the king wanted nothing to do with Weizmann who had impugned his 'honour, patriotism and religion' with a bribe which he regarded as a 'gross insult'.[43] Gaining western Palestine by agreement with the Arabs had always been a desert mirage, enticing its viewers into taking false steps. So it would have to be partition imposed by the Great Powers, Weizmann's first option, which, in truth, he had never abandoned.

Weizmann included the Soviet Union in these calculations. On 2 March 1942 he addressed a memorandum on the 'USSR and Zionism' to Ivan Maisky, the sociable Soviet ambassador to London, in which he elaborated on Palestine's role in solving the Jewish question, hoping that the terrible experiences suffered by both the Jewish and Russian peoples during the war would soften traditional Soviet hostility to Zionism. To Maisky he outlined their community of purpose, explaining,

> Three of the most fundamental aspects of the Soviet social philosophy [are also] embodied in the national system which is being built up in Palestine. Collective welfare and not economic gain is the guiding principle and goal of the economic structure; equality of standing is established in the community between manual and intellectual workers; and consequently the fullest scope is provided for the intellectual life and the development of labour.

Both societies were inspired by a joint aim: to transform backward countries into fully developed modern societies; and as 'no fundamental psychological barriers' separated them, and the 'Zionist Movement has never felt antagonistic to the Soviet social philosophy', the path was clear to 'a mutual understanding'.[44]

No dramatic breakthrough resulted from this appeal. The Soviet Union remained basically hostile to Zionism; and it was only after the war that the Soviet government startled the Zionists, and its erstwhile allies, by registering support for partition—not, needless to say, out of a sudden passion for Zionism or even because its ideologues had adopted Weizmann's speciously argued community of purpose.

Weizmann's frequent trips to America concerned not only Zionist business. Before Pearl Harbor, the British encouraged his visits because they believed that his presence, the symbol of persecuted Jewry, would foster sympathy for Britain, which was standing alone against Nazi Germany. But he also went to advance his scientific work. From the outbreak of war, Weizmann had placed his scientific expertise at the service of the British government. In the autumn of 1939 he had gone to Switzerland to confer with Richard Willstaetter about German secret weapons, particularly new forms of gas. In June 1940, Herbert Morrison, then Minister of Supply, offered him the post of honorary chemical adviser to the director of scientific research. Weizmann accepted. He was provided with a laboratory, 'a large matchbox' in a Knightsbridge mews close to Hyde Park Corner. There he gathered round him a group of chemists, which included his team of Harold Davies and Ernst Bergmann, and set to work. By official decree they were required to cease work during air raids; but these became so frequent in the winter of 1940–41 that Weizmann decided to turn a deaf ear. By a odd quirk of fate, he was working in his laboratory when his designated shelter received a direct hit, which probably saved his life.

As always, he found great mental and physical relaxation in scientific research. It absorbed much of his time and energy—in the view of his Zionist colleagues too much. On more than one occasion he was berated, behind his back, for neglecting his Zionist tasks. At times, this criticism caught his attention, but he shrugged it off as short-sighted. The lessons of the First World War loomed once again before him. Could he now translate his scientific talents into political advantages for his people? With magnificent achievements already to his credit, his reputation secure, his prestige high, he would not be deterred this time from putting forward a definite claim for a sovereign Jewish state.

His current work was in the main a continuation of his previous researches, developing methods, from his fermentation processes, of producing large quantities of high-octane aviation fuel and synthetic rubber. At the Sieff Institute, much work had been done on pharmaceutics under his direction, and his research into medicinal drugs was extended. He was also preoccupied with the novel concept of substitute foodstuffs, which yielded, eventually, a 'Blitz Broth' to sustain the wartime hungry. (When paratroop regiments were dropped over Normandy on D Day, they were issued this refreshment.)[45]

Despite the obvious benefits of these researches, they brought him no breakthrough comparable to that of his acetone production methods, though he received much encouragement. In America, Vice-President Henry Wallace and Sumner Welles were extremely receptive to his ideas. And Roosevelt, whom he saw for twenty-five minutes on 7 July 1942, was as pliant as ever and wished to exploit his knowledge. But he could make no real progress in securing the administration's support, and his efforts were smothered by bureaucratic in-fighting. Vested interests, especially the almighty oil companies, saw in his processes a threat to their profits. A high-powered United States government committee, headed by Bernard Baruch and including some well-respected scientists, investigated his schemes for the production of synthetic rubber and high-octane aviation fuel and found against him. He found himself caught in the machinations of rival lobbies, a Washington game whose rules were unfamiliar to him. Eventually he turned his processes over to a private firm in Philadelphia, which exploited them for the duration of the war and continued to do so afterward.

In Britain, it was the same kind of story. Influential figures—Lord Mountbatten, Lord Lloyd, Leo Amery, and Ernest Bevin—were impressed by Weizmann's ideas, 'but things moved very slowly'. At the end of 1943, a commission, which included Walter Elliot, was sent to West Africa to investigate the exploitation of new sources of raw materials for fuel. Before the commission left, Bevin, then minister of labour and a member of the war cabinet, sought Weizmann's advice. Weizmann suggested exploring the possibilities of growing vast quantities of root starches and cane sugar, which, through fermentation, would produce bountiful supplies of high-octane fuel, enough to make Britain self-sufficient in this vital commodity. These ideas, too, were shelved.[46]

Perhaps Weizmann's reputation, real and imagined, had run too far ahead of him. After the complications resulting from the Balfour Declaration, no politician, on either side of the Atlantic, could have wished to put himself too heavily in Weizmann's debt. His projects were listened to attentively but acted upon gingerly, if at all. Nevertheless, no less an authority than Henry Wallace remarked, 'The world will never know what a significant contribution Weizmann made toward the success of the synthetic rubber programme at a time when it was badly bogged down and going too slowly.'[47]

On 9 May 1942, an Extraordinary Zionist Conference opened at the Biltmore Hotel, New York City. It resolved 'that the gates of Palestine be opened; that the Jewish Agency be invested with control of immigration . . . and that Palestine be established as a Jewish Commonwealth integrated in the structure of the new democratic world'. This platform was broad enough to encompass the mainstream of Zionist thought. Before the year had passed, the three major forces of world

Zionism—American and British Jewry and the *Yishuv*—were committed to the Biltmore programme.

The genesis of the programme can now hardly be disputed. It was drafted by Meyer Weisgal and Louis Lipsky, Weizmann's trusted aides, and embodied, in more 'solemn terms', the essential points of a well-known article written by Weizmann and published in *Foreign Affairs* in February 1942. Weizmann had called for a Jewish state in unequivocal terms, but his formulation of its eventual boundaries and constitution was sufficiently ambiguous to leave several options open. He wrote of 'a Jewish Palestine' and 'a Jewish State in Palestine': at times he envisaged a completely independent state, unencumbered by association with the mandatory power; at others he toyed with the idea of 'the inclusion of the Jewish State within the British Commonwealth of Nations' or even of its being linked with an Arab federation. As to Weizmann's own preference, he would surely have preferred a Jewish state in all of western Palestine, in some form of close association with the British Empire. Whether he believed this goal to be attainable or not in existing circumstances is another matter. This was a maximalist aim; he would settle for less—an improved Peel line if no other feasible alternative presented itself. The Biltmore programme reflected, in appropriate conference jargon, views he had been formulating since 1937.

The furious controversy that later arose stemmed from Ben Gurion's fierce and passionate advocacy of the programme in Palestine during the autumn of 1942. As he barnstormed the *Yishuv*, almost browbeating it into agreement, Weizmann sourly noted: '[he conveyed] the idea that it is the triumph of his policy as against my moderate formulation of the same aims'.[48] In fact, the policy differences between them at the time were slight, for both were severely limited in their options by the actions of the great powers, and both were wise enough to know it. Commentators with a sense of the dramatic have read too much into this incident. A clash between these two almost diametrically opposite personalities there undoubtedly was, but it was a clash based more on differences in temperament than on broad lines of actual policy. Here, after all, was the classic confrontation in politics: between a young, capable, abrasive leader, anxious to get on, and an older statesman blocking his path and reluctant to relinquish his own grip.

Ben Gurion's criticism of Weizmann's methods had begun long before the war, an expression, often in an exaggerated form, of a general uneasiness prevalent in Mapai circles. When the land regulations were promulgated in February 1940, he called for 'a fighting Zionism' to replace the discredited 'talking Zionism', a broad hint aimed at Weizmann. And as the negotiations for a Jewish fighting force ran into the ground, the shrillness of his tone increased. He demanded the right to shepherd Weizmann at all his meetings—a preposterous request for Weizmann to agree to, particularly as Ben Gurion was in any case an active participant in many of them. Also he laid down as a prerequisite that the JFF must fight in Palestine, for Weizmann an impossible starting-point for the negotiations. When thwarted, Weizmann noticed, he resigned, 'grumbling and grousing', and sulked 'like Achilles', only to return later having gained nothing except a reputation for irascibility. In all his wartime confrontations with Weizmann, whether in the forums of American Jewry or in his own, private fiefdom, the Jewish Agency Executive in Jerusalem, he failed to muster sufficient support to consummate his anti-Weizmann crusade.[49]

Immediately after the Biltmore conference, Ben Gurion accused Weizmann of acting autocratically, of consulting only those whom he knew were in agreement with his views. Weizmann, he cried, who could never say 'no' to an Englishman, had now bungled the JFF negotiations; he still adhered to the Ahad Ha'am school of thought, remote from the practicalities of day-to-day politics, and this was sure proof of his fossilized approach. Since he could no longer be trusted to conduct political negotiations, he should be asked to resign. In short, Ben Gurion attributed all the disappointments of Zionist policy to Weizmann's 'sins and shortcomings', and all its failures were loaded onto Weizmann's weary shoulders.

It was true, of course, that in London Weizmann was surrounded by an admiring court, but it was equally true that the Palestinians—Locker, Shertok, and Ben Gurion himself—were party to the negotiations with the British and involved in all their twists and turns. Weizmann had little difficulty in refuting Ben Gurion's 'histrionic display' as 'political assassination' when they clashed at a meeting of Zionist leaders in New York at the end of June 1942. Ben Gurion had overplayed his hand, for his was a solitary voice. In a hard-hitting letter to the executive in Jerusalem, which he drafted twice but did not send, Weizmann wrote:

I have watched Mr. Ben Gurion carefully during his stay here. His conduct and deportment were painfully reminiscent of the petty dictator, a type one meets with so often in public life now. They are all shaped on a definite pattern: they are humorless, thin-lipped, morally stunted, fanatical and stubborn, apparently frustrated in some ambition, and nothing is more dangerous than a small man nursing his grievances introspectively.

Yet Weizmann attempted a reconciliation with his tempestuous rival—'I have tried, two or three times, to have a quiet talk with him'— but failed: 'It is perfectly useless to try and argue with him as I think the man suffers from some mental aberrations.' To Berl Locker, he was even more unrestrained: 'I'm quite certain that he is developing fascist tendencies and megolamania coupled with political hysteria.' No amount of mediation sufficed to allay Ben Gurion's suspicions or to appease Weizmann's temper. Finally Weizmann advised Ben Gurion to return to Palestine, as 'your presence [there], especially in these trying days, is of infinitely greater importance than anywhere else'.[50]

This ordeal, the most serious challenge to his leadership yet, exhausted Weizmann. His doctors ordered him to rest, and, in September 1942, he retired to Ross Cottage at Grossingers, a resort in the Catskills, *hors de combat* for six weeks. But Ben Gurion harried him throughout the war. In October 1943 he resigned from the executive, fearing that Weizmann might accept a defective partition plan and reject the Biltmore programme. Effective co-operation between them was at a minimum. Ben Gurion refused to come to London to repeat his charges, and Weizmann refused to go to Palestine 'to fight a madman on his own ground'. 'Ben Gurion . . . seems to have gone quite *meshuga* in his dislike of Chaim and distrust of him,' Baffy recorded in July 1943; 'Chaim says he will never sit with him on the same Executive again. This is a terrible misfortune at this juncture, just when unity is most needed.'[51]

But in the autumn of 1942, having neutralized Ben Gurion's opposition, Weizmann set up an *ad hoc* committee of his own with the participation of Stephen Wise, Louis Lipsky, and Nahum Goldmann, to centralize political work in the United States. In October, this body underwent a metamorphosis to emerge as a branch of the World Zionist Executive. Packed with Weizmann's men (with the notable exception of Abba Silver) and without Ben Gurion's foreboding presence, it enabled Weizmann to pursue his political aims in his own manner.[52]

He continued his controversy with Ben Gurion in a long letter to Baffy in January 1943.[53] Particularly troubled by the lack of Jewish unity in America, he claimed that Ben Gurion, who had done little to advance this aim, was unduly optimistic, chasing one of his 'chimeras'. In fact, relations with non-Zionists were in a state of 'suspended animation' or, more brutally, 'practically broken up'. To make matters worse, Magnes was up to his old tricks again, he reported, and had gathered round him those powerful groups in American Jewry opposed to a Jewish state. 'So the line-up is quite clear, and history repeats itself once more,' referring to his past struggles and victories against Montagu and Montefiore in 1917.

He turned to Ben Gurion's pessimistic evaluation of the future role of the British Empire in world affairs. Was it truly 'doomed'? And was the United States destined to emerge as 'the greatest force in the world'? And should, therefore, the emphasis of Zionist work be focussed on the United States? Weizmann was frank enough to admit that he did not know.

> It is quite true that America will rise as a very great force in the world, I hope for the good; but whether the United States, after the war, will take an interest in Middle East politics, or whether it will again retire from continental and European entanglements—that is a very moot question, and in view of the present tendencies . . . it would be a great mistake to discount Great Britain and overemphasize the importance of America for our cause. I think both are important, and our work must go on with equal fervour on both sides of the Atlantic.

He foresaw a new balance of forces within the British Empire. India would acquire 'a new political status after the war', a development of revolutionary significance that would lead to a restructuring of the Empire and a re-ordering of British priorities. The weight of British imperial activity would henceforth concentrate on Africa, and here 'The vicinity of Palestine, just across the Suez Canal, may prove a great boon'. Within this new constellation, he saw the 'possibility of co-operation which might give most beneficial results to both parties': a new, brighter dawn would break in Anglo-Zionist relations. 'I believe, as I always did, that our fate is bound up with England. They will have to develop Africa to the maximum, just as we would have to do the same in Palestine, and here both sides meet.'* He was especially

---

*Weizmann wrote these words in January 1943. In March 1946, Hugh Dalton, then Chancellor of the Exchequer, noted in his diary: 'Attlee is pressing on the Chiefs of Staff and the Defence Committee a large view of his own, aiming at considerable disengagement from areas where there is a risk of clashing with the Russians. We should pull out, he thinks, from all the Middle East including Egypt and Greece,

keyed up because he believed that the so-called Lowdermilk plan held the key to the absorption of at least 4 million people in Palestine. This plan, propounded by Walter Lowdermilk, a world authority on soil conservation and reclamation who had visited Palestine in 1938, called for the establishment of a Jordan Valley Authority on similar lines to the Tennessee Valley Authority in the United States, to develop the economy and regional capabilities on both banks of the Jordan.[54] Now being seriously considered by the American administration, if adopted by the Jews it would have immense political repercussions.

> Thus we can assert: [a] that Palestine can hold a vast population; [b] that we can dissipate the fears of the Arabs lest they will be ousted, also [c] we would set an example of how to develop empty spaces for the benefit of oppressed populations, and such a plan could not be held up by chauvinistic tendencies of fascist Arabs. Liberal opinion in this country would favour us against the chauvinism of the Arab leaders.

Here was the cement that would bind liberal, progressive opinion in the West—for were they not also fighting for lofty ideals?—to the enlightened aims of Zionism.

This cold, logical analysis was perceptive in parts, even if a little too academic for some tastes, and eminently reasonable in the context of international politics in the winter of 1942–43. But, Weizmann believed, it would all come to naught for the Jews unless Ben Gurion ceased his splitting tactics. In his own mind, Weizmann returned Ben Gurion's compliment: he saw him as an intolerable bugbear and the chief obstacle to a rational Zionist policy that would unite the diverse elements of world Jewry. Ben Gurion had stolen his clothes at the Biltmore hotel and made off with them to Palestine, and this gave him no rest. Once again, he unburdened himself to Baffy:

> I would like to say a word about the Biltmore declaration, of which such a fuss has been made by Ben-Gurion on his return to Palestine. It has become, as far as I can see, a new Decalogue, or certainly, a new Basel programme, and would have thought that it has emerged out of deliberations which occupied months of serious study. Let me tell you that it is nothing of the kind. . . . [It] is just a resolution, like the hundred and one resolutions usually passed at great meetings. . . . It embodied, in somewhat solemn terms, the chief points as laid down in my article in *Foreign Affairs*. But Ben Gurion, after his stay here of

---

make a line of defence across Africa from Lagos to Kenya, and concentrate a large part of our forces in the latter.' Quoted in Kenneth Harris, *Attlee* (1982), 299.

eight or nine months, had absolutely nothing to show by way of achievement, and so he stuck to the Biltmore resolution, more or less conveying the idea that it is the triumph of his policy as against my moderate formulation of the same aims, and he injected into it all of his own extreme views.[55]

Yet, having made allowance for all of Ben Gurion's tantrums, the question must be asked whether his vision of the future was clearer than Weizmann's. Perhaps Ben Gurion's strictures may be interpreted as a rallying-call for an independent Zionist policy that was willing to accept the implications of an anti-British line? According to Weizmann, his 'so-called new revolutionary programme' argued that

> It is no use to wait until the end of the war. We have to do things now. The sort of constructive work which we have been doing in the last twenty years has been valuable in its time, but now it is of secondary importance. . . . Governments do not keep any promises. Of course the British Government will play only a secondary part in the future settlement, and the American Government, however, is the prop on which one has to lean (in spite of the fact that it might not keep its promises).

To see Ben Gurion's aims realized, it would be necessary to effect a great immigration of two million Jews in one fell swoop, in 'a year or two' (Weizmann was thinking in terms of the same total, but at the more modest rate of 100,000 a year), and to build up 'a great defence force to fight either the Arabs or the British or both'. In short, the Jews could rely on no one but themselves; and once the immeasurable power and influence of American Jewry had been harnessed to Zionism, it would be possible not only to demand a Jewish state but to create one.

At the time, these sounded as 'fantastic utterances' to Weizmann,[56] as they did to a majority of mainstream Zionists. What was the point of promoting Ben Gurion's revolutionary programme in the winter of 1942–43? With Britain's fortunes at their lowest point, would this not be totally counter-productive? Was it not morally reprehensible to attack Britain in public when she was still engaged in a titanic struggle against Hitler, one that would also settle the fate of the Jews? Would not every anti-Zionist official in Whitehall pounce on this opportunity to sabotage the Zionist enterprise, perhaps fatally? But the Revisionists were already stirring up American opinion against Britain. Stooping on occasion to blatant vilification, their propaganda campaign caused Weizmann much embarrassment in his public duties. Nor was he helped by the 'thunder and lightning' of the formidable Rabbi Silver, who terminated one speech with the defiant words, 'Agitate! Agitate! Agitate!'[57] Demagogues and so-called revolutionaries, he thought, were recklessly mortgaging Zionism's future for the sake of cheap, popular successes, bringing it into disrepute, and deflecting it from the path he had chosen for it — that of firm but patient diplomacy.

Perhaps there was a deeper reason for Weizmann's rejection of Ben Gurion's programme, one that he instinctively recognized but could not acknowledge. Could Weizmann himself lead the movement if ever the conditions should ripen for implementing it? Was it not so foreign to his political outlook that he would shrink from executing it? Had he, in his declining years, the necessary reserves of energy and strength to see it through? He must have sensed that time was working against him, that the cruel realities of the years had unleashed forces beyond his control, impervious to his powers of persuasion, that his long period of leadership was finally drawing to a close. Yet, by one of the strange ironies of history, when in December 1946 Ben Gurion and his allies had their way and Weizmann was removed from the Zionist presidency, they then found themselves impaled on the horns of the same dilemma that had plagued Weizmann: how to conduct their relations with Britain. They found salvation in semantics, digging out the formula of 'informal negotiations'. Even without Weizmann, Weizmannism lived on in the field of Zionist diplomacy. This was as true in the 1940s as it had been in earlier periods. In the final analysis, it was not the Zionists who abandoned Britain, but Britain who abandoned Zionism.

EIGHTEEN

SCHE'ERIT HAPLETA —ONLY A REMNANT SHALL SURVIVE

On 17 December 1942, an incredulous House of Commons listened as the Foreign Secretary, Anthony Eden, read out an official Allied statement telling of the systematic mass killings of Jews in Nazi-occupied Europe. When he had finished, the shocked members rose and, with bowed heads, stood in silent tribute to the massacred Jews.[1]

For some time now, information had been reaching the West recounting Nazi atrocities, sometimes in the most horrifying detail. These reports had been received with varying degrees of bewilderment, scepticism, reserve, disbelief, on occasion even derision: the enormity of the crimes was too frightful for the human mind to grasp. Journalists of Hebrew newspapers in Palestine regarded the reports as 'rumours' and not 'fully reliable'. State Department officials wished away the allegations as 'fantastic', 'unsubstantiated', 'wild rumours inspired by Jewish fears', while a Foreign Office official coldly minuted, 'Familiar stuff. The Jews have spoilt their case by laying it on too thick for years past.' Even to Nahum Goldmann it was not clear how 'the Germans could do it in such an orderly and systematic manner'.[2]

Ever since his prophetic warning to the Peel Commission about the doomed 'six million Jews', Weizmann had been consumed by the thought of the fate that awaited European Jewry. In *Trial and Error* he was to write that already by January 1940 he had received information that 'if Hitler overran Europe Zionism would lose all its meaning because no Jew would be left alive'. Either his memory had misled him as to the date or he was giving free vent to his finely tuned intuition, for the mass killings by gas in the death camps had not yet begun. But exactly a year later, with mass deportations and with the Jews of eastern Europe locked up in ghettos where thousands were dying of starvation and disease, Weizmann recorded:

> The position of the Jews in Europe has, in my opinion, been irretrievably destroyed, and when the pall is lifted, we shall find only remnants of misery and wretchedness. I dread to think of the problems which will then face those to whom it may be given to survive this catastrophe.

By March 1942, with the actions of the *Einsatzgruppen* a horrible reality (by January 1942, it has been estimated, they had already butchered 500,000–600,000 Jews) and the main extermination camps about to become fully operational, Weizmann told Lord Cranborne, the Colonial Secretary, that 'in the matter of exterminating the Jews Hitler is as good as his word'.[3]

As 1942 passed, the scale of the tragedy unfolded until the Allied declaration of December at last officially acknowledged the horrible truth. Short of protesting, of publicizing the true nature of Nazi barbarism and its consequences for humanity in general and the Jews in particular, there was little of substance the Zionist leaders could do while the Jewish communities that had nourished them, among them Motol and Pinsk, were ruthlessly decimated.[4] The mass destruction of their people enveloped them like a funeral shroud: they could not escape it, and it conditioned their behaviour and activity. It was most poignantly expressed in their struggle to relieve the agony of the 'remnants of misery and wretchedness' who were making their way to Palestine in a ghastly procession of 'death-ships', defying the clauses of the May white paper.

In mid-November 1940 the *Pacific* and the *Milos*, two dilapidated vessels, carrying 1724 Jewish refugees, crawled into Haifa bay escorted by British naval patrols. They had spent a wretched month at sea, having set sail from Tulcea, a Rumanian port near the mouth of the Danube, on 11 September. The passengers, hoping they had at last reached safety, were greatly disillusioned when they were greeted by High Commissioner Sir Harold MacMichael's communiqué that they would not be allowed into Palestine, and were re-embarked on the *Patria* for deportation to Mauritius. Some days later they were joined by another hulk, the *Atlantic* with an additional 1700 survivors: they too were destined for re-settlement in Mauritius.

The *Yishuv*, outraged by the prohibition, responded with a general strike. In London, the Zionists began to petition the British government to reverse the decision. Baffy Dugdale recorded that when the news of this imbroglio reached Weizmann he was 'absorbed in his laboratory' and arrived at the office 'very cross'. His initial inclination was to play the issue down; perhaps, he suggested, the refugees would be safer in Mauritius. But his mood changed dramatically on 25 November when he heard the appalling news that the *Patria* had blown up, with a death toll of 267, as it lay at anchor off Haifa. Stories circulated that here was a case of mass suicide, an act of despair spawned by Britain's inhumane policies. Weizmann might well have believed this version, but the truth was more prosaic: far from being an act of despair, the explosion was the result of an unforeseen error on the part of the Haganah. In an effort to immobilize the ship's engines in order to keep the refugees in Haifa, thereby exerting political pressure on the authorities to allow them entry into Palestine, and miscalculating the amount of explosives required, the Haganah's plan had miscarried with the most tragic consequences.

Weizmann, believing the British guilty of an awful injustice, considered them ultimately responsible for this senseless loss of Jewish lives. He stormed into Lord Lloyd's office 'in his most agitated mood', according to Sir John Shuckburg, a high Colonial Office figure who witnessed the encounter. The government's policy was 'beyond endurance'; cooperation between them was no longer possible. He 'hinted darkly at the reaction of the Jews in America and on the length of Lord Lloyd's future tenure of his present office'. Then he saw Attlee, but Attlee seemed to have withstood Weizmann's fury, for his reaction reminded Weizmann of Lord Passfield's unsympathetic attitude during the crisis of 1929–31. To Halifax Weizmann blasted MacMichael's 'vindictiveness', threatening to 'fight this thing until they sent him to a concentration camp'. This bitter anger must cumulatively have left an impression, for the survivors from the *Patria* were eventually allowed to remain in Palestine 'as a special act of clemency', despite the opposition of the Colonial and Foreign Offices.[5]

It was not possible, except by force, to impose the immigration restrictions of the May white paper, a policy that coldly elevated political calculation above humanitarian principles. The agony of European Jewry at once compounded and simplified the problem. Some British officials appeared incapable of grasping the true dimensions of the tragedy, seeing the root of the problem as being Zionist perfidy, classifying those who pleaded for help as 'wailing Jews'. The 'illegals', in their estimation, constituted not 'a genuine refugee movement' but a 'political conspiracy' designed 'to fill Palestine with Jews and secure domination over the country'.[6] This was sheer fantasy, impossible to rationalize except by the most convoluted mental gymnastics. If the Zionists on occasion exploited the situation, as they undoubtedly did, the responsible parties in the British government had only themselves to blame. In the last resort they defeated their own policy, for it was 'illegal immigration', more than any other issue, that finally destroyed the white paper policy.

No administrative statute could prevent the boats from running the British blockade—*Patria, Darien, Struma, Mekfure, Nyasa, Salvador, Exodus*—names of vessels engraved on the Jewish conscience as bearing martyrs to the Jewish state. The sinkings, the drownings, the internments, the expulsions served as a permanent reminder to Zionist leaders that after the war a political solution would have to be found for the survivors. Weizmann was now talking freely of two or three million Jews who would enter the Jewish state once hostilities had ceased.

Yet the future of Palestine was still to be determined by the provisions of the white paper: the establishment of a Palestinian state in treaty relations with Britain after a transitionary period of not more than ten years. But as both Jews and Arabs had rejected the document, there was no chance of implementing it. On 29 May 1941, Eden, in a well-publicized speech at the Mansion House, London, pledged government support for the concept of greater Arab unity in any scheme that commanded 'general approval'. Generally interpreted as supporting pan-Arabism and foretelling an extension of Arab independence and unity, his speech conspicuously failed to mention the future of the Jewish National Home. Weizmann, *en route* to Los Angeles at the time, wrote to Dorothy Thompson, 'It is inconceivable to me how any statesman fighting against the common enemy can for even a brief moment forget the first victims of these dark forces.' Oliver Harvey, Weizmann's friend and Eden's usually admiring private secretary, had a plausible explanation. His chief, he asserted in his diary, had never resisted the blind pro-Arabism of the Foreign Office. 'He is hopelessly prejudiced. The Arab myth clouds his mind. . . . Unfortunately A.E. is immovable on the subject of Palestine. He loves Arabs and hates Jews.'

Weizmann, convinced that Eden was a sworn enemy and had 'deliberately omitted' to mention the Jews, would not have faulted Harvey's verdict. In fact, although Eden might have loved the Arabs, he had not excluded the possibility of a Jewish state in an Arab federation. Nor had his fellow ministers. But lacking adequate time to discuss Eden's views before his speech, the cabinet had approved its contents four days after it was delivered, a rather casual approach to what was generally considered to be a major foreign policy statement.[7]

Ben Gurion reacted in typical fashion, describing the speech as 'the worst that has happened to them since the war broke out', while the Jewish Agency Executive in Jerusalem decided to launch a propaganda campaign in the United States to foil Eden's alleged machinations. It was left to Weizmann's aides in London, Namier and Locker, to register a formal protest. Lord Moyne pacified them: the phrase 'general approval', he claimed, also covered Jewish rights. But this was totally unsatisfactory. What were the British up to? While still adhering to the white paper, they were now flaunting Arab unity in public. The Arabs, a reliable press report claimed, had already interpreted Eden's reference to Syrian aspirations for independence to include northern and southern Syria, a clear hint as to the fate that awaited Palestine, for 'southern Syria' was a well-known euphemism for Palestine in the vocabulary of Syrian nationalists.[8] The Mansion House speech left Weizmann apprehensive that the destiny of the Middle East, including Palestine, was being decided without taking the Zionist interest into account. In August 1941 he revealed his thoughts to Smuts:

> After the war, the Jewish people will need a territory large enough to receive the bulk of the Jewish immigration to be expected, and to form the foundation of a sound and self-supporting Jewish commonwealth . . . [which] must have such degree of sovereignty as will secure its independence and freedom from outside interference. The Jewish people can never agree to being a permanent minority in one Arab State (as envisaged in the 1939 white paper), nor yet to be subject to a combination of Arab States so far as its vital interests . . . are concerned.[9]

This was clear-cut; yet equally, the pundits in government employ — learned experts in the Foreign Office, the Colonial Office, the Palestine administration, the Middle East political and military command, and many of their political masters — were fearful of the repercussions of any change in policy that favoured the Zionists.

Churchill, on the other hand, had fought the white paper in 1939 and the land regulations in 1940, and time had not eroded his well-attested views on the topic. 'If Britain and the United States emerge victorious from the war,' he had remarked in October 1941, 'the creation of a great Jewish State in Palestine inhabited by millions of Jews will be one of the leading features of the Peace Conference discussions.' Do not make me angry and argue with me, he commanded a bewildered General Sir Edward Louis Spears: 'he [Churchill] had formed an opinion which nothing could change [and] intended to see to it that there was a Jewish State.'[10] By early 1943, when any number of schemes were being floated—from Philby's fantasy to the Biltmore programme, or from strict observance of the white paper to the chimera of Arab unity—Weizmann appealed to Churchill to 'arrest the fatal process and open the way for a new dispensation in Palestine'. Damning the white paper once again, he reminded Churchill, 'The present activities run counter to your attitude,' and concluded, 'The slaughter of European Jews can be redeemed only by establishing Palestine as a Jewish country.'[11]

Weizmann's appeal reactivated Churchill. Churchill, like Weizmann in Washington in May, was too busy to meet Weizmann, but he informed his colleagues that his administration was now free to review, and if necessary revise, the entire Palestine question. He had written to his colonial secretary, Oliver Stanley:

> I cannot agree that the White Paper of 1939 is 'the firmly established policy' of His Majesty's present Government. I have always regarded it as a gross breach of faith committed by the Chamberlain Government in respect of obligations to which I was personally a party. . . . My position remains strictly that set forth in the speech I made in the House of Commons in the debate on the White Paper. I am sure that the majority of the present War Cabinet would never agree to any positive endorsement of the White Paper. It runs until it is superseded.[12]

The following weeks saw the cabinet inundated with papers relating to Palestine. None of them disputed Churchill's basic contention, but equally none of them displayed the slightest sympathy for the aims of Zionism as expressed in the Biltmore programme. There was a faintly hysterical tone in this war of words. In the grimmest of pictures, the Zionist leadership was portrayed as a band of fanatics and extremists who were bent on political, and if necessary military, confrontation with the British and the Arabs. The military authorities expressed these sentiments in the most lurid phrases, visualizing 'a highly organized military machine on Nazi lines' which, having chosen its moment carefully, would prosecute 'by force . . . [its] policy of establishing an exclusively Jewish State in Palestine'. These appraisals were highly colourful. There was in fact very little chance of a Zionist *coup de main* in Palestine.[13] But the first response to Churchill's initiative held out little promise for an annulment, or even a revision, of the white-paper policy.

Nevertheless, as a consequence of these soundings a cabinet committee on Palestine was set up in July which, according to the Foreign Office, had a pro-Zionist bias. Chaired by Herbert Morrison, it included also Leo Amery and Archie Sinclair, two well-known gentile Zionists. Oliver Stanley, the Colonial Secretary, untainted by Zionist ardour, was no match for this combination or, apparently, for any other. (Churchill was once reported to have told him that 'he had not enough drive or initiative to carry anything through, but he was a Stanley and might do for the Dominions'.) Toward the end of July, Amery leaked the good news to Weizmann: the white paper was to be discarded. 'Two ideas hold the field. *One*, a Jewish State in an undivided Palestine, *two*, in a Palestine excluding Samaria.' Weizmann told Amery he would have nothing to do with any plan for the partition of Palestine, having been let down too badly by the government last time. Still, he must have been overjoyed. Amery's message was the first true ray of hope since the start of the war. At the same time, Zionist pressure in Washington helped quash an American initiative, backed by the British, which would have frozen the Palestine question until the end of hostilities. The path was open for a revision of British policy, and partition was again in the air.[14]

Despite his caveat to Amery, Weizmann was in fact as strongly committed to partition as ever. But the forces in the government that had sabotaged partition in 1937 were still thriving and just as powerful: he knew them well, and he knew they would not hesitate to intervene a second time should the opportunity arise. As for the Palestinian Arabs, partition was wholly unacceptable to them; all previous experience had shown that such a solution could be imposed on them only by force. But the most intriguing question mark hung over Churchill himself, the key to Weizmann's manoeuvres to induce Britain to re-adopt a Zionist-oriented policy. In 1937, he had been an anti-partitionist, not out of lack of sympathy for the Zionists but because he was unable to countenance a great imperial power abdicating its pledges in the face of violence. Would he not, upon victory, when Britain's imperial role was likely to be enlarged and his own personal prestige and authority immensely strengthened, be encouraged in this attitude? When Weizmann lunched with Churchill and Attlee at the end of October 1943, the Prime Minister told him not to worry: '[you] have a wonderful case'. Hinting that the Negev, and possibly Transjordan, would be included in a Jewish state, he assured Weizmann that following Hitler's defeat the Jews would be established in their rightful position. The meaning of Churchill's remarks could not have been clearer, and Weizmann came away 'much cheered and encouraged'.[15]

But he was faced with no less serious problems in his own camp. In October Ben Gurion, fearing that Weizmann might abandon the Biltmore programme in favour of an inferior partition scheme, resigned from the executive. 'He is an old man who has suffered much through the death of his son, and he would like to live to see the creation of a Jewish State,' remarked Ben Gurion of Weizmann. 'His political activity today, therefore, is still based on the old Partition Plan, and in this lies our difference of opinion.' And, touching on a sore point, not without a characteristic exaggeration, he went on: 'I see the same difficulties as he does, but he has lost all personal feelings for the *Yishuv*. He is not impregnated with the Zionist ideals of our Jewish youth in Palestine. He sees problems where we see facts.'[16]

Ever since their clash in America, Ben Gurion's crotchety behaviour, tinged with a personal animosity, had greatly distressed Weizmann. Once again, he contemplated resignation, and it was only after long and wearisome negotiations that a compromise was patched together. Ben Gurion accepted that there could be no rules governing the question of who accompanied Weizmann to official meetings, while Weizmann reconciled himself to the permanent stationing of another member of the Jerusalem Executive in London.[17] Still, the break lasted until February 1944 when Ben Gurion agreed to return to the leadership. His defection during these crucial months seriously weakened the Zionists and adversely effected their capacity to negotiate from a position of relative strength.

Ben Gurion's huffiness apart, Weizmann knew that securing a consensus for partition among his own people would be a huge task. Time had not mellowed the oppositionists' views; if anything, the experience of the war had served only to harden them. In 1937–38 the Zionists had veered off on an anti-partitionist tack, overstating in public their opposition to partition and thereby encouraging its enemies. Now they faced the same acute dilemma. Weizmann and his entourage would undoubtedly accept the right kind of partition, but it had to be forced on them. '[Weizmann] asked us,' Baffy reported, 'whether if partition is suggested, we would back him in considering it. Lewis [Namier] and [Selig] Brodetsky said *yes, on condition only* (said Lewis) that no one knows at this stage that Chaim would even consider it.'[18] Weizmann, having cast himself as the shrinking bride dragged reluctantly to the altar, would have to play the role with consummate skill; his conversation with Amery and luncheon party with Churchill was as a kind of gala dress rehearsal.

In January 1944, the cabinet agreed in principle to adopt partition on a modified Peel line: most of Galilee was excluded from the Jewish state, though minor territorial gains were made elsewhere, and, of greater importance, there was hope of eventually including the Negev area. Only Eden voiced dissent from the general view. He wished to defer judgement about Palestine until he had canvassed the opinions of his ambassadors in Cairo and Baghdad.[19] So once again, as in 1937, the Foreign Office was afforded sufficient breathing space to orchestrate an anti-partition campaign. During the coming months the officials, backed by the chiefs of staff, mounted a concerted attack against the concept of partition, which they considered ruinous to British policy. But there were two surprising deviationists: Sir Harold MacMichael, the high commissioner, and Lord Moyne, now minister resident in the Middle East, who emerged during 1944 as staunch defenders of partition.[20]

These preliminary skirmishes were inconclusive, but clearly the seeds of doubt had been extensively sown. A massive effort would be required on the part of the government, and in particular from Churchill, to overcome the combined wisdom of the officials and their political controllers. Weizmann and his circle scarcely concealed their favour of partition, provided it conformed with Zionist requirements. Government leakages, though at times contradictory, left him with sufficient hope that such indeed would be the case.[21] He was more perplexed by the activities of the American Zionists, who appeared to be charging through Congress like bulls in a china shop. An attempt to introduce militantly pro-Zionist resolutions in the Senate and the House of Representatives had sadly backfired, resulting in an innocuous statement by Roosevelt that neither added to nor subtracted from what was previously known of his opinions. But leading members of Roosevelt's administration—George Marshall, Cordell Hull, Henry Stimson, possibly Roosevelt himself—were much put out at this clumsy effort to railroad the administration. Silver, the main culprit—who, Nahum Goldmann recorded, had 'bullied' Wise and others into taking this badly timed and amateurish initiative—failed to comprehend why 'everybody is not shouting "Hurrah"'.[22] If this was the face of 'activism', there was still no substitute for Weizmann's patient and constructive diplomacy.

In the midst of these transactions, news reached Weizmann of an 'extraordinary offer' regarding the fate of European Jewry, which continued to engross his thoughts. In February 1943, he had pleaded with Halifax to take seriously a report in *The New York Times* that the Rumanian government would be prepared to transfer 70,000 Jews to a place of safety, perhaps to Palestine. Unwilling to exceed the limits of the white paper, and fearful of creating a precedent for the Axis powers to unload their 'unwanted nationals', the British rejected his plea. Two weeks later, on 1 March, in a speech at Madison Square Garden, he appealed to the conscience of the world.

> When the historian of the future assembles the bleak record of our days he will find two things unbelievable; first the crime itself, second the reaction of the world to that crime. . . . He will be puzzled by the apathy of the civilized world in the face of this immense, systematic carnage of human beings. . . . Above all, he will not be able to understand why the free nations, in arms against a resurgent, organized barbarism, required appeals to give sanctuary to the first and chief victim of that barbarism. Two million Jews have already been exterminated. The world can no longer plead that the ghastly facts are unknown or unconfirmed.[22]

This appeal had no substantial effect. A month later an Anglo-American conference on refugees, convened at Bermuda, failed to reach agreement; in any case, to Weizmann's immense chagrin, the British representatives expressly excluded Palestine from the conference programme.[24] And now came the Brandt mission.

Joel Brandt, a Hungarian Zionist functionary, had arrived in Istanbul in May 1944 carrying a German offer to exchange the remnants of Hungarian Jewry, and possibly the surrounding countries—in all, a million Jews—for ten thousand trucks to be used on the eastern front, and quantities of tea, coffee, cocoa, and soap. Weizmann first heard the story, '[which] gave me a great and most painful shock', on 2 June. On 7 June he suggested to Eden that the British government 'play for time' to explore thoroughly this fantastic proposal; that it inform the Soviet Union of the result of the exploration; and, if the affair proved to be a false starter, that it give it the fullest publicity. Shertok, who was the main Zionist agent in this macabre incident, took the offer seriously; the British, equally, had serious reservations.

Already suspicious of Brandt's credentials, they were not prepared to submit to blackmail, speculating that it would lead to further shady schemes and the 'unloading' of more Jews into the West. But more practically, the allocation of 10,000 lorries to the East just after D-Day would cause major logistical dislocations in the general war effort. Suspecting a German ploy to split the Allies, the British decided, after due consultation with the United States and the Soviet Union (which adamantly opposed any talks with the Germans), to reject the 'goods for blood' deal.[25]

While Weizmann and Shertok were pursuing the Brandt affair with Eden, on 6 July they raised another possibility for aiding European Jewry: the bombing of Birkenau, part of the great complex at the Auschwitz camp where the gas chambers and crematoria were located, and the railways lines leading to it. Eden replied that this idea had already been examined and rejected, but that owing to the 'appalling slaughter' at Auschwitz he would re-open the matter. The Zionists realized that bombing the camps would have little practical value, but they considered that it would have a 'far-reaching moral effect', demonstrating the Allied resolve to wage 'direct war on the extermination of the victims of Nazi oppression'. Both Eden and Churchill were inclined to support the proposal. But it, too, was rejected, the experts claiming technical difficulties (which, on examination, proved to be of highly dubious validity) and making the specious suggestion that the deportations to the death camps had in any case ceased. In these attempts to galvanize the Allies to greater efforts to rescue European Jewry, the Zionists were always led back to the same starting-point. 'The Jewish question,' Sir Ronald Campbell, minister at the Washington embassy, wrote to Weizmann, 'can only be dealt with completely by an Allied victory, and any step calculated to prejudice this is not in the real interests of the Jews of Europe.' From the German occupation of Greater Hungary in March 1944 until its liberation by the Russians in February 1945, 450,000 Jews either were deported, were murdered, or simply died.[26]

'Sunk in deep despair' at the fate awaiting Hungarian Jewry, Weizmann and Vera left London for a short holiday at Monkton Coombe, near Bath, in mid-July. On 20 July Vera, 'very hysterical', telephoned the office in London to report that Weizmann had collapsed: '[she] spoke of bleeding from the lungs and pneumonia'. But his situation was less serious than it seemed at first. He had succumbed to a severe attack of bronchitis and was confined to his bed for three weeks. 'I am feeling better, but not too bright,' was his eventual verdict. But one piece of good news pierced his gloom. At long last he could rejoice at the formation of a Jewish Brigade Group, finally settled after five years of broken promises and soft nothings. By the beginning of September he was back in London, preparing for his first visit to Palestine since the outbreak of war. And another pleasant surprise awaited him. Before his departure, he was entertained by his closest friends and aides at 'a very gay and happy luncheon-party' at the Savoy Grill to mark a grand event: the liberation of Pinsk. But what is left of it? they all wondered.[27]

On 4 November, a week before he was due to leave for Palestine, he drove to Chequers for a talk with Churchill. It was a most satisfactory interview, lasting two hours. Weizmann later recounted proudly how on this occasion, instead of listening to the usual Churchillian monologue, he managed to conduct a genuine discussion. He handed the Prime Minister a memorandum arguing against partition, and enquired: '[would it] be merely a beach-head, a bathing beach in Tel Aviv?' Churchill, friendly as usual, frankly told him it would be wonderful 'if you could get the whole of Palestine... but I feel that if it comes to a choice between the white paper and partition you should take partition'. There could not, however, be any definite statement until the termination of hostilities, a period, Churchill envisaged, about six months off. He did not flinch when Weizmann spoke of bringing 'something like one-and-a-half million Jews' into Palestine in fifteen years. Disturbed at the elements hostile to Zionism within his own party, he assured Weizmann that 'we had many friends in the Labour and Liberal camps'. As for the Americans, they 'must give active support, and not merely criticism'. He was perturbed at rich and prominent Jews' opposition to Zionism, singling out Bernard Baruch, but, 'If he and Roosevelt met at the conference table they would get what they wanted.' Go and see Lord Moyne on your way to Palestine, he urged Weizmann, '[he has] changed and developed in the past two years'. 'If the United States would also sponsor it,' he continued, 'they could get the whole of western Palestine.' These words gave Weizmann much encouragement, but he had suffered too many disappointments to be carried away by rhetoric or enthusiasm.[28]

The following evening, a Sunday, he received a frightening message from Oliver Stanley's secretary summoning him to an urgent meeting:

'something terrible has happened'. Stanley sent his car to the Dorchester to bring Weizmann to the colonial office; there he imparted the dreadful news that Lord Moyne, the most prominent British official in the Middle East, had been assassinated. It transpired later that the gunmen were members of the Stern gang, young Jews who had witnessed the *Patria* tragedy and were now devoted to carrying out extremist acts against British authority. So fanatics had murdered a partitionist—just as their associates, two months earlier, had made an abortive attempt on the life of MacMichael, who inclined to similar views. Weizmann left Stanley's room 'white as a sheet'. (He never forgave him for the brutal manner in which he had conducted the talk. 'Colonel Stanley is only half my age,' he told John Martin, Churchill's private secretary, 'but if he lives to be a hundred he will not have done half what I have in my life-time.') To Churchill, he wrote of 'the abyss to which terrorism leads' and vowed that the representative bodies of the *Yishuv* would 'go to the utmost limit in its power to cut out, root and branch, this evil from its midst'. But the depth of his revulsion from this senseless, barbarous act can best be gauged from a reference he made to it in a speech delivered to the Actions Committee in Jerusalem shortly afterward:

> You all know my personal tragedy in losing my son. You can imagine how great was the shock to me. But the shock when I heard of the murder of Lord Moyne was not less. When my son was killed it was my personal tragedy—*Hashem natan, Hashem lakach* [God gives, God takes]—but here is the tragedy of the entire nation.[29]

Weizmann's views on terrorism had not altered since the 1930s, and his convictions would strengthen as this malignant disease spread in the 1940s.

As a result of Moyne's assassination Churchill suspended cabinet ratification of partition. Moyne had been numbered among Churchill's particular friends, and the Prime Minister, in a forthright statement to the House of Commons on 17 November, gave vent to his emotions:

> If our dreams for Zionism are to end in the smoke of assassins' pistols, and our labours for its future to produce only a new set of gangsters worthy of Nazi Germany, many like myself will have to reconsider the position we have maintained so consistently and so long in the past.

Yet Churchill had not washed his hands of Zionism. In a more cautious mood, he sent a message to Stanley, on the same day he made his statement to the Commons, doubting the wisdom of taking extreme anti-Zionist measures, arguing that they 'may well unite the whole forces of Zionism, and even Jewry throughout the world, against us instead of against the terrorist bands'. Let Weizmann's 'counsels of moderation' prevail, and direct whatever action may be necessary against those directly responsible.[30] But by freezing partition until the end of the war, Churchill made it possible for the anti-partitionist, anti-Zionist forces in government to gather momentum. A British-inspired partition was now dead, and Weizmann's 'counsels of moderation' fell on deaf ears.

The Weizmanns arrived in Palestine on 15 November 1944. 'I fear to enter the house,' recorded Vera in her diary. 'It is so full of sweet memories never to return'—memories of Michael, of more carefree days spent in the company of friends. Beset by the same haunting thoughts, Weizmann was equally apprehensive at the reception the *Yishuv* would accord him. For five years he had conducted the affairs of the Zionist movement from London and Washington, leaving Palestine in the restless, dynamic hands of Ben Gurion. Weizmann's influence was on the wane. he sensed it, and was uncertain how the new breed of Palestinian Jews would welcome him home.

He need not have worried. Abba Eban, who was a witness to Weizmann's reception, has recorded: 'The Hebrew press poured out its affection in words of stately tribute. The community surrounded him with the emblems and ceremonies befitting a beloved Head of State.' At Rehovot, a unit of the Jewish brigade paraded for his inspection, and 'the little township puffed out its chest and almost exploded with pride.'[31] Weizmann wrote of his home-coming as 'warm, generous and spontaneous'; but it was also dangerously deceptive. It meant little in terms of political power. The *Yishuv* greeted him as the venerable head of the movement whose past achievements had resounded throughout the world. At the age of seventy, he was being groomed for the role of an elder statesman, courtly, urbane, sagacious, whose advice would be heard though not necessarily listened to, and whose political usefulness was strictly limited.

Contemporary observers testified that Weizmann had 'perceptibly aged', his lined face showing 'the ravages' wreaked by the tragedies of the past five years.[32] Ill health would pursue him here. While walking in the garden with his doctor, he suddenly cried out: 'I can't see you.' He had endured these black-outs before and believed they resulted from the severe headaches that frequently attacked him. Dr. Joel suggested that he see an eye specialist. Weizmann was reluctant, but Joel insisted in the strongest terms. 'You have frightened me,' Weizmann replied, finally acceding to his request. He was found to be suffering from glaucoma, a condition that would gradually worsen and lead to near blindness.[33]

Yet the tranquil beauty of his Rehovot home, in such contrast to the tensions of wartime London, brought him contentment. His birthday celebrations extended to a week of festivities. The farmers of Nahalal brought him in tribute seventy olive trees, much to his delight, though Vera would have preferred decorative shrubs or flowers.[34] Meyer Weisgal presented him with a dutiful volume of essays from his admirers, *Chaim Weizmann, Statesman and Scientist: Builder of the Jewish Commonwealth*. (Please, Meyer, Weizmann had entreated, 'you know my nature. I feel rather shy and humble and I abhor overstatement and praise . . . make molehills out of mountains which I prefer to the other way.'[35]) Perhaps most satisfying of all (though the idea developed only by chance at the time of the celebrations), Weisgal hatched a scheme to create a Weizmann Institute, to include the Sieff complex, in order to ensure the financial viability of an institution about which Weizmann had so long worried. A special Weizmann birthday fund to raise money for the Sieff Institute had proved 'a dismal failure', but Weisgal turned these efforts into an American Committee of the Weizmann Institute, with a goal of raising $1 million; its first board meeting had been held on 2 November 1944, on the eve of Weizmann's arrival in Palestine.[36]

Weizmann toured the country extensively. He found it extraordinary that in Upper Galilee, 'the end of the world', he should discover a precision-instruments factory. At Athlit, the refugee internment camp, he was brought face to face with a grimmer reality, a traumatic experience for him and his entourage. He was also depressed by the general political situation. The Jewish Agency promise to assist in the eradication of the terrorist organizations, which he had endorsed, was now being executed, and Weizmann reported on the results to Churchill: 500 names handed over to the authorities, leading to 250 arrests. He met with the leaders of all the political parties in the *Yishuv*, complaining of its 'political cantonisation', with the exception of the Revisionists. He referred to Menachem Begin, commander of its military wing, the Irgun Zvai Leumi (National Military Organization), as 'a megalomaniac suffering from a Messianic complex. Whether he is a fanatic or a charlatan or both is difficult to say.'[37]

He felt strongly at odds with new, disturbing phenomena that he encountered in the *Yishuv* and that distanced him from its youth. For Baffy, he painted 'a dark picture of psychology of rising generation in the *Yishuv*, said B.G. is much to blame and is perhaps frightened now of the devils he has failed to discourage.' In his memoirs, he noted

> Here and there a relaxation of the old, traditional Zionist purity of ethics, a touch of militarization, and a weakness for its trappings; here and there something worse—the tragic, futile un-Jewish resort to terrorism, a perversion of the purely defensive function of Haganah; and worst of all, in certain circles, a readiness to compound with the evil, to play politics with it, to condemn and not to condemn it, to treat it not as the thing it was, namely, an unmitigated curse to the National Home, but as a phenomenon which might have its advantages.[38]

Still, despite these misgivings, the overall impression he carried away was one that gave him confidence and pride. The war years had knit the *Yishuv* into 'a powerful, self-conscious organism' and had bestowed upon it 'a heightened self-reliance, a justified sense of merit and achievement, a renewed claim on the democratic world, and a high degree of technical development'. 'The National Home was in fact here,' Weizmann proclaimed, even though it was 'unrecognized' and hence 'frustrated in the fulfillment of its task'.[39]

He summed up his political feelings in a lengthy address to the Zionist General Council in Jerusalem in March 1945, ignoring his own maxim not to make prophecies in Palestine. Speaking in Yiddish, to avoid any 'possibility of misunderstanding', he told them: 'Something was cooking. . . . That is why I am in a hurry to return to England, because I think a decision is going to be made.' As if to immortalize his guiding philosophy, he continued:

> But whatever happens our fate lies with England, not with Stalin or Roosevelt. The others may help or hinder, but the decisive factor is still England, because the British Empire will continue to exist, despite much suggestion here that it has already been eliminated or is about to be.[40]

The British Empire staggered on for another few years. But Zionist policy was being determined more and more in the *Yishuv*, where Weizmann's authority was at a low premium, and in the United States, which was too remote for him to influence. Weizmann was left stranded in London, negotiating with Britain, for she was still the mandatory power, but a victim of events that spun out of his control.

NINETEEN

THE LINE OF LEAST INJUSTICE

On 7 May 1945 Germany surrendered unconditionally to the Allied powers. The war in Europe was over, but, contrary to Weizmann's premonition that 'something was cooking', there had been no movement in Zionist affairs. Rumours were afoot that at Yalta the Big Three had promised Palestine to the Jews; but this was 'pure moonshine', as one British official put it. Stalin remained adamantly anti-Zionist. Weizmann had attempted to breach Soviet hostility during the war and had even sought a meeting with Stalin after Yalta, but was discouraged from doing so by the British on the grounds that it was 'impracticable'. [1]

The last months of war had shown ominous signs of an erosion in the Zionist position. A British-sponsored Arab League was formed in March which, Weizmann surmised, would prejudice decisions regarding the future of Palestine. And the myth of Ibn Saud underwriting an Arab-Zionist understanding was finally punctured. Roosevelt was proclaiming that he had learned more about 'the whole problem, the Muslim problem, the Jewish problem, by talking with Ibn Saud for five minutes [aboard an American warship in the Suez Canal on his return from Yalta] than I could have learned in an exchange of two or three dozen letters'. Roosevelt told Wise, who reported the message to Weizmann, 'The one failure of his mission was with Ibn Saud. . . . Every time I mentioned the Jews he would shrink.' Had not the Jews reclaimed Palestine? persisted Roosevelt. 'My people don't like trees,' Ibn Saud retorted. 'We are desert dwellers.' Even Churchill's persuasive tongue, Roosevelt added, had failed to dent the desert king's hostility. [2]

Weizmann spent the first days of May in a nursing home, convalescing after an operation on his eyes. On 22 May he approached Churchill. The plight of his people was 'desperate', he said; if no positive move was made immediately, his personal position as president of the Jewish Agency would become 'untenable'. He continued:

> Your word could never carry greater weight than it does now. The White Paper still stands. It is prolonging the agony of the Jewish survivors. Will you not say the word which is to right wrongs and set the people free? . . . This is the hour to eliminate the White Paper, to open the doors of Palestine, and to proclaim the Jewish State.

Churchill's concise and unambiguous reply shattered Weizmann: 'There can I fear be no possibility of the question being effectively considered until the victorious Allies are definitely seated at the Peace table.' How many times during the war had Churchill promised to see him through? Together with Roosevelt, they would sail over all barriers, taking Weizmann with them. Now Roosevelt was dead, his successor was an unknown quantity, and Churchill, at the moment of truth, fobbed him off with an inexplicable insensitivity to his political fortunes. 'I stand before young Jews today,' Weizmann reflected a year later, 'as a leader who failed to achieve anything by peaceful means.'[3]

Weizmann might well have recalled his conversation with Smuts some months earlier, when he had remarked: 'You and I started from opposite poles. You began as an enemy of the British, I as their staunchest friend. But it seems they do not want my friendship or that of my people. Hitler has won this war as far as the Jews are concerned.'[4] In any event, he planned to tender his resignation at the forthcoming Zionist conference in August, and when he dined with Meinertzhagen on 3 July, he painted the future in dark colours. Palestine was like a volcano, he observed, and his resignation would be the signal for it to erupt. A revolt directed against the British would have catastrophic consequences, but he was powerless to prevent it. He had failed personally. Convinced that 'God's promise would eventually come true', he was equally convinced that he was not destined 'to act as the Almighty's agent on earth. Somebody else must try.' 'Poor Weizmann,' Meinertzhagen wrote. 'It must be heartbreaking for him to see twenty-five years' hard work made futile.'[5]

Then on 26 July the Labour Party was returned to office in a landslide victory at the polls. The change in government brought some hope to the Zionists. In opposition, Labour had consistently registered its commitment to Zionism; at its party conference in December 1944 it had adopted an extreme pro-Zionist resolution (which caused much embarrassment in moderate Zionist circles) calling for mass Jewish immigration and the transfer of populations: 'Let the Arabs be encouraged to move out as the Jews move in.' It also suggested extending 'the present Palestinian frontiers by agreement with Egypt, Syria and Transjordan'. The question must have crossed Weizmann's mind whether the Labour Party would remain bound by its earlier extravagant pledges or whether Ernest Bevin, the new Foreign Secretary, would be a new version of Passfield. In the event, to Weizmann's everlasting sorrow, the latter alternative prevailed.

It would be altogether too facile to attribute Britain's Palestine policy to Bevin's alleged anti-semitism. Bevin's record on behalf of Zionism was better than most, and both Weizmann and Ben Gurion had counted him among Zionist sympathizers. As his biographer has pointed out, a man of sixty-five, of known strong prejudices and opinions, is hardly likely to become an anti-semite overnight.[6] When he entered the Foreign Office, Bevin was already suffering from a serious heart condition, which at times caused him to black out and often left him thoroughly exhausted, a condition that helps to explain his short temper and violent outbursts when confronted by opposition to his policies. He was certainly guilty of tactlessness, of adopting a hectoring, bullying tone, of unleashing a coarse tongue, of articulating unfortunate phrases, with anti-semitic connotations, best left unsaid. A street fighter, he paid back Zionist attacks on his person—they often compared him to Hitler—in the same coin. Having foolishly staked his reputation on resolving the Palestine issue, he vented his anger and frustration against those whom he believed were willfully thwarting him. Still, for a modern politician, style is all-important; and Bevin fell victim to his image of himself as a blunt, no-nonsense working man at last running the foreign affairs of his country.

But his fundamental error in regard to Palestine was far more grievous: it was a failure to evaluate correctly the temper of the nationalist forces at work in the Middle East, and in particular in the Jewish world. Bevin, together with Attlee and others, held that Jewish survivors from the holocaust still had a future in Europe. They kept excellent company: Churchill announced to the House of Commons in August 1946 that he did not believe that the Jewish problem could be resolved by 'a vast dumping of the Jews of Europe into Palestine', continuing, 'I am not absolutely sure that we should be in too great a hurry to give up the idea that European Jews may live in the countries where they belong.' For the Zionists, this was akin to sacrilege. Nearly six million Jews had been slaughtered in Europe; and even after the end of hostilities Jews were still being killed in eastern Europe by anti-semites. Only Palestine could offer them a safe haven, they believed. 'Are you suggesting that Europe as a home for Jews is really finished?' Richard Crossman asked Weizmann. Weizmann nodded his assent. 'But if the Jews left Europe, would it not be an admission that de-mocracy is through in Europe?' persisted Crossman. 'It would be an admission that Europeans are sick, and it will take a long time to get rid of the sickness,' Weizmann replied. 'The presence of Jews in Eu-rope today might exaggerate the sickness.'[7] The Zionists never deviated from this view; and if, in retrospect, it may be judged as simplistic, at the time its firmness of purpose and boldness of spirit won the day, helped along by the clumsy British.

No doubt relying on his experience as a trade-union boss, Bevin sincerely believed that two sides to a dispute, no matter how far apart at the outset, would gradually draw together in a mutual compromise prompted by common sense and joint interests. But the Zionists were demanding full implementation of the Biltmore programme, while the Arabs were threatening a 'new crusader's war'. This unbridgeable gap defeated Bevin, as it had others before him. The Anglo-Zionist alliance that Weizmann had helped forge no longer held. British and Zionist interests were at variance, pulling in opposite directions. Britain— virtually bankrupt, her economy run down, saddled with added re-sponsibilities in Europe, her empire rent by belligerent nationalisms, dependent upon American aid—sought stubbornly to maintain her position in the Arab and Muslim worlds, a desperate holding action in view of her shrinking resources. The Zionists figured marginally in this dismal story, their demands for justice merely aggravating an already complicated situation.

These differences surfaced immediately after the Labour govern-ment had assessed the situation. In early September, the cabinet, fearing the repercussions in the Arab world, decided to persist with the white paper policy: Jewish immigration into Palestine would be allowed to continue on a limited basis of 1500 per month. Although nothing was announced officially, the Zionists soon learned of this decision through one of their friends in the government. Weizmann appealed to Attlee but was put off with a noncommittal reply.[8] He was under considerable pressure from his Zionist colleagues, who had severely criticized him at the London conference in August, where they had not only reconfirmed the Biltmore programme and reiterated their demands for mass immigration but also raised the cry for active resistance against the mandatory power. Hoping to annul the white paper as a first step toward creating their state, the Zionists worked assiduously to secure the immediate admission into Palestine of 100,000 immigrants: this magic figure came to symbolize the Zionist struggle, to be the focal point for a formidable propaganda campaign to win world sympathy and destroy Britain's Palestine policy. And it was given an unexpected fillip when President Truman publicly announced his support for it at the end of September, leaving the British bitterly resentful at his intervention.[9]

Despite his consistent advocacy of mass immigration, Weizmann now stood before his people, six months after the end of the war, with empty hands. In Palestine, this lack of concrete results led to increased violence. Weizmann's prediction was coming true. The Haganah and the dissident groups, the Irgun and the Stern gang, were coordinating their activities in the Jewish Resistance Movement, a development Weizmann viewed with extreme trepidation. His definition of activism was a rigid one: it should be limited to operations that directly undermined the white paper: illegal immigration or the establishment of new settlements. He opposed direct action against British military or police forces, which he deemed as 'aggressive', believing that the present conflict with Britain was 'only partial and temporary' and that eventually saner councils would prevail in the British government, a view most leaders of the Jewish Agency and the Haganah emphatically rejected.[10] At odds with the Jewish Agency leadership and convinced that Ben Gurion was leading them down a slippery path, he was, as Sir Alan Cunningham, the latest high commissioner, bluntly put it later, 'deliberately kept in ignorance of the seamy side of Jewish political activities', an assessment later confirmed by Moshe Sneh, commander-in-chief of the Haganah.[11] All too often, he learned of the spectacular actions of the resistance movement from the newspapers. Was this not the first stage in ousting him from effective leadership of the Zionist movement?

In this volatile atmosphere Weizmann met Bevin for the first time. The British had got wind of what was going on in Palestine, which may account for Bevin's bellicose attitude. 'What do you mean by refusing the white paper certificates?' he asked Weizmann. 'Are you trying to force my hand? If you want a fight you can have it.' In any case, there was no question of admitting 100,000 refugees. Five days later, on 10 October, they renewed their talk, but the impasse remained. They met again on 1 November, by which time the *Palmach*, the élite corps of the Haganah, had broken into an internment camp at Athlit and freed 200 immigrants; in a finely coordinated action, the resistance movement simultaneously attacked British installations throughout Palestine. Bevin, a muscle twitching at the side of his mouth, accused the *Yishuv* of declaring war against Britain. Weizmann protested, but to no effect. Bevin would not negotiate under the threat of violence:

> I cannot bear English Tommies being killed. They are innocent. . . . I do not want any Jews killed either, but I love the British soldiers. They belong to my class. They are working people. . . . The problem is intolerably difficult . . . but we are honestly trying to find a way out.

Weizmann was deeply hurt by what he considered Bevin's 'overbearing, quarrelsome' manner, but he found even more disturbing Bevin's ignorance of Palestinian matters and his inability to perceive the true dimensions of the Jewish problem. '[He] could not see them,' Bevin's biographer writes, 'as a separate nationality.'[12]

On 13 November Bevin made public his 'way out'. In a statement to the House of Commons he refused to rescind the white paper but announced the appointment of an Anglo-American Committee of Inquiry to investigate the condition of European Jewry and to make recommendations to alleviate their plight. Convinced that Truman was cynically exploiting British difficulties for internal political reasons and alarmed by the adverse effect that anti-British agitation in the United States was having on relations between the two powers, Bevin hoped that the joint initiative would tone down the Americans' criticism and force them to behave more responsibly. But this was to misjudge Truman's motives. Truman was, of course, sensitive to the Jewish vote, as American politicians must be; but he was also moved by a deep and genuine sympathy for the sufferings of the Jewish refugees, and his support, though at times sorely tried by over-enthusiastic Zionist lobbyists, stood firm. Nor did Bevin succeed in calming American opinion—quite the contrary. At a press conference held in the Foreign Office immediately after his announcement to the Commons, he remarked:

> I am very anxious that Jews shall not in Europe over-emphasize their racial position. . . . I want the suppression of racial warfare, and there-

fore if the Jews, with all their sufferings, want to get too much at the head of the queue, you have the danger of another anti-Semitic reaction through it all.

This reference to pushy Jews was taken by many as decisive proof of Bevin's anti-semitism. Weizmann, who was then in America, reacted forthwith: 'It is brutal, vulgar and anti-semitic, but I suppose that such is the nature of the gentleman.' In Atlantic City, he told an American Zionist conference that not so long ago, 'Jews had the highest priority in the queues which led to the crematoria of Auschwitz and Treblinka'. But Bevin, as though possessed by a *dybbuk*, seemed to have lost control of his tongue. Barely a year later, he attributed to the American campaign for the 100,000 immigrants 'the purest of motives. They did not want too many Jews in New York.'[13]

Weizmann's predictable observations were representative of outraged world Jewry. Of more consequence, however, was his attitude toward the Anglo-American Committee. For years he had aimed at American involvement in the Palestinian question. Had he not dreamed of Roosevelt and Churchill imposing a pro-Zionist solution on the Arabs? But he had not bargained for another inquiry, particularly if its terms of reference did not exclude solutions other than Palestine. Suspicious of a British trick to sidetrack the Americans, he strived to retain Palestine as the only viable option. This was the gist of his message to Truman, whom he saw for the first time on 4 December: 100,000 certificates; the abrogation of the white paper; and the creation of a 'Jewish democratic commonwealth'.

The meeting had been arranged by David Niles, Truman's influential aide and specialist in minority affairs, known to be a Zionist sympathizer. Lord Halifax, ambassador in Washington, escorted Weizmann at Truman's request. Before they entered the Oval Office, Weizmann told him: 'If you think you will prevail over us through committees, or that you will coerce the *Yishuv*, you are very much mistaken. We have a hundred thousand boys who will fight to the death, and we are with them.' Halifax wisely remained silent, as he did throughout the interview, even though Weizmann severely criticized British policy, on one occasion comparing Bevin's approach to that of Alfred Rosenberg's. Truman barely responded to Weizmann's claim for a Jewish state that would absorb four million Jews, except to ask whether it would be a religious state, to which Weizmann answered an emphatic 'No'. Nor did he react to Weizmann's pooh-poohing the Moslem-Arab threat or his playing down the importance of the Anglo-American Committee: 'What have they to investigate?' he argued. 'Nothing is hidden, everything is known.' He had less cause for concern than he imagined, for Truman, despite his reticence, had already given instructions that Palestine 'be the focus of the inquiry'.[14]

On 8 March 1946, at the YMCA building in Jerusalem, Weizmann appeared before the committee. Richard Crossman, a Labour intellectual and formerly a philosophy don at Oxford, who at the beginning of his work as a committeeman confessed to 'a blankness toward the philosophy of Zionism which is virtually anti-Zionist', noted the event in his diary:

> Today we had Weizmann, who looks like a weary and more humane version of Lenin, very tired, very ill, too old and too pro-British to control his extremists. He spoke for two hours with a magnificent mixture of passion and scientific detachment. Here is a Jew who frankly admits that every Jew carries the virus of anti-semitism with him and founded his case for a Jewish Commonwealth on that fact. He is the first witness who has frankly and openly admitted that the issue is not between right and wrong but between the greater and lesser injustice.

When Weizmann admitted that he did not know whether it would take one or two years to absorb 100,000 immigrants, there was great consternation among the Zionist politicians listening. Had he given something away?

> They don't understand that Weizmann's extraordinary hold on Britain depends entirely on an integrity which refuses to say 'I know' when he does not know. He made a far greater impression on the committee by his candour than if he had merely made the routine propaganda speech which we have heard so often.[15]

Take 'the line of least injustice', Weizmann had urged, which in current circumstances could mean only the establishment of a Jewish state. In private, he made no secret that he would accept a workable partition. He carefully cultivated the commissioners, inviting them in turn to his home in Rehovot. Crum thought him 'a towering figure', but his greatest conquest was Crossman. Himself gifted with a sharp, analytical mind and a wonderful power of expression, he found Weizmann's flair for conveying profound wisdom through humourous anecdotes captivating. Crossman would later say, 'He was the only truly great statesman I have known.' It must have been nearly impossible to withstand Weizmann's alluring blend of charm and innocence and guile:

> I went on chatting with the old man in his library until he suggested a walk in the garden. He is seventy-two and nearly blind from cataract, and as we stepped out of doors he slipped his arm into mine. We strolled out, and the scent of orange blossom streamed up from the grove below like a sweet mist. [16]

Crossman remained a devoted friend, the last of Weizmann's converts among English gentiles.

The Anglo-American Committee's report, published on 20 April 1946, was unanimous. It called for the immediate admission of 100,000 immigrants and the annulment of the land restriction, but it rejected the claim for either a Jewish or an Arab state, proposing instead that the Palestine mandate make way for a United Nations trusteeship. The Zionists had hoped for more: the fact that no Jewish state was recommended was certainly a punishing blow. But could they range themselves against a joint Anglo-American policy? In any case, it was clear that implementation of the report spelled the end of the white paper; and would not the entry of 100,000 Jews pave the way for a Jewish majority and, inevitably, a Jewish state? This was Weizmann's view, and it was upheld by a majority of the Zionist leaders. Others, notably Ben Gurion, played up the negative aspects of the report. [17]

The Zionist dilemma was resolved by the interplay between British and American policies. Truman, succumbing to pressure, had enthusiastically endorsed the admission of 100,000 Jewish immigrants to Palestine, but he had not consulted the British beforehand, which greatly angered Bevin and Attlee. Attlee stressed to the House of Commons the difficulties in absorbing 100,000 immigrants, of the mandatory power's shouldering the burden alone, and declared that the implementation of the report would be made conditional on the disarming of the *Yishuv*. [18] Anglo-American contacts continued to devise other schemes, but Attlee's statement killed the committee's report.

Was this the last chance for a negotiated settlement in Palestine? Weizmann might have clung to his Zionist leadership position by manipulating the recommendations of the committee; as one of his advisers put it, 'The obvious tactics are to accept in generous spirit, and proceed to argue specific points.' [19] But in view of the hostility of the

Arabs there was no question of the *Yishuv* disarming itself or of allowing itself to be disarmed. And with immigration still controlled and 'illegals' still running the British blockade, Palestine was like a tinder-box waiting for a spark. Weizmann was acutely aware of the dangers, but he could not fathom British motives. Were 'sinister forces' at work, 'bent on the liquidation of the National Home', or was it 'mere muddle-headedness'? Whatever the explanation, he warned Attlee that if 'there is further delay and the issue is again thrown into the melting pot, there is certain to be trouble both from the Arabs who will be encouraged by this to back up their threats by action, and from Jewish extremists prepared to resort to violence.'[20]

Weizmann's fears were only too well-founded. Since the autumn of 1945, with the establishment of the Jewish Resistance Movement, violence in Palestine had been escalating steadily, and it would reach a bloody climax in the coming months. Weizmann, who watched these events with mounting horror, was not a silent spectator. He appealed to the British commander in Palestine, General Sir Evelyn Barker, to commute the death sentences imposed on two Irgun members: 'However wrong or misguided these young men may be, they have not acted from criminal motives, but because of a deep-seated feeling of a great injustice done to their people.'[21] (The sentences were later commuted, but only after the Irgun had kidnapped six British officers as hostages.) But the actions against the British mounted in intensity. On 17 June 1946 the Palmach blew up eleven bridges linking Palestine with her neighbours; at the same time the Stern gang attacked the Haifa oil refineries, and the Irgun carried out its kidnapping of six British officers. It was a virtual declaration of war.

It was also, Weizmann believed, an act of defiance against him. After admonishing Sneh—'You are doing foolish things and I have to take responsibility'—he went to see the high commissioner on 24 June. 'You have a brilliant army, brilliant fighters and staff officers,' Sir Alan Cunningham told him, 'but you have to understand that no government can tolerate the existence of an army outside its control.' 'Our youth can no longer suffer government policy and keep their emotions in check,' Weizmann retorted. 'The Haganah operates with deference for human life,' he explained. 'The other groups are different on that point. But resistance is inevitable to such policy.'[22]

Three days later he composed a letter to Shertok. Explaining his tiredness, having carried the burden 'for so many years', he stressed the 'profound differences' that separated him from his colleagues. No longer could he keep quiet, for he dreaded 'to think of what may happen in the coming six months'. 'I am emphatically opposed to political violence, and it is also, I fear, becoming clear that my power to restrain it is very small.' Referring to the abduction of the British officers as a 'vile and hideous crime', he went on: 'In the eyes of all men of good will, our movement is sinking to the level of gangsterdom.' Of course, he appreciated the intolerable provocation driving the Jews to such actions. The British government, he claimed, 'has clearly abdicated its moral position, and intends to rule here in Palestine by the sword and the hangman's rope. But it is not for us to imitate its methods.' Nor those of the Arabs or the Boers or the Irish, totally 'fallacious' and 'immoral' analogies.

> *Our* only force is moral force—as we showed during all the years of the 'troubles'. It is the duty of our leaders to point out to our young people—the only valuable asset we possess—that they must concentrate on constructive achievement, however difficult that may seem. A policy of destruction can rebound only on ourselves, and it is we who, in the end, will be destroyed.
>
> Political violence is one and indivisible. It is a method; and it is both inconsistent and useless to condemn one single act unless the whole method is discarded. . . . The events of the last few days indicate either a complete loss of control over the forces of destruction, or a change of policy (of which I know nothing). . . .
>
> I cannot continue to play the part of a respectable façade screening things which I abhor, but for which I must bear responsibility in the eyes of the world.

Unless the Irgun and the Stern gang were brought to heel, unless they gave evidence of 'obedience' and 'moral discipline', and unless political violence was 'definitely abandoned', he would have no option but to leave office immediately, he wrote. 'As I told you personally yesterday, this letter serves notice that the very next act of sabotage will automatically bring about my resignation.'[23]

Owing to Weizmann's ill health, the delivery of this letter was delayed, and it remained locked in his drawer, perhaps forgotten, until January 1947 when, rankled by his defeat at the Zionist Congress, he finally sent it off. By that time, events had overtaken its contents.

The British Army, already straining at the leash, was now allowed its head, and on 29 June Operation Agatha, known to the Jews as 'Black Sabbath', was put into effect, an action that effectively crippled the Resistance Movement. Leaders of the Jewish Agency were rounded up and confined in a detention camp at Latrun: settlements were searched, buildings ransacked, and secret documents procured. In all, some 2700 suspects were detained. Not all the leaders were apprehended. Ben Gurion was in Paris and Moshe Sneh escaped capture. Weizmann was left alone, in despair at the British action. That day a message reached him that the British would consider releasing the internees if he would intervene. Suffering from a chill and running a high temperature, he motored to Jerusalem to interview the high commissioner. Vera pointedly remained in the car outside Government House, refusing the light refreshments offered her.

The stormy meeting was barren of results. Mutual accusations were exchanged that each side had declared hostilities against the other. The Jewish Agency is working behind your back, Cunningham reminded a 'very distressed' Weizmann: lay down your arms and help suppress the dissidents, the Irgun and the Sternists. This struck a sensitive nerve, and Cunningham reported that Weizmann was receptive to the 'idea of negotiation in regard to the Jewish armed forces'. But he failed to drive a wedge between Weizmann the moderate and the extremists he could no longer control. Whatever his private thoughts, and even while engaged in a battle with his executive on these very issues, he preserved Jewish solidarity in his public duels. Arrest me also, he invited the high commissioner, telling him that one can never rule Jews by force. At a further confrontation with Cunningham, on 14 July, Weizmann claimed that the British had created an impossible situation. He warned that the *Yishuv* was at the end of its tether, ready to risk all in open rebellion in which thousands of Jews would die. Cooperation had become a dirty word, and the moderates, with himself at their head, were fighting a losing battle. He argued that the release of the Latrun detainees as a gesture of good intent would clear the air. But his plea was met by a flat negative. Cunningham made clear that he was neither open to bargaining nor impressed by threats.[24]

Something had snapped in Weizmann's attitude toward Britain, and he now drew upon the cruelest analogy his memory allowed. Speaking to the executive in Jerusalem on 9 July, he claimed, 'Nothing could be further from my mind than to suggest comparisons between the Tsarist regime and the British Government of today, but one's memory is sometimes irrational. . . . Ours is no less a struggle— Let my people go!' A few days later, from London, he wrote to the Chief Rabbi of Palestine, Isaac Herzog: 'Palestine today is not merely a police state: it is the worst form of military dictatorship', a country where 'the writ of *habeas corpus* does not run'. The dictator, General Barker, he continued, was consumed by anti-semitism and had vowed to 'uproot every Jew in Palestine'; his troops were taught to regard the Jews as 'the enemy'. When they pillaged Givat Brenner, a communal settlement just outside Rehovot, they behaved like conquering invaders. Swastikas and slogans—'"What we need is gas-chambers!" "Hitler didn't finish the job!'"—were chalked or painted on walls; 'and also even on the pavements of Rehovot—where I have seen them with my own eyes!' In order to avoid open war between the *Yishuv* and the British, Weizmann had proposed a three-point programme: the immediate release of the detainees at Latrun; the admission of the 100,000; and the re-establishment of civil authority in Palestine. But he waited in vain for its implementation. 'Black Sabbath', Weizmann concluded, had fundamentally altered the ground rules: 'What has been destroyed is so deep, so vital, and of such moral significance, that it cannot be restored by projects, resolutions, and kind words. . . . What has happened in Palestine has been burnt into the soul of every man, woman and child in the *Yishuv*.' Trust, understanding, co-operation had been swept away. The British, bereft of moral authority, had forfeited the right to rule over the Jews. Only partition, 'an independent Jewish State in treaty relations with Great Britain', would provide an honourable way out of this dreadful impasse and eventually lead to a *rapprochement* between Arabs and Jews.[25]

Weizmann's anger was turned not only against the British. Incensed that the Haganah had again defied him, now by provocatively raiding a British army camp to retrieve its confiscated arms, he sent word, through Meyer Weisgal, to 'Committee X' (the body responsible to the Jewish Agency and the Vaad Leumi, which coordinated activities with the Irgun and the Stern group) that he would resign forthwith unless all violent actions against British military and police installations were suspended until the Jewish Agency executive could meet to decide on an agreed policy:

I am President of the World Zionist Organization. In every democratic State the President is commander of the army. Nobody knows better than you [Sneh] that I have never used this privilege of mine. This time I must. If you continue military resistance to the British, this would endanger the very existence of all we have achieved in two generations. Black Sabbath signifies for me that the British have resolved to destroy us if we continue with our military struggle. I am not ready or able to bear this responsibility on my shoulders. So if you continue I must resign and of course I must publish the reasons for my resignation. I don't want to do this as it would split our people. But the continuation of the military struggle will force my hand. Therefore I appeal to you to stop all military action until a plenary session of the Jewish Agency Executive when a collective decision will be taken and the responsibility will be on the elected body. You and I are only individuals.

Sneh disagreed, but Weizmann's ultimatum carried sufficient weight to convince a majority of his comrades. Orders were issued to the Haganah to suspend its military actions. An attack on a British arms dump was abandoned, and the Haganah withdrew from a joint operation planned with the Irgun against the British military headquarters housed in the King David hotel, Jerusalem. The united Jewish Resistance Movement dissolved. In August 1946 the Jewish Agency Executive meeting in Paris (though without Weizmann, who was too ill to attend) postponed a final decision until December when the twenty-second Zionist Congress was due to convene. Sneh resigned in protest. Weizmann told him, 'our ways have parted, but you have always behaved like a gentleman'.[26] At last, Weizmann had imposed his moral authority upon the Haganah; the Irgun and the Stern gang went their own way, dragging the movement down to the level of the Mufti and his cohorts.

Perhaps Weizmann was seeking the impossible: a pure 'activism', guided by the old moral precepts. Yigal Allon, the young commander of the Palmach, representative of the new generation of Palestinian Jews, was chosen to sound him out:

This was the first time in my life that I had approached Weizmann directly. I had some highly ambivalent attitudes toward Weizmann. On the one hand, there was great admiration: from childhood, I had regarded him as King of the Jews. On the other hand, there were whispers that he was too great a compromiser. . . . I had an unforgettable conversation with the man, who then told me: 'This ceasefire is only temporary.' 'It is permitted,' he said, 'in a national struggle, to act when necessary and also to refrain from action when necessary. I have determined that now is the time to refrain.'[27]

He was not, apparently, all restraint. Meyer Weisgal recalls that, in the summer of 1946, Weizmann hinted to his aide-de-camp that a radar station employed in detecting immigrant boats might be cleared 'out of the way'; it was. Henceforth, the Haganah centered its struggle on settlements and 'illegal' immigration, and if on occasion its deeds stretched Weizmann's definition of activism, he tolerated these transgressions.[28]

Weizmann left Palestine on 17 July for London. On 22 July the Irgun blew up the King David hotel, destroying the wing that housed the headquarters of the British administration: the casualties, ninety-one dead and forty-five wounded, included British, Jews, and Arabs. Weizmann first heard of the incident over the radio in his rooms at the Dorchester. Baffy, who recorded his reaction, noted that he would not 'come near the office, nor discuss anything calmly on telephone'. Convinced that he had been deceived, that the Haganah had broken its pledge, his pent-up feelings burst into an 'irrational frenzy of anger', a 'wild rage' directed against even his closest associates—Locker, Shertok, and especially Ben Gurion. In fact, although the Haganah had initially approved of the operation, they had, at the last moment, withdrawn from the action, largely owing to Weizmann's intervention. But even if the precise details of this dreadful affair were known to him, what did it matter? Public opinion tarred them all with the same brush, he believed, which no doubt was why the government made public documents that incriminated Jewish Agency leaders, including Weizmann, in the violence of recent months.

When Richard Crossman visited him, he gave expression to an unmentionable but popular after-thought:

> He put his arm round me. 'You are the first Goy who has been here,' he said. 'All my old friends refuse to see me now—Winston and the other Conservatives as well as your Labour people.' And a little later he muttered below his breath, 'I detest terrorism, but, you know, if it had been a German headquarters they'd have got the V.C.'[29]

The British reacted in hot fury. Twenty thousand troops descended on Tel Aviv, imposing curfews and conducting searches, often brutally. General Barker issued a notorious non-fraternization *ukaz* to punish 'the Jews in a way the race dislikes as much as any, by striking at their pockets and showing our contempt [and loathing] for them'. In a colder, no less menacing mood, the authorities intensified their campaign against the 'illegals', now transferring these new immigrants to camps in Cyprus. These days were a ghastly nightmare for Weizmann. 'Where we shall find the courage and strength to live through them I hardly know.'[30]

Weizmann had returned to Europe to undergo treatment for his eyes, and this prevented him from attending a meeting of the Jewish Agency Executive in Paris in August. It was a crucial gathering, and a special messenger was despatched imploring him to attend, if only for twenty-four hours. But he refused, with Vera's blessing. 'It is a fatal mistake,' Baffy recorded, 'and equivalent to abdication'.[31] Yet in fact the executive adopted Weizmann's partition policy; though Ben Gurion declared that he had lost faith in Weizmann's ability to negotiate on behalf of the movement, he too argued for partition, then abstained on the vote, and finally refused to accompany Nahum Goldmann to Washington to put the Zionist case to Congress.[32] At the same time, the Zionists debated the conditions necessary for them to enter into discussions with the government. They rejected the so-called Morrison–Grady scheme for provincial autonomy, as had the Arabs, consenting to negotiate only if a viable partition plan was on the agenda. Gradually their terms were raised to include the freedom to choose their own delegates: in other words, the release of the men arrested and detained at Latrun. With the Zionists still debating these fine points in Paris, a conference of sorts opened in London on 9 September, but it included only the delegates from three Arab states and their British hosts.

All along Weizmann had kept an open mind in regard to the Morrison–Grady scheme, which included the interesting proposal that 100,000 immigrants be admitted to the Jewish province within a year. Even Bevin had not excluded the notion that it could eventually evolve into the partition of Palestine, and for once Weizmann agreed with him. Now that the Palestine conference had proved a false starter and the Jewish Agency had clearly defined its terms, Weizmann wanted to push ahead. He wrote to Ben Gurion:

> While agreeing with the course taken I have always felt—I made no secret of it—and I feel it more strongly today, that if we could find a decent and honourable way to go into the Conference, it would be our duty to do so. . . . We shall be committing a sin against the movement and against the *Yishuv* if we do not explore even the slightest possibility of reaching a solution acceptable to us.

Politics, he explained to Locker, 'is a matter of *Fingerspitzengefühl* [instinct, intuition]': opportunities, he insisted, should be exploited, not wasted. After considerable pressure and repeated threats of resignation, Weizmann got his way.[33] Informal talks, a semantic nicety, began on 1 October.

They were indecisive. Having for the moment made no progress with either the Jews or the Arabs, the British postponed the conference until the new year, pending the deliberations of the forthcoming Zionist Congress. As for Weizmann, his position had strengthened over the past months. Not only had he liberated the Jewish Agency from its corruptive pact with terrorism, but he had guided the executive back to the commitment to a plan for partition. Yet, at the end of October, Ben Gurion harked back to the differences between them. He wanted nothing to do with the provincial autonomy scheme, he said, or with any conference that placed it at the centre of its deliberations. In a letter to Weizmann, touchingly written in especially large script so that Weizmann could read it, he stated, 'Our line should be the Mandate—or a State. . . . If Britain is unable or unwilling to carry out the Mandate, she should agree to the establishment of a Jewish State, even if not in the whole of Palestine, but at once.' In effusive, laudatory language, he went on:

> Whatever your views are on all this you remain for me the elect of Jewish history, representing beyond compare the suffering and the glory of the Jews. And wherever you go you will be attended by the love and faithful esteem of me and my colleagues. We are the generation that comes after you and which has been tried, perhaps, by crueller and greater sufferings, and we sometimes, for this reason, see things differently—but fundamentally we draw from the same reservoir of inspiration—that of sorely tried Russian Jewry—the qualities of tenacity, faith, and persistent striving which yields to no adversary or foe.

Weizmann was moved by Ben Gurion's kindness and by his 'charming and friendly' letter. But he would not budge from his position. He replied: 'I think it would be wrong to abstain from the conference, even if our point of view is not accepted beforehand. I believe the others will eventually come round to it. . . . I can't help feeling that the inexorable logic of facts will drive them [Byrnes and Bevin] towards partition.'[34]

What did these differences amount to in fact? Were they not tactical at best? And could not some compromise formula have been found, as in the past? Fundamental principles were not at stake here. The crucial issue was who would lead the Zionist movement if it was now engaged in a remorseless struggle against British rule. His detractors had no faith that Weizmann was suited for such a role. It was of small consequence that Weizmann was now as disillusioned with Britain as his critics were. As Abba Eban has pointed out, 'A statesman remains a symbol of an attitude long after the attitude has passed away'.[35] His carefully, proudly fostered image as an Anglophile led to his political downfall. His ill health must also have influenced opinion against him: he had aged markedly, his sight was failing, and he was confined for longer periods to his sick-bed. Did he possess the necessary strength and energy to lead the movement through these tumultuous times?

These questions were very much to the fore when the delegates gathered at Basel in December 1946 for the twenty-second Zionist Congress. Weizmann arrived on 5 December from Lugano, where he had spent a few days recuperating from yet another eye operation. As he walked through the lobby of the Hotel Drei Könige, Baffy thought he looked 'very well'.[36] But he sadly over-estimated the degree of support he commanded, perhaps misled by the effect of Britain's conciliatory gesture in freeing the Latrun detainees a month before. In fact, his position was abysmally weak. He had no party machine to fall back on, and relied on the lobbying of Simon Marks and Harry Sacher— a poor substitute—to rally his forces. With few exceptions, the American and the Palestinian delegates were solidly ranged against him. There was little Weizmann could do to break the Silver–Ben Gurion combination, certainly not by speeches alone, however impassioned and dramatic.

His opening address, read in English, lacked the necessary fire.[37] He spoke of the holocaust, of the war, of broken British promises, of the rupture with Britain: '[It] is not of our making, and cannot be healed by ourselves alone. Neither is it necessary or an inevitable breach.' He touched on the Arab problem: 'How can it be moderate for them to claim seven states, and extreme for us to claim one', and reaffirmed his belief in a Jewish state, rejecting the autonomy scheme. But his strongest, most impassioned words were reserved to condemn terrorism:

> Assassination, ambush, kidnapping, the murder of innocent men, are alien to the spirit of our movement. We came to Palestine to build, not to destroy; terror distorts the essence of Zionism. It insults our history; it mocks the ideals for which a Jewish society must stand; it sullies our banner. . . . Nor must our judgement be dazzled by the glare of self-

conscious heroism. Massada, for all its heroism, was a disaster in our history. It is not our purpose or our right to plunge to destruction in order to bequeath a legend of martyrdom to posterity. Zionism was to mark the end of our glorious deaths and the beginning of a new path leading to life.

The sessions dragged on without issue. Speaker after speaker rose to solemnly recite known, entrenched positions. On 16 December, Weizmann mounted the rostrum to reply to the general debate. Did he sense that he was appearing for the last time before a Zionist Congress? He pulled no punches, made no concessions, sought no compromises. With a careless disregard for his own political future, he aimed his oratorical shafts with skill, conviction, great passion, and to tremendous effect at those who irresponsibly preached activism and resistance at any price. Speaking in Yiddish, the language that had always given him greatest freedom of expression, he addressed a keyed-up audience. Admitting that mistakes had been made—'My grandfather used to say, "I never make mistakes in the letters I don't write"'—he explained that 'the political work which we are doing is empirical. Such work is not an exact science, but based on experiment, on trial and error.' Again, he condemned terror, the 'cancer in the body politic of Palestine Jewry, *And thou shalt burn out the evil from thy midst.*' He warned against following 'false paths', invoking Ahad Ha'am, '*Lo zu haderech*—this is not the road,' and restating his belief in practical Zionism.

I am going to say something which this Congress may find unpopular—of building, of laying brick upon brick and stone upon stone. These eleven new settlements in the Negev [established on the evening after Yom Kippur, 1946] will, in my opinion, have greater political significance than a hundred speeches about resistance, especially when the speeches are made in Washington and New York, while it is intended that the resistance shall take place in Jerusalem or Tel Aviv. We must stop being intoxicated by our own words.

Had he gone too far? Had he overstepped the bounds of propriety? In the midst of this discourse, Emanuel Neumann, a Silverite, shouted out: 'This is demagoguery.' Weizmann paused, stunned at the rebuke, and then reacted with a spontaneous fury that riveted his audience.

Somebody has called me a demagogue. I do not know who. I hope I never learn the man's name. I—a demagogue! I who have borne all the ills and travails of this movement! The person who flung this word in my face should know that in every house and every stable in Nahalal, in every workshop in Tel Aviv or Haifa there is a drop of my blood [the delegates, except the *Mizrachi* and the Revisionists, rose to their feet in applause]. You know that I am telling you the truth. Some people don't like to hear it—but you will hear me. I warn you against false prophets, against facile generalization, against distortion of historical facts.

And if you have lost your faith that better times may come, and wish to secure redemption through means which are not Jewish, means which do not accord with Jewish morale, with Jewish ethics or Jewish history, I say to you that you are worshipping false gods. And you endanger everything we have built up. Do not be dazzled. Would that my tongue were tipped with flame, and my soul touched with the strength of our great prophets, when they warned against following the paths of Babylon and Egypt which always led Jewry to failure. I fear that we stand before such dangers today. . . . Go and re-read Isaiah, Jeremiah and Ezekiel, and test that which we do and wish to do in the light of the teachings of our great prophets and wise men. . . . *Zion will be redeemed through righteousness*—and not by any other means.

As Weizmann, half-blind and aged, slowly made his way from the hall to the rapturous acclaim of the delegates, he must have been conscious of the high drama surrounding his person. Some days later, after the vote had gone against him, he appeared again: 'If I have said harsh things to anyone, I did not intend to hurt. The Jewish people, especially those waiting in the camps, look to you to open the gates. I thank you all.' Without exception, the delegates rose to him and sang the Zionist anthem, *Hatikvah*. Weizmann left the rostrum, never again to return to Zionist Congress politics.

'The greatest speech of his life. Perhaps the greatest I have ever heard,' enthused Baffy Dugdale, and then added, more soberly, 'But speeches seldom change opinions.' And so it was. The Zionist Congress voted 171–154 against attending the London conference, while reiterating the Jews' claim for all western Palestine as their Jewish state. No president was nominated to replace Weizmann, nor was he elected to the Jewish Agency Executive. Instead, Silver led the movement from New York, Ben Gurion from Jerusalem—not the happiest of marriages. Over the weeks Weizmann watched, sadly but knowingly, as those who had claimed his position stole his policy. At the end of January 1947, the new leadership entered into 'informal talks' with the British government on a revamped version of the autonomy scheme, known as 'Bevin's plan', only to come away empty-handed.[38]

As Weizmann learned of the wire-pulling and manipulations that had defeated him, his bitterness grew. 'They applauded me and they fired me,' was his acid verdict. Even Paula Ben Gurion had waylaid Baffy at Basel, imploring her to persuade Weizmann to accept an honorary presidency. 'It is an age of pygmies, and so much squalor, spite, folly and party hatreds seem to be devouring Zionist politics. I think the day is done for Zionists of the old school,' Baffy concluded.[39] Weizmann himself professed to 'feel full of hope', having finally emerged from the 'slime' of the Congress. He referred disparagingly to the 'filibustering Rabbi from Cleveland [Silver]' and compared the new executive with Noah's Ark: 'two each of all the animals—clean and unclean (and I very much fear that the unclean ones have the upper hand). Unfortunately, I am obliged to class David [Ben Gurion] with the unclean ones as a result of the role he played.' He returned to London in January, where he toyed with the idea of forming his own progressive group, but wisely abandoned this rash venture.[40] By February, he was back in Rehovot, hoping to relax in the familiar comforts of his home.

TWENTY

A ZIONIST OF THE OLD SCHOOL

Having been freed of the burdens of office, Weizmann could look forward to picking up the threads of his private affairs. Over the past months he had known few moments of real pleasure. One of them, certainly, was the laying of the foundation-stone of the Weizmann Institute in June 1946, the culminating event of an international symposium on 'Trends in Modern Science'. But, although he began to renew his scientific activities, the months ahead were to be among the most crowded and dramatic of his political career. The times were not conducive to detached academic investigations. In Palestine, terrorist groups and the mandate authorities battled each other, trapped in an escalating cycle of violence. In London, the break-down of the informal talks in February led the government to wash its hands of Palestine and turn the problem over to the United Nations. This was not a device by which Britain intended to return to Palestine through the back door. Withdrawal had always been on the public agenda. Churchill had told the House of Commons on 1 August 1946, 'If the United States will not come and share the burden of the Zionist cause . . . we should now give notice that we will return our mandate . . . and will evacuate Palestine within a specified period.'[1] When Bevin met Truman in December 1946, he had found the President more receptive to Britain's predicament, but there had been no indication that the United States was prepared to help shoulder the burden. Britain would have to either negotiate an agreed settlement or else impose her own solution. The first alternative was beyond her wit (and perhaps anyone's), the second beyond her resources.

The winter of 1946–47 was unprecedented in its severity. 'All Britain Freezes,' proclaimed The Times. With rising unemployment, industries crippled through lack of fuel, power cuts, intense cold followed by floods, Britain was in the throes of an economic crisis of the first order, her plans for post-war recovery gone awry. 'This poor country is undergoing afflictions like the Ten Plagues,' Baffy recorded. 'Could the reason be the same? Too fantastic an idea to utter!' But she did: 'Let my People go.'[2]

More down to earth, American political observers pointed out that the Labour government was forced into 'a contest between foreign and domestic policies'.[3] Its decision on Palestine was accompanied by a general retreat from overseas commitments: Greece; Turkey; India above all. Britain's world role was diminishing and her scale of priorities changing. Palestine had proved too intractable a problem, too costly in blood and money and reputation. Bevin told Attlee: 'I am at the end of my tether.' By February 1947, as the young Zionist diplomat Abba Eban observed, Britain was prepared to abandon Palestine, even if in the minds of some officials the decision was not irrevocable.[4]

Weizmann heard of the British decision to refer the Palestine issue to the United Nations while he was in Rehovot. He immediately grasped its implications. On 21 February, he wrote to his friend and scientific collaborator in Chicago, Albert Epstein:

> The strategic position of Palestine under these circumstances loses almost entirely its importance, and if relations between Jews and Arabs become more acute, I have no doubt that the Labour Government will decide to pull out of Palestine, as it does from every part of the Empire. Great Britain has neither the money nor the desire to keep armies, and the present situation in England is such that every penny is required for domestic purposes.

Removing Palestine from Britain's jurisdiction alone and taking it into the international arena gave the movement 'a great chance . . . our last chance'. He was less confident in his correspondence with Crossman, but perhaps he shied from committing himself to an Englishman, even a friendly one. Despite Bevin's recent statement that partition was not practical politics and the news that it had been 'relegated to the back bench', Weizmann remained as firm an advocate as ever, quite certain, as he wrote to his friend John Martin, Deputy Under Secretary of State, that 'they will have to come back to it.'[5]

On 14 May 1947 Weizmann noted, 'We shall have the eighteenth or nineteenth commission coming to investigate and look us over'. He was referring to the United Nations Special Committee on Palestine

(UNSCOP), appointed that day by the General Assembly. Still, despite his weary comment, the astonishing news from New York that the Soviet Union would not exclude partition as a solution to the Palestine dispute must have boosted his morale. Rarely has a deposed politician been placed in such a false position. The policies he had advocated and for which he had been ostensibly removed from office were now being adopted by all and sundry. In London and Washington, authoritative voices were calling for partition; and now Moscow had joined them. The Jewish Agency Executive had long agreed with his logic, even though it went through the motions of publicly demanding a Jewish state in an undivided Palestine. And when the time came for the movement to plead its case before the world, it turned to Weizmann. Even though he was forcibly retired, the Jewish Agency dared not forego his services. It must, therefore, have been particularly galling for him to suffer the vicious campaign of vilification waged against his person and policies by the terrorist groups and their minions. Scurrilous leaflets were circulated accusing him of having sold out to the British; walls were daubed with slogans 'Weizmann—Petain'.[6] This was the dark side of Zionist politics, which cast a shadow also on him.

He appeared before UNSCOP in Palestine on 8 July 1947. 'I speak in my private capacity,' he told the members of the committee, 'but I believe I speak the mind of the overwhelming majority of Jewish people everywhere.' How many times over the past decade had he repeated the same speech? But never did he speak out more clearly. Avoiding any ambiguity, he insisted on a clean cut: partition would combine the three qualities of 'finality, equality and justice'. He insisted on the territorial arrangements made in the Peel proposals of 1937, plus the Negev desert in southern Palestine, as the minimum territory required for a Jewish state. His eloquence and restrained passion, his dignity and inner strength made a profound impression on the committee, disarming even the most hostile of its members, the Indian delegate Sir Abdur Rahman. As was his wont, Weizmann entertained the committee at his Rehovot home, where, in his own special environment, he blossomed. At these informal gatherings Weizmann 'sparkled'; his 'wit and delicate irony' as he reviewed Jewish history, illustrating his narrative with personal anecdotes, left his guests spellbound. David Horowitz, Jewish Agency liaison officer to UNSCOP, who was present, observed the impressions of his charges:

Dr. Bunche [the committee's secretary], who was greatly moved, referred to his feelings as a Negro and the emotional identity that Dr.
Weizmann's description of Jewish destiny aroused in him. . . . Driving
back to Jerusalem they sat silent and meditative, and only murmured.
'Well, that's really a great man.'[7]

On 18 July, at four o'clock in the afternoon, Emil Sandstrom and
Valado Simic, the UNSCOP members from Sweden and Yugoslavia,
watched as a ship named the *Exodus*, jammed with 4500 immigrants
from Europe, was towed into the port of Haifa. British marines had
boarded her on the high seas (to accusations of piracy) and, after a
fierce and bloody struggle in which three Jews had been killed, had
wrested control of the unfortunate vessel from its Haganah defenders.
At Haifa, the UNSCOP members witnessed harrowing scenes as the
refugees were forcibly disembarked for transfer back to Europe. Barely
twelve hours after their arrival, the wretched passengers were shipped
back to West Germany, where they were eventually confined in internment camps near Lübeck.

The *Exodus* affair, which no dramatist could have improved upon,
was enacted in the full glare of the world's newsreels, press, and radio;
and the Zionist propaganda machine exploited it to devastating effect,
offering it as decisive proof of British depravity, callousness, and moral
bankruptcy. The Zionists won a stunning victory in the eyes of world
public opinion; and the British, in their folly and anger and frustration,
allowed them to do so. Simic later commented: 'This is the best testimony of all.' For British policy, the *Exodus* affair was a total catastrophe.

Less than two weeks later, the bodies of two British sergeants were
found hanging in a eucalyptus grove near Natanya, the ground beneath
their dangling feet having been booby-trapped. The sergeants had been
killed by the Irgun in retaliation for the hanging of three of their
comrades (captured during the storming of Acre prison in May, a raid
staged by the Irgun that freed scores of Jewish prisoners). The next
day, a photograph of this ghastly scene—'a picture that will shock the
world'—appeared in the London *Daily Express*. This horrific deed was
condemned in the most outspoken fashion by the representative bodies
of the *Yishuv*. The Haganah declared: 'The separatists have carried
out one of the most abominable crimes of all.' The Jewish Agency
denounced 'the dastardly murder of two innocent men by a set of
criminals', while a journalist wrote: 'If there were such a thing as a

Streicher medal, the Irgun leaders would surely deserve it for services rendered to anti-semitism.' In Britain, anti-semitic disturbances broke out in London, Glasgow, Manchester, and Liverpool: synagogues were daubed with swastikas, and Jewish shop windows were smashed. In Palestine, British troops and policemen sought revenge: vehicles were overturned, shops broken into, Jews assaulted and shot at; by the end of the rioting, five Jews had been killed. Relations between the *Yishuv* and the British authorities had deteriorated to a point of no return.[8]

These incidents provided a gruesome setting for UNSCOP as it deliberated in Geneva. They must have demonstrated beyond any reasonable doubt that the mandate was not only unworkable but had in fact collapsed. On 1 September it recommended unanimously that the mandate be terminated as soon as possible, while a majority proposed that Palestine be partitioned into Jewish and Arab states. Weizmann heard this news in London, whither he had returned after spending August at Flims, Switzerland. The following month he was in New York, at the request of the Jewish Agency, to present the Zionist case before the United Nations. Once again, his presence was considered indispensable if the political struggle to attain a Jewish state was to succeed. Even out of office, his majestic personality still swayed Zionist affairs, and he remained Zionism's most potent and persuasive voice to the non-Jewish world.

Although the Zionists had welcomed the committee's report, it was by no means a foregone conclusion that the United Nations would accept its recommendations. True, the Russians and the Americans had indicated their support, but Bevin had called the majority proposal 'manifestly unjust', and, naturally, the Arabs had rejected it out of hand. It would need a mammoth effort on the part of the Zionists to command the two-thirds majority in the General Assembly necessary to carry through a viable partition scheme. Weizmann was groomed by his ex-colleagues to lead the assault to counter Arab pressure, to capture the floating votes, and to stiffen the resolve of the committed. His address to the United Nations was prepared with painstaking care. Abba Eban recalled:

> Saw Chief after he lunched with Henry M[organthau, formerly secretary to the treasury, now chairman of the United Jewish Appeal]. Worked on draft for four steady hours. After each sentence was written in huge letters and agreed, he would go to lamp-stand and bring the text right to his eyes, endeavouring to learn it by heart. By the end of the session his eyes were watering as if in tears. Finally he said: 'We'll

make this do—but how about a *posuk* [biblical verse] for the ending?'
We looked for a Bible and eventually found one supplied by the hotel
in the bedside table. Spent a half-hour on Isaiah, looking for 'Return
to Zion' passages. Finally his mind was caught by the prophecy of 'an
ensign for the nations'. As I left he said: 'Well, this is it. Over the top
for the last time!'[9]

On 16 October Weizmann addressed the United Nations, then in
session at Lake Success. He recalled the council room that had ratified
the mandate twenty-five years before with the express purpose of
establishing 'the Jews as a nation amongst the nations of the world'.
He flattered UNSCOP—a most 'judicial and distinguished tribunal'—
and mocked the Arabs: 'I do not dispute their right to speak with
authority and intimacy on the nature of Nazism'. He paid his debt to
Britain, hoping that 'the traditional British–Jewish friendship will
once again become evident. . . The great services which Britain rendered in helping to lay the foundations of Jewish independence will
be remembered with appreciation while the sordid consequences of
the white paper pass into history.'

What alternatives lay before them? The mandate was dead, buried
by the very power that had given it life. A Jewish minority in an Arab
state? Ask 'the Jews of Iraq, of Yemen and Tripoli—and the Christian
Assyrians of Iraq'. Only partition that promised 'finality', 'equality',
would resolve the issue, and only then would true Arab–Jewish cooperation be attained. He was not bothered by the smallness of the
future Jewish state: 'Athens was only one small city and the whole
world is still its debtor.' For all that, he pleaded for viable borders, for
the inclusion of western Galilee and the Jewish districts of Jerusalem
and the Negev. He concluded with his quotation from Isaiah, the
greatest of the prophets.

The Lord shall set His hand again the second time to recover the
remnants of His people. And He shall set up an ensign for the nations,
and shall assemble the outcast of Israel and gather together the dispersed
of Judah from the four corners of the earth.[10]

And so began one of the most intricate and dramatic lobbying
exercises in modern diplomatic history. Stationed in a suite at the
Plaza Hotel, Weizmann, frequently sick and unable to read, indulged
in the kind of private, individual diplomacy that best suited his style.
He was still estranged from the American Zionist leaders, Silver and
Neumann in particular. For them, he ironically noted, Zionist history

began after the 1946 Basel Congress; and was not this typical of 'dictators', for had not Italian history begun after the March on Rome? He had most contact with the younger generation of Zionist diplomats—Abba Eban, Eliyahu Eilat, Arthur Lourie. The attitude of the United States and the Soviet Union pleased him: 'excellent so far', he commented, 'it is almost tantamount to a miracle that these two countries should have agreed on our problem'. But the hostility of Britain bewildered him. He had not forgotten the debt that Zionism owed to Britain, though other Zionists had: 'Gratitude has always been a trait of the Jews,' he wrote to Joseph Linton, political secretary to the World Zionist Organization, 'but their manners have deteriorated like everybody else's.' He hoped for improved relations, but saw little evidence of it in Britain's statement at the United Nations that British troops would not enforce any decision in Palestine against the wishes of one of the parties.

The petitioning went on. France's vote was uncertain, and Weizmann, fearing this would influence the stand of Holland, Belgium, and Luxembourg, appealed to Leon Blum to intervene. He turned to Samuel Zemurray, an old friend and head of the United Fruit Corporation, to use his influence with the smaller republics of Central America, since 'the vote of Nicaragua weighs as much as that of the United States'. He solicited the aid of the Philippine people. He conducted many long and searching talks with the Indian delegation. Impressed by their positive attitude toward Zionism, he enthusiastically adopted their proposal that he visit India to sound out areas of cooperation beneficial to both countries. Thus began his correspondence with Nehru, not merely to win his political support but to propose scientific and technological collaboration between their two peoples. While the fate of the Jewish state was still hanging in the balance, his mind was already exploring cultural and scientific relations among sovereign states. On the whole, he was satisfied with the Zionists' position. To Doris May, his secretary, he observed that 'we might get a Jewish State quite soon', adding, typically, 'with Silver as president and Ben Gurion as prime minister—God help us!' But what kind of state?[11]

It soon became apparent that the American delegation, although committed to partition, had succumbed to Arab pressure and wished to exclude the southern Negev from the proposed Jewish state. At this critical moment, on 19 November, Weizmann, sick with fever, travelled to Washington to convince Truman that the Negev, with its sea outlet to the Far East, was essential to the viability of a Jewish state. Armed with a formidable memorandum, he was received with 'the utmost cordiality' by the President, and he put his case skillfully and persuasively. Weizmann said, 'It is the first time in my life that I have met a President who can read and understand maps.' An amused Truman replied, 'Don't worry. Go home, and before you reach your hotel I will have put it right.' He was as good as his word. At three o'clock the same day, Truman telephoned his representatives at the United Nations instructing them to leave the Negev in the partition proposal. Somewhat embarrassed, for they had been about to impart a contrary decision, they informed the anxious Jewish Agency delegates that there were 'no changes' in the American position. 'We sighed with relief. Dr. Weizmann's talk had been successful. The struggle for the frontiers ended in victory.'[12]

The United Nations was due to vote on partition on 26 November. As the debate progressed, it became clear that the proposal would not command the required majority. The Jewish Agency representatives adopted desperate filibustering measures. Nahum Goldmann instructed their friends to request the floor again: 'Read from the Bible . . . read the Psalms, the promises of the prophet Isaiah.' Read anything, in fact, to postpone the session. The tactic succeeded, and 'Black Wednesday' passed; the crucial vote would take place three days later, on 29 November. Abba Eban recalls:

> We took the list of undecided countries and began to seek ways of influencing them. How shall we influence Liberia? They say that the American Firestone Company carries weight there. How to reach Firestone? How shall we approach the President of the Philippines? Is there any Jew who knows him? How can we influence Haiti, which was still straddling the fence?

Weizmann played his part, despatching last-minute appeals to the French, the Indians, and the Filipinos. 'Our fate is still hanging in the balance,' he wrote to Henry Morganthau, Jr. 'Could [you] help us with Greece or with the Philippines or with Haiti. Mr. Sumner Welles has promised to do something with Greece.' The pressure was intense, perhaps too much so. Weizmann hastened to assure Truman that the Zionists were not overplaying their hand and had kept within the limits of 'legitimate and moderate persuasion'.[13]

The roll call was taken on 29 November 1947. That afternoon, with the issue still in doubt, Arthur Lourie and other close friends visited Weizmann in his rooms at the Plaza Hotel: 'He pressed our hands and, as we left, he suddenly broke down and burst into heart-rending sobs.'[14] His emotions strained to the limit, he would not witness the historic session at the United Nations. The vote, broadcast all over the world, lasted three minutes: partition was adopted 33 – 13, with 10 abstentions. After the decision, the Jewish delegates, led by Moshe Sharett and Yosef Sprinzak, went to Weizmann and 'found him profoundly moved'. The Jewish state had received the blessing of the international community. That evening, escorted by Weisgal and the New York police, Weizmann attended a mass Labour Zionist rally at the St. Nicholas Arena. As he entered, 'the cheering engulfed the building. He was lifted out of my [Weisgal's] protective grasp on to the shoulders of his people and carried into the hall.' The ecstatic crowd sung *Hatikvah*. He stood before them silent, his hands raised in ac-knowledgement, his eyes, concealed by dark glasses, glistening with tears.[15]

On the following day, exalted by the historic decision but deeply con-scious that the future of the Jewish state lay precariously balanced on a razor's edge, Weizmann jotted down some thoughts on 'The Chal-lenge' facing the Jewish people and in particular the Zionists.[16] Though perhaps not intended as such, it reads, in retrospect, as his political testament. His first priority was to achieve the 'tremendous task' of securing a yearly immigration of 70,000 – 100,000 Jews into the new state; a 'destitute' *aliyah*, possessing nothing, robbed of everything, the tiny population of the *Yishuv*—not more than 650,000—would have to absorb these new Israelis productively and painlessly. This alone would be a crushing financial burden, but the new state would have to develop an economic and social infra-structure to guarantee its future; of most immediate urgency, it would have to secure its defence requirements, running at an estimated £6 million per annum. It was not, however, 'solely a question of finance', of introducing taxes, raising loans, or raiding the treasure-chests of American and European Jewry. Human resources—experienced, with fresh ideas, eager to help—were in desperately short supply. Yet they could be found in the West, and they should be encouraged to make their contribution even though it would provide 'a very severe test' for the veteran, tested Zionists who, despite their glorious record, sometimes lacked the talents nec-essary to run a modern state. 'They must recognize that it is in the interest of the State to bring new forces and new points of view to bear on the whole situation.'

And what of the constitution, upon which a 'great deal will also depend'? Weizmann deplored fashioning 'the new republic' in the image of the Zionist Organization. Proportional representation, which inevitably spawns splinter parties and sectarian politics, would have to make way for a new, more stable system. Once again, he fell back upon his western experience. 'I think it would be sounder to have a constitution like the American, or almost no constitution, like the British, at any rate for the beginning, and to feel our way for the first few years before laying down hard and fast rules.'

But these matters, although of prime importance, related to the 'externals' of statehood'. Weizmann looked beyond them: 'As the State is merely a means to an end . . . merely a vessel into which the contents still have to be poured . . it is necessary to know what the contents are likely to be.' Certainly the educational system was in need of radical surgery. At present based on 'class divisions' which made for 'inefficiency' and produced 'a bias in the mind and soul of the child', it was imperative to replace it with a unified, state system: 'Instead of partisanship there must be citizenship, which of course transcends party interests.' Higher education would also have to be expanded. But it was not simply a matter of acquiring the technical skills necessary to compete in the outside world. The 'get rich quick' mentality had to be eradicated. Producing 'shabby stuff' might corner soft markets and rake in easy profits, initially; 'but this sort of production corrupts the producer, who in the end becomes unable to improve himself'. A new, a more honest, a loftier and more dignified work ethic had to be achieved: 'integrity in commercial and industrial relations, efficiency and the desire to produce the best and the most beautiful, are the essential props on which a great industry can be built even in a small country.' 'One may, indeed, speak of moral industrial development.'

And here Weizmann, expressing that Tolstoyan streak in him, believed that the new Jewish state would have a positive advantage if it knew how to exploit wisely its unique system of 'agricultural colonization', using it, so to speak, as a bridgehead from which to launch out and conquer other areas of life.

Civilization is based more on the village and on God's earth than on the town, however attractive certain features of our town life may be. It is in the quiet nooks and corners of the village that the language, the poetry and literature of a country are enriched. The stability of the country does not depend so much on the towns as on the rural population.

Adding a personal note, he admitted, 'If I had to begin my life over again, and educate my children again, I would perhaps emulate the example of our peasants in Nahalal or Deganiah'—a touching confession, in view of the tragic history of his relationship with Michael and Benji.

He turned to the perennial problem of religion and its place in the state to be. He did not fear 'the really religious people', for they, like 'our saintly rabbis and sages in olden times', sought 'no power' and were 'modest and retiring' in their ways and ambitions. But a new menace had appeared: 'the secularized type of rabbi . . . who will make a heavy bid for power by parading his religious convictions'; and if given even a little leeway, he will shatter the social cohesion of the state with incalculable consequences for all.

> I think it is our duty to make it clear to them from the very beginning that whereas the state will treat with the highest respect the true religious feelings of the community, it cannot put the clock back by making religion the cardinal principle in the conduct of the state. Religion should be relegated to the synagogue and the homes of those families that want it; it should occupy a special place in the schools; but it shall not control the ministries of state.

He would remind the Jewish clerics that they transgressed a fundamental principle of their sages—'Thou shalt not make of the Torah a crown to glory in, or a spade to dig with'—though he suspected that, in their overweening arrogance, they would choose to ignore it.

> There will be a great struggle. I foresee something which will perhaps be reminiscent of the *Kulturkampf* in Germany, but we must be firm if we are to survive; we must have a clear line of demarcation between legitimate religious aspirations and the duty of the state toward preserving such aspirations, on the one hand, and on the other hand the lust for power which is sometimes exhibited by pseudo-religious groups.

Above all, he saw the concept of 'justice' not as an abstract principle, but as 'the very lifeblood of a stable society' and as something that if meted out expeditiously and to all on an equal basis would guarantee a healthy and thriving body politic.

Weizmann discerned that the creation of a Jewish state in a hostile environment posed a most agonizing moral problem. Justice was indivisible: but would it, could it, be applied also to the state's Arab population? He, at least, had no doubt.

> There must not be one law for the Jews and another for the Arabs. We must stand firm by the ancient principle enunciated in our Torah: 'One law and one manner shall be for you and for the stranger that sojourneth with you.' In saying this, I do not assume that there are tendencies toward inequality or discrimination. It is merely a timely warning which is particularly necessary because we shall have a very large Arab minority.

'I am certain,' he went on, 'that the world will judge the Jewish state by what it will do with the Arabs'.

But the implications were even more far-reaching, for the Jewish state could not rely on the sword alone to defend its future.

> It is such an extraordinary phenomenon that it will no doubt be the sensation of the century, and both our friends and our enemies—the latter more than the former—will be watching us carefully. . . . Our security will to a great extent depend not only on the armies and navies which we can create, but on the internal moral stability of the country, which will in turn influence its external political stability.

And what of the 'arduous task of achieving understanding and cooperation with the Arabs of the Middle East? Two factors were necessary:

> First, the Arabs must be given the feeling that the decision of the United Nations is final, and that the Jews will not trespass on any territory outside the boundaries assigned to them. . . . Second, . . . they must see from the outset that their brethren within the Jewish State are treated exactly like the Jewish citizens.

Given 'tact, understanding, human sympathy and a great deal of political wisdom', Weizmann did not think the task insuperable. He also looked farther afield, to India and the Orient, and saw 'a mighty opportunity to build a bridge between the East and the West', a task the Jewish state was eminently suited to accomplish. Palestine, he enthused, 'can become a modern Phoenecia, and her ships can trade as far as the coasts of America.'

These ideas, Weizmann concluded, were not intended as a programmatic statement. Much would have to be left to 'trial and error, and we shall have to learn the hard way—by experience'. They should be regarded more as indications and signposts pointing along the road which in my opinion must be followed if we are to reach our goal. This goal is the building of a high civilization based on the austere standards of Jewish ethics. From these standards we must not swerve, as some elements have done during the short period of the National Home, by bending the knee to strange gods. The Prophets have always chastised the Jewish people with the utmost severity for this tendency; and whenever it slipped back into paganism, whenever it reverted, it was punished by the stern God of Israel. Whether Prophets will once more arise among the Jews in the near future it is difficult to say. But if they choose the way of honest and hard and clean living, on the land in settlements built on the old principles, and in cities cleansed of the dross which has been sometimes mistaken for civilization; if they centre their activities on genuine values, whether in industry, agriculture, science, literature or art; then God will look down benignly on His children who after a long wandering have come home to serve Him with a psalm on their lips and a spade in their hands, reviving their old country and making it a centre of human civilization.

Weizmann sailed for England in mid-December. He planned to rest in London for a month, and then to continue to Rehovot where he would remain 'until the State is set up and the first elections carried through'. Outside forces intervened to wreck these plans. As he noted: 'These are indeed days of mighty events—but they don't bring us to the end of our troubles; only to the beginning of another phase.'[17] In Palestine, Arab violence against partition flared up: demonstrations, riots, ambushes along the main highways, attacks against Jewish settlements and urban centres. In January 1948, an 'Army of Liberation' crossed the border into northern Palestine bent on destroying the United Nations decision, while in the Jerusalem hills Arab irregulars roamed at will, subjecting the countryside to their violence.

In the face of this challenge to their authority, the British took no effective action to maintain order. Quite the reverse; by their contrary interpretation of their mandatory obligations they appeared determined to prevent a smooth take-over by the Jewish Agency authorities, if not to strangle the Jewish state at birth. In this deteriorating situation, the Haganah deployed its forces to defend the *Yishuv*, but their convoys were searched, their members arrested, and their arms confiscated. A United Nations committee meant to implement the partition decision was refused entry into Palestine, leaving its members, the 'Five Lonely Pilgrims', stranded in New York awaiting His Majesty's Government's pleasure. Content to stand by and defend their positions, British troops finally retreated into heavily guarded, barbed-wire compounds, the notorious 'Bevingrads', leaving the combatants to fight it out. It was a humiliating and ignominious finale to British rule in Palestine.

With the Arabs fighting to undo the partition plan and Palestine in chaos, many delegates to the United Nations began to doubt the wisdom of their original decision. Could the Jews hold the situation? Or were the Arabs too strong for them? Would their brave resolution disappear in an orgy of bloodletting, a victim of good intentions but bad judgement? In Washington, a formidable coalition emerged to reverse the partition plan. Rumours abounded that Truman himself was entertaining second thoughts, fearful of Russian intervention in the Palestine uprising. Nor, apparently, was there any way of appealing to him, for he had cut off contact with the Zionist leaders, indignant about their disrespectful lobbying tactics. George Marshall, Secretary of State, whose reputation stood high, was reported to be disappointed with the Haganah's showing and now thought partition a mistake, a view sustained by James Forrestal, Secretary of Defence, and a generous battery of officials who held that the United States could afford no longer to compromise her Arab interests. Their thoughts revolved around abandoning partition and returning Palestine to the trusteeship of the United Nations. Weizmann's friends in New York, alarmed at the rapid collapse of their position, though not without some voices of protest from the official leadership, decided to call for his help.[18]

Weizmann was resting quietly at the Dorchester when their summons arrived. He had been settling a backlog of private affairs: checking his investments with Marks and Spencer, correcting his memoirs, arranging a dinner party with Baffy. Not entirely neglecting politics, he had written to Churchill, emphasizing the importance of re-establishing sound Anglo-Jewish relations. But his mind was also focussed on the Far East. Planning a visit to Burma and India later in the year, he had already approached the Burmese government with pilot schemes for scientific, agricultural, and industrial co-operation. These plans were rudely disrupted by frantic telephone calls from America. 'We have just left New York,' he exploded with anger to Vera, 'and the idiots now want us to go back.' He received Abba Eban's urgent telegram: 'Most crucial phase of all now approaches here in which we sorely miss your presence advice activity influence'.[19] But he still refused to budge until an official invitation was sent from the Jewish Agency. It arrived post-haste.

Weizmann, still in bad health, sailed on the *Queen Mary* and arrived in New York on 4 February in the midst of a blizzard. That evening, at dinner at the Waldorf Astoria, he snapped at Abba Eban:

> 'Why in heaven did you drag me to this frozen waste when I might have been in Rehovot?' Told him of our danger at Lake Success and our position in Washington where not a single contact on high level had been possible since November. Truman furious with Zionist leaders and won't even see them. Chief's contact with President our only hope at UN and Washington. Chief decided to seek interview with Truman this month.[20]

In an age of mass politics, Weizmann's reliance on personal contacts, his emphasis on the special *rapport* he forged with leading politicians, had seemed faintly anachronistic. Yet his unique qualities could not so easily be consigned to the pages of a political-science textbook. Only Weizmann, the pundits held, could persuade Truman to countermand the anti-Zionist bias of his administration.

To arrange a meeting with Truman proved more difficult than anticipated. Weizmann, ill and weak, needed time to recover his strength, but also the President's schedule was crowded. He was due to leave Washington on a Caribbean cruise, and his aides claimed he had no time to fit Weizmann in. But this was only partially accurate. Truman had left strict instructions that he was not to be approached by 'spokesmen for the extreme Zionist cause'. So annoyed was he at their belligerent methods that he also put off Weizmann.

At this moment, fate intervened in the improbable figure of a haberdasher from Kansas City, Eddie Jacobson, Truman's former business partner. As a last resort, Frank Goldman, head of the B'nai Brith organization, approached Jacobson to intervene with the President. Although not a Zionist, Jacobson regarded Weizmann with awe and reverence, and he responded without hesitation. He flew to Washington and saw Truman on 13 March. At first, the President remained indifferent, even hostile, to Jacobson's pleas: 'let these subjects take their course through the United Nations'. Dejected, Jacobson's eyes came to rest on a statuette of Andrew Jackson mounted on a horse. In a flight of inspiration, he told Truman:

> Harry, all your life you have had a hero. You are probably the best-read man in America on the life of Andrew Jackson.... Well, Harry, I too have a hero, a man I never met, but who is, I think, the greatest Jew who ever lived. I too have studied his past and I agree with you, as you have often told me, that he is a gentleman and a great statesman as

well. I am talking about Chaim Weizmann; he is a very sick man, almost broken in health, but he travelled thousands of miles just to see you and plead the cause of my people. Now you refuse to see him because you were insulted by some of our American Jewish leaders, even though you know that Weizmann had absolutely nothing to do with these insults and would be the last man to be a party to them. It doesn't sound like you, Harry, because I thought that you could take this stuff they have been handing out to you. I wouldn't be here if I didn't know that, if you will see him, you will be properly and accurately informed on the situation as it exists in Palestine, and yet you refuse to see him.

Truman listened in silence, gazing through the windows at the Rose Garden as he contemplated the words of his friend. Suddenly, he turned to Jacobson. '"You win, you baldheaded son of a bitch. I will see him. Tell Matt [Connelly, his personal secretary] to arrange the meeting as soon as possible."' [21]

Weizmann arrived at the White House on 18 March. To avoid any media coverage of the meeting, he was smuggled in through the East Gate. Truman recalled:

We talked for almost three-quarters of an hour. He talked about the possibilities of development in Palestine, about the scientific work that he and his assistants had done that would some day be translated into industrial activity in the Jewish state that he envisaged. He spoke of the need for land if future immigrants were to be cared for, and he impressed on me the importance . . . of the Negeb area in the south.

By the time they parted they had reached a full understanding: Weizmann left convinced that Truman remained personally committed to partition. [22] But the following day, 'Black Friday', the American representative to the United Nations, Warren Austin, threw a bombshell: he informed the Security Council that his country now supported a United Nations trusteeship for Palestine—partition had been jettisoned.

Truman was the first to express astonishment at this amazing *volte-face*. 'How could this have happened?' he questioned one of his assistants. 'I assured Chaim Weizmann that we were for partition and would stick to it. He must think I am a plain liar. Find out how this could have happened.' There was a ready explanation, for he later described in his memoirs the overtly hostile attitude of certain State Department officials which, at times, he believed inclined to anti-semitism. [23]

Austin's announcement rocked the Jewish world. Weizmann immediately phoned Jacobson:

> Don't be disappointed and do not feel badly. I do not believe that President Truman knew what was going to happen.... I am seventy-two years old, and all my life I have had one disappointment after another. This is just another letdown for me.... You have a job to do; so keep the White House doors open.

Truman was clearly perturbed at the implied slur on his integrity. His spokesman intimated that trusteeship would not necessarily prejudice the final settlement. He sent Weizmann an indirect message through Jacobson that there would be no change in American policy. But it was not until the eve of Passover, 23 April, that Weizmann learned from the lips of Judge Samuel Rosenman, Truman's special counsel, that the President would not renege on his promise. He would grant immediate recognition to the Jewish state: 'I have Dr. Weizmann on my conscience,' he confessed to Rosenman.[24]

Truman's message confirmed for Weizmann what he had known all along. At this critical stage, there could be no turning back. The Jewish state was in the making and would be made. There could be no more doubts or vacillations. A false step, a hesitant move could prove fatal. He hammered this theme home with all the iron determination that had characterized his early career and an intransigence that surprised his listeners, whether Jew or gentile. He ironically dismissed trusteeship as 'a still-born project produced on the spur of the moment by some fertile brain in the American State Department'. In a public statement, he called for an independent Jewish state as the only solution. As for British policy, in 'exposing everything and everybody in the country to lawless hordes, the Mandatory Government has acted against its own best traditions, and left a tragic legacy to the country's future'.

> As you may know [he wrote to Truman] I have cherished the British–Jewish relationship all my life. I have upheld it in difficult times. I have been grievously disappointed by its recent decline. It is because I hope for its renewal that I tremble to think of the wave of violence and repression which would sweep Palestine if the conditions and auspices of the recent unhappy years were to be continued under British, or indeed any foreign, rule.... Should your administration, despite all this, press for any prolongation of British tenure, it would incur a responsibility for terrible events and, almost certainly, the equal resentment of the British and Jewish peoples.

In a dramatic cry, he presented the stark alternatives: 'The choice for our people, Mr. President, is between statehood and extermination. History and providence have placed this issue in your hands, and I am confident that you will decide it in the spirit of the moral law.'[25]

It would have been out of character had Weizmann not complained about his anomalous position. It still rankled that he had been deprived of his leadership role and that he was subject to the whims of those less competent than he. He objected to being shunted from pillar to post at the arbitrary commands of others. His mood was particularly grim because he had just been informed that the executive in Jerusalem wished him to remain in New York, whereas he yearned for the comfort of his home in Rehovot and fretted at being outside Palestine at this critical juncture in her fortunes. In a typical display of defiance, he hit out blindly in every direction, at friends and enemies alike:

> My stay here . . . was the most heart-breaking and futile waste of time. . . . I [have] had comparatively little to do except occasionally seeing some people and trying to instill some ideas into their block-heads. . . . I am definitely under the impression that probably Mr. Silver and Mr. Neumann didn't want me at all to take part in their work, and Moshe [Shertok] and other friends were too cowardly to assert their point of view. . . . When the show is all over, we shall have spent a great deal of money, wasted a great deal of time, made quite a number of speeches, but the result will be very small.[26]

For all his pessimism at the political campaign orchestrated by others but conducted by himself, he maintained a healthy optimism regarding the ability of the *Yishuv* to maintain itself in the face of Arab violence. He lunched with Alexandre Parodi, chief French delegate to the United Nations, who feared that the Jews would be massacred by superior Arab forces. 'How can a few hundred thousands of you stand up against millions?' Parodi asked. 'The trouble with the Egyptian army,' Weizmann replied, 'is that its soldiers are too lean and its officers too fat.' And as the news of Jewish victories reached him in early May, his confidence seemed more than justified: 'All the threats which were held over our heads for so many years were merely the inventions of our enemies who used [them] in order to keep Jewish activities down'.[27]

As 15 May approached, the day the British would terminate the mandate, Weizmann's anxiety grew. American officials were pressing the Jewish Agency (threatening, according to Shertok) to postpone the declaration of independence or at least to declare a temporary truce, which amounted to much the same thing. In a weird situation involving clandestine, nocturnal parleys between Russian and Zionist diplomats, a strange covenant emerged between the Soviet Union and the Jews to ensure the implementation of the November resolution, to force the United States 'to return to the logic of partition'.[28]

Weizmann had planned to return to Palestine in April, but the momentum of the political struggle kept him in New York. Whatever the Soviet Union's motives, the United States still remained the key factor, and Weizmann's special relationship with Truman could not be squandered. So he stayed. But as he watched developments from New York, he realized that, however the political struggle resolved itself at the United Nations, the *Yishuv* had to declare nationhood now. 'Our only chance now, as in the past, was to create facts, to confront the world with these facts, and to build on their foundation. Independence is never given to a people; it has to be earned; and having been earned, it has to be defended.'[29] Would Ben Gurion and company lose their nerve and waver at the last moment? He could not be certain. As Shertok was about to board a plane for Palestine, Weizmann told him, 'Don't let them weaken, Moshe, it is now or never.' Ben Gurion himself badly needed the benefit of Weizmann's experience and judgement. He cornered Weisgal, who was in Palestine 'to spy out the land' for Weizmann: 'I must know *at once* what Weizmann thinks about declaring independence'. Weisgal left immediately, stopping off at Nice where he could make an untapped phone call to his chief. Weizmann's reply, in Yiddish, was blunt and in style: 'What are they waiting for, the idiots?' Weisgal relayed the answer back to Ben Gurion. On 12 May, by a 6–4 vote, the *Yishuv*'s provisional cabinet decided in favour of statehood.[30]

There was little else Weizmann could do. On 13 May he addressed a final appeal to Truman, urging him to recognize the provisional government of the new Jewish state. The following afternoon, at a tense ceremony at the Tel Aviv museum, Ben Gurion declared the establishment of the state of Israel. The news reached Truman while he and his aides were considering Weizmann's request. Overriding last-minute protests from many of his leading officials, Truman authorized the recognition of Israel to take effect from 6 p.m. 'The old Doctor will believe me now,' he remarked.[31]

Exhausted by the labours of the past weeks, Weizmann remained in his rooms at the Waldorf Astoria, resting in bed, too indisposed to attend a mass rally at Madison Square Garden. The news from Israel was distressing. Tel Aviv had been bombed and the armies of six Arab countries had invaded the infant state. He sent off a telegram of encouragement to Prime Minister Ben Gurion and his government and to 'our fighters and workers who have borne burden building Jewish Palestine and who now sustain brunt and sacrifice of its defense'. Owing to the interruption of communications from Tel Aviv, he waited, practically incommunicado, twenty-four hours for an answer, resentment building up at those he thought were ignoring him. At long last, on 16 May, a bell-boy disturbed his troubled rest to deliver a cable from Ben Gurion:

> Greetings to you upon establishment of the Hebrew State. Of all those living, no one contributed as much as you to its creation. Your position and help at this stage in our struggle encouraged all of us. Looking to the day when we shall be privileged to see you at the head of the State — when it enjoys the blessings of peace. May we go from strength to ever greater strength.

That evening, Weizmann spent a quiet evening with Vera. He had already retired when she received a telephone call: a journalist informed her that a despatch had arrived from Tel Aviv stating that Weizmann had been elected President of the provisional council. 'I went into the bedroom and said to my husband, "Congratulations, Chaimchik. You are now President!" He looked up at me. "What nonsense are you talking?" he asked.' The news, however, spread like wildfire. Shortly afterward, his aides invaded his suite, where they celebrated the great occasion with champagne.[32]

The following day, Ben Gurion's official telegram arrived informing him that the provisional council of the state of Israel had elected him its president. 'Mine eyes have seen the coming of the glory of the Lord,' Felix Frankfurter rejoiced: 'Happily you can now say that — and can say what Moses could not. I salute you with a full heart — full of glad sadness, or rather, sad gladness.'[33]

One can only speculate on Weizmann's feelings. Perhaps all one can say is that it is given to few men to live out their dreams. Against the most colossal odds, he had realized the vision he had first glimpsed as a child in Motol. How characteristic, then, that he should end his first message to his people as President of Israel with his favourite verse from Isaiah, words that had served him as a lodestar throughout his career:

I regret that at this moment I am not with our people, but my thoughts and prayers are especially with those who are bearing the brunt and sacrifice of Israel's defense. Future of Israel will not be unworthy of those who have fallen, and Zion shall be redeemed in justice.

That day the flag of Israel (allegedly stitched together from a blue and white dress belonging to Lady Melchett) flew, beside the Stars and Stripes, above the Waldorf Astoria, a remarkable sight for thousands of New Yorkers who gathered in the streets below, faces raised upward.[34]

On 25 May, Weizmann accepted Truman's invitation to go to the White House on a state visit. The occasion had been planned with meticulous care. Some days earlier Weizmann had asked Jacobson to see Truman again in order to impress upon him three points: the need for a development loan for Israel—a sum of $100 million was mentioned; a relaxation of the arms embargo against Israel; and help in neutralizing British intrigues against the fledgling state. Truman made no definite promises, but Jacobson reported that he revealed great 'sympathy and understanding', and invited Weizmann to meet him at the White House. The Weizmanns travelled to Washington with all the pomp and circumstance due the president of a sovereign state. They drove up Pennsylvania Avenue, bedecked with the flags of Israel and the United States, and stayed at the official guest residence, Blair House. In a warm ceremony on the South Portico of the White House, Weizmann presented Truman with a scroll of the Torah, symbolizing Jewish tradition. But they also pursued in greater detail the more material matters broached earlier by Jacobson. Again, Truman demonstrated his friendship and promised to do everything in his power to accede to these requests. Two days later, well satisfied with his first outing as President, Weizmann and Vera sailed for Europe aboard the *Mauretania*. Weizmann had intended stopping off in London. But he felt, in present circumstances, that he had no place in Bevin's England. With the British-trained and officered Arab Legion spearheading an assault on Jerusalem, he considered that Britain was engaged in 'bloody conflict' with the ideals of Israel.[35] In any case, his links with Britain had become more tenuous. One of his dearest friends, Baffy Dugdale, had died suddenly, on 15 May, in her native Scotland. He mourned her loss: 'We still cannot reconcile ourselves to the thought that we shall not see her again. London will not be the same for us without her,' he wrote to Baffy's son-in-law, Sir James Fergusson.[36] He was estranged from another old comrade, Lewis Namier;[37] and as his political contacts were at a minimum and he no longer maintained a home in London, there was little to attract him there. He moved on to France and Switzerland to recuperate and to put his affairs in order.

He and Vera moved from hotel to hotel. She reckoned that they had slept in nineteen different places since leaving Rehovot in July 1947. In Paris, they were entertained at a state dinner at the Élysée Palace by Vincent Auriol. Later, in a warm, emotional reunion, they visited Leon Blum at his country home outside Versailles. By July, they were ensconced in their favourite resorts by the Lake of Geneva, Glion and Vevey. Weizmann's mind would not leave politics alone. He was already considering his future role in the new state. What kind of a president would he be? A mere figurehead? Or would he be endowed with some powers? And what kind of constitution would govern Israel? He did not favour a 'fully fledged' one, but something more general: 'let experience teach us what is the best form suitable to our conditions'. While he was willing to learn from British political experience, he was disgusted with the machinations of the Foreign Office, which, having abandoned its aim of annihilating the Jewish state, was now working hard to amputate the Negev from Israel. He appealed to Truman to make it abundantly clear that the United States 'views with disfavour these hostilities toward Israel'. In September, with much sadness, he returned his British passport to the Home Office.[38]

Weizmann was disturbed not only by the aggressiveness of British policy. In Israel, too, he glimpsed 'a byzantine display of power and quasi-military strength'. 'I realize that we are at war,' he wrote to Meyer Weisgal, 'but it seems to me, that the moloch of militarism is having everything and everybody in its grip.' When, in September, he learned of the assassination in Jerusalem of Count Bernadotte, the United Nations mediator, by Jewish extremists, his suspicions appeared fully justified. He denounced this 'cowardly and . . . criminal act'. 'The fatal series which began with Moyne seems to continue,' he reflected, 'and it is no use to try to apportion blame, as we are paying for all the sins to some extent.'

These features of the new state filled him with foreboding. But how typical of him that even during these troubled times he should be thinking of launching another 'spiritual dreadnought'. With the Hebrew University cut off on Mount Scopus, besieged by the Arab Legion, he proposed a second university. Not that he would ever renounce Jerusalem, but in two years there would be one million Jews in Israel: had not the time arrived to establish a university in Tel Aviv?[39]

In August he entered a sanitarium near Geneva for further surgery on his eyes; on 30 September, early in the morning, he and his party boarded an El Al plane. Ten hours later, they landed at the Tel Nof military airfield. He had returned to Israel as its first President.

TWENTY-ONE

THE PRISONER OF REHOVOT

From the outset Weizmann attempted to elicit some indication of the powers he would have and the role he would play as president. He was unwilling to be a mere figurehead. He envisaged something on the Czech model, recalling the late Tomáš Masaryk, an old acquaintance. But his enquiries were neatly stonewalled, and this increased his suspicions of what lay ahead. Soon he was threatening resignation, severing connection with 'the office which has been foisted on me'. In Israel he was told that the presidency was to be a symbol, but until his last days he claimed to be unable to fathom what this 'vague statement' meant; in his heart, he knew. Although he was informed of cabinet decisions, met with ministers, ruminated the issues, voiced his opinions, his participation in decision-making was limited; he was now simply an elder statesman whose words are listened to with the utmost respect but not necessarily acted upon.

Weizmann must also have harboured a humiliating feeling of being patronized. As late as January 1951, he said the only thing that prevented him from resigning was 'the international repercussion'. His figurehead position rankled, and he would often react with the bitter sarcasm for which he was celebrated. Once, being led to the rostrum during a state ceremony, he dropped his handkerchief. Someone retrieved it. 'Thank you,' he acknowledged politely, 'I haven't words enough to express my thanks. Nowadays, this handkerchief is the only thing I am allowed to poke my nose into.'[1]

There was probably no alternative. Weizmann was too ill to play anything other than a supporting role, and while the government might have shown more tact and understanding for an old man's dreams, it was inconceivable that Ben Gurion would have deliberately fostered Weizmann as a potential centre of opposition. These two dominant but diametrically opposite personalities had clashed so often in the past that further collisions could not be ruled out. It was precisely to avoid such a disastrous occurrence that Weizmann was turned into a 'symbol'. He had accepted the presidency but he had ruled for too long to accept its restraints, and his inability to do so soured his last years.

Another cut to his wounded pride was that his name had not been included among the signatories of the Declaration of Independence. He brooded on the reasons, some imaginary, some real, as to why this was so. Was he not the most eminent of those who had struggled for Israel's independence? Had not Ben Gurion, Moshe Shertok, Golda Meir, and the other leaders admitted that 'no one contributed as much as you to its creation'? Running his finger down the list of names he stumbled on non-entities, mere party hacks raised to such heights only through political wire-pulling. He heard the lawyers and pedants arguing that he was a member of neither the Vaad Leumi nor the Jewish Agency Executive, nor even in Tel Aviv at the time, and so was ineligible for inclusion among the chosen. But only pettifogging quill-pushers whose minds did not extend beyond their legal jargon would accept this as sufficient cause for his exclusion. Surely these legal niceties were as nothing when thrown into the balance against his record? Was this not, then, a deliberate slight to his person? Weizmann's suspicious nature would not exclude such an explanation. But he was too stiff-necked to beg the authorities to rectify the injustice. Yigal Allon, the young commander of the Palmach who had struck up a warm friendship with him, recalls: 'At the time I was intimate with B. G. and could easily have got him to act. But when I suggested doing this, he [Weizmann] always said no. He was too proud.'[2] It remains one of the great ironies of Israel's history that Weizmann's name still does not adorn its Declaration of Independence.*

For all his grievances, Weizmann took justifiable pride in the achievements of the state. Naturally, he was concerned at the consequences of a mass immigration 'not imbued with the *chalutz* spirit,

---

*On 2 November 1967, the fiftieth anniversary of the Balfour Declaration, President Shazar signed a proclamation, at Weisgal's urging, wherein some amends were made. The scroll emphasised Weizmann's role in the establishment of Israel and is kept together with the Declaration of Independence in the State Archives. A copy is on display at the Weizmann Archives in Rehovot.

like the previous generation', for the character of Israeli society; but on the whole he was moved by a new optimism.

> Considering the enormous difficulties with which we are faced, . . . state affairs are running remarkably smoothly, and sometimes I think we are all day-dreaming. . . . One feels for once that the Almighty is on the side of the Jews, and one realizes how good a partner he can be if he chooses to.

Even Ben Gurion appeared in a different guise, now as the sheet anchor of Israel's struggle.

> B. G. as Prime Minister and Minister of Defence has proved a great success. Whether he will be the same success in peace time I am not prepared to say; he reminds me somewhat of Winston who is good in war and less so in peace. However, it is too early to draw any conclusions. He is thoughtful, calm, resolute and a man of enormous courage.[3]

Weizmann's buoyancy fed off the remarkable victories of the Israel Defence Forces, which, throughout 1948, had taken the initiative to drive Arab invaders to and beyond the partition frontiers. Like the simplest Jew in the Lower East Side or Whitechapel, Weizmann too swelled with pride at these triumphs. After the conquest of Eilath, he was delighted when Yigal Allon escorted him to review his victorious troops in the Negev. 'This is the first time I have had the feeling of being royalty,' he told the young general. He became quite an 'activist' in his remaining years, startling his entourage with his militancy. Yigal Yadin, the thirty-two-year-old chief-of-staff, used to report regularly to Weizmann and found him 'rather hawkish' in his attitude toward military questions. Exploiting his contacts in Switzerland, Weizmann set about procuring anti-aircraft guns to defend the country from Egyptian attacks. 'Let us know whether and how many guns we can get, and what are the conditions of payment', he requested. 'If we would have the necessary equipment, we could finish the job in about a month.' He rejected all claims, whether inspired by the late Count Bernadotte or by the British Foreign Office, to revise the frontiers: all Galilee and the Negev would remain in the Jewish state. 'We shall not agree to [revision] on any account and I am most anxious that this matter should be made perfectly clear in the most authoritative form, both to the President and Mr. Marshall [Secretary of State],' he wrote to David Ginsberg, a politically influential Washington attorney. 'Akaba will be a dagger in our backs if it falls into the others' hands,' he expounded to Ben Gurion and Shertok. To Leo Amery, another pugnacious character, he wrote in October 1948:

> I do not think that an inch of territory will be yielded by the Armies of Israel to anybody. The conquest of the Negev has cost us many hundreds of dead and many thousands of wounded, and the account is not yet closed, and the Jews are not prepared to shed their blood either for Mr. Bevin or Mr. Abdullah.

Two months later, his nephew, Ezer Weizmann, now an Israel Air Force commander, visited him at Rehovot. In an excited mood, he told of Israeli victories in the Sinai. 'Uncle Chaim listened attentively, his wise eyes sparkling with a kind of moistness, and then he asked, "Ezer, why don't we go to Cairo?"' Ezer never worked out whether it was said in jest or in earnest.[4]

Foreign affairs offered Weizmann the greatest scope for contributing to the well-being of Israel. Here he could rely on his vast experience and innumerable contacts, confident that his name and reputation would open doors. He was particularly eager to repair Anglo-Jewish relations, but wherever he turned he found Bevin blocking his path. Apart from Leo Amery and Walter Elliot, both in opposition, and Richard Crossman, a Labour back-bench rebel, he found few British politicians he could talk to, even among his old friends. Churchill, his main hope, had sent his warmest personal regards, but 'The Palestine position now, as concerns Great Britain, is simply such a hell-disaster that I cannot take it up or renew my efforts of twenty years. It is a situation which I myself cannot help in, and must, as far as I can, put out of my mind.'[5]

The bloodshed of the past years had roused the strongest passions. Lady Violet Bonham Carter, Asquith's daughter and one of the most feared controversialists in British public life, gave vent to her own in a frank letter to Weizmann.

> I think you know how deeply I have felt the tragic wrongs and sufferings of the Jewish people. You know that I have always tried to fight their battle both in public and private life. Yet to-day, alas! I can feel no friendship for the new State of Israel.

She deplored the general amnesty recently awarded to members of the Stern gang, for she condemned terrorism and murder 'as much when it is practiced by Jews as by anyone else', and pitied the Arab refugees, innocent people 'chosen' by the Jews as their victims. 'Israel will no doubt in time be "recognized"—*de facto* and *de jure*. But it has lost the *hearts* of all its truest friends in this country. . . . I think it is right that you should know the bitter disillusionment some of us are living through.'

Weizmann had no need to be reminded by Lady Violet of the iniquities of terrorism. In a fiercely worded reply, he proved just how deadly a polemicist he could be when provoked.

> I am very sorry that you should have fallen victim to the campaign of vilification that is now being waged against our young state. British people have a reputation of being able to see the other side even in times of conflict and tension. There is little evidence of this where we are concerned. You use strong language about our terrorists and their deeds. Has it occurred to you that there might be grievous reasons for the appearance of so unbelievable and unprecedented a phenomenon as 'Jewish terrorism'?
>
> The Jews are not a people given to violence. For many centuries force has not been our weapon. Our colonization in Palestine was an outstanding example of non-violence.

He went on to relate how 'Arab gunmen' had won the battle of the white paper. Only then did Jews begin to think 'that violence paid with the British Government'. Six million Jews were done to death in Europe while the doors of Palestine remained 'bolted by the white paper'. As for the Arab refugees, he blamed those who had encouraged them to fight, and had actually aided them—the British.

> Whose responsibility is it? Did we declare war on the Arabs and drive them out of the country? I cannot help feeling that a good deal of the self-righteous indignation with which the British press abounds in these days springs from an uneasy awareness—perhaps only subconscious—that the guilt rests with the accusers.
>
> You are annoyed with Israel . . . for having declared a general amnesty which benefited also the terrorists. It so happens that I had nothing to do with this matter because it is outside my province, although I share the responsibility for it, but you are very much mistaken if you think this decision implies any truckling to terrorism or any fear of its agents. . . . If [the] Government . . . have decided now to proclaim a general amnesty, it is because they felt—and presumably had good reason to feel—that that was the most effective way of liquidating, not the terrorists, but terrorism. It may be that they were mistaken; only the future can tell. But if the assumption is correct that this evil thing

was the result of a holocaust such as the world has not seen and of the heartless policy of those who bolted the doors of Palestine against the victims, there may be ground for hoping that the normalization of our national life may eradicate this cancer more effectively than savage punishment, however well deserved by ordinary standards. The hangman and the jailer, on whom the British administration relied for fighting terrorism, have as you know certainly not produced results. This is not an age of humanists, but speaking for myself I still believe that there is boundless wisdom in Goethe's dictum that if you want to change the hearts of men, treat them as though they were already what you want them to become.

Something very great and significant has happened here during these twelve months. The spirit of freedom is alive again in this ancient land, and it is producing miracles as in the days of old. There is a great hope in this, not only for us, but also for our neighbours, and certainly for those Arabs who are staying with us or those who intend to come back. It is sad that all this is hidden from your vision which is usually so clear.[6]

On 7 January 1949, as Israeli–Egyptian armistice talks were about to commence, British reconnaissance planes crossed the frontier into the western Negev. They were engaged by Israeli Spitfires commanded by Ezer Weizmann, and in three dogfights five British aircraft were shot down. With British troops deployed at Akaba, and the BBC reporting that the fleet at Malta had been put on alert, how would the British react? Richard Crossman, who was staying at Rehovot, found Weizmann in his library closeted with Shertok and other aides. 'Will Tel Aviv be bombarded tonight?' he was asked. 'No!' replied Crossman. 'This is good news. Bevin has overreached himself and this will bring you British recognition.' Bevin's policy had been savaged in the House of Commons in December. During the debate, Anthony Eden had demanded *de facto* recognition, while Churchill had reviewed 'the lamentable tale of prejudice and incapacity. . . . Israel cannot be ignored or treated as if she does not exist'. He renewed his relationship with Weizmann: 'I look back with much pleasure on our long association,' adding, 'The light grows.' At the end of January 1949, Bevin granted *de facto* recognition, according *de jure* status in April 1950.[7]

Relations with the United States were not so stormy. Weizmann built on his friendship with Truman. He congratulated the President on his unexpected re-election in November 1948. Truman replied: 'We had both been abandoned by the so-called realistic experts to our supposedly forlorn lost causes. Yet we both kept pressing for what we were sure was right—and we were both proven to be right.' Weizmann happily concurred: 'We may indeed say in the words of the Psalmist: "The stone which the builders rejected is become the chief corner-stone".' In January 1949, the U.S. Export-Import Bank extended the long-awaited $100 million loan.[8] All in all, Weizmann had much cause for satisfaction at the state of Israel's foreign relations: recognition by the Soviet Union and France, and finally by Britain, buttressed by a special relationship with the United States. Just as Zionism had flourished when it enjoyed the support and recognition of the Powers, so too would Israel. He eagerly lent his support to Israel's early policy of non-identification, 'a policy of friendship to all the nations', anxious not to get involved in the passions of the Cold War. There was one exception to this rule: Germany. Nothing could exonerate Germany from the heinous crimes committed against the Jewish people. He favoured reparations, but as a token gesture on Germany's part and as a Jewish right. But he would not forget. He refused point-blank to meet West German Chancellor Konrad Adenauer when they chanced to stay at the same hotel at Glion in Switzerland, though Adenauer was more than anxious to see Weizmann.[9]

Although Weizmann's official election to the presidency by the first *Knesseth Israel* (Parliament) was a foregone conclusion, the occasion was marred for him by *Herut*'s (the political successors to the Irgun) running a rival candidate, to loud cries of 'shame' from offended legislators from other parties. Weizmann waited for the result in Rehovot (it was 13 February 1949) but soon lost patience with the proceedings. At ten o'clock he announced to his guests, 'I am going to bed. You may sit and wait if you wish.' At midnight, they told him that his election was confirmed. The following morning a delegation of twelve Knesseth members, symbolizing the twelve tribes of Israel, headed by its speaker, Yosef Sprinzak, escorted Weizmann to Jerusalem, where he was sworn in. Sprinzak ended the ceremony with the words '*Yechi Hanassi!*' (Long live the President); a small voice from the audience replied, '*Yechi Hamelech!*' (Long live the King).[10]

Two months later Weizmann was in New York. He had left home reluctantly, for he wished to be present at the celebrations for the first anniversary of Israel's independence, but his visit, his last to the United

States, had been planned long in advance. Illness had delayed his arrival, but he could no longer evade the obligations Weisgal had undertaken on his behalf. He was billed as the star attraction at a campaign dinner for the Weizmann Institute, but pressures from American Jewish leaders to exploit his presence for more general fund-raising purposes had eventually prevailed—'We must use the visit for bigger things,' they nagged—wearing down even Weisgal's substantial powers of resistance. Intensive negotiations resulted in an agreement whereby the takings would be divided between the state and the institute. The dinner, at the Waldorf Astoria, was an unprecedented success. Weizmann sat on the platform with a large basket in front of him into which poured cash, checks, and pledges, until, by the end of the evening, the staggering sum of $18 million had been collected. A few days later, he met a more select group and raised an additional $5 million. For days afterward Weizmann's hand was bruised, put out of action by the furious handshakes of the masses of Jews who had come to greet him, 'the *Hinterfolk* of the State of Israel', he affectionately noted.

As usual, his itinerary was exhausting. Some time was devoted to high politics, but his main efforts were directed at American Jewry. He spoke at many gatherings, still able to delight his listeners with a brilliant turn of phrase, telling one audience that 'always and steadily we are narrowing the confines of the impossible'. By the end of his stay, homesick and angry at being dragged away from Israel on her first anniversary, he succumbed to one of his 'fogs'. He obstinately refused to attend a mass rally in New York. 'For once I am going to make a liar of you,' he warned Weisgal. But he could not resist the call and relented when he heard the reports that Joshua Harlap, his bodyguard, and Weisgal brought him: in Madison Square Garden, 'they're standing packed like herring in a barrel', and outside 150,000 Jews were waiting impatiently in the streets, refusing to disperse until they had seen and heard Weizmann. When he arrived under police escort, two hours late, the crowds surged forward, cheering, clapping, touching him as he passed. The last New York Zionist demonstration he would attend was also its most splendid, a fitting finale to his relationship with American Jewry. The following day, 5 May, he sailed for Europe.[11]

*   *   *

On 2 November 1949 the Weizmann Institute of Science was officially inaugurated. Plans made in 1944 for its expansion had now been completed. As Weizmann sat on the ceremonial stage clad in his academic robes, he saw laid out before him a fully fledged research institute such as he had dreamed of. Surrounded by eminent scientists, many of them Nobel laureates, and distinguished guests and friends who had gathered from all over the world, he savoured this moment with special pleasure. In a generous, sincere mood, Ben Gurion, the principal speaker, referred to Weizmann's 'two crowns, the crown of statehood and the crown of learning'. When Weizmann rose to reply, he ignored his notes, as was his wont, and spoke impromptu.

> We live, as you know, in a pioneering country. We are pioneering in the wilderness, in agriculture, and in industry. But here in Rehovot we are also engaged in a peculiar kind of pioneer work—we are pioneering in science. There are many problems to be solved in our land, and many difficulties to be overcome. There are also many dangers still to be met. But to meet them, we must not rely only or chiefly on physical force. We have a mighty weapon which we must utilize with ingenuity and skill, and with every means available to us. Science is that weapon, our vessel of strength and our source of defence.

Immediately after the celebrations were over he withdrew to his home, physically exhausted by the effort. Early that evening he sent for Weisgal. In his dimly lit study, he made Weisgal promise never to abandon the institute. 'It has only been born. It still has to be nurtured and brought up to manhood.' The ever faithful Weisgal solemnly gave his word; and the institute continued to flourish under his dynamic and stormy leadership. [12]

Weizmann's dramatic request expressed a passionate concern for the future of the institute. During the years of his absence, and under the direction of Ernst Bergmann, the institute had moved into war-oriented research (a process that had begun during the Second World War and had intensified during Israel's war of independence), and the question whether this was right or not came to obsess Weizmann. Of course, he realized that no scientific institution, or scientist, could remain immune from the pressures of war. His own record was there to prove it. But he believed that under Bergmann's guidance the process had been taken too far, with too much enthusiasm, and, above all, without his prior consent and knowledge. Was the empire he had built up so painstakingly—all that remained to him in his declining years and which he had come to consider as his most lasting legacy to the State of Israel—to slip out of grasp? Bergmann's intoxication with his current projects was spoiling the reputation of the institute, Weizmann thought, and he expected from him 'a clear answer' to his questions. They were not forthcoming, at least not to his satisfaction. He wrote to Weisgal:

> I am quite certain that Dr. Bergmann could carry on without me, and if one day he reverts back to science he would probably do quite well whether I am connected or not.
>
> My hatred for all these military performances is so profound and ingrained in me since my childhood that it literally hurts me to feel that the institute to which I have devoted so much energy and so many hours of endeavor should be desecrated in a manner which I can neither explain nor acquiesce in.

Into this principled debate intruded a personal element. Over the years Bergmann had come to occupy a special place in Weizmann's life. He had long been considered Weizmann's scientific heir-apparent, and many years of close collaboration had cemented a strong bond between them. When Weizmann's eyesight began to deteriorate, it was Bergmann who supervised his laboratory work. But their relationship extended far beyond the laboratory. In time, and particularly after Michael's death, Bergmann assumed the role of a surrogate son for the Weizmanns. This was especially so for Vera, who clung to Bergmann as a substitute for her lost and beloved Michael and defended him fervently against attack and scurrilous gossip, which, unfortunately, Weizmann was only too ready to believe. He would never forgive Bergmann for not only attempting to alter the character of his institute but also for daring to serve as Ben Gurion's scientific adviser. In these matters he lacked magnanimity. He nursed his grudges, brooding on them endlessly. Bergmann, eventually relegated to the status of an apostate, had betrayed him. '[He] behaves like a Prussian junker,' Weizmann scornfully remarked. 'War seems to be his primary consideration.' By mid-1951, Weizmann terminated his duties as scientific director of the institute. Weisgal, who followed this wretched affair closely and from the inside, observed in July, a week after Bergmann had been sacked, that Weizmann 'has suffered more deeply about this thing than about anything else in the last few years, leaving its deep impress on his state of health', and described the atmosphere in the Weizmann House as 'beyond endurance'.[13]

* * *

Weizmann's memoirs, *Trial and Error*, published in February 1949, were immediately acclaimed. The critics were dazzled: 'the self-portrait of a most remarkable man', 'immensely dramatic', 'Dr. Weizmann, one of the great figures of our age, has written a deeply moving account of his life', 'a heroic story by a heroic man', 'a book of absorbing interest'. Richard Crossman wrote in the *New Statesman*: 'Not only the autobiography of the greatest practical Zionist, but the first account of Zionism which elucidates it in terms intelligible to the gentile mind.' Weizmann had first considered this project in the early 1930s, following his defeat at the Congress of 1931. Reputable publishers—The Viking Press for one—had turned down the proposition, and other houses were rejected by the author and his agents; finally a contract was signed with Harper Brothers in the United States and Hamish Hamilton in Britain.[14]

The book was written over a long period, owing to Weizmann's many other preoccupations. By the summer of 1947 he was revising the final draft with the help of Maurice Samuel, author and translator. Samuel recalls those days:

> He was in poor physical condition, but his mind was as vigorous and supple as ever, and it was amazing to hear him pour forth his recollections and reflections . . . in ordered paragraphs, with witty and pungent interpolations. . . . When we came to some particularly murderous sideswipe at someone, I would ask: 'You don't really want that to stay, Dr. Weizmann, or do you?' His face would light up. 'No, Maur-r-rice, I think we can do a little p-r-runing.' Then he might add, in Yiddish: 'He was, to be sure a *mamzer* [a bastard: implying grudging admiration of a clever rascal as well as detestation of a low, mean character], but that wasn't his fault.'
>
> He indulged in another kind of private savagery in the first draft, directed at political opponents with unchallengeably honest motives. He would pour out his old resentments; the heat of long-since fought-out battles would return to his blood, and he would remember his frustrations. Then, the emotion having subsided, he would wink, adding: 'He was—or is—a decent fellow, you know.'[15]

Despite the pruning, the book caused a lot of heart-ache. Old comrades complained that their contributions had been diminished or overlooked. Gaps in the narrative were noted, as were inconsistencies and inaccuracies. Lord Wavell threatened legal action, withdrawing his suit only when he received public and private apologies.[16] Yet for all this criticism, some of it legitimate, *Trial and Error* remains a most fascinating document: Weizmann's account of his childhood and life in the Pale remains a classic of its kind; it is highly readable, informative, rich in humour, and punctuated by unforgettable pen-portraits. For professional historians, it is as reliable a source as most autobiographies and, despite the carping, undoubtedly constitutes an authentic contribution to contemporary history.

Its success stirred Weizmann's imagination. *Trial and Error* would be the first brick in a greater edifice raised for historical scholarship. Was he not duty bound to preserve his papers for the sake of the generations to come? To set the record straight regarding his past battles, his triumphs as well as his defeats? By all means let posterity judge him, but let it do so honestly and accurately, according also to his truth. As usual in matters of this nature, he turned to Meyer Weisgal.

> Now that *Trial and Error* is published and is in process of translation into the *shiv'im leshonot* [Hebrew: seventy tongues], I have been thinking about the many unpublished documents and letters of the past forty years and more that might be of some public interest. These letters and documents are scattered all over the world and in many hands. . . . I should very much like to see them collected in one place and prepared for proper editing and publication. Would you be willing to undertake this task?

He had made a similar request in 1940, but now Weisgal took it up with all of his characteristic volcanic energy. Approximately twenty-three thousand Weizmann letters, together with countless other documents, photographs, and other Weizmann memorabilia, now lie in array in the Weizmann Archives at Rehovot. And, after a mammoth organizational and logistic operation, twenty-three carefully annotated volumes of Weizmann's letters and two volumes of his speeches are, at the time of this writing, at the disposal of any interested reader.[17]

On 27 November 1949 a public banquet was held in London to celebrate Weizmann's seventy-fifth birthday. Smuts, who had come from South Africa especially for the occasion, addressed the distinguished guests. Bracketing the Battle of Britain and the creation of the State of Israel 'as among the human highlights of our epoch', he continued:

Let us repeat that supreme effort and our European civilization will enter upon perhaps its most glorious epoch of history. We thank Israel for having once more reminded us of that last, that only, way to salvation. And especially do we think of Chaim Weizmann tonight in honour and gratitude for his great leadership and inspiration to the world looking for leadership and inspiration.

That evening plans were set afoot to plant a Weizmann forest in the Jerusalem hills.[18]

By 1950, owing to the state of his health, Weizmann's public duties — mainly of a ceremonial, symbolic nature against which his entire personality rebelled — were reduced to a minimum. Although in physical decline, he was still mentally alert, and this aggravated an already painful situation. His thoughts turned to those who had placed him in this intolerable position, particularly Ben Gurion whom he now referred to as not being 'fit to be a shoemaker, never mind a prime minister'. Always prone to his 'fogs', he yielded to them with increasing frequency as his health faded. His doctor noted that 'the changes of mood were linked with the ups and downs in his physical health and his illness took on ever more obsessive forms'. Captive to his own prejudices and physically restricted to his home, he began to refer to himself as 'the prisoner of Rehovot'.[19]

Otherwise his routine was fairly relaxed. At times, he would surprise the staff of his laboratory with a snap visit, pumping them for all the latest gossip. During the day he might watch the birds at play in the bird-bath he had installed on the balcony outside his room, while at dusk he would relax on his favourite bench among the trees, sipping lemon tea and watching the sunset. He still took an abiding interest in the landscaping of his gardens, and he would while away the hours gossiping with the gardeners. Once he summoned Yehiel Paldi, the chief gardener, to tell him 'how beautiful the institute looks', though by now he was almost totally blind. Distinguished visitors waited on him; old comrades came to chat and reminisce. There were luncheon and dinner parties, but Weizmann could no longer enjoy his favourite foods — radishes or pickled herring or haddock or kippers or even toast — for he had been put on a strict diet, though, like a naughty boy, he tried to avoid these restrictions when Vera's eagle eye was turned. On fine days he might go for a drive, riding up front, in his spanking new Lincoln limousine, presented to him by Henry Ford II; there were only two of its kind in existence, the other being in the possession of Harry Truman. But most of all, he delighted in the visits, all too infrequent, of his daughter-in-law, Maidie, and grandson, David, and forever enquired after David's progress at school.[20]

In November 1951 Weizmann fell dangerously ill. There was genuine concern for his life. Weisgal, who was summoned urgently to the Weizmann house and feared the worst, was astonished to find him sitting up in a chair surrounded by his doctors and Vera, all 'purring over him'. He asked Weisgal to cheer him up, to tell him funny stories in Yiddish. Later, the conversation took a more serious note, and Weisgal recorded his chief's thoughts.

'My greatest difficulty in lying here in this helpless condition is to watch and see all the mistakes that are being made in this country. You see, the Jews are a small people, a very small people quantitatively, but also a great people qualitatively. An ugly people, but also a beautiful people, a people that builds and destroys. A people of genius and, at the same time, a people of enormous stupidity. With their obstinacy they will drive through a wall, but the breach in the wall . . . always remains gaping at you. Those who strive consciously to reach the mountain top remain chained to the bottom of the hill.' As if to illustrate this point, he suddenly turned to science and said: 'Those who set out to achieve something specific in science, never achieve it. But those who work *lishmoh* [for its own sake] usually reach the top of the mountain.' . . . He spoke of the Jewish people and then paused, and after a few seconds said, 'I want to tell you something about Ben Gurion.' I made a gesture with my hand, as if to say, this is not the time. I was afraid that the subject would over-excite him. But he continued: 'No, no, listen,' and he went on. 'Ben Gurion did something which I could never have done, no matter what the circumstances. He sent Jewish boys and girls to the front to die for the State of Israel. It was probably necessary and history will accord him his place for this. But,' he added after a long, long pause, 'I would not like to be around when he himself will try to destroy the very things he helped to create.'

Then he turned to me and in an almost pleading voice said: 'Meyer, you have been a loyal friend all the years I have known you. I have other loyal friends, perhaps many more than I deserve. Tell them not to permit the destruction of the thing we have laboured over for years.' I tried to comfort him and say a few words to the effect that things were not as bad as he thought. Then he gave me a big *krechts* [groan] and said '*Alevai*' [I hope so].[21]

For the remaining months of his life Weizmann was almost entirely bedridden, his doctor sleeping in a room adjoining his, always in attendance. From his sick-bed he issued a message to the people of Israel on the occasion of the fourth anniversary of the establishment of the state: 'On this solemn day I would say this to all my brethren: the future of Israel rests on three foundations—brotherly love, constructive effort and peace near and far.' The people of Rehovot came to wish him well, and, in his last public appearance, he greeted them from his balcony. He was sinking slowly. Often in pain, he was given morphia to relieve his distress. Toward the end, he contracted a severe inflammation of the lungs, a recurrent complaint since his student days. One day Vera entered his room and heard him singing softly to himself: 'Chaimchik, is it Beethoven?' 'No,' he replied, 'it's a psalm.' Vera recorded in her diary: 'burying himself'.

> Then he asked me for a needle and cotton, but I could not make out for what purpose. It was to sew his own shroud. Then turning to the nurse, he said, 'I am going on a very, very long journey. Prepare everything.'

The following day, in the early hours of 9 November 1952, he drifted into a coma, suffered two heart attacks, and died at 5.55 in the morning, a few days before his seventy-eighth birthday.[22]

EPILOGUE

Weizmann's body was laid to rest in the grove of olive and fruit trees that had been presented to him by the farmers of Nahalal and Mishmar HaEmek, in the grounds of the Weizmann Institute, on the slope of a hill that faces east toward Jerusalem. His coffin, wrapped in a silk-tassled blue and white Israeli flag, stood in state on a black-draped catafalque under a blue and white canopy while for two days an estimated 250,000 Israelis passed by, many weeping openly, to pay their last respects. After the funeral ceremony, sirens sounded throughout the country and the people of Israel stood in silence for two minutes. The cabinet gathered for an extraordinary meeting, and the Knesseth went into special session, thousands crowding the streets outside. Ben Gurion paid respect to him in a munificent panegyric:

> Chaim Weizmann was a Prince of the Jewish Nation. . . . [He] will take his place in the eternal history of the Jewish people alongside the great figures of the past—the Patriarchs and Kings, Judges, Prophets and spiritual leaders who have woven the fabric of our national life for four thousand years. The entire Jewish people will join in our deep mourning for the passing of the last President of the Zionist Organization and the First President of the State of Israel.

World Jewry paid tribute to his memory as services and demonstrations were held in every Jewish centre. In New York, the United Nations General Assembly observed a minute's silence in respect. Heads of state and politicians throughout the world registered their condolences and voiced their appreciations, as did countless ordinary folk everywhere. Renowned scientists grieved the loss of an eminent colleague. The feeling was general that one of the great, formative personalities of the twentieth century had passed away. Let Sir Isaiah Berlin, who had come to know him well, render the final judgement: 'Chaim Weizmann was the first totally free Jew of the modern world, and the state of Israel was constructed, whether or not he knows it, in his image. No man has ever had a comparable monument built to him in his own lifetime.'[1]

BIBLIOGRAPHY

The Weizmann papers are located at the Weizmann Institute, Rehovot. Some 23,000 letters, apart from photographs, assorted documents, and other Weizmann memorabilia, are arranged in chronological order and ready for inspection by any interested person. A selection of them, approximately 15,000 letters, has been published in twenty-three volumes under the title *The Letters and Papers of Chaim Weizmann. Series A. Letters* (Oxford University Press–Transaction Books–Rutgers University–Israel Universities Press, 1968–80), cited in the notes as WL. Two volumes of his speeches have also appeared under the title *The Letters and Papers of Chaim Weizmann. Series B. Papers* (Israel Universities Press–Transaction Books–Rutgers University, 1983–84), cited in the notes as WP. All students of Weizmann must be grateful for these carefully annotated and scholarly collections. They constituted the main source material from which this study was drawn. I was also allowed to draw upon the late Richard Crossman's 'Notes' (now located at the Weizmann Archives, and indicated in the notes as WA), which he wrote while engaged on the official biography of Weizmann. Although extremely interesting and useful, Crossman's Notes are fragmentary in nature, consisting of two transcripts of interviews and two draft chapters; his untimely death prevented him from completing the biography. The Passfield Papers (indicated in the notes as PP), which include Beatrice Webb's diaries and the Webbs' correspondence, are deposited at the London School of Economics, where I examined them. Papers from the Central Zionist Archives (S24, S25, and A312 series), the (British) Public Record Office (FO.371, CO.733, CAB, PREM, and WP (G) series), other archives and libraries (see Acknowledgements), and interviews and private correspondence (also acknowledged) augmented the primary sources. I have also used *Hansard Parliamentary Debates*, Lords and Commons; British Parliamentary Papers, Cmd. series (1919–56, listed in notes); and the British Museum Newspaper Collection at Colindale.

The first volume of Jehuda Reinharz's biography *Chaim Weizmann: The Making of a Zionist Leader* (1985), came into my hands after my own manuscript had been completed, so that I was unable to benefit from this important piece of research.

This bibliography lists only those works which I used directly in writing this book, or those I found especially useful in providing background material. It makes no pretence at being a comprehensive bibliography of the Weizmann era. The places of publication, unless stated otherwise, are London and/or New York.

Abella, I., and H. Troper. *None Is Too Many* (1983).

Adelson, Roger. *Mark Sykes: Portrait of an Amateur* (1975).

Adler-Rudel, S. *The Evian Conference* (1968).

Aleichem, Sholem. *The Best of Sholem Aleichem*, eds. Irving House and Ruth Wise (1979).

Alsberg, Avraham. 'Delimitation of the Eastern Border of Palestine,' *Zionism* (Tel Aviv, Spring 1981).

Amery, Leo. *The Leo Amery Diaries*, eds. John Barnes and David Nicholson (1980).

Anonymous. 'Chaim Weizmann in Los Angeles 50 Years Ago,' *Western States Jewish Historical Journal* (Los Angeles, 1974). A reprint of a report in *B'nai B'rith Messenger*, 18 April 1924.

Asquith, H. H. (Earl of Oxford). *Memories and Reflections*, 2 vols. (1928).

Ayerst, David. *Guardian: Biography of a Newspaper* (1971).

Barzilay, Dvorah. 'Crisis as Turning Point: Chaim Weizmann in World War 1,' *Studies in Zionism* (Tel Aviv, Autumn 1982).

Bar Zohar, Michael. *Ben Gurion* (1978).

Beer, F. J. 'Chaim Weizmann et Fritz Haber,' *Amitiés Franco-Israel* (Paris, 1978).

Bein, Alex. *Theodor Herzl* (Philadelphia, Pa., 1962).

Ben Gurion, David. *Letters to Paula* (1971).

———. *Letters*, 3 vols. (Tel Aviv, 1971–74, in Hebrew).

———. *Memoirs*, 5 vols. (Tel Aviv, 1971–82, in Hebrew).

Bergmann, Ernst. 'Dr. Weizmann's Scientific Work (and Bibliography),' *Bulletin of the Research Council of Israel* (Jerusalem, June–September 1953).

Berlin, George L. 'The Brandeis-Weizmann Dispute,' *American Jewish Historical Quarterly* (September 1970–June 1971).

Berlin, Isaiah. 'Anatomy of Leadership,' *Jewish Frontier* (December 1954).

———. *Zionist Politics in Wartime Washington: A Fragment of Personal Reminiscences* (Jerusalem, 1972).

———. *Personal Impressions* (1982).

Berlin, Isaiah, and Kollat, Israel. *The Leadership of Chaim Weizmann* (Jerusalem, 1970, in Hebrew).

Bertie of Thame, Lord. *The Diaries of Lord Bertie of Thame*, ed. Lady Algernon Gordon Lennox, 2 vols. (1924).

Bethell, Nicholas. *The Palestine Triangle* (1979).

Bowle, John. *Viscount Samuel* (1957).

Brandt, Joel. *Desperate Mission* (1962).

Bullock, Alan. *The Life and Times of Ernest Bevin* (1960).

———. *Ernest Bevin: Foreign Secretary* (1983).

Caplan, Neil. *Palestine Jewry and the Arab Question* (1978).

Carpi, D. 'Weizmann's Political Activity in Italy,' *Zionism*, vol. 1 (Tel Aviv, 1975).

Churchill, Winston. *The Second World War*, vols. iii, vi (1950–51).

Clark, Ronald. *Albert Einstein* (1971).

Cohen, Amnon, and Gabriel Baer, eds. *Egypt and Palestine: A Millennium of Association, 868–1948* (1984).

Cohen, Gabi. 'Harold MacMichael and Palestine's Future', *Zionism* (Tel Aviv, Spring 1981).

Cohen, Michael J. *Palestine: Retreat from the Mandate* (1978).

————. *Palestine and the Great Powers, 1945–48* (Princeton, N.J., 1982).

————. 'Churchill and Palestine: At the Exchequer, 1928,' *Studies in Zionism* (Tel Aviv, Autumn 1983).

Cohen, Stuart. *English Zionists and British Jews: The Communal Politics of Anglo-Jewry, 1895–1920* (Princeton, N.J., 1982).

Cowling, Maurice. *The Impact of Labour: 1920–1924* (1971).

Crossman, Richard. *Palestine Mission* (1947).

————. 'Chaim Weizmann,' *New Statesman and Nation* (15 November 1952).

————. 'The Young Weizmann,' *Encounter* (November 1952).

————. *A Nation Reborn* (1960).

Crum, Bartley. *Behind the Silken Curtain* (1947).

Cust, Archer. 'Cantonization: A Plan for Palestine,' *Journal of Royal Central Asian Society* (April 1936).

Dalton, Hugh. *Memoirs: High Time and After* (1967).

Daniels, Jonathan. *The Man of Independence* (1950).

David, Edward. *Inside Asquith's Cabinet* (1977).

Dawidowicz, Lucy. *The War Against the Jews, 1933–1945* (1976).

Dugdale, Blanche. *Arthur James Balfour* 2 vols. (1936).

————. *Baffy: The Diaries of Blanche Dugdale, 1936–1947,* ed. Norman Rose (1973).

Eban, Abba. *An Autobiography* (1978).

Eliav, Mordecai. *David Wolffsohn: The Man and His Times* (Tel Aviv, 1977, in Hebrew).

Elon, Amos. *Herzl* (1975).

ESCO Foundation. *A Study of Jewish, Arab, and British Policies* (New Haven, Conn., 1947).

Farrer, David. *The Warburgs* (1975).

Forrestal, James. *The Forrestal Diaries,* ed. Walter Mills (1951).

Fraenkel, Josef. 'Chaim Weizmann and Haham Moses Gaster,' *Herzl Year Book* (1964–65).

Frankfurter, Felix. *Reminiscences* (1960).

Friedman, Isaiah. *The Question of Palestine: 1914–1918* (1973).

————. *Germany, Turkey, and Zionism: 1897–1918* (1977).

Friedman, Maurice. *Martin Buber's Life and Works,* 3 vols. (1981).

Friezal, E. *Zionist Policy After the Balfour Declaration: 1917–22* (Tel Aviv, 1977, in Hebrew).

Fry, Michael. *Lloyd George and Foreign Policy* (1977).

Fyvel, T. R. 'My Father's Jewish Renaissance,' *Jewish Chronicle Literary Supplement* (10 June 1983).

Gal, Allon. 'Brandeis's View of the Upbuilding of Palestine, 1914–1923,' *Studies in Zionism* (Tel Aviv, Autumn, 1982).

Garcia-Granados, J. *The Birth of Israel* (1949).

Gilbert, Martin. *Churchill,* vol. 4 and companion volumes (1975).

————. *Auschwitz and the Allies* (1981).

Gilhar, Y. *The Separation of Transjordan from Palestine* (Jerusalem, 1979, in Hebrew).

Goldmann, Nahum. *Autobiography* (1969).

Goodman, Paul, ed. *Chaim Weizmann: A Tribute on His Seventieth Birthday* (1945).

Gorni, Josef. *Partnership and Conflict: Chaim Weizmann and the Jewish Labour Movement in Palestine* (Tel Aviv, 1976, in Hebrew).

————. *The British Labour Movement and Zionism, 1917–1948* (1983).

Gorni, Josef, and Gedalia Yogev, eds. *A Statesman in Times of Crisis* (Tel Aviv, 1977 in Hebrew).

Guriel, Boris. 'Lenin and Weizmann. Records of One Meeting,' *Ha'aretz* (3 November 1967).

Gwynn, Major-General Sir Charles. *Imperial Policing* (1939).

Halperin, S. *The Political World of American Zionism* (Detroit, 1961).

Halpern, Ben. 'Brandeis and the Origins of the Balfour Declaration,' *Studies in Zionism* (Tel Aviv, Spring 1983).

Harris, Kenneth. *Attlee* (1982).

Harvey, Oliver. *The War Diaries of Oliver Harvey, 1941–1945*, ed. John Harvey (1978).

Heller, Josef. 'Roosevelt, Stalin and the Palestine Problem at Yalta,' *Weiner Library Bulletin* (1977).

————. *The Struggle for the Jewish State: Zionist Politics, 1936–1948* (Jerusalem, 1984, in Hebrew).

Hermoni, A. *In the Footsteps of the Biluim* (Jerusalem, 1952, in Hebrew).

Herzl, Theodor. *The Complete Diaries of Theodor Herzl*, ed. Raphael Patai, 5 vols. (1960).

Heymann, M., ed. *The Uganda Controversy* (Jerusalem, 1970).

Her Majesty's Stationery Office. *Documents on British Foreign Policy, 1918–1939* (BD), First Series, vols. iv, viii.

Horowitz, David. *State in the Making* (Tel Aviv, 1951, in Hebrew; English translation, 1953).

Hull, Cordell. *Memoirs* (1948).

Hurewitz, J. C. *The Struggle for Palestine* (1950).

Ingrams, Doreen. *Palestine Papers, 1917–1922: Seeds of Conflict* (1972).

Jacobson, Eddie. 'Two Presidents and a Haberdasher,' *American Jewish Archives* (April 1968).

Jaffe, Jean. 'Recollections of Chaim Weizmann's Childhood' (copy in Weizmann Archives).

————. 'The House of Weizmann,' *Israel Life and Letters* (November 1952).

————. 'From Motele to Haifa,' *The Pioneer Women* (December 1952).

Joll, James. *The Origins of the First World War* (1984).

Kedem, Menecham. *Chaim Weizmann in the Second World War* (Tel Aviv, 1983, in Hebrew).

Kedourie, Eli. *The Chatham House Version and Other Middle Eastern Studies* (1970).

————. *In the Anglo-Arab Labyrinth* (1976).

Kehanovitch, Y. *From Homel to Tel Aviv* (Tel Aviv, 1952, in Hebrew).

Kisch, Frederick. *Palestine Diary* (1938).

Kleimann, Aaron. *Foundations of British Foreign Policy in the Arab World: The Cairo Conference* (Baltimore, 1970).

Knightley, Phillip, and Colin Simpson. *The Secret Lives of Lawrence of Arabia* (1969).

Knox, D. E. 'Weizmann's First Visit to Palestine,' *Wiener Library Bulletin* (1975).

L. M. [?] 'Chaim Weizmann: The Late President's Contribution to Israel's Economic Development,' *Israel Economic Bulletin* (Tel Aviv, October 1952).

Laqueur, Walter. *A History of Zionism* (1976).

————. *The Terrible Secret* (1982).

Lebow, R. N. 'The Morgenthau Peace Mission of 1917,' *Jewish Social Studies* (October 1970).

Levin, Schmarya. *Youth in Revolt* (1939).

————. *Forward from Exile* (Philadelphia, Pa., 1967).

Lichtenstein, Haya (Weizmann). *In the Shadow of Our Roof* (Tel Aviv, 1947, in Hebrew).

Lipsky, Louis. *Memoirs in Profile* (Philadelphia, Pa., 1975).

Litvinoff, Barnet. *Weizmann: Last of the Patriarchs* (1976).

Lloyd George, David. *The Truth About the Peace Treaties* (1938).

————. *War Memoirs*, 6 vols. (1938).

Louis, William Roger. *The British Empire and the Middle East, 1945–1951: Arab Nationalism, the United States, and Postwar Imperialism* (1984).

Lourie, Arthur. 'Chaim Weizmann: The Man and the Statesman,' *The Reconstructionist* (26 December 1952).

Lowdermilk, Walter. *Palestine, Land of Promise* (1944).

MacDonald, James G. *My Mission in Israel* (1951).

Manuel, F. E. *The Realities of American-Palestine Relations* (Washington, D.C., 1949).

Marshall, Louis. *Louis Marshall, Champion of Liberty: Selected Papers and Addresses*, 2 vols., ed. C. Reznikoff (1957).

Meinerzthagen, Richard. *Middle East Diary, 1917–1956* (1959).

Meyer, I. S., ed. *The Early History of Zionism in America* (1958).

Miller, M. *Plain Speaking: An Oral Biography of Harry S. Truman* (1974).

Minney, R. *The Private Papers of Hore-Belisha* (1960).

Monroe, Elizabeth. *Britain's Moment in the Middle East, 1914–1956* (1963).

————. *Philby of Arabia* (1973).

Mossek, M. *Palestine Immigration Policy under Sir Herbert Samuel* (1978).

Nachmani, Amikam. *Great Power Discord in Palestine: The Anglo-American Committee of Inquiry into the Problems of European Jewry and Palestine, 1945–46* (1986).

Namier, Lewis. 'Zionism,' in *New Statesman* (5 November 1927); subsequently published in *Skyscrapers and Other Essays* (1931).

————. *Diplomatic Prelude* (1948).

Neumann, Emanuel. *In the Arena* (1976).

Nevakiki, Jukka. *Britain, France and the Arab Middle East, 1914–1920* (1969).

Nicolson, Harold. *Peacemaking 1919* (1964).

Niv, David. *The Irgun Zvai Leumi*, 6 vols. (Tel Aviv, 1965–80, in Hebrew).

Ofer, Pincus. 'The Role of the High Commissioner in British Policy in Palestine: Sir John Chancellor' (unpublished PhD thesis, London, 1972).

Ovendale, Ritchie. 'The Palestine Policy of the British Government, 1945–46,' *International Affairs* (July 1979).

————. 'The Palestine Policy of the British Government, 1947,' *International Affairs* (January 1980).

Panitz, Esther. 'Louis Dembitz Brandeis and the Cleveland Conference,' *American Jewish Historical Quarterly* (September 1975).

————. '"Washington v. Pinsk": The Brandeis-Weizmann Dispute,' *Herzl Year Book* (1978).

Parzen, Herbert. 'The Magnes-Weizmann-Einstein Controversy,' *Jewish Social Studies* (July 1970).

Pearlman, Moshe. *Ben Gurion Looks Back* (1965).

Philby, Harry St. John. *Arabian Jubilee* (1952).

Playfair, I. S. O. *History of Second World War. U.K. Military Series: The Mediterranean and Middle East* (1954).

Porat, Yehoshua. *The Emergence of the Palestinian-Arab National Movement, 1918–1929* (1974).

———. *The Palestinian Arab National Movement, 1929–39: From Riots to Rebellion* (1977).

———. 'The Philby Episode,' *Zionuth* (Tel Aviv, 1984, in Hebrew).

Rabinowicz, Oskar. *Fifty Years of Zionism* (1950).

Reading, Marchioness of. *For the Record* (1973).

Richards, Bernard. 'Dr. Weizmann at Versailles,' *Congress Weekly* (December 1952).

Rose, Norman. 'The Arab Rulers and Palestine, 1936: The British Reaction,' *Journal of Modern History* (June 1972).

———. *The Gentile Zionists* (1973).

———. *Vansittart: Study of a Diplomat* (1978).

———. *Lewis Namier and Zionism* (1980).

Roskill, Stephen. *Hankey: Man of Secrets*, 3 vols. (1970–74).

Rothschild, Miriam. *Dear Lord Rothschild* (1984).

Ruppin, Arthur. *Memoirs, Diaries, and Letters*, ed. Alex Bein (1971).

Sacher, Harry. *Zionist Portraits and Other Essays* (1959).

Samuel, Sir Herbert. *Report to Colonial Office on Administration of Palestine, 1920–25* (HMSO, July 1925).

———. *Memoirs* (1945).

Samuel, Horace. *Unholy Memories of the Holy Land* (1930).

Samuel, Maurice. *Little Did I Know* (1963).

Sanders, Ronald. *The High Walls of Jerusalem* (1983).

Schama, Simon. *Two Rothschilds and the Land of Israel* (1978).

Schechtman, J. B. *Fighter and Prophet: The Vladimir Jabotinsky Story*, 2 vols. (1961).

Scott, C. P. *The Political Diaries of C. P. Scott, 1911–1928*, ed. Trevor Wilson (1970).

Shapiro, Anita. *Berl*, 2 vols. (Tel Aviv, 1980, in Hebrew).

Shapiro, Y. 'The Controversy Between Chaim Weizmann and Louis Brandeis,' *Zionuth* (Tel Aviv, 1973, in Hebrew).

Sharett (Shertok), Moshe. *Political Diaries*, 5 vols. (Tel Aviv, 1968–79, in Hebrew).

Shavit, Ya'akov. 'Fire and Water: Ze'ev Jabotinsky and the Revisionist Movement,' *Studies in Zionism* (Tel Aviv, October 1981).

Sherman, A. J. *Island Refuge: Britain and Refugees from the Third Reich* (1973).

Shihor, Samuel. *Hollow Glory* (1960).

Sieff, Israel. *Memoirs* (1970).

Silver, Eric. *Begin* (1984).

Simon, Julius. *Certain Days* (1971).

Slutsky, Yehuda. *History of the Haganah*, vols. 2 and 3 (Tel Aviv, 1964–73, in Hebrew).

Sokolow, N. *History of Zionism* (1919).

Stein, Leonard. *The Balfour Declaration* (1961).

Stone, Norman. *Europe Transformed, 1878–1919* (1983).

Storrs, Ronald. *Orientations* (1939).

Sykes, Christopher. *Two Studies in Virtue* (1953).
———. *Orde Wingate* (1959).
———. *Crossroads to Israel* (1965).
Taylor, A. J. P. *Beaverbrook* (1972).
Tevet, Shab'tai. *Ben Gurion*, 2 vols. (Jerusalem, 1976–80, in Hebrew).
———. *The Arlosoroff Murder* (Tel Aviv, 1982, in Hebrew).
Tibawi, A. L. 'T. E. Lawrence, Faisal and Weizmann: The 1919 Attempt to Secure an Arab Balfour Declaration,' *Royal Central Asian Journal* (1959).
Tolkowsky, Samuel. *Zionist Political Diary, London 1915–1919*, ed. Dvora Barzilay (Jerusalem, 1981, in Hebrew).
Truman, Harry S. *Memoirs: Years of Trial and Hope*, vol. 2 (1956).
U.S. Government Printing Office. *Foreign Relations of the United States* (FRUS).
Vansittart, Lord. *The Mist Procession* (1958).
Verete, Meir. 'The Idea of the Restoration of the Jews in English Protestant Thought, 1790–1840,' *Zion* (Jerusalem), nos. 3–4 (1968).
———. 'The Balfour Declaration and Its Makers,' *Middle Eastern Studies* (January 1970).
———. 'Why Was a British Consulate Established in Jerusalem,' *English Historical Review*, April 1970.
Vital, David. *The Origins of Zionism* (1975).
———. *Zionism: The Formative Years* (1982).
Voss, C. H. *Selected Letters of Stephen Wise* (Philadelphia, Pa., 1969).
Wasserstein, Bernard. *Britain and the Jews of Europe, 1939–1945* (1979).
Webster, Sir Charles. *The Art and Practice of Diplomacy* (1961).
Wedgwood, J. C. *The Seventh Dominion* (1928).
Weisgal, Meyer. . . . *So Far* (1971).
Weisgal, Meyer, ed. *Chaim Weizmann: Statesman and Scientist* (1944).
Weisgal, Meyer, and Joel Carmichael, eds. *A Biography By Several Hands* (1964). Containing essays by: Sir Isaiah Berlin, 'The Biographical Facts'; Maurice Samuel, 'The Road from Motol'; Israel Sieff, 'The Manchester Period'; Selman Waksman, 'Chaim Weizmann as Bacteriologist'; Ritchie Calder, 'The Secret of Life'; Aharon Katzir-Katchalsky, 'Vision versus Fantasy'; T. R. Fyvel, 'Weizmann and the Balfour Declaration'; Robert Weltsch, 'The Fabian Decade'; Louis Lipsky, 'A Portrait in Action'; J. Meltzer, 'Towards the Precipice'; Abba Eban, 'Tragedy and Triumph'; Jon Kimche, 'Bridge to Statehood'; and Richard Crossman, 'Prisoner of Rehovoth'.
Weizman, Ezer. *On Eagles' Wings* (1976).
Weizmann, Chaim. 'Palestine's Role in the Solution of the Jewish Problem,' *Foreign Affairs* (January 1942).
———. 'The Right to Survive: Testimony Before the Anglo-American Committee of Enquiry,' *Jewish Agency*. (Jerusalem and London, 1946).
———. *Trial and Error* (1950), cited in notes as *T&E*.
———. *The Essential Chaim Weizmann*, ed. Barnet Litvinoff (1982).
Weizmann, Vera. *The Impossible Takes Longer* (1967).
Wise, Stephen. *Challenging Years* (1949).
———. 'In the Great Tradition,' *Opinion* (November 1952).

Yogev, Gedalia. 'Weizmann as Leader of the Opposition Faction,' in Gorni and Yogev, eds., *A Statesman in Times of Crisis* (Tel Aviv, 1977, in Hebrew).

Yossin, Yigal. *Pillar of Fire* (Jerusalem, 1983).

Zweig, Ronald. *Britain and Palestine During the Second World War* (1986).

NOTES

PROLOGUE

1 The account of events here, except where stated otherwise, is based on *Ha'aretz, The Palestine Post, The Times* (London), and *The New York Times.*

   The use of the Skymaster was in itself a daring piece of improvisation. It had been briefly demobilized from service in Israel's war of independence for the express purpose of bringing Weizmann to Israel. Once its mission was accomplished, the aircraft was stripped of its colours and furnishings and returned to active service.

2 See V. Weizmann, *Impossible,* 241.
3 From his speech at the eleventh Zionist Congress. WP, 1:104.
4 See MacDonald, *My Mission,* 30.
5 Ibid., 94.
6 See WL, 1, no. 1.
7 See Isaiah Berlin's essay in Weisgal and Carmichael, *A Biography,* 56.

1: FAIR BEGINNINGS

1 See *T&E,* 12, 28.
2 Quoted in Vital, *Zionism,* 170. Maj. W. E. Evans-Gordon was on a fact-finding mission for the Royal Commission on Alien Immigration set up by Balfour's government in 1902.
3 *T&E,* 40.
4 See Vital, *Origins,* 55.
5 See Lichtenstein, *In the Shadow,* 86.
6 See Vital, *Origins,* 58–59.
7 From the recollections of M. Ussishkin, quoted in Vital, *Origins,* 75–76.
8 Ibid., 155, 157, 167.
9 *T&F,* 30.
10 See Namier, 'Zionism.'
11 The date of Weizmann's birth cannot be determined with absolute certainty. The above date, now generally accepted, is registered in Weizmann's Israel passport. By an interesting coincidence, Vera Weizmann's fell on 26 November, though she was seven years younger. See WL, 1:xxix, and V. Weizmann, *Impossible,* 4.
12 Lichtenstein, *In the Shadow,* 74.
13 These ages necessarily involve some guesswork. Their ages, Ozer (1850?–1911) and Rachel (1852?–1939) are given in WL, 1:427.
14 *T&E,* 21–22.
15 See Sacher, *Zionist Portraits,* 2.
16 *T&E,* 25.
17 *T&E,* 23–24.
18 Lichtenstein, *In the Shadow,* 36.

19 Interview with Sir Isaiah Berlin, May 1983.
20 *T&E*, 26.
21 See Jaffe, *'Recollections.'*
22 See E. Weizman, *On Eagles' Wings*, 9.
23 Lichtenstein, *In the Shadow*, 75–76.
24 Ibid., 72–73, 75–76.
25 E. Weizman, *On Eagles' Wings*, 9.
26 *T&E*, 23.
27 Lichtenstein, *In the Shadow*, 76.
28 See Jaffe, 'The House of Weizmann.'
29 WL, 5, no. 332.
30 Quoted in Weisgal and Carmichael, *A Biography*, 68.
31 *T&E*, 20.
32 *T&E*, 13.
33 From Sholem Aleichem, 'Mottel the Cantor's Son', in *The Best of Sholem Aleichem*, 200.
34 See Lichtenstein, *In the Shadow*, 32, 48–51; and *T&E*, 14.
35 The following passage is based on Lichtenstein, *In the Shadow*, 32–34; Jaffe, 'Recollections'; and *T&E*, 16–17, 21–22.
36 Lichtenstein, *In the Shadow*, 45.
37 WL, 6, no. 43; *T&E*, 19.
38 The above passage is based on Lichtenstein, *In the Shadow*, 11, 22–23, 31, 34–37, 94, 137, 139; and *T&E*, 15, 22.
39 WL, 4, no. 139.

2: APPRENTICESHIP

1 WL, 10, no. 68.
2 See WL, 1, no. 1.
3 *T&E*, 21.
4 WL, 6, no. 305.
5 Vital, *Origins*, 157.
6 *T&E*, 31–32; and WL, 1:38.
7 Lichtenstein, *In the Shadow*, 44.
8 See Jaffe, 'Recollections,' and Lichtenstein, *In the Shadow*, 44–46.
9 From Jaffe, 'Recollections.'
10 See *T&E*, 40.

11 WL, 1, nos. 3–8.
12 *T&E*, 34–35.
13 See his record of studies in WA.
14 *T&E*, 45.
15 *T&E*, 38.
16 *T&E*, 54–55, 83, 87–90.
17 See Namier's pen portrait of him cited in Rose, *Lewis Namier*, Appendix 1.
18 See *T&E*, 45–49, and Lichtenstein, *In the Shadow*, 54.
19 See transcript of courses in WA.
20 See Lichtenstein, *In the Shadow*, 54–57; and *T&E*, 48.
21 *T&E*, 47, 48.
22 *T&E*, 47. See also M. Samuel, *Little*, 190, and Litvinoff, *Essential*, 53.
23 *T&E*, 49.
24 See Lichtenstein, *In the Shadow*, 67–68.
25 Ibid., 92–97, and Sacher, *Zionist Portraits*, 3. The precise details of this incident are impossible to ascertain. His sister places it well before the first Zionist Congress in 1897, and this is confirmed by Sacher, probably by hearsay. WL offers no further explanation.
26 See *T&E*, 52, 55, and WL, 1, no. 11 n4.
27 See Levin, *Youth*, 247; *T&E*, 54.
28 *T&E*, 57–58. Also, interview with Yisraela Lichtenstein Margalith, June 1983.
29 Levin, *Youth*, 248–49.
30 WL, 1, no. 11 n4.
31 *T&E*, 54.
32 WL, 1, no. 260.
33 WL, 1, no. 225.
34 WL, 1, no. 9 n1, and 25; *T&E*, 34, 55.
35 This passage, unless stated otherwise, is based on WL, 1, nos. 11–21.
36 See Jaffe, 'From Motele,' and Lichtenstein, *In the Shadow*, 98.
37 *T&E*, 24.

38 *T&E*, 49–50, and Lichtenstein, *In the Shadow*, 89–92.

39 *T&E*, 58–60, and Lichtenstein, *In the Shadow*, 85.

40 See WL, 1, no. 18.

41 See WL, 1, nos. 11–21 passim.

42 *T&E*, 52.

43 *T&E*, 82–83.

44 See WL, 1, nos. 61, 279, 308, 311.

45 *T&E*, 52–54.

46 WL, 1, no. 16 *n*2.

47 Quoted in Vital, *Origins*, 196.

48 See Lipsky, *Memoirs*, 133.

49 WL, 1, no. 22, and 7, no. 57; V. Weizmann, *Impossible*, 49.

50 See, for example, WL, 1:395, and 7, no. 58.

51 *T&E*, 52.

52 *T&E*, 69.

53 His Ph.D. thesis, *Elektrolytische Reduktion von 1 Nitroanthrachinon. Über die Kondensation von Phenanthrenchinon U 1-Nitroanthrachinon mit einegen Phenolen* (certificate in WA), showed that by a process of de-oxygenation through electrolysis it was possible to produce amino-anthraquinones, an essential of dyestuffs.

54 See WL, 1, no. 36; his letter of appointment as *privat-docent* in WA; and *T&E*, 76–77.

3: THE REBEL

1 See Bein, *Herzl*, 232, and Elon, *Herzl*, 240.

2 Herzl, *Diaries*, 2:581.

3 Ibid., 1:248.

4 Elon, *Herzl*, 17–63, 87–88, 106–22, 126–29.

5 Ibid., 128.

6 Its full title reads *Der Judenstaat: Versuch einer modernen Lösung der Judenfrage*, commonly rendered *The Jewish State* but literally *The Jews' State: An Attempt at a Modern Solution to the Jewish Question*.

7 The book eventually ran through seventeen editions in Herzl's lifetime and was translated into Russian, Yiddish, English, French, Rumanian, and Bulgarian. See Vital, *Origins*, 260 *n*43; also Elon, *Herzl*, 175.

8 Herzl, *Diaries*, 281–82, entries for 25 November 1895 and 5–6 July 1896; also WL, 7, no. 128 *n*8.

9 Vital, *Origins*, quoting Herzl, *Diaries*, 1:299.

10 Elon, *Herzl*, 182.

11 *T&E*, 61.

12 *T&E*, 67–68, and Lichtenstein, *In the Shadow*, 99–101; also WL, 1:65.

13 *T&E*, 62, 63, 75; WL, 3, no. 253.

14 Quoted in Wise, 'Great Tradition.'

15 WL, 1:19.

16 WL, 1, nos 40, 160.

17 WL, 1, nos. 320, 247.

18 See WP, 1:3–4; WL, 1, no. 48; and *T&E*, 78.

19 Among them: Catherine Dorfmann, Anne Koenigsberg, Esther Shneerson, and Rosa Grinblatt. See WL, 1, no. 87 *n*7.

20 WL, 1, nos. 73, 77, 80.

21 WL, 1, no. 100 *n*21.

22 WL, 1, no. 107.

23 WL, 1, nos. 103, 124.

24 WL, 1, no. 134.

25 WL, 1, no. 111 *n*3.

26 WL, 1, no. 72 *n*1; also M. Friedman, *Buber's Life*, 1:57.

27 Ibid., 2. WL, 1:395.

28 WL, 1, no. 144.

29 See, for example, Yogev, 'Weizmann as Leader.'

30 WL, 1, no. 127.

31 WL, 1, no. 152.

32 See WL, 1, nos. 177, 278, and WL, 2, no. 187.

33 WL, 2, nos. 308, 311, 313.

34 See V. Weizmann, *Impossible* 1–2, *T&E*, 95–96.

35 See WL, 1, nos. 63, 85, 95. His terms of endearment for Vera

included Verchik; Verochka; Veronchik; Verunka; Verusenka; Verussik; Verusya.

36 See WL, 2, no. 297.

37 WL, 1, nos. 105, 245. Some 230 letters from Weizmann to Sophia Getsova, at present in the possession of a family resident in the United States, have not been released to the Weizmann Archives and so are not available to scholars. See WL, 1:xx.

38 See WL, 1, nos. 23, 73, 133, 140, 152, 206, 230, 274, 318; and 5, no. 13.

39 T&E, 96.

40 See, for example, WL, 5, no. 335, and V. Weizmann, *Impossible*, 2, 38–39.

41 WL, 1, no. 256.

42 WL, 1, nos. 257, 266.

43 V. Weizmann, *Impossible*, 46.

44 WL, 1, nos. 251 n1, 256.

45 See Stone, *Europe Transformed*, 160–61.

46 See WL, 1, nos. 55, 87; and T&E, 77.

47 WL, 1, nos. 165, 234, 238.

48 See WL, 1, nos. 35, 44, 55 n15, 87, 95 n17, 130, 165, 234, 238; nos. 96 n11, 293, 294; 3, no. 318. A number of his papers were published in the *Bulletin of the German Chemical Society*, vol. 36 (1903).

49 See WL, 1, nos. 260, 280; 4, no. 128; 5, no. 263.

50 WL, 1, no. 256; 3, no. 305.

51 See WL, 4, no. 65.

52 See WL, 2, no. 314 n21.

53 See Lichtenstein, *In the Shadow*, 85–88; and WL, 1, no. 135.

54 WL, 2, no. 314.

55 T&E, 70.

56 WL, 1, no. 44, and 4, no. 180.

57 WL, 1, no. 144; Hermoni, *Footsteps*, 91–92; and T&E, 71.

58 Hermoni, *Footsteps*, 89, 93.

59 See WL, 1, nos. 157–59; also T&E,

70–72. Weizmann's memoir merges these events into one performance.

60 WL, 1, no. 156.

61 See WL, 1, nos. 156, 199, 202, 204, 240, 257, 260, 298, 308, 316, 320; 2, nos. 13, 57, 87, 108, 203, 210, 292, 295. For his contacts with Evans-Gordon, 2, nos. 22, 36, 38; for his preference for either England or Switzerland, 2, nos. 161, 281, 385; and for bureau closing down, 3:213.

62 WL, 1, nos. 222, 238, 278.

63 T&E, 87–88.

64 WL, 1, nos. 100, 299.

65 See WL, 2, no. 272.

66 See Joll, *Origins*, 187–88.

67 Lichtenstein, *In the Shadow*, 154.

68 See WL, 7, no. 45; and T&E, 107.

69 WL, 2, nos. 307, 310.

70 WL, 1, no. 320.

71 Elon, *Herzl*, 350–51.

72 See WL, 2, no. 292 ns10, 11.

73 WL, 2, no. 316, for Weizmann's essay; and WL, 3, no. 67, for refinement of his argument.

74 WL, 2, no. 413.

75 WL, 2, no. 336 n3.

76 WL, 2, no. 295.

77 See his article 'The Torso of Greatness' in *Encounter*, November 1972.

78 WL, 1:31.

79 See WL, 5, no. 294; and 3, no. 47 n2, where, in July 1903, he writes of his readiness to settle in England or the U.S. for a number of years. See also T&E, 123–24.

80 WL, 2, nos. 414, 415.

4: UGANDA AND MANCHESTER

1 Herzl, *Diaries*, 4:1547.

2 For Herzl's Russian visit, see Vital, *Zionism*, 248–64, and Elon, *Herzl*, 377–84; and for the El Arish proposal, Vital, *Zionism*, 146–54, and WL, 2, no. 309 n5.

3 Extracts from Herzl's speech quoted in Vital, *Zionism*, 283–84.

4 *The Jewish Chronicle*, 21 August 1903, had hinted that a dramatic proposal by a Great Power would be placed before Congress. See also *T&E*, 110.

5 See Vital, *Zionism*, 301 n6 for text of resolution, and 302 for voting figures.

6 See Elon, *Herzl*, 388.

7 See Vital, *Zionism*, 318–21, and Elon, *Herzl*, 392.

8 See Herzl's comments, Herzl, *Diaries*, 4:1571.

9 See *T&E*, 110–17.

10 See WL, 3:xxv–ix, and no. 1. His resolution read: 'Congress does not conceive the action in Africa as the ultimate aim of the Zionists, but deems it necessary to regulate emigration and consequently finds that the Zionists must unify all colonization societies or convene a Congress in order to decide on East Africa.'

11 See WL, 3:xxv, and Vital, *Zionism*, 291.

12 *T&E*, 113.

13 *T&E*, 114.

14 Quoted in Vital, *Zionism*, 305; see also WL, 3:xxvi, and WP, 1:35–64.

15 WL, 3, nos. 10, 29.

16 WL, 3, no. 12.

17 WL, 3, no. 22 n1. The directive (in WA), unsigned and undated, bears the hallmark of Weizmann's style.

18 WL, 3, nos. 12, 20.

19 WL, 3, no. 4.

20 WL, 3, nos. 25, 39.

21 WL, 3, nos. 43, 44.

22 See WL, 3, nos. 44, 55, 56, 66. Weizmann's memoirs are somewhat misleading (*T&E*, 117–20) as he telescoped two visits to London, in October 1903 and July 1904, into one.

23 WL, 3, nos. 60, 66.

24 WL, 18, no. 185.

25 WL, 3, no. 47. See also Fraenkel, 'Chaim Weizmann.'

26 For a full list of the courses offered, see WL, 3, nos. 56, 66.

27 See WL, 3, nos. 45, 47.

28 WL, 3, no. 47.

29 WL, 3, nos. 53, 56.

30 WL, 3, nos. 38, 61.

31 WL, 3, no. 106 n2.

32 WL, 3, no. 109.

33 WL, 3, no. 161.

34 Elon, *Herzl*, 393.

35 See WL, 3, no. 160 n4.

36 WL, 4, no. 4.

37 Elon, *Herzl*, 325.

38 WL, 3, no. 47.

39 See an early essay in Sykes, *Two Studies*, and a more recent work, Verete, 'Idea of Restoration.'

40 Wedgwood, *Seventh Dominion*, 119–21.

41. See Verete, 'British Consulate.'

42 WL, 3, no. 55.

43 WL, 3, nos. 146, 148, 158.

44 WL, 3, nos. 29, 65, 81 n1, 158, 179; and Yogev, 'Weizmann as Leader', 23.

45 WL, 3, no. 77.

46 WL, 3, no. 146.

47 WL, 3, no. 93.

48 WL, 3, no. 224.

49 WL, 3, nos. 210, 220, 230, 231.

50 WL, 3, no. 204.

51 WL, 3, no. 230.

52 WL, 3, nos. 242, 244 n1.

53 WL, 3, no. 244.

54 *T&E*, 123.

55 WL, 3, no. 203.

56 WL, 3, nos. 247, 249, 251.

57 Quoted in Elon, *Herzl*, 402.

58 Quoted in Sykes, *Two Studies*, 122.

59 WL, 3, no. 253.

60 WL, 3, no. 255.

61 WL, 3, no. 258.

62 WL, 3, nos. 259, and 5, no. 294.

5: NEW BEGINNINGS

1 See WL, 3, nos. 261, 262.

2 WL, 3, no. 267.

3 WL, 3, no. 261.

4 The motion, on whether there was a danger to peace in East Africa arising out of the proposal, was debated on 20 June 1904. See *Parliamentary Debates*, Commons [hereafter cited as *H.C. Deb.*], 4th ser., vol. 136, cols. 561–79.

5 For Weizmann's account see WL, 3, no. 285; for Percy and Hill's record, see FO.2/848. Weizmann's memoirs, *T&E*, 118–19, are hazy on these meetings. He has telescoped his meetings of October 1903 with those of July 1904, and he puts, for example, Hill's words into Percy's mouth.

6 See WL, 3, no. 286.

7 WL, 3, no. 284.

8 From a note by Lord Robert Cecil in FO.800/95.

9 See WL, 3, no. 294.

10 See FO.2/848; also Fraenkel, 'Chaim Weizmann.'

11 WL, 3, nos. 271, 280, 331, 332.

12 WL, 3, nos. 284, 295; and *T&E*, 127–30.

13 WL, 3, no. 328; *T&E*, 129; WL, 4, no. 274.

14 See WL, 3, no. 331, and 4, nos. 4, 39, 166.

15 WL, 4, nos. 6, 21.

16 WL, 4, no. 248.

17 WL, 4, nos. 33, 124.

18 *T&E*, 125.

19 See M. Samuel, *Little*, 182.

20 WL, 4, no. 131.

21 WL, 4, no. 143 $n1$.

22 V. Weizmann, *Impossible*, 30.

23 WL, 3, nos. 266, 315 $n1$.

24 WL, 3, nos. 290, 309, and 4, nos. 30, 37.

25 WL, 4, no. 241.

26 WL, 3, no. 305.

27 See WL, 4, nos. 67, 68.

28 WL, 4, nos. 76 $n2$, 77, 78.

29 WL, 4, no. 79.

30 WL, 4, no. 79 $n5$.

31 V. Weizmann, *Impossible*, 29.

32 *T&E*, 146.

33 See *T&E*, 146, and V. Weizmann, *Impossible*, 29.

34 V. Weizmann, *Impossible*, 31.

35 WL, 4, no. 306.

36 WL, 4, no. 32.

37 WL, 4, no. 299.

38 V. Weizmann, *Impossible*, 31.

39 WL, 3, nos. 318, 331; 4, no. 93 $n3$.

40 See WL, 3, nos. 109 $n1$, 289, 312 $n4$, 347; 4, no. 9; 5, no. 126; and *T&E*, 133.

41 Cited in Weisgal, *Weizmann*, 265.

42 See M. Samuel, *Little*, 181–82; and author's interview with Norah Schuster Nicholls, September 1983.

43 See WL, 4, nos. 52, 168, 209, 224.

44 WL, 4, no. 288.

45 WL, 3, no. 344.

46 See Sacher, *Zionist Portraits*, 17.

47 WL, 3, nos. 299, 304.

48 WL, 4:xxi–xxii and nos. 4, 9, 69.

49 See WL, 4, nos. 216, 239, 290.

50 For example, WL, 4, no. 53.

51 See WL, 3, no. 66; 4, nos. 64, 226; and 5, no. 3.

52 WL, 4, no. 53.

53 WL, 4, nos. 91, 176.

54 See WL, 4, nos. 174, 176, 185, 216.

55 WL, 4, no. 53.

56 See WL, 4, nos. 191, 196.

57 See WL, 4, nos. 195, 304.

58 See Dugdale, *Balfour*, 1:325–27, and *T&E*, 142–44.

59 Quoted in Stein, *Balfour Declaration*, 152.

60 Dugdale, *Balfour*, 1:327, and Stein, *Balfour Declaration*, 157. See also Balfour's introduction to Sokolow's *History*, where he wrote that it was his conversation with Weizmann in

1906 which convinced him that only Palestine would serve as a home for the Jewish people.

61 See, for example, WL, 5, no. 5; *T&E*, 158.

62 See Goodman, *Weizmann*, 147–48; also WP, 1:65–71.

63 WL, 5, no. 47.

64 V. Weizmann, *Impossible*, 35; and WL, 5:xviii.

65 See WL, 5, nos. 20, 22, 26.

66 WL, 5, nos. 50, 52, 55.

67 WL, 5, no. 56.

68 See his speech to a Manchester audience as reported in the *Jewish Chronicle*, 25 October 1907, quoted in WL, 5:xxi.

69 See WL, 5, nos. 58, 60 n7.

70 V. Weizmann, *Impossible*, 36.

71 WL, 5, nos. 60, 71.

72 See WL, 5, no. 65 n4.

73 See WL, 5:xxv and no. 81.

74 See WL, 5, nos. 155 n3, 158.

75 WL, 5, no. 363.

76 WL, 5, no. 96.

77 See WL, 5, nos. 102, 105.

78 See S. Cohen, *English Zionists*, 116.

79 WL, 5, no. 114.

80 For a sympathetic treatment of Wolffsohn, see Eliav, *Wolffsohn*, 189–92.

The gist of Weizmann's proposals was to depose Wolffsohn and to ensure the election of a 'practical' as president of the Zionist Organization. This turned on a motion of the Standing Committee that the president be elected by the SAC, which would be expanded to include a majority of 'practicals', and not, as previously, by the Congress itself. See WL, 5, nos. 160 n1, 173.

81 WL, 5, no. 174 ns11 and 12, and *Jewish Chronicle*, 7 January 1910.

82 WL, 5, nos. 164, 173.

83 WL, 5, no. 175.

84 See WL, 5, no. 201 ns4 and 7; and

Eliav, *Wolffsohn*, 260–61.

85 See WL, 5, nos. 204, 206 n7, 234.

86 WL, 5, no. 173.

87 WL, 5, no. 206.

88 WL, 5, no. 115.

89 See WL, 5:241; also S. Cohen, *English Zionists*, 122–23.

6: PERSONAL CRISIS— AND RECOVERY

1 See Weisgal and Carmichael, *A Biography*, 95.

2 *T&E*, 147; WL, 6, no. 144; and interview with present residents, September 1983.

3 See WL, 5, no. 341; *T&E*, 148; and V. Weizmann, *Impossible*, 33–34.

4 See WL, 5, nos. 32, 33, 36; 235, 295, 349 n2.

5 WL, 5, no. 344.

6 WL, 5, nos. 232, 239.

7 WL, 5, nos. 238, 239, 244.

8 See, for example, *T&E*, 151.

9 WL, 5, no. 306.

10 WL, 5, no. 316.

11 *T&E*, 152.

12 WL, 5, no. 316.

13 Interview with Nora Schuster Nicholls and a private communication, September 1983; WL, 6, no. 34.

14 Interview with Norah Schuster Nicholls and a private communication; and Crossman's Notes.

15 See WL, 5, no. 352.

16 See WL, 5, no. 361.

17 WL, 5, nos. 361, 363.

18 See, for example, his letter to Norah, WL, 5, no. 367.

19 Interview with Norah Schuster Nicholls.

20 WL, 5, no. 269.

21 WL, 5, no. 324.

22 WL, 5, no. 350.

23 See WL, 5, no. 159, and 6, no. 339.

24 See WL, 5, nos. 68 n2, 92 n3, 147,

153, 346 *n*3; and Weisgal, *Weizmann*, 289–91.

25 See WL, 5, nos. 109 *n*1, 187–94.

26 WL, 5, no. 185 *n*3.

27 WL, 5, nos. 215 *n*2, 226 *n*7.

28 See WL, 5, no. 225 *n*9; and Crossman Notes; also *T&E*, 172.

29 For these events, see WL, 5, nos. 280, 317 *n*3; and Crossman Notes.

30 Strange to Perkin, 1 June 1912, WA; and Crossman Notes.

31 See WL, 5, nos. 288 *n*4, 293, 297.

32 For this passage, see WL, 5, nos. 312, 323, 338; Crossman Notes; and interview with Norah Schuster Nicholls.

33 See WL, 5, no. 321, and 6, no. 51.

34 See WL, 6, nos. 47, 83, 194.

35 See Simon, *Certain Days*, 52–53; and WL, 6, no. 67.

36 WL, 5, no. 156.

37 WL, 5, nos. 227 *n*3, 229 *n*1. His certificate bears the date 17 December 1910.

38 WL, 5, nos. 227, 338, and 6, no. 51.

39 WL, 5, no. 263.

40 WL, 6, no. 51.

41 WL, 6, no. 350.

42 WL, 6, nos. 3, 4.

43 WL, 5, no. 263.

44 *T&E*, 173–74, and V. Weizmann, *Impossible*, 39.

45 For an account of the meeting, see *Ha'aretz*, 3 November 1967, and WL, 5, no. 191 *n*7.

46 WL, 6, no. 5.

47 See WL, 6:142–43 and nos. 7, 9, 16, 29, 43, 121; and *T&E*, 179–81. Also WP, 1:101–110, and Goodman, *Weizmann*, 149–52.

48 See WL, 6:143.

49 WL, 6, nos. 165, 209.

50 WL, 6, nos. 121, 156.

51 WL, 6, nos. 9, 134 *n*10, 147, 155.

52 WL, 6, nos. 150 *n*4, 259.

53 Quoted in Goodman, *Weizmann*, 152.

54 See WL, 6, no. 231 *n*6.

55 WL, 6, no. 183.

56 See Schama, *Two Rothschilds*.

57 *T&E*, 177.

58 WL, 6, nos. 287, 288.

59 WL, 6, no. 192.

60 WL, 6, nos. 192, 213, 300.

61 WL, 6, no. 349.

62 WL, 6, nos. 205, 298, 300.

63 WL, 6, nos. 192 *n*14, 258, 263, 286, 289, 298, 315 *n*9, 363.

64 WL, 6, nos. 298, 300.

65 WL, 6, nos. 192 *n*19, 310 *n*s3 and 4.

66 WL, 6, nos. 310 *n*3, 315 *n*3, 321.

67 WL, 6, no. 310.

68 WL, 6, no. 317.

69 WL, 6, nos. 323, 338 *n*3, 350. The talks were later postponed to 10 August. See no. 373.

70 WL, 6, nos. 325, 334.

71 WL, 6, no. 350.

72 See Lipsky, *Memoirs*, 103.

73 See WL, 6, no. 385.

74 *T&E*, 188–89.

7: TOWARD THE CHARTER

1 See Stein, *Balfour Declaration*, 101; Laqueur, *History*, 174–75; and *T&E*, 210.

2 See WL, 7, no. 21; Stein, *Balfour Declaration*, 99; and *T&E*, 210–11.

3 WL, 7, nos. 19, 21, 34; Stein, *Balfour Declaration*, 18.

4 WL, 5, no. 257.

5 See WL, 7, nos. 4, 5, 22, 33, 121. For letter to Zangwill, 9 October 1914, see WL, 7, no. 22.

6 Rabinowicz, *Fifty Years*, 67. See also WL, 7, no. 12 *n*1, and *T&E*, 212–15.

7 For the above passage, see Meyer, *Early History*; Laqueur, *History*, 158–59, 179; Stein, *Balfour Declaration*, 188–190; and WL, 7, nos. 4, 11, 21, 35, 36, 37.

8 For Asquith's speech, see *The Times*, 10 November 1914. See also *Daily Chronicle*, 4–7 November 1914 and

15 January 1915, quoted in WL, 7, nos. 31, 95, 103 n7.

9 WL, 7, no. 95.

10 WL, 7, no. 95.

11 WL, 7, nos. 22, 42.

12 Full text in Stein, *Balfour Declaration*, 222.

13 WL, 7, no. 48; also Stein, *Balfour Declaration*, 176–77.

14 WL, 7, no. 128.

15 WL, 7, no. 120.

16 WL, 7, no. 13.

17 For this incident, see WL, 7, nos. 100, 103, 106, 114, 126, 220.

18 See Ayerst, *Guardian*, 381; *T&E*, 190–91; and WL, 7, no. 9.

19 See WL, 7, no. 128.

20 WL, 7, no. 33.

21 WL, 7, no. 39.

22 Scott to Sacher, 16 January 1915, quoted in Ayerst, *Guardian*, 382, also in Stein, *Balfour Declaration*, 132.

23 See Ayerst, *Guardian*, 382–86; and WL, 7, nos. 177 n1, 218 n2.

24 See WL, 7:127, and *T&E*, 192, 194; also Lloyd George, *War Memoirs*, 1:348, and Stein, *Balfour Declaration*, 140. No contemporary record of the meeting has yet come to light. Weizmann dated it 3 December and included as participants Josiah Wedgwood as well as Samuel. But he evidently compressed his separate meetings with Samuel and Lloyd George into one.

25 See WL, 7, nos. 65, 95.

26 See Viscount Samuel, *Memoirs*, 140–42.

27 Copy of Viscount Samuel's memorandum, 21 January 1915, in CAB.37/123/43 and FO.800/100; see also his paper, 11 March 1915, CAB.27/126; and *Memoirs*, 140–42. See also I. Friedman, *Question*, 9–10; Stein, *Balfour Declaration*, 109–110.

28 Asquith, *Memories*, 2:59–60, 65–66.

29 See WL, 7, nos. 68, 95; *T&E*, 195–96; and Dugdale, *Balfour*, 2:165.

30 On Dorothy de Rothschild, see WL, 7, nos. 45, 95. W. to D. Rothschild, 22 November 1914; no. 95 contains accounts of his meetings with D. Rothschild. See also Schama, *Two Rothschilds*, 198, and *T&E*, 206.

31 WL, 7, no. 95.

32 See WL, 7, no. 95; also Bertie of Thame, *Diaries*, 1:105–6; and Verete, 'Balfour Declaration,' for more indications of the Foreign Office's scepticism about the aims of Zionism.

33 See WL, 7, no. 41 n1; also Verete, 'Balfour Declaration,' n7; V. Weizmann, *Impossible*, 57.

34 See WL, 7, no. 176, and V. Weizmann, *Impossible*, 57.

35 See WL, 7, nos. 196, 198. Cecil's note is in FO.800/95. See also Sanders, *High Walls*, 318–19.

36 V. Weizmann, *Impossible*, 68.

37 See Stein, *Balfour Declaration*, 321–22.

38 See David, *Inside*, 227.

39 *T&E*, 218.

40 See WL, 7, nos. 46, 241.

41 See WL, 7, nos. 115, 124, 152, 158, 159, and *T&E*, 219.

42 See WL, 7, nos. 159, 160, and *T&E*, 220. No contemporary record exists of his meeting with Churchill, but it must have been during the last days of Churchill's tenure as First Lord, for he left the Admiralty on 26 May 1915.

43 See Weisgal and Carmichael, *A Biography*, 108. See also Weisgal, *Weizmann*, 266–69, and Crossman Notes.

44 See WL, 7, nos. 160, 169, 195, 229, 234, 245, 277, 318.

45 See WL, 7, nos. 245, 387; *T&E*, 222; and V. Weizmann, *Impossible*, 54.

46 See WL, 7, nos. 199 n8, 234, 282.

67, Addison Road still stands, and I am grateful to its present occupants, Mr. and Mrs. Strage, for allowing me to wander through it; 16, Addison Crescent has been converted into a number of self-contained apartments, reputedly under Arab ownership.

47 See WL, 7, nos. 193 n2, 199, 245; and T&E, 222; also V. Weizmann, *Impossible*, 54.

48 WL, 7, no. 190.

49 See WL, 7, nos. 221, 224, 229. See also Scott, *Political Diaries*, 159.

50 Scott, *Political Diaries*, 205; WL, 7, nos. 254, 289, 318.

51 See WL, 7, nos. 289 n2, 509, and T&E, 222. The official *U.K. History of the Ministry of Munitions* (1922) sheds little extra light on this topic; see its vol. 7, pt. 4, ch. 4.

52 WL, 7, no. 261.

53 See WL, 7, nos. 255, 260, 261, 274, 436; 12, nos. 405, 407, 408; and 13, no. 1 ns3 and 4.

54 See Lloyd George, *War Memoirs*, 1:349; and T&E, 192.

55 See *U.K. History of Ministry of Munitions*, vol. 7, pt. 4, ch. 4.

56 Scott, *Political Diaries*, 255.

57 See *Report of the Committee on Asiatic Turkey*, 30 June 1915, in CAB.27/1.

58 See Cmd. 5957, which contains the text of the correspondence between McMahon and Husayn, and Cmd. 5974, the report of an investigation into that correspondence. See also McMahon to Sir John Shuckburgh, 12 March 1922, CO.733/38/13471. For the latest and most authoritative contribution to this debate, see Kedourie, *Labyrinth*.

59 See his latest biography, Adelson, *Sykes*.

60 See Verete, 'Balfour Declaration'; Stein, *Balfour Declaration*, 218 passim; I. Friedman, *Question*, 65 passim.

61 See Verete, 'Balfour Declaration.'

62 Quoted in Stein, *Balfour Declaration*, 224.

63 See WL, 7, no. 237 n1, pp. 543–44.

64 WL, 7, no. 271.

65 WL, 7, no. 276 n4 and, for the Programmatic Statement and Memorandum, pp. 543–44.

66 WL, 7, no. 269.

8: THE CHARTER

1 Asquith, *Memories*, 2:66.

2 Quoted in Fry, *Lloyd George*, 263.

3 See PRO CAB.24/9.

4 Quoted in Dugdale, *Balfour*, 2:200.

5 See Amery, *Diaries*, 1:177.

6 See WL, 7, nos. 306, 307, 480 n1, 490, 493.

7 Quoted in Sanders, *High Walls*, 419.

8 See WL, 7, nos. 303, 311, 329.

9 See WL, 7, 306, and Stein, *Balfour Declaration*, 367–74.

10 Quoted in Stein, *Balfour Declaration*, 370–71.

11 See WL, 7, no. 306 n3; Stein, *Balfour Declaration*, 370–74; and T&E, 238–40.

12 See WL, 7, nos. 302, 303, and Sanders, *High Walls*, 472.

13 WL, 7, nos. 321, 334 n2, 345 n5; and Ayerst, *Guardian*, 385.

14 WL, 7, nos. 323, 325, 336. See also Stein, *Balfour Declaration*, 380–81, and Vansittart, *Mist Procession*, 232.

15 See WL, 7, nos. 329, 336; Stein, *Balfour Declaration*, 379–84; Sanders, *High Walls*, 485; and V. Weizmann, *Impossible*, 67–68. For Weizmann's conversation with Lloyd George, see Scott, *Political Diaries*, 274. The deliberations of the Committee on Territorial Desiderata on the Terms of Peace, which reported on 28 April 1917, are in CAB.21/77; it was chaired by Curzon, and its members included Cecil and Smuts.

16 See WL, 7, no. 334 *n*2, and *T&E*, 241.

17 See WL, 7, no. 356, a note of Weizmann's interview with Lord Robert Cecil, 25 April 1917.

18 WL, 7, no. 351.

19 See the note on Wilson in the *Encyclopaedia Britannica* by Paul Freund.

20 Stein, *Balfour Declaration*, 196–97, 422–28.

21 Dugdale, *Balfour*, 2:17.

22 See WL, 7, no. 356. Cecil's version of the meeting, which took place on 25 April 1917, does not differ materially from Weizmann's; it may be found in FO.371/3053.

23 See WL, 7, nos. 343, 349, 350, 364 *n*3, 378, 380, 382, 391; FO.371/ 3083; Stein, *Balfour Declaration*, 394–421; *T&E*, 240.

24 See, for example, WL, 7, nos. 343, 360, 365, and *T&E*, 240.

25 *T&E*, 252.

26 For a report of the speech, see *Jewish Chronicle*, 25 May 1917; WP, 1:154–59; also WL, 7, no. 402 *n*1.

27 See WL, 7, nos. 284, 287.

28 See WL, 7, nos. 404, 405; also Stein, *Balfour Declaration*, 448–49.

29 See *The Times* (London), 28 May 1917; and *T&E*, 255.

30 See WL, 7, no. 434; and *Jewish Chronicle*, 22 June 1917.

31 *T&E*, 246.

32 See WL, 7, no. 431.

33 See WL, 7, nos. 419, 431, 432, 435, 516 *n*13; and I. Friedman, *Germany, Turkey*, pt.3

34 For the Gibraltar incident, see WL, 7, nos. 431, 441–43, 446–49, 451–54, 456, 461, 466; and *T&E*, 246–51.

35 WL, 7, nos. 463, 466.

36 WL, 7, nos. 465, 482.

37 The drafts and final text of the declaration may be found in Stein, *Balfour Declaration*, 664.

38 For cabinet meeting, see CAB.23/24; and Lloyd George, *Truth*, 2:1117.

39 WL, 7, no. 502.

40 WL, 7, no. 417; and Stein, *Balfour Declaration*, 437.

41 WL, 7, no. 489.

42 See WL, 7, no. 489.

43 See *The Times*, 28 July 1917, and Stein, *Balfour Declaration*, 486, 492.

44 Quoted in Stein, *Balfour Declaration*, 491.

45 Ibid., 494.

46 WL, 7, nos. 480, 481.

47 WL, 7, nos. 490, 491.

48 See Berlin and Kollat, *Leadership*, 33; Stein, *Balfour Declaration*, 495; and WL, 7, no. 492 *n*20.

49 WL, 7, no. 490.

50 Quoted in Stein, *Balfour Declaration*, 495–96; and WL, 7, no. 505 *n*2.

51 WL, 7, no. 501.

52 WL, 7, nos. 496, 497, 505.

53 WL, 7, nos. 507, 509; and Stein, *Balfour Declaration*, 480, 511, 514

54 See Scott, *Political Diaries*, 28 September 1917.

55 WL, 7, no. 514.

56 Cabinet minutes in CAB.21/58. Also WL, 7, no. 516, Stein, *Balfour Declaration*, 500, 514–32, and *T&E*, 259.

57 Quoted in Stein, *Balfour Declaration*, 500.

58 See CAB.23/4; WL, 7, nos. 524, 529, 531; and Stein, *Balfour Declaration*, 520. See also Curzon's paper 'The Future of Palestine,' 26 October 1917, CAB.24/4.

59 *T&E*, 262; V. Weizmann, *Impossible*, 78.

60 Quoted in Weisgal and Carmichael, *A Biography*, 37.

61 See WL, 7, no. 534; also WP, 1:257, *T&E*, 261, and Sanders, *High Walls*, 616.

62 *T&E*, 261.

63 See Stein, *Balfour Declaration*, 559 passim.

64 See Lloyd George, *War Memoirs*, 2:1451.

65 See Dugdale, *Diaries*, 216.

66 Quoted in Weisgal and Carmichael, *A Biography*, 143.

67 See Webster, *Art and Practice*, 114–15, 118.

9: PALESTINE AGAIN

1 For full report of meeting, see *Jewish Chronicle*, 7 December 1917; also Sanders, *High Walls*, 620.

2 WL, 8, nos. 6, 23, 34, 63, 68, 103.

3 See *T&E*, 267.

4 See WL, 8, nos. 66, 121; and *T&E*, 268–69.

5 WL, 8, no. 138, and Horace Samuel, *Unholy Memories*, 15–16.

6 See Kedourie, 'Cairo and Khartoum on the Arab Question, 1915–18,' in *Chatham House Version*.

7 *T&E*, 273.

8 Storrs, *Orientations*, 375.

9 See WL, 8, nos. 175, 200, 208.

10 *T&E*, 280–81.

11 WL, 7, no. 166, and *T&E*, 278–81.

12 *T&E*, 274.

13 See Ormsby-Gore to Hankey, 19 April 1918, in CAB.21/58.

14 Cited in Simon, *Certain Days*, 69.

15 Storrs, *Orientations*, 353–54; see WP, 1:182–86; WL, 8, no. 181.

16 WL, 8, no. 161.

17 For details see Kedourie, *Labyrinth*, 190–93.

18 WL, 8, no. 213, and *T&E*, 292.

19 See WL, 9, no. 31 n6.

20 WL, 8, no. 217.

21 From his speech to the Zionist Congress in August 1925, see WL, 1:466.

22 For his speech, see WP, 1:191–95.

23 See *T&E*, 295–97.

24 WL, 8, no. 213.

25 WL, 8, no. 232. See the reports of Ormsby-Gore to Balfour, 7 April 1918, and Clayton to Balfour, 16 June 1918, in FO.371/3394, 3395.

26 WL, 8, no. 213.

27 See Simon, *Certain Days*, 111, and Levin, *Youth*, 184.

28 WL, 8, nos. 163, 236.

29 Quoted in Tevet, *Ben Gurion*, 2:78.

30 See WL, 8:286; and for an example of his correspondence with Bella, 9, no. 202.

31 WL, 8, no. 213.

32 WL, 8, no. 258.

33 WL, 8, nos. 243, 255.

34 See Scott, *Political Diaries*, 360–61; *T&E*, 298–99; and WL, 9, nos. 4, 52, 53, 80. Also Weizmann's despatches to Louis Mallet, 18 June 1919, and Curzon, 2 February 1920, WL, 9, nos. 170, 279, 280, summarizing the work of the Zionist Commission and urging the development of the Jewish National Home. For minutes of interview, see FO.371/3385, and CZA.A36/113.

35 Roskill, *Hankey*, 2:28–29.

36 Text in WL, 9:86–87, also nos. 61, 70; and WP, 1:218–20.

37 See Kedourie, *Labyrinth*, 225; and Knightley and Simpson, *Lawrence of Arabia*, 116–19.

38 See WL, 9, no. 124, and WP, 1:236–37.

39 WL, 9, no. 100 n5.

40 See WL, 9, app. 11.

41 See CMD.1500.

42 WL, 9, no. 100.

43 See WL, 9, no. 108 n20. Also Meinertzhagen, *Middle East Diary*, 15, and Nicolson, *Peacemaking*, 237.

44 See WL, 9, no. 123; also WP, 1:221–32, and *T&E*, 304–6.

45 Meinertzhagen, *Middle East Diary*, 47–48, 57–58; and WL, 9, nos. 252, 265.

46 WL, 9, no. 297.

47 WL, 9, nos. 299, 302–3, 306, 318.

48 Quoted in Ingrams, *Palestine Papers*, 84, 86. For further details, see FO.371/5117.

49 See WL, 9, nos. 320, 335, 351; and interview with Sir Isaiah Berlin, September 1983.

50 See his note to Allenby in FO.371/5035.

51 WL, 9, nos. 201, 299, 313, 317, 318.

52 Bowle, *Viscount Samuel*, 199.

53 See WL, 9, no. 81, and Sieff, *Memoirs*, 126.

54 WL, 9, no. 300.

10: BETWEEN PALESTINE, PINSK, AND WASHINGTON

1 WL, 9, no. 171.

2 For this passage, see WL, 9, nos. 198, 204, minutes of GAC meeting in CZA, Z4/251/4, 5, and Simon, *Certain Days*, 93–95.

3 Quoted in Berlin and Kollat, *Leadership*, 30–31.

4 Ibid; also Tevet, *Ben Gurion*, 82–85; and A. Shapiro, *Berl*, 1:173. Also *Jewish Chronicle*, 16 July 1920; and Yossin, *Pillar of Fire*, 85.

5 See Simon, *Certain Days*, 100, 343.

6 WP, 1:292.

7 Quoted in Shihor, *Hollow Glory*, 204.

8 See Simon, *Certain Days*, 98–100. The literature on this topic is rich; see, for example, G. Berlin, 'Brandeis-Weizmann Dispute,' Y. Shapiro, 'Controversy,' and Gal, 'Brandeis's View.'

9 Simon, *Certain Days*, 103.

10 See Simon, *Certain Days*, 104.

11 WL, 10, no. 7, and p. 139; and Simon, *Certain Days*, 104, 353.

12 WL, 10, nos. 83, 93, 108.

13 See WP, 1:328.

14 See Neumann, *Arena*, 56; Weisgal, *So Far*, 59–60; and *T&E*, 331–32.

15 Neumann, *Arena*, 58.

16 WL, 10, no. 180.

17 See WL, 10, no. 205.

18 WL, 10, nos. 180 *n*9, 204 *n*2.

19 See WL, 11, no. 16.

20 See WL, 10, no. 204.

21 WL, 10:200.

22 WL, 10, no. 1 *n*5.

23 Weizmann's definition of San Remo in WL, 9, no. 318.

24 *Documents on British Foreign Policy* [hereafter cited as BD], series 1, v. xiii, nos. 301, 302, 305.

25 See WL, 10, nos. 17 *n*2, 135; and Gilbert, *Churchill*, iv, 541.

26 For details of Churchill's visit, see WL, 10, nos. 138, 140; and Gilbert, *Churchill*, 558–75.

27 See WL, 10:202.

28 WL, 10, no. 211.

29 WP, 1:331.

30 WL, 10, nos. 213, 228.

31 See WL, 10:227; also Meinertzhagen, *Middle East Diary*, 103–6, and Gilbert, *Churchill*, 621–22.

32 See WP, 1:326.

33 See Cmd.1540.

34 See WL, 10, nos. 230, 240, 243, 278, p. 305. Also CO.733/15/287, 290, 855, and Cmd.1700.

35 See Cmd.1500; WP, 1:326; and *T&E*, 347–48.

36 See *T&E*, 348, and Rose, *Vansittart*, 51–52.

37 See Cmd.1700.

38 See *H. L. Deb.* 5s, 50:263–1034; *H. C. Deb.* 5s, 156:263–1034.

39 WL, 11, nos. 169, 199.

40 See V. Weizmann, *Impossible*, 104.

41 From his speech at a conference of the EZF, 21 September 1919, see WP 1:256–57.

42 For this passage, see WL, 11:xii, and nos. 21 *ns*3–5, 22, 142, 233 *n*1; *Daily Express*, 28 October 1922; *T&E*, 351–52; Taylor, *Beaverbrook*, 200, 206; and Cowling, *Impact*, 81.

43 See WL, 10:254 and no. 315; 11, no.

33 n5; and his speech at the Carlsbad Congress, 5 September 1921, in WP, 1:324–33.

44 See his opening speech to the thirteenth Zionist Congress at Carlsbad on 6 August 1923, WP, 1:393–400.

11: THE BENEVOLENT DESPOT

1 See L.M.[?], 'Chaim Weizmann.'
2 WL, 11, no. 112; and Cmd.1500.
3 WL, 11, nos. 185, 194.
4 Quoted in Lourie, 'Chaim Weizmann.'
5 See WL, 11, nos. 309, 310, 382; 13, nos. 115, 364, 366. Also T&E, 337–38.
6 WL, 12, no. 77.
7 WL, 10:139, and 13, nos. 116, 137.
8 T&E, 386–87.
9 See T&E, 381–86; also Farrer, *Warburgs*, and Reznikoff, *Louis Marshall*.
10 WL, 11, nos. 353, 363, 364, 369, and p. 335; also T&E, 382–85.
11 WL, 11, no. 370.
12 See WL, 11, no. 359; 12:xv and no. 2; WP, 1:400–4; T&E, 404.
13 WL, 12, nos. 61, 63.
14 See WL, 11, no. 276, and 13, nos. 108, 113, 183; and T&E, 405.
15 WL, 12, nos. 298, 347, 350; WP, 1:468 n17; and Ruppin, *Diaries*, 210.
16 See Ruppin, *Diaries*, 209.
17 WL, 12, no. 85.
18 WL, 11, no. 294 n8.
19 WL, 13, nos. 14, 100, and 14, no. 93.
20 WL, 12, nos. 317, 345; WP, 1:451–68.
21 See Cmd.1889, *Papers Relating to Elections for the Legislative Council* (1923); and Cmd.1989, *Correspondence with the High Commissioner on the Proposed Formation of an Arab Agency* (1923); also WL, 12, nos. 11, 27, 77.

22 See cabinet minutes for 27 June and 31 July 1923, CAB.23/46; and CAB.24/161, CP.351.
23 See his sympathetic article 'In Palestine Now' in *Awakening Palestine*; also WL, 11, no. 22 n5, and 12, nos. 170, 171 n6.
24 WL, 12, no. 191, and 18, no. 285.
25 WL, 9, no. 240.
26 See WP, 1:454, and T&E, 344–46.
27 See Mossek, *Palestine Immigration Policy*, 44, 107–8.
28 WL, 13, nos. 11, 24, 439, 446; and T&E, 342–43.
29 See WL, 10, nos. 77, 157, and 11, no. 2, also 12, nos. 159, 170. See also Simon, *Certain Days*, 109–10, 159.
30 WP, 1:425–34; Kisch, *Palestine Diary*, 144–45; and Ruppin, *Diaries*, 214–15.
31 WL, 7, nos. 101, 267; 12, nos. 82, 267; WP, 1:422–45; Dugdale, *Balfour*, 2:268–70; Horace Samuel, *Unholy Memories*, 89–90; Ruppin, *Diaries*, 217; Kisch, *Palestine Diary*, 170–71; T&E, 390–96.
32 WL, 12, no. 252.
33 WL, 13, no. 8.
34 WL, 12, nos. 333, 337.
35 WL, 12, no. 341.
36 WL, 12, no. 367.
37 WL, 13, nos. 63, 68.
38 For this passage, see WL, 13, nos. 182, 183, 191, 195; and interviews with Mrs. Kitty Stein and Mrs. Hahn-Warburg, October 1983, also transcript of interview with Yeheskiel Sahar, 4 December 1971, WA.
39 See Rose, *Namier*, 28–30.
40 WL, 13, nos. 1, 20.
41 See Samuel, *Report*, 15; for Weizmann's dissatisfaction with him, see WL, 10, nos. 201, 213; 11, no. 16; 12, nos. 157, 210.
42 See Samuel, *Report*; also Bowle, *Viscount Samuel*, 230–34, and Samuel, *Memoirs*, 177–78.

43 Quoted in Sykes, *Crossroads*, 105.
44 WL, 12, no. 319.
45 Sykes, *Crossroads*, 107–9.
46 WP, 1:391.
47 WL, 13, no. 70; 14, nos. 85, 97.
48 WL, 12, nos. 7, 21 *n*4, 77 *n*9, 170;
   see also transcript of interview with
   Yeheskiel Sahar, 4 December 1971,
   WA.
49 See Yossin, *Pillar of Fire*, 135, and
   Kisch, *Palestine Diary*, 236.
50 WL, 13, no. 253.
51 WL, 13, nos. 279, 281; also
   Laqueur, *History*, 316–17, 466.
52 WL, 13, no. 227.
53 WL, 13, nos. 235, 308, 310, 322,
   378. See also Amery, *Diaries*, 1:538,

541, 546; and M. J. Cohen,
   'Churchill and Palestine.'
54 WL, 13, nos. 304 *n*3, 452.
55 *T&E*, 406.
56 WL, 12, no. 116; 13, no. 116.
57 WL, 12, no. 170.
58 WL, 13, nos. 136, 143, 145, 390;
   and Farrer, *Warburgs*, 149.
59 WL, 12, no. 412; 13, nos. 390 *n*1,
   429, 430.
60 WL, 13, nos. 390 *n*1, 429, 430.
61 WL, 13, nos. 390, 480–85.
62 WP, 1:554.
63 Ruppin, *Diaries*, 246.
64 See Cmd.3530, *Shaw Report on the
   Disturbances of August 1929* (March
   1930); and *T&E*, 409–10.

12: THE CHIEF

I have not cited specific references for quotations in this chapter. To have done so
would have been cumbersome and tiresome, as practically every sentence would have
deserved at least one reference, possibly more. Much of the information came from
interviews (see Acknowledgments), as well as a multiplicity of other sources. I have
listed the main ones below.

The Letters and Papers of Chaim Weizmann, Series A, 23 vols. [WL]
The Letters and Papers of Chaim Weizmann, Series B, 2 vols. [WP]
Crossman, Richard. 'Notes,' WA.
Goldmann, Nahum. 'Chaim Weizmann: An Evaluation' (Zionist Archives, New York).
New York Post, 25 June 1940.
Schuster (Nicholls), Norah, to Vera Weizmann, 17 October 1923, WA.
Weizmann, Benji, to Vera Weizmann, 10 January 1937, WA.

Berlin, Isaiah. *Personal Impressions* (1982).
Brodetsky, Selig. *Memoirs* (1960).
Boothby, Robert. 'The Weizmann I Knew,' *Jewish Observer and Middle East Review*
   (15 November 1974).
Crossman, Richard. *Palestine Mission* (1947).
———. *A Nation Reborn* (1960).
Dugdale, Blanche. *Baffy: The Diaries of Blanche Dugdale, 1936–1947*, ed. Norman
   Rose (1973).
Frankfurter, Felix. *From the Diaries of Felix Frankfurter*, ed. J. P. Lash (1975).
Goldmann, Nahum. *Autobiography* (1969).
———. 'Realities and Illusions,' *Jewish Quarterly* (Winter 1975).
Gorni, Joseph. *Partnership and Conflict: Chaim Weizmann and the Jewish Labour Move-
   ment in Palestine* (1976).

486 • Notes

Halifax, Lord. *Fulness of Days* (1957).

Hay (Paterson), Alice Ivy. *There Was a Man of Genius* (1963).

James, Robert Rhodes. *Victor Cazalet* (1976).

Kollek, Teddy. *For Jerusalem* (1976).

Lawrence, T. E. *Selected Letters of T. E. Lawrence*, ed. David Garnett (1952).

Lipsky, Louis. *Memoirs in Profile* (1975).

Lourie, Arthur. 'Chaim Weizmann: The Man and the Statesman,' *The Reconstructionist* (26 December 1952).

MacDonald, James G. *My Mission in Israel* (1951).

Meinertzhagen, Richard. *Middle East Diary: 1917–1956* (1959).

Neumann, Emanuel. *In the Arena* (1976).

Reading, Marchioness of. *For the Record* (1973).

Rezzori, Gregor von. *Memoirs of an Anti-Semite: A Novel* (1982).

Rose, Norman. *Lewis Namier and Zionism* (1980).

Sacher, Harry. *Zionist Portraits and Other Essays* (1959).

Samuel, Horace. *Unholy Memories of the Holy Land* (1930).

Samuel, Maurice. *Little Did I Know* (1963).

Shertok, Moshe. *Political Diaries* (1968–79).

Shihor, Samuel. *Hollow Glory* (1960).

Sidebotham, Herbert. *Great Britain and Palestine* (1937).

Sieff, Israel. *Memoirs* (1970).

Simon, Julius. *Certain Days* (1971).

Stein, Leonard. *Weizmann and England* (1964).

———. *The Balfour Declaration* (1961).

Storrs, Ronald. *Orientations* (1939).

Weisgal, Meyer. . . . *So Far* (1971).

Weizmann, Chaim. *The Essential Chaim Weizmann*, ed. Barnet Litvinoff (1982).

———. *Trial and Error* (1950).

Weizmann, Ezer. *On Eagles' Wings* (1976).

Weizmann, Vera. *The Impossible Takes Longer* (1967).

13: YOU HAVE SAT TOO LONG AT ENGLISH FEASTS

1 See Cmd.3229, A *Memorandum . . . on the Wailing Wall* (November 1928); and Cmd.3530.

2 Weisgal, *So Far*, 90–91; WL, 14, nos. 9, 10.

3 Minutes of Zionist Executive, 28 August 1929, WA; WL, 14, nos. 14, 17, 19; Passfield to Weizmann, 30 August 1929, WA; notes of an interview between Smuts and Weizmann, 3 December 1929, WA; Beatrice Webb, *Diaries*, xliv, 5 February 1930, at the London School of Economics [hereafter cited as LSE]; notes of a meeting between R. MacDonald and Weizmann, 6 November 1930, WA; and *T&E*, 411.

4 See Rose, *Gentile Zionists*, 2.

5 WL, 14, nos. 23, 27.

6 WL, 14, no. 58; and notes of an interview between Passfield, Weizmann, and Brodetsky, 27 September 1929, WA.

7 See Dugdale, *Balfour*, 2:301.

8 See Cmd.3530. The commission was particularly critical of the manner of selecting new immigrants, and claimed that no more land was available for settlement unless new agricultural methods were

introduced. The conclusions of the commission were challenged, in a minority report, by Lord Snell.

9 See notes of a meeting of 28 March 1930, WA. Those present included Felix Warburg, Lord Melchett, and Lord Reading.

10 WL, 13, no. 439; notes of interview between Smuts and Weizmann, 3 December 1929, WA.

11 Weizmann's appointment diary [hereafter cited as WD], 11 April 1930; and WL, 14, no. 272.

12 See Namier to Kisch, 8 May 1930, WA.

13 T&E, 412.

14 WL, 14, nos. 274–76.

15 WL, 14, nos. 272, 328; and WD, 15 May 1930, WA.

16 See Cmd. 3852.

17 WL, 14, no. 291.

18 See minutes of J.A. Executive, 19 June 1930, WA; minutes of Passfield–Weizmann meeting, 7 July 1930, WA. For details of Rutenberg proposals, see Rose, *Gentile Zionists*, 14–15, and WL, 14, nos. 272 n20, 340, 341.

19 See Ofer, 'Role of High Commissioner.'

20 WL, 14, no. 340.

21 See Cabinet Conclusions for 10 and 24 September 1930, Cab.23/65; Sidney to Beatrice Webb, 24 September and 1 October 1930, Passfield Papers at LSE [hereafter cited as PP]; minutes of interview between Passfield, Weizmann, and Namier, 1 October 1930, WA.

22 Namier to M. MacDonald, 14 October 1930, WA; and Rose, *Namier*, 47–48.

23 See Cmd. 3686 (the Hope Simpson report) and Cmd. 3692 (the Statement of Policy).

24 B. Webb, *Diaries*, 26 October 1930; also WL, 14, nos. 364–65 and p. 390.

25 See Sidney to Beatrice Webb, 28 October 1930, PP.

26 See Rose, *Gentile Zionists*, 17–18, 37; and Bullock, *Life and Times of Bevin*, 1:455–57.

27 See Sidney to Beatrice Webb, 28 October 1930, PP; and R. MacDonald to Weizmann, 31 October 1930, WA.

28 See minutes of meeting, 6 November 1930, WA.

29 WL, 15, no. 38; *H. C. Deb.*, vol. 245, cols. 78–210.

30 For details see Rose, *Gentile Zionists*, 22–25.

31 R. MacDonald to M. Marcus (Labour M.P.), 10 June 1930, WA.

32 See minutes of a telephone conversation between MacDonald and Weizmann, at 9.30 p.m., 11 February 1931, WA.; and *H. C. Deb.*, vol. 248, cols. 599, 751–57.

33 WL, 14, no. 133; see also, for example, notes on an interview between R. MacDonald, Ben Gurion, and Namier, 12 July 1931, WA.

34 WL, 14, nos. 129, 143, 246, 357.

35 See WL, 14, nos. 20, 78, 89, 122, 184 n24, 366; and interview with Abba Eban, July 1983.

36 WL, 14, nos. 97, 122, 366.

37 See WL, 15, nos. 76 n2, 92, 113, 132. See also Thomas Mayer, 'Dreams and Opportunities: Abbas Hilmi's Peace Initiative in Palestine, 1930–1931,' in Cohen and Baer, eds., *Egypt and Palestine*.

38 For his stormy relationship with Warburg, see WL, 14, nos. 89, 105, 133, 143, 184.

39 T&E, 419.

40 WL, 14, nos. 184, 187.

41 See WL, 14, nos. 276, 286, 302; and 15:38 and nos. 74, 111, 140, 149. Also Ben Gurion, *Letters*, 3:202; Goldmann, *Autobiography*, 114; Rose, *Namier*, 54.

42 WP, 1:613–41.

43 See WL, 15, nos. 167, 168; also Laqueur, *History*, 49.

44 WP, 1:641–42.

45 For details see Rose, *Gentile Zionists*, 51–52.

46 See WL, 15:xviii–xxi, and no. 170; Goldmann, 115–117; V. Weizmann, *Impossible*, 120; T&E, 418–20.

47 Weisgal, *So Far*, 96.

48 WL, 15, no. 192.

49 WL, 15, nos. 171, 175, 178.

14: ENFORCED RETIREMENT

1 WL, 15:xxiii, xxv, and nos. 152, 213, 283.

2 See WL, 13, nos. 13, 36, 48, 168, 312, 313, 414; and 15, no. 251.

3 See WL, 15: xxv, and nos. 251 $n1$, 298, 305 $n2$, 334, 346.

4 Sieff, *Memoirs*, 132.

5 WP, 2:43; WL, 16, nos. 204, 257.

6 See WP, 2:34.

7 WL, 17, nos. 60 $n2$, 176, 197, 239.

8 WL, 16, no. 158; and 17, nos. 65, 70, 102, 125, 199, 321, 331, 324 $n5$.

9 For the following passage on his relations with the Hebrew University, see WL, 15, nos. 350, 366, 409, 416, and 16, nos. 145, 197 $n6$, 204, 317, 319, 348, 375, 389, 390.

10 WL, 16, nos. 363, 369, 370, 388; and Rose, *Namier*, 68–69.

11 WL, 16, no. 363.

12 See V. Weizmann, *Impossible*, 138–40; and WL, 16, nos. 352, 397; 17, no. 325 $n5$; 18, no. 240.

13 See V. Weizmann, *Impossible*, 139–40, and interview with Yehiel Paldi, December 1983, and Dugdale, *Diaries*, entry for 10 January 1938. The material about Weizmann House is in WA.

14 See Rose, *Namier*, 58; and WL, 15, no. 93.

15 See WL, 15:186 and nos. 235, 236, 274; and T&E, 423–24, 427–30.

16 See WL, 15, no. 393, and 16, no. 7; also T&E, 425, 427–30; Weisgal, *So Far*, 111–12.

17 See WL, 16, no. 13.

18 See WL, 16, nos. 340 $n2$, 342; WP, 2:24–26; T&E, 441–42; Weisgal and Carmichael, *A Biography*, 232.

19 WL, 16, no. 134.

20 See WL, 16, nos. 223, 262, 321; Cmd.5479, *The Peel Report*, 279; T&E, 442–44.

21 See WL, 15, nos. 360, 383; T&E, 432–38; V. Weizmann, *Impossible*, 137; and Litvinoff, *Weizmann*, 177.

22 See WL, 15:428–29 and 16, nos. 40, 57.

23 See his two Reports, WL, 16, nos. 291, 334.

24 WL, 16, nos. 134, 162.

25 See WL, 16, no. 273; T&E, 450–52.

26 WL, 15:404 and nos. 421, 427; 16, nos. 249 $n1$, 297, 361; 17, no. 290; also WP, 2:38–41. See also Carpi, 'Weizmann's Political Activity'; and 'Notes on Italian Ambitions in the Eastern Mediterranean,' WA.; and T&E, 455–59.

27 See WL, 15, nos. 48, 240, 245, 293, 340, 369.

28 WL, 16, no. 1.

29 Two members of the *Brit Habiryonim*, an extremist Revisionist offshoot, were arrested but were subsequently acquitted. The identity of the assailants remains unknown. For the latest examination of this affair, see Tevet, *Arlosoroff Murder*.

30 WL, 15, nos. 300 $n2$, 301, and 16, nos. 2, 29, 35.

31 WL, 16, nos. 29, 34.

32 See WL, 16, no. 253; Schechtman, *Fighter and Prophet*, 2:245–55; also Shavit, 'Fire and Water.'

33 Ben Gurion, *Letters to Paula*, 81.

34 Ibid.

35 See Gorni, *Partnership and Conflict,* 16.

36 See Ben Gurion, *Letters to Paula,* 82–84.

37 See WL, 17:ix–x; Ben Gurion, *Letters to Paula,* 84–85, and Laqueur, *History,* 513.

38 WL, 16, nos. 369, 388.

39 Ben Gurion, *Letters to Paula,* 82–85.

15: STANDING ROOM ONLY

1 WL, 18, no. 337.

2 See, for example, WL, 17, nos. 51, 65, 78, 102, 199, 300, 324 *n*5, 344.

3 See WL, 17, nos. 115, 120, 124, 166, 189, 190.

4 WL, 17, nos. 32, 84; see Rose *Gentile Zionists,* 104.

5 See minutes of meeting between MacDonald, Ben Gurion, and Namier at Chequers, 12 July 1931, WA.

6 WL, 17, nos. 142, 154, 174; see Cabinet Minutes for 15 January 1936, Cab.23/83; minutes of an interview with Wauchope, 26 January 1936, WA; and Sharett, *Diaries,* 1:27–36.

7 WL, 17, no. 180.

8 *H. L. Deb.,* vol. 99, cols. 750–93; and *H C. Deb.,* vol. 310, cols. 1079–1173.

9 Mrs. Dugdale to Cecil, 17 February 1936, Cecil Papers, ms.51157, British Museum. See Cab.23/83, 1 April 1936.

10 See WL, 17, nos. 213, 214, 218; *H. C. Deb.,* vol. 312, cols. 837; Sharett, *Diaries,* 1:92–93; Dugdale, *Diaries,* 2 May 1936. For his interview with Baldwin, 19 May 1936, WA, and Minutes of London Political Advisory Committee, 8 June 1936, WA.

11 See Cmd.5479, *The Report of the Palestine Royal Commission* (July 1937), the Peel Report.

12 See Dugdale, *Diaries,* entries for 10 and 29 June 1936; and WL, 17, nos. 268, 269.

13 See Sharett, *Diaries,* 1:196.

14 WL, 17:xxi and no. 327; and Sharett, *Diaries,* 1:347.

15 WL, 17, nos. 215, 306. See Rose, 'Arab Rulers.'

16 See Minutes of Public Sessions, Colonial No. 134 (HMSO, 1937); and WP, 2:100–25; A. Shapiro, *Berl,* 2:532.

17 Vera Weizmann's diaries, WA, quoted in *Impossible,* 148; Dugdale, *Diaries,* 3 March 1937; Weisgal and Carmichael, *A Biography,* 3–4.

18 See report of in camera session, 26 November 1936, WA, and Vera Weizmann's diaries, WA, quoted in *Impossible,* 148.

19 Verbatim reports of the sessions, 23 December 1936 and 8 January 1937, WA.

20 For Weizmann's immediate reaction to Coupland's proposal, see Sykes, *Crossroads,* 201–2, and transcript of interview with Yeheskiel Sahar (Saharoff), 4 December 1971, WA. And for Weizmann's meeting with Coupland, see Weisgal and Carmichael, *A Biography,* 240–41. This account is based on Coupland's recollection of the meeting as told to Abba Eban.

21 See Rose, *Gentile Zionists,* 128–30.

22 See WL, 18, no. 21, and Sharett, *Diaries,* 2:24.

23 Minutes of Zionist meeting, 1 March 1937, WA; Sharett, *Diaries,* 2:16.

24 See Ben Gurion, *Memoirs,* 4:55–75, 130–31, for the minutes of the Mapai central committee's deliberations, 5–6 February and 10 April 1937; also Dugdale, *Diaries,* 2 March and 29 June 1937; and transcript of interview with Ben Gurion, 4 December 1971, WA.

25 See WL, 18, no. 114; and *Jewish Chronicle*, 30 April 1937. For his differences with Warburg, see also WL, 18, nos. 10, 19, 33, 41, 64, 320.

26 WL, 18, no. 121.

27 Notes of the dinner party, 8 June 1937, WA, and Dugdale, *Diaries*, 9 June 1937.

28 Dugdale, *Diaries*, 22 June 1937.

29 WL, 18, no. 130. Peel proposed that the Jewish state consist of the coastal strip from Haifa to a point just south of Rehovot and the Galilee, leaving various strategic areas, including a land corridor from Jerusalem to the sea, in the hands of the British. See Cmd. 5479.

30 See notes of telephone conversation between Weizmann and Ormsby-Gore, 1 July 1937, and Ormsby-Gore to Weizmann, 20 July 1937, WA; Cmd. 5513; Dugdale, *Diaries*, 7 July 1937; and WL, 18, nos. 107, 108, 138, 139, 140, 159.

31 WL, 18, no. 156.

32 See Dugdale, *Diaries*, 11 July 1937; and *H. L. Deb.*, vol. 106, cols. 599–674, and *H C. Deb.*, vol. 326, cols. 2235–2367.

33 Dugdale, *Diaries*, 13 September 1937.

34 WP, 2:276–87; and report in *Manchester Guardian*, 9 August 1937.

35 Dugdale, *Diaries*, 4 August 1937.

36 See Dugdale, *Diaries*, 10 August 1937, and transcript of interview with Yeheskiel Sahar, 4 December 1971, WA.

37 See Weisgal and Carmichael, *A Biography*, 5–7; also Ben Gurion, *Memoirs*, 4:422–24.

38 See Eden's memorandum, 19 November 1937, CP. 28 (37), CAB. 24/273; minutes of CID from February 1937, CP. 65 (37), CAB. 24/268; I. S. O. Playfair, *Second World War*, 1:11; and Dugdale, *Diaries*, 23 November 1937.

39 See accounts in *The Times*, 10 and 27 September 1937.

40 Cazalet to Ormsby-Gore, 16 January 1938, WA.

41 WL, 18, nos. 243, 257; and Weizmann to Lipsky and Wise, 21 December 1937, WA.

42 WL, 18, no. 264.

16: THE DOCTRINE OF TEMPORARY EXPEDIENCY

1 WL, 18, nos. 232, 233.

2 WL, 18, no. 231; Sharett, *Diaries*, 23 March 1939; and Dugdale, *Diaries*, vii.

3 See V. Weizmann, *Impossible*, 155.

4 WL, 18, no. 364.

5 WL, 18, no. 364; *Irgun*, 2:78–80, and a report in *Manchester Guardian*, 25 July 1937.

6 See Sharett, *Diaries*, 2:66.

7 See WL, 10, nos. 249, 260; 11, no. 279; 15, no. 215; 16, no. 242; and transcript of interview with Yeheskiel Sahar, 4 December 1971, WA.

8 See Sykes, *Wingate*, 33, 83, 130–31; and Sharett, *Diaries*, vol. 2, 3 June 1937, and Dugdale, *Diaries*, 23 January 1938.

9 See Sykes, *Wingate*, 173.

10 See Dugdale, *Diaries*, 10 March 1938, and minutes of Weizmann's interview with Chamberlain, 10 March 1938, WA.

11 WL, 18, no. 337.

12 WL, 18, no. 285.

13 Cazalet to Weizmann, 2 February 1938; *Jewish Chronicle*, 4 February 1938; Dugdale, *Diaries*, 11 February 1938; and WL, 18, no. 323.

14 WL, 18, no. 323.

15 See WL, 18, nos. 347 *n*3, 365, 371, 426; and Sherman, *Island Refuge*, 112–36.

16 See Abella and Troper, *None Is Too Many*.

17 See WL, 18, nos. 375–83.

18 Minutes of the interview, 22 June 1938, WA, and CP190 (38), CAB.24/278; and minutes of Woodhead Commission's sessions, WA.

19 See record of Anglo-French conversations, 28 April 1938, BD, 3d ser., 1:201, 208–9; Minney, *Private Papers of Hore-Belisha*, 101-3; and Gwynn, *Imperial Policing*, 374.

20 See his report to the Cabinet, 24 August 1938, CP.193 (38), CAB.24/278.

21 Notes of his appearance before the commission, 30 August 1938, WA.

22 MacDonald's despatch to the high commissioner, Sir H. MacMichael, 24 September 1938, FO.371/2186/1/5603.

23 Notes of two conversations with 'B' (MacDonald), 13 and 14 September 1938, WA, and Dugdale, *Diaries*, 19 September 1938.

24 Dugdale, *Diaries*, 30 September 1938; WL, 18, nos. 401, 403; and A. Shapiro, *Berl*, 2:570.

25 See Cmd.5854 and Cmd.5893, and minutes of interview with MacDonald, 9 November 1938, WA.

26 See notes of his speech, 10 November 1938, and report in *Jewish Chronicle*, 18 November 1938.

27 This episode may be followed in: Dugdale, *Diaries*, 28 June, 13 October, and 12 December 1938; notes of an interview between Weizmann, MacDonald, and Halifax, 17 October 1938, WA, and between Halifax and Weizmann, 24 January 1939, WA; minutes of Weizmann's conversations in Turkey, 29 November 1938, WA; FO.371/21880/10/5239; and BD, 3d ser., 6:353–55, 567–68.

28 See Dugdale, *Diaries*, 2 March 1937; 23 September 1937 [unpublished]; 17 October 1938 [unpublished]; 31 August 1939.

29 Dugdale, *Diaries*, 16 and 20 December 1938.

30 See Dugdale, *Diaries*, 11 December 1938; notes of a Zionist meeting, 16 December 1938, CZA A.312/23; and MacDonald's Note, 16 December 1938, FO.371/21869, E.7200/1/1.

31 See Dugdale, *Diaries*, 11, 20, 21, and 25 February 1939; and Rose, *Namier*, 89.

32 See Cabinet minutes for 14 and 21 December 1938, CAB.23/96; and notes of a Zionist meeting, 5 February 1939, WA.

33 See Cabinet minutes, 1 and 15 February 1939, CAB.23/97; CP.4 and CP.7 in CAB.24/282; FO.371/22963, C.1292/15/18; and Dugdale, *Diaries*, 10 January 1939.

34 Namier, *Diplomatic Prelude*, 3.

35 Minutes of the 'Panel', 5 February 1939, WA. The Panel was the chief Jewish deliberative body. It included representatives of the Jewish Agency, the religious groups, and Anglo-Jewry, known fondly as 'the Lords'.

36 See WP, 2:341–60; MacDonald's memorandum, CP.4, CAB.24/282; minutes of a meeting between MacDonald, Weizmann, and Ben Gurion, 25 February 1939, WA; Cabinet minutes of 8 March 1939, CAB.23/97; Dugdale, *Diaries*, 11 February and 8 March 1939; A. Shapiro, 2:575; and *T&E*, 499.

37 See Dugdale, *Diaries*, 4 and 8 March 1939; WL, 19, nos. 24, 27; W. Bullit to C. Hull, 10 March 1939, 4 FRUS 731 (1939); *The Times* (London) and *Manchester Guardian*, 14 March 1939; Cabinet minutes for 8 March 1939, CAB.23/97; Weizmann's report to J.A. Executive, 15 March 1939, WA.

38 See minutes of the final session of

conference, 15 March 1939, CZA, S25/7633; Minutes of the Panel, 16 March 1939, WA; WL, 19, no. 35.

39 See 4 FRUS 737–38 (1939); correspondence between Hull, Welles, and Kennedy, 19–20 March 1939; Cazalet to Moore-Brabazon, 31 March 1939, WA; WL, 19, no. 37; and Cabinet minutes for 3 and 10 May 1939, CAB.23/99.

40 WL, 19, no. 46.

41 WL, 19, no. 47; see also Dugdale, Diaries, 10 January, 7 and 9 February 1938.

42 See notes of the conversation, 11 May 1939, WA; report to J.A. Executive, 15 March 1939, WA; and Dugdale, Diaries, 11 February 1939.

43 Notes of a conversation with Mrs. A. Paterson, 13 May 1939, WA; WL, 19, no. 64; Dugdale, Diaries, 14 May 1939.

44 Cmd.6109.

45 See Manchester Guardian, 18, 19, and 22 May 1939; The Times (London), 17–20 May 1939; The Daily Telegraph, 18 May 1939; The Daily Herald, 18 May 1939; and Wasserstein, Britain and Jews, 23–24.

46 See memorandum to Hull, 15 May 1938, and Roosevelt to Hull, 17 May 1939, 4 FRUS 756–58 (1939).

47 See WL, 19, nos. 65, 70, 71, 73, 74, 77; the letter in The Times (London) signed by four of the Peel Commissioners, Rumbold, Carter, Morris, and Coupland, calling for a 'federal solution'; and H. C. Deb., vol. 347, cols. 1937–2056, 2129–90, and H. L. Deb., vol. 113, cols. 81–145.

48 See H. C. Deb., vol. 347, cols. 1937–2056, 22 May 1939, and cols. 2129–90, 23 May 1939. Although most historical comparisons are misleading, it is worth noting that the government majority on the white paper was only eight more than in the debate over the Norwegian debacle a year later, a vote that led to the fall of the Chamberlain administration and elevated Churchill to power.

49 WL, 19, no. 80; Dugdale, Diaries, 22 May 1939.

50 Remarks to the Panel, 24 February 1939, WA.

51 Address to the English Zionists, 18 May 1939, WP, 2:364–70; and speech at the Kingsway Hall, Jewish Chronicle, 26 May 1939.

52 WL, 19, nos. 84, 91, 97, 110; The Times (London), 18 July 1939; Dugdale, Diaries, 3 July 1939; Mrs. Dugdale to Weizmann, 6 July 1939, WA; T&E, 463–64.

53 See Cmd.6109, 5–6; WL, 19, no. 110; Lugard to Weizmann, 23 June 1939, WA; The Times (London), 22 May 1939.

54 See WL, 19, nos. 38, 104, 110; Sharett to Amery, 22 May 1939, CZA, Z4/17125; Weizmann, diaries, 20–21 June 1939, WA (these list only his engagements and contain little additional information); and Dugdale, Diaries, 23 June and 10 August 1939.

55 WL, 19, nos. 120–22.

56 Report of Proceedings of Congress, New Judaea (September 1939); Heller, 264–66; Dugdale, Diaries, 20 August 1939; and A. Shapiro, Berl, 2:580–81. Also T&E, 508–9.

57 Dugdale, Diaries, 20 August 1939.

58 See Proceedings of Congress, and Dugdale, Diaries, 20–24 August 1939.

59 Dugdale, Diaries, 24–28 August 1939; WL, 19, no. 123; and Weisgal and Carmichael, A Biography, 253.

60 Chamberlain to Weizmann, 2 September 1939, WA.

17: ONLY REBUFFS AND HUMILIATIONS

1 See WL, 19, no. 123; T&E, 512; I. Berlin, Zionist Politics; and Sykes, Wingate, 233.

2 See Rose, Namier, 96–97; WL, 19:185 and nos. 123, 153; Dugdale, Diaries, 18 September 1939.

3 Lord Moyne reported to the Cabinet on 2 October 1941 that Weizmann had mentioned the figure of three million Jews. See CAB.65/19.

4 See Dugdale, Diaries, 19 December 1939; WL, 19, nos. 173, 191; Halifax to Weizmann, 19 December 1939, WA.

5 See T&E, 514; minutes of meeting, WA.

6 Dugdale, Diaries, 28 and 31 December 1939; Namier to Mrs. Dugdale, 2 January 1940, CZA.A312/44.

7 For the struggle in Cabinet, see discussions for 27 December 1939, and 16 January and 12 February 1940 in CAB.65/2,5; Churchill's anti–White Paper memorandum of 25 December 1939, and MacDonald's answer of 5 January 1940, CAB.67/3.

8 See Jewish Agency reports in CZA.312/16,30, and WL, 19, no. 224.

9 See ESCO Foundation, Study, 940–41; Zweig, Britain and Palestine, 2; and Wasserstein, Britain and Jews, 19.

10 See Dugdale, Diaries, 21 December 1940.

11 V. Weizmann, Impossible, 184; Dugdale, Diaries, 6 December 1939 and 28 May 1940; WL, 19, nos. 283, 291; and Weisgal and Carmichael, A Biography, 238.

12 WL, 19, no. 272.

13 See Sharett, Diaries, 14 May 1940; Dugdale, Diaries, 10 May 1940 and 10 February 1941; and Weisgal and Carmichael, A Biography, 258.

14 Dugdale, Diaries, 16 May 1940.

15 See minutes of meeting in WA; also WL, 19, no. 201.

16 See WL, 19, no. 273; the Jewish Agency memoranda, dated 10 and 13 May, in WA; and a paper by the Jewish Agency, 'War Effort and War Potentialities of Palestinian Jewry,' CZA.A312/8.

17 See WL, 19, no. 281.

18 These figures are taken from 'War Effort' CZA.A312/8.

19 WL, 19, no. 174; see Dugdale, Diaries, 14 November 1939.

20 See WL, 19, nos. 124, 136.

21 Minutes of the Barker–Ben Gurion interview, 9 November 1939, WA; also Brooke to Dill, 19 April 1942, PREM.3/492/2. I am grateful to Tuvia Ben Moshe for bringing this reference to my attention.

22 See records of their discussions, 24 May and 18 June 1940, in WA and 'War Effort'; also WL, 19, nos. 270, 281, 286.

23 Dugdale, Diaries, 6 and 13 September 1940; see Weizmann's report, 4 September 1940, in WA, and report of 16 September 1940 in CZA.Z4/302/24.

24 See Lloyd to Weizmann, 17 October 1940, WA; for details of proposals see 'Recruitment of Jewish Units', 8 October 1940, CAB.66/12; Cabinet decisions of 10 October 1940, CAB.65/9; and Dugdale, Diaries, 13, 14 September and 11 October 1940.

25 See WL, 20:xi, and Dugdale, Diaries, 18 September 1940.

26 Dugdale, Diaries, 6–7 November 1940; minutes of Namier–Lloyd meeting, 7 January 1941, WA, and Namier to Mrs. Dugdale, 8 January 1941, CZA.A312/44.

27 See Churchill, Second World War,

3:658. Churchill's instructions to Moyne, 1 March 1941, PREM.4/51/9; Moyne's letter to Weizmann, 4 March 1941, WA.

28 See WL, 20, nos. 143, 152.

29 See Dugdale, *Diaries*, 5 and 11 March 1941, and Namier to Mrs. Dugdale, 12 March 1941, CZA.A312/44.

30 WL, 20, no. 129, and *T&E*, 525–26.

31 WL, 20, no. 129, and *T&E*, 525–26.

32 See minutes of interviews with Moyne and Sir Archibald Sinclair, 6 and 26 May 1941, and Namier to Moyne, 22 April 1941, CZA.A312/35, 55.

33 For these events, see WL, 20, nos. 172, 182, 198; Cabinet minutes, 13 October 1941, in CAB.65/19; Moyne's memorandum of 9 October 1941, in CAB.67/7; Moyne to Weizmann, 28 August, 15 and 29 October, and 5 December 1941, WA; and Dugdale, *Diaries*, 5 and 23 October 1941.

34 See WL, 21, nos. 184, 190, 201, 220; Cabinet minutes of 5 August 1942, CAB.65/27; the government statement of 6 August 1941, *H C. Deb.*, vol. 382, cols. 1271–72; Namier to Mrs. Dugdale, 24 August and 8 September 1944, CZA A312/44; and Pearlman, *Ben Gurion*, 15, 105.

35 See V. Weizmann, *Impossible*, 183, 189–90; Dugdale, *Diaries*, 13 February 1942; E. Weizmann, *On Eagles' Wings*, 38; WL, 20, no. 307.

36 See WL, 19, nos. 235, 272; and I. Berlin, *Zionist Politics*.

37 Meinertzhagen, *Middle East Diary*, 183; WL, 19, nos. 193–241.

38 WL, 20, no. 152, also nos. 130–66.

39 See WL, 9, no. 326, and 14, nos. 89, 91, 187.

40 See records of meetings, 26 September and 6 October 1939, CZA.A312/27.

41 See WL, 20, no. 129, and 21, no. 38. Also Porat's detailed examination of this topic, 'The Philby Episode'. He claims that Weizmann considered the implementation of the Philby plan as 'his main task during the first years of the war', surely a lop-sided evaluation of Weizmann's wartime activities.

42 See WL, 20:42.

43 For Philby's account see *Arabian Jubilee*, 212–13, and Monroe, *Philby of Arabia*, 219. See also WL, 4, no. 106; and Prime Minister's [Churchill's] telegram, 12 September 1943, serial no. T.1333/3, PRO. I am grateful to Martin Gilbert for bringing this reference to my attention.

44 WL, 20, no. 267.

45 See *T&E*, 519–20; Weisgal and Carmichael, *A Biography*, 118; and WL, 17, nos. 65, 199, 324; 18, nos. 67, 210 n3, 298; 19:xv and nos. 129, 150, 178, 185, 236, 247; 20, nos. 18, 47, 155, 156, 193, 238, 239, 265, 281, 291, 323.

46 See, for his activity in the United States, WL, 20, nos. 281, 291, 296, 310 n2, 312, and 21:2 n5; for the Bevin initiative, WL, 21, no. 133; and in general, *T&E*, 516, 519–20, 527–29, 545–47.

47 Quoted by Eban, 'Tragedy and Triumph,' in Weisgal and Carmichael, *A Biography*, 264.

48 See Weisgal, *So Far*, 173–74, and WL, 20, no. 364; also C. Weizmann, 'Palestine's Role'.

49 WL, 20, nos. 298, 301, 304, 312, 364, and 21, nos. 88 n4, p. 125; also Dugdale, *Diaries*, 6 and 11 September 1940; and M. J. Cohen, *Palestine: Retreat*, 128, 134, 137–38.

50 On the Ben Gurion dispute, see WL, 20, nos. 292, 295, 298, 301, 304, 317, 321 *n*1, 329, 339 *n*7, 340, 364.

51 See WL, 21, nos. 88, 96; and Dugdale, *Diaries*, 16 July and 14 November 1943.

52 See WL, 20, nos. 312 *n*8, 331 *n*1, 364.

53 WL, 20, no. 364.

54 See Lowdermilk, *Palestine*.

55 WL, 20, no. 364.

56 WL, 20, no. 340.

57 Quoted in I. Berlin, *Zionist Politics*.

18: SCHE'ERIT HAPLETA— ONLY A REMNANT SHALL SURVIVE

1 See Laqueur, *Terrible Secret*, 224–28; also Gilbert, *Auschwitz*, 103–4.

2 See Yoslin, *Pillar of Fire*, 319, 339, 341, 343; also Gilbert, *Auschwitz*, 99.

3 *T&E*, 515; WL, 20, nos. 88, 268; see Laqueur, *Terrible Secret*, 11–15.

4 Laqueur, *Terrible Secret*, 109.

5 See Wasserstein, *Britain and Jews*, 60–71; Dugdale, *Diaries*, 12, 15, 22, and 25–28 November 1940; Rose, *Namier*, 132.

6 See Gilbert, *Auschwitz*, 312, and Zweig, *Britain and Palestine*, 57.

7 See *The Times* (London), 30 May 1941; WL, 20, nos. 146, 152, 170; Harvey, *War Diaries*, 30 November 1942 and 21 April 1943; and M. J. Cohen, *Palestine: Retreat*, 142.

8 See Namier to Moyne, 10 June 1941, CZA.A312/16; Zweig, *Britain and Palestine*, 68; and *Manchester Guardian* report from Cairo, 2 June 1941.

9 WL, 20, no. 170.

10 Churchill's minutes of 1 October 1941, PREM.4/52/5 pt. 2; Spears quoted in Zweig, *Britain and Palestine*, 174 *n*107.

11 WL, 21, no. 20.

12 See his paper, 27 April 1943, in CAB.66/36; also Harvey, *War Diaries*, 21 April 1943; and Churchill, *Second World War*, 4:849.

13 The memoranda may be found in CAB.66/36, 37, 38; also Zweig, *Britain and Palestine*, 169–76.

14 See Cabinet minutes of 2 July 1943, CAB.65/39; for Churchill's remark about Stanley, Dugdale, *Diaries*, 14 May 1940; for Amery's conversation with Weizmann, Dugdale, *Diaries*, 21 July 1943; for the American initiative, the so-called Hoskins mission, WL, 21, no. 55 *n*2.

15 Weizmann's note of the meeting, 26 October 1943, WA; also WL, 21, no. 86.

16 Quoted by M. J. Cohen, *Retreat*, 135.

17 See WL, 21:125.

18 Dugdale, *Diaries*, 20 October 1943.

19 See Cabinet committee's report of 20 December 1943, in CAB.63/44; and Cabinet minutes for 25 January 1944, CAB.65/45.

20 See, in particular, Eden's memorandum, 15 May 1944, containing reports from Sir Miles Lampson from Cairo, and Sir Kinahan Cornwallis from Baghdad, in CAB.66/50; also a report by the chiefs of staff, 22 January 1944, CAB.66/45. See also G. Cohen, 'Harold MacMichael.'

21 See Dugdale, *Diaries*, for this period.

22 See WL, 21, no. 131; I. *Zionist Politics*, Berlin, 48; and Weisgal, *So Far*, 186–88.

23 WL, 21, no. 9; see also Laqueur, *History*, 551.

24 See WL, 21, nos. 23, 49; Wasserstein, *Britain and Jews*, 188–98.

25 See WL, 21:185, nos. 165–67; Wasserstein, *Britain and Jews*, 253–59; Dugdale, *Diaries*, June and 10

July 1944. Joel Brandt left his own account in *Desperate Mission*.

26 See a note by Weizmann and Sharett, 6 July 1944, WA, for Eden; also Wasserstein, *Britain and Jews*, 309–20; Gilbert, *Auschwitz*; and Dawidowicz, *War Against Jews*, 517.

27 See WL, 21, nos. 181, 184, 188, 190, 201; and Dugdale, *Diaries*, 20 and 21 July 1944; for luncheon-party, Dugdale, *Diaries*, 4 October 1944.

28 This account of their meeting may be followed in WL, 21, nos. 207, 225; WP, 2:540–43; also Heller, *Struggle*, 411–15, and *T&E*, 536–37.

29 See Dugdale, *Diaries*, 5 and 9 November 1944; WL, 21, no. 226; Heller, *Struggle*, 411–15; and *Jewish Chronicle*, 24 November 1944.

30 See report in *The Times* (London), 18 November 1944, and Churchill, *Second World War*, 6:612.

31 See Eban, 'Tragedy and Triumph,' in Weisgal and Carmichael, *A Biography*, 275–76.

32 See report in *The New York Times*, 26 November 1944, and in WP, 2:543–46.

33 See videotaped interview with Dr. Joel, WA.

34 Interviews with Joel and Paldi.

35 WL, 21, no. 188.

36 See WL, 21, nos. 157, 261; also Weisgal, *So Far*, 214–16.

37 For his tour of the country, see WP, 2:546–55; for his visit to Athlit, V. Weizmann, *Impossible*, 196–98, and Weisgal, *So Far*, 205–6; for the action against the terrorists, WL, 21, nos. 235, 239; for Begin, WL, 22, no. 292.

38 Dugdale, *Diaries*, 17 March 1945, and *T&E*, 539.

39 *T&E*, 538.

40 For his speech to the Zionist Council, see WP, 2:546–55.

19: THE LINE OF LEAST INJUSTICE

1 See Heller, 'Roosevelt, Stalin,' and WL, 20, no. 267, for Weizmann's memorandum to Maisky, Soviet ambassador in London; see also WL, 21:xi and no. 263 *n*3.

2 See WL, 21, no. 285, for the Arab League; for Ibn Saud's views, WL, 21, nos. 283, 293, and Notes of the Wise–Roosevelt interview, 16 March 1945, WA.

3 The correspondence is in WL, 22, no. 10; Weizmann's reflection in Crum, *Behind*, 169.

4 Dugdale, *Diaries*, 14 October 1943.

5 Meinertzhagen, *Middle East Diary*, 3 July 1945; see Dugdale, *Diaries*, 27 June and 23 July 1945.

6 See Bullock, *Bevin: Foreign Secretary*, 165, 182–83. Also Louis, *British Empire*, 383–96.

7 See Harris, *Attlee*, 390; Bullock, *Bevin: Foreign Secretary*, 167–68; and Crum, *Behind*, 171. For Churchill's statement in the Commons on 1 August 1946, see *H C. Deb.*, vol. 426, col. 1252.

8 See Dugdale, *Diaries*, 20 September 1945, and WL, 22, nos. 63, 69.

9 For London conference, WL, xxii, nos. 10, 45, 47. See Truman, *Memoirs*, 145–48, and Bullock, *Bevin: Foreign Secretary*, 175–76.

10 See transcript of interview with Moshe Sneh, commander-in-chief of the Haganah, 6 December 1971, WA.

11 WL, 22:xvii; and transcript of interview with Moshe Sneh, 6 December 1971, WA.

12 See WL, xxii: xii, nos. 71, 80 *n*3. The action of the Jewish resistance

movement took place on 1 November, but Bevin was already in receipt of the news when he met with Weizmann. Also Bullock, *Bevin: Foreign Secretary*, 167, 173, 178; also *T&E*, 541.

13 See WL, 22, nos. 88, 89 *n*2; and Bullock, *Bevin: Foreign Secretary*, 181, 277; also *T&E*, 541.

14 See WL, 22, no. 97, and Truman, *Memoirs*, 151; also Heller, *Struggle*, 471–73.

15 The text of his speech is in WP, 2:576–620. Also Crossman, *Palestine Mission*, 25, 133, and Crum, *Behind*, 168–71; for Zionist consternation, see WL, 22, no. 126.

16 See WP, 2:576–620; Crum, *Behind*, 65; Crossman, *Palestine Mission*, 138; and a private communication.

17 This discussion may be followed in Nachmani, *Great Power Discord*, 357–61.

18 See Truman, *Memoirs*, 155–59, and Bullock, *Bevin: Foreign Secretary*, 257–58.

19 Dugdale, *Diaries*, 26 April 1946.

20 WL, 22, nos. 158, 161, 163.

21 WL, 22, no. 179.

22 Interview with Moshe Sneh, 6 December 1971, WA, which also includes an account of his meeting with Cunningham.

23 WL, 22, no. 254, Weizmann to Shertok, 27 June 1946.

24 See WL, 22:xviii–xix, and no. 191 *n*2; minutes of Weizmann–Cunningham meeting of 14 July 1946 in WA; also Horowitz, *State in the Making*, 137–40; V. Weizmann, *Impossible*, 205.

25 See Weisgal and Carmichael, *A Biography*, 285, and WL, 22, no. 193.

26 Interview with Moshe Sneh, 6

December 1971, WA; WL, 22:xii, xix.

27 Quoted in Yossin, *Pillar of Fire*, 443.

28 Yossin, *Pillar of Fire*, 443; and Weisgal, *So Far*, 232–33; and the interview with Sneh in which he mentions Weizmann's justifying attacks on radar stations.

29 See Crossman, 'Chaim Weizmann'; also E. Weizman, *On Eagles' Wings*, 46–47; Dugdale, *Diaries*, 23 July 1946; and Silver, *Begin*, 66–69.

30 See Bethell, *Palestine Triangle*, 267; and WL, 22, no. 196.

31 Dugdale, *Diaries*, 5 August 1946.

32 See M. J. Cohen, *Palestine and Great Powers*, 141.

33 See WL, 22, nos. 197 *n*3, 213, 215, 216–17, 219, 220, and Dugdale, *Diaries*, 25 September 1946.

34 For the failure of the informal talks, see WP, 2:622–26, and Dugdale, *Diaries*, 1 and 9 October 1946; and for the Weizmann–Ben Gurion exchange, Weisgal and Carmichael, *A Biography*, 287–89, and WL, 22, no. 231.

35 Weisgal and Carmichael, *A Biography*, 291.

36 Dugdale, *Diaries*, 5 December 1946.

37 The passage on the Congress is based on WP, 2:629–51; Dugdale, *Diaries*, 7, 9, 10–12, 14, and 16 December 1946; Laqueur, *History*, 575; V. Weizmann, *Impossible*, 213; and Weisgal and Carmichael, *A Biography*, 291–93.

38 Bullock, *Bevin: Foreign Secretary*, 366–67. Also WL, xxii; xxiv, no. 266 *n*3.

39 Dugdale, *Diaries*, 18 December 1946; and interview with Abba Eban, 22 July 1983.

40 See WL, 22, nos. 235, 237–39, 242; and Dugdale, *Diaries*, 4 January 1947.

20: A ZIONIST OF THE OLD SCHOOL

1 *H. C. Deb.*, vol. 426, col. 1252.

2 Dugdale, *Diaries*, 11 March 1946.

3 Quoted in Bullock, *Bevin: Foreign Secretary*, 362.

4 See Harris, *Attlee*, 397, and Bethell, *Palestine Triangle*, 312.

5 See WL, 22, nos. 268, 269, 271, 283, 284.

6 See M. Samuel, *Little*, 196.

7 See Garcia-Granados, *Birth of Israel*, 140–45; Horowitz, *State*, 206–7; Weisgal and Carmichael, *A Biography*, 297–98.

8 These episodes may be followed in greater detail in Bethell, *Palestine Triangle*, 316–43, and Sykes, *Crossroads*, 381–84.

9 Abba Eban in Weisgal and Carmichael, *A Biography*, 300.

10 See WP, 2:672–80, and Isaiah, 11:12.

11 These activities may be followed in WL, 23, nos. 16–57, and *T&E*, 570.

12 See *T&E*, 561–63; V. Weizmann, *Impossible*, 219–20; WL, 23, no. 40 n3; Eban in Weisgal and Carmichael, *A Biography*, 301–2.

13 See Yossin, *Pillar of Fire*, 489, and WL, 23, nos. 48, 50, 51, 54.

14 Lourie, 'Chaim Weizmann.'

15 Eban in Weisgal and Carmichael, *A Biography*, 302; Weisgal, *So Far*, 251.

16 See *T&E*, 564–71.

17 WL, 23, nos. 101, 102.

18 See WL, 23:85; Weisgal and Carmichael, *A Biography*, 304–5; Bullock, *Bevin: Foreign Secretary*, 559–60; Truman, *Memoirs*, 168–69, 170–71; and Forrestal, *Diaries*, 358–64.

19 See WL, 23, nos. 106–09; and Eban in Weisgal and Carmichael, *A Biography*, 304; V. Weizmann, *Impossible*, 221.

20 See Abba Eban, 'Tragedy and Triumph,' in Weisgal and Carmichael, *A Biography*, 304–5.

21 Jacobson, 'Two Presidents'; see also Truman, *Memoirs*, 170–71; and for a livelier version, Miller, *Plain Speaking*, 217.

22 See Truman, *Memoirs*, 171–72; and *T&E*, 577.

23 See Truman, *Memoirs*, 173–74; also Daniels, *Man of Independence*, 317–18.

24 See Truman, *Memoirs*, 172; Jacobson, 'Two Presidents'; WL, 23, nos. 137 n2, 146 n3; and Weisgal and Carmichael, *A Biography*, 309–10.

25 See WL, 23, nos. 127, 137, pp. 92–93.

26 See WL, 23, nos. 148, 149.

27 Quoted by Eban in Weisgal and Carmichael, *A Biography*, 309; and WL, 23, no. 153; also *T&E*, 579–80.

28 See Eban's evidence in Yossin, *Pillar of Fire*, 535.

29 *T&E*, 582.

30 See Weisgal, *So Far*, 256, 263; Weisgal and Carmichael, *A Biography*, 310–11; and M. J. Cohen, *Palestine and the Great Powers*, 376–77.

31 See WL, 23, no. 154; Truman, *Memoirs*, 174–76; M. J. Cohen, *Palestine and Great Powers*, 384–87; and Weisgal and Carmichael, *A Biography*, 312.

32 See WL, 23, no. 155, and V. Weizmann, *Impossible*, 235.

33 WL, 23, no. 161; Weisgal and Carmichael, *A Biography*, 327; and *T&E*, 587.

34 See WL, 23, no. 161; Reading, *For the Record*, 188; and Jacobson, 'Two Presidents.'

35 See WL, 23, no. 173, and *T&E*, 587–88.

36 WL, 23, no. 171.

37 See Rose, *Namier*, 146–47.

38 WL, 23, nos. 201, 206, 208, 260; Weisgal and Carmichael, *A Biography*, 328–29; and V. Weizmann, *Impossible*, 241.

39 See WL, 23, nos. 232, 238, 240, 253, 257.

21: THE PRISONER OF REHOVOT

1 See WL, 23, nos. 201, 238, 241, 343; and videotaped interview with Joel, WA.

2 See Weisgal and Carmichael, *A Biography*, 332–33; also Weisgal, *So Far*, 260–62.

3 WL, 23:xvi, and nos. 264, 305.

4 See WL, 23, nos. 179, 189, 201, 215, 262, 263; interview with Yigal Yadin, 7 December 1971, WA; E. Weizmann, *On Eagles' Wings*, 47.

5 WL, 23, no. 241 n1.

6 WL, 23, no. 308; Weisgal and Carmichael, *A Biography*, 337–38.

7 See WL, 23, nos. 290, 291, 295; Weisgal and Carmichael, *A Biography*, 336.

8 See WL, 23, nos. 269, 290, 292.

9 WP, 2:711; and videotaped interview with Josef Cohn, WA.

10 See *New York Post*, 17 February 1949, and Weisgal, *So Far*, 268.

11 For the American visit, see WL, 23:274 and nos. 320–21A; also Weisgal, *So Far*, 269–70; Weisgal and Carmichael, *A Biography*, 339–40; Shihor, *Hollow Glory*, 198, 207–9; and *The New York Times*, 17 February 1949.

12 See WL, 23:284; Weisgal, *So Far*, 271–74; and Weisgal and Carmichael, *A Biography*, 351–52.

13 This episode may be followed in WL, 23, nos. 238, 242, 247, 349; and Weisgal, *So Far*, 274–75. See also interviews with Ernst Simon, 30 November 1971, and Ernst Bergmann, 7 December 1971, WA.

14 See WL, 18, no. 129, and 23, no. 6 n3.

15 See M. Samuel, *Little Did I Know*, 194–95.

16 See WL, 23, nos. 306, 326.

17 See WL, 1:ix–xvii, xx; 19, no. 291; 23, no. 300; and Weisgal, *So Far*, 275–76.

18 See WL, 23:284, and Weisgal and Carmichael, *A Biography*, 352.

19 Crossman, 'Prisoner of Rehovoth,' in Weisgal and Carmichael, *A Biography*, 354; also videotaped interview with Joel, and interview with Joseph Joffe, 2 December 1971, WA.

20 See videotaped interviews with Joel and Y. Sahar, WA; and interviews with Mrs. Maidie Weizmann, 22 July 1982 and April 1983, Mrs. Batia Abromovitch, 20 June 1982, and Mr. Y. Paldi, 26 December 1983.

21 Weisgal, *So Far*, 277–78.

22 *The New York Times* and *Jerusalem Post*, 9–14 November 1952; and V. Weizmann, *Impossible*, 250.

Epilogue

1 See *The New York Times*, *The Times* (London), and *Jerusalem Post*, 9–14 November 1952; and I. Berlin, *Personal Impressions*, 62.

INDEX

FOR THE BEST IN PAPERBACKS, LOOK FOR THE 🐧

In every corner of the world, on every subject under the sun, Penguin represents quality and variety—the very best in publishing today.

For complete information about books available from Penguin—including Pelicans, Puffins, Peregrines, and Penguin Classics—and how to order them, write to us at the appropriate address below. Please note that for copyright reasons the selection of books varies from country to country.

In the United Kingdom: For a complete list of books available from Penguin in the U.K., please write to *Dept E.P., Penguin Books Ltd, Harmondsworth, Middlesex, UB7 0DA.*

In the United States: For a complete list of books available from Penguin in the U.S., please write to *Dept BA, Penguin,* Box 120, Bergenfield, New Jersey 07621-0120.

In Canada: For a complete list of books available from Penguin in Canada, please write to *Penguin Books Ltd, 2801 John Street, Markham, Ontario L3R 1B4.*

In Australia: For a complete list of books available from Penguin in Australia, please write to the *Marketing Department, Penguin Books Ltd, P.O. Box 257, Ringwood, Victoria 3134.*

In New Zealand: For a complete list of books available from Penguin in New Zealand, please write to the *Marketing Department, Penguin Books (NZ) Ltd, Private Bag, Takapuna, Auckland 9.*

In India: For a complete list of books available from Penguin, please write to *Penguin Overseas Ltd, 706 Eros Apartments, 56 Nehru Place, New Delhi, 110019.*

In Holland: For a complete list of books available from Penguin in Holland, please write to *Penguin Books Nederland B.V., Postbus 195, NL-1380AD Weesp, Netherlands.*

In Germany: For a complete list of books available from Penguin, please write to *Penguin Books Ltd, Friedrichstrasse 10-12, D-6000 Frankfurt Main 1, Federal Republic of Germany.*

In Spain: For a complete list of books available from Penguin in Spain, please write to *Longman, Penguin España, Calle San Nicolas 15, E-28013 Madrid, Spain.*

In Japan: For a complete list of books available from Penguin in Japan, please write to *Longman Penguin Japan Co Ltd, Yamaguchi Building, 2-12-9 Kanda Jimbocho, Chiyoda-Ku, Tokyo 101, Japan.*